W9-AOQ-218

NEW WEBSTER'S

SPELLER

STAFF

EXECUITIVE EDITOR
Edward G. Finnegan

ADMINISTRATION EDITOR
Thomas Vadakelalam

EDITORS
Marilyn Finnegan
Rhonda Heisler
Judy Van Wie
McVey Associates

Copyright © 1982, 1980
This edition by DPC, 1987
All rights reserved under the international and
Pan American Copyright Conventions.
Manufactured in the U.S.A.

ISBN: 0-8326-0041-5

FOREWORD

This book is compiled with your convenience in mind. It is intended to give you the information you seek about dividing words simply and clearly. It is based on NEW WEBSTER'S DICTIONARY OF THE ENGLISH LANGUAGE, copyright 1975 by Consolidated Book Publishers.

A centered dot (•) is used throughout to indicate where words may be broken. Words should be broken only as indicated even though the word may have additional syllables. For example, "abra•sion" has three syllables, but it would be bad practice to break it after the initial "a."

The one exception to the above rule is the orthographic hyphen. This is a hyphen that is part of the spelling of a word: "about-face." This hyphen may never be eliminated and the word, except when absolutely necessary, should be broken only at the hyphen.

Some common proper names are included in this book. Generally, it is better practice not to break proper names but, when necessary, they may be broken as indicated.

aard·vark
Aa·ron
aback
ab·a·cus
  ab·a·cus·es
  ab·a·ci
abaft
ab·a·lo·ne
aban·don
  aban·doned
  aban·don·er
  aban·don·ment
abase
  abased
  abas·ing
  abase·ment
abash
  abash·ment
abate
  abat·ed
  abat·ing
  abat·a·ble
  abate·ment
ab·at·toir
ab·ba·cy
ab·ba·tial
ab·bey
  ab·beys
ab·bre·vi·a·tion
  ab·bre·vi·ate
  ab·bre·vi·at·ed
  ab·bre·vi·at·ing
  ab·bre·vi·a·tor
ab·di·cate
  ab·di·cat·ed
  ab·di·cat·ing
  ab·di·ca·tion
ab·do·men
  ab·dom·i·nal
  ab·dom·i·nal·ly
ab·duct
  ab·duc·tion
  ab·duc·tor
abeam
abed
Ab·e·lard
Ab·er·deen
ab·er·rance
ab·er·ran·cy
ab·er·rant
  ab·er·rant·ly
ab·er·ra·tion
  ab·er·ra·tion·al
abet
  abet·ted
  abet·ting
  abet·ment
  abet·tor
  abet·ter
abey·ance
ab·hor
  ab·horred
  ab·hor·ring
  ab·hor·rence
  ab·hor·er

ab·hor·rent
  ab·hor·rent·ly
abide
abode
abi·ded
abid·ing
abid·ance
abid·ing
  abid·ing·ly
Abid·jan
Ab·i·gail
Ab·i·lene
abil·i·ty
  abil·i·ties
ab·ject
  ab·ject·ly
  ab·ject·ness
ab·jure
  ab·jured
  ab·jur·ing
  ab·ju·ra·tion
  ab·jur·er
ab·late
  ab·lat·ed
  ab·lat·ing
  ab·la·tion
  ab·la·tive
ablaze
able
ably
able-bod·ied
abloom
ab·lu·tion
  ab·lu·tion·ary
ab·ne·gate
  ab·ne·gat·ed
  ab·ne·gat·ing
ab·nor·mal
  ab·nor·mal·i·ty
  ab·nor·mal·i·ties
aboard
abode
abol·ish
  abol·ish·a·ble
  abol·ish·er
  abol·ish·ment
ab·o·li·tion
  ab·o·li·tion·ism
  ab·o·li·tion·ist
A-bomb
abom·i·na·ble
  abom·i·na·bly
abom·i·nate
  abom·i·nat·ed
  abom·i·nat·ing
  abom·i·na·tion
ab·o·rig·i·ne
  ab·o·rig·i·nal
abort
abor·tion
  abor·tion·ist
  abor·tive
abound
about
about-face

above
above-board
ab·ra·ca·dab·ra
abrade
  abrad·ed
  abrad·ing
Abra·ham
abra·sion
abra·sive
abreast
abridge
  abridged
  abridg·ing
  abridg·er
  abridg·a·ble
  abridge·a·ble
  abridg·ment
  abridge·ment
abroad
ab·ro·gate
  ab·ro·gat·ed
  ab·ro·gat·ing
  ab·ro·ga·tion
ab·rupt
Ab·sa·lom
ab·scess
  ab·scessed
ab·scis·sa
  ab·scis·sas
  ab·scis·sae
ab·scis·sion
ab·scond
ab·sence
ab·sent
ab·sen·tee
  ab·sen·tee·ism
ab·sent-mind·ed
ab·sinthe
ab·so·lute
  ab·so·lute·ly
ab·so·lu·tion
ab·so·lut·ism
  ab·so·lut·ist
ab·solve
  ab·solved
  ab·solv·ing
  ab·solv·a·ble
  ab·solv·er
ab·sorb
  ab·sorb·a·bil·i·ty
  ab·sorb·a·ble
  ab·sorb·en·cy
  ab·sorb·ent
  ab·sorp·tion
  ab·sorp·tive
  ab·sorp·tiv·i·ty
  ab·sorb·ing
ab·stain
ab·sten·tion
ab·sti·nence
  ab·sti·nent
ab·ste·mi·ous
ab·stract
  ab·strac·tion
  ab·strac·tive

ab·stract·ed
  ab·stract·ed·ly
ab·struse
ab·surd
  ab·surd·i·ty
  ab·surd·i·ties
  ab·surd·ly
abun·dance
abun·dant
  abun·dant·ly
abuse
  abused
  abus·ing
  abus·er
abu·sive
  abu·sive·ly
  abu·sive·ness
abut
  abut·ted
  abut·ting
abut·ment
abysm
abys·mal
abyss
Ab·ys·sin·ia
aca·cia
ac·a·deme
ac·a·dem·ic
  ac·a·dem·i·cal·ly
ac·a·dem·i·cal
acad·e·mi·cian
acad·e·my
  acad·e·mies
Aca·dia
acan·thus
  acan·thus·es
  acan·thi
a cap·pel·la
Aca·pul·co
ac·cede
  ac·ced·ed
  ac·ced·ing
ac·cel·er·ate
  ac·cel·er·at·ed
  ac·cel·er·at·ing
  ac·cel·er·a·tive
  ac·cel·er·a·tion
  ac·cel·er·a·tor
ac·cent
ac·cen·tu·al
ac·cen·tu·ate
  ac·cen·tu·at·ed
  ac·cen·tu·at·ing
  ac·cen·tu·a·tion
ac·cept
  ac·cept·ance
  ac·cept·er
  ac·cept·or
ac·cept·a·ble
  ac·cept·a·bil·i·ty
  ac·cept·ed
ac·cess
ac·ces·si·ble
  ac·ces·si·bil·i·ty
ac·ces·sion

ac·ces·so·ry
  ac·ces·so·ri·ly
  ac·ces·so·ri·ness
ac·ci·dent
ac·ci·den·tal
  ac·ci·den·tal·ly
ac·claim
ac·cla·ma·tion
  ac·clam·a·to·ry
ac·cli·mate
  ac·cli·mat·ed
  ac·cli·mat·ing
  ac·cli·ma·tion
  ac·cli·ma·tize
  ac·cli·ma·tized
  ac·cli·ma·tiz·ing
  ac·cli·ma·ti·za·tion
ac·cliv·i·ty
  ac·cliv·i·ties
ac·co·lade
ac·com·mo·date
  ac·com·mo·dat·ed
  ac·com·mo·dat·ing
  ac·com·mo·da·tive
  ac·com·mo·da·tion
ac·com·pa·ni·ment
ac·com·pa·nist
ac·com·pa·ny
  ac·com·pa·nied
  ac·com·pa·ny·ing
ac·com·plice
ac·com·plish
  ac·com·plish·a·ble
  ac·com·plish·ment
  ac·com·plished
ac·cord
  ac·cord·ance
  ac·cord·ing
  ac·cord·ing·ly
ac·cor·di·on
  ac·cor·di·on·ist
ac·cost
ac·couche·ment
ac·count
  ac·count·a·ble
  ac·count·a·bil·i·ty
  ac·count·a·bly
  ac·count·an·cy
  ac·count·ant
  ac·count·ing
Ac·cra
ac·cred·it
ac·cre·tion
  ac·cre·tive
ac·cru·al
ac·crue
  ac·crued
  ac·cru·ing
ac·cum·u·late
  ac·cum·u·lat·ed
  ac·cum·u·lat·ing
  ac·cum·u·la·tion
  ac·cu·mu·la·tive
  ac·cum·u·la·tor
ac·cu·ra·cy

ac·cu·rate
  ac·cu·rate·ly
  ac·cu·rate·ness
ac·curs·ed
ac·curst
ac·cu·sa·tive
ac·cuse
  ac·cused
  ac·cus·ing
  ac·cu·sa·tion
  ac·cu·sa·to·ry
  ac·cus·ing·ly
ac·cus·tom
  ac·cus·tomed
acer·bi·ty
ac·e·tate
ace·tic
acet·i·fy
  acet·i·fied
  acet·i·fy·ing
ac·e·tone
acet·y·lene
ache
  ached
  ach·ing
achieve
  achieved
  achiev·ing
  achiev·a·ble
  achiev·er
  achieve·ment
Ach·il·le·an
Achil·les' heel
ach·ro·mat·ic
ac·id
acid·ic
acid·i·fy
  acid·i·fied
  acid·i·fy·ing
  acid·i·fi·ca·tion
  acid·i·fi·er
acid·i·ty
ac·i·do·sis
acid·u·late
  acid·u·lat·ed
  acid·u·lat·ing
  acid·u·la·tion
acid·u·lous
ac·knowl·edge
  ac·knowl·edged
  ac·knowl·edg·ing
  ac·knowl·edge·a·ble
  ac·knowl·edg·er
  ac·knowl·edg·ment
  ac·knowl·edge·ment
ac·me
ac·ne
ac·o·lyte
ac·o·nite
acorn
acous·tic
  acous·ti·cal
  acous·ti·cal·ly
acous·tics
ac·quaint

ac·quaint·ance
ac·quaint·ance·ship
ac·qui·esce
ac·qui·esced
ac·qui·esc·ing
ac·qui·es·cence
ac·qui·es·cent
ac·quire
ac·quired
ac·quir·ing
ac·quir·er
ac·quir·a·ble
ac·quire·ment
ac·qui·si·tion
ac·quit
ac·quit·ted
ac·quit·ting
ac·quit·tal
acre
acre·age
ac·rid
acrid·i·ty
ac·ri·mo·ni·ous
ac·ri·mo·ny
ac·ro·bat
ac·ro·bat·ic
ac·ro·nym
ac·ro·pho·bia
acrop·o·lis
across
acros·tic
acros·ti·cal·ly
acryl·ic
ac·ry·lo·ni·trile
act·ing
ac·tin·ic
ac·tin·ism
ac·tin·i·um
ac·ti·nom·e·ter
ac·ti·non
ac·ti·no·zo·an
ac·tion
ac·tion·a·ble
ac·tion·a·bly
ac·ti·vate
ac·ti·vat·ed
ac·ti·vat·ing
ac·ti·va·tion
ac·ti·va·tor
ac·tive
ac·tive·ly
ac·tive·ness
ac·tiv·ism
ac·tiv·ist
ac·tiv·i·ty
ac·tiv·i·ties
ac·tor
ac·tress
ac·tu·al
ac·tu·al·ly
ac·tu·al·i·ty
ac·tu·al·i·ties
ac·tu·al·ize
ac·tu·al·ized
ac·tu·al·iz·ing

ac·tu·al·i·za·tion
ac·tu·ary
ac·tu·ar·ies
ac·tu·ar·i·al
ac·tu·ate
ac·tu·at·ed
ac·tu·at·ing
ac·tu·a·tion
ac·tu·a·tor
acu·i·ty
acu·men
ac·u·punc·ture
acute
acute·ly
acute·ness
ad·age
ada·gio
Ad·am
Ad·ams
ad·a·mant
ad·a·mant·ly
ad·a·man·tine
adapt
adapt·er
adapt·a·ble
adapt·a·bil·i·ty
ad·ap·ta·tion
adap·tive
adap·tive·ly
add
add·a·ble
add·i·ble
ad·dend
ad·den·dum
ad·den·da
ad·der
ad·dict
ad·dic·tion
ad·dict·ed
ad·dic·tive
Ad·dis Ab·a·ba
Ad·di·son
ad·di·tion
ad·di·tion·al
ad·di·tion·al·ly
ad·di·tive
ad·dle
ad·dress
ad·dress·ee
ad·duce
ad·duct
ad·duc·tion
ad·duc·tive
ad·e·noid
ad·e·noi·dal
adept
adept·ly
adept·ness
ad·e·qua·cy
ad·e·quate
ad·e·quate·ly
ad·here
ad·hered
ad·her·ing
ad·her·ence

ad·her·ent
ad·he·sion
ad·he·sive
ad·he·sive·ly
ad·he·sive·ness
ad hoc
ad ho·mi·nem
ad·i·a·bat·ic
adieu
ad in·fi·ni·tum
adi·os
ad·i·pose
Ad·i·ron·dack
ad·ja·cen·cy
ad·ja·cen·cies
ad·ja·cent
ad·ja·cent·ly
ad·jec·tive
ad·jec·ti·val
ad·join
ad·join·ing
ad·journ
ad·journ·ment
ad·judge
ad·judged
ad·judg·ing
ad·ju·di·cate
ad·ju·di·cat·ed
ad·ju·di·cat·ing
ad·ju·di·ca·tion
ad·ju·di·ca·tor
ad·junct
ad·junc·tive
ad·jure
ad·jured
ad·jur·ing
ad·ju·ra·tion
ad·ju·ra·to·ry
ad·jur·er
ad·just
ad·just·a·ble
ad·just·er
ad·just·or
ad·just·ment
ad·ju·tan·cy
ad·ju·tant
ad·lib
ad·libbed
ad·lib·bing
ad·man
ad·men
ad·min·is·ter
ad·min·is·trate
ad·min·is·tra·tion
ad·min·is·tra·tive
ad·min·is·tra·tor
ad·mi·ral
ad·mi·ral·ty
ad·mire
ad·mired
ad·mir·ing
ad·mi·ra·ble
ad·mi·ra·bly
ad·mi·ra·tion
ad·mi·rer

ad·mir·ing·ly
ad·mis·si·ble
ad·mis·si·bil·i·ty
ad·mis·sion
ad·mit
ad·mit·ted
ad·mit·ting
ad·mit·ted·ly
ad·mit·tance
ad·mix
ad·mix·ture
ad·mon·ish
ad·mon·ish·er
ad·mo·ni·tion
ad·mon·i·to·ry
ado
ado·be
ad·o·les·cence
ad·o·les·cent
Ad·olph
Adon·is
adopt
adopt·a·ble
adopt·er
adop·tion
adop·tive
adore
adored
ador·ing
ador·a·ble
ad·o·ra·tion
ador·ing·ly
adorn
adorn·ment
ad·re·nal
adren·a·line
Adri·an
adrift
adroit
adroit·ly
adroit·ness
ad·sorb
ad·sor·bent
ad·sorp·tion
ad·u·la·tion
ad·u·late
ad·u·lat·ed
ad·u·lat·ing
ad·u·la·tor
ad·u·la·to·ry
adult
adult·hood
adul·ter·ate
adul·ter·at·ed
adul·ter·at·ing
adul·ter·ant
adul·ter·a·tion
adul·tery
adul·ter·er
adul·ter·ess
adul·ter·ous
ad·um·brate
ad·um·brat·ed
ad·um·brat·ing
ad va·lo·rem

ad·vance
ad·vanced
ad·vanc·ing
ad·vanced
ad·vance·ment
ad·van·tage
ad·van·taged
ad·van·tag·ing
ad·van·ta·geous
ad·van·ta·geous·ly
ad·vent
ad·ven·ti·tious
ad·ven·tive
ad·ven·ture
ad·ven·tured
ad·ven·tur·ing
ad·ven·tur·er
ad·ven·tur·ess
ad·ven·tur·ous
ad·ven·ture·some
ad·verb
ad·ver·bi·al
ad·ver·sary
ad·ver·sar·ies
ad·verse
ad·verse·ly
ad·verse·ness
ad·ver·si·ty
ad·ver·si·ties
ad·vert
ad·vert·ence
ad·vert·ent
ad·ver·tise
ad·ver·tised
ad·ver·tis·ing
ad·ver·tis·er
ad·ver·tise·ment
ad·vice
ad·vise
ad·vised
ad·vis·ing
ad·vis·a·bil·i·ty
ad·vis·a·ble
ad·vis·a·bly
ad·vis·er
ad·vis·ed·ly
ad·vise·ment
ad·vi·so·ry
ad·vo·ca·cy
ad·vo·ca·cies
ad·vo·cate
ad·vo·cat·ed
ad·vo·cat·ing
ad·vo·ca·tion
Ae·ge·an
Ae·gi·na
ae·gis
Ae·ne·as
Ae·ne·id
Ae·o·lus
ae·on
aer·ate
aer·at·ed
aer·at·ing
aer·a·tion

aer·a·tor
aer·i·al
aer·i·al·ly
aer·i·al·ist
aer·ie
aer·i·fy
aer·i·fi·ca·tion
aer·obe
aer·o·me·chan·ics
aer·o·naut·ics
aer·o·nau·ti·cal
aer·o·plane
aer·o·sol
aer·o·space
Aes·chy·lus
Aes·cu·la·pi·us
Ae·sop
aes·thete
aes·thet·ic
aes·thet·i·cal·ly
Aet·na
afar
af·fa·ble
af·fa·bil·i·ty
af·fa·bly
af·fair
af·fect
af·fect·ing
af·fect·ing·ly
af·fect·ive
af·fec·ta·tion
af·fect·ed
af·fect·ed·ly
af·fect·ed·ness
af·fec·tion
af·fec·tion·ate
af·fec·tion·ate·ly
af·fec·tion·ate·ness
af·fer·ent
af·fi·ance
af·fi·anced
af·fi·anc·ing
af·fi·da·vit
af·fil·i·ate
af·fil·i·at·ed
af·fil·i·at·ing
af·fin·i·ty
af·fin·i·ties
af·firm
af·firm·a·ble
af·firm·a·bly
af·fir·ma·tion
af·firm·a·tive
af·fix
af·fla·tus
af·flict
af·flic·tion
af·flu·ence
af·flu·ent
af·flu·ent·ly
af·ford
af·fray
af·front
af·ghan
Af·ghan·i·stan

afield
afire
aflame
afloat
afoot
afore·men·tioned
afore·said
afore·thought
afoul
afraid
afresh
Af·ri·ca
Af·ri·can
Af·ri·kan·der
af·ter
af·ter·birth
af·ter·burn·er
af·ter·ef·fect
af·ter·glow
af·ter·life
af·ter·math
af·ter·noon
af·ter·taste
af·ter·thought
af·ter·ward
 af·ter·wards
again
against
Ag·a·mem·non
agape
agar
Ag·as·siz
ag·ate
aga·ve
age
 aged
 ag·ing
 age·ing
aged
age·less
age·long
agen·cy
 agen·cies
agen·da
agent
 agen·tial
ag·glom·er·ate
 ag·glom·er·at·ed
 ag·glom·er·at·ing
 ag·glom·er·a·tion
 ag·glom·er·a·tive
ag·glu·ti·nate
 ag·glu·ti·nat·ed
 ag·glu·ti·nat·ing
 ag·glu·ti·na·tion
 ag·glu·ti·na·tive
ag·gran·dize
 ag·gran·dized
 ag·gran·diz·ing
 ag·gran·dize·ment
 ag·gran·diz·er
ag·gra·vate
 ag·gra·vat·ed
 ag·gra·vat·ing
 ag·gra·va·tion

ag·gre·gate
 ag·gre·gat·ed
 ag·gre·gat·ing
 ag·gre·ga·tion
 ag·gre·ga·tive
ag·gress
 ag·gress·ive
 ag·gress·ive·ly
 ag·gress·ive·ness
 ag·gress·or
ag·gres·sion
ag·grieve
 ag·grieved
 ag·griev·ing
aghast
ag·ile
 ag·ile·ly
agil·i·ty
ag·i·tate
 ag·i·tat·ed
 ag·i·tat·ing
 ag·i·tat·ed·ly
 ag·i·ta·tion
 ag·i·ta·tor
agleam
aglow
ag·no·men
 ag·nom·i·na
ag·nos·tic
 ag·nos·ti·cism
ago
agog
agon·ic
ag·o·nize
 ag·o·nized
 ag·o·niz·ing
ag·o·ny
 ag·o·nies
ag·o·ra·pho·bia
agrar·i·an
 agrar·i·an·ism
agree
 agreed
 agree·ing
 agree·a·bil·i·ty
agree·a·ble
 agree·a·ble·ness
 agree·a·bly
agreed
agree·ment
ag·ri·cul·ture
 ag·ri·cul·tur·al
 ag·ri·cul·tur·ist
Agrip·pa
agron·o·my
 ag·ro·nom·ic
 ag·ro·nom·i·cal
 agron·o·mist
aground
Aguas·ca·lien·tes
ague
 agu·ish
aha
ahead
ahem

ahoy
Ai-da
aide-de-camp
ai-grette
ail
  ail-ing
ail-ment
ai-lan-thus
ai-ler-on
aim-less
air-less
air-borne
air-brush
air-con-di-tion
  air-con-di-tioned
air con-di-tion-er
air con-di-tion-ing
air-craft
air-craft car-ri-er
air-drome
air-drop
  air-dropped
  air-drop-ping
Aire-dale
air-field
air-foil
air-mail
air-man
  air-men
air-plane
air-port
air pres-sure
air-ship
air-sick-ness
air-space
air-speed
air-strip
air-tight
air-wave
air-way
airy
  air-i-er
  air-i-est
  air-i-ness
  air-i-ly
aisle
Aix-la-Cha-pelle
ajar
akim-bo
akin
Ak-ron
Al-a-bama
al-a-bas-ter
a la carte
alac-ri-ty
Alad-din
Al-a-me-da
Al-a-mo
Alar-cón
alarm
  alarm-ing
  alarm-ing-ly
alarm-ist
  alarm-ism
alas

Alas-ka
alate
  alat-ed
al-ba-core
Al-ba-nia
Al-ba-ny
al-ba-tross
al-be-it
Al-be-marle
Al-ber-ta
Al-bi-gen-ses
al-bi-no
  al-bi-nos
  al-bi-nism
Al-bi-on
al-bum
al-bu-men
al-bu-min
  al-bu-mi-nous
Al-bu-quer-que
Al-cae-us
Al-ca-traz
Al-ces-tis
al-che-my
  al-che-mist
Al-ci-bi-a-des
Al-ci-des
al-co-hol
  al-co-hol-ic
  al-co-hol-ism
Al-cott
al-cove
al-der
al-der-man
  al-der-man-ic
Al-der-ney
Al-drich
ale-a-to-ry
alee
alert
  alert-ness
Ales-san-dria
Aleu-tian
ale-wife
  ale-wives
Al-ex-an-der
Al-ex-an-dria
al-ex-an-drine
al-fal-fa
al-fres-co
al-ga
  al-gae
al-ge-bra
  al-ge-bra-ic
  al-ge-bra-ic-al
  al-ge-bra-ic-al-ly
Al-ge-ria
Al-giers
Al-gon-qui-an
Al-gon-quin
al-go-ri-thm
Al-ham-bra
ali-as
  ali-as-es
Ali Ba-ba

al-i-bi
al-ien
  al-ien-a-ble
  al-ien-a-bil-i-ty
al-ien-ate
  al-ien-at-ed
  al-ien-at-ing
al-ien-ist
  al-ien-ism
al-i-form
alight
  alight-ed
alit
  alight-ing
align
align-ment
aline-ment
alike
al-i-ment
  al-i-men-tal
  al-i-men-tal-ly
  al-i-men-ta-tion
  al-i-men-ta-ry
  al-i-men-ta-ry ca-nal
al-i-mo-ny
al-i-quant
al-i-quot
Al-i-son
alive
al-ka-li
  al-ka-lies
  al-ka-lis
al-ka-line
  al-ka-lin-i-ty
al-ka-lize
  al-ka-lized
  al-ka-liz-ing
  al-ka-li-za-tion
al-ka-loid
  al-ka-loi-dal
Al-lah
all-A-mer-i-can
all-a-round
al-lay
  al-layed
  al-lay-ing
  al-lay-er
al-le-ga-tion
al-lege
  al-leged
  al-leg-ing
  al-lege-a-ble
Al-le-ghe-nies
Al-le-ghe-ny
al-le-giance
al-le-go-ry
  al-le-go-ries
  al-le-gor-ic
  al-le-gor-i-cal
  al-le-gor-i-cal-ly
  al-le-gor-ist
al-le-gret-to
al-le-gro
Al-len-town
al-ler-gen

al·ler·gy
al·ler·gies
al·ler·gic
al·ler·gist
al·le·vi·ate
al·le·vi·at·ed
al·le·vi·at·ing
al·le·vi·a·tion
al·le·vi·a·tor
al·le·vi·a·tive
al·le·vi·a·to·ry
al·ley
al·leys
All·hal·lows
al·li·ance
al·lied
al·li·ga·tor
al·lit·er·ate
al·lit·er·at·ed
al·lit·er·at·ing
al·lit·er·a·tive
al·lit·er·a·tive·ly
al·lit·er·a·tive·ness
al·lit·er·a·tion
al·lo·cate
al·lo·cat·ed
al·lo·cat·ing
al·lo·ca·tion
al·lop·a·thy
al·lo·path·ic
al·lo·path·i·cal·ly
al·lop·a·thist
al·lo·phone
al·lot
al·lot·ted
al·lot·ting
al·lot·ment
al·lot·ta·ble
al·lot·ro·py
al·lot·ro·pism
al·lo·trope
al·lo·trop·ic
al·lo·trop·i·cal·ly
al·low
al·low·a·ble
al·low·a·bly
al·low·ed·ly
al·low·ance
al·low·anced
al·low·anc·ing
al·loy
all right
all·spice
al·lude
al·lud·ed
al·lud·ing
al·lure
al·lured
al·lur·ing
al·lure·ment
al·lur·er
al·lur·ing·ly
al·lu·sion
al·lu·sive
al·lu·sive·ly

al·lu·sive·ness
al·lu·vi·al
al·lu·vi·um
al·lu·vi·ums
al·lu·via
al·ly
al·lied
al·ly·ing
al·ly
al·lies
al·ma ma·ter
al·ma·nac
al·mighty
al·mond
al·most
alms·giv·er
alms·giv·ing
alms·house
al·ni·co
al·oe
aloft
alo·ha
alone
alone·ness
along
along·shore
along·side
aloof
aloof·ly
aloof·ness
al·pen·stock
al·pha
al·pha·bet
al·pha·bet·ic
al·pha·bet·i·cal
al·pha·bet·i·cal·ly
al·pha·bet·i·za·tion
al·pha·bet·ize
al·pha·bet·ized
al·pha·bet·iz·ing
Al·phe·us
Al·phon·so
Al·pine
al·ready
Al·sace-Lor·raine
al·so
al·tar
al·ter
al·ter·a·bil·i·ty
al·ter·a·ble
al·ter·ant
al·ter·a·tion
al·ter·a·tive
al·ter·ca·tion
al·ter e·go
al·ter·nate
al·ter·nat·ed
al·ter·nat·ing
al·ter·nate·ly
al·ter·na·tion
al·ter·na·tive
al·ter·na·tive·ly
al·ter·na·tive·ness
al·ter·na·tor
al·though

al·tim·e·ter
al·tim·e·try
al·ti·pla·no
al·ti·tude
al·to
al·to·cu·mu·lus
al·to·gether
Al·too·na
al·to·re·lie·vo
al·to·stra·tus
al·tru·ism
al·tru·is·tic
al·lu·mi·na
alu·mi·nif·er·ous
alu·mi·nous
alu·mi·num
alum·na
alum·nae
alum·nus
alum·ni
al·ve·o·lar
al·ve·o·lus
al·ve·o·li
al·ways
amal·gam
amal·gam·a·ble
amal·gam·ate
amal·gam·at·ed
amal·gam·at·ing
amal·gam·a·tion
aman·u·en·sis
aman·u·en·ses
Am·a·ril·lo
am·a·ryl·lis
amass
amass·ment
am·a·teur
am·a·teur·ism
am·a·teur·ish
am·a·teur·ish·ly
am·a·teur·ish·ness
am·a·tive
am·a·tive·ness
am·a·to·ry
amaze
amazed
amaz·ing
amaz·ed·ly
amaz·ed·ness
amaze·ment
Am·a·zon
Am·a·zo·ni·an
am·bas·sa·dor
am·bas·sa·do·ri·al
am·ber
am·ber·gris
am·bi·dex·trous
am·bi·ance
am·bi·ence
am·bi·ent
am·big·u·ous
am·big·u·ous·ly
am·big·u·ous·ness
am·bi·gu·i·ty
am·bit

am·bi·tion
am·bi·tious
am·bi·tious·ly
am·bi·tious·ness
am·biv·a·lence
am·biv·a·lent
am·ble
am·bled
am·bling
am·bler
am·bro·sia
am·bro·sial
am·bro·sial·ly
am·bu·lance
am·bu·la·to·ry
am·bu·lant
am·bu·late
am·bu·lat·ed
am·bu·lat·ing
am·bus·cade
am·bus·cad·ed
am·bus·cad·ing
am·bush
am·bush·ment
ame·ba
amel·io·rate
amel·io·rat·ed
amel·io·rat·ing
amel·io·ra·ble
amel·io·ra·tion
amel·ior·a·tive
amel·io·ra·tor
amen
ame·na·ble
ame·na·bil·i·ty
ame·na·ble·ness
ame·na·bly
amend
amend·a·ble
amend·er
amend·ment
amends
amen·i·ty
amerce
amerced
amerc·ing
amerce·a·ble
amerce·ment
amerc·er
Amer·i·ca
Amer·i·can
Amer·i·cana
Amer·i·can·ism
am·e·thyst
am·e·thys·tine
Am·herst
ami·a·ble
ami·a·bil·i·ty
ami·a·bly
am·i·ca·ble
am·i·ca·bil·i·ty
am·i·ca·bly
am·ice
amid
amidst

am·ide
amid·ships
Am·i·ens
ami·go
amine
ami·no ac·id
amir
Amish
amiss
am·i·to·sis
am·i·tot·ic
am·i·tot·i·cal·ly
am·i·ty
Am·man
am·me·ter
Am·mon
am·mo·nia
am·mon·ic
am·mo·ni·ac
am·mo·ni·um
am·mo·ni·un chlo·ride
am·mo·ni·um hy·drox·ide
am·mu·ni·tion
am·ne·sia
am·ne·sic
am·nes·tic
am·nes·ty
am·ni·on
am·ni·ons
am·nia
am·ni·on·ic
am·ni·ot·ic
amoe·ba
amoe·bae
amoe·bas
amoe·bic
amoe·boid
amok
among
amongst
Amon·til·la·do
amor·al
am·o·rous
am·o·rous·ly
am·o·rous·ness
amor·phism
amor·phous
am·or·tize
am·or·tized
am·or·tiz·ing
am·or·ti·za·tion
amount
amour
am·per·age
am·pere
am·per·sand
am·phet·a·mine
Am·phib·ia
am·phib·i·an
am·phib·i·ous
am·phi·the·a·ter
am·phi·the·at·ric
am·pho·ra
am·pho·rae
am·pho·ras

am·ple
 am·pler
 am·plest
 am·ple·ness
 am·ply
am·pli·fy
 am·pli·fied
 am·pli·fy·ing
 am·pli·fi·ca·tion
am·pli·fi·er
am·pli·tude
am·pul
am·pu·tate
 am·pu·tat·ed
 am·pu·tat·ing
 am·pu·ta·tion
am·pu·tee
Am·ster·dam
Am·trak
amuck
am·u·let
amuse
 amused
 amus·ing
amuse·ment
am·yl·ase
An·a·bap·tist
anach·ro·nism
 anach·ro·nis·tik
 anach·ro·nis·ti·cal·ly
 anach·ro·nous
an·a·con·da
an·aer·obe
an·aes·the·sia
an·aes·thet·ic
an·a·gram
 an·a·gram·mat·ic
 an·a·gram·mat·i·cal
ana·gram·ma·tize
 ana·gram·ma·tized
 ana·gram·ma·tiz·ing
anal
an·a·lects
an·al·ge·sia
an·al·ge·sic
an·a·log
 an·a·log·i·cal
 an·a·log·i·cal·ly
anal·o·gize
 anal·o·gized
 anal·o·giz·ing
anal·o·gy
 anal·o·gies
 anal·o·gous
anal·y·sis
 anal·y·ses
an·a·lyst
 an·a·lyt·ic
an·a·lyt·ics
an·a·lyze
 an·a·lyzed
 an·a·lyz·ing
 an·a·lyz·a·ble
 an·a·ly·za·tion
 an·a·lyz·er

An·a·ni·as
an·a·pest
 an·a·pes·tic
an·ar·chism
an·ar·chist
 an·ar·chis·tic
an·ar·chy
 an·ar·chic
 an·ar·chi·cal
anath·e·ma
 anath·e·mas
anath·e·ma·tize
 anath·e·ma·tized
 anath·e·ma·tiz·ing
 anath·e·mat·iz·a·tion
An·a·to·lia
anat·o·mize
 anat·o·mized
 anat·o·mizing
 anat·o·mi·za·tion
anat·o·my
 anat·o·mies
 an·a·tom·i·cal
 an·a·tom·i·cal·ly
 anat·o·mist
an·ces·tor
 an·ces·tral
an·ces·tress
an·ces·try
An·chi·ses
an·chor
an·chor·age
an·cho·ress
an·cho·rite
an·cho·vy
an·cient
 an·cient·ly
 an·cient·ness
an·cil·lary
An·co·na
An·da·lu·sia
an·dan·te
An·de·an
An·der·son
An·des
and·i·ron
An·dor·ra
An·do·ver
an·dro·gen
an·drog·y·nous
 an·drog·y·nal
 an·drog·y·ny
An·drom·a·che
An·drom·e·da
An·dros
an·dros·ter·one
an·ec·dote
an·ec·dot·age
 an·ec·do·tal
 an·ec·dot·ist
ane·mia
 ane·mic
an·e·mom·e·ter
an·e·mom·e·try
anem·o·ne

13

an·er·oid
an·es·the·sia
an·es·thet·ic
an·es·the·tist
an·es·the·tize
an·es·the·tized
an·es·the·tiz·ing
an·eu·rysm
an·eu·rism
an·eu·rys·mal
anew
an·ga·ry
an·gel
an·gel·ic
an·gel·i·cal
an·gel·i·cal·ly
an·gel·i·ca
An·ge·lus
an·ger
an·gi·na
an·gi·na pec·to·ris
an·gi·o·sperm
an·gi·o·sper·mous
Ang·kor
an·gle
an·gler
an·gle·worm
An·gli·can
An·gli·can·ism
An·gli·cism
An·gli·cize
An·gli·cized
An·gli·ciz·ing
An·gli·ci·za·tion
an·gling
An·glo·phile
An·glo·phobe
An·glo-Sax·on
An·go·la
an·go·ra
an·gos·tu·ra bark
an·gry
an·gri·ly
an·gri·ness
ang·strom unit
an·guish
an·gu·lar
an·gu·lar·i·ty
an·gu·lar·ly
an·gu·lar·ness
An·gus
an·hy·dride
an·hy·drous
an·i·line
an·i·mad·vert
an·i·mad·ver·sion
an·i·mal
an·i·mal·cule
an·i·mal·cu·lar
an·i·mal·ism
an·i·mal·i·ty
an·i·mal·ize
an·i·mal·ized
an·i·mal·iz·ing
an·i·mate

an·i·mat·ed
an·i·mat·ing
an·i·ma·tion
ani·ma·to
an·i·mism
an·i·mis·tic
an·i·mos·i·ty
an·i·mus
an·i·on
an·ise
an·i·seed
an·i·sette
An·jou
An·ka·ra
an·kle
an·kle-bone
an·klet
an·ky·lose
an·ky·losed
an·ky·los·ing
an·ky·lo·sis
an·ky·lot·ic
an·nal·ist
an·nal·is·tic
an·nals
An·nam
An·nap·o·lis
Ann Arbor
an·neal
an·ne·lid
an·nel·i·dan
an·nex
an·nex·a·tion
an·nex·a·tion·ist
an·ni·hi·late
an·ni·hi·lat·ed
an·ni·hi·lat·ing
an·ni·hi·la·tion
an·ni·hi·la·tor
An·nis·ton
an·ni·ver·sa·ry
an·ni·ver·sa·ries
an·no Dom·i·ni
an·no·tate
an·no·tat·ed
an·no·tat·ing
an·no·ta·tion
an·no·ta·tor
an·nounce
an·nounced
an·nounc·ing
an·nounce·ment
an·nounc·er
an·noy
an·noy·ance
an·noy·er
an·nu·al
an·nu·i·ty
an·nu·i·tant
an·nul
an·nulled
an·nul·ling
an·nul·ment
an·nu·lar
an·nu·lar·i·ty

an·nu·lar·ly
an·nu·late
an·nu·let
an·nu·lus
an·nu·lus·es
an·nun·ci·a·tion
an·nun·ci·ate
an·nun·ci·at·ed
an·nun·ci·at·ing
an·nun·ci·a·tor
an·ode
an·od·ic
an·o·dyne
anoint
anoint·er
anoint·ment
anom·a·ly
anom·a·lism
anom·a·lous
anom·a·lous·ly
anom·a·lous·ness
an·o·mie
an·o·my
an·o·nym
anon·y·mous
an·o·nym·i·ty
anon·y·mous·ly
anon·y·mous·ness
anoph·e·les
an·oth·er
an·ox·ia
An·schluss
an·ser·ine
an·swer
an·swer·a·ble
ant·ac·id
An·tae·us
an·tag·o·nist
an·tag·o·nism
an·tag·o·nis·tic
an·tag·o·nis·ti·cal·ly
an·tag·o·nize
an·tag·o·nized
an·tag·o·niz·ing
ant·arc·tic
Ant·arc·ti·ca
An·tar·es
an·te
an·ted
an·te·ing
ant·eat·er
an·te·bel·lum
an·te·ced·ence
an·te·ced·ent
an·te·cede
an·te·ced·ed
an·te·ced·ing
an·te·ce·dent·ly
an·te·cham·ber
an·te·choir
an·te·date
an·te·dat·ed
an·te·dat·ing
an·te·di·lu·vi·an
an·te·lope

an·te·lopes
an·te me·rid·i·em
an·ten·na
an·ten·nae
an·ten·nas
an·te·pe·nult
an·te·pe·nul·ti·mate
an·te·ri·or
an·te·room
an·them
an·ther
an·ther·id·i·um
an·thol·o·gy
an·thol·o·gies
an·thol·o·gist
an·thol·o·gize
an·thol·o·gized
an·thol·o·giz·ing
an·tho·zo·an
an·thra·cene
an·thra·cite
an·thra·cit·ic
an·thrax
an·thra·ces
an·thro·po·cen·tric
an·thro·po·gen·e·sis
an·thro·poid
an·thro·pol·o·gy
an·thro·po·log·ic
an·thro·po·log·i·cal
an·thro·pol·o·gist
an·thro·pom·e·try
an·thro·po·met·ric
an·thro·po·mor·phic
an·thro·po·mor·phi·cal·ly
an·thro·po·mor·phize
an·thro·po·mor·phized
an·thro·po·mor·phiz·ing
an·thro·po·mor·phism
an·thro·po·mor·phist
an·ti·air·craft
an·ti·bi·o·sis
an·ti·bi·ot·ic
an·ti·body
an·ti·bod·ies
an·tic
an·ti·christ
an·tic·i·pate
an·tic·i·pat·ed
an·tic·i·pat·ing
an·tic·i·pa·tion
an·tic·i·pa·tive
an·tic·i·pa·to·ry
an·ti·cler·i·cal
an·ti·cler·i·cal·ism
an·ti·cli·max
an·ti·cli·mac·tic
an·ti·cli·nal
an·ti·cline
an·ti·cy·clone
an·ti·dote
an·ti·dot·al
An·tie·tam
an·ti·fed·er·al
an·ti·fed·er·al·ist

an·ti·fed·er·al·ism
an·ti·freeze
an·ti·gen
An·tig·o·ne
An·tig·o·nus
An·ti·gua
an·ti·he·ro
an·ti·his·ta·mine
An·til·les
an·ti·log·a·rithm
an·ti·ma·cas·sar
an·ti·mis·sile
an·ti·mo·ny
An·ti·och
an·ti·pas·to
an·tip·a·thy
an·ti·phon
an·tiph·o·nal
an·ti·pode
an·ti·quar·i·an
an·ti·quary
an·ti·quar·ies
an·ti·quate
an·ti·quat·ed
an·ti·quat·ing
an·ti·quat·ed
an·tique
an·tiqued
an·tiq·uing
an·tique·ly
an·tique·ness
an·tiq·ui·ty
an·tiq·ui·ties
an·ti-Sem·i·tism
an·ti·sep·sis
an·ti·sep·tic
an·ti·se·rum
an·ti·slav·ery
an·ti·so·cial
an·tith·e·sis
an·tith·e·ses
an·ti·thet·i·cal
an·ti·tox·in
an·ti·tox·ic
an·ti·trust
ant·ler
ant·lered
An·toi·nette
An·to·ny
an·to·nym
an·trum
an·tra
An·trim
Ant·werp
anus
an·vil
anx·i·e·ty
anx·i·e·ties
anx·ious
anx·ious·ness
any
an·y·body
an·y·bod·ies
an·y·how
an·y·more

an·y·one
an·y·place
an·y·thing
an·y·way
an·y·where
an·y·wise
aor·ta
aor·tas
aor·tae
aor·tal
aor·tic
apace
apache
apart
apart·heid
apart·ment
ap·a·thy
ap·a·thet·ic
ap·a·thet·i·cal·ly
ape
aped
ap·ing
Ap·en·nines
aper·ri·tif
ap·er·ture
apex
apex·es
api·ces
ap·i·cal
apha·sia
aphe·li·on
aphe·lia
aphid
aphis
aphi·des
aph·o·rism
aph·o·rist
aph·o·ris·tic
aph·ro·dis·i·ac
Aph·ro·di·te
api·an
api·ar·i·an
api·a·rist
api·ary
api·ar·ies
api·cul·ture
api·cul·tur·al
api·cul·tur·ist
apiece
ap·ish
ap·ish·ly
ap·ish·ness
aplomb
apoc·a·lypse
apoc·a·lyp·tic
apoc·o·pe
Apoc·ry·pha
apoc·ry·phal
Ap·o·des
ap·o·gee
apo·lit·i·cal
Apol·li·nar·is
Apol·lo
apol·o·get·ics
apol·o·gist

apol·o·gize
apol·o·gized
apol·o·giz·ing
apol·o·gy
apol·o·gies
apol·o·get·ic
apol·o·get·i·cal
Ap·o·lo·ni·us
ap·o·plec·tic
ap·o·plex·y
aport
apos·ta·sy
apos·ta·sies
apos·tate
apos·ta·tize
apos·ta·tized
apos·ta·tiz·ing
a pos·te·ri·o·ri
apos·tle
apos·tle·ship
apos·to·late
ap·os·tol·ic
ap·os·tol·i·cal
apos·tro·phe
apoth·e·cary
apoth·e·car·ies
ap·o·thegm
ap·o·phthegm
ap·o·theg·mat·ic
apoth·e·o·sis
apoth·e·o·ses
apoth·e·o·size
apoth·e·o·sized
apoth·e·o·siz·ing
Ap·pa·la·chi·an
ap·pall
ap·palled
ap·pal·ling
ap·pal·ling·ly
ap·pa·rat·us
ap·pa·rat·us
ap·pa·rat·us·es
ap·par·el
ap·par·ent
ap·pa·ri·tion
ap·pa·ri·tion·al
ap·peal
ap·peal·a·ble
ap·peal·er
ap·peal·ing·ly
ap·pear
ap·pear·ance
ap·pease
ap·peased
ap·peasing
ap·pease·ment
ap·peas·a·ble
ap·peas·er
ap·pel·lant
ap·pel·late
ap·pel·la·tion
ap·pel·la·tive
ap·pend
ad·pen·dage
ap·pend·ant

ap·pen·dec·to·my
ap·pen·di·ci·tis
ap·pen·dix
ap·pen·dix·es
ap·pen·di·ces
ap·per·cep·tion
ap·per·cep·tive
ap·per·tain
ap·pe·tite
ap·pe·tiz·er
ap·pe·tiz·ing
Ap·pi·an
ap·plaud
ap·plause
ap·ple
ap·ple·jack
Ap·ple·ton
ap·pli·ance
ap·pli·ca·ble
ap·pli·ca·bil·i·ty
ap·pli·ca·ble·ness
ap·pli·cant
ap·pli·ca·tion
ap·pli·ca·tive
ap·pli·ca·to·ry
ap·pli·ca·tor
ap·plied
ap·pli·qué
ap·ply
ap·plied
ap·ply·ing
ap·point
ap·point·a·ble
ap·point·er
ap·point·ee
ap·poin·tive
ap·point·ment
Ap·po·mat·tox
ap·por·tion
ap·por·tion·ment
ap·pose
ap·posed
ap·pos·ing
ap·po·site
ap·po·si·tion
ap·po·si·tion·al
ap·pos·i·tive
ap·praise
ap·praised
ap·prais·ing
ap·prais·er
ap·prais·al
ap·pre·ci·a·ble
ap·pre·ci·a·bly
ap·pre·ci·ate
ap·pre·ci·at·ed
ap·pre·ci·at·ing
ap·pre·ci·a·tion
ap·pre·ci·a·tive
ap·pre·hend
ap·pre·hen·si·ble
ap·pre·hen·si·bil·i·ty
ap·pre·hen·sion
ap·pre·hen·sive
ap·pre·hen·sive·ly

ap·pre·hen·sive·ness
ap·pren·tice
ap·pren·ticed
ap·pren·tic·ing
ap·pren·tice·ship
ap·prise
ap·prize
ap·prised
ap·pris·ing
ap·proach
ap·proach·a·bil·i·ty
ap·proach·a·ble
ap·pro·ba·tion
ap·pro·ba·tive
ap·pro·ba·to·ry
ap·pro·pri·ate
ap·pro·pri·at·ed
ap·pro·pri·at·ing
ap·pro·pri·ate·ly
ap·pro·pri·ate·ness
ap·pro·pri·a·tor
ap·pro·pri·a·tion
ap·pro·pri·a·tive
ap·prov·al
ap·prove
ap·proved
ap·prov·ing
ap·prov·a·ble
ap·prov·er
ap·prov·ing·ly
ap·prox·i·mate
ap·prox·i·mate·ly
ap·prox·i·ma·tion
ap·pur·te·nance
ap·pur·te·nant
ap·ri·cot
April
a pri·o·ri
apron
ap·ro·pos
apt
apt·ly
apt·ness
ap·ter·ous
ap·ti·tude
aq·ua
aq·uas
aq·uae
aqua·cul·ture
Aq·ua·lung
aq·ua·ma·rine
aq·ua·naut
aq·ua·plane
aquar·i·um
aquar·i·ums
aquar·ia
Aquar·i·us
aquat·ic
aq·ua·tint
aq·ue·duct
aque·ous
Aq·ui·la
aq·ui·line
Aqui·nas
Aq·ui·taine

Ar·ab
Ara·bia
 Ara·bi·an
ar·a·besque
Ar·a·bic
Ar·ab·ist
ar·a·ble
Arach·ne
arach·nid
 arach·ni·dan
Ar·a·gon
Ar·al
Ar·a·ma·ic
Ar·a·min·ta
Arap·a·ho
Ar·a·rat
Ar·as
ar·ba·lest
 ar·ba·list
 ar·ba·lest·er
ar·bi·ter
ar·bi·tral
ar·bit·ra·ment
ar·bi·trary
 ar·bi·trar·i·ly
 ar·bi·trar·i·ness
ar·bi·trate
 ar·bi·trat·ed
 ar·bi·trat·ing
 ar·bi·tra·ble
 ar·bi·tra·tor
 ar·bi·tra·tion
ar·bor
ar·bo·re·al
ar·bo·res·cent
ar·bo·re·tum
 ar·bo·re·tums
 ar·bo·re·ta
ar·bor·vi·tae
ar·bu·tus
arc
 arced
 arcked
 arc·ing
 arck·ing
ar·cade
Ar·ca·dia
ar·cane
arch
 arch·ly
 arch·ness
ar·chae·ol·o·gy
ar·che·ol·o·gy
ar·chae·o·log·i·cal
ar·che·o·log·i·cal
ar·chae·ol·o·gist
ar·che·ol·o·gist
Ar·chae·o·zo·ic
Ar·che·o·zo·ic
ar·cha·ic
ar·cha·ism
ar·cha·ist
ar·cha·is·tic
arch·an·gel
arch·bish·op

arch·bish·op·ric
arch·dea·con
arch·di·o·cese
 arch·di·oc·e·san
arch·du·cal
arch·duch·ess
arch·duchy
 arch·duch·ies
arch·duke
Ar·che·an
arch·en·e·my
 arch·en·e·mies
arch·er
ar·chery
ar·che·type
 ar·che·typ·al
 ar·che·typ·i·cal
arch·fiend
ar·chi·e·pis·co·pate
 ar·chi·e·pis·co·pal
Ar·chi·me·de·an
Ar·chi·me·des
ar·chi·pel·a·go
 ar·chi·pel·a·goes
 ar·chi·pel·a·gos
ar·chi·tect
ar·chi·tec·ton·ic
ar·chi·tec·ture
 ar·chi·tec·tur·al
ar·chi·trave
ar·chive
 ar·chi·val
ar·chi·vist
ar·chon
arch·priest
arch·way
arc·tic
 arc·tic cir·cle
Arc·tu·rus
ar·dent
 ar·dent·ly
ar·dor
ar·du·ous
 ar·du·ous·ly
 ar·du·ous·ness
ar·ea
ar·e·al
are·a·way
are·na
are·o·la
 are·o·lae
 are·o·las
Ar·e·op·a·gus
Ar·e·thu·sa
ar·gent
Ar·gen·ti·na
ar·gen·tine
ar·gil
Ar·give
Ar·go·lis
ar·gon
Ar·go·naut
Ar·gonne
Ar·gos
ar·go·sy

ar·go·sies
ar·got
ar·got·ic
ar·gue
 ar·gued
 ar·gu·ing
 ar·gu·a·ble
 ar·gu·er
ar·gu·ment
ar·gu·men·ta·tion
ar·gu·men·ta·tive
Ar·gus
ar·gyle
ar·gyll
aria
Ar·i·an
ar·id
 arid·i·ty
Ar·i·el
A·ri·es
aright
arise
 arose
aris·en
aris·ing
Ar·is·ti·des
ar·is·toc·ra·cy
 ar·is·toc·ra·cies
aris·to·crat
aris·to·crat·ic
Ar·is·toph·a·nes
Ar·is·tot·le
arith·me·tic
 ar·ith·met·i·cal
 ar·ith·met·i·cal·ly
arith·me·ti·cian
Ar·i·zo·na
Ar·kan·sas
Ar·ling·ton
ar·ma·da
ar·ma·dil·lo
Ar·ma·ged·don
ar·ma·ment
ar·ma·ture
arm·chair
armed forc·es
Ar·me·nia
Ar·men·tieres
arm·ful
arm·hole
ar·mi·stice
arm·let
ar·moire
ar·mor
ar·mored
ar·mor·er
ar·mory
 ar·mor·ies
arm·pit
Arm·strong
ar·my
 ar·mies
ar·ni·ca
Ar·nold
aro·ma

ar·o·mat·ic
ar·o·mat·i·cal
around
arouse
aroused
arous·ing
arous·al
ar·peg·gio
ar·peg·gi·os
ar·raign
ar·raign·ment
ar·range
ar·ranged
ar·rang·ing
ar·rang·er
ar·range·ment
ar·rant
ar·rant·ly
ar·ras
ar·ray
ar·rear
ar·rest
ar·rest·er
ar·rest·or
ar·ri·val
ar·rive
ar·rived
ar·riv·ing
ar·ro·gant
ar·ro·gance
ar·ro·gant·ly
ar·ro·gate
ar·ro·gat·ed
ar·ro·gat·ing
ar·ro·ga·tion
ar·row
ar·row·head
ar·row·root
ar·royo
ar·roy·os
ar·se·nal
ar·se·nate
ar·se·nic
ar·son
ar·son·ist
Ar·te·mis
ar·te·ri·al
ar·te·ri·o·scle·ro·sis
ar·tery
ar·ter·ies
ar·te·sian well
art·ful
art·ful·ly
art·ful·ness
ar·thri·tis
ar·thrit·ic
ar·thro·pod
ar·throp·o·dal
ar·throp·o·dous
Ar·thur
Ar·thu·ri·an
ar·ti·choke
ar·ti·cle
ar·tic·u·lar
ar·tic·u·late

ar·tic·u·lat·ed
ar·tic·u·lat·ing
ar·tic·u·late·ly
ar·tic·u·late·ness
ar·tic·u·la·tor
ar·tic·u·la·tion
ar·tic·u·la·to·ry
ar·ti·fact
ar·te·fact
ar·ti·fice
ar·tif·i·cer
ar·ti·fi·cial
ar·ti·fi·ci·al·i·ty
ar·ti·fi·cial·ly
ar·ti·fi·cial·ness
ar·ti·fi·cial res·pi·ra·tion
ar·til·lery
ar·til·ler·ist
ar·ti·san
art·ist
ar·tiste
ar·tis·tic
ar·tis·ti·cal·ly
art·ist·ry
art·less
art·less·ly
art·less·ness
arty
ar·ti·ness
Ar·y·an
as·bes·tos
as·bes·tus
As·bu·ry
as·cend
as·cend·ance
as·cend·ence
as·cend·an·cy
as·cend·en·cy
as·cend·ant
as·cend·ent
as·cen·sion
as·cent
as·cer·tain
as·cer·tain·a·ble
as·cer·tain·ment
as·cet·ic
as·cet·i·cal
as·cet·i·cism
As·cham
as·cot
as·cribe
as·cribed
as·crib·ing
as·crib·a·ble
as·crip·tion
asep·sis
asep·tic
asex·u·al
asex·u·al·i·ty
asex·u·al·ly
As·gard
ashamed
asham·ed·ly
ash·en
Ashe·ville

ash·lar
ash·ler
ashore
ashy
Asi·at·ic
aside
as·i·nine
askance
askew
aslant
asleep
aslope
aso·cial
as·par·a·gus
as·pect
as·pen
as·per·i·ty
as·perse
as·persed
as·pers·ing
as·per·sion
as·phalt
as·phal·tic
as·pho·del
as·phyx·ia
as·phyx·i·ate
as·phyx·i·at·ed
as·phyx·i·at·ing
as·phyx·i·a·tion
as·pic
as·pi·dis·tra
as·pir·ant
as·pi·rate
as·pi·rat·ed
as·pi·rat·ing
as·pi·ra·tion
as·pi·ra·tor
as·pire
as·pired
as·pir·ing
as·pir·er
as·pi·rin
as·sail
as·sail·a·ble
as·sail·ant
As·sam
as·sas·sin
as·sas·si·nate
as·sas·si·nat·ed
as·sas·si·nat·ing
as·sas·si·na·tion
as·sas·si·na·tor
as·sault
as·say
as·say·er
as·sem·blage
as·sem·ble
as·sem·bled
as·sem·bling
as·sem·bler
as·sem·bly
as·sem·blies
as·sem·bly·man
as·sem·bly·men
as·sent

as·sent·er
as·sert
　as·ser·tion
　as·sert·er
　as·ser·tive
　as·ser·tive·ly
　as·ser·tive·ness
as·sess
　as·sess·a·ble
　as·sess·ment
　as·sess·or
as·set
as·sev·er·ate
　as·sev·er·at·ed
　as·sev·er·at·ing
　as·sev·er·a·tion
as·si·du·i·ty
as·sid·u·ous
　as·sid·u·ous·ly
　as·sid·u·ous·ness
as·sign
　as·sign·a·bil·i·ty
　as·sign·a·ble
　as·sign·a·bly
　as·sig·na·tion
　as·sign·ee
　as·sign·ment
as·sim·i·late
　as·sim·i·lat·ed
　as·sim·i·lat·ing
　as·sim·i·la·bil·i·ty
　as·sim·i·la·ble
　as·sim·i·la·tion
　as·sim·i·la·tive
　as·sim·i·la·tor
as·sist
　as·sist·ance
　as·sis·tant
as·size
as·so·ci·ate
　as·so·ci·at·ed
　as·so·ci·at·ing
　as·so·ci·a·tion
　as·so·ci·a·tive
as·so·nance
as·sort
　as·sort·ed
　as·sort·ment
as·suage
　as·suaged
　as·suag·ing
　as·suage·ment
as·sume
　as·sumed
　as·sum·ing
as·sump·tion
　as·sump·tive
as·sur·ance
as·sure
　as·sured
　as·sur·ing
　as·sur·er
　as·sur·ed·ly
　as·sur·ed·ness
As·syr·ia

as·ter
　as·ter·isk
astern
　as·ter·oid
　as·ter·oi·dal
asth·ma
asth·mat·ic
astig·ma·tism
　as·tig·mat·ic
astir
as·ton·ish
　as·ton·ish·ing
　as·ton·ish·ing·ly
　as·ton·ish·ment
As·tor
As·to·ria
as·tound
　as·tound·ing
astrad·dle
as·tra·khan
as·tral
astray
astride
as·trin·gent
　as·trin·gen·cy
as·tro·dome
as·tro·labe
as·trol·o·gy
　as·trol·o·ger
as·tro·log·ic
　as·tro·log·i·cal
　as·tro·log·i·cal·ly
as·tro·naut
as·tro·nau·tics
　as·tro·nau·ti·cal
as·tro·nom·ic
　as·tro·nom·i·cal·ly
as·tron·o·my
　as·tron·o·mer
as·tro·phys·ics
　as·tro·phys·i·cist
as·tute
　as·tute·ly
　as·tute·ness
asun·der
asy·lum
asym·me·try
　asym·met·ric
　asym·met·ri·cal
　asym·met·ri·cal·ly
at·a·vism
　at·a·vist
　at·a·vis·tic
atax·ia
　atax·ic
Atch·i·son
at·el·ier
Ath·a·na·si·us
athe·ism
　athe·ist
　athe·is·tic
　athe·is·ti·cal
　athe·is·ti·cal·ly
Athe·na
Ath·ens

ath·er·o·scle·ro·sis
athirst
ath·lete
ath·let·ic
ath·let·ics
Ath·os
athwart
atilt
At·lan·ta
At·lan·tic
at·las
　at·las·es
at·mos·phere
　at·mos·pher·ic
　at·mos·pher·i·cal
　at·mos·pher·i·cal·ly
　at·mos·pher·ics
at·oll
at·om
　atom·ic
　atom·i·cal
　atom·i·cal·ly
at·om·ize
　at·om·ized
　at·om·iz·ing
　at·om·iz·er
ato·nal·i·ty
ato·nal
　ato·nal·ly
atone
　atoned
　aton·ing
atone·ment
aton·er
atop
atri·um
atro·cious
　atro·cious·ly
　atro·cious·ness
atroc·i·ty
　atroc·i·ties
at·ro·phy
　at·ro·phies
　at·ro·phied
　at·ro·phy·ing
atroph·ic
at·ro·pine
At·ro·pos
at·tach
　at·tach·a·ble
　at·tach·ment
at·ta·ché
at·tack
at·tain
　at·tain·a·ble
　at·tain·a·bil·i·ty
　at·tain·a·ble·ness
　at·tain·ment
at·tain·der
at·taint
at·tar
at·tempt
　at·tempt·a·ble
at·tend
　at·tend·ance

at·tend·ant
at·ten·tion
at·ten·tive
at·ten·u·ate
at·ten·u·at·ed
at·ten·u·at·ing
at·ten·u·a·tion
at·test
at·tes·ta·tion
at·tic
At·ti·ca
At·ti·la
at·tire
at·tired
at·tir·ing
at·ti·tude
at·ti·tu·di·nize
at·ti·tu·di·nized
at·ti·tu·di·niz·ing
at·tor·ney
at·tor·neys
at·tor·ney gen·er·al
at·tract
at·tract·a·ble
at·trac·tive
at·tract·or
at·trac·tion
at·tri·bute
at·tri·but·ed
at·tri·but·ing
at·tri·but·a·ble
at·tri·bu·tion
at·trib·u·tive
at·tri·tion
at·tune
at·tuned
at·tun·ing
atyp·i·cal
atyp·ic
atyp·i·cal·ly
au·burn
au cou·rant
auc·tion
auc·tion·eer
au·da·cious
au·da·cious·ness
au·dac·i·ty
au·di·ble
au·di·ble·ness
au·di·bly
au·di·ence
au·dio
au·di·o·vis·u·al
au·dit
au·di·tion
au·dit·or
au·di·to·ri·um
au·di·to·ry
Au·du·bon
au·ger
aug·ment
aug·ment·a·ble
aug·ment·er
aug·men·ta·tion
aug·ment·a·tive

au grat·in
Augs·burg
au·gur
au·gu·ry
au·gu·ries
au·gust
au·gust·ly
au·gust·ness
Au·gust
Au·gus·ta
Au·gus·tine
Au·gus·tus
auk
auld lang syne
au na·tu·rel
aunt
au·ra
au·ras
au·rae
au·ral
au·ral·ly
au·re·ate
au·re·ole
Au·re·o·my·cin
au re·voir
au·ri·cle
au·ric·u·lar
au·rif·er·ous
au·ro·ra
au·ro·ra bor·e·al·is
aus·cul·tate
aus·cul·tat·ed
aus·cul·tat·ing
aus·cul·ta·tion
aus·pice
aus·pic·es
aus·pi·cious
aus·pi·cious·ly
aus·pi·cious·ness
aus·tere
aus·ter·i·ty
aus·ter·i·ties
Aus·ter·litz
Aus·tin
aus·tral
Aus·tra·lia
Aus·tra·lian
Aus·tria
Aus·tri·an
au·then·tic
au·then·ti·cate
au·then·ti·cat·ed
au·then·ti·cat·ing
au·then·ti·ca·tion
au·then·tic·i·ty
au·then·ti·ca·tor
au·thor
au·thor·i·tar·i·an
au·thor·i·tar·i·an·ism
au·thor·i·ta·tive
au·thor·i·ta·tive·ness
au·thor·i·ty
au·thor·i·ties
au·thor·ize
au·thor·ized

au·thor·iz·ing
au·thor·i·za·tion
au·thor·ship
au·to
au·to·bi·og·ra·phy
au·to·bi·og·ra·phies
au·to·bi·og·ra·pher
au·to·bi·o·graph·ic
au·to·bi·o·graph·i·cal
au·to·bi·o·graph·i·cal·ly
au·toc·ra·cy
au·toc·ra·cies
au·to·crat
au·to·crat·ic
au·to·crat·i·cal
au·to·crat·i·cal·ly
au·to-da-fé
au·tos-da-fé
au·to·graph
au·to·mat
au·to·mat·ic
au·to·ma·tion
au·to·mate
au·to·mat·ed
au·to·mat·ing
au·tom·a·tism
au·tom·a·ton
au·tom·a·tons
au·tom·a·ta
au·to·mo·bile
au·to·mo·tive
au·to·nom·ic
au·to·nom·i·cal·ly
au·ton·o·mous
au·ton·o·mous·ly
au·ton·o·my
au·ton·o·mies
au·ton·o·mist
au·top·sy
au·to·sug·ges·tion
au·tumn
au·tum·nal
Au·vergne
aux·il·ia·ry
aux·il·ia·ries
avail
avail·a·bil·i·ty
avail·a·ble
avail·a·ble·ness
avail·a·bly
av·a·lanche
av·a·lanched
av·a·lanch·ing
Av·a·lon
avant-garde
av·a·rice
av·a·ri·cious
av·a·ri·cious·ly
av·a·ri·cious·ness
avast
av·a·tar
ave
Ave Ma·ria
avenge
avenged

aveng·ing
aveng·er
Av·en·tine
av·e·nue
aver
averred
aver·ring
aver·ment
av·er·age
av·er·aged
av·er·ag·ing
averse
averse·ly
averse·ness
aver·sion
avert
avi·ary
avi·ar·ies
avi·a·rist
avi·a·tion
avi·a·tor
av·id
avid·i·ty
av·id·ly
Avi·gnon
avi·on·ics
av·o·ca·do
av·o·ca·dos
av·o·ca·tion
avoid
avoid·a·ble
avoid·ance
av·oir·du·pois
avouch
avow
avow·er
avow·al
avowed
avun·cu·lar
await
awake
awoke
awaked
awak·ing
awak·en
awak·en·ing
award
award·a·ble
award·er
aware
aware·ness
awash
away
awe
awed
aw·ing
aweigh
awe·some
awe·some·ly
awe·some·ness
awe·strick·en
awe·struck
aw·ful
aw·ful·ly
aw·ful·ness

awhile
awk·ward
awk·ward·ly
awk·ward·ness
awn
awned
awn·less
awn·ing
awry
ax
ax·es
ax·i·al
ax·i·al·ly
ax·i·om
ax·i·o·mat·ic
ax·i·o·mat·i·cal
ax·i·o·mat·i·cal·ly
ax·is
ax·es
ax·le
Ayr·shire
azal·ea
az·i·muth
az·i·muth·al
Az·tec
az·ure
Ba·al
bab·bitt
bab·ble
bab·bled
bab·bling
bab·bler
ba·bel
ba·boon
ba·bush·ka
ba·by
ba·bies
ba·bied
ba·by·ing
ba·by·hood
ba·by·ish
Bab·y·lon
Bab·y·lo·nia
ba·by·sit
ba·by·sat
ba·by·sit·ting
ba·by·sit·ter
bac·ca·lau·re·ate
bac·ca·rat
bac·cha·nal
bac·cha·na·li·an
bac·chant
bac·chan·te
Bac·chus
bach·e·lor
bach·e·lor·hood
bac·il·lary
ba·cil·lus
ba·cil·li
back·bite
back·bit
back·bit·ten
back·bit·ing
back·bit·er
back·board

back·bone
back·drop
back·er
back·field
back·fire
back·fired
back·fir·ing
back·gam·mon
back·ground
back·hand
back·hand·ed
back·ing
back·lash
back·log
back·side
back·slide
back·slid
back·slid·den
back·slid·ing
back·slid·er
back·spin
back·stage
back·stairs
back·stay
back·stop
back·stretch
back·stroke
back·talk
back·track
back·up
back·ward
back·wards
back·ward·ness
back·wash
back·wa·ter
back·woods
back·woods·man
ba·con
bac·te·ria
bac·ter·i·um
bac·te·ri·al
bac·te·ri·al·ly
bac·te·ri·cide
bac·te·ri·ci·dal
bac·te·ri·ol·o·gy
bac·te·ri·ol·o·gist
bac·te·ri·o·log·i·cal
bac·te·ri·o·phage
bad
worse
worst
badge
badged
badg·ing
badg·er
bad·i·nage
bad·land
bad·lands
bad·ly
bad·min·ton
Bae·de·ker
baf·fle
baf·fled
baf·fling
baf·fler

bag	bal·kan·ized	band·mas·ter
bagged	bal·kan·iz·ing	ban·do·leer
bag·ging	bal·kan·i·za·tion	ban·do·lier
ba·gasse	balky	bands·man
bag·a·telle	balk·i·er	bands·men
Bag·dad	balk·i·est	band·stand
ba·gel	bal·lad	band·wag·on
bag·gage	bal·lade	ban·dy
bag·gy	bal·lad·ry	ban·died
bag·gi·er	bal·last	ban·dy·ing
bag·gi·est	ball bear·ing	ban·dy·leg·ged
Bagh·dad	bal·le·ri·na	bane·ful
bag·man	bal·let	bane·ful·ness
ba·gnio	Bal·li·ol	Bang·kok
bag·pipe	bal·lis·tic	Ban·gla·desh
bag·pi·per	bal·lis·tics	ban·gle
ba·guette	bal·lis·ti·cian	Ban·gor
Ba·hai	bal·loon	Ban·gui
Ba·ha·ma	bal·lot	ban·ish
Ba·hia	bal·lot·ed	ban·ish·ment
Bah·rain	bal·lot·ing	ban·is·ter
bail·iff	ball·room	ban·nis·ter
bail·i·wick	bal·ly·hoo	ban·jo
bails·man	balm	Ban·jul
bails·men	Bal·mor·al	bank
bake	balmy	bank·book
baked	balm·i·er	bank·er
bak·ing	balm·i·est	bank·ing
Ba·ke·lite	balm·i·ly	bank·roll
bak·er	balm·i·ness	bank·rupt
bak·er·y	ba·lo·ney	bank·rupt·cy
bak·er·ies	bal·sa	bank·rupt·cies
bak·ing pow·der	bal·sam	ban·ner
bak·ing so·da	Bal·tic	ban·quet
bak·sheesh	Bal·ti·more	ban·quet·er
bak·shish	Ba·lu·chi·stan	ban·quette
Ba·laam	bal·us·ter	Ban·quo
bal·a·lai·ka	bal·us·trade	ban·shee
bal·ance	Bal·zac	ban·tam
bal·anced	Ba·ma·ko	ban·tam·weight
bal·anc·ing	bam·bi·no	ban·ter
bal·anc·er	bam·bi·nos	ban·ter·er
Bal·boa	bam·boo	ban·ter·ing·ly
bal·brig·gan	bam·boo·zle	Ban·ting
bal·co·ny	bam·boo·zled	Ban·tu
bal·co·nies	bam·boo·zling	ban·yan
bald	bam·boo·zler	ban·ian
bald·ly	ban	ban·zal
bald·ness	banned	ba·o·bab
bal·der·dash	ban·ning	bap·tism
bald·head	ba·nal	bap·tis·mal
bal·dric	ba·nal·i·ty	bap·tist
Bald·win	ba·nana	bap·tis·tery
bale	band·age	bap·tis·ter·ies
baled	band·aged	bap·tize
bal·ing	band·ag·ing	bap·tized
ba·leen	ban·dana	bap·tiz·ing
bale·ful	ban·dan·na	bar
bale·ful·ly	ban·deau	barred
Bal·four	ban·deaux	bar·ring
Ba·li	ban·de·role	Bar·ab·bas
balk	ban·dit	Ba·raca
balk·er	ban·dits	Bar·ba·dos
Bal·kan	ban·dit·ti	bar·bar·i·an
bal·kan·ize	ban·dit·ry	bar·bar·ic

bar·ba·rism
bar·bar·i·ty
  bar·bar·i·ties
bar·ba·rize
  bar·ba·rized
  bar·ba·riz·ing
Bar·ba·ros·sa
bar·ba·rous
Bar·ba·ry
bar·be·cue
  bar·be·cued
  bar·be·cu·ing
bar·ber
bar·ber·ry
  bar·ber·ries
bar·ber·shop
bar·bi·tal
bar·bi·tu·rate
bar·bi·tur·ic
Bar·bi·zon
Bar·busse
bar·ca·role
Bar·ce·lo·na
bare
  bar·er
  bar·est
  bare·ness
bare·back
bare·faced
bare·foot
bare·hand·ed
bare·head·ed
bare·ly
bar·gain
  bar·gain·er
barge
  barged
  barg·ing
bar·i·tone
bar·i·um
bar·keep·er
bar·ken·tine
bark·er
bar·ley
  bar·leys
bar·maid
bar·man
  bar·men
bar mitz·vah
barmy
Bar·na·bas
bar·na·cle
barn·storm
  barn·storm·er
  barn·storm·ing
Bar·num
barn·yard
bar·o·graph
ba·rom·et·er
bar·o·met·ric
  bar·o·met·ric·al
bar·on
ba·ro·ni·al
bar·on·age
bar·on·ess

bar·on·et
  bar·on·et·age
  bar·on·et·cy
bar·o·ny
  bar·o·nies
ba·roque
barque
bar·quen·tine
bar·rack
bar·ra·cu·da
  bar·ra·cu·das
bar·rage
  bar·raged
  bar·rag·ing
bar·ra·try
  bar·ra·tries
bar·ra·tor
bar·ra·trous
bar·rel
  bar·reled
  bar·relled
  bar·rel·ing
  bar·rel·ling
bar·ren
  bar·ren·ly
  bar·ren·ness
bar·rette
bar·ri·cade
  bar·ri·cad·ed
  bar·ri·cad·ing
bar·ri·er
bar·ring
bar·rio
  bar·ri·os
bar·ris·ter
bar·room
bar·row
bar·ten·der
bar·ter
  bar·ter·er
Bar·thol·o·mew
Bar·uch
ba·sai
bas·al·ly
ba·salt
base
  based
  bas·ing
base·ball
base·board
base·born
Ba·sel
base·less
base·ment
bash·ful
  bash·ful·ly
  bash·ful·ness
ba·sic
  ba·si·cal·ly
ba·sil
ba·sil·i·ca
bas·i·lisk
ba·sin
ba·sis
  ba·ses

bas·ket
bas·ket·ball
bas·ket·ry
bas-re·lief
bas·si·net
bas·so
  bas·sos
bas·soon
bass·wood
bas·tard
  bas·tard·ize
  bas·tard·ized
  bas·tard·iz·ing
  bas·tard·ly
baste
  bast·ed
  bast·ing
bas·tille
bas·ti·on
  bas·ti·oned
Ba·su·to·land
bat
  bat·ted
  bat·ting
  bat·ter
Ba·ta·via
bate
  bat·ed
  bat·ing
bathe
  bathed
  bath·ing
  bath·er
bath·robe
Bath·she·ba
Bath·urst
bath·y·scaphe
bath·y·sphere
ba·tik
ba·tiste
bat·on
Bat·on Rouge
bat·tal·ion
bat·ten
bat·ter
bat·tery
bat·tle
  bat·tled
  bat·tling
bat·tle·field
bat·tle·ment
bat·ty
  bat·ti·er
  bat·ti·est
Bat·um
bau·ble
Bau·douin
baux·ite
Ba·va·ria
bawdy
  bawd·i·er
  bawd·i·est
Ba·yeux
bay·o·net
  bay·o·net·ed

bay·o·net·ing
Ba·yonne
bay·ou
Bay·reuth
ba·zaar
ba·zoo·ka
beach
beach·comb·er
beach·head
bea·con
bead
 bead·ed
 bead·like
beady
 bead·i·er
 bead·i·est
beak
 beaked
beak·er
beam
 beamed
bear
 bore
 borne
 bear·ing
 bear·a·ble
 bear·a·bly
 bear·er
beard
 beard·ed
 beard·less
bear·ing
bear·ish
bear·skin
beast
 beast·li·ness
 beast·ly
 beast·li·er
 beast·li·est
beat
 beat·en
 beat·ing
 beat·er
be·a·tif·ic
be·at·i·fy
 be·at·i·fied
 be·at·i·fy·ing
 be·at·i·fi·ca·tion
be·at·i·tude
beat·nik
beau
 beaus
 beaux
Beau·fort
beau geste
 beaux gestes
Beau·mar·chais
Beau·mont
Beau·re·gard
beau·te·ous
 beau·te·ous·ly
beau·ti·cian
beau·ti·fy
 beau·ti·fied
 beau·ti·fy·ing

beau·ti·fi·ca·tion
 beau·ti·fi·er
beauty
 beau·ti·ful
 beau·ti·ful·ly
beaux-arts
bea·ver
be·calm
be·cause
Bech·u·an·a·land
Beck·et
beck·on
be·cloud
be·qome
 be·came
 be·com·ing
 be·com·ing·ly
bed
 bed·ded
 bed·ding
be·daub
be·daz·zle
 be·daz·zled
 be·daz·zling
 be·daz·zle·ment
bed·bug
bed·clothes
be·deck
be·dev·il
 be·dev·iled
 be·dev·il·ing
 be·dev·il·ment
be·dew
bed·fast
bed·fel·low
Bed·ford
be·dim
 be·dimmed
 be·dim·ming
bed·lam
Bed·ou·in
bed·pan
be·drag·gle
 be·drag·gled
 be·drag·gling
bed·rid·den
bed·rock
bed·room
bed·side
bed·sore
bed·spread
bed·spring
bed·stead
bed·time
bee·bread
beech
beef
 beefs
 beeves
beef·eat·er
beef·steak
beefy
 beef·i·er
 beef·i·est
bee·hive

bee·line
Beel·ze·bub
Beer·she·ba
beery
 beer·i·er
 beer·i·est
beest·ings
bees·wax
Bee·tho·ven
bee·tle
 bee·tled
 bee·tling
bee·tle-browed
be·fall
 be·fell
 be·fall·en
 be·fall·ing
be·fit
 be·fit·ted
 be·fit·ting
be·fog
 be·fogged
 be·fog·ging
be·fore
 be·fore·hand
be·foul
be·friend
be·fud·dle
 be·fud·dled
 be·fud·dling
beg
 begged
 beg·ging
be·get
 be·got
 be·got·ten
 be·get·ter
beg·gar
 beg·gar·dom
 beg·gar·hood
 beg·gar·ly
be·gin
 be·gan
 be·gun
 be·gin·ning
 be·gin·ner
be·go·nia
be·grime
 be·grimed
 be·grim·ing
be·grudge
 be·grudged
 be·grudg·ing
 be·grudg·ing·ly
be·guile
 be·guiled
 be·guil·ing
 be·guil·er
be·half
be·have
 be·haved
 be·hav·ing
be·hav·ior
 be·hav·ior·ism
 be·hav·ior·ist

24

be·hav·ior·is·tic
be·head
be·he·moth
be·hest
be·hind
be·hind-hand
be·hold
be·held
be·hold·ing
be·hold·er
be·hold·en
be·hoove
be·hooved
be·hoov·ing
Beh·ring
beige
be·ing
Bei·rut
be·la·bor
be·lat·ed
be·lat·ed·ly
be·lat·ed·ness
be·lay
be·layed
be·lay·ing
belch
be·lea·guer
Bel·fast
Bel·fort
bel·fry
bel·fries
Bel·gian
Bel·gium
Bel·grade
be·lie
be·lied
be·ly·ing
be·lief
be·lieve
be·lieved
be·liev·ing
be·liev·a·ble
be·liev·er
be·lit·tle
be·lit·tled
be·lit·tling
bel·la·don·na
bell·boy
Bel·leau
belles let·tres
bell·hop
bel·li·cose
bel·li·cos·i·ty
bel·lig·er·ence
bel·lig·er·en·cy
bel·lig·er·ent
bel·lig·er·ent·ly
Bel·loc
bel·low
bel·lows
bell·weth·er
bel·ly
bel·lies
bel·lied
bel·ly·ing

bel·ly·ache
bel·ly·ached
bel·ly·ach·ing
bel·ly·but·ton
Bel·mont
be·long
be·long·ings
be·loved
be·low
Bel·shaz·zar
belt
belt·ed
belt·way
be·lu·ga
Be·midji
be·mire
be·mired
be·mir·ing
be·moan
be·muse
be·mused
be·mus·ing
be·mused
Be·na·res
bench
bend
bent
bend·ing
bend·er
be·neath
ben·e·dict
Ben·e·dic·tine
ben·e·dic·tion
ben·e·dic·to·ry
ben·e·fac·tion
ben·e·fac·tor
ben·e·fac·tress
be·nef·ic
ben·e·fice
ben·e·ficed
ben·e·fic·ing
be·nef·i·cent
be·nef·i·cence
ben·e·fi·cial
ben·e·fi·cial·ly
ben·e·fi·ci·ar·y
ben·e·fi·ci·ar·ies
ben·e·fit
ben·e·fit·ed
ben·e·fit·ing
Be·nes
be·nev·o·lence
be·nev·o·lent
be·nev·o·lent·ly
Ben·gal
Ben-Gu·rion
be·night·ed
be·nign
be·nig·ni·ty
be·nig·ni·ties
be·nign·ly
be·nig·nant
be·nig·nan·cy
be·nig·nan·cies
ben·i·son

Ben·ja·min
Ben·ning·ton
ben·ny
ben·nies
be·numb
Be·o·wulf
ben·zene
ben·zine
ben·zo·ate
ben·zo·in
ben·zol
be·queath
be·quest
be·rate
be·rat·ed
be·rat·ing
Ber·ber
ber·ceuse
be·reave
be·reaved
be·reft
be·reav·ing
Ber·es·ford
be·ret
ber·ga·mot
Ber·gen
Ber·ge·rac
ber·i·beri
Ber·ing
Berke·ley
berke·li·um
Berk·ley
Berk·shire
Ber·lin
Ber·mu·das
Bern·hardt
ber·ry
ber·ries
ber·ried
ber·ry·ing
ber·serk
berth
ber·tha
ber·yl
be·ryl·li·um
be·seech
be·sought
be·seeched
be·seech·ing
be·seech·ing·ly
be·set
be·set·ting
be·side
be·sides
be·siege
be·sieged
be·sieg·ing
be·sieg·er
be·smear
be·smirch
bes·om
be·sot
be·sot·ted
be·sot·ting
be·spat·ter

be·speak
be·spoke
be·spok·en
be·speak·ing
Bes·sa·ra·bia
Bes·se·mer
best
bes·tial
bes·tial·ly
bes·ti·al·i·ty
bes·ti·al·i·ties
be·stir
be·stirred
be·stir·ring
be·stow
be·stow·al
be·strew
be·stride
be·strode
be·strid·den
be·strid·ing
bet
bet·ted
bet·ting
be·ta
be·take
be·took
be·tak·en
be·tak·ing
be·ta·tron
be·tel
Be·tel·geuse
Beth·a·ny
beth·el
Be·thes·da
Beth·le·hem
Beth·sa·i·da
be·tide
be·tid·ed
be·tid·ing
be·to·ken
be·tray
be·tray·al
be·tray·er
be·troth
be·troth·al
be·trothed
bet·ter
bet·ter·ment
bet·tor
be·tween
be·twixt
bev·el
bev·eled
bev·el·ing
bev·er·age
bevy
bev·ies
be·wail
be·ware
be·wil·der
be·wil·der·ing·ly
be·wil·der·ment
be·witch
be·witch·er

be·witch·ery
be·witch·ing
be·witch·ing·ly
be·witch·ment
be·yond
be·zique
Bhu·tan
bi·an·nu·al
bi·as
bi·ased
bi·as·ing
bi·ax·i·al
bi·ax·i·al·ly
bi·be·lot
Bi·ble
Bib·li·cal
Bib·li·cal·ly
bib·li·og·ra·phy
bib·li·og·ra·phies
bib·li·og·ra·pher
bib·li·o·graph·ic
bib·li·o·ma·nia
bib·li·o·ma·ni·ac
bib·li·o·phile
bib·u·lous
bi·cam·er·al
bi·car·bo·nate
bi·cen·te·nary
bi·cen·te·nar·ies
bi·cen·ten·ni·al
bi·ceps
bi·chlo·ride
bick·er
bi·con·cave
bi·con·vex
bi·cus·pid
bi·cus·pi·dal
bi·cus·pi·date
bi·cy·cle
bi·cy·cled
bi·cy·cling
bi·cy·cler
bi·cy·clist
bid
bade
bid·den
bid·ding
bid·da·ble
bid·der
Bid·de·ford
bid·dy
bid·dies
bide
bid·ed
bid·ing
Bid·e·ford
bi·en·ni·al
bi·en·ni·al·ly
bier
bi·fid
bi·fo·cal
bi·fo·cals
bi·fur·cate
bi·fur·cat·ed
bi·fur·cat·ing

bi·fur·ca·tion
big
big·ger
big·gest
big·a·my
big·a·mies
big·a·mist
big·a·mous
big·heart·ed
big·horn
big·no·nia
big·ot
big·ot·ed
big·ot·ed·ly
big·ot·ry
big·ot·ries
bi·jou
bi·joux
bi·ju·gous
bi·ki·ni
bi·la·bi·al
bi·la·bi·ate
bi·lat·er·al
bi·lat·er·al·ly
Bil·bao
bil·ber·ry
bil·ber·ries
bil·i·ary
bi·lin·gual
bil·ious
bill
billed
bill·ing
bil·la·bong
bill·board
bil·let
bil·let-doux
bill·fold
bill·hook
bil·liards
bil·lings·gate
bil·lion
bil·lion·aire
bil·low
bil·low·y
bil·low·i·er
bil·low·i·est
bi·met·al·lism
bi·met·al·list
bi·me·tal·lic
bi·month·ly
bi·month·lies
bi·na·ry
bi·nate
bin·au·ral
bind
bound
bind·ing
bind·er
bind·ery
bind·er·ies
Bi·net
binge
Bing·ham·ton
bin·go

bin·na·cle
bi·noc·u·lar
bi·no·mi·al
bi·o·chem·is·try
bi·o·chem·i·cal
bi·o·chem·ist
bi·o·e·col·o·gy
bi·o·en·gi·neer·ing
bi·o·gen·e·sis
bi·o·ge·net·ic
bi·og·ra·phy
bi·og·ra·pher
bi·o·graph·ic
bi·o·graph·i·cal
bi·o·graph·i·cal·ly
bi·ol·o·gy
bi·o·log·i·cal
bi·ol·o·gist
bi·o·met·rics
bi·om·e·try
bi·o·met·rics
bi·o·nom·ics
bi·o·phys·ics
bi·o·phys·i·cal
bi·o·phys·i·cist
bi·op·sy
bi·op·sies
bi·o·sphere
bi·o·tin
bi·par·ti·san
bi·par·tite
bi·par·ti·tion
bi·ped
bi·ped·al
bi·plane
bi·po·lar
bi·po·lar·i·ty
birch
birch·en
bird·bath
bird·brain
bird·brained
bird·call
bird·ie
bird·lime
bird·man
bird's-eye
bi·ret·ta
Bir·ming·ham
birth·day
birth·mark
birth·place
birth·right
birth·stone
Bis·cay
bis·cuit
bi·sect
bi·sec·tion
bi·sec·tor
bi·sex·u·al
bish·op
bish·op·ric
Bis·marck
bis·muth
bi·son

bisque
Bis·sau
bis·ter
bis·tered
bis·tro
bis·tros
bi·sul·fide
bitch
bite
bit
bit·ten
bit·ing
bit·ing·ly
bit·stock
bit·ter
bit·ter·ish
bit·ter·ly
bit·ter·ness
bit·tern
bit·ter·root
bit·ters
bit·ter·sweet
bi·tu·men
bi·tu·mi·nous
bi·va·lent
bi·va·lence
bi·valve
bi·val·vu·lar
biv·ou·ac
biv·ou·acked
biv·ou·ack·ing
bi·week·ly
bi·week·lies
bi·year·ly
bi·zarre
bi·zarre·ly
bi·zarre·ness
Bi·zet
blab
blabbed
blab·bing
blab·ber
blab·ber·mouth
black·ball
black·ber·ry
black·ber·ries
black·bird
black·board
black·body
black·cap
black·en
black·eyed Su·san
Black·feet
Black·foot
black·guard
black·head
black·ing
black·jack
black·list
black·ly
black·mail
black·out
black·smith
black·snake
black·thorn

black·top
blad·der
blade
blad·ed
blame
blamed
blam·ing
blam·a·ble
blame·a·ble
blame·ful
blame·less
blame·less·ly
blame·less·ness
blame·wor·thy
blame·wor·thi·ness
blanch
blanch·er
blanch·ing
blanc·mange
bland
bland·ly
bland·ness
blan·dish
blan·dish·er
blan·dish·ment
blank
blank·ly
blank·ness
blan·ket
blare
blared
blar·ing
blar·ney
bla·sé
blas·pheme
blas·phemed
blas·phem·ing
blas·phem·er
blas·phem·ous
blas·phemy
blas·phem·ies
blast·ed
blas·tu·la
blat
blat·ted
blat·ting
bla·tant
bla·tan·cy
bla·tant·ly
blath·er·skite
blaze
blazed
blaz·ing
bla·zer
bleach
bleach·er
bleak
bleak·ly
bleak·ness
blear
bleary
blear·i·ness
bleed
bled
bleed·ing

bleed·er
blem·ish
blend
 blend·ed
 blend·ing
 blend·er
Blen·heim
bless
 bless·ed
 blest
 bles·sing
bless·ed·ness
blind
 blind·ing
 blind·ing·ly
 blind·ly
 blind·ness
blind·er
blind·fold
blind·man's buff
blink·er
bliss
 bliss·ful
 bliss·ful·ly
 bliss·ful·ness
blis·ter
 blis·tery
blithe
 blithe·ly
 blithe·some
 blithe·some·ly
blitz·krieg
bliz·zard
block
 block·er
block·ade
 block·ad·ed
 block·ad·ing
 block·ad·er
block·bus·ter
block·head
block·house
block·ish
 block·ish·ly
blocky
blond
blond·ness
blood·curd·ling
blood·ed
blood·hound
blood·less
 blood·less·ly
 blood·less·ness
blood·let·ting
blood·shed
blood·shot
blood·stained
blood·stone
blood·suck·er
blood·thirsty
 blood·thirst·i·ly
bloody
 blood·i·er
 blood·i·est
 blood·ied

blood·y·ing
blood·i·ly
blood·i·ness
bloom·ers
bloom·ing
 bloom·ing·ly
bloop·er
blos·som
blot
 blot·ted
 blot·ting
blotch
 blotchy
blot·ter
blow
 blew
 blown
 blow·ing
 blow·er
blow·fly
 blow·flies
blow·gun
blow·hole
blow·out
blow·pipe
blow·torch
blow·up
blowy
blowzy
blub·ber
 blub·bery
bludg·eon
blue
 blu·er
 blu·est
 blu·ing
 blue·ness
Blue·beard
blue·bell
blue·ber·ry
 blue·ber·ries
blue·bird
blue·blood·ed
blue·bon·net
blue·coat
blue·col·lar
blue·fish
blue·grass
blue·gum
blue·jack·et
blue·nose
blue·pen·cil
blue·print
blue·stock·ing
blu·et
 blu·ing
blun·der
 blun·der·er
 blun·der·ing·ly
 blun·der·buss
blunt
 blunt·ly
 blunt·ness
blur
 blurred

blur·ring
blur·ry
blush
 blushed
 blush·ing
 blush·ing·ly
blus·ter
 blus·ter·er
 blus·ter·ing·ly
 blus·ter·ous
 blus·tery
boa
board·er
board·walk
boast
 boas·ter
 boast·ful
 boast·ful·ness
 boast·ing·ly
boat·house
boat·man
 boat·men
boat·swain
bob
 bobbed
 bob·bing
bob·bin
bob·ble
 bob·bled
 bob·bling
bob·by pin
bob·cat
bob·o·link
bob·sled
bob·tail
bob·white
Boc·cac·cio
bode
 bod·ed
 bod·ing
bod·ice
 bod·i·ly
bod·kin
bod·y
 bod·ied
 bod·y·ing
bod·y·guard
Bo·e·thi·us
bog
 bog·gy
 bog·ging
bo·gey
bog·gle
 bog·gled
 bog·gling
 bog·gler
Bo·go·ta
bo·gus
bo·gy
Bo·he·mia
bo·he·mi·an
boil·er
Boi·se
bois·ter·ous
 bois·ter·ous·ly

28

bois·ter·ous·ness
bo·la
 bo·las
bold
 bold·ly
 bold·ness
bold·face
bo·le·ro
Bo·li·var
Bo·liv·ia
bol·lix
boll·worm
bo·lo
bo·lo·gna
bo·lo·ney
Bol·she·vik
Bol·she·vism
bol·ster
 bol·ster·er
bolt
 bolt·ed
 bolt·er
bom·bard
 bom·bard·ment
 bom·bar·dier
bom·bast
 bom·bas·tic
 bom·bas·ti·cal·ly
Bom·bay
bomb·er
bomb·proof
 bomb·shell
 bomb·sight
bo·na fide
bo·nan·za
Bo·na·parte
Bo·na·ven·tu·ra
bon·bon
bond·age
bond·ed
bond·man
 bond·men
bonds·man
 bonds·men
bone
 boned
 bon·ing
bone·head
bon·er
bon·fire
bon·go
 bon·gos
 bon·goes
bon·ho·mie
Bon·i·face
bon·net
bon·ny
bo·nus
 bo·nus·es
bon voy·age
bony
 bon·i·er
 bon·i·est
boo
 booed

boo·ing
boo·by
 boo·bies
 boo·by trap
boo·dle
boo·hoo
 boo·hooed
 boo·hoo·ing
book
 book·bind·er
 book·case
 book·end
 book·ie
 book·ish
 book·ish·ness
 book·keep·ing
 book·keep·er
 book·let
 book·mak·er
 book·mark
 book·mo·bile
 book·plate
 book·sell·er
 book·sell·ing
 book·stall
 book·worm
boo·me·rang
boon·dog·gle
boor
 boor·ish
 boor·ish·ness
boost
 boost·er
boot·black
boot·ee
boot·jack
boot·leg
 boot·legged
 boot·leg·ging
 boot·leg·ger
boot·less
 boot·less·ly
 boot·less·ness
boot·lick
 boot·lick·er
boot·ty
boo·ties
booze
 booz·er
boozy
 booz·i·er
 booz·i·est
bo·rax
Bor·deaux
bor·der
 bor·dered
 bor·der·land
 bor·der·line
bore
 bored
 bor·ing
 bor·er
bo·re·al
bore·dom
Bor·gia

bo·ric
Bor·neo
bo·ron
bor·ough
bor·row
 bor·row·er
Bos·nia
bos·om
boss·ism
bossy
 boss·i·er
 boss·i·est
 boss·i·ness
Bos·ton
bo·sun
Bos·well
bot·a·ny
 bo·tan·i·cal
 bot·a·nist
 bot·a·nize
botch
botchy
 botch·i·er
 botch·i·est
both·er
 both·er·some
Bot·swa·na
Bot·ti·cel·li
bot·tle
 bot·tled
 bot·tling
 bot·tle·ful
 bot·tler
 bot·tle·neck
bot·tom
 bot·tom·less
bot·u·lism
bou·doir
bouf·fant
bough
bought
bouil·lon
boul·der
boul·e·vard
Bou·logne
bounce
 bounced
 bounc·ing
bound
bound·a·ry
 bound·a·ries
bound·less
 bound·less·ness
boun·te·ous
 boun·te·ous·ness
boun·ti·ful
boun·ty
 boun·ties
bou·quet
bour·bon
bour·geois
bour·geoi·sie
bou·tique
bou·ton·niere
bo·vine

29

bow·el	brais·ing	break·down
bow·er	brake	break·er
bow·ery	braked	break·fast
bow·ie	brak·ing	break·neck
bow·ing	brake·man	break·out
bow·knot	brake·men	break·through
bowl	bram·ble	break·up
bow·leg	bram·bly	break·wa·ter
bow·leg·ged	branch	breast·bone
bowl·er	branch·ed	breast·plate
bow·line	brand	breath
bow·ling	brand·er	breathe
bow·man	Bran·deis	breathed
bow·men	Bran·den·burg	breath·ing
bow·string	bran·dish	breath·er
box	brand-new	breath·ing
box·ful	bran·dy	breath·tak·ing
box·fuls	bran·dies	breath·tak·ing·ly
box·car	bran·died	breathy
box·er	bran·dy·ing	breath·i·er
box·ing	Bran·dy·wine	breath·i·est
boy	bra·sier	breech·es
boy·hood	Bra·si·lia	breech·load·er
boy·ish	bras·se·rie	breed
boy·ish·ly	bras·se·ries	bred
boy·ish·ness	bras·siere	breed·ing
boy·cott	brassy	breeze
boy·friend	brass·i·er	breeze·way
boy·sen·ber·ry	brass·i·est	breezy
boy·sen·ber·ries	brat	breez·i·er
brace	brat·tish	breez·i·est
braced	brat·ty	breez·i·ness
brac·ing	bra·va·do	breth·ren
brace·let	brave	Bret·on
brac·er	braved	bre·vet
bra·ces	brav·ing	bre·vet·ted
brack·en	brave·ness	bre·vet·ting
brack·et	brav·ery	bre·vi·a·ry
brack·ish	brav·er·ies	bre·vi·a·ries
brack·ish·ness	bra·vo	brev·i·ty
brad	bra·vos	brew
brad·ded	bra·vu·ra	brew·er
brad·ding	brawl	brew·ery
brag	brawl·er	brew·er·ies
bragged	brawn	Bri·and
brag·ging	brawn·i·ness	bri·ar
brag·gart	brawny	bri·ary
Brah·ma	brawn·i·er	bribe
Brah·min	brawn·i·est	bribed
Brahms	bra·zen	brib·ing
braid	bra·zier	brib·a·ble
braid·er	Bra·zil	brib·ery
braid·ing	Braz·za·ville	brib·er·ies
braille	breach	bric-a-brac
brain·child	bread	brick·lay·er
brain·less	bread·ed	brick·lay·ing
brain·pow·er	breadth·ways	brick·work
brain·storm	bread·win·ner	brick·yard
brain·storm·ing	break	bride
brain·wash·ing	broke	brid·al
brainy	bro·ken	bride·groom
brain·i·er	break·ing	brides·maid
brain·i·est	break·a·ble	bridge
braise	break·age	Bridge·port
braised	break·a·way	Bridge·town

Bridge·wa·ter
bridge·work
bri·dle
  bri·dled
  bri·dling
brief
  brief·ly
brief·ing
bri·er
bri·gade
brig·a·dier
brig·an·tine
bright
  bright·ly
  bright·ness
bright·en
Brigh·ton
bril·liance
  bril·lian·cy
  bril·liant
brim
  brimmed
  brim·ming
brim·stone
brine
  briny
bring
  brought
  bring·ing
brink
bri·oche
bri·quette
  bri·quet
brisk
  brisk·ly
  brisk·ness
bris·ket
bris·tle
  bris·tled
Bris·tol
Brit·ain
Bri·tan·nia
britch·es
Brit·ish
Brit·on
Brit·ta·ny
brit·tle
broach
  broached
  broach·ing
broad·cast
  broad·cast·ed
  broad·cast·ing
broad·cloth
broad·mind·ed
broad·side
Broad·way
bro·cade
  bro·cad·ed
  bro·cad·ing
broc·co·li
bro·chure
Brock·ton
broil·er
bro·ken

bro·ken-down
bro·ken-heart·ed
bro·ker
bro·ker·age
bro·mide
bro·mine
bron·chi
bron·chi·al
bron·chi·tis
bron·chus
bron·co
  bron·cos
Bron·te
bron·to·saur
bronze
  bronzed
  bronz·ing
brooch
brood
  brood·ing
brook
Brook·line
Brook·lyn
broom·stick
broth·el
broth·er
broth·er·hood
broth·er-in-law
  broth·ers-in-law
broth·er·ly
brow·beat
  brow·beat·en
  brow·beat·ing
brown
brown·ie
brown·out
brown·stone
Browns·ville
browse
  browsed
  brows·ing
bru·in
bruise
  bruised
  bruis·ing
bruis·er
brunch
bru·net
Bruns·wick
brush-off
brusque
Brus·sels
bru·tal
  bru·tal·i·ty
  bru·tal·ize
    bru·tal·ized
    bru·tal·iz·ing
    bru·tal·i·za·tion
brut·ish
Bru·tus
bub·ble
  bub·bled
  bub·bling
bub·bler
bu·bon·ic

buc·ca·neer
Bu·chan·an
Bu·cha·rest
buck·a·roo
buck·board
buck·et
  buck·et·ed
  buck·et·ing
buck·eye
Buck·ing·ham
buck·le
buck·ram
buck·saw
buck·shot
buck·skin
buck·tooth
  buck·teeth
  buck·toothed
buck·wheat
bu·col·ic
bud
  bud·ded
  bud·ding
Bu·da·pest
Bud·dha
Bud·dhism
Bud·dhist
bud·dy
budge
budg·et
Bue·na Vis·ta
Bue·nos Ai·res
buf·fa·lo
  buf·fa·loes
  buf·fa·los
  buf·fa·loed
  buf·fa·lo·ing
buff·er
buf·fet
  buf·fet·ed
  buf·fet·ing
buf·foon
  buf·foon·ery
  buf·foon·er·ies
  buf·foon·ish
bug
  bugged
  bug·ging
bug·a·boo
bug·gy
bug·gi·er
bug·gi·est
bu·gle
  bu·gled
  bu·gling
  bu·gler
build
  build·er
  build·ing
  build-up
built-in
built-up
Bu·jum·bu·ra
bulb
  bul·ba·ceous

bul·bar
bul·bous
Bul·gar·ia
bulge
  bulged
  bulg·ing
  bulgy
bulk·head
bulky
  bulk·i·er
  bulk·i·est
  bulk·i·ly
  bulk·i·ness
bull·dog
bull·doze
  bull·dozed
  bull·doz·ing
  bull·doz·er
bul·let
bul·le·tin
bul·let·proof
bull·fight
  bull·fight·er
  bull·fight·ing
bull·finch
bull·frog
bull·head·ed
bull·horn
bul·lion
bull·ock
bull·pen
bull's-eye
bull·whip
bul·ly
  bul·lies
  bul·lied
  bul·ly·ing
bul·rush
bul·wark
bum
  bum·mer
  bum·mest
bum·ble·bee
bump·er
bump·kin
bump·tious
  bump·tious·ness
bumpy
  bump·i·er
  bump·i·est
  bump·i·ly
  bump·i·ness
bunch
  bunchy
  bunch·i·er
  bunch·i·est
bun·co
bun·combe
bun·dle
  bun·dled
  bun·dling
bun·ga·low
bun·gle
  bun·gled
  bun·gling

bun·gler
bun·ion
bunk·er
bunk·house
bun·ko
bun·kum
bun·ny
  bun·nies
Bun·sen
bun·ting
Bun·yan
bu·oy
buoy·an·cy
  buoy·ant
  buoy·ant·ly
Bur·bank
bur·ble
bur·den
bur·den·some
bur·dock
bu·reau
  bu·reaus
  bu·reaux
bu·reauc·ra·cy
  bu·reauc·ra·cies
  bu·reau·crat
  bu·reau·crat·ic
bu·rette
bur·geon
burg·er
bur·gess
bur·glar
bur·glar·ize
  bur·glar·ized
  bur·glar·iz·ing
bur·gla·ry
  bur·gla·ries
bur·gle
  bur·gled
  bur·gling
Bur·goyne
Bur·gun·dy
bur·i·al
bur·lap
Bur·leigh
bur·lesque
  bur·lesqued
  bur·les·quing
  bur·les·quer
Bur·ling·ton
bur·ly
  bur·li·er
  bur·li·est
  bur·li·ness
Bur·ma
burn
  burned
  burnt
  burn·ing
  burn·a·ble
burn·er
bur·nish
  bur·nish·er
bur·noose
burn·sides

burp
burr
  burred
  bur·ring
bur·ro
  bur·ros
Bur·roughs
bur·row
  bur·row·er
bur·sa
  bur·sae
bur·sal
bur·sar
  bur·sa·ri·al
bur·sa·ry
  bur·sa·ries
bur·si·tis
burst
  burst·ing
  burst·er
Bu·run·di
bury
  bur·ied
  bur·y·ing
bus
  bus·es
  bused
  bus·ing
bus·boy
bus·by
  bus·bies
bushed
bush·el
bu·shi·do
bush·ing
bush·man
  bush·men
bush·mas·ter
bush·rang·er
bush·whack
  bush·whack·er
  bush·whack·ing
bushy
  bush·i·er
  bush·i·est
  bush·i·ness
bus·i·ly
busi·ness
busi·ness·like
busi·ness·man
  busi·ness·men
busi·ness·wom·an
  busi·ness·wom·en
bus·kin
bus·kined
bus·tard
bus·tle
  bus·tled
  bus·tling
  bus·tler
busy
  bus·i·er
  bus·i·est
  bus·ied
  bus·y·ing

bus·y·body
bu·ta·di·ene
bu·tane
butch·er
  butch·er·er
butch·er·bird
butch·er's-broom
butch·ery
  butch·er·ies
but·ler
  but·ler·ship
butte
but·ter
but·ter·cup
but·ter·fat
but·ter·fin·gered
  but·ter·fin·gers
but·ter·fish
but·ter·fly
  but·ter·flies
but·ter·milk
but·ter·nut
but·ter·scotch
but·tery
  but·ter·ies
but·tock
but·ton
but·ton·hole
  but·ton·holed
  but·ton·hol·ing
  but·ton·hol·er
but·ton·wood
but·tress
bu·ty·ric
bux·om
  bux·om·ly
  bux·om·ness
buy
  bought
  buy·ing
  buy·a·ble
buy·er
buz·zard
buzz·er
by-e·lec·tion
by·gone
by·law
by·line
by·pass
by·path
by·play
by·prod·uct
by·road
By·ron
by·stand·er
byte
by·way
by·word
Byz·an·tine
By·zan·tium
ca·bal
  ca·balled
  ca·ball·ing
cab·a·la
  cab·a·lis·tic

cab·a·lis·ti·cal
ca·bal·le·ro
ca·ba·na
cab·a·ret
cab·bage
  cab·baged
  cab·bag·ing
cab·by
  cab·bies
ca·ber
cab·in
cab·i·net
cab·i·net·mak·er
  cab·i·net·mak·ing
cab·i·net·work
ca·ble
  ca·bled
  ca·bling
ca·ble·gram
cab·o·chon
ca·boo·dle
ca·boose
Cab·ot
cab·ri·o·let
cab·stand
ca·cao
cach·a·lot
cache
  cached
  cach·ing
ca·chet
ca·cique
cack·le
  cack·led
  cack·ling
  cack·ler
ca·coph·o·ny
  ca·coph·o·nies
cac·tus
  cac·tus·es
  cac·ti
cad
  cad·dish
ca·dav·er
  ca·dav·er·ous
cad·die
  cad·died
  cad·dy·ing
cad·dis fly
cad·dy
  cad·dies
ca·dence
ca·den·za
ca·det
cadge
  cadged
  cadg·ing
Cad·il·lac
Ca·diz
cad·mi·um
Cad·mus
ca·dre
ca·du·ce·us
  ca·du·cei
Cae·sar

Cae·sa·rea
Cae·sar·e·an
cae·su·ra
  cae·su·ras
  cae·su·rae
ca·fe
caf·e·te·ria
caf·feine
caf·tan
Ca·ga·yan
cage
  caged
  cag·ing
cai·man
cairn
Cai·ro
cais·son
cai·tiff
Ca·ius
ca·jole
  ca·joled
  ca·jol·ing
  ca·jol·ery
  ca·jol·ing·ly
Ca·jun
cake
  caked
  cak·ing
cake·walk
cal·a·bash
cal·a·boose
Ca·la·bria
Ca·lais
cal·a·mine
ca·lam·i·ty
  ca·lam·i·ties
  ca·lam·i·tous
cal·cic
cal·ci·fy
  cal·ci·fied
  cal·ci·fy·ing
  cal·ci·fi·ca·tion
cal·ci·mine
cal·cite
cal·ci·um
cal·cu·la·ble
cal·cu·la·bil·i·ty
cal·cu·late
  cal·cu·lat·ed
  cal·cu·lat·ing
  cal·cu·la·tion
cal·cu·la·tor
cal·cu·lus
  cal·cu·lus·es
Cal·cut·ta
Cal·de·ron
cal·dron
Ca·leb
Cal·e·do·nia
cal·en·dar
cal·ends
calf
  calves
calf·skin
Cal·ga·ry

Cal·houn
cal·i·ber
cal·i·brate
cal·i·brat·ed
cal·i·brat·ing
cal·i·bra·tion
cal·i·co
cal·i·coes
Cal·i·for·nia
Ca·lig·u·la
cal·i·per
ca·liph
cal·iph·ate
cal·is·then·ics
Cal·lao
Cal·les
cal·lig·ra·pher
cal·lig·ra·phy
call·ing
cal·li·o·pe
Cal·lis·to
cal·lous
cal·loused
cal·low
cal·lus
cal·lus·es
calm
ca·lor·ic
cal·o·rie
cal·o·ries
cal·o·rif·ic
cal·u·met
cal·um·ny
cal·um·nies
ca·lum·ni·ate
ca·lum·ni·at·ed
ca·lum·ni·at·ing
ca·lum·ni·a·tion
Cal·va·ry
calve
calved
calv·ing
Cal·vert
Cal·vin
Cal·vin·ism
Cal·y·don
ca·lyp·so
ca·lyp·sos
ca·lyx
ca·lyx·es
cal·y·ces
ca·ma·ra·de·rie
cam·ber
cam·bi·um
Cam·bo·dia
Cam·bria
cam·bric
Cam·bridge
Cam·den
cam·el
ca·mel·lia
Cam·e·lot
Cam·em·bert
cam·eo
cam·era

cam·er·a·man
Cam·er·oon
cam·i·sole
cam·o·mile
Ca·mor·ra
cam·ou·flage
cam·ou·flaged
cam·ou·flag·ing
Cam·pa·gna
cam·paign
cam·paign·er
cam·pa·ni·le
cam·pa·ni·les
camp·er
camp·fire
cam·phor
cam·pus
cam·pus·es
campy
camp·i·er
camp·i·est
cam·shaft
can
canned
can·ning
Ca·naan
Can·a·da
ca·nal
ca·naled
ca·nal·ing
can·a·pé
ca·nard
ca·nary
ca·nas·ta
Can·ber·ra
can·can
can·cel
can·celed
can·cel·ing
can·cel·la·tion
can·cer
can·de·la·brum
can·de·la·bra
can·de·la·brums
can·did
can·di·da·cy
can·di·da·cies
can·di·date
can·died
can·dle
can·dled
can·dling
can·dle·light
Can·dle·mas
can·dle·pow·er
can·dle·stick
can·dor
can·dy
can·dies
can·died
can·dy·ing
cane
caned
can·ing
ca·nine

Ca·nis
can·is·ter
can·ker
can·ker·ous
can·na·bis
canned
can·ner
can·nery
can·ner·ies
Cannes
can·ni·bal
can·ni·bal·ism
can·ni·bal·ize
can·ni·bal·ized
can·ni·bal·iz·ing
can·non
can·not
can·ny
can·ni·er
can·ni·est
can·ni·ly
can·ni·ness
ca·noe
ca·noed
ca·noe·ing
ca·noe·ist
can·on
ca·non·i·cal
can·on·ize
can·on·ized
can·on·iz·ing
can·on·i·za·tion
can·o·py
can·o·pies
can·o·pied
can·o·py·ing
can·ta·loup
can·ta·loupe
can·ta·lope
can·tan·ker·ous
can·ta·ta
can·teen
can·ter
Can·ter·bury
can·ti·cle
Can·ti·gny
can·ti·lev·er
can·to
can·tos
can·ton
can·tor
Ca·nuck
Ca·nute
can·vas
can·vass
can·vass·er
can·yon
caou·tchouc
cap
capped
cap·ping
ca·pa·bil·i·ty
ca·pa·bil·i·ties
ca·pa·ble
ca·pa·bly

34

ca·pa·cious
ca·pac·i·tate
  ca·pac·i·tat·ed
  ca·pac·i·tat·ing
ca·pac·i·ty
  ca·pac·i·ties
Ca·pel·la
ca·per
Ca·per·na·um
Ca·pet
ca·pi·as
cap·il·lar·i·ty
cap·il·lary
  cap·il·lar·ies
cap·i·tal
cap·i·tal·ism
  cap·i·tal·is·tic
cap·i·tal·ist
cap·i·tal·ize
  cap·i·tal·i·za·tion
cap·i·tal·ly
cap·i·ta·tion
ca·pit·u·late
  ca·pit·u·lat·ed
  ca·pit·u·lat·ing
  ca·pit·u·la·tor
ca·pon
ca·pote
Cap·pa·do·cia
Ca·pri
ca·pric·cio
ca·price
  ca·pri·cious
  ca·pri·cious·ly
  ca·pri·cious·ness
Cap·ri·con
cap·ri·ole
  cap·ri·oled
  cap·ri·ol·ing
cap·size
  cap·sized
  cap·siz·ing
cap·stan
cap·stone
cap·sule
  cap·su·lar
cap·tain
  cap·tain·cy
  cap·tain·ship
cap·tion
cap·tious
  cap·tious·ness
cap·ti·vate
  cap·ti·vat·ed
  cap·ti·vat·ing
  cap·ti·vat·ing·ly
  cap·ti·va·tion
  cap·ti·va·tor
cap·tive
  cap·tiv·i·ty
  cap·tiv·i·ties
cap·tor
cap·ture
  cap·tured
  cap·tur·ing

  cap·tur·er
Cap·u·let
Car·a·cal·la
Ca·ra·cas
car·a·cole
  car·a·coled
  car·a·col·ing
car·a·cul
ca·rafe
car·a·mel
car·a·pace
car·at
car·a·van
car·a·van·sa·ry
  car·a·van·sa·ries
car·a·vel
car·a·way
car·bide
car·bine
car·bo·hy·drate
car·bo·lat·ed
car·bol·ic
car·bon
car·bo·na·ceous
car·bo·nate
  car·bo·na·tion
car·bon di·ox·ide
car·bon·if·er·ous
car·bon·ize
  car·bon·ized
  car·bon·iz·ing
  car·bon·i·za·tion
car·bon mon·ox·ide
Car·bo·run·dum
car·boy
car·bun·cle
car·bu·re·tor
car·ca·jou
car·cass
car·cin·o·gen
  car·cin·o·gen·ic
car·ci·no·ma
  car·ci·no·mas
  car·ci·no·ma·ta
card
  card·er
car·da·mom
card·board
Cár·de·nas
car·di·ac
Car·diff
car·di·gan
car·di·nal
car·di·o·graph
  car·di·og·ra·phy
card·sharp
care
  cared
  car·ing
ca·reen
ca·reer
care·free
care·ful
  care·ful·ly
  care·ful·ness

care·less
  care·less·ly
  care·less·ness
ca·ress
  ca·ress·ing·ly
car·et
care·tak·er
Ca·rew
care·worn
car·fare
car·go
  car·goes
  car·gos
car·hop
Car·ib·be·an
car·i·bou
car·i·ca·ture
  car·i·ca·tured
  car·i·ca·tur·ing
  car·i·ca·tur·ist
car·ies
car·il·lon
  car·il·lonned
  car·il·lon·ning
  car·il·lon·neur
car·load
Carls·bad
Car·mel
car·mine
car·nage
car·nal
  car·nal·i·ty
  car·nal·ly
car·na·tion
Car·ne·gie
car·nel·ian
car·ni·val
car·ni·vore
car·niv·o·rous
  car·niv·o·rous·ly
  car·niv·o·rous·ness
car·ol
  car·oled
  car·ol·ing
  car·ol·er
Car·o·li·na
car·om
ca·rot·id
ca·rous·al
ca·rouse
  ca·roused
  ca·rous·ing
  ca·rous·er
car·ou·sel
carp
car·pal
Car·pa·thi·an
car·pen·ter
  car·pen·try
car·pet
car·pet·bag·ger
car·pet·ing
car·port
car·pus
car·riage

car·ri·er
car·ri·ole
car·ri·on
car·rot
car·roty
car·ry
  car·ried
  car·ry·ing
car·ry·all
car·ry·o·ver
car·sick·ness
  car·sick
Car·son
cart
  car·ter
cart·age
Car·ta·ge·na
carte blanche
car·tel
Car·ter
Car·thage
Car·thu·sian
Car·tier
car·ti·lage
car·ti·lag·i·nous
car·tog·ra·phy
  car·tog·ra·pher
  car·to·graph·ic
car·ton
car·toon
  car·toon·ist
car·tridge
cart·wheel
Ca·ru·so
carve
  carved
  carv·ing
  carv·er
car·vel
car·y·at·id
  car·y·at·ids
  car·y·at·i·des
ca·sa·ba
Ca·sa·blan·ca
Ca·sals
Cas·a·no·va
cas·cade
  cas·cad·ed
  cas·cad·ing
case
  cased
  cas·ing
case·hard·en
ca·sein
case·mate
  case·mat·ed
case·ment
  case·ment·ed
case·work·er
  case·work
cash·book
cash·ew
cash·ier
cash·mere
cas·ing

ca·si·no
  ca·si·nos
cas·ket
Cas·pi·an
cas·sa·ba
Cas·san·dra
cas·sa·va
cas·se·role
cas·sette
cas·si·no
Cas·sius
cas·sock
  cas·socked
cas·so·wary
  cas·so·war·ies
cast
  cast·ing
cas·ta·net
cast·a·way
caste
cas·tel·lat·ed
cast·er
cas·ti·gate
  cas·ti·gat·ed
  cas·ti·gat·ing
  cas·ti·ga·tion
  cas·ti·ga·tor
Cas·tile
cast i·ron
cas·tle
  cas·tled
  cas·tling
cast·off
cas·tor
cas·trate
  cas·trat·ed
  cas·trat·ing
  cas·trat·er
  cas·tra·tion
Cas·tro
cas·u·al
  cas·u·al·ly
  cas·u·al·ness
cas·u·al·ty
  cas·u·al·ties
cas·u·ist
  cas·u·is·tic
  cas·u·ist·ry
  cas·u·ist·ries
cat
  cat·ted
  cat·ting
cat·a·clysm
  cat·a·clys·mal
cat·a·comb
cat·a·falque
cat·a·lep·sy
  cat·a·lep·tic
Cat·a·li·na
cat·a·log
  cat·a·loged
  cat·a·log·ing
  cat·a·log·er
  cat·a·log·ist
ca·tal·pa

ca·tal·y·sis
ca·tal·y·ses
cat·a·lyt·ic
cat·a·lyst
cat·a·lyze
  cat·a·lyzed
  cat·a·lyz·ing
cat·a·ma·ran
cat·a·mount
cat·a·pult
cat·a·ract
ca·tarrh
ca·tas·tro·phe
  cat·as·troph·ic
Ca·taw·ba
cat·bird
cat·boat
cat·call
catch
  caught
  catch·ing
catch·all
catch·er
  catch·ing
catch·up
catch·word
catchy
  catch·i·er
  catch·i·est
cat·e·chism
  cat·e·chis·mal
cat·e·chize
  cat·e·chized
  cat·e·chiz·ing
  cat·e·chi·za·tion
  cat·e·chist
  cat·e·chiz·er
cat·e·chu·men
cat·e·gor·i·cal
  cat·e·gor·i·cal·ly
cat·e·go·ry
  cat·e·go·ries
cat·e·gor·ize
  cat·e·gor·ized
  cat·e·gor·iz·ing
ca·ter
ca·ter·er
cat·er·pil·lar
cat·er·waul
cat·fish
  cat·fish·es
cat·gut
ca·thar·sis
  ca·thar·ses
ca·thar·tic
Ca·thay
ca·the·dral
Cath·er
cath·e·ter
cath·ode
cath·o·lic
  cath·o·lic·i·ty
ca·thol·i·cize
  ca·thol·i·cized
  ca·thol·i·ciz·ing

Ca·thol·i·cism
cat·i·on
cat·kin
cat·mint
cat·nap
  cat·napped
  cat·nap·ping
cat·nip
Ca·to
cat-o'-nine-tails
Cats·kill
cat's-paw
cat·sup
cat·tail
cat·tle
cat·tle·man
cat·ty
  cat·ti·er
  cat·ti·est
  cat·ti·ly
  cat·ti·ness
cat·ty-cor·ner
  cat·ty-cor·nered
cat·walk
Cau·ca·sian
cau·cus
  cau·cus·es
  cau·cused
  cau·cus·ing
cau·dal
cau·date
  cau·dat·ed
cau·dle
caul·dron
cau·li·flow·er
caulk
  caulk·er
caus·al
  caus·al·ly
cau·sal·i·ty
  cau·sal·i·ties
cause
  caused
  caus·ing
  cau·sa·tion
  caus·a·tive
  cause·less
  caus·er
cause·way
caus·tic
  caus·ti·cal·ly
cau·ter·ize
  cau·ter·ized
  cau·ter·iz·ing
  cau·ter·i·za·tion
cau·tery
  cau·ter·ies
cau·tion
  cau·tion·ary
cau·tious
cav·al·cade
cav·a·lier
  cav·a·lier·ly
cav·al·ry
  cav·al·ry·man

cav·al·ry·men
cave
caved
cav·ing
ca·ve·at
cave-in
cav·ern
  cav·ern·ous
cav·i·ar
cav·il
  cav·iled
  cav·il·ing
cav·i·ty
  cav·i·ties
ca·vort
cay·enne
cay·man
  cay·mans
cay·use
cease
ceased
ceas·ing
cease-fire
ce·cum
ce·dar
cede
  ced·ed
  ced·ing
ce·dil·la
ceil·ing
cel·an·dine
cel·e·brant
cel·e·brate
  cel·e·brat·ed
  cel·e·brat·ing
  cel·e·bra·tion
  cel·e·bra·tor
ce·leb·ri·ty
  ce·leb·ri·ties
ce·ler·i·ty
cel·ery
ce·les·tial
ce·li·ac
cel·i·ba·cy
  cel·i·bate
cel·lar
cel·lo
cel·los
cel·list
cel·lo·phane
cel·lu·lar
cel·lule
Cel·lu·loid
cel·lu·lose
Celt·ic
ce·ment
cem·e·tery
  cem·e·ter·ies
ce·no·bite
cen·o·taph
Ce·no·zo·ic
cen·ser
cen·sor
  cen·so·ri·al
  cen·sor·ship

cen·so·ri·ous
  cen·so·ri·ous·ly
  cen·so·ri·ous·ness
cen·sure
  cen·sured
  cen·sur·ing
  cen·sur·er
  cen·sur·a·ble
  cen·sur·a·bly
cen·sus
  cen·sus·es
  cen·sused
  cen·sus·ing
cen·tare
cen·taur
cen·te·nar·i·an
cen·te·na·ry
  cen·te·na·ries
cen·ten·ni·al
cen·ter
cen·ter·board
cen·ter·piece
cen·ti·are
cen·ti·grade
cen·ti·gram
cen·ti·li·ter
cen·ti·me·ter
cen·tral
cen·tral·ize
  cen·tral·ized
  cen·tral·iz·ing
cen·trif·u·gal
cen·tri·fuge
cen·trip·e·tal
cen·tu·ri·on
cen·tu·ry
  cen·tu·ries
ce·ram·ic
ce·ram·ics
Cer·ber·us
ce·re·al
cer·e·bel·lum
cer·e·bral
cer·e·brum
cer·e·mo·ni·al
  cer·e·mo·ni·al·ism
cer·e·mo·ni·ous
cer·e·mo·ny
  cer·e·mo·nies
Ce·res
ce·rise
ce·ri·um
ce·ric
cer·tain
  cer·tain·ly
  cer·tain·ty
  cer·tain·ties
cer·tif·i·cate
cer·ti·fi·ca·tion
cer·ti·fy
  cer·ti·fied
  cer·ti·fy·ing
  cer·ti·fi·a·ble
  cer·ti·fi·a·bly
  cer·ti·fi·er

cer·ti·tude
ce·ru·le·an
Cer·van·tes
cer·vi·cal
cer·vix
  cer·vix·es
  cer·vi·ces
ces·sa·tion
ces·sion
cess·pool
ce·ta·cean
  ce·ta·ceous
Cey·lon
Cha·blis
Cha·co
chafe
  chafed
  chaf·ing
chaf·er
chaff
  chaf·fer
  chaff·er·er
Cha·gall
Cha·gres
cha·grin
  cha·grined
  cha·grin·ing
chain re·ac·tion
chair·man
  chair·men
chair·man·ship
chair·per·son
chair·wom·an
  chair·wom·en
chaise longue
Chal·ce·don
Chal·dea
chal·et
chal·ice
chalk
  chalky
chal·lenge
  chal·lenged
  chal·leng·ing
cham·ber
cham·ber·maid
cha·me·le·on
cham·ois
cham·pagne
cham·pi·on
  cham·pi·on·ship
Cham·plain
Champs Ely·sées
chance·ful
chan·cel·lor
Chan·cel·lors·ville
chancy
  chanc·i·er
  chanc·i·est
chan·de·lier
change
  changed
  chang·ing
change·a·ble
change·ful

chan·nel
chan·ti·cleer
cha·os
cha·ot·ic
chap
  chapped
  chap·ping
cha·pa·re·jos
chap·ar·ral
cha·peau
  cha·peaux
chap·el
chap·e·ron
chap·fall·en
chap·lain
chap·let
Chap·lin
chap·ter
char
  charred
  char·ring
char·ac·ter
char·ac·ter·is·tic
  char·ac·ter·is·ti·cal·ly
char·ac·ter·ize
  char·ac·ter·ized
  char·ac·ter·iz·ing
  char·ac·ter·i·za·tion
  char·ac·ter·iz·er
cha·rade
char·coal
charge
  charged
  char·ging
char·gé d'af·faires
charg·er
char·i·ot
  char·i·ot·eer
cha·ris·ma
char·i·ta·ble
  char·i·ta·ble·ness
  char·i·ta·bly
char·i·ty
  char·i·ties
cha·riv·a·ri
char·la·tan
  char·la·tan·ism
Char·le·magne
Charles·ton
Charles·town
char·ley horse
Char·lotte
Char·lottes·ville
Char·lotte·town
charm·er
char·nel
char·ter
char·treuse
char·wom·an
chary
  char·i·er
  char·i·est
Cha·ryb·di·an
Cha·ryb·dis
chase

chased
chas·ing
chas·er
chasm
chas·sis
chaste
chaste·ly
chas·ten
chas·tise
chas·tised
chas·tis·ing
chas·tise·ment
chas·tis·er
chas·ti·ty
chat
chat·ted
chat·ting
cha·teau
cha·teaux
Cha·teau·bri·and
Châ·teau-Thier·ry
chat·e·laine
Chat·ham
Chat·ta·hoo·chee
Chat·ta·noo·ga
chat·tel
chat·ter
chat·ter·box
Chat·ter·ton
chat·ty
chat·ti·er
chat·ti·est
chat·ti·ly
chat·ti·ness
Chau·cer
chauf·feur
chau·vin·ist
chau·vin·ism
chau·vin·is·tic
cheap
cheap·ly
cheap·ness
cheap·en
cheap·skate
cheat
check·book
check·er
check·er·board
check·list
check·mate
check·mat·ed
check·mat·ing
check·out
check·point
check·room
check·up
ched·dar
cheek·bone
cheeky
cheek·i·er
cheek·i·est
cheek·i·ly
cheek·i·ness
cheer·ful
cheer·ful·ly

cheer·ful·ness
cheer·lead·er
cheer·less
cheer·less·ly
cheer·less·ness
cheery
cheer·i·er
cheer·i·est
cheer·i·ly
cheer·i·ness
cheese·burg·er
cheese·cake
cheese·cloth
cheesy
chees·i·er
chees·i·est
chees·i·ness
chee·tah
Chel·sea
chem·i·cal
chem·i·cal·ly
che·mise
chem·ist
chem·is·try
chem·o·ther·a·py
che·nille
Cher·bourg
cher·ish
Cher·o·kee
che·root
cher·ry
cher·ries
cher·ub
cher·ubs
cher·u·bim
che·ru·bic
cher·vil
Ches·a·peake
Chesh·ire
chess·man
chess·men
Ches·ter·field
Ches·ter·ton
chest·nut
chesty
chest·i·er
chest·i·est
Chev·ro·let
chev·ron
chew
chew·er
Chey·enne
Chiang Kai·shek
Chi·an·ti
chi·a·ro·scu·ro
Chi·ca·go
chi·can·ery
chi·can·er·ies
Chi·ca·no
chi·chi
chick·a·dee
Chick·a·hom·i·ny
Chick·a·mau·ga
Chick·a·saw
chic·ken

chic·ken·heart·ed
chic·le
chic·o·ry
chic·o·ries
chide
chid·ed
chid·ing
chief
chief·ly
chief·tain
chif·fon
chif·fo·nier
chi·gnon
Chi·hua·hua
chil·blain
chil·dren
child·bear·ing
child·birth
child·hood
child·ish
child·ish·ly
child·like
chili
chil·ies
chill
chill·ing·ly
Chil·lon
chilly
chill·i·er
chill·i·est
chill·i·ness
chi·me·ra
chi·mer·ic
chi·mer·i·cal
chi·mer·i·cal·ly
chi·mer·i·cal·ness
chim·ney
chim·pan·zee
chin
chinned
chin·ning
chi·na
Chi·na·town
chin·chil·la
Chi·nese
Chin·kiang
chi·no
chi·nos
chi·noi·se·rie
chintzy
chintz·i·er
chintz·i·est
chip
chipped
chip·ping
chip·munk
Chip·pen·dale
chip·per
Chip·pe·wa
chi·rog·ra·pher
chi·rog·ra·phy
chi·rop·o·dist
chi·ro·prac·tic
chi·ro·prac·tor
chis·el

chis·eled
chis·el·ing
chis·el·er
chit·chat
chi·tin
chit·ter·ling
chiv·al·ry
chiv·al·ries
chiv·al·ric
chiv·al·rous
chiv·al·rous·ly
chiv·al·rous·ness
chlo·rine
chlo·ro·form
chlo·ro·phyll
chock·full
choc·o·late
Choc·taw
choice
choice·ly
choice·ness
choir·boy
choke
choked
chok·ing
chok·er
chol·er
chol·era
chol·er·ic
cho·les·te·rol
choose
chose
cho·sen
choos·ing
choosy
choos·i·er
choos·i·est
chop
chopped
chop·ping
Cho·pin
chop·per
chop·pi·ness
chop·py
chop·pi·er
chop·pi·est
chop·sticks
chop su·ey
cho·ral
cho·ral·ly
cho·rale
chord
chord·al
cho·rea
cho·re·og·ra·phy
cho·re·og·ra·pher
cho·re·o·graph·ic
cho·ric
chor·is·ter
chor·tle
chor·tled
chor·tling
cho·rus
cho·rus·es
cho·rused

cho·rus·ing
chos·en
chow·der
chow mein
chrism
Christ
Chris·ta·bel
chris·ten
chris·ten·ing
Chris·ten·dom
Chris·tian
Chris·ti·an·i·ty
Chris·ti·an·i·ties
Chris·tian·ize
Chris·tian·ized
Chris·tian·iz·ing
Christ·like
Christ·mas
Christ·mas·tide
chro·mate
chro·mat·ic
chro·mat·i·cal·ly
chro·mat·ics
chro·ma·tin
chro·mic
chro·mi·um
chro·mo
chro·mos
chro·mo·lith·o·graph
chro·mo·li·thog·ra·pher
chro·mo·lith·o·graph·ic
chro·mo·some
chro·mo·sphere
chron·ic
chron·i·cal·ly
chron·i·cle
chron·i·cled
chron·i·cling
chron·i·cler
chron·o·log·i·cal
chron·o·log·i·cal·ly
chro·nol·o·gy
chro·nol·o·gies
chro·nol·o·gist
chro·nom·e·ter
chron·o·met·ric
chrys·a·lis
chrys·a·lis·es
chry·sal·i·des
chry·san·the·mum
chrys·o·lite
chub·by
chub·bi·er
chub·bi·est
chub·bi·ness
chuck·full
chuck·le
chuck·led
chuck·ling
chuk·ker
chum·my
chum·mi·er
chum·mi·est
Chung·king
chunk

chunky
chunk·i·er
chunk·i·est
church
church·li·ness
church·ly
church·go·er
Church·ill
church·man
church·men
church·war·den
church·yard
churl·ish
churl·ish·ly
churl·ish·ness
churn·er
chut·ney
chutz·pah
ci·bo·ri·um
ci·bo·ria
ci·ca·da
ci·ca·das
ci·ca·dae
cic·a·trix
cic·a·tri·ces
cic·a·trize
cic·a·trized
cic·a·triz·ing
Cic·e·ro
cic·e·ro·ne
ci·der
ci·gar
cig·a·rette
cil·ia
cil·i·ar·y
cil·i·ate
Ci·li·cia
cin·cho·na
Cin·cin·nati
cinc·ture
cin·der
Cin·der·el·la
cin·e·ma
cin·e·mas
cin·e·mat·ic
cin·e·mat·o·graph
cin·e·ma·tog·ra·pher
cin·e·ma·tog·ra·phy
cin·e·rar·i·um
cin·na·bar
cin·na·mon
cinque·foil
ci·on
ci·pher
cir·ca
cir·ca·di·an
Cir·ce
cir·cle
cir·cled
cir·cling
cir·clet
cir·cuit
cir·cu·i·tous
cir·cu·i·tous·ly
cir·cu·i·tous·ness

cir·cu·lar
cir·cu·lar·ize
  cir·cu·lar·ized
  cir·cu·lar·iz·ing
  cir·cu·lar·i·za·tion
cir·cu·la·tion
  cir·cu·late
  cir·cu·lat·ed
  cir·cu·lat·ing
  cir·cu·la·tive
  cir·cu·la·tor
  cir·cu·la·to·ry
cir·cum·am·bi·ent
cir·cum·cise
  cir·cum·cised
  cir·cum·cis·ing
  cir·cum·cis·er
  cir·cum·ci·sion
cir·cum·fer·ence
  cir·cum·fer·en·tial
cir·cum·flex
cir·cum·flu·ent
cir·cum·fuse
  cir·cum·fused
  cir·cum·fus·ing
  cir·cum·fu·sion
cir·cum·lo·cu·tion
  cir·cum·lo·cu·to·ry
cir·cum·nav·i·gate
  cir·cum·nav·i·gat·ed
  cir·cum·nav·i·gat·ing
  cir·cum·nav·i·ga·tion
  cir·cum·nav·i·ga·tor
cir·cum·scribe
  cir·cum·scribed
  cir·cum·scrib·ing
  cir·cum·scrib·er
  cir·cum·scrip·tion
  cir·cum·scrip·tive
cir·cum·spect
cir·cum·stance
cir·cum·stan·tial
  cir·cum·stan·ti·al·i·ty
cir·cum·stan·ti·ate
  cir·cum·stan·ti·at·ed
  cir·cum·stan·ti·at·ing
  cir·cum·stan·ti·a·tion
cir·cum·vent
  cir·cum·ven·tion
  cir·cum·ven·tive
cir·cus
  cir·cus·es
cir·rho·sis
  cir·rhot·ic
cir·rus
Cis·ter·cian
cis·tern
cit·a·del
cite
  cit·ed
  cit·ing
  ci·ta·tion
cith·a·ra
cit·i·zen
  cit·i·zen·ship

cit·i·zen·ry
  cit·i·zen·ries
cit·rate
cit·ric
cit·ron
cit·ron·el·la
cit·rus
cit·tern
city
  cit·ies
ci·ty-state
civ·et
civ·ic
civ·ics
civ·il
ci·vil·ian
ci·vil·i·ty
  ci·vil·i·ties
civ·i·li·za·tion
civ·i·lize
  civ·i·lized
  civ·i·liz·ing
clab·ber
claim
  claim·a·ble
  claim·ant
  claim·er
clair·voy·ance
  clair·voy·ant
clam
  clammed
  clam·ming
clam·bake
clam·bar
clam·my
  clam·mi·er
  clam·mi·est
  clam·mi·ly
  clam·mi·ness
clam·or
  clam·or·ous
clan
  clan·nish
clan·des·tine
clang·or
  clang·or·ous
clans·man
  clans·men
clap
  clapped
  clap·ping
clap·board
clap·per
clap·trap
claque
clar·et
clar·i·fy
  clar·i·fied
  clar·i·fy·ing
  clar·i·fi·ca·tion
clar·i·net
  clar·i·net·ist
clar·i·on
clar·i·ty
class·a·ble

clas·sic
clas·si·cal
  clas·si·cal·ly
clas·si·cism
  clas·si·cist
clas·si·fied
clas·si·fy
  clas·si·fied
  clas·si·fy·ing
  clas·si·fi·er
  clas·si·fi·ca·tion
class·mate
class·room
classy
  class·i·er
  class·i·est
clat·ter
Clau·di·us
clause
  claus·al
claus·tro·pho·bia
clav·i·chord
clav·i·cle
cla·vier
clay
  clay·ey
clay·more
clean-cut
clean·er
clean·ly
  clean·li·er
  clean·li·est
  clean·li·ness
cleanse
  cleansed
  cleans·ing
  cleans·er
clean·up
clear
  clear·ly
  clear·ness
clear·ance
clear-cut
clear·ing
clear-sight·ed
cleav·age
cleave
  cleaved
  cleav·ing
cleav·er
clef
cleft
Cle·men·ceau
clem·en·cy
  clem·ent
Clem·ens
Cle·o·pat·ra
clere·sto·ry
  clere·sto·ries
cler·gy
  cler·gies
cler·gy·man
  cler·gy·men
cler·ic
cler·i·cal

cler·i·cal·ism
cler·i·cal·ist
Cler·mont
Cleve·land
clev·er
clev·er·ly
clev·er·ness
clev·is
clev·is·es
clew
cli·ché
cli·ent
cli·en·tele
cliff·hang·er
cli·mac·ter·ic
cli·mate
cli·mat·ic
cli·mat·i·cal
cli·max
cli·mac·tic
climb
climb·a·ble
climb·er
clinch·er
cling
clung
cling·ing
cling·ing·ly
cling·er
clin·ic
clin·i·cal
clin·i·cal·ly
clink·er
Clin·ton
clip
clipped
clip·ping
clip·per
clique
cliqu·ey
cliqu·ish
clit·o·ris
clo·a·ca
clo·a·cae
clo·a·cal
clob·ber
clock·wise
clock·work
clod
clod·dish
clod·dy
clog
clogged
clog·ging
clois·ter
clois·tral
close
closed
clos·ing
clos·er
clos·est
close·ly
close·ness
close·fist·ed
close-mouthed

clos·et
clos·et·ed
clos·et·ing
close-up
clo·sure
clot
clot·ted
clot·ting
clothe
clothed
cloth·ing
clothes·horse
clothes·line
clothes·pin
cloth·ier
cloth·ing
clo·ture
cloud·burst
cloudy
cloud·i·er
cloud·i·est
cloud·i·ly
cloud·i·ness
clo·ven
clo·ver
clo·ver·leaf
Clo·vis
clown
clown·ish
cloy
cloy·ing·ly
club
clubbed
club·bing
club·foot
club·house
clump
clumpy
clum·sy
clum·si·er
clum·si·est
clum·si·ly
clum·si·ness
Clu·ny
clus·ter
clut·ter
Clydes·dale
coach·man
coach·men
co·ag·u·late
co·ag·u·lat·ed
co·ag·u·lat·ing
co·ag·u·la·tion
co·a·lesce
co·a·lesced
co·a·les·cing
co·a·les·cence
co·a·les·cent
co·a·li·tion
coarse
coars·er
coars·est
coars·en
coarse·ly
coast·er

coast·line
coat·ing
co·au·thor
coax
coax·ing·ly
co·balt
cob·ble
cob·bled
cob·bling
cob·bler
cob·ble·stone
co·bra
cob·web
cob·webbed
cob·web·by
co·ca
co·caine
coc·cyx
coc·cy·ges
coc·cyg·e·al
coch·le·a
cock·ade
cock·a·too
cock·crow
cocker·er span·iel
cock·eyed
cock·fight
cock·le
cock·le·bur
cock·le·shell
cock·ney
cock·neys
cock·pit
cock·roach
cocks·comb
cock·sure
cock·tail
cocky
cock·i·er
cock·i·est
cock·i·ly
cock·i·ness
co·coa
co·co·nut
co·coon
cod
cod·fish
cod·dle
cod·dled
cod·dling
code
cod·ed
cod·ing
co·deine
codg·er
cod·i·cil
cod·i·fy
cod·i·fied
cod·i·fy·ing
cod·i·fi·ca·tion
cod-liv·er oil
co·ed
co·ed·u·ca·tion
co·ef·fi·cient
coe·len·ter·ate

co·e·qual
co·erce
  co·erced
  co·er·cing
  co·er·ci·ble
  co·er·cion
  co·er·cive
co·ex·ist
  co·ex·ist·ence
  co·ex·ist·ent
cof·fee
cof·fee·house
cof·fee·pot
cof·fer
cof·fin
co·gent
  co·gen·cy
  co·gent·ly
cog·i·tate
  cog·i·tat·ed
  cog·i·tat·ing
  cog·i·ta·ble
  cog·i·ta·tive
cog·nac
cog·nate
cog·ni·tion
  cog·ni·tive
cog·ni·zance
cog·ni·zant
cog·wheel
co·hab·it
  co·hab·i·ta·tion
co·here
  co·hered
  co·her·ing
co·her·ent
  co·her·ence
  co·her·en·cy
  co·her·ent·ly
co·he·sion
  co·he·sive
  co·he·sive·ly
  co·he·sive·ness
co·hort
coif·feur
coif·fure
  coif·fured
  coif·fur·ing
coin·age
co·in·cide
  co·in·cid·ed
  co·in·cid·ing
  co·in·ci·dence
  co·in·ci·dent
  co·in·ci·den·tal
    co·in·ci·den·tal·ly
co·i·tion
co·i·tus
  co·i·tal
coke
  coked
  cok·ing
co·la
col·an·der
Col·chis

cold·blood·ed
cole·slaw
col·ic
  col·icky
col·i·se·um
co·li·tis
col·lab·o·rate
  col·lab·o·rat·ed
  col·lab·o·rat·ing
  col·lab·o·ra·tion
  col·lab·o·ra·tor
col·lage
col·lapse
  col·lapsed
  col·laps·ing
  col·lap·si·ble
col·lar
col·lar·bone
col·late
  col·lat·ed
  col·lat·ing
  col·la·tion
  col·la·tor
col·lat·er·al
col·league
col·lect
  col·lect·i·ble
  col·lect·or
  col·lect·ed
  col·lec·tion
  col·lec·tive
  col·lec·tive·ly
  col·lec·tiv·i·ty
  col·lec·tiv·ism
  col·lec·tiv·ize
  col·lec·tiv·ized
  col·lec·tiv·iz·ing
  col·lec·tiv·i·za·tion
col·lege
  col·le·gi·al
  col·le·gian
  col·le·giate
col·lide
  col·lid·ed
  col·lid·ing
  col·li·sion
col·li·mate
  col·li·mat·ed
  col·li·mat·ing
  col·li·ma·tion
col·lo·cate
  col·lo·cat·ed
  col·lo·cat·ing
  col·lo·ca·tion
col·loid
col·lo·qui·al
  col·lo·qui·al·ly
  col·lo·qui·al·ism
col·lo·quy
  col·lo·quies
col·lu·sion
  col·lu·sive
co·logne
Co·lom·bia
Co·lom·bo

co·lon
colo·nel
co·lo·ni·al
co·lo·ni·al·ism
  co·lo·ni·al·ist
col·o·nist
col·on·nade
col·o·ny
  col·o·nies
col·o·nize
  col·o·nized
  col·o·niz·ing
  col·o·niz·er
  col·o·ni·za·tion
col·or
  col·or·er
  col·or·less
Col·o·rado
  col·or·a·tion
  col·or·blind
  col·or·blind·ness
  col·or·cast
  col·ored
  col·or·fast
  col·or·ful
  col·or·ing
co·los·sal
Col·os·se·um
Co·los·si·an
co·los·sus
  co·los·si
colt·ish
Co·lum·bia
col·um·bine
Co·lum·bus
col·umn
  co·lum·nar
  col·umned
  col·um·nist
co·ma
  co·mas
  co·ma·tose
Co·man·che
com·bat
  com·bat·ed
  com·bat·ing
  com·bat·ant
  com·ba·tive
comb·er
com·bi·na·tion
  com·bi·na·tion·al
  com·bi·na·tive
com·bine
  com·bined
  com·bin·ing
  com·bin·a·ble
  com·bin·er
com·ic
  com·i·cal
com·ing
com·i·ty
  com·i·ties
com·ma
  com·mas
com·mand

com·man·dant
com·man·deer
com·mand·er
  com·mand·er·ship
com·mand·ment
com·man·do
  com·man·dos
com·mem·o·rate
  com·mem·o·rat·ed
  com·mem·o·rat·ing
  com·mem·o·ra·ble
  com·mem·o·ra·tion
  com·mem·o·ra·tive
  com·mem·o·ra·to·ry
com·mence
  com·menced
  com·menc·ing
com·mence·ment
com·mend
  com·mend·a·ble
  com·mend·a·bly
com·men·da·tion
  com·mend·a·to·ry
com·men·su·rate
  com·men·su·rate·ly
  com·men·su·ra·tion
com·ment
com·men·tary
  com·men·tar·ies
com·men·ta·tor
com·merce
com·mer·cial
  com·mer·cial·ism
  com·mer·cial·ize
  com·mer·cial·ized
  com·mer·cial·iz·ing
  com·mer·cial·i·za·tion
com·mie
com·mis·er·ate
  com·mis·er·at·ed
  com·mis·er·at·ing
  com·mis·er·a·tion
  com·mis·er·a·tive
com·mis·sar
com·mis·sary
  com·mis·sar·ies
com·mis·sion
  com·mis·sioned
com·mis·sion·er
com·bo
  com·bos
com·bus·ti·ble
  com·bus·ti·bil·i·ty
com·bus·tion
  com·bus·tive
come
  com·ing
come·back
co·me·di·an
  co·me·di·enne
come·down
com·e·dy
  com·e·dies
come·ly
  come·li·ness

come-on
com·er
com·et
come-up·pance
com·fort
com·fort·a·ble
  com·fort·a·bly
com·fort·er
com·fy
  com·fi·er
  com·fi·est
com·mit
  com·mit·ted
  com·mit·ting
com·mit·ment
com·mit·tee
  com·mit·tee·man
  com·mit·tee·wo·man
com·mode
com·mo·di·ous
com·mod·i·ty
  com·mod·i·ties
com·mo·dore
com·mon
com·mon·al·ty
  com·mon·al·ties
com·mon·place
com·mons
com·mon·weal
com·mon·wealth
com·mo·tion
com·mu·nal
  com·mu·nal·i·ty
com·mune
  com·muned
  com·mun·ing
com·mu·ni·cant
com·mu·ni·cate
  com·mu·ni·cat·ed
  com·mu·ni·cat·ing
  com·mu·ni·ca·ble
  com·mu·ni·ca·tive
com·mu·ni·ca·tion
com·mun·ion
com·mu·ni·qué
com·mun·ism
com·mu·nist
com·mu·ni·ty
  com·mu·ni·ties
com·mu·nize
  com·mu·nized
  com·mu·niz·ing
com·mu·ta·tion
com·mu·ta·tor
com·mute
  com·mut·ed
  com·mut·ing
  com·mut·a·ble
com·mut·er
Co·mo·ra
com·pact
com·pan·ion
com·pan·ion·a·ble
com·pan·ion·ship
com·pa·ny

com·pa·nies
com·pa·ra·ble
  com·pa·ra·bil·ity
com·par·a·tive
com·pare
  com·pared
  com·par·ing
com·par·i·son
com·part·ment
  com·part·men·tal
  com·part·ment·ed
  com·part·men·tal·ize
com·pass
com·pas·sion
  com·pas·sion·ate
com·pat·i·ble
  com·pat·i·bly
  com·pat·i·bil·i·ty
com·pa·tri·ot
com·peer
com·pel
  com·pelled
  com·pel·ling
com·pen·di·ous
com·pen·di·um
com·pen·sate
  com·pen·sat·ed
  com·pen·sat·ing
  com·pen·sa·tive
  com·pen·sa·tor
  com·pen·sa·to·ry
com·pen·sa·tion
com·pete
  com·pet·ed
  com·pet·ing
  com·pet·i·tor
com·pe·tence
com·pe·ten·cy
com·pe·tent
com·pe·ti·tion
com·pet·i·tive
com·pile
  com·piled
  com·pil·ing
  com·pi·la·tion
com·pla·cence
  com·pla·cen·cy
  com·pla·cent
com·plain
com·plain·ant
com·plaint
com·plai·sance
  com·plai·sant
com·plect·ed
com·ple·ment
  com·ple·men·tal
  com·ple·men·ta·ry
com·plete
  com·plet·ed
  com·plet·ing
  com·plet·a·ble
com·ple·tion
com·plex
com·plex·ion
  com·plex·ioned

com·plex·i·ty
com·plex·i·ties
com·pli·ance
com·pli·an·cy
com·pli·ant
com·pli·cate
com·pli·cat·ed
com·pli·cat·ing
com·pli·ca·tion
com·plic·i·ty
com·plic·i·ties
com·pli·ment
com·pli·men·ta·ry
com·pli·men·ta·ri·ly
com·ply
com·plied
com·ply·ing
com·po·nent
com·port
com·port·ment
com·pose
com·posed
com·pos·ing
com·pos·er
com·pos·ite
com·po·si·tion
com·post
com·po·sure
com·pote
com·pound
com·pre·hend
com·pre·hend·i·ble
com·pre·hen·si·ble
com·pre·hen·si·bil·i·ty
com·pre·hen·si·bly
com·pre·hen·sion
com·pre·hen·sive
com·press
com·pressed
com·press·i·ble
com·press·i·bil·i·ty
com·pres·sion
com·pres·sor
com·prise
com·prised
com·pris·ing
com·pro·mise
com·pro·mised
com·pro·mis·ing
comp·trol·ler
com·pul·sion
com·pul·sive
com·pul·so·ry
com·punc·tion
com·pute
com·put·ed
com·put·ing
com·put·a·ble
com·pu·ta·tion
com·put·er
com·put·er·ize
com·put·er·ized
com·put·er·iz·ing
com·put·er·i·za·tion
com·rade

com·rade·ship
com·sat
con
conned
con·ning
Co·na·kry
con·cave
con·ceal
con·ceal·a·ble
con·ceal·ment
con·cede
con·ced·ed
con·ced·ing
con·ceit
con·ceit·ed
con·ceive
con·ceived
con·ceiv·ing
con·ceiv·a·ble
con·ceiv·a·bly
con·cen·trate
con·cen·trat·ed
con·cen·trat·ing
con·cen·tra·tive
con·cen·tra·tor
con·cen·tra·tion
con·cen·tric
con·cen·tri·cal
con·cen·tric·i·ty
con·cept
con·cep·tu·al
con·cep·tion
con·cep·tive
con·cep·tu·al·ize
con·cep·tu·al·ized
con·cep·tu·al·iz·ing
con·cep·tu·al·i·za·tion
con·cern
con·cerned
con·cern·ing
con·cert
con·cert·ed
con·cer·ti·na
con·cert·mas·ter
con·cer·to
con·ces·sion
con·ces·sion·aire
conch
conchs
con·cil·i·ate
con·cil·i·at·ed
con·cil·i·at·ing
con·cil·i·a·tion
con·cil·i·a·to·ry
con·cise
con·cise·ness
con·cise·ly
con·clave
con·clude
con·clud·ed
con·clud·ing
con·clu·sion
con·clu·sive
con·coct
con·coc·tion

con-com-i-tant
con-com-i-tance
con-cord
con-cord-ance
con-cord-ant
con-course
con-crete
con-cret-ed
con-cret-ing
con-cre-tion
con-cre-tive
con-cu-bine
con-cur
con-curred
con-cur-ring
con-cur-rence
con-cur-rent
con-cus-sion
con-cus-sive
con-demn
con-dem-na-ble
con-dem-na-tion
con-dem-na-to-ry
con-dense
con-densed
con-dens-ing
con-den-sa-ble
con-den-sa-tion
con-dens-er
con-de-scend
con-de-scend-ing
con-de-scen-sion
con-di-ment
con-di-tion
con-di-tion-al
con-di-tion-er
con-di-tioned
con-dole
con-doled
con-dol-ing
con-do-la-to-ry
con-do-ler
con-do-lence
con-dom
con-do-min-i-um
con-done
con-doned
con-don-ing
con-do-na-tion
con-dor
con-duce
con-duced
con-duc-ing
con-du-cive
con-duct
con-duct-i-bil-i-ty
con-duct-i-ble
con-duct-ance
con-duc-tion
con-fer-ence
con-fer-en-tial
con-fess
con-fess-ed-ly
con-fes-sion
con-fes-sion-al

con-fes-sor
con-fet-ti
con-fi-dant
con-fi-dante
con-fide
con-fid-ed
con-fid-ing
con-fi-dence
con-fi-dent
con-fi-den-tial
con-fig-u-ra-tion
con-fig-u-ra-tion-al
con-fine
con-fined
con-fin-ing
con-fine-ment
con-firm
con-firm-a-ble
con-fir-ma-tion
con-fir-ma-tive
con-fir-ma-to-ry
con-firmed
con-firm-ed-ly
con-firm-ed-ness
con-fis-cate
con-fis-cat-ed
con-fis-cat-ing
con-fis-ca-tion
con-fis-ca-tor
con-fis-ca-to-ry
con-fla-gra-tion
con-flict
con-flict-ing
con-flic-tive
con-flic-tion
con-flu-ence
con-flu-ent
con-flux
con-form
con-form-ist
con-form-ism
con-form-a-ble
con-form-a-bly
con-form-ance
con-for-ma-tion
con-form-i-ty
con-form-i-ties
con-found
con-found-ed
con-found-ed-ly
con-front
con-fron-ta-tion
Con-fu-cius
con-fuse
con-fused
con-fus-ing
con-fus-ed-ly
con-fus-ed-ness
con-fu-sion
con-fute
con-fut-ed
con-fut-ing
con-fu-ta-tion
con-ga
con-gas

con-geal
con-geal-ment
con-gen-ial
con-ge-ni-al-i-ty
con-gen-ial-ly
con-gen-i-tal
con-ger
con-ge-ries
con-gest
con-ges-tion
con-ges-tive
con-glom-er-ate
con-glom-er-at-ed
con-glom-er-at-ing
con-glom-er-a-tion
Con-go
con-grat-u-late
con-grat-u-lat-ed
con-grat-u-lat-ing
con-grat-u-la-tor
con-grat-u-la-to-ry
con-grat-u-la-tion
con-gre-gate
con-gre-gat-ed
con-gre-gat-ing
con-gre-ga-tion
con-gre-ga-tion-al
con-gress
con-gres-sion-al
con-gress-man
con-gress-men
con-gress-wom-an
con-gress-wom-en
con-gru-ent
con-gru-ent-ly
con-gru-ence
con-gru-en-cy
con-gru-en-cies
con-gru-ous
con-gru-ous-ly
con-gru-ous-ness
con-gru-i-ty
con-gru-i-ties
con-ic
con-i-cal
co-ni-fer
con-jec-ture
con-jec-tured
con-jec-tur-ing
con-jec-tur-al
con-join
con-joint
con-joint-ly
con-ju-gal
con-ju-gal-ly
con-ju-gate
con-ju-gat-ed
con-ju-gat-ing
con-ju-ga-tion
con-ju-ga-tive
con-junc-tion
con-junc-tive
con-jur-a-tion
con-jure
con-jured

con·jur·ing
con·jur·er
con·nect
con·nec·tor
Con·nect·i·cut
con·nec·tion
con·nec·tive
con·nip·tion
con·nive
con·nived
con·niv·ing
con·niv·ance
con·nois·seur
con·note
con·not·ed
con·not·ing
con·no·ta·tion
con·no·ta·tive
con·nu·bi·al
con·nu·bi·al·ly
con·quer
con·quer·a·ble
con·quer·or
con·quest
con·quis·ta·dor
con·quis·ta·dors
con·quis·ta·dor·es
con·san·guin·e·ous
con·san·guin·i·ty
con·science
con·sci·en·tious
con·sci·en·tious·ly
con·scious
con·scious·ly
con·scious·ness
con·script
con·scrip·tion
con·se·crate
con·se·crat·ed
con·se·crat·ing
con·se·cra·tive
con·se·cra·tor
con·se·cra·tion
con·sec·u·tive
con·sec·u·tive·ly
con·sen·sus
con·sent
con·sent·er
con·se·quence
con·se·quent
con·se·quent·ly
con·se·quen·tial
con·se·quen·ti·al·i·ty
con·se·quen·tial·ly
con·ser·va·tion
con·ser·va·tion·al
con·ser·va·tion·ist
con·ser·va·tive
con·serv·a·tism
con·serv·a·tive·ly
con·serv·a·to·ry
con·serv·a·to·ries
con·serve
con·served
con·serv·ing

con·serv·a·ble
con·serv·er
con·sid·er
con·sid·er·a·ble
con·sid·er·a·bly
con·sid·er·ate
con·sid·er·a·tion
con·sid·er·ing
con·sign
con·sign·er
con·sign·or
con·sign·ment
con·sign·ee
con·sist
con·sist·en·cy
con·sist·en·cies
con·sist·ence
con·sist·ent
con·sist·ent·ly
con·sis·to·ry
con·sis·to·ries
con·so·la·tion
con·sol·a·to·ry
con·sole
con·soled
con·sol·ing
con·sol·a·ble
con·sol·i·date
con·sol·i·dat·ed
con·sol·i·dat·ing
con·sol·i·da·tion
con·som·mé
con·so·nant
con·so·nance
con·so·nant·ly
con·so·nan·tal
con·sort
con·sor·ti·um
con·sor·tia
con·spic·u·ous
con·spic·u·ous·ly
con·spic·u·ous·ness
con·spire
con·spired
con·spir·ing
con·spir·a·cy
con·spir·a·cies
con·spir·a·tor
con·spir·a·to·ri·al
con·spir·er
con·spir·ing·ly
con·sta·ble
con·sta·ble·ship
con·stab·u·lary
con·stab·u·lar·ies
con·stant
con·stan·cy
Con·stan·tine
Con·stan·ti·no·ple
con·stant·ly
con·stel·la·tion
con·ster·na·tion
con·sti·pa·tion
con·sti·pate
con·stit·u·en·cy

con·stit·u·en·cies
con·stit·u·ent
con·sti·tute
con·sti·tu·tion
con·sti·tu·tion·al
con·sti·tu·tion·al·i·ty
con·sti·tu·tion·al·ly
con·strain
con·strain·a·ble
con·strained
con·straint
con·strict
con·stric·tive
con·stric·tion
con·stric·tor
con·struct
con·struc·tor
con·struc·tion
con·struc·tion·al
con·struc·tive
con·struc·tive·ly
con·struc·tive·ness
con·strue
con·strued
con·stru·ing
con·stru·a·ble
con·stru·er
con·sul
con·su·lar
con·sul·ship
con·su·late
con·sult
con·sul·ta·tion
con·sult·ant
con·sume
con·sumed
con·sum·ing
con·sum·a·ble
con·sum·er
con·sum·mate
con·sum·mat·ed
con·sum·mat·ing
con·sum·mate·ly
con·sum·ma·tion
con·sump·tion
con·sump·tive
con·tact
con·ta·gion
con·ta·gious
con·ta·gious·ness
con·tain
con·tain·a·ble
con·tain·er
con·tain·ment
con·tam·i·nate
con·tam·i·nat·ed
con·tam·i·nat·ing
con·tam·i·nant
con·tam·i·na·tion
con·tam·i·na·tive
con·tam·i·na·tor
con·tem·plate
con·tem·plat·ed
con·tem·plat·ing
con·tem·pla·tion

con·tem·pla·tive
con·tem·po·ra·ne·ous
con·tem·po·rary
  con·tem·po·rar·ies
con·tempt
con·tempt·i·ble
  con·tempt·i·bly
con·temp·tu·ous
  con·temp·tu·ous·ly
con·tend
  con·tend·er
con·tent
  con·tent·ment
con·tent·ed
  con·tent·ed·ly
  con·tent·ed·ness
con·ten·tion
con·ten·tious
  con·ten·tious·ly
  con·ten·tious·ness
con·ter·mi·nous
con·test
  con·test·a·ble
  con·test·er
  con·test·ant
con·text
con·tig·u·ous
  con·ti·gu·i·ty
  con·ti·gu·i·ties
  con·tig·u·ous·ly
  con·tig·u·ous·ness
con·ti·nence
  con·ti·nen·cy
  con·ti·nent
  con·ti·nent·ly
con·ti·nent
con·ti·nen·tal
con·tin·gent
  con·tin·gen·cy
  con·tin·gen·cies
  con·tin·gent·ly
con·tin·u·al
  con·tin·u·al·ly
  con·tin·u·ance
con·tin·ue
  con·tin·ued
  con·tin·u·ing
  con·tin·u·a·tion
  con·tin·u·er
con·ti·nu·i·ty
  con·ti·nu·i·ties
con·tin·u·ous
  con·tin·u·ous·ly
con·tin·u·um
  con·tin·ua
con·tort
  con·tor·tion
  con·tor·tive
  con·tor·tion·ist
con·tour
con·tra·band
con·tra·cep·tive
  con·tra·cep·tion
con·tract
  con·tract·ed

con·tract·i·ble
con·trac·tu·al
con·trac·tion
  con·trac·tive
  con·trac·tile
con·trac·tor
con·tra·dict
  con·tra·dict·a·ble
  con·tra·dic·tion
  con·tra·dic·to·ry
  con·tra·dis·tinc·tion
con·trail
con·tral·to
  con·tral·tos
  con·tral·ti
con·trap·tion
con·tra·pun·tal
con·tra·ri·wise
con·tra·ry
  con·tra·ries
  con·tra·ri·ly
  con·tra·ri·ness
con·trast
  con·trast·a·ble
  con·trast·ing·ly
con·tra·vene
  con·tra·vened
  con·tra·ven·ing
  con·tra·ven·er
  con·tra·ven·tion
con·trib·ute
  con·trib·ut·ed
  con·trib·ut·ing
  con·trib·ut·a·ble
  con·trib·u·tor
  con·trib·u·tory
con·tri·bu·tion
con·trite
  con·trite·ly
  con·trite·ness
con·tri·tion
con·trive
  con·trived
  con·triv·ing
  con·triv·ance
con·trol
  con·trolled
  con·trol·ling
  con·trol·la·ble
con·trol·ler
  con·trol·ler·ship
con·tro·ver·sy
  con·tro·ver·sies
  con·tro·ver·sial
  con·tro·ver·sial·ly
con·tro·vert
con·tu·me·ly
  con·tu·me·lies
con·tuse
  con·tused
  con·tus·ing
  con·tu·sion
co·nun·drum
con·va·lesce
  con·va·lesced

con·va·les·cing
con·va·les·cence
con·va·les·cent
con·vec·tion
con·vene
  con·vened
  con·ven·ing
  con·ven·er
con·ven·ience
con·ven·ient
  con·ven·ient·ly
con·vent
con·ven·tion
con·ven·tion·al
  con·ven·tion·al·ism
  con·ven·tion·al·ist
  con·ven·tion·al·i·ty
  con·ven·tion·al·i·ties
con·ven·tion·al·ize
  con·ven·tion·al·ized
  con·ven·tion·al·iz·ing
con·verge
  con·verged
  con·verg·ing
con·ver·gence
con·ver·gen·cy
con·ver·gent
con·ver·sant
con·ver·sa·tion
  con·ver·sa·tion·al
  con·ver·sa·tion·al·ist
con·verse
  con·versed
  con·vers·ing
  con·verse·ly
con·ver·sion
con·vert
con·vert·er
con·vert·i·ble
  con·vert·i·bil·i·ty
  con·vert·i·bly
con·vex
  con·vex·ly
  con·vex·i·ty
con·vey
  con·vey·a·ble
con·vey·ance
con·vey·er
con·vey·or
con·vict
con·vic·tion
  con·vic·tion·al
con·vince
  con·vinced
  con·vinc·ing
  con·vinc·er
  con·vinc·i·ble
con·viv·i·al
  con·viv·i·al·i·ty
  con·viv·i·al·ly
con·vo·ca·tion
  con·vo·ca·tion·al
con·voke
  con·voked
  con·vok·ing

con·vok·er
con·vo·lute
 con·vo·lut·ed
 con·vo·lut·ing
 con·vo·lute·ly
con·vo·lu·tion
con·voy
con·vulse
 con·vulsed
 con·vuls·ing
con·vul·sion
 con·vul·sive
 con·vul·sive·ly
co·ny
coo
 cooed
 coo·ing
 coo·ing·ly
cook·book
cook·e·ry
 cook·e·ries
cook·ie
 cook·ies
cook·out
cool
 cool·ish
 cool·ly
 cool·ness
cool·ant
cool·er
Coo·lidge
coo·lie
 coo·lies
coon·skin
coop·er
coop·er·age
co·op·er·ate
 co·op·er·at·ed
 co·op·er·at·ing
co·op·er·a·tion
co·op·er·a·tive
 co·op·er·a·tive·ly
co·opt
 co·op·ta·tion
co·or·di·nate
 co·or·di·nat·ed
 co·or·di·nat·ing
 co·or·di·nate·ly
 co·or·di·na·tor
 co·or·di·na·tion
coot·ie
cop
 copped
 cop·ping
co·pa·cet·ic
co·part·ner
 co·part·ner·ship
cope
 coped
 cop·ing
Co·pen·ha·gen
Co·per·ni·cus
cope·stone
cop·i·er
co·pi·lot

co·pi·ous
 co·pi·ous·ly
 co·pi·ous·ness
cop·out
cop·per
 cop·pery
 cop·per·head
 cop·per·plate
cop·pice
cop·ra
copse
Cop·tic
cop·u·la
 cop·u·las
 cop·u·lae
 cop·u·lar
cop·u·late
 cop·u·lat·ed
 cop·u·lat·ing
 cop·u·la·tion
cop·u·la·tive
 cop·u·la·tive·ly
copy
 cop·ies
 cop·ied
 cop·y·ing
cop·y·book
cop·y·cat
cop·y·ist
cop·y·right
co·quet
 co·quet·ted
 co·quet·ting
 co·quet·ry
 co·quet·ries
co·quette
 co·quet·tish
 co·quet·tish·ly
cor·a·cle
cor·al
cor·bel
cord·age
cor·date
 cor·date·ly
cor·dial
 cor·dial·i·ty
 cor·dial·ness
 cor·dial·ly
cor·dil·le·ra
cord·ite
Cor·do·ba
cor·don
cor·do·van
cor·du·roy
cord·wood
core
 cored
 cor·ing
co·re·la·tion
co·re·spond·ent
co·ri·an·der
Cor·inth
Co·rin·thi·an
cor·ker
cork·screw

corn·cob
cor·nea
cor·ne·al
cor·ner
cor·ner·stone
cor·net
 cor·net·ist
corn·flow·er
cor·nice
Cor·nish
corn·starch
cor·nu·co·pia
Corn·wall
Corn·wal·lis
corny
 corn·i·er
 corn·i·est
co·rol·la
cor·ol·lary
 cor·ol·lar·ies
co·ro·na
 co·ro·nas
 co·ro·nae
Cor·o·na·do
cor·o·nary
cor·o·na·tion
cor·o·ner
 cor·o·ner·ship
cor·o·net
 cor·o·net·ed
cor·po·ral
cor·po·rate
 cor·po·rate·ly
 cor·po·ra·tive
cor·po·ra·tion
cor·po·rat·ism
cor·po·re·al
 cor·po·re·al·i·ty
 cor·po·re·al·ness
corps
corpse
corps·man
 corps·men
cor·pu·lent
 cor·pu·lence
 cor·pu·len·cy
cor·pus
Corpus Chris·ti
cor·pus·cle
 cor·pus·cu·lar
cor·ral
 cor·ralled
 cor·ral·ling
cor·rect
 cor·rect·a·ble
 cor·rect·i·ble
 cor·rect·ness
cor·rec·tor
cor·rec·tion
 cor·rec·tion·al
cor·rec·tive
Cor·reg·i·dor
cor·re·late
 cor·re·lat·ed
 cor·re·lat·ing

cor·re·la·tion
cor·rel·a·tive
cor·re·spond
 cor·re·spond·ing
 cor·re·spond·ing·ly
cor·re·spond·ence
cor·re·spond·ent
cor·ri·dor
cor·ri·gi·ble
 cor·ri·gi·bil·i·ty
 cor·ri·gi·bly
cor·rob·o·rate
 cor·rob·o·rat·ed
 cor·rob·o·rat·ing
 cor·rob·o·ra·tion
 cor·rob·o·ra·tive
 cor·rob·o·ra·to·ry
cor·rode
 cor·rod·ed
 cor·rod·ing
 cor·rod·i·ble
cor·ro·sion
cor·ro·sive
cor·ru·gate
 cor·ru·gat·ed
 cor·ru·gat·ing
 cor·ru·ga·tion
cor·rupt
 cor·rupt·er
 cor·rup·ti·ble
 cor·rup·ti·bil·i·ty
 cor·rupt·ly
 cor·rupt·ness
cor·rup·tion
cor·sage
cor·sair
cor·set
 cor·set·ed
Cor·si·ca
cor·tex
 cor·ti·ces
cor·ti·cal
cor·ti·sone
co·run·dum
co·sig·na·to·ry
cos·met·ic
cos·mic
 cos·mi·cal·ly
cos·mog·o·ny
 cos·mog·o·nies
cos·mo·gon·ic
cos·mog·o·nist
cos·mog·ra·phy
 cos·mog·ra·phies
 cos·mog·ra·pher
 cos·mo·graph·ic
cos·mol·o·gy
 cos·mol·o·gies
 cos·mo·log·ic
 cos·mo·log·i·cal
 cos·mol·o·gist
cos·mo·naut
cos·mo·pol·i·tan
 cos·mo·pol·i·tan·ism
cos·mop·o·lite

cos·mos
Cos·sack
Cos·ta Ri·ca
cost·ly
 cost·li·er
 cost·li·est
 cost·li·ness
cost-plus
cos·tume
 cos·tumed
 cos·tum·ing
 cos·tum·er
co·sy
 co·si·er
 co·si·est
co·te·rie
co·ter·mi·nous
co·til·lion
cot·tage
cot·ter
cot·ton
 cot·tony
cot·ton·mouth
cot·ton·seed
cot·ton·tail
cot·ton·wood
couch
cough
cou·lée
coun·cil
 coun·cil·or
 coun·cil·man
 coun·cil·lor·ship
coun·sel
 coun·seled
 coun·sel·ing
coun·se·lor
 coun·se·lor·ship
count
 count·a·ble
 count·down
coun·te·nance
 coun·te·nanced
 coun·te·nanc·ing
 coun·te·nanc·er
count·er
coun·ter·act
 coun·ter·ac·tion
 coun·ter·ac·tive
coun·ter·at·tack
coun·ter·charge
 coun·ter·charged
 coun·ter·char·ging
coun·ter·claim
 coun·ter·claim·ant
coun·ter·clock·wise
coun·ter·cul·ture
coun·ter·es·pi·o·nage
coun·ter·feit
 coun·ter·feit·er
coun·ter·in·tel·li·gence
coun·ter·mand
coun·ter·meas·ure
coun·ter·of·fen·sive
coun·ter·pane

coun·ter·part
coun·ter·point
coun·ter·poise
 coun·ter·poised
 coun·ter·pois·ing
coun·ter·rev·o·lu·tion
coun·ter·sign
 coun·ter·sig·na·ture
coun·ter·sink
 coun·ter·sank
 coun·ter·sunk
coun·ter·spy
 coun·ter·spies
coun·ter·weight
coun·tess
count·less
coun·tri·fied
coun·try
 coun·tries
 coun·try·man
 coun·try·men
 coun·try·wo·man
 coun·try·wo·men
 coun·try·side
coun·ty
 coun·ties
coup
 coups
cou·pé
coup·le
 coup·led
 coup·ling
coup·ler
cou·pon
cour·age
 cou·ra·geous
cour·i·er
course
 coursed
 cours·ing
cours·er
cour·te·ous
 cour·te·ous·ly
cour·te·sy
 cour·te·sies
court·house
cour·ti·er
court·ly
 court·li·er
 court·li·est
 court·li·ness
court-mar·tial
 courts-mar·tial
 court-mar·tialed
 court-mar·tial·ing
court·room
court·ship
court·yard
cous·in
 cous·in·hood
cous·in·ly
cou·tu·rier
cov·e·nant
 cov·e·nan·ter
 cov·e·nan·tor

Cov·en·try
cov·er
 cov·ered
 cov·er·ing
 cov·er·less
cov·er·age
cov·er·all
cov·er·let
cov·ert
 cov·ert·ly
 cov·ert·ness
cov·er·up
cov·et
 cov·et·a·ble
 cov·et·er
cov·et·ous
 cov·et·ous·ly
cov·ey
cow·ard
 cow·ard·ly
 cow·ard·li·ness
cow·ard·ice
cow·boy
cow·er
 cow·er·ing·ly
cow·hide
cowl
 cowled
cow·lick
cowl·ing
cow·man
 cow·men
co-work·er
cow·poke
cow·pox
cow·ry
 cow·rie
 cow·ries
cox·swain
coy
 coy·ly
 coy·ness
coy·o·te
coz·en
 coz·en·age
 coz·en·er
co·zy
 co·zi·er
 co·zi·est
 co·zi·ly
 co·zi·ness
crab
 crabbed
 crab·bing
 crab·by
 crab·bed·ly
 crab·bed·ness
crack·down
crack·er
crack·ing
crack·le
 crack·led
 crack·ling
crack·up
Cra·cow

cra·dle
 cra·dled
 cra·dling
crafts·man
 crafts·man·ship
crafty
 craft·i·er
 craft·i·est
 craft·i·ly
 craft·i·ness
crag
 crag·ged
 crag·gy
 crag·gi·ness
cram
 crammed
 cram·ming
 cram·mer
cran·ber·ry
 cran·ber·ries
crane
 craned
 cran·ing
cra·ni·um
 cra·ni·ums
 cra·nia
 cra·ni·al
 cra·ni·ate
 cra·ni·al·ly
crank·case
crank·shaft
cranky
 crank·i·er
 crank·i·est
 crank·i·ly
 crank·i·ness
Cran·mer
cran·ny
 cran·nies
 cran·nied
crash-land
crass
 crass·ly
 crass·ness
Cras·sus
crate
 crat·ed
 crat·ing
cra·ter
 cra·ter·al
 cra·tered
cra·vat
crave
 craved
 crav·ing
 crav·er
 crav·ing·ly
craw·fish
crawl
 crawly
 crawl·ing·ly
 crawl·er
cray·fish
cray·on
craze

crazed
craz·ing
cra·zy
 cra·zi·er
 cra·zi·est
 cra·zi·ly
 cra·zi·ness
creak
 creak·i·ly
 creak·i·ness
 creaky
 creak·i·er
 creak·i·est
cream
 cream·i·ly
 cream·i·ness
 creamy
 cream·i·er
 cream·i·est
 cream·er
 cream·ery
 cream·er·ies
crease
 creased
 creas·ing
 creasy
 creas·i·er
 creas·i·est
cre·ate
 cre·at·ed
 cre·at·ing
cre·a·tion
 cre·a·tion·al
cre·a·tive
 cre·a·tiv·i·ty
cre·a·tor
crea·ture
cre·dence
cre·den·tial
cre·den·za
cred·i·ble
 cred·i·bil·i·ty
 cred·i·bly
cred·it
 cred·it·a·ble
 cred·it·a·bil·i·ty
 cred·it·a·bly
cred·i·tor
cre·do
cre·dos
cred·u·lous
creek
creel
creep
 crept
 creep·ing
 creepy
 creep·i·er
 creep·i·est
 creep·i·ness
creep·er
cre·mate
 cre·mat·ed
 cre·mat·ing
cre·ma·tion

cre·ma·ter
cre·ma·to·ry
  cre·ma·to·ri·um
Cre·ole
cre·o·sote
crêpe
crepe
  creped
  crep·ing
cre·pus·cu·lar
cres·cen·do
  cres·cen·dos
cres·cent
crest
  crest·ed
  crest·less
crest·fall·en
cre·ta·ceous
Cre·tan
cre·tin·ism
cre·tonne
cre·vasse
crev·ice
crew·el
crib
  cribbed
  crib·bing
  crib·ber
crib·bage
crick·et
cri·er
Cri·mea
crim·i·nal
  crim·i·nal·i·ty
  crim·i·nal·ly
crim·i·nol·o·gy
crim·i·nol·o·gist
crimpy
  crimp·i·er
  crimp·i·est
crim·son
cringe
  cringed
  cring·ing
crin·kle
  crin·kled
  crin·kling
  crin·kly
  crin·kli·er
  crin·kli·est
crip·ple
  crip·pled
  crip·pling
cri·sis
  cri·ses
crisp
  crisp·er
  crisp·ness
  crispy
  crisp·i·er
  crisp·i·est
criss·cross
Cris·to·bal
cri·te·ri·on
  cri·te·ria

crit·ic
crit·i·cal
  crit·i·cal·ly
  crit·i·cal·ness
crit·i·cism
crit·i·cize
  crit·i·cized
  crit·i·ciz·ing
  crit·i·ciz·a·ble
cri·tique
crit·ter
croaky
  croak·i·er
  croak·i·est
  croak·er
Cro·a·tia
cro·chet
  cro·cheted
  cro·chet·ing
  cro·chet·er
crock·ery
Crock·ett
croc·o·dile
cro·cus
  cro·cus·es
crois·sant
Cro-Mag·non
cro·ny
  cro·nies
crook·ed
croon·er
crop
  cropped
  crop·ping
crop·per
cro·quet
cro·quette
cross·bar
cross·bones
cross·bow
cross·bred
  cross·breed
  cross·breed·ing
cross-coun·try
cross·cut
cross-ex·am·ine
  cross-ex·am·ined
  cross-ex·am·in·ing
cross-fer·ti·li·za·tion
cross·hatch
cross·ing
cross-pol·li·na·tion
  cross-pol·li·nate
cross-pur·pose
cross-ref·er·ence
cross·road
cross-stitch
cross·tie
cross·walk
cross·wise
  cross·ways
crotch·ety
  crotch·et·i·ness
crouch
croup

croupy
crou·pi·er
crou·ton
crow·bar
crow's-foot
crow's-feet
crow's-nest
cru·cial
cru·ci·al·i·ty
cru·cial·ly
cru·ci·ble
cru·ci·fix
cru·ci·fix·ion
cru·ci·form
cru·ci·fy
cru·ci·fied
cru·ci·fy·ing
crude
  crud·er
  crud·est
  crude·ly
  crude·ness
cru·di·ty
  cru·di·ties
cru·el
  cru·el·ly
  cru·el·ness
  cru·el·ty
cru·et
cruise
  cruised
  cruis·ing
  cruis·er
crul·ler
crum·ble
  crum·bled
  crum·bling
  crum·bly
crum·my
  crum·mi·er
  crum·mi·est
crum·pet
crum·ple
  crum·pled
  crum·pling
  crum·pler
  crum·ply
  crum·pli·er
  crum·pli·est
crunchy
  crunch·i·er
  crunch·i·est
cru·sade
cru·sad·er
crush·er
crush·ing
crush·ing·ly
Cru·soe
crus·ta·cean
crusty
  crust·i·er
  crust·i·est
  crust·i·ly
  crust·i·ness
crux

crux·es
cru·ces
cry
  cried
  cry·ing
cry·ba·by
cry·o·gen·ics
cry·o·sur·gery
crypt
  crypt·al
crypt·a·nal·y·sis
cryp·tic
  cryp·ti·cal
  cryp·ti·cal·ly
cryp·to·gram
cryp·to·graph
  cryp·tog·ra·phy
  cryp·to·graph·ic
  cryp·tog·ra·pher
crys·tal
crys·tal·line
crys·tal·lize
  crys·tal·lized
  crys·tal·liz·ing
  crys·tal·liz·er
  crys·tal·liz·a·ble
  crys·tal·li·za·tion
Cu·ba
cub·by
  cub·bies
cub·by·hole
cube
  cubed
  cub·ing
cu·bic
cu·bi·cle
cub·ism
cu·bit
cuck·old
  cuck·old·ry
cuck·oo
  cuck·oos
  cuck·ooed
  cuck·oo·ing
cu·cum·ber
cud·dle
  cud·dled
  cud·dling
  cud·dle·some
  cud·dly
  cud·dli·er
  cud·dli·est
cudg·el
  cudg·eled
  cudg·el·ing
cue
  cued
  cu·ing
cui·sine
cul-de-sac
  culs-de-sac
cu·li·nary
cul·mi·nant
cul·mi·nate
  cul·mi·nat·ed

cul·mi·nat·ing
cul·mi·na·tion
cu·lottes
cul·pa·ble
  cul·pa·bil·i·ty
  cul·pa·bly
cul·prit
cult
  cul·tic
cul·ti·vate
  cul·ti·vat·ed
  cul·ti·vat·ing
  cul·ti·va·tion
  cul·ti·va·ble
  cul·ti·vat·a·ble
  cul·ti·va·tor
cul·tur·al
cul·ture
  cul·tured
  cul·tur·ing
cul·vert
cum·ber
  cum·ber·some
Cum·ber·land
cum·brance
cum lau·de
cum·mer·bund
cu·mu·late
  cu·mu·lat·ed
  cu·mu·lat·ing
  cu·mu·la·tion
  cu·mu·la·tive
  cu·mu·lo·nim·bus
  cu·mu·lo·nim·bus·es
  cu·mu·lus
  cu·mu·lous
cu·ne·i·form
cun·ni·lin·gus
cun·ning
  cun·ning·ly
  cun·ning·ness
cup
  cupped
  cup·ping
cup·board
cup·cake
cup·ful
  cup·fuls
Cu·pid
cu·pid·i·ty
cu·po·la
cur·a·ble
  cur·a·bil·i·ty
  cur·a·bly
Cu·ra·cao
cu·rate
cur·a·tive
cu·ra·tor
  cu·ra·to·ri·al
  cu·ra·tor·ship
curb·ing
curb·stone
cur·dle
  cur·dled
  cur·dling

cure
  cured
  cur·ing
  cur·er
cure-all
cur·few
cu·ria
  cu·ri·ae
cu·ri·al
cu·rie
cu·rio
cu·ri·os
cu·ri·os·i·ty
  cu·ri·os·i·ties
cu·ri·ous
cu·ri·um
curl
  curl·er
curl·i·cue
curl·ing
curly
  curl·i·er
  curl·i·est
  curl·i·ness
cur·rant
cur·ren·cy
  cur·ren·cies
cur·rent
cur·ric·u·lum
  cur·ric·u·lums
  cur·ric·u·la
  cur·ric·u·lar
cur·rish
cur·ry
  cur·ries
  cur·ried
  cur·ry·ing
  cur·ri·er
cur·ry·comb
curse
  cursed
  curs·ing
  curs·ed·ly
  curs·ed·ness
cur·sive
  cur·sive·ly
cur·so·ry
  cur·so·ri·ly
  cur·so·ri·ness
curt
  curt·ly
  curt·ness
cur·tail
  cur·tail·ment
cur·tain
curt·sy
  curt·sies
  curt·sied
  curt·sy·ing
cur·va·ceous
cur·va·ture
curve
  curved
  curv·ing
  curv·ed·ness

cur·vi·lin·e·ar
cush·ion
cushy
 cush·i·er
 cush·i·est
cus·pid
 cus·pi·dal
cus·pi·date
cus·pi·dor
cuss·ed
 cuss·ed·ly
 cuss·ed·ness
cus·tard
Cus·ter
cus·to·di·an
 cus·to·di·an·ship
cus·to·dy
 cus·to·dies
 cus·to·di·al
cus·tom
cus·tom·ary
 cus·tom·ar·ies
 cus·tom·ar·i·ly
 cus·tom·ar·i·ness
cus·tom-built
cus·tom·er
cus·tom·house
cus·tom·ize
 cus·tom·ized
 cus·tom·iz·ing
cus·tom-made
cu·ta·ne·ous
cut·back
cute
 cut·er
 cut·est
 cute·ly
 cute·ness
cu·ti·cle
cut·lass
cut·lery
cut·let
cut·off
cut·out
cut·rate
cut·ter
cut·throat
cut·ting
 cut·ting·ly
cut·tle
cut·tle·fish
cut·up
cut·worm
cy·an·ic
cy·a·nide
cy·a·no·sis
cy·ber·na·tion
cy·ber·net·ics
cyc·la·men
cy·cle
 cy·cled
 cy·cling
 cy·clist
cy·clic
 cy·cli·cal

cy·cli·cal·ly
cy·clom·e·ter
cy·clone
cy·clo·rama
 cy·clo·ram·ic
cy·clo·tron
cyg·net
cyl·in·der
 cy·lin·dric
 cy·lin·dri·cal
cym·bal
 cym·bal·ist
cyn·ic
 cyn·i·cism
 cyn·i·cal
 cyn·i·cal·ly
cy·no·sure
cy·pher
cy·press
Cy·prus
cyst
 cys·tic
 cys·tic fi·bro·sis
cy·tol·o·gy
 cy·tol·o·gist
czar
czar·e·vitch
cza·ri·na
Czech·o·slo·va·kia
dab
 dabbed
 dab·bing
dab·ble
 dab·bled
 dab·bling
 dab·bler
Dac·ca
Da·cron
dac·tyl
 dac·tyl·ic
dad·dy-long·legs
daf·fo·dil
daf·fy
 daf·fi·er
 daf·fi·est
dag·ger
Da·guerre
da·guerre·o·type
dahl·ia
Da·ho·mey
dai·ly
 dai·lies
dain·ty
 dain·ti·er
 dain·ti·est
 dain·ties
 dain·ti·ly
 dain·ti·ness
dai·qui·ri
dairy
 dair·ies
 dair·y·man
 dair·y·men
da·is
dai·sy

dai·sies
Da·kar
Da·ko·ta
Dal·las
dal·ly
 dal·lied
 dal·ly·ing
 dal·li·ance
Dal·ma·tia
dam
 dammed
 dam·ming
dam·age
 dam·aged
 dam·ag·ing
 dam·age·a·ble
dam·a·scene
 dam·a·scened
 dam·a·scen·ing
Da·mas·cus
dam·ask
damn
dam·na·ble
 dam·na·ble·ness
 dam·na·bly
dam·na·tion
damned
damp·en
damp·er
dam·sel
dam·son
dance
 danced
 danc·ing
 dan·cer
dan·de·li·on
dan·der
dan·dle
 dan·dled
 dan·dling
dan·druff
dan·dy
 dan·dies
 dan·di·er
 dan·di·est
 dan·dy·ism
dan·ger
dan·ger·ous
 dan·ger·ous·ly
 dan·ger·ous·ness
dan·gle
 dan·gled
 dan·gling
 dan·gler
Dan·ish
dank
 dank·ly
 dank·ness
dan·seuse
 dan·seus·es
Dan·te
Dan·ube
Dan·ville
Dan·zig
dap·per

dap·ple
  dap·pled
  dap·pling
Dar·da·nelles
dare
  dared
  dar·ing
dare·dev·il
Dar·i·en
dar·ing·ly
dark
  dark·ish
  dark·ly
  dark·ness
Dark Ag·es
dark·en
dark·ling
dark·room
dar·ling
  dar·ling·ly
  dar·ling·ness
Darm·stadt
darn·er
dart·er
Dart·mouth
Dar·win
Dar·win·ism
  Dar·win·ist
dash·board
dash·ing
das·tard
  das·tard·li·ness
  das·tard·ly
da·ta
date
  dat·ed
  dat·ing
  dat·a·ble
  dat·er
date·less
date·line
da·tive
da·tum
  da·ta
daub
  daub·er
daugh·ter
  daugh·ter·ly
daugh·ter·in·law
  daugh·ters·in·law
daunt·less
  daunt·less·ly
  daunt·less·ness
dau·phin
dav·en·port
Da·vid
dav·it
daw·dle
  daw·dled
  daw·dling
  daw·dler
dawn
day·break
day·dream
  day·dream·er

day·light
day·light·sav·ing time
day·time
Day·ton
Day·to·na
daze
  dazed
  daz·ing
  daz·ed·ly
daz·zle
  daz·zled
  daz·zling
  daz·zler
  daz·zling·ly
D-day
dea·con
  dea·con·ry
  dea·con·ship
  dea·con·ess
dead·beat
dead·en
  dead·en·er
dead·end
dead·line
dead·lock
dead·ly
  dead·li·er
  dead·li·est
  dead·li·ness
dead·pan
dead·wood
deaf
  deaf·ly
  deaf·ness
deaf·en
  deaf·en·ing·ly
deaf·mute
deal
  dealt
  deal·ing
  deal·er
dean·ship
dear
  dear·ly
  dear·ness
Dear·born
dearth
death
  death·less
  death·ly
death·blow
death's·head
death·trap
death·watch
de·ba·cle
de·bar
  de·barred
  de·bar·ring
  de·bar·ment
de·bark
  de·bar·ka·tion
de·base
  de·based
  de·bas·ing
  de·base·ment

de·bas·er
de·bate
  de·bat·ed
  de·bat·ing
  de·bat·a·ble
  de·bat·er
de·bauch
  de·bauch·er
  de·bauch·ment
  de·bauch·ery
  de·bauch·er·ies
deb·au·chee
de·ben·ture
de·bil·i·tate
  de·bil·i·tat·ed
  de·bil·i·tat·ing
  de·bil·i·ta·tion
de·bil·i·ty
  de·bil·i·ties
deb·it
deb·o·nair
Deb·o·rah
de·bris
debt·or
de·bunk
  de·bunk·er
de·but
deb·u·tante
de·cade
dec·a·dent
  dec·a·dence
  dec·a·dent·ly
dec·a·gon
dec·a·gram
dec·a·he·dron
  dec·a·he·drons
de·cal
Dec·a·logue
de·camp
  de·camp·ment
de·cant
  de·cant·er
de·cap·i·tate
  de·cap·i·tat·ed
  de·cap·i·tat·ing
  de·cap·i·ta·tion
dec·a·pod
Dec·ap·o·lis
de·cath·lon
De·ca·tur
de·cay
Dec·can
de·cease
  de·ceased
de·ceit
  de·ceit·ful
  de·ceit·ful·ly
  de·ceit·ful·ness
de·ceive
  de·ceived
  de·ceiv·ing
  de·ceiv·er
  de·ceiv·ing·ly
  de·ceiv·a·ble
de·cel·er·ate

de·cel·er·at·ed
de·cel·er·at·ing
de·cel·er·a·tion
De·cem·ber
de·cen·cy
de·cen·cies
de·cen·ni·al
de·cen·ni·al·ly
de·cent
de·cent·ly
de·cen·tral·ize
de·cen·tral·ized
de·cen·tral·iz·ing
de·cen·tral·i·za·tion
de·cep·tion
de·cep·tive
de·cep·tive·ly
de·cep·tive·ness
dec·i·bel
de·cide
de·cid·ed
de·cid·ing
de·cid·a·ble
de·cid·ed·ly
de·cid·ed·ness
de·cid·u·ous
de·cid·u·ous·ly
dec·i·mal
dec·i·mate
dec·i·mat·ed
dec·i·mat·ing
dec·i·ma·tion
de·ci·pher
de·ci·pher·a·ble
de·ci·sion
de·ci·sive
de·ci·sive·ly
de·ci·sive·ness
deck·le
de·claim
dec·la·ma·tion
de·clam·a·tory
de·clare
de·clared
de·clar·ing
de·clar·a·tive
de·clar·a·to·ry
de·clar·er
dec·la·ra·tion
de·clas·si·fy
de·clas·si·fied
de·clas·si·fy·ing
de·clen·sion
dec·li·na·tion
de·cline
de·clined
de·clin·ing
de·clin·a·ble
de·cliv·i·ty
de·cliv·i·ties
de·code
de·cod·ed
de·cod·ing
de·cod·er
dé·colle·tage

de·com·pose
de·com·posed
de·com·pos·ing
de·com·po·si·tion
de·com·press
de·com·pres·sion
de·con·tam·i·nate
de·con·tam·i·nat·ed
de·con·tam·i·nat·ing
de·con·tam·i·na·tion
de·con·trol
de·con·trolled
de·con·trol·ling
de·cor
dec·o·rate
dec·o·rat·ed
dec·o·rat·ing
dec·o·ra·tion
dec·o·ra·tive
dec·o·ra·tive·ly
dec·o·ra·tor
dec·o·rous
dec·o·rous·ly
de·co·rum
de·coy
de·crease
de·creased
de·creas·ing
de·creas·ing·ly
de·cree
de·creed
de·cree·ing
de·crep·it
de·crep·i·tude
de·crep·it·ly
de·cre·scen·do
de·cre·scen·dos
de·cry
de·cried
de·cry·ing
de·cri·al
ded·i·cate
ded·i·cat·ed
ded·i·cat·ing
ded·i·ca·to·ry
ded·i·ca·tive
ded·i·ca·tion
de·duce
de·duc·i·ble
de·duct
de·duct·i·ble
de·duc·tion
de·duc·tive
de·duc·tive·ly
deep
deep·ly
deep·ness
deep·en
deep-root·ed
deep-seat·ed
deer·skin
de-es·ca·late
de-es·ca·lat·ed
de-es·ca·lat·ing
de-es·ca·la·tion

de·face
  de·faced
  de·fac·ing
  de·face·ment
  de·fac·er
de fac·to
de·fame
  de·famed
  de·fam·ing
  def·a·ma·tion
  de·fam·a·to·ry
  de·fam·er
de·fault
  de·fault·er
de·feat
  de·feat·ism
  de·feat·ist
def·e·cate
  def·e·cat·ed
  def·e·cat·ing
  def·e·ca·tion
de·fect
  de·fec·tion
  de·fec·tor
de·fec·tive
  de·fec·tive·ly
  de·fec·tive·ness
de·fend
  de·fend·er
  de·fend·ant
de·fense
  de·fense·less
  de·fense·less·ly
  de·fense·less·ness
  de·fen·si·ble
  de·fen·si·bil·i·ty
  de·fen·si·bly
de·fen·sive
  de·fen·sive·ly
de·fer
  de·ferred
  de·fer·ring
  de·fer·ment
def·er·ence
  def·er·en·tial
  def·er·en·tial·ly
de·fi·ance
  de·fi·ant
  de·fi·ant·ly
de·fi·cient
  de·fi·cien·cy
  de·fi·cien·cies
  de·fi·cient·ly
def·i·cit
de·file
  de·filed
  de·fil·ing
de·fine
  de·fined
  de·fin·ing
  de·fin·er
  de·fin·a·ble
  de·fin·a·bly
def·i·nite
  def·i·nite·ly

def·i·nite·ness
def·i·ni·tion
de·fin·i·tive
  de·fin·i·tive·ly
de·flate
  de·flat·ed
  de·flat·ing
  de·fla·tion
  de·fla·tion·ary
de·flect
  de·flec·tion
  de·flec·tive
  de·flec·tor
de·flow·er
De·foe
de·fo·li·ate
  de·fo·li·at·ed
  de·fo·li·at·ing
de·for·est
  de·for·est·a·tion
de·form
  de·for·ma·tion
  de·formed
  de·form·i·ty
  de·form·i·ties
de·fraud
de·fray
  de·fray·al
  de·fray·ment
  de·fray·a·ble
de·frost
  de·frost·er
deft
  deft·ly
  deft·ness
de·funct
de·fy
  de·fied
  de·fy·ing
  de·fi·er
de·gen·er·ate
  de·gen·er·at·ed
  de·gen·er·at·ing
  de·gen·er·ate·ly
  de·gen·er·a·cy
  de·gen·er·a·tion
  de·gen·er·a·tive
de·grade
  de·grad·ed
  de·grad·ing
  deg·ra·da·tion
de·gree
de·his·cence
  de·his·cent
de·hy·drate
  de·hy·drat·ed
  de·hy·drat·ing
  de·hy·dra·tion
de·i·fy
  de·i·fied
  de·i·fy·ing
  de·i·fi·ca·tion
  de·i·fi·er
deign
de·ist

de·ism
  de·is·tic
  de·is·ti·cal
de·i·ty
  de·i·ties
de·ject·ed
  de·jec·ted·ly
  de·jec·tion
de ju·re
Del·a·ware
de·lay
  de·lay·er
de·lec·ta·ble
  de·lec·ta·ble·ness
  de·lec·ta·bly
  de·lec·ta·tion
del·e·gate
  del·e·gat·ed
  del·e·gat·ing
  del·e·ga·tion
de·lete
  de·let·ed
  de·let·ing
  de·le·tion
del·e·te·ri·ous
Del·hi
de·lib·er·ate
  de·lib·er·at·ed
  de·lib·er·at·ing
  de·lib·er·ate·ly
  de·lib·er·ate·ness
  de·lib·er·a·tion
  de·lib·er·a·tive
  de·lib·er·a·tor
del·i·ca·cy
  del·i·ca·cies
del·i·cate
  del·i·cate·ly
  del·i·cate·ness
  del·i·ca·tes·sen
de·li·cious
  de·li·cious·ly
  de·li·cious·ness
de·light
  de·light·ed
  de·light·ed·ly
  de·light·ful
  de·light·ful·ly
  de·light·ful·ness
De·li·lah
de·lim·it
  de·lim·i·ta·tion
de·lin·e·ate
  de·lin·e·at·ed
  de·lin·e·at·ing
  de·lin·e·a·tion
  de·lin·e·a·tor
de·lin·quent
  de·lin·quen·cy
  de·lin·quen·cies
de·lir·i·um
  de·lir·i·ums
  de·lir·ia
  de·lir·i·ous
  de·lir·i·ous·ly

de·liv·er
 de·liv·er·a·ble
 de·liv·er·er
de·liv·er·ance
de·liv·ery
 de·liv·er·ies
de·louse
 de·loused
 de·lous·ing
Del·phi
del·phin·i·um
del·ta
del·toid
de·lude
 de·lud·ed
 de·lud·ing
 de·lud·er
de·lu·sive
de·lu·so·ry
 de·lu·sive·ly
del·uge
 del·uged
 del·ug·ing
de·lu·sion
de·luxe
delve
 delved
delv·ing
dem·a·gogue
 dem·a·gogu·ery
 dem·a·gog·ic
 dem·a·gog·i·cal
de·mand
 de·mand·er
de·mar·ca·tion
de·mean
 de·mean·or
de·ment·ed
de·men·tia
de·mer·it
De·me·tri·us
dem·i·god
dem·i·john
de·mise
 de·mised
 de·mis·ing
dem·i·tasse
de·mo·bi·lize
 de·mo·bi·lized
 de·mo·bi·liz·ing
 de·mo·bi·li·za·tion
de·moc·ra·cy
 de·moc·ra·cies
dem·o·crat
dem·o·crat·ic
 dem·o·crat·i·cal·ly
de·moc·ra·tize
 de·moc·ra·tized
 de·moc·ra·tiz·ing
 de·moc·ra·ti·za·tion
De·moc·ri·tus
de·mog·ra·phy
 de·mog·ra·pher
 dem·o·graph·ic
de·mol·ish

de·mol·ish·er
dem·o·li·tion
de·mon
 de·mon·ic
de·mon·e·tize
 de·mon·e·tized
 de·mon·e·tiz·ing
 de·mon·e·ti·za·tion
de·mo·ni·ac
 de·mo·ni·a·cal
de·mon·ol·o·gy
 de·mon·ol·o·gist
dem·on·strate
 dem·on·strat·ed
 dem·on·strat·ing
 dem·on·stra·ble
 dem·on·stra·bly
 dem·on·stra·tion
de·mon·stra·tive
 de·mon·stra·tive·ly
 de·mon·stra·tive·ness
 dem·on·stra·tor
de·mor·al·ize
 de·mor·al·ized
 de·mor·al·iz·ing
 de·mor·al·i·za·tion
 de·mor·al·iz·er
De·mos·the·nes
de·mote
 de·mot·ed
 de·mot·ing
 de·mo·tion
de·mur
 de·murred
 de·mur·ring
de·mur·ral
 de·mur·er
 de·mur·est
 de·mure·ly
 de·mure·ness
de·mur·rage
de·nat·u·ral·ize
 de·nat·u·ral·ized
 de·nat·u·ral·iz·ing
 de·nat·u·ral·i·za·tion
de·na·ture
 de·na·tured
 de·na·tur·ing
den·drite
den·dro·lite
den·drol·o·gy
den·e·ga·tion
de·ni·al
de·ni·er
den·im
den·i·zen
Den·mark
de·nom·i·nate
 de·nom·i·nat·ed
 de·nom·i·nat·ing
 de·nom·i·na·tion
 de·nom·i·na·tion·al
 de·nom·i·na·tion·al·ism
 de·nom·i·na·tive
 de·nom·i·na·tor

de·note
 de·not·ed
 de·not·ing
 de·no·ta·tion
de·noue·ment
de·nounce
 de·nounced
 de·noun·cing
 de·nounce·ment
de·nun·ci·a·tion
 de·nun·ci·a·to·ry
dense
 den·ser
 den·sest
 dense·ly
 dense·ness
den·si·ty
 den·si·ties
den·tal
den·tate
den·ti·frice
den·tin
den·tist
den·tist·ry
den·ti·tion
den·ture
de·nude
 de·nud·ed
 de·nud·ing
den·u·da·tion
de·nun·ci·ate
 de·nun·ci·at·ed
 de·nun·ci·at·ing
 de·nun·ci·a·tion
 de·nun·ci·a·to·ry
Den·ver
de·ny
 de·nied
 de·ny·ing
de·o·dor·ant
de·o·dor·ize
 de·o·dor·ized
 de·o·dor·iz·ing
de·part
 de·part·ed
 de·part·ment
 de·part·men·tal
de·par·ture
de·pend
 de·pend·ence
 de·pend·a·ble
 de·pend·a·bly
 de·pend·a·bil·i·ty
 de·pend·en·cy
 de·pend·en·cies
 de·pend·ent
de·pict
 de·pic·tion
de·pil·a·to·ry
 de·pil·a·to·ries
de·plete
 de·plet·ed
 de·plet·ing
 de·ple·tion
de·plor·a·ble

de·plor·a·bly
de·plore
de·plored
de·plor·ing
de·ploy
de·ploy·ment
de·po·nent
de·pop·u·late
de·pop·u·lat·ed
de·pop·u·lat·ing
de·pop·u·la·tion
de·port
de·por·ta·tion
de·port·ment
de·pose
de·posed
de·pos·ing
de·pos·a·ble
de·pos·it
de·pos·i·tor
dep·o·si·tion
de·pos·i·to·ry
de·pot
de·prave
de·praved
de·prav·ing
de·prav·i·ty
dep·re·cate
dep·re·cat·ed
dep·re·cat·ing
dep·re·cat·ing·ly
dep·re·ca·tion
dep·re·ca·to·ry
de·pre·ci·ate
de·pre·ci·at·ed
de·pre·ci·at·ing
de·pre·ci·a·tion
de·pre·ci·a·to·ry
de·pre·ci·a·tor
dep·re·date
dep·re·dat·ed
dep·re·dat·ing
dep·re·da·tion
de·press
de·pres·sant
de·pressed
de·pres·sion
de·prive
de·prived
de·priv·ing
dep·ri·va·tion
depth
dep·u·ta·tion
de·pute
de·put·ed
de·put·ing
dep·u·tize
dep·u·tized
dep·u·tiz·ing
dep·u·ty
dep·u·ties
dep·u·ty·ship
de·rail
de·rail·ment
de·range

de·ranged
de·rang·ing
de·range·ment
Der·by
Der·bies
Der·by·shire
der·e·lict
der·e·lic·tion
de·ride
de·rid·ed
de·rid·ing
de·ri·sion
de·ri·sive
de·ri·sive·ly
de·ri·so·ry
der·i·va·tion
de·riv·a·tive
de·rive
de·rived
de·riv·ing
de·riv·a·ble
der·ma
der·mal
der·ma·tol·o·gy
der·ma·to·log·i·cal
der·ma·tol·o·gist
der·mis
der·o·gate
der·o·gat·ed
der·o·gat·ing
der·o·ga·tion
de·rog·a·to·ry
de·rog·a·to·ri·ly
der·rick
der·rin·ger
der·vish
des·cant
Des·cartes
de·scend
de·scend·a·ble
de·scend·ant
de·scent
de·scribe
de·scribed
de·scrib·ing
de·scrib·a·ble
de·scrib·er
de·scrip·tion
de·scrip·tive
de·scrip·tive·ly
de·scrip·tive·ness
de·scry
de·scried
de·scry·ing
des·e·crate
des·e·crat·ed
des·e·crat·ing
des·e·cra·tion
de·seg·re·gate
de·seg·re·gat·ed
de·seg·re·gat·ing
de·seg·re·ga·tion
des·ert
de·sert
de·sert·er

de·ser·tion
de·serve
de·served
de·serv·ing
de·serv·ed·ly
des·ha·bille
des·ic·cate
des·ic·cat·ed
des·ic·cat·ing
des·ic·ca·tion
des·ic·ca·tive
de·sid·er·a·tum
de·sign
des·ig·nate
des·ig·nat·ed
des·ig·nat·ing
des·ig·na·tion
des·ig·na·tive
des·ig·na·tor
de·sign·ed·ly
de·sign·er
de·sign·ing
de·sire
de·sired
de·sir·ing
de·sir·a·ble
de·sir·a·bil·i·ty
de·sir·a·bly
de·sir·ous
de·sist
Des Moines
des·o·late
des·o·lat·ed
des·o·lat·ing
des·o·late·ly
des·o·la·tion
De So·to
de·spair
de·spair·ing
de·spair·ing·ly
des·per·a·do
des·per·a·does
des·per·ate
des·per·ate·ly
des·per·ate·ness
des·per·a·tion
des·pi·ca·ble
des·pi·ca·bly
de·spise
de·spised
de·spis·ing
de·spite
de·spoil
de·spoil·er
de·spo·li·a·tion
de·spond
de·spond·en·cy
de·spond·ence
de·spond·ent
de·spond·ent·ly
des·pot
des·pot·ic
des·pot·i·cal·ly
des·pot·ism
des·sert

des·ti·na·tion
des·tine
des·tined
des·tin·ing
des·ti·ny
des·ti·nies
des·ti·tute
des·ti·tu·tion
de·stroy
de·stroy·er
de·struc·tion
de·struct·i·ble
de·struct·i·bil·i·ty
de·struc·tive
de·struc·tive·ly
de·struc·tive·ness
des·ue·tude
des·ul·to·ry
des·ul·to·ri·ly
de·tach
de·tach·a·ble
de·tached
de·tach·ment
de·tail
de·tailed
de·tain
de·tain·ment
de·tain·er
de·tect
de·tect·a·ble
de·tec·tion
de·tec·tive
de·tec·tor
dé·tente
dé·tentes
de·ten·tion
de·ter
de·terred
de·ter·ring
de·ter·gent
de·te·ri·o·rate
de·te·ri·o·rat·ed
de·te·ri·o·rat·ing
de·te·ri·o·ra·tion
de·ter·mi·na·ble
de·ter·mi·nant
de·ter·mi·nate
de·ter·mi·na·tion
de·ter·mi·na·tive
de·ter·mine
de·ter·mined
de·ter·min·ing
de·ter·min·er
de·ter·mined
de·ter·mined·ly
de·ter·min·ism
de·ter·min·ist
de·ter·rent
de·ter·rence
de·test
de·test·a·ble
de·test·a·bly
de·tes·ta·tion
de·throne
de·throned

de·thron·ing
de·throne·ment
det·o·nate
det·o·nat·ed
det·o·nat·ing
det·o·na·tion
det·o·na·tor
de·tour
de·tract
de·trac·tion
de·trac·tor
det·ri·ment
det·ri·men·tal
det·ri·men·tal·ly
de·tri·tus
De·troit
deuce
deu·te·ri·um
Deu·ter·on·o·my
Deutsch·land
de·val·u·ate
de·val·u·at·ed
de·val·u·at·ing
de·val·u·a·tion
dev·as·tate
dev·as·tat·ed
dev·as·tat·ing
dev·as·ta·tion
de·vel·op
de·vel·op·ment
de·vel·op·er
de·vi·ate
de·vi·at·ed
de·vi·at·ing
de·vi·ant
de·vi·a·tion
de·vice
dev·il
dev·il·ment
dev·il·try
dev·il·tries
dev·il·ry
dev·il·ish
dev·il·ish·ly
dev·il·ish·ness
dev·il-may-care
de·vi·ous
de·vi·ous·ly
de·vi·ous·ness
de·vise
de·vised
de·vis·ing
de·vis·a·ble
de·vis·al
de·vi·see
de·vi·sor
de·void
de·volve
de·volved
de·volv·ing
dev·o·lu·tion
Dev·on
Dev·on·shire
de·vote
de·vot·ed

de·vot·ing
de·vot·ed
de·vot·ed·ly
dev·o·tee
de·vo·tion
de·vo·tion·al
de·vour
de·vour·er
de·vour·ing·ly
de·vout
de·vout·ly
de·vout·ness
dew·ber·ry
dew·ber·ries
dew·drop
Dew·ey
dew·lap
dewy
dew·i·er
dew·i·est
dew·i·ness
dew·y-eyed
dex·ter·ous
dex·ter·i·ty
dex·ter·ous·ly
dex·trose
di·a·be·tes
di·a·bet·ic
di·a·bol·ic
di·a·bol·i·cal
di·a·bol·i·cal·ly
di·a·crit·ic
di·a·crit·i·cal
di·a·crit·i·cal·ly
di·a·dem
di·ag·nose
di·ag·nosed
di·ag·nos·ing
di·ag·no·sis
di·ag·no·ses
di·ag·nos·tic
di·ag·nos·ti·cian
di·ag·o·nal
di·ag·o·nal·ly
di·a·gram
di·a·gramed
di·a·gram·ing
di·a·gram·mat·ic
di·a·gram·mat·i·cal
di·al
di·aled
di·al·ing
di·a·lect
di·a·lec·tal
di·a·lec·tic
di·a·lec·ti·cal
di·a·lec·ti·cian
di·a·logue
di·am·e·ter
di·a·met·ric
di·a·met·ric·al
di·a·met·ric·al·ly
dia·mond
Di·ana
dia·per

di·aph·a·nous
di·a·phragm
di·ar·rhea
di·a·ry
  di·a·ries
  di·a·rist
di·as·to·le
  di·as·tol·ic
di·a·ther·mic
di·a·ther·my
di·a·tom
di·a·ton·ic
di·a·tribe
Di·az
dib·ble
  dib·bled
  dib·bling
dice
  diced
  dic·ing
di·chot·o·my
  di·chot·o·mies
  di·chot·o·mous
  di·cho·tom·ic
dick·ens
dick·er
dick·ey
  dick·eys
Dick·in·son
Dic·ta·phone
dic·tate
  dic·tat·ed
  dic·tat·ing
  dic·ta·tion
dic·ta·tor
  dic·ta·tor·ship
  dic·ta·to·ri·al
  dic·ta·to·ri·al·ly
dic·tion
dic·tion·ar·y
  dic·tion·ar·ies
dic·tum
  dic·tums
  dic·ta
di·dac·tic
  di·dac·ti·cal
  di·dac·ti·cal·ly
did·dle
  did·dled
  did·dling
Di·de·rot
die
  died
  dy·ing
di·e·cious
Di·e·go
die-hard
di·e·lec·tric
di·er·e·sis
  di·er·e·ses
die·sel
die·sink·er
  die·sink·ing
di·et
  di·et·er

di·e·tary
  di·e·tar·ies
di·e·tet·ic
  di·e·tet·i·cal
  di·e·tet·i·cal·ly
di·e·tet·ics
di·e·ti·cian
dif·fer
  dif·fer·ence
  dif·fer·enced
  dif·fer·en·cing
dif·fer·ent
  dif·fer·ent·ly
dif·fer·en·tial
  dif·fer·en·tial·ly
  dif·fer·en·ti·ate
  dif·fer·en·ti·at·ed
  dif·fer·en·ti·at·ing
  dif·fer·en·ti·a·tion
dif·fi·cult
  dif·fi·cult·ly
dif·fi·cul·ty
  dif·fi·cul·ties
dif·fi·dence
dif·fi·dent
  dif·fi·dent·ly
dif·fuse
  dif·fused
  dif·fus·ing
  dif·fuse·ly
  dif·fuse·ness
  dif·fu·sion
  dif·fu·sive·ly
  dif·fu·sive·ness
dig
  dig·ging
di·gest
  di·gest·er
  di·gest·i·ble
  di·gest·i·bil·i·ty
  di·ges·tion
  di·ges·tive
dig·ger
  dig·gings
dig·it
  dig·it·al
  dig·i·tal·is
dig·ni·fied
dig·ni·fy
  dig·ni·fied
  dig·ni·fy·ing
dig·ni·tary
  dig·ni·tar·ies
dig·ni·ty
  dig·ni·ties
di·graph
di·gress
  di·gres·sion
  di·gres·sive
  di·gres·sive·ly
di·he·dral
dike
  diked
  dik·ing
di·lap·i·dat·ed

di·lap·i·da·tion
dil·a·ta·tion
di·late
  di·lat·ed
  di·lat·ing
  di·lat·a·bil·i·ty
  di·lat·a·ble
  di·la·tion
dil·a·to·ry
  dil·a·to·ri·ly
di·lem·ma
dil·et·tan·te
  dil·et·tan·tes
dil·i·gence
dil·i·gent
  dil·i·gent·ly
dil·ly-dal·ly
  dil·ly-dal·lied
  dil·ly-dal·ly·ing
di·lute
  di·lut·ed
  di·lut·ing
  di·lute·ness
  di·lu·tion
dim
  dim·mer
  dim·mest
  dimmed
  dim·ming
  dim·ly
  dim·ness
di·men·sion
  di·men·sion·less
  di·men·sion·al
di·min·ish
  di·min·ish·a·ble
di·min·u·en·do
  di·min·u·en·dos
dim·i·nu·tion
di·min·u·tive
  di·min·u·tive·ly
  di·min·u·tive·ness
dim-out
dim·ple
  dim·pled
  dim·pling
dim·wit
  dim·wit·ted
din
  dinned
  din·ning
dine
  dined
  din·ing
din·er
di·nette
ding-dong
din·ghy
  din·ghies
din·gy
  din·gi·er
  din·gi·est
  din·gi·ness
dinky
  dink·i·er

dink·i·est
din·ner
di·no·saur
di·o·cese
di·oc·e·san
Di·o·cle·tian
Di·og·e·nes
Di·o·me·des
di·o·rama
dip
  dipped
  dip·ping
diph·the·ria
diph·thong
di·plo·ma
di·plo·ma·cy
  di·plo·ma·cies
dip·lo·mat
  dip·lo·mat·ic
  dip·lo·mat·i·cal·ly
dip·per
dip·so·ma·nia
  dip·so·ma·ni·ac
dip·stick
dire
  dir·er
  dir·est
  dire·ly
  dire·ness
di·rect
  di·rect·ness
di·rec·tion
  di·rec·tion·al
di·rec·tive
di·rect·ly
di·rec·tor
  di·rec·to·ri·al
  di·rec·tor·ship
di·rec·to·rate
di·rec·to·ry
  di·rec·to·ries
dirge
dirty
  dirt·i·er
  dirt·i·est
  dirt·ied
  dirt·y·ing
  dirt·i·ly
  dirt·i·ness
dis·a·ble
  dis·a·bled
  dis·a·bling
  dis·a·bil·i·ty
  dis·a·bil·i·ties
  dis·a·ble·ment
dis·a·buse
  dis·a·bused
  dis·a·bus·ing
dis·ad·van·tage
  dis·ad·van·taged
  dis·ad·van·tag·ing
  dis·ad·van·ta·geous
  dis·ad·van·ta·geous·ly
dis·af·fect
  dis·af·fec·tion

dis·af·fect·ed
dis·a·gree
  dis·a·greed
  dis·a·gree·ing
  dis·a·gree·a·ble
  dis·a·gree·a·ble·ness
  dis·a·gree·a·bly
  dis·a·gree·ment
dis·al·low
  dis·al·low·ance
dis·ap·pear
  dis·ap·pear·ance
dis·ap·point
  dis·ap·point·ment
dis·ap·pro·ba·tion
dis·ap·prove
  dis·ap·proved
  dis·ap·prov·ing
  dis·ap·prov·al
  dis·ap·prov·ing·ly
dis·arm
  dis·ar·ma·ment
dis·ar·range
  dis·ar·ranged
  dis·ar·rang·ing
  dis·ar·range·ment
dis·ar·ray
dis·as·sem·ble
dis·as·ter
  dis·as·trous
  dis·as·trous·ly
dis·a·vow
  dis·a·vow·al
dis·band
  dis·band·ment
dis·bar
  dis·barred
  dis·bar·ring
dis·be·lieve
  dis·be·lieved
  dis·be·liev·ing
  dis·be·lief
  dis·be·liev·er
dis·burse
  dis·bursed
  dis·burs·ing
  dis·burse·ment
  dis·burs·er
dis·card
dis·cern
  dis·cern·er
  dis·cern·i·ble
  dis·cern·i·bly
  dis·cern·ing
  dis·cern·ing·ly
  dis·cern·ment
dis·charge
  dis·charged
  dis·charg·ing
  dis·charge·a·ble
  dis·char·ger
dis·ci·ple
  dis·ci·ple·ship
dis·ci·pli·nar·i·an
dis·ci·pline

dis·ci·plined
  dis·ci·plin·ing
  dis·ci·pli·nary
dis·claim
  dis·claim·er
dis·close
  dis·closed
  dis·clos·ing
  dis·clos·er
  dis·clo·sure
dis·coid
dis·col·or
  dis·col·or·a·tion
dis·com·fit
  dis·com·fi·ture
dis·com·fort
dis·com·mode
  dis·com·mod·ed
  dis·com·mod·ing
dis·com·pose
  dis·com·posed
  dis·com·pos·ing
  dis·com·po·sure
dis·con·cert
  dis·con·cert·ing
  dis·con·cert·ed
dis·con·nect
  dis·con·nec·tion
  dis·con·nect·ed
  dis·con·nect·ed·ness
dis·con·so·late
  dis·con·so·late·ly
dis·con·tent
  dis·con·tent·ment
  dis·con·tent·ed
  dis·con·tent·ed·ly
dis·con·tin·ue
  dis·con·tin·ued
  dis·con·tin·u·ing
  dis·con·tin·u·ance
  dis·con·tin·u·a·tion
  dis·con·tin·u·ous
  dis·con·ti·nu·i·ty
dis·cord
  dis·cord·ance
  dis·cor·dan·cy
  dis·cord·ant·ly
dis·co·thèque
dis·count
dis·cour·age
  dis·cour·aged
  dis·cour·ag·ing
  dis·cour·age·ment
  dis·cour·ag·ing
dis·course
  dis·coursed
  dis·cours·ing
dis·cour·te·ous
  dis·cour·te·ous·ly
  dis·cour·te·ous·ness
  dis·cour·te·sy
  dis·cour·te·sies
dis·cov·er
  dis·cov·er·a·ble
  dis·cov·er·er

dis·cov·ery
  dis·cov·er·ies
dis·cred·it
  dis·cred·it·a·ble
  dis·cred·it·a·bly
dis·creet
  dis·creet·ly
dis·crep·an·cy
  dis·crep·an·cies
dis·crete
dis·cre·tion
  dis·cre·tion·ary
dis·crim·i·nate
  dis·crim·i·nat·ed
  dis·crim·i·nat·ing
  dis·crim·i·nate·ly
  dis·crim·i·na·tion
  dis·crim·i·na·tive
  dis·crim·i·na·to·ry
  dis·crim·i·na·tor
dis·cur·sive
  dis·cur·sive·ly
  dis·cur·sive·ness
dis·cus
  dis·cus·es
dis·cuss
  dis·cuss·i·ble
  dis·cus·sion
dis·dain
  dis·dain·ful
  dis·dain·ful·ly
dis·ease
  dis·eased
  dis·eas·ing
dis·em·bark
  dis·em·bar·ka·tion
  dis·em·bark·ment
dis·em·body
  dis·em·bod·ied
  dis·em·bod·y·ing
  dis·em·bod·i·ment
dis·em·bow·el
  dis·em·bow·eled
  dis·em·bow·el·ing
  dis·em·bow·el·ment
dis·en·chant
  dis·en·chant·ment
dis·en·cum·ber
dis·en·fran·chise
  dis·en·fran·chised
  dis·en·fran·chis·ing
dis·en·gage
  dis·en·gaged
  dis·en·gag·ing
  dis·en·gage·ment
dis·en·tan·gle
  dis·en·tan·gled
  dis·en·tan·gling
  dis·en·tan·gle·ment
dis·es·tab·lish
  dis·es·tab·lish·ment
dis·fa·vor
dis·fig·ure
  dis·fig·ured
  dis·fig·ur·ing

dis·fig·ure·ment
dis·fran·chise
  dis·fran·chised
  dis·fran·chis·ing
  dis·fran·chise·ment
dis·gorge
  dis·gorged
  dis·gorg·ing
dis·grace
  dis·graced
  dis·grac·ing
dis·grace·ful
  dis·grace·ful·ly
  dis·grace·ful·ness
dis·grun·tle
  dis·grun·tled
  dis·grun·tling
dis·guise
  dis·guised
  dis·guis·ing
  dis·guis·er
dis·gust
  dis·gust·ed
  dis·gust·ing
dis·ha·bille
dis·har·mo·ny
  dis·har·mo·nies
dis·heart·en
  dis·heart·en·ing
di·shev·eled
dis·hon·est
  dis·hon·est·ly
  dis·hon·es·ty
  dis·hon·es·ties
dis·hon·or
  dis·hon·or·a·ble
  dis·hon·or·a·bly
dis·il·lu·sion
  dis·il·lu·sion·ment
dis·in·cline
  dis·in·clined
  dis·in·clin·ing
  dis·in·cli·na·tion
dis·in·fect
  dis·in·fect·ant
  dis·in·fec·tion
dis·in·her·it
  dis·in·her·i·tance
dis·in·te·grate
  dis·in·te·grat·ed
  dis·in·te·grat·ing
  dis·in·te·gra·tion
  dis·in·te·gra·tor
dis·in·ter
  dis·in·terred
  dis·in·ter·ring
  dis·in·ter·ment
dis·in·ter·est
  dis·in·ter·es·ted
  dis·in·ter·est·ed·ly
dis·join
dis·joint
  dis·joint·ed
  dis·joint·ed·ness
  dis·joint·ed·ly

dis·junc·tion
disk
 disk·like
dis·like
 dis·liked
 dis·lik·ing
 dis·lik·a·ble
dis·lo·cate
 dis·lo·cat·ed
 dis·lo·cat·ing
 dis·lo·ca·tion
dis·lodge
 dis·lodged
 dis·lodg·ing
dis·loy·al
 dis·loy·al·ly
 dis·loy·al·ty
 dis·loy·al·ties
dis·mal
 dis·mal·ly
dis·man·tle
 dis·man·tled
 dis·man·tling
dis·may
dis·mem·ber
 dis·mem·ber·ment
dis·miss
 dis·mis·sal
dis·mount
dis·o·be·di·ence
 dis·o·be·di·ent
 dis·o·be·di·ent·ly
dis·o·bey
 dis·o·bey·er
dis·or·der
 dis·or·dered
 dis·or·der·ly
 dis·or·der·li·ness
dis·or·gan·ize
 dis·or·gan·ized
 dis·or·gan·iz·ing
 dis·or·gan·i·za·tion
dis·o·ri·ent
 dis·o·ri·en·ta·tion
dis·own
dis·par·age
 dis·par·aged
 dis·par·ag·ing
 dis·par·age·ment
 dis·par·ag·ing·ly
dis·pa·rate
 dis·pa·rate·ly
 dis·pa·rate·ness
dis·par·i·ty
 dis·par·i·ties
dis·pas·sion
 dis·pas·sion·ate·ness
 dis·pas·sion·ate
 dis·pas·sion·ate·ly
dis·patch
dis·patch·er
dis·pel
 dis·pelled
 dis·pel·ling
dis·pen·sa·ble

dis·pen·sa·bil·i·ty
dis·pen·sa·ry
 dis·pen·sa·ries
dis·pen·sa·tion
dis·pense
 dis·pensed
 dis·pens·ing
dis·perse
 dis·persed
 dis·pers·ing
dis·place
 dis·placed
 dis·plac·ing
dis·play
dis·please
 dis·pleased
 dis·pleas·ing
 dis·pleas·ure
dis·port
dis·pos·a·ble
dis·pose
 dis·posed
 dis·pos·ing
dis·po·si·tion
dis·pro·por·tion
 dis·pro·por·tion·ate·ness
dis·prove
 dis·proved
 dis·prov·ing
dis·pute
 dis·put·ed
 dis·put·ing
 dis·put·a·ble
dis·qual·i·fy
 dis·qual·i·fied
 dis·qual·i·fy·ing
 dis·qual·i·fi·ca·tion
dis·qui·et
Dis·rae·li
dis·re·gard
dis·re·pair
dis·rep·u·ta·ble
dis·re·spect
 dis·re·spect·ful
 dis·re·spect·a·ble
dis·robe
 dis·robed
 dis·rob·ing
dis·rupt
dis·rup·tion
dis·rup·tive
 dis·rup·tive·ly
 dis·rup·tive·ness
 dis·rupt·er
dis·sat·is·fac·tion
dis·sat·is·fac·to·ry
dis·sat·is·fy
 dis·sat·is·fied
 dis·sat·is·fy·ing
dis·sect
 dis·sect·ed
 dis·sec·tion
dis·sem·blance
dis·sem·ble
 dis·sem·bled

dis·sem·bling
dis·sem·bler
dis·sem·i·nate
dis·sem·i·nat·ed
dis·sem·i·nat·ing
dis·sem·i·na·tion
dis·sem·i·na·tive
dis·sem·i·na·tor
dis·sent
dis·sent·ing
dis·sen·sion
dis·sen·tious
dis·sent·er
dis·ser·tate
dis·ser·ta·ted
dis·ser·ta·ting
dis·ser·ta·tion
dis·ser·ta·tor
dis·serve
dis·served
dis·serv·ing
dis·serv·ice
dis·si·dence
dis·si·dent
dis·sim·i·lar
dis·sim·i·lar·i·ty
dis·sim·i·lar·ly
dis·sim·i·late
dis·sim·i·lat·ed
dis·sim·i·lat·ing
dis·sim·i·la·tion
dis·sim·i·la·tive
dis·sim·i·la·to·ry
dis·si·mil·i·tude
dis·sim·u·late
dis·sim·u·lat·ed
dis·sim·u·lat·ing
dis·sim·u·la·tion
dis·sim·u·la·tive
dis·sim·u·la·tor
dis·si·pate
dis·si·pat·ed
dis·si·pat·ing
dis·si·pat·ed
dis·si·pa·ted·ly
dis·si·pat·ed·ness
dis·si·pa·tive
dis·si·pa·tor
dis·si·pa·tion
dis·so·ci·ate
dis·so·ci·at·ed
dis·so·ci·at·ing
dis·so·ci·a·tive
dis·so·ci·a·tion
dis·so·lute
dis·so·lute·ly
dis·so·lu·tion
dis·solve
dis·solved
dis·solv·ing
dis·solv·er
dis·solv·a·ble
dis·so·nance
dis·so·nant
dis·so·nant·ly

dis·suade
dis·suad·ed
dis·suad·ing
dis·suad·er
dis·sua·sion
dis·sua·sive
dis·taff
dis·tal
dis·tance
dis·tant
dis·tant·ly
dis·taste
dis·taste·ful
dis·taste·ful·ly
dis·taste·ful·ness
dis·tem·per
dis·tend
dis·ten·sion
dis·ten·tion
dis·till
dis·tilled
dis·till·ing
dis·till·a·ble
dis·til·la·tion
dis·til·late
dis·till·er
dis·till·ery
dis·till·er·ies
dis·tinct
dis·tinct·ly
dis·tinct·ness
dis·tinc·tion
dis·tinc·tive
dis·tin·guish
dis·tin·guish·a·ble
dis·tin·guished
dis·tort
dis·tor·tion
dis·tor·tion·al
dis·tort·ed
dis·tract
dis·tract·ing
dis·tract·ing·ly
dis·tract·ed
dis·tract·ed·ly
dis·trac·tion
dis·trac·tive
dis·trait
dis·traught
dis·tress
dis·tress·ful
dis·tress·ful·ly
dis·tress·ful·ness
dis·tress·ing
dis·tress·ing·ly
dis·trib·ute
dis·trib·ut·ed
dis·trib·ut·ing
dis·trib·ut·a·ble
dis·tri·bu·tion
dis·trib·u·tor
dis·trict
dis·trict at·tor·ney
dis·trust
dis·trust·ful

dis·trust·ful·ly
dis·trust·ful·ness
dis·turb
dis·turb·ance
dis·turbed
dis·un·ion
dis·u·nite
dis·u·ni·ted
dis·u·ni·ting
dis·u·ni·ty
dis·u·ni·ties
dis·use
dis·used
dis·us·ing
ditch
ditch·er
dith·er
dit·to
dit·tos
dit·toed
dit·to·ing
dit·ty
dit·ties
di·u·ret·ic
di·ur·nal
di·ur·nal·ly
di·van
dive
dived
dove
div·ing
div·er
di·verge
di·verged
di·verg·ing
di·ver·gence
di·ver·gen·cy
di·ver·gent
di·vers
di·verse
di·ver·si·fi·ca·tion
di·ver·si·fy
di·ver·si·fied
di·ver·si·fy·ing
di·ver·sion
di·ver·sion·ary
di·ver·si·ty
di·ver·si·ties
di·vert
Di·ves
di·vide
di·vid·ed
di·vid·ing
div·i·dend
di·vine
di·vined
di·vin·ing
di·vin·i·ty
di·vin·i·ties
di·vis·i·ble
di·vis·i·bly
di·vi·sion
di·vi·sive
di·vi·sor
di·vorce

di·vorced
di·vorc·ing
di·vor·cé
di·vor·cee
di·vulge
di·vulged
di·vulg·ing
di·vul·gence
Dix·ie
Dix·on
diz·zy
diz·zi·er
diz·zi·est
diz·zied
diz·zy·ing
diz·zi·ly
diz·zi·ness
Dja·kar·ta
do·a·ble
Do·ber·man
doc·ile
dock·yard
doc·tor
doc·tor·al
doc·tor·ate
doc·trine
doc·tri·nal
doc·u·ment
doc·u·men·ta·ry
doc·u·men·ta·ries
doc·u·men·ta·ri·ly
doc·u·men·ta·tion
dod·der
dod·dered
dodge
dodged
dodg·ing
dodg·er
do·do
do·dos
do·er
doe·skin
doesn't
dog
dogged
dog·ging
dog-eared
dog·fight
dog·ged
dog·ged·ly
dog·ged·ness
dog·gone
dog·goned
dog·gon·ing
dog·house
dog·ma
dog·mas
dog·ma·ta
dog·mat·ic
dog·mat·i·cal
dog·mat·i·cal·ly
dog·ma·tism
dog·ma·tist
dog·ma·tize
dog·ma·tized

dog·ma·tiz·ing
do-good·er
dog·wood
Do·ha
doi·ly
doi·lies
do·ing
do-it-your·self
dol·drums
dole
doled
dol·ing
dole·ful
dol·lar
dol·ly
dol·lies
dol·lied
dol·ly·ing
dol·or·ous
dol·phin
dolt
dolt·ish
do·main
dome
domed
dom·ing
Domes·day
do·mes·tic
do·mes·ti·cal·ly
do·mes·ti·cate
do·mes·ti·cat·ed
do·mes·ti·cat·ing
do·mes·ti·ca·ble
do·mes·ti·ca·tion
do·mes·tic·i·ty
do·mes·tic·i·ties
dom·i·cile
dom·i·ciled
dom·i·cil·ing
dom·i·nance
dom·i·nan·cy
dom·i·nant
dom·i·nate
dom·i·nat·ed
dom·i·nat·ing
dom·i·na·tion
dom·i·na·tor
dom·i·neer
dom·i·neer·ing
Do·min·i·can
do·min·ion
dom·i·no
dom·i·noes
don
donned
don·ning
do·nate
do·nat·ed
do·nat·ing
do·na·tor
do·na·tion
do·nee
Don·e·gal
don·key
don·keys

do·nor
do-noth·ing
Don Qui·xo·te
don't
doo·dad
doo·dle
doo·dled
doo·dling
dooms·day
door·bell
door·jamb
door·knob
door·mat
door·step
door·way
dope
doped
dop·ing
dop·ey
dop·i·er
dop·i·est
dop·i·ness
Dor·ches·ter
Dor·ic
dor·mant
dor·man·cy
dor·mer
dor·mered
dor·mi·to·ry
dor·mi·to·ries
dor·sal
Dor·set·shire
dory
dor·ies
dos·age
dose
dosed
dos·ing
dos·si·er
dot
dot·ted
dot·ting
dot·age
dot·ard
dote
dot·ed
dot·ing
dot·er
dot·ing·ly
dot·ty
dot·ti·er
dot·ti·est
dou·ble
dou·bled
dou·bling
doub·ly
dou·ble-breast·ed
dou·ble-cross
dou·ble-deck·er
dou·ble-faced
dou·ble-head·er
dou·ble-joint·ed
dou·ble·take
dou·ble·time
dou·ble-timed

dou·ble-tim·ing
doubt
doubt·a·ble
doubt·ful
  doubt·ful·ly
doubt·less
douche
  douched
  douch·ing
dough
dough·nut
dough·ty
  dough·ti·er
  dough·ti·est
  dough·ti·ly
  dough·ti·ness
dour
  dour·ly
  dour·ness
douse
  doused
  dous·ing
dove·cote
Do·ver
dove·tail
dow·a·ger
dow·dy
  dow·di·er
  dow·di·est
  dow·di·ness
dow·el
  dow·eled
  dow·el·ing
dow·er
down
  down·i·ness
  downy
down·cast
down·fall
  down·fall·en
down·grade
  down·grad·ed
  down·grad·ing
down·heart·ed
down·hill
down·pour
down·right
down·stairs
down·stream
down-to-earth
down·town
down·trod·den
down·ward
  down·ward·ly
down·wind
dow·ry
  dow·ries
dox·ol·o·gy
doze
  dozed
  doz·ing
doz·en
  doz·enth
drab
  drab·ber

drab·best
drab·ly
drab·ness
draft
  draft·er
  draft·ee
drafts·man
  drafts·men
  drafts·man·ship
drafty
  draft·i·er
  draft·i·est
  draft·i·ly
drag
  dragged
  drag·ging
  drag·ging·ly
drag·gle
drag·net
drag·on
  drag·on·fly
  drag·on·flies
drain
  drain·a·ble
  drain·er
  drain·age
  drain·pipe
drake
dra·ma
  dra·mat·ic
  dra·mat·i·cal·ly
  dra·mat·ics
dram·a·tist
dram·a·tize
  dram·a·tized
  dram·a·tiz·ing
  dram·a·ti·za·tion
drape
  draped
  drap·ing
  drap·er
  dra·pery
  dra·per·ies
dras·tic
  drast·i·cal·ly
draught
draw
  drawn
  draw·ing
draw·back
draw·bridge
draw·er
  draw·ers
  draw·ing
drawl
drawn
dread
  dread·ful
  dread·ful·ly
dream
  dreamed
  dreamt
  dream·ing
  dream·er
  dream·ful·ly

dream·like
dreamy
  dream·i·er
  dream·i·est
dreary
  drear·i·er
  drear·i·est
  drear·i·ly
  drear·i·ness
dredge
  dredged
  dredg·ing
  dredg·er
dreg
  dreg·gy
drench
Dres·den
dress
  dressed
  dres·sing
  dress·er
  dress·mak·er
dressy
  dress·i·er
  dress·i·est
Drey·fus
drib·ble
  drib·bled
  drib·bling
  drib·bler
drib·let
dri·er
drift
  drift·age
  drift·er
  drift·wood
drill·ing
dri·ly
drink
  drank
  drunk
  drink·ing
  drink·a·ble
  drink·er
Drink·wa·ter
drip
  dripped
  drip·ping
  drip·py
drip-dry
  drip-dried
  drip-dry·ing
drive
  drove
  driv·en
  driv·ing
driv·el
  driv·eled
  driv·el·ing
  driv·el·er
driv·er
drive·way
driz·zle
  driz·zled
  driz·zling

driz·zly
droll
droll·ery
droll·er·ies
drom·e·dary
drom·e·dar·ies
drone
droned
dron·ing
drool
droop
droop·ing·ly
droop·y
droop·i·er
droop·i·est
drop
dropped
drop·ping
drop·let
drop·out
drop·per
drop·sy
dross
drought
droughty
drought·i·er
drought·i·est
drowned
drowse
drowsed
drows·ing
drow·si·ly
drow·si·ness
drow·sy
drow·si·er
drow·si·est
drub
drubbed
drub·bing
drudge
drudged
drudg·ing
drudg·ery
drudg·er·ies
drudg·ing·ly
drug
drugged
drug·ging
drug·gist
drug·store
dru·id
drum
drummed
drum·ming
drum·mer
drum·stick
drunk·ard
drunk·en
drunk·en·ly
drunk·en·ness
dry
dri·er
dri·est
dried
dry·ing

dry·ly
dry·ness
dry·ad
dry·ads
dry·a·des
dry goods
du·al
du·al·i·ty
du·al·ism
du·al·ist
du·al·is·tic
dub
dubbed
dub·bing
dub·ber
du·bi·ous
du·bi·e·ty
du·bi·ous·ly
du·bi·ous·ness
Dub·lin
Du·buque
du·cal
du·cal·ly
du·cat
duch·ess
duchy
duch·ies
duck·bill
duck·ling
ducky
duck·i·er
duck·i·est
duct·less
duc·tile
du·el
du·eled
du·el·ing
du·el·ist
du·en·na
du·et
duf·fel bag
duff·er
dug·out
duke·dom
dul·cet
dull
dull·ard
dull·ish
dull·ness
Dul·les
Du·luth
du·ly
dumb
dumb·ly
dumb·ness
dumb·bell
dumb·struck
dumb·wait·er
dum·dum
dum·found
dum·my
dum·mies
dump·i·ness
dump·ling
dumpy

dump·i·er
dump·i·est
dump·i·ness
dun
dunned
dun·ning
dunce
Dun·dee
dune
dung
dungy
dun·ga·ree
dun·geon
dung·hill
dunk·er
Dun·kirk
dun·nage
duo
du·o·dec·i·mal
du·o·de·num
du·o·de·na
du·o·de·nal
dupe
duped
dup·ing
du·plex
du·pli·cate
du·pli·cat·ed
du·pli·cat·ing
du·pli·ca·tion
du·pli·ca·tor
du·plic·i·ty
du·plic·i·ties
Du·quesne
du·ra·ble
du·ra·bil·i·ty
du·ra·bly
dur·ance
du·ra·tion
du·ress
Dur·ham
dur·ing
dusk
dusk·i·ly
dusk·i·ness
dusky
dusk·i·er
dusk·i·est
dust·er
dust·pan
dusty
dust·i·er
dust·i·est
dust·i·ly
dust·i·ness
Dutch·man
du·ti·a·ble
du·ti·ful
du·ti·ful·ly
du·ti·ful·ness
du·ty
du·ties
dwarf
dwarf·ish
dwell

68

dwelt
dwelled
dwell·ing
dwin·dle
dwin·dled
dwin·dling
dye
dyed
dye·ing
dyed-in-the-wool
dye·stuff
dy·ing
dyke
dy·nam·ic
dy·nam·i·cal
dy·nam·i·cal·ly
dy·na·mism
dy·nam·ics
dy·na·mite
dy·na·mo
dy·na·mos
dy·na·mo·e·lec·tric
dy·nas·ty
dy·nas·ties
dyne
dys·en·tery
dys·func·tion
dys·pep·sia
dys·pep·tic
dys·pep·ti·cal
dys·pep·ti·cal·ly
dys·tro·phy
ea·ger
ea·ger·ly
ea·ger·ness
ea·gle
ea·gle-eyed
ea·glet
ear·ache
ear·drum
Ear·hart
earl·dom
ear·ly
ear·li·er
ear·li·est
ear·li·ness
ear·mark
ear·muff
earn
earn·er
ear·nest
ear·nest·ly
ear·nest·ness
earn·ings
ear·phone
ear·ring
ear·shot
earth·bound
earth·en
earth·en·ware
earth·ly
earth·li·er
earth·li·est
earth·quake
earth·ward

earth·work
earth·worm
earthy
earth·i·er
earth·i·est
earth·i·ness
ear·wax
ease
eased
eas·ing
ea·sel
ease·ment
eas·i·ly
eas·i·ness
East·er
east·er·ly
east·ern
East·ern·er
east·ern·most
Eas·ter·tide
Eas·ton
east·ward
east·wards
easy
eas·i·er
eas·i·est
eas·y-go·ing
eat
ate
eat·en
eat·ing
eat·a·ble
eat·er
eau de co·logne
eaves·drop
eaves·dropped
eaves·drop·ping
eaves·drop·per
ebb
Eb·e·ne·zer
Eber·hart
eb·ony
eb·on·ies
ebul·lience
ebul·lient
eb·ul·li·tion
ec·cen·tric
ec·cen·tri·cal·ly
ec·cen·tric·i·ty
ec·cen·tric·i·ties
Ec·cle·si·as·tes
ec·cle·si·as·tic
ec·cle·si·as·ti·cal
ec·cle·si·as·ti·cal·ly
ech·e·lon
echi·no·derm
echo
ech·oes
ech·oed
ech·o·ing
ech·o·er
echo·ic
eclair
ec·lec·tic
ec·lec·ti·cal·ly

ec·lec·ti·cism
eclipse
eclipsed
eclips·ing
eclip·tic
ecol·o·gy
ec·o·log·ic
ec·o·log·i·cal
ecol·o·gist
eco·nom·ic
eco·nom·i·cal
eco·nom·ics
econ·o·mist
econ·o·mize
econ·o·mized
econ·o·miz·ing
econ·o·miz·er
econ·o·my
econ·o·mies
ec·o·sys·tem
ec·ru
ec·sta·sy
ec·sta·sies
ec·stat·ic
ec·stat·i·cal
ec·to·morph
ec·to·mor·phic
ec·to·plasm
Ec·ua·dor
ec·u·men·i·cal
ec·u·men·ic
ec·u·men·i·cal·ly
ec·u·men·ism
ec·ze·ma
ed·dy
ed·dies
ed·died
ed·dy·ing
ede·ma
ede·ma·ta
Eden
eden·tate
edge
edged
edg·ing
edge·wise
Edge·worth
edgy
edg·i·er
edg·i·est
edg·i·ness
ed·i·ble
edict
ed·i·fice
ed·i·fy
ed·i·fied
ed·i·fy·ing
ed·i·fi·ca·tion
Ed·in·burgh
ed·it
edi·tion
ed·i·tor
ed·i·tor·ship
ed·i·to·ri·al
ed·i·to·ri·al·ly

ed·i·to·ri·al·ize
ed·i·to·ri·al·ized
ed·i·to·ri·al·iz·ing
ed·u·cate
ed·u·cat·ed
ed·u·cat·ing
ed·u·ca·ble
ed·u·ca·tive
ed·u·ca·tor
ed·u·ca·tion
ed·u·ca·tion·al
educe
educed
educ·ing
educ·i·ble
educ·tion
eel
eel-like
eely
ee·rie
ee·ri·er
ee·ri·est
ee·ri·ly
ee·ri·ness
ef·face
ef·faced
ef·fac·ing
ef·face·ment
ef·fac·er
ef·fect
ef·fec·tive
ef·fec·tive·ness
ef·fec·tive·ly
ef·fec·tive·ness
ef·fec·tu·al
ef·fec·tu·al·i·ty
ef·fec·tu·ate
ef·fec·tu·at·ed
ef·fec·tu·at·ing
ef·fem·i·nate
ef·fem·i·na·cy
ef·fem·i·na·cies
ef·fem·i·nate·ly
ef·fer·vesce
ef·fer·vesced
ef·fer·vesc·ing
ef·fer·ves·cence
ef·fer·ves·cent
ef·fete
ef·fi·ca·cious
ef·fi·ca·cy
ef·fi·ca·cies
ef·fi·cien·cy
ef·fi·cien·cies
ef·fi·cient
ef·fi·cient·ly
ef·fi·gy
ef·fi·gies
ef·flo·resce
ef·flo·resced
ef·flo·resc·ing
ef·flo·res·cence
ef·flo·res·cent
ef·flu·ent
ef·flu·ence

ef·flu·vi·um
ef·flu·via
ef·flu·vi·ums
ef·flu·vi·al
ef·fort
ef·fort·less
ef·fort·less·ly
ef·fort·less·ness
ef·fron·tery
ef·fron·ter·ies
ef·ful·gent
ef·ful·gence
ef·fuse
ef·fused
ef·fus·ing
ef·fu·sion
ef·fu·sive
ef·fu·sive·ly
ef·fu·sive·ness
egal·i·tar·i·an
egal·i·tar·i·an·ism
egg·head
egg·nog
egg·plant
egg·shell
ego
egos
ego·cen·tric
ego·ism
ego·ist
ego·is·tic
ego·tism
ego·tist
ego·tis·tic
ego·tis·ti·cal
egre·gious
egre·gious·ly
egress
egret
Egypt
Egyp·tian
ei·der·down
Eif·fel
eight
eighth
eight-ball
eight·een
eight·eenth
eight·fold
eighty
eight·ies
eight·i·eth
Ein·stein
Ei·sen·how·er
ei·ther
ejac·u·late
ejac·u·lat·ed
ejac·u·lat·ing
ejac·u·la·tion
ejac·u·la·to·ry
eject
ejec·tion
eject·ment
ejec·tor
eke

eked
ek·ing
elab·o·rate
elab·o·rat·ed
elab·o·rat·ing
elab·o·rate·ly
elab·o·rate·ness
elab·o·ra·tion
élan
elapse
elapsed
elaps·ing
elas·tic
elas·ti·cal·ly
elas·tic·i·ty
elate
elat·ed
elat·ing
ela·tion
El·ba
el·bow
el·bow-room
el·der
eld·er
eld·er·ship
el·der·ly
eld·er·li·ness
eld·est
El Do·ra·do
El·e·a·zar
elect
elec·tion
elec·tion·eer
elec·tive
elec·tor
elec·tor·al
elec·tor·ate
elec·tric
elec·tri·cal
elec·tri·cal·ly
elec·tri·cian
elec·tric·i·ty
elec·tri·fy
elec·tri·fied
elec·tri·fy·ing
elec·tri·fi·ca·tion
elec·tri·fi·er
elec·tro·car·di·o·graph
elec·tro·cute
elec·tro·cut·ed
elec·tro·cut·ing
elec·tro·cu·tion
elec·trode
elec·tro·dy·nam·ics
elec·trol·y·sis
elec·tro·lyze
elec·tro·lyzed
elec·tro·lyz·ing
elec·tro·lyte
elec·tro·lyt·ic
elec·tro·mag·net
elec·tro·mag·net·ism
elec·tro·mag·net·ic
elec·tron
elec·tron·ics

elec·tron·ic
elec·tron·i·cal·ly
elec·tro·plate
elec·tro·plat·ed
elec·tro·plat·ing
elec·tro·ther·a·py
elec·trum
el·ee·mos·y·nary
el·e·gant
el·e·gance
el·e·gan·cy
el·e·gant·ly
el·e·gy
el·e·gies
el·e·gi·ac
el·e·gist
el·e·gize
el·e·gized
el·e·giz·ing
el·e·ment
el·e·men·tal
el·e·men·tal·ly
el·e·men·ta·ry
el·e·men·ta·ri·ly
el·e·phant
el·e·phan·tine
el·e·vate
el·e·vat·ed
el·e·vat·ing
el·e·va·tion
el·e·va·tor
elev·en
elev·enth
elf
elves
elf·in
elf·ish
El·gin
Eli·as
elic·it
el·i·gi·ble
el·i·gi·bil·i·ty
el·i·gi·bly
Eli·jah
elim·i·nate
elim·i·nat·ed
elim·i·nat·ing
elim·i·na·tion
elim·i·na·tor
Eli·sha
elite
elit·ism
elit·ist
elix·ir
Eliz·a·beth·an
el·lipse
el·lip·sis
el·lip·ses
el·lip·ti·cal
el·lip·tic
el·lip·ti·cal·ly
El·mi·ra
el·o·cu·tion
el·o·cu·tion·ary
el·o·cu·tion·ist

elon·gate
elon·gat·ed
elon·gat·ing
elon·ga·tion
elope
eloped
elop·ing
elope·ment
elop·er
el·o·quence
el·o·quent
el·o·quent·ly
El Paso
else·where
elu·ci·date
elu·ci·dat·ed
elu·ci·dat·ing
elu·ci·da·tion
elu·ci·da·tor
elude
elud·ed
elud·ing
elu·sion
elu·sive
elu·so·ry
elu·sive·ly
elu·sive·ness
elv·ish
Ely·see
ema·ci·ate
ema·ci·at·ed
ema·ci·at·ing
ema·ci·a·tion
em·a·nate
em·a·nat·ed
em·a·nat·ing
em·a·na·tion
eman·ci·pate
eman·ci·pat·ed
eman·ci·pat·ing
eman·ci·pa·tor
emas·cu·late
emas·cu·lat·ed
emas·cu·lat·ing
emas·cu·la·tion
em·balm
em·balm·er
em·balm·ment
em·bank·ment
em·bar·go
em·bar·goes
em·bar·goed
em·bar·go·ing
em·bark
em·bar·ka·tion
em·bark·ment
em·bar·rass
em·bar·rass·ing·ly
em·bar·rass·ment
em·bas·sy
em·bas·sies
em·bat·tle
em·bat·tled
em·bat·tling
em·bat·tle·ment

em·bed
em·bed·ded
em·bed·ding
em·bel·lish
em·bel·lish·ment
em·ber
em·bez·zle
em·bez·zled
em·bez·zling
em·bez·zle·ment
em·bez·zler
em·bit·ter
em·bit·ter·ment
em·bla·zon
em·bla·zon·er
em·blaz·on·ment
em·bla·zon·ry
em·blem
em·blem·at·ic
em·blem·at·i·cal
em·bod·y
em·bod·ied
em·bod·y·ing
em·bod·i·ment
em·bold·en
em·bo·lism
em·bo·lus
em·bos·om
em·boss
em·boss·ment
em·bou·chure
em·brace
em·braced
em·brac·ing
em·broi·der
em·broi·dery
em·broi·der·ies
em·broil
em·broil·ment
em·bryo
em·bry·os
em·bry·on·ic
em·bry·ol·o·gy
em·cee
em·ceed
em·cee·ing
emend
em·er·ald
emerge
emerged
emerg·ing
emer·gence
emer·gent
emer·gen·cy
emer·gen·cies
emer·i·tus
Em·er·son
em·ery
emet·ic
em·i·grant
em·i·grate
em·i·grat·ed
em·i·grat·ing
em·i·gra·tion
émi·gré

émi·grés
em·i·nence
em·i·nent
em·i·ent·ly
em·i·nent do·main
em·is·sary
em·is·sar·ies
emis·sion
emis·sive
emit
emit·ted
emit·ting
emit·ter
Em·man·u·el
emol·lient
emol·u·ment
emote
emot·ed
emot·ing
emo·tive
emo·tion
emo·tion·al
emo·tion·al·ly
emo·tion·al·ism
em·pan·el
em·pa·thize
em·pa·thized
em·pa·thiz·ing
em·pa·thy
em·pa·thet·ic
em·path·ic
em·per·or
em·pha·sis
em·pha·ses
em·pha·size
em·pha·sized
em·pha·siz·ing
em·phat·ic
em·phat·i·cal·ly
em·phy·se·ma
em·pire
em·pir·i·cal
em·pir·i·cal·ly
em·pir·i·cism
em·pir·i·cist
em·place·ment
em·ploy
em·ploy·a·ble
em·ploy·ee
em·ploy·er
em·ploy·ment
em·po·ri·um
em·po·ri·ums
em·po·ria
em·pow·er
em·press
emp·ty
emp·ti·er
emp·ti·est
emp·tied
emp·ty·ing
emp·ti·ly
emp·ti·ness
emp·ty-hand·ed
emp·ty-head·ed

emu
em·u·late
em·u·lat·ed
em·u·lat·ing
em·u·la·tion
emul·si·fy
emul·si·fied
emul·si·fy·ing
emul·si·fi·ca·tion
emul·si·fi·er
emul·sion
emul·sive
en·a·ble
en·a·bled
en·a·bling
en·act
enam·el
enam·eled
enam·el·ing
enam·el·er
enam·el·ware
en·am·or
en·am·ored·ness
en·camp
en·camp·ment
en·cap·su·late
en·cap·su·lat·ed
en·cap·su·lat·ing
en·cap·sule
en·case
en·cased
en·cas·ing
en·ceinte
en·ceph·a·li·tis
en·ceph·a·lit·ic
en·ceph·a·lon
en·ceph·a·la
en·chant
en·chant·er
en·chant·ress
en·chant·ing
en·chant·ing·ly
en·chant·ment
en·chi·la·da
en·cir·cle
en·cir·cled
en·cir·cling
en·cir·cle·ment
en·clave
en·close
en·closed
en·clos·ing
en·clo·sure
en·code
en·cod·ed
en·cod·ing
en·co·mi·ast
en·com·pass
en·com·pass·ment
en·core
en·coun·ter
en·cour·age
en·cour·aged
en·cour·ag·ing
en·cour·ag·ing·ly

en·croach
en·croach·er
en·croach·ment
en·crust
en·crus·ta·tion
en·cum·ber
en·cum·brance
en·cy·clo·pe·dia
en·cy·clo·pe·dic
en·cy·clo·pe·di·cal
en·cy·clo·pe·di·cal·ly
en·cyst
en·dan·ger
en·dan·ger·ment
en·dear
en·dear·ment
en·deav·or
en·dem·ic
en·dem·i·cal
en·dem·i·cal·ly
end·ing
end·less
end·less·ly
end·less·ness
end·most
en·do·crine
en·do·cri·nol·o·gy
en·do·crin·o·log·ic
en·do·crin·o·log·i·cal
en·do·cri·nol·o·gist
en·dog·e·nous
en·dorse
en·dorsed
en·dors·ing
en·dor·see
en·dor·ser
en·dorse·ment
en·do·sperm
en·dow
en·dow·ment
en·due
en·dued
en·du·ing
en·dur·ance
en·dure
en·dured
en·dur·ing
en·dur·a·ble
en·dur·a·bly
en·dur·ing·ness
end·ways
en·e·ma
en·e·my
en·e·mies
en·er·get·ic
en·er·get·i·cal
en·er·get·i·cal·ly
en·er·gize
en·er·gized
en·er·giz·ing
en·er·giz·er
en·er·gy
en·er·gies
en·er·vate
en·er·vat·ed

en·er·vat·ing
en·er·va·tion
en·fee·ble
en·fee·bled
en·fee·bling
en·fee·ble·ment
en·fi·lade
en·fi·lad·ed
en·fi·lad·ing
en·fold
en·force
en·forced
en·forc·ing
en·force·a·ble
en·force·ment
en·forc·er
en·fran·chise
en·fran·chised
en·fran·chis·ing
en·fran·chise·ment
en·gage
en·gaged
en·gag·ing
en·gage·ment
en·gen·der
en·gine
en·gi·neer
en·gi·neer·ing
En·gland
En·glish
en·gorge
en·gorged
en·gorg·ing
en·gorge·ment
en·grave
en·graved
en·grav·ing
en·grav·er
en·gross
en·grossed
en·gross·er
en·gross·ing
en·gross·ing·ly
en·gross·ment
en·gulf
en·gulf·ment
en·hance
en·hanced
en·hanc·ing
en·hance·ment
enig·ma
en·ig·mat·ic
en·ig·mat·i·cal
en·ig·mat·i·cal·ly
en·join
en·join·er
en·join·ment
en·joy
en·joy·a·ble
en·joy·a·ble·ness
en·joy·a·bly
en·joy·ment
en·large
en·larged
en·larg·ing

en·large·a·ble
en·larg·er
en·large·ment
en·light·en
en·light·en·ment
en·list
en·list·ed
en·list·ment
en·liv·en
en·liv·en·er
en·mesh
en·mi·ty
en·mi·ties
en·no·ble
en·no·bled
en·no·bling
en·no·ble·ment
en·no·bler
en·nui
enor·mi·ty
enor·mi·ties
enor·mous
enor·mous·ly
enor·mous·ness
enough
en·plane
en·planed
en·plan·ing
en·rage
en·raged
en·rag·ing
en·rap·ture
en·rap·tured
en·rap·tur·ing
en·rapt
en·rich
en·rich·er
en·rich·ment
en·roll
en·roll·ment
en route
en·sconce
en·sconced
en·sconc·ing
en·sem·ble
en·shrine
en·shrined
en·shrin·ing
en·shroud
en·sign
en·si·lage
en·si·laged
en·si·lag·ing
en·slave
en·slaved
en·slav·ing
en·slave·ment
en·slav·er
en·snare
en·snared
en·snar·ing
en·snare·ment
en·snar·er
en·snar·ing·ly
en·sue

en·sued
en·su·ing
en·su·ing·ly
en·sure
en·sured
en·sur·ing
en·sur·er
en·tail
en·tail·er
en·tail·ment
en·tan·gle
en·tan·gled
en·tan·gling
en·tan·gle·ment
en·tan·gler
en·tente
en·ter
en·ter·a·ble
en·ter·i·tis
en·ter·prise
en·ter·pris·ing
en·ter·pris·ing·ly
en·ter·tain
en·ter·tain·er
en·ter·tain·ing
en·ter·tain·ing·ly
en·ter·tain·ment
en·thrall
en·thralled
en·thrall·ing
en·thrall·ment
en·throne
en·throned
en·thron·ing
en·throne·ment
en·thuse
en·thused
en·thus·ing
en·thu·si·asm
en·thu·si·ast
en·thu·si·as·tic
en·thu·si·as·ti·cal·ly
en·tice
en·ticed
en·tic·ing
en·tice·ment
en·tic·er
en·tic·ing·ly
en·tire
en·tire·ly
en·tire·ness
en·tire·ty
en·tire·ties
en·ti·tle
en·ti·tled
en·ti·tling
en·ti·tle·ment
en·ti·ty
en·ti·ties
en·to·mol·o·gy
en·to·mol·o·gies
en·to·mo·log·ic
en·to·mo·log·i·cal
en·to·mo·log·i·cal·ly
en·to·mol·o·gist

en·tou·rage
en·trails
en·train
en·train·er
en·trance
en·trance·way
en·trance
en·tranced
en·tranc·ing
en·trance·ment
en·tranc·ing·ly
en·trant
en·trap
en·trapped
en·trap·ping
en·trap·ment
en·treat
en·treat·ing·ly
en·treat·ment
en·treaty
en·tree
en·trench
en·trench·ment
en·tre·pre·neur
en·tre·pre·neur·i·al
en·tre·pre·neur·ship
en·tro·py
en·trust
en·trust·ment
en·try
en·tries
en·twine
en·twined
en·twin·ing
enu·mer·ate
enu·mer·at·ed
enu·mer·at·ing
enu·mer·a·tion
enu·mer·a·tive
enu·mer·a·tor
enun·ci·ate
enun·ci·at·ed
enun·ci·at·ing
enun·ci·a·tion
enun·ci·a·tive
enun·ci·a·tor
en·u·re·sis
en·u·ret·ic
en·vel·op
en·vel·oped
en·vel·op·ing
en·ve·lope
en·vi·a·ble
en·vi·a·ble·ness
en·vi·a·bly
en·vi·ous
en·vi·ous·ly
en·vi·ous·ness
en·vi·ron
en·vi·ron·ment
en·vi·ron·men·tal
en·vi·ron·men·tal·ly
en·vi·rons
en·vis·age
en·vis·aged

en·vis·ag·ing
en·vi·sion
en·voy
en·vy
en·vies
en·vied
en·vy·ing
en·vi·er
en·vy·ing·ly
en·zyme
en·zy·mat·ic
en·zy·mat·i·cal·ly
eon
ep·au·let
épée
épée·ist
ephed·rine
ephem·er·al
ephem·er·al·ness
ephem·er·al·ly
Ephe·sian
Eph·e·sus
Ephra·im
Eph·ra·ta
ep·ic
ep·i·cal
ep·i·cen·ter
ep·i·cure
epi·cu·re·an
ep·i·dem·ic
ep·i·dem·i·cal·ly
ep·i·der·mis
ep·i·der·mal
ep·i·der·mic
ep·i·glot·tis
ep·i·gram
ep·i·gram·mat·ic
ep·i·gram·mat·i·cal
ep·i·gram·mat·i·cal·ly
ep·i·gram·ma·tist
ep·i·gram·ma·tize
ep·i·gram·ma·tized
ep·i·gram·ma·tiz·ing
ep·i·lep·sy
ep·i·lep·tic
ep·i·logue
ep·i·log
Epiph·a·ny
Epiph·a·nies
epis·co·pa·cy
epis·co·pa·cies
epis·co·pal
epis·co·pa·lian
epis·co·pa·lian·ism
epis·co·pate
ep·i·sode
ep·i·sod·ic
ep·i·sod·i·cal
ep·i·sod·i·cal·ly
epis·te·mol·o·gy
epis·te·mo·log·i·cal
epis·te·mol·o·gist
epis·tle
epis·to·lary
ep·i·taph

ep·i·taph·ic
ep·i·taph·ist
ep·i·thet
ep·i·thet·ic
ep·i·thet·i·cal
epit·o·me
epit·o·mize
epit·o·mized
epit·o·miz·ing
ep·och
ep·och·al
ep·oxy
ep·oxy res·in
ep·si·lon
Ep·som
eq·ua·ble
eq·ua·bil·i·ty
eq·ua·ble·ness
eq·ua·bly
equal
equaled
equal·ling
equal·ly
equal·ness
equal·i·tar·i·an
equal·i·tar·i·an·ism
equal·i·ty
equal·i·ties
equal·ize
equal·ized
equal·iz·ing
equal·i·za·tion
equal·iz·er
equa·nim·i·ty
equate
equat·ed
equat·ing
equa·tion
equa·tion·al
equa·tion·al·ly
equa·tor
equa·to·ri·al
equa·to·ri·al·ly
eques·tri·an
eques·tri·enne
equi·dis·tance
equi·dis·tant
equi·dis·tant·ly
equi·lat·er·al
equi·li·brate
equi·li·brat·ed
equi·li·brat·ing
equi·li·bra·tion
equi·li·bra·tor
equi·lib·ri·um
equi·lib·ri·ums
equi·lib·ria
equine
equi·noc·tial
equi·nox
equip
equipped
equip·ping
equip·per
eq·ui·page

equip·ment
equi·poise
eq·ui·ta·ble
  eq·ui·ta·ble·ness
  eq·ui·ta·bly
eq·ui·ty
  eq·ui·ties
equiv·a·lence
  equiv·a·len·cy
equiv·a·lent
  equiv·a·lent·ly
equiv·o·cal
  equiv·o·cal·ly
  equiv·o·cal·ness
equiv·o·cate
  equiv·o·cat·ed
  equiv·o·cat·ing
  equiv·o·ca·tor
  equiv·o·ca·tion
era
erad·i·cate
  erad·i·cat·ed
  erad·i·cat·ing
  erad·i·ca·ble
  erad·i·ca·tion
  erad·i·ca·tive
  erad·i·ca·tor
erase
  erased
  eras·ing
  eras·a·bil·i·ty
  eras·a·ble
eras·er
Eras·mus
eras·ure
Er·a·tos·the·nes
erect
  erect·a·ble
  erect·er
  erec·tive
  erect·ly
  erect·ness
erec·tile
  erec·til·i·ty
erec·tion
erec·tor
er·go
Er·hard
Er·ic·son
Er·in
Er·i·trea
er·mine
erode
  erod·ed
  erod·ing
erog·e·nous
Er·os
ero·sion
erot·ic
  erot·i·cal·ly
erot·i·cism
err
  err·ing·ly
er·rand
er·rant

er·rant·ly
er·rat·ic
  er·rat·i·cal·ly
er·ra·tum
  er·ra·ta
er·ro·ne·ous
  er·ro·ne·ous·ly
  er·ro·ne·ous·ness
er·ror
  er·ror·less
er·satz
erst·while
er·u·dite
  er·u·dite·ly
  er·u·dite·ness
er·u·di·tion
erupt
  erup·tion
  erup·tive
  erup·tive·ly
  erup·tive·ness
es·ca·lade
  es·ca·lad·ed
  es·ca·lad·ing
  es·ca·lad·er
es·ca·late
  es·ca·lat·ed
  es·ca·lat·ing
  es·ca·la·tion
  es·ca·la·tor
es·cal·lop
es·ca·pade
es·cape
  es·caped
  es·cap·ing
  es·cap·er
es·ca·pee
es·cap·ist
  es·cap·ism
es·carp·ment
es·chew
  es·chew·al
  es·chew·er
es·cort
es·cri·toire
es·crow
es·cutch·eon
  es·cutch·eoned
Es·ki·mo
  Es·ki·mos
esoph·a·gus
es·o·ter·ic
  es·o·ter·i·cal
  es·o·ter·i·cal·ly
es·pal·ier
es·pe·cial
  es·pe·cial·ly
  es·pe·cial·ness
Es·pe·ran·to
es·pi·o·nage
es·pla·nade
es·pouse
  es·poused
  es·pous·ing
  es·pous·er

es·pous·al
es·pres·so
es·prit
es·prit de corps
es·py
  es·pied
  es·py·ing
es·quire
  es·quired
  es·quir·ing
es·say
  es·say·er
  es·say·ist
es·sence
es·sen·tial
  es·sen·ti·al·i·ty
  es·sen·tial·ly
  es·sen·tial·ness
Es·sex
es·tab·lish
  es·tab·lish·er
  es·tab·lish·ment
es·tate
es·teem
es·thete
  es·thet·ic
es·ti·ma·ble
  es·ti·ma·ble·ness
  es·ti·ma·bly
es·ti·mate
  es·ti·mat·ed
  es·ti·mat·ing
  es·ti·ma·tive
  es·ti·ma·tor
  es·ti·ma·tion
Es·to·nia
es·trange
  es·tranged
  es·trang·ing
  es·trange·ment
  es·tran·ger
es·trus
es·tu·ary
  es·tu·ar·ies
  es·tu·ar·i·al
et cet·era
etch
  etch·er
  etch·ing
eter·nal
  eter·nal·ly
eter·ni·ty
eter·nize
  eter·nized
  eter·niz·ing
  eter·ni·za·tion
eth·a·nol
ether
ethe·re·al
  ethe·re·al·i·ty
  ethe·re·al·ly
  ethe·re·al·ness
ethe·re·al·ize
  ethe·re·al·ized
  ethe·re·al·iz·ing

ethe·re·al·i·za·tion
eth·ic
eth·i·cal
  eth·i·cal·ly
eth·ics
Ethi·o·pia
eth·nic
  eth·ni·cal
  eth·ni·cal·ly
eth·nol·o·gy
eth·yl
eti·ol·o·gy
  eti·o·lo·gist
  eti·o·log·i·cal
  eti·o·log·i·cal·ly
et·i·quette
Etrus·can
etude
et·y·mol·o·gy
  et·y·mol·o·gies
  et·y·mo·log·ic
  et·y·mo·log·i·cal
  et·y·mol·o·gist
eu·ca·lyp·tus
  eu·ca·lyp·tus·es
  eu·ca·lyp·ti
Eu·cha·rist
  Eu·cha·ris·tic
  Eu·cha·ris·ti·cal
Eu·clid
Eu·clid·e·an
eu·gen·ic
  eu·gen·i·cal·ly
eu·gen·ics
eu·lo·gize
  eu·lo·gized
  eu·lo·giz·ing
  eu·lo·giz·er
eu·lo·gy
  eu·lo·gies
  eu·lo·gist
  eu·lo·gis·tic
  eu·lo·gis·ti·cal·ly
eu·nuch
eu·phe·mism
  eu·phe·mist
  eu·phe·mis·tic
  eu·phe·mis·ti·cal
  eu·phe·mis·ti·cal·ly
eu·phe·mize
  eu·phe·mized
  eu·phe·miz·ing
eu·pho·ni·ous
  eu·pho·ni·ous·ly
  eu·pho·ni·ous·ness
eu·pho·ny
  eu·phon·ic
  eu·phon·i·cal
  eu·phon·i·cal·ly
eu·pho·ria
  eu·phor·ic
Eu·phra·tes
Eur·asia
Eur·a·sian
eu·re·ka

Eu·rip·i·des
Eu·rope
Eu·ro·pe·an
Eu·ro·pe·an·ize
  Eu·ro·pe·an·ized
  Eu·ro·pe·an·iz·ing
  Eu·ro·pe·an·i·za·tion
Eu·sta·chian
eu·tha·na·sia
evac·u·ate
  evac·u·at·ed
  evac·u·at·ing
  evac·u·a·tion
  evac·u·a·tive
  evac·u·a·tor
evac·u·ee
evade
  evad·ed
  evad·ing
  evad·a·ble
  evad·er
  evad·ing·ly
eval·u·ate
  eval·u·at·ed
  eval·u·at·ing
  eval·u·a·tion
  eval·u·a·tor
ev·a·nesce
  ev·a·nesced
  ev·a·nesc·ing
  ev·a·nes·cent
  ev·a·nes·cence
  ev·a·nes·cent·ly
evan·gel
evan·gel·i·cal
  evan·gel·ic
  evan·gel·i·cal·ism
  evan·gel·i·cal·ly
  evan·gel·i·cal·ness
Evan·ge·line
evan·ge·lism
  evan·ge·lis·tic
  evan·ge·lis·ti·cal·ly
evan·ge·list
evan·ge·lize
  evan·ge·lized
  evan·ge·liz·ing
  evan·ge·li·za·tion
  evan·ge·liz·er
Ev·ans·ton
Ev·ans·ville
evap·o·rate
  evap·o·rat·ed
  evap·o·rat·ing
  evap·o·ra·ble
  evap·o·ra·tion
  evap·o·ra·tive
  evap·o·ra·tor
eva·sion
eva·sive
  eva·sive·ly
  eva·sive·ness
even
  even·ly
  even·ness

even-hand·ed
eve·ning
event
event·ful
  event·ful·ly
  event·ful·ness
even·tu·al
  even·tu·al·ly
  even·tu·al·i·ty
  even·tu·al·i·ties
even·tu·ate
  even·tu·at·ed
  even·tu·at·ing
ev·er
Ev·er·est
Ev·er·ett
Ev·er·glades
ev·er·green
ev·er·last·ing
  ev·er·last·ing·ly
  ev·er·last·ing·ness
ev·er·more
evert
  ever·si·ble
  ever·sion
ev·ery
ev·ery·body
ev·ery·day
ev·ery·one
ev·ery·thing
ev·ery·where
evict
  evic·tion
  evic·tor
ev·i·dence
  ev·i·denced
  ev·i·denc·ing
ev·i·dent
  ev·i·dent·ly
ev·i·den·tial
  ev·i·den·tial·ly
evil
  evil·do·er
  evil·do·ing
  evil·ly
  evil·ness
evil-mind·ed
  evil-mind·ed·ly
  evil-mind·ed·ness
evince
  evinced
  evinc·ing
evin·ci·ble
evis·cer·ate
  evis·cer·at·ed
  evis·cer·at·ing
  evis·cer·a·tion
evoke
  evoked
  evok·ing
  ev·o·ca·tion
ev·o·lu·tion
  ev·o·lu·tion·al
  ev·o·lu·tion·ary
  ev·o·lu·tion·ism

ev·o·lu·tion·ist
evolve
 evolved
 evolv·ing
 evolv·a·ble
 evolve·ment
 evolv·er
ew·er
ex·ac·er·bate
 ex·ac·er·bat·ed
 ex·ac·er·bat·ing
 ex·ac·er·ba·tion
ex·act
 ex·act·a·ble
 ex·ac·tor
ex·act·ing
 ex·act·ing·ly
 ex·act·ing·ness
ex·act·i·tude
ex·act·ly
ex·ag·ger·ate
 ex·ag·ger·at·ed
 ex·ag·ger·at·ing
 ex·ag·ger·a·tion
 ex·ag·ger·a·tor
ex·alt
 ex·alt·er
ex·al·ta·tion
ex·alt·ed
 ex·alt·ed·ly
 ex·alt·ed·ness
ex·am
ex·am·i·na·tion
ex·am·ine
 ex·am·ined
 ex·am·in·ing
 ex·am·in·a·ble
 ex·am·i·nant
 ex·am·in·er
 ex·am·i·nee
ex·am·ple
 ex·am·pled
 ex·am·pling
ex·as·per·ate
 ex·as·per·at·ed
 ex·as·per·at·ing
 ex·as·per·a·tion
Ex·cal·i·bur
ex·ca·vate
 ex·ca·vat·ed
 ex·ca·vat·ing
 ex·ca·va·tion
 ex·ca·va·tor
ex·ceed
ex·ceed·ing
 ex·ceed·ing·ly
ex·cel
 ex·celled
 ex·cel·ling
ex·cel·lence
ex·cel·len·cy
 ex·cel·len·cies
ex·cel·lent
 ex·cel·lent·ly
ex·cel·si·or

ex·cept
ex·cept·ing
ex·cep·tion
 ex·cep·tion·a·ble
 ex·cep·tion·al
ex·cerpt
ex·cess
ex·ces·sive
 ex·ces·sive·ly
 ex·ces·sive·ness
ex·change
 ex·changed
 ex·chang·ing
 ex·change·a·bil·i·ty
 ex·change·a·ble
 ex·chan·ger
ex·cheq·uer
ex·cise
 ex·cised
 ex·cis·ing
 ex·cis·a·ble
 ex·ci·sion
ex·cit·a·ble
 ex·cit·a·bil·i·ty
 ex·cit·a·bly
ex·ci·ta·tion
ex·cite
 ex·cit·ed
 ex·cit·ing
ex·cit·ed
 ex·cit·ed·ly
 ex·cit·ed·ness
ex·cite·ment
ex·cit·ing
 ex·cit·ing·ly
ex·claim
ex·cla·ma·tion
ex·clam·a·to·ry
 ex·clam·a·to·ri·ly
ex·clude
 ex·clud·ed
 ex·clud·ing
 ex·clud·a·bil·i·ty
 ex·clud·a·ble
 ex·clud·er
ex·clu·sion
ex·clu·sive
 ex·clu·sive·ly
 ex·clu·sive·ness
 ex·clu·siv·i·ty
ex·com·mu·ni·cate
 ex·com·mu·ni·cat·ed
 ex·com·mu·ni·cat·ing
 ex·com·mu·ni·cant
 ex·com·mu·ni·ca·ble
 ex·com·mu·ni·ca·tion
 ex·com·mu·ni·ca·tive
 ex·com·mu·ni·ca·to·ry
ex·co·ri·ate
 ex·co·ri·at·ed
 ex·co·ri·at·ing
 ex·co·ri·a·tion
ex·cre·ment
 ex·cre·men·tal
ex·cres·cense

ex·cres·cent
ex·cre·ta
 ex·cre·tal
ex·crete
 ex·cret·ed
 ex·cret·ing
ex·cre·tion
ex·cru·ci·ate
 ex·cru·ci·at·ed
 ex·cru·ci·at·ing
 ex·cru·ci·at·ing·ly
 ex·cru·ci·a·tion
ex·cul·pate
 ex·cul·pat·ed
 ex·cul·pat·ing
 ex·cul·pa·tion
 ex·cul·pa·to·ry
ex·cur·sion
 ex·cur·sion·al
 ex·cur·sion·ary
 ex·cur·sion·ist
ex·cur·sive
 ex·cur·sive·ly
 ex·cur·sive·ness
ex·cus·a·to·ry
ex·cuse
 ex·cused
 ex·cus·ing
 ex·cus·a·ble
 ex·cus·a·bly
 ex·cus·er
ex·cuse
 ex·cuse·less
 ex·cus·ing·ly
ex·e·cra·ble
 ex·e·cra·ble·ness
 ex·e·cra·bly
ex·e·crate
 ex·e·crat·ed
 ex·e·crat·ing
 ex·e·cra·tive
 ex·e·cra·tor
ex·e·cra·tion
ex·e·cute
 ex·e·cut·ed
 ex·e·cut·ing
 ex·e·cut·a·ble
 ex·e·cut·er
ex·e·cu·tion
ex·e·cu·tion·er
ex·ec·u·tive
 ex·ec·u·tive·ly
ex·ec·u·tor
 ex·ec·u·tor·ship
ex·e·ge·sis
 ex·e·ge·ses
ex·em·plar
ex·em·pla·ry
 ex·em·pla·ri·ly
 ex·em·pla·ri·ness
ex·em·pli·fy
 ex·em·pli·fied
 ex·em·pli·fy·ing
 ex·em·pli·fi·a·ble
 ex·em·pli·fi·ca·tion

ex·empt
ex·emp·tion
ex·er·cise
  ex·er·cised
  ex·er·cis·ing
  ex·er·cis·er
  ex·er·cis·a·ble
ex·ert
ex·er·tion
Ex·e·ter
ex·fo·li·ate
  ex·fo·li·at·ed
  ex·fo·li·at·ing
  ex·fo·li·a·tion
ex·ha·la·tion
ex·hale
  ex·haled
  ex·hal·ing
  ex·hal·ant
ex·haust
  ex·haust·er
  ex·haust·i·bil·i·ty
  ex·haust·i·ble
  ex·haust·ed
  ex·haust·ed·ly
  ex·haus·tion
  ex·haust·ing
  ex·haus·tive
  ex·haus·tive·ly
  ex·haus·tive·ness
ex·hib·it
  ex·hib·it·a·ble
  ex·hib·i·tor
  ex·hib·i·to·ry
ex·hi·bi·tion
  ex·hi·bi·tion·ism
  ex·hi·bi·tion·ist
  ex·hi·bi·tion·is·tic
ex·hil·a·rate
  ex·hil·a·rat·ed
  ex·hil·a·rat·ing
  ex·hil·a·ra·tion
  ex·hil·a·ra·tive
  ex·hil·a·ra·to·ry
ex·hort
  ex·hor·ta·tive
  ex·hor·ta·to·ry
  ex·hort·er
  ex·hort·ing·ly
ex·hor·ta·tion
ex·hume
  ex·humed
  ex·hum·ing
ex·i·gen·cy
  ex·i·gen·cies
ex·i·gent
  ex·i·gent·ly
ex·ile
  ex·iled
  ex·il·ing
  ex·il·a·ble
  ex·il·er
ex·ist
  ex·ist·ence
  ex·ist·ent

ex·is·ten·tial
  ex·is·ten·tial·ly
ex·it
ex li·bris
ex·o·dus
ex of·fi·cio
ex·og·a·my
  ex·og·a·mous
ex·og·e·nous
  ex·og·e·nous·ly
ex·on·er·ate
  ex·on·er·at·ed
  ex·on·er·at·ing
  ex·on·er·a·tion
  ex·on·er·a·tive
ex·or·bi·tant
  ex·or·bi·tance
  ex·or·bi·tant·ly
ex·or·cise
  ex·or·cised
  ex·or·cis·ing
  ex·or·cism
  ex·or·cist
ex·o·tic
  ex·ot·i·cal·ly
  ex·ot·i·cism
ex·pand
  ex·pand·er
ex·panse
ex·pan·si·ble
  ex·pan·si·bil·i·ty
ex·pan·sion
  ex·pan·sion·ism
  ex·pan·sion·ist
ex·pan·sive
  ex·pan·sive·ly
  ex·pan·sive·ness
ex·pa·ti·ate
  ex·pa·ti·at·ed
  ex·pa·ti·at·ing
  ex·pa·ti·a·tion
ex·pa·tri·ate
  ex·pa·tri·at·ed
  ex·pa·tri·at·ing
  ex·pa·tri·a·tion
ex·pect
  ex·pect·a·ble
  ex·pect·a·bly
  ex·pect·ing·ly
  ex·pect·an·cy
  ex·pect·an·cies
  ex·pect·ant
  ex·pect·ant·ly
  ex·pec·ta·tion
ex·pec·to·rate
  ex·pec·to·rat·ed
  ex·pec·to·rat·ing
  ex·pec·to·ra·tion
ex·pe·di·en·cy
ex·pe·di·ent
  ex·pe·di·ent·ly
ex·pe·dite
  ex·pe·dit·ed
  ex·pe·dit·ing
  ex·pe·dit·er

ex·pe·di·tion
  ex·pe·di·tion·ary
ex·pe·di·tious
  ex·pe·di·tious·ly
  ex·pe·di·tious·ness
ex·pel
  ex·pelled
  ex·pel·ling
ex·pend
  ex·pend·a·ble
  ex·pend·a·bil·i·ty
  ex·pend·i·ture
ex·pense
ex·pen·sive
  ex·pen·sive·ly
  ex·pen·sive·ness
ex·pe·ri·ence
  ex·pe·ri·enced
  ex·pe·ri·enc·ing
ex·pe·ri·en·tial
  ex·pe·ri·en·tial·ly
ex·per·i·ment
  ex·per·i·men·ta·tion
ex·per·i·men·tal
  ex·per·i·men·tal·ism
  ex·per·i·men·tal·ist
  ex·per·i·men·tal·ly
ex·pert
  ex·pert·ly
  ex·pert·ness
  ex·per·tise
ex·pi·ate
  ex·pi·at·ed
  ex·pi·at·ing
  ex·pi·a·ble
  ex·pi·a·tion
  ex·pi·a·tor
  ex·pi·a·to·ry
ex·pi·ra·tion
  ex·pir·a·to·ry
ex·pire
  ex·pired
  ex·pir·ing
ex·plain
  ex·plain·a·ble
  ex·plain·er
ex·pla·na·tion
  ex·plan·a·to·ry
  ex·plan·a·to·ri·ly
ex·ple·tive
ex·pli·ca·ble
ex·pli·cate
  ex·pli·cat·ed
  ex·pli·cat·ing
  ex·pli·ca·tion
  ex·pli·ca·tive
  ex·pli·ca·tor
ex·plic·it
  ex·plic·it·ly
  ex·plic·it·ness
ex·plode
  ex·plod·ed
  ex·plod·ing
  ex·plod·er
ex·ploit

ex·ploit·a·ble
ex·ploi·ta·tion
ex·ploit·er
ex·ploit·ive
ex·plore
ex·plo·ra·tion
ex·plor·a·to·ry
ex·plor·er
ex·plo·sion
ex·plo·sive
ex·plo·sive·ly
ex·plo·sive·ness
ex·po·nent
ex·po·nen·tial
ex·po·nen·tial·ly
ex·port
ex·port·a·ble
ex·por·ta·tion
ex·port·er
ex·pose
ex·posed
ex·pos·ing
ex·pos·er
ex·po·sé
ex·po·si·tion
ex·pos·i·tor
ex·pos·i·to·ry
ex post fac·to
ex·pos·tu·late
ex·pos·tu·lat·ed
ex·pos·tu·lat·ing
ex·pos·tu·la·tion
ex·pos·tu·la·tive
ex·pos·tu·la·to·ry
ex·po·sure
ex·pound
ex·pound·er
ex·press
ex·press·er
ex·press·i·ble
ex·pres·sion
ex·pres·sive
ex·pres·sive·ly
ex·pres·sive·ness
ex·press·ly
ex·press·way
ex·pro·pri·ate
ex·pro·pri·at·ed
ex·pro·pri·at·ing
ex·pro·pri·a·tor
ex·pro·pri·a·tion
ex·pul·sion
ex·pul·sive
ex·punge
ex·punged
ex·pung·ing
ex·pung·er
ex·pur·gate
ex·pur·gat·ed
ex·pur·gat·ing
ex·pur·ga·tion
ex·pur·ga·tor
ex·pur·ga·to·ry
ex·pur·ga·to·ri·al
ex·qui·site

ex·qui·site·ly
ex·qui·site·ness
ex·tant
ex·tem·po·ra·ne·ous
ex·tem·po·ra·ne·ous·ly
ex·tem·po·ra·ne·ous·ne
ex·tem·po·rize
ex·tem·po·rized
ex·tem·po·riz·ing
ex·tem·po·ri·za·tion
ex·tem·po·riz·er
ex·tend
ex·tend·i·bil·i·ty
ex·tend·i·ble
ex·tend·ed
ex·tend·ed·ly
ex·tend·ed·ness
ex·tend·er
ex·ten·si·ble
ex·ten·si·bil·i·ty
ex·ten·sion
ex·ten·sion·al
ex·ten·sive
ex·ten·sive·ly
ex·ten·sive·ness
ex·tent
ex·ten·u·ate
ex·ten·u·at·ed
ex·ten·u·at·ing
ex·ten·u·a·tion
ex·ten·u·a·tor
ex·te·ri·or
ex·te·ri·or·ly
ex·ter·mi·nate
ex·ter·mi·nat·ed
ex·ter·mi·nat·ing
ex·ter·mi·na·tion
ex·ter·mi·na·tor
ex·ter·mi·na·to·ry
ex·ter·nal
ex·ter·nal·ly
ex·tinct
ex·tinc·tion
ex·tin·guish
ex·tin·guish·a·ble
ex·tin·guish·er
ex·tin·guish·ment
ex·tir·pate
ex·tir·pat·ed
ex·tir·pat·ing
ex·tir·pa·tion
ex·tir·pa·tive
ex·tol
ex·tolled
ex·tol·ling
ex·tol·ler
ex·tol·ling·ly
ex·tol·ment
ex·tort
ex·tor·ter
ex·tor·tive
ex·tor·tion
ex·tor·tion·ary
ex·tor·tion·ate
ex·tor·tion·er

ex·tor·tion·ist
ex·tra
ex·tract
ex·tract·a·ble
ex·trac·tive
ex·trac·tor
ex·trac·tion
ex·tra·cur·ric·u·lar
ex·tra·dite
ex·tra·dit·ed
ex·tra·dit·ing
ex·tra·dit·a·ble
ex·tra·di·tion
ex·tra·ne·ous
ex·tra·ne·ous·ly
ex·tra·ne·ous·ness
ex·traor·di·nary
ex·traor·di·nar·i·ly
ex·trap·o·late
ex·trap·o·lat·ed
ex·trap·o·lat·ing
ex·trap·o·la·tion
ex·tra·sen·so·ry
ex·tra·ter·res·tri·al
ex·tra·ter·ri·to·ri·al
ex·tra·ter·ri·to·ri·al·i·ty
ex·trav·a·gance
ex·trav·a·gan·cy
ex·trav·a·gant
ex·trav·a·gant·ly
ex·trav·a·gan·za
ex·treme
ex·treme·ly
ex·treme·ness
ex·trem·ist
ex·trem·ism
ex·trem·i·ty
ex·trem·i·ties
ex·tri·cate
ex·tri·cat·ed
ex·tri·cat·ing
ex·tri·ca·ble
ex·tri·ca·tion
ex·trin·sic
ex·tro·vert
ex·tro·ver·sion
ex·trude
ex·trud·ed
ex·trud·ing
ex·tru·sion
ex·tru·sive
ex·u·ber·ance
ex·u·ber·ant
ex·u·ber·ant·ly
ex·ude
ex·ud·ed
ex·ud·ing
ex·u·da·tion
ex·ult
ex·ult·ant
ex·ult·ant·ly
ex·ul·ta·tion
ex·ult·ing·ly
ex·ur·ban·ite
eye

eyed
eye·ing
eye·ball
eye·bright
eye·brow
eye·cup
eye·ful
  eye·fuls
eye·glass
  eye·glass·es
eye·hole
eye·lash
eye·let
eye·lid
eye·o·pen·er
  eye·o·pen·ing
eye·piece
eye·shade
eye·sight
eye·sore
eye·strain
eye·tooth
  eye·teeth
eye·wash
eye·wa·ter
eye·wink
eye·wit·ness
ey·rie
  ey·ry
  ey·ries
Eze·ki·el
Ez·ra
Fa·bi·an
Fa·bi·us
fa·ble
  fa·bled
fab·ric
fab·ri·cate
  fab·ri·cat·ed
  fab·ri·cat·ing
  fab·ri·ca·tion
  fab·ri·ca·tive
  fab·ri·ca·tor
fab·u·lous
  fab·u·lous·ly
  fab·u·lous·ness
fa·cade
  fa·cades
face
  faced
  fac·ing
fac·et
fa·ce·tious
  fa·ce·tious·ly
  fa·ce·tious·ness
fa·cial
  fa·cial·ly
fac·ile
  fac·ile·ly
  fac·ile·ness
fa·cil·i·tate
  fa·cil·i·tat·ed
  fa·cil·i·tat·ing
fa·cil·i·ty
  fa·cil·i·ties

fac·sim·i·le
fac·tion
fac·tion·al
fac·tion·al·ism
fac·tion·al·ly
fac·ti·tious
  fac·ti·tious·ly
  fac·ti·tious·ness
fac·tor
fac·fo·ry
  fac·to·ries
fac·to·tum
fac·tu·al
  fac·tu·al·ly
fac·ul·ty
fad
fad·dish
fad·dism
fad·dist
fade
  fad·ed
  fad·ing
fa·er·ie
fa·ery
fa·er·ies
fag
fagged
fag·ging
fag·got
Fa·gin
Fahr·en·heit
fail·ing
  fail·ing·ly
fail·safe
fail·ure
faint
  faint·ly
  faint·ness
faint·heart·ed
  faint·heart·ed·ly
  faint·heart·ed·ness
fair
  fair·ness
Fair·fax
fair·ground
fair·ly
fair·mind·ed
  fair·mind·ed·ness
fairy
  fair·ies
  fair·y·like
faith·ful
faith·less
  faith·less·ly
  faith·less·ness
fake
  faked
  fak·ing
  fak·er
fal·con
fal·con·ry
Falk·land
fall
  fall·en
  fall·ing

fal·la·cious
  fal·la·cious·ly
  fal·la·cious·ness
fal·la·cy
fal·li·ble
  fal·li·bil·i·ty
  fal·li·bly
Fal·lo·pi·an
fall·out
fal·low
  fal·low·ness
false
  fals·er
  fals·est
  false·ly
  false·ness
false·hood
fal·si·fy
  fal·si·fied
  fal·si·fy·ing
  fal·si·fi·ca·tion
  fal·si·fi·er
fal·si·ty
Fal·staff
fal·ter
  fal·ter·er
  fal·ter·ing·ly
famed
fa·mil·ial
fa·mil·iar
  fa·mil·iar·ly
  fa·mil·i·ar·i·ty
  fa·mil·i·ar·i·ties
  fa·mil·iar·ize
  fa·mil·iar·ized
  fa·mil·iar·iz·ing
  fa·mil·iar·i·za·tion
fam·i·ly
  fam·i·lies
fam·ine
fam·ish
  fam·ished
fa·mous
  fa·mous·ly
fan
  fan·like
  fan·ner
  fanned
  fan·ning
fa·nat·ic
  fa·nat·i·cal
  fa·nat·i·cal·ly
  fa·nat·i·cism
  fa·nat·i·cize
  fa·nat·i·cized
  fa·nat·i·ciz·ing
fan·ci·er
fan·ci·ful
  fan·ci·ful·ly
  fan·ci·ful·ness
fan·cy
  fan·cies
  fan·ci·er
  fan·ci·est
  fan·cied

fan·cy·ing
fan·ci·ly
fan·ci·ness
fan·cy·work
Fan·euil
fan·fare
fanged
fan·light
fan·tas·tic
fan·tas·ti·cal
fan·tas·ti·cal·ly
fan·tas·ti·cal·i·ty
fan·tas·ti·cal·ness
fan·ta·sy
fan·ta·sies
far
far·ther
far·thest
Far·a·day
far·a·way
farce
farced
farc·ing
far·ci·cal
far·ci·cal·i·ty
far·ci·cal·ly
fare
fared
far·ing
far·er
fare·well
far·fetched
far·flung
Far·go
farm·er
farm·hand
farm·house
farm·ing
farm·yard
far·off
Fa·rouk
Far·ra·gut
far·reach·ing
far·reach·ing·ly
far·reach·ing·ness
far·see·ing
far·sight·ed
far·sight·ed·ly
far·sight·ed·ness
far·ther·most
fas·cia
fas·ci·ae
fas·ci·as
fas·ci·al
fas·ci·cle
fas·ci·cled
fas·ci·nate
fas·ci·nat·ed
fas·ci·nat·ing
fas·ci·nat·ing·ly
fas·ci·na·tion
fas·cism
fas·cist
fa·scis·tic
fa·scis·ti·cal·ly

fash·ion
fash·ion·a·ble
fash·ion·a·ble·ness
fash·ion·a·bly
fas·ten
fas·ten·er
fas·ten·ing
fas·tid·i·ous
fas·tid·i·ous·ly
fas·tid·i·ous·ness
fat
fat·ter
fat·test
fat·ted
fat·ting
fat·ly
fat·ness
fa·tal
fa·tal·ly
fa·tal·ism
fa·tal·ist
fa·tal·is·tic
fa·tal·is·ti·cal·ly
fa·tal·i·ty
fa·tal·i·ties
fate
fat·ed
fat·ing
fate·ful
fate·ful·ly
fate·ful·ness
fa·ther
fa·ther·hood
fa·ther·li·ness
fa·ther·ly
fa·ther·in·law
fa·thers·in·law
fa·ther·land
fath·om
fath·om·a·ble
fath·om·less
fa·tigue
fa·tigued
fa·tig·uing
fat·i·ga·ble
fat·i·ga·bil·i·ty
Fat·i·ma
fat·ten
fat·ten·er
fat·ty
fat·ti·er
fat·ti·est
fat·ti·ness
fat·tish
fa·tu·i·ty
fa·tu·i·ties
fat·u·ous
fat·u·ous·ly
fat·u·ous·ness
fau·cet
Faulk·ner
fault
fault·find·er
fault·find·ing
fault·less

fault·less·ly
fault·less·ness
faulty
fault·i·er
fault·i·est
fault·i·ly
fault·i·ness
fau·na
fau·nas
fau·nae
faux pas
fa·vor
fa·vor·ing·ly
fa·vor·a·ble
fa·vor·a·ble·ness
fa·vor·a·bly
fa·vored
fa·vored·ly
fa·vored·ness
fa·vor·ite
fa·vor·it·ism
fawn
faze
fazed
faz·ing
fe·al·ty
fear·ful
fear·ful·ly
fear·ful·ness
fear·less
fear·less·ly
fear·less·ness
fear·some
fear·some·ly
fear·some·ness
fea·si·ble
fea·si·bil·i·ty
fea·si·ble·ness
fea·si·bly
feath·er
feath·ered
feath·er·bed·ding
fea·ture
fea·tured
fea·tur·ing
fea·ture·less
fe·brile
Feb·ru·ary
Feb·ru·ar·ies
fe·ces
fe·cal
feck·less
fe·cund
fe·cun·di·ty
fe·cun·date
fe·cun·dat·ed
fe·cun·dat·ing
fe·cun·da·tion
fed·er·al
fed·er·al·ism
fed·er·al·ist
fed·er·al·ize
fed·er·al·ized
fed·er·al·iz·ing
fed·er·al·i·za·tion

fed·er·al·ly
fed·er·ate
fed·er·at·ed
fed·er·at·ing
fee·ble
fee·bler
fee·blest
fee·bly
fee·ble-mind·ed
fee·ble-mind·ed·ness
feed
fed
feed·ing
feed·er
feed·back
feel
felt
feel·ing
feel·er
feel·ing
feel·ing·ly
feel·ing·ness
feign
feigned
feign·ed·ly
feign·er
feign·ing·ly
feint
feisty
feist·i·er
feist·i·est
fe·lic·i·tate
fe·lic·i·tat·ed
fe·lic·i·tat·ing
fe·lic·i·ta·tion
fe·lic·i·tous
fe·lic·i·tous·ly
fe·lic·i·tous·ness
fe·lic·i·ty
fe·lic·i·ties
fe·line
fe·line·ly
fe·lin·i·ty
fel·la·tio
fel·low
fel·low·ship
fel·on
fel·o·ny
fel·o·nies
fe·lo·ni·ous
fe·lo·ni·ous·ly
fe·lo·ni·ous·ness
fe·male
fem·i·nine
fem·i·nine·ly
fem·i·nine·ness
fem·i·nin·i·ty
fem·i·nism
fem·i·nist
fem·i·nis·tic
fem·i·nize
fem·i·nized
fem·i·niz·ing
fem·i·ni·za·tion
fe·mur

fe·murs
fem·o·ra
fem·o·ral
fen
fen·ny
fen·ni·er
fen·ni·est
fence
fenced
fenc·ing
fenc·er
fen·der
fe·ral
Fer·di·nand
fer·ment
fer·ment·a·ble
fer·men·ta·tion
Fer·nan·dez
fern·ery
fern·er·ies
fe·ro·cious
fe·ro·cious·ness
fe·ro·cious·ly
fe·ro·ci·ty
fer·ret
fer·ret·er
Fer·ris wheel
fer·ro-con·crete
fer·ro-mag·net·ic
fer·ru·gi·nous
fer·rule
fer·ry
fer·ries
fer·ry·boat
fer·ry·man
fer·tile
fer·tile·ly
fer·tile·ness
fer·til·i·ty
fer·ti·li·za·tion
fer·ti·li·za·tion·al
fer·ti·lize
fer·ti·lized
fer·ti·liz·ing
fer·ti·liz·a·ble
fer·ti·liz·er
fer·vent
fer·ven·cy
fer·vent·ly
fer·vid
fer·vid·ly
fer·vid·ness
fer·vor
fes·ter
fes·ti·val
fes·tive
fes·tive·ly
fes·tive·ness
fes·tiv·i·ty
fes·toon
fes·toon·ery
fes·toon·er·ies
fe·tal
fetch
fetch·er

fetch·ing
fetch·ing·ly
fete
fet·id
fet·id·ly
fet·id·ness
fet·ish
fet·ish·ism
fet·ish·ist
fet·ish·is·tic
fet·lock
fet·ter
fet·tle
fe·tus
fe·tus·es
feud
feud·ist
feu·dal
feu·dal·ism
feu·dal·ist
feu·dal·is·tic
feu·dal·i·za·tion
feu·dal·ize
feu·dal·ized
feu·dal·iz·ing
fe·ver
fe·ver·ish
fe·ver·ish·ly
fe·ver·ish·ness
fe·ver·ous
fe·ver·ous·ly
few·ness
fez·zes
fi·an·cé
fi·an·cée
fi·as·co
fi·as·cos
fi·as·coes
fi·at
fib
fib·ber
fib·ster
fi·ber
fi·bered
fi·ber·board
fi·ber·glass
fi·bril
fi·bril·la·tion
fi·broid
fi·brous
fib·u·la
fib·u·las
fib·u·lae
fib·u·lar
fick·le
fick·le·ness
fic·tion
fic·tion·al
fic·tion·al·ly
fic·ti·tious
fic·ti·tious·ly
fic·ti·tious·ness
fid·dle
fid·dler
fid·dled

fid·dling
fi·del·i·ty
fidg·et
  fidg·ety
  fidg·et·i·er
  fidg·et·i·est
fi·du·ci·ary
fief
field day
field·er
field·er's choice
field glass
field house
field mar·shal
field·work
fiend
  fiend·ish
  fiend·ish·ly
  fiend·ish·ness
fierce
  fierce·ly
  fierce·ness
fiery
  fier·i·er
  fier·i·est
  fier·i·ly
  fier·i·ness
fif·teen
fif·teenth
fif·ti·eth
fif·ty
  fif·ties
Fig·a·ro
fight·er
fig·ment
fig·u·ra·tion
fig·u·ra·tive
  fig·ur·a·tive·ly
  fig·ur·a·tive·ness
fig·ure
  fig·ured
  fig·ur·ing
  fig·ure·less
  fig·ur·er
fig·ure·head
fig·ur·ine
Fi·ji
fil·a·ment
  fil·a·men·ta·ry
  fil·a·ment·ed
  fil·a·men·tous
filch·er
file
  filed
  fil·ing
fi·let
fi·let mi·gnon
fil·i·al
  fil·i·al·ly
fil·i·bus·ter
fil·i·gree
  fil·i·greed
  fil·i·gree·ing
fil·lings
Fil·i·pi·no

fill·er
fil·let
fill·ing
fil·lip
fil·ly
  fil·lies
film·strip
filmy
  film·i·er
  film·i·est
  film·i·ness
fil·ter
filth
  filth·i·ness
filthy
  filth·i·er
  filth·i·est
fin
  finned
  fin·ning
  fin·less
  fin·like
fi·na·gle
  fi·na·gled
  fi·na·gling
  fi·na·gler
fi·nal
fi·na·le
fi·nal·ist
fi·nal·i·ty
  fi·nal·i·ties
fi·nal·ize
  fi·nal·ized
  fi·nal·iz·ing
fi·nal·ly
fi·nance
  fi·nanced
  fi·nanc·ing
fi·nan·cial
  fi·nan·cial·ly
fin·an·cier
finch
find
  found
  find·ing
  find·er
fine
  fin·er
  fin·est
  fine·ly
  fine·ness
fin·ery
  fin·er·ies
fi·nesse
  fi·nessed
  fi·nes·sing
Fin·gal
fin·ger
  fin·ger·bowl
  fin·ger·ing
  fin·ger·nail
  fin·ger·print
fin·i·al
fin·i·cal
  fin·i·cal·ly

fin·icky
  fin·ick·ing
fin·is
  fin·is·es
fin·ish
  fin·ished
  fin·ish·er
fi·nite
  fi·nite·ly
  fi·nite·ness
Fin·land
Finn·ish
fire
  fired
  fir·ing
  fir·er
fire·arm
fire·ball
fire·brand
fire·bug
fire·crack·er
fire·fight·er
fire·fly
  fire·flies
fire·man
fire·place
fire·plug
fire·pow·er
fire·proof
fire·side
fire·trap
fire·wa·ter
fire·wood
fire·works
fir·ing squad
firm
  firm·ly
  firm·ness
fir·ma·ment
first-born
first-hand
first·ling
first·ly
first-rate
first-string
fis·cal
  fis·cal·ly
fish·er
fish·er·man
  fish·er·men
fish·ery
  fish·er·ies
fish·hook
fish·ing
fish·wife
  fish·wives
fishy
  fish·i·er
  fish·i·est
fis·sile
fis·sion
fis·sure
  fis·sured
  fis·sur·ing
fist·ic

fist·i·cuff
fit
  fit·ter
  fit·test
  fit·ted
  fit·ting
  fit·ly
  fit·ness
fit·ful
  fit·ful·ly
  fit·ful·ness
fit·ting
  fit·ting·ly
  fit·ting·ness
five·fold
five-and-ten
fix
  fix·a·ble
  fixed
  fix·ed·ly
  fix·er
fix·a·tion
fix·a·tive
fix·ings
fix·i·ty
  fix·i·ties
fix·ture
fiz·zle
  fiz·zled
  fiz·zling
fiz·zy
  fiz·zi·er
  fiz·zi·est
flab·ber·gast
flab·by
  flab·bi·er
  flab·bi·est
  flab·bi·ly
  flab·bi·ness
flac·cid
flag
  flagged
  flag·ging
flag·el·lant
flag·el·late
  flag·el·lat·ed
  flag·el·lat·ing
  flag·el·la·tion
fla·gi·tious
  fla·gi·tious·ly
flag-on
flag·pole
flag·rank
fla·grant
  fla·grant·ly
flag·ship
flag·stone
flail
flair
flake
  flaked
  flak·ing
flaky
  flak·i·er
  flak·i·est

flak·i·ness
flam·boy·ant
  flam·boy·ance
  flam·boy·an·cy
  flam·boy·ant·ly
flame
  flamed
  flam·ing
  flam·ing·ly
flam·ma·ble
Flan·a·gan
Flan·ders
flange
flank
  flank·er
flan·nel·ette
flap
  flapped
  flap·ping
  flap·per
flap·jack
flare
  flared
  flar·ing
flare-up
flash·back
flash·light
flashy
  flash·i·er
  flash·i·est
  flash·i·ly
  flash·i·ness
flask
flat
  flat·ly
  flat·ted
  flat·ting
  flat·ness
flat·car
flat·foot
  flat-foot·ed
  flat-foot·ed·ly
  flat-foot·ed·ness
flat·ten
  flat·ten·er
flat·ter
  flat·ter·er
  flat·ter·ing·ly
flat·tery
  flat·ter·ies
flat·u·lent
  flat·u·lence
  flat·u·len·cy
  flat·u·lent·ly
flat·ware
flaunt
  flaunt·er
  flaunt·ing·ly
  flaunty
  flaunt·i·er
  flaunt·i·est
flau·tist
fla·vor
  fla·vored
  fla·vor·less

fla·vor·ing
flaw·less
flax·en
flax·seed
flay·er
flea·bite
flea-bit·ten
fleck
flec·tion
fledge
  fledged
  fledg·ing
  fledg·ling
flee
  fled
  flee·ing
fleece
  fleeced
  fleec·ing
fleecy
  fleec·i·er
  fleec·i·est
  fleec·i·ness
fleet
  fleet·ly
  fleet·ness
fleet·ing
  fleet·ing·ly
  fleet·ing·ness
Flem·ish
flesh·ly
  flesh·li·er
  flesh·li·est
flesh·pots
fleshy
  flesh·i·er
  flesh·i·est
  flesh·i·ness
Fleu·ry
flex·i·ble
  flex·i·bil·i·ty
  flex·i·bly
flex·ion
flex·or
flex·ure
flib·ber·ti·gib·bet
flick·er
  flick·er·ing
fli·er
flight
  flight·less
flighty
  flight·i·er
  flight·i·est
  flight·i·ly
  flight·i·ness
flim·flam
  flim·flammed
  flim·flam·ming
flim·sy
  flim·si·er
  flim·si·est
  flim·si·ly
  flim·si·ness
flinch

flinch·er
flinch·ing·ly
flin·ders
fling
flung
fling·ing
flinty
flint·i·er
flint·i·est
flint·i·ness
flip
flipped
flip·ping
flip-flop
flip·pant
flip·pan·cy
flip·pant·ly
flip·per
flirt·er
flir·ta·tion
flir·ta·tious
flit
flit·ted
flit·ting
flit·ter
float·a·ble
float·a·tion
float·er
float·ing
floc·cu·lent
floc·cu·lence
flocked
flocky
flog
flogged
flog·ging
flog·ger
flood-gate
flood·light
flood·light·ed
flood·lit
flood·light·ing
floor·ing
floor·walk·er
floo·zy
floo·zies
flop
flopped
flop·ping
flop·per
flop-house
flop·py
flop·pi·er
flop·pi·est
flop·pi·ly
flop·pi·ness
flo·ra
flo·ras
flo·rae
flo·ral
Flor·ence
Flor·en·tine
flo·res·cence
flo·res·cent
flo·ret

flo·ri·cul·ture
flo·ri·cul·tur·al
flo·ri·cul·tur·ist
flor·id
flo·rid·i·ty
flor·id·ly
flor·id·ness
Flor·i·da
flo·rist
floss
flossy
floss·i·er
floss·i·est
flo·ta·tion
flo·til·la
flot·sam
flounce
flounced
flounc·ing
floun·der
floury
flour·i·er
flour·i·est
flour·ish
flour·ish·ing
flout·er
flow·er
flow·ered
flow·er·ing
flow·ery
flow·er·i·ness
flub
flubbed
flub·bing
fluc·tu·ate
fluc·tu·at·ed
fluc·tu·at·ing
fluc·tu·a·tion
flue
flu·ent
flu·en·cy
flu·ent·ly
fluff
fluff·i·ness
fluffy
fluff·i·er
fluff·i·est
flu·id
flu·id·ly
flu·id·ness
fluke
fluky
fluk·i·er
fluk·i·est
flum·mery
flum·mer·ies
flun·ky
flun·kies
flu·o·resce
flu·o·resced
flu·o·resc·ing
flu·o·res·cence
flu·o·res·cent
fluor·i·da·tion
fluor·i·date

fluor·i·dat·ed
fluor·i·dat·ing
fluor·o·scope
flur·ry
flur·ries
flur·ried
flur·ry·ing
Flush·ing
flus·ter
flute
flut·ed
flut·ing
flut·ist
flut·ter
flut·ter·er
flut·ter·ing·ly
flut·tery
flut·ter·i·er
flut·ter·i·est
flux·ion
fly-blown
fly-by-night
fly·er
fly·ing
fly·leaf
fly·leaves
fly·pa·per
fly·speck
fly·wheel
foal
foam
foam·i·ness
foamy
foam·i·er
foam·i·est
fob
fobbed
fob·bing
fo·cal
fo·cal·ly
fo·cal·ize
fo·cal·ized
fo·cal·iz·ing
fo·cus
fo·cus·es
fo·cused
fo·cus·ing
fo·cus·er
fod·der
foe·tus
foe·tal
fog
fogged
fog·ging
fog·gy
fog·gi·er
fog·gi·est
fog·gi·ly
fog·gi·ness
fog·horn
fo·gy
fo·gies
fo·gy·ish
foi·ble
fold·er

fol·de·rol
fo·li·a·ceous
fo·li·age
fo·li·ate
  fo·li·at·ed
  fo·li·at·ing
  fo·li·a·tion
fo·lio
  fo·li·os
  fo·li·oed
  fo·li·o·ing
folk·lore
  folk·lor·ist
folk·sy
  folk·si·er
  folk·si·est
  folk·si·ness
folk·ways
fol·li·cle
  fol·lic·u·lar
fol·low
  fol·low·er
  fol·low·ing
fol·ly
  fol·lies
fo·ment
  fo·men·ta·tion
  fo·ment·er
fon·dant
fon·dle
  fon·dled
  fon·dling
  fon·dler
  fond·ly
  fond·ness
fon·due
Fon·taine·bleau
Foo·chow
food·stuff
fool·ery
  fool·er·ies
fool·har·dy
  fool·har·di·ness
fool·proof
fools·cap
foot·age
foot·ball
foot·board
foot·can·dle
foot·ed
foot·fall
foot·hill
foot·hold
foot·ing
foot·lights
foot·loose
foot·note
  foot·not·ed
  foot·not·ing
foot·path
foot·print
foot·sore
foot·step
foot·stool
foot·wear

foot·work
foo·zle
  foo·zled
  foo·zling
fop
  fop·pery
  fop·per·ies
  fop·pish
  fop·pish·ly
  fop·pish·ness
for·age
  for·aged
  for·ag·ing
for·ay
for·bear
  for·bore
  for·borne
  for·bear·ing
  for·bear·ance
  for·bear·ing·ly
for·bid
  for·bade
  for·bid·den
  for·bid·ding
  for·bid·dance
for·bid·ding
  for·bid·ding·ly
  for·bid·ding·ness
force
  forced
  forc·ing
  force·a·ble
  force·less
  forc·er
force·ful
  force·ful·ly
  force·ful·ness
for·ceps
for·ci·ble
  for·ci·bly
ford·a·ble
fore·arm
fore·bear
fore·bode
  fore·bod·ed
  fore·bod·ing
  fore·bod·er
  fore·bod·ing
fore·brain
fore·cast
  fore·cast·ed
  fore·cast·ing
  fore·cast·er
fore·close
  fore·closed
  fore·clos·ing
  fore·clo·sure
fore·fa·ther
fore·fin·ger
fore·foot
  fore·feet
fore·front
fore·gath·er
fore·go
  fore·went

fore·gone
fore·go·ing
fore·gone
fore·ground
fore·hand
fore·hand·ed
  fore·hand·ed·ness
fore·head
for·eign
  for·eign·er
  for·eign·ness
fore·know
  fore·knew
  fore·known
  fore·know·ing
  fore·knowl·edge
fore·leg
fore·lock
fore·man
  fore·men
fore·most
fore·noon
fo·ren·sic
fore·or·dain
fore·quar·ter
fore·run
  fore·ran
  fore·run·ning
  fore·run·ner
fore·see
  fore·saw
  fore·seen
  fore·see·ing
  fore·see·a·ble
  fore·se·er
fore·shad·ow
  fore·shad·ow·er
fore·short·en
fore·sight
  fore·sight·ed
  fore·sight·ed·ness
fore·skin
for·est
fore·stall
for·est·a·tion
for·es·ter
for·est·ry
fore·taste
  fore·tast·ed
  fore·tast·ing
fore·tell
  fore·told
  fore·tell·ing
  fore·tell·er
fore·thought
for·ev·er
for·ev·er·more
fore·warn
fore·word
for·feit
  for·feit·er
  for·fei·ture
for·gath·er
forge
  forged

forg·ing
forg·er
for·gery
for·ger·ies
for·get
for·got
for·got·ten
for·get·ting
for·get·ta·ble
for·get·ter
for·get·ful
for·get·ful·ly
for·get·ful·ness
for·give
for·gave
for·giv·en
for·giv·ing
for·giv·a·ble
for·give·ness
for·giv·er
for·go
for·went
for·gone
for·go·ing
for·go·er
fork·lift
for·lorn
for·lorn·ly
for·lorn·ness
for·mal
for·mal·ly
for·mal·ism
for·mal·i·ty
for·mal·i·ties
for·mal·ize
for·mal·ized
for·mal·iz·ing
for·mal·i·za·tion
for·mat
for·ma·tion
form·a·tive
for·mer
for·mer·ly
For·mi·ca
for·mi·da·ble
for·mi·da·ble·ness
for·mi·da·bly
form·less
form·less·ly
form·less·ness
For·mo·sa
for·mu·la
for·mu·las
for·mu·lae
for·mu·lary
for·mu·lar·ies
for·mu·late
for·mu·lat·ed
for·mu·lat·ing
for·mu·la·tion
for·mu·la·tor
for·ni·cate
for·ni·cat·ed
for·ni·cat·ing
for·ni·cat·or

for·ni·ca·tion
for·sake
for·sook
for·sak·en
for·sak·ing
for·sak·en
for·sak·en·ly
for·swear
for·swore
for·sworn
for·swear·ing
for·swear·er
fort
forte
for·te
forth·com·ing
forth·right
forth·right·ness
forth·with
for·ti·fi·ca·tion
for·ti·fy
for·ti·fied
for·ti·fy·ing
for·ti·fi·er
for·tis·si·mo
for·ti·tude
fort·night
fort·night·ly
fort·night·lies
for·tress
for·tu·i·tous
for·tu·i·tous·ly
for·tu·i·tous·ness
for·tu·nate
for·tu·nate·ly
for·tune
for·tune·tell·er
for·tune·tell·ing
for·ty
for·ties
for·ty·nin·er
fo·rum
fo·rums
fo·ra
for·ward
for·ward·er
for·ward·ly
for·ward·ness
fos·sil
fos·sil·ize
fos·sil·ized
fos·sil·iz·ing
fos·sil·i·za·tion
fos·ter
fos·tered
fos·ter·ing
fought
fou·lard
found
foun·da·tion
foun·da·tion·al
found·er
found·ling
found·ry
found·ries

foun·tain
foun·tain·head
four·flush·er
four·fold
four·post·er
four·score
four·some
four·square
four·teen
four·teenth
fourth
fourth·ly
fowl
fowl·er
fox·hole
fox·hound
fox·tail
foxy
fox·i·er
fox·i·est
fox·i·ly
fox·i·ness
foy·er
fra·cas
fra·cas·es
frac·tion
frac·tion·al
frac·tious
frac·tious·ly
frac·ture
frac·tured
frac·tur·ing
frag·ile
fra·gil·i·ty
frag·ment
frag·men·tal
frag·men·tar·i·ness
frag·men·tary
frag·men·ta·tion
frag·ment·ize
frag·ment·ized
frag·ment·iz·ing
fra·grance
fra·grant
fra·grant·ly
frail
frail·ty
frail·ness
frail·ty
frail·ties
frame
framed
fram·ing
fram·er
frame-up
frame·work
franc
fran·chise
fran·chised
fran·chis·ing
fran·chise·ment
Fran·cis·can
Fran·co·phile
Fran·co·pho·bia
fran·gi·ble

frank
  frank·er
  frank·ly
  frank·ness
Frank·en·stein
Frank·fort
frank·furt·er
frank·in·cense
Frank·lin
fran·tic
  fran·ti·cal·ly
fra·ter·nal
  fra·ter·nal·ly
fra·ter·ni·ty
  fra·ter·ni·ties
frat·er·nize
  frat·er·nized
  frat·er·niz·ing
  frat·er·niz·er
frat·ri·cide
  frat·ri·cid·al
fraud·u·lent
  fraud·u·lence
  fraud·u·lent·ly
fraught
Fra·zer
fraz·zle
  fraz·zled
  fraz·zling
freak
  freak·ish
  freak·ish·ness
freaky
  freak·i·er
  freak·i·est
freck·le
  freck·led
  freck·ling
  freck·led
  freck·ly
  freck·li·er
  freck·li·est
Fred·er·ick
Fred·er·icks·burg
free
  fre·er
  fre·est
  free·ly
free·bie
free·boot·er
free·dom
free·hand
free·hand·ed
free·lance
  free·lanced
  free·lanc·ing
Free·ma·son
  Free·ma·son·ry
free·spo·ken
  free·spo·ken·ness
free·stone
free·think·er
  free·think·ing
Free·town
free·way

free·wheel
freeze
  froze
  fro·zen
  freez·ing
freeze-dry
  freeze-dried
  freeze-dry·ing
freez·er
freight·age
freight·er
Fre·mont
French·man
Fre·neau
fre·net·ic
  fre·net·i·cal·ly
fren·zy
  fren·zies
  fren·zied
  fren·zy·ing
Fre·on
fre·quen·cy
  fre·quen·cies
fre·quent
  fre·quent·er
  fre·quent·ly
fre·quen·ta·tive
fres·co
  fres·coes
  fres·cos
  fres·coed
  fres·co·ing
fresh
  fresh·ly
  fresh·ness
fresh·en
  fresh·en·er
fresh·et
fresh·man
  fresh·men
Fres·no
fret
  fret·ted
  fret·ting
fret·ful
  fret·ful·ly
fret·work
Freud·i·an
fri·a·ble
fri·ar
fri·ary
  fri·ar·ies
Fri·bourg
fric·as·see
  fric·as·seed
  fric·as·see·ing
fric·tion
fric·tion·al
  fric·tion·less
Fri·day
friend
  friend·less
  friend·less·ness
  friend·ship
  friend·ly

friend·li·er
friend·li·est
friend·li·ly
friend·li·ness
Fries·land
frieze
fright·en
  fright·en·ing·ly
fright·ful
  fright·ful·ly
  fright·ful·ness
frig·id
  fri·gid·i·ty
  frig·id·ly
  frig·id·ness
Frig·i·daire
frilly
  frill·i·er
  frill·i·est
fringe
  fringed
  fring·ing
frip·pery
  frip·per·ies
Fris·co
frisky
  frisk·i·er
  frisk·i·est
  frisk·i·ly
  frisk·i·ness
frit·ter
friv·o·lous
  fri·vol·i·ty
  fri·vol·i·ties
  friv·o·lous·ly
frizz
  friz·zi·ness
  friz·zy
  friz·zi·er
  friz·zi·est
friz·zle
  friz·zled
  friz·zling
  friz·zly
  friz·zli·er
  friz·zli·est
Fro·bish·er
frog
  frogged
  frog·ging
frog·man
frol·ic
  frol·icked
  frol·ick·ing
  frol·ic·some
front·age
fron·tal
  fron·tal·ly
fron·tier
  fron·tiers·man
  fron·tiers·men
fron·tis·piece
frost
  frost·ed
frost·bite

frost·bit
frost·bit·ten
frost·bit·ing
frost·ing
frosty
　frost·i·er
　frost·i·est
　frost·i·ly
　frost·i·ness
froth
　froth·i·ness
frothy
　froth·i·er
　froth·i·est
frou·frou
fro·ward
frown
　frown·ing·ly
frow·zy
　frow·zi·er
　frow·zi·est
fro·zen
　fro·zen·ly
　fro·zen·ness
fruc·ti·fy
　fruc·ti·fied
　fruc·ti·fy·ing
　fruc·ti·fi·ca·tion
fru·gal
　fru·gal·i·ty
　fru·gal·i·ties
　fru·gal·ly
fruit·ful
　fruit·ful·ly
　fruit·ful·ness
fru·i·tion
fruit·less
　fruit·less·ly
　fruit·less·ness
fruity
frump
　frump·ish
　frumpy
　frump·i·er
　frump·i·est
frus·trate
　frus·trat·ed
　frus·trat·ing
　frus·tra·tion
fry
　fried
　fry·ing
fry·er
fud·dle
　fud·dled
　fud·dling
fud·dy-dud·dy
　fud·dy-dud·dies
fudge
　fudged
　fudg·ing
fu·el
　fu·eled
　fu·el·ing
fu·gi·tive

fu·gi·tive·ly
Füh·rer
Fu·ji·ya·ma
ful·crum
　ful·crums
　ful·cra
ful·fill
　ful·filled
　ful·fil·ling
　ful·fill·ment
full
　full·ness
　ful·ly
full·back
full-blood·ed
full-blown
Full·er
full-fledged
full-scale
ful·mi·nate
　ful·mi·nat·ed
　ful·mi·nat·ing
　ful·mi·na·tion
ful·some
　ful·some·ly
Ful·ton
fum·ble
　fum·bled
　fum·bling
　fum·bler
fume
　fumed
　fum·ing
　fum·ing·ly
fu·mi·gate
　fu·mi·gat·ed
　fu·mi·gat·ing
　fu·mi·ga·tion
　fu·mi·ga·tor
func·tion
　func·tion·less
　func·tion·al
　func·tion·al·ly
　func·tion·ary
　func·tion·ar·ies
fun·da·men·tal
　fun·da·men·tal·ly
　fun·da·men·tal·ism
　fun·da·men·tal·ist
Fun·dy
fu·ner·al
fu·ne·re·al
fun·gi·cide
　fun·gi·cid·al
　fun·gi·cid·al·ly
fun·gous
fun·gus
　fun·gi
　fun·gus·es
fu·nic·u·lar
funky
　funk·i·er
　funk·i·est
fun·nel
　fun·neled

fun·nel·ing
fun·ny
　fun·ni·er
　fun·ni·est
　fun·nies
　fun·ni·ly
　fun·ni·ness
fur
　furred
　fur·ring
fur·bish
fu·ri·ous
　fu·ri·ous·ly
fur·long
fur·lough
fur·nace
fur·nish
　fur·nish·ings
fur·ni·ture
fu·ror
fur·ri·er
fur·row
fur·ry
　fur·ri·er
　fur·ri·est
fur·ther
　fur·ther·more
　fur·ther·most
　fur·thest
fur·tive
　fur·tive·ly
fu·ry
　fu·ries
fuse
　fused
　fus·ing
fu·see
fu·se·lage
fu·si·bil·i·ty
fu·si·ble
fu·si·form
fu·sil·lade
　fu·sil·lad·ed
　fu·sil·lad·ing
fu·sion
fussy
　fuss·i·er
　fuss·i·est
　fuss·i·ly
　fuss·i·ness
fus·tian
fus·ty
　fus·ti·er
　fus·ti·est
　fus·ti·ly
　fus·ti·ness
fu·tile
　fu·til·i·ty
　fu·til·i·ties
fu·ture
　fu·tur·ism
　fu·tur·is·tic
　fu·tu·ri·ty
　fu·tu·ri·ties
fu·zee

fuzzy
 fuzz·i·er
 fuzz·i·est
 fuzz·i·ly
 fuzz·i·ness
gab
 gabbed
 gab·bing
 gab·ber
gab·ar·dine
gab·ble
 gab·bled
 gab·bling
 gab‚bler
gab·by
 gab·bi·er
 gab·bi·est
ga·ble
 ga·bled
 ga·bling
Ga·bon
Ga·bri·el
gad
 gad·ded
 gad·ding
gad·a·bout
gad·fly
 gad·flies
gad·get
 gad·get·ry
Gad·ite
Gads·den
Gael·ic
gaffe
gaf·fer
gag
 gagged
 gag·ging
ga·ga
gai·e·ty
 gai·e·ties
gai·ly
gain·er
gain·ful
gain·say
 gain·said
 gain·say·ing
Gains·bor·ough
gait
Ga·ius
ga·la
ga·lac·tic
Gal·a·had
Ga·la·pa·gos
Gal·a·tea
Ga·la·tia
gal·axy
 gal·ax·ies
Gal·i·lee
Gal·i·leo
gal·lant
gal·lant·ry
 gal·lant·ries
gal·lery
 gal·ler·ies

gal·ley
Gal·lic
gal·li·cism
Gal·li·e·nus
gal·li·mau·fry
 gal·li·mau·fries
gall·ing
gal·li·vant
gal·lon
gal·lop
gal·lows
 gal·lows·es
gall·stone
ga·loot
ga·lore
ga·losh
ga·lumph
gal·van·ic
gal·va·nism
gal·va·nize
 gal·va·nized
 gal·va·niz·ing
gal·va·nom·e·ter
Gal·ves·ton
Gal·way
Gam·bia
gam·bit
gam·ble
 gam·bled
 gam·bling
gam·bol
gam·brel
game
 gam·er
 gam·est
gamed
gam·ing
game·keep·er
games·man·ship
game·some
game·ster
gam·ete
ga·met·ic
gam·in
gam·ma
gam·ma glob·u·lin
gam·mon
gam·ut
gamy
 gam·i·er
 gam·i·est
 gam·i·ly
 gam·i·ness
gan·der
Gan·dha·ra
Gan·dhi
Gan·ges
gang·land
gan·gling
gan·gli·on
gan·glia
gan·gli·ons
gan·gly
gan·gli·er
gan·gli·est

gang·plank
gan·grene
 gan·grened
 gan·gren·ing
 gan·gre·nous
gang·ster
gang·way
gant·let
gan·try
 gan·tries
gaol
gap
 gapped
 gap·ping
ga·rage
 ga·raged
 ga·rag·ing
gar·bage
gar·ble
 gar·bled
 gar·bling
gar·den
Gar·di·ner
Gard·ner
Gar·field
Gar·gan·tua
gar·gan·tu·an
gar·gle
 gar·gled
 gar·gling
gar·goyle
Gar·i·bal·di
gar·ish
gar·land
gar·ment
gar·ner
gar·net
gar·nish
 gar·nish·eed
 gar·nish·ee·ing
gar·nish·ment
gar·ni·ture
gar·ret
gar·ri·son
gar·rote
 gar·rot·ed
 gar·rot·ing
 gar·rot·er
gar·ru·lous
gar·ter
gas
 gassed
 gas·sing
Gas·co·ny
gas·e·ous
gas·i·fy
 gas·i·fied
 gas·i·fy·ing
 gas·i·fi·ca·tion
 gas·i·fi·er
gas·ket
gas·light
gas·lit
gas·o·line

gas·ser
gas·sy
  gas·si·er
  gas·si·est
  gas·si·ness
gas·tric
gas·tri·tis
gas·tro·in·tes·ti·nal
gas·tron·o·my
  gas·tro·nom·ic
  gas·tro·nom·i·cal
  gas·tro·nom·i·cal·ly
gas·works
gate·crash·er
  gate·crash·ing
gate·house
gate·keep·er
gate·post
gate·way
gath·er
gath·er·ing
Gat·ling
Ga·tun
gauche
gau·cho
gaudy
  gaud·i·er
  gaud·i·est
  gaud·i·ly
  gaud·i·ness
gauge
  gauged
  gaug·ing
Gau·guin
Gaull·ist
gaunt·let
gauze
  gauz·i·ness
gauzy
  gauz·i·er
  gauz·i·est
gav·el
Ga·wain
gawky
  gawk·i·er
  gawk·i·est
  gawk·i·ly
  gawk·i·ness
gay·e·ty
gay·ly
Ga·za
gaze
  gazed
  gaz·ing
  gaz·er
ga·ze·bo
  ga·ze·bos
  ga·ze·boes
ga·zelle
ga·zette
gaz·et·teer
gear·box
gear·ing
gear·shift
gear·wheel

gee
  geed
  gee·ing
gee·zer
Ge·hen·na
Gei·ger count·er
gei·sha
Geiss·ler
gel
  gelled
  gel·ling
gel·a·tin
ge·lat·i·nous
ge·la·tion
geld
  geld·ed
  gelt
  geld·ing
gel·id
gem
  gemmed
  gem·ming
gem·i·nate
  gem·i·nat·ed
  gem·i·nat·ing
  gem·i·nate·ly
  gem·i·na·tion
Gem·i·ni
gem·ol·o·gy
  gem·o·log·i·cal
  gem·ol·o·gist
gem·stone
gen·darme
gen·der
gene
ge·ne·al·o·gy
  ge·ne·a·log·i·cal
  ge·ne·al·o·gist
gen·er·al
gen·er·al·is·si·mo
  gen·er·al·is·si·mos
gen·er·al·ist
gen·er·al·i·ty
  gen·er·al·i·ties
gen·er·al·ize
  gen·er·al·ized
  gen·er·al·iz·ing
  gen·er·al·i·za·tion
  gen·er·al·iz·er
gen·er·ate
  gen·er·at·ed
  gen·er·at·ing
  gen·er·a·tive
  gen·er·a·tive·ly
gen·er·a·tion
gen·er·a·tor
ge·ner·ic
  ge·ner·i·cal
  ge·ner·i·cal·ly
gen·er·ous
  gen·er·os·i·ty
  gen·er·os·i·ties
gen·e·sis
  gen·e·ses
ge·net·ic

  ge·net·i·cal·ly
ge·net·ics
  ge·net·i·cist
Ge·ne·va
Gen·ghis Khan
gen·ial
  ge·ni·al·i·ty
ge·nie
  ge·nies
  ge·nii
gen·i·tal
gen·i·ta·lia
gen·i·tals
gen·ius
  gen·ius·es
Gen·oa
gen·o·cide
  gen·o·ci·dal
gen·re
gen·teel
gen·tian
gen·tile
gen·til·i·ty
  gen·til·i·ties
gen·tle
gen·tler
gen·tlest
gen·tly
gen·tle·folk
gen·tle·man
  gen·tle·men
gen·tle·wom·an
  gen·tle·wom·en
gen·try
gen·u·flect
  gen·u·flec·tion
  gen·u·flec·tor
gen·u·ine
ge·nus
  gen·e·ra
  ge·nus·es
ge·o·cen·tric
  ge·o·cen·tri·cal·ly
ge·o·chem·is·try
  ge·o·chem·i·cal
  ge·o·chem·ist
ge·ode
ge·o·des·ic
ge·og·ra·phy
  ge·og·ra·phies
  ge·og·ra·pher
  ge·o·graph·ic
  ge·o·graph·i·cal
ge·ol·o·gy
  ge·ol·o·gies
  ge·o·log·ic
  ge·o·log·i·cal
  ge·o·log·i·cal·ly
  ge·ol·o·gist
ge·o·mag·net·ic
  ge·o·mag·ne·tism
ge·o·met·ric
ge·om·e·try
  ge·om·e·tries
ge·o·phys·ics

ge·o·phys·i·cal
ge·o·phys·i·cist
ge·o·pol·i·tics
ge·o·pol·i·tic
ge·o·po·lit·i·cal
ge·o·po·lit·i·cal·ly
George·town
Geor·gia
ge·o·ther·mal
ger·bil
Ger·hard
ger·i·at·rics
  ger·i·at·ric
  ger·i·a·tri·cian
  ger·i·at·rist
ger·mane
Ger·man
Ger·ma·ny
ger·mi·cide
  ger·mi·cid·al
ger·mi·nate
  ger·mi·nat·ed
  ger·mi·nat·ing
  ger·mi·na·tion
Ge·ron·i·mo
ger·on·tol·o·gy
  ger·on·tol·o·gist
ger·ry·man·der
Gersh·win
ger·und
ges·so
Ge·stalt
ges·tate
  ges·tat·ed
  ges·tat·ing
  ges·ta·tion
ges·tic·u·late
  ges·tic·u·lat·ed
  ges·tic·u·lat·ing
  ges·tic·u·la·tion
  ges·tic·u·la·tive
  ges·tic·u·la·to·ry
  ges·tic·u·la·tor
ges·ture
  ges·tured
  ges·tur·ing
  ges·tur·er
ge·sund·heit
get·a·way
Geth·sem·a·ne
get·to·geth·er
Get·tys·burg
get·up
gew·gaw
gey·ser
Gha·na
ghast·ly
  ghast·li·er
  ghast·li·est
  ghast·li·ness
gher·kin
ghet·to
  ghet·tos
  ghet·toes
Ghi·ber·ti

ghost·ly
  ghost·li·er
  ghost·li·est
  ghost·li·ness
ghost·write
  ghost·wrote
  ghost·writ·ten
  ghost·writ·ing
ghoul
gi·ant
gib·ber·ish
gib·bon
gibe
  gib·er
  gib·ing·ly
Gib·e·on·ite
gib·let
Gi·bral·tar
Gib·son
gid·dy
  gid·di·er
  gid·di·est
  gid·di·ly
  gid·di·ness
Gid·e·on
gi·gan·tic
  gi·gan·tism
gig·gle
  gig·gled
  gig·gling
  gig·gler
  gig·gly
  gig·gli·er
  gig·gli·est
gig·o·lo
Gi·la
Gil·bert
gild·ed
Gil·e·ad
gilt-edged
gim·crack
gim·let
gim·mick
gin·ger
gin·ger·bread
gin·ger·ly
  gin·ger·li·ness
gin·ger·snap
gin·ger·y
ging·ham
Giot·to
Gio·van·ni
Gip·sy
  gip·sy
  gip·sies
Gi·rard
gird·er
gir·dle
  gir·dled
  gir·dling
girl·hood
girl·ish
girth
gist
give

gave
giv·en
giv·ing
give-and-take
give·a·way
giz·zard
gla·cial
gla·cier
glad
  glad·der
  glad·dest
  glad·ly
  glad·ness
glad·den
glad·i·a·tor
  glad·i·a·to·ri·al
glad·i·o·lus
  glad·i·o·lus·es
  glad·i·o·la
glad·some
Glad·stone
glam·or·ize
  glam·or·ized
  glam·or·iz·ing
  glam·or·i·za·tion
  glam·or·iz·er
glam·or·ous
  glam·or·ous·ly
  glam·or·ous·ness
glam·our
glance
  glanced
  glanc·ing
glan·du·lar
glare
  glared
  glar·ing
  glar·i·ness
glary
  glar·i·er
  glar·i·est
Glas·gow
glass·blow·ing
  glass·blow·er
glass·ful
glass·ware
glassy
  glass·i·er
  glass·i·est
  glass·i·ly
  glass·i·ness
glau·co·ma
glaze
  glazed
  glaz·ing
gla·zier
gleam
  gleam·ing
  gleamy
glean
  glean·er
  glean·ing
glee
  glee·ful
  glee·ful·ly

glee·ful·ness
Gleich·schal·tung
Glen·gar·ry
glib
  glib·ber
  glib·best
  glib·ly
  glib·ness
glide
  glid·ed
  glid·ing
glim·mer
glimpse
  glimpsed
  glimps·ing
glis·san·do
  glis·san·di
  glis·san·dos
glis·ten
glit·ter
gloam·ing
gloat
  gloat·er
  gloat·ing
glob
glob·al
  glob·al·ly
globe·trot·ter
  globe·trot·ting
glob·u·lar
  glob·ule
glock·en·spiel
gloomy
  gloom·i·er
  gloom·i·est
  gloom·i·ly
  gloom·i·ness
glo·ri·fy
  glo·ri·fied
  glo·ri·fy·ing
  glo·ri·fi·ca·tion
  glo·ri·fi·er
glo·ri·ous
  glo·ri·ous·ly
  glo·ri·ous·ness
glo·ry
  glo·ries
  glo·ried
  glo·ry·ing
glos·sa·ry
  glos·sa·ries
glossy
  gloss·i·er
  gloss·i·est
  gloss·i·ly
  gloss·i·ness
glot·tis
  glot·tis·es
  glot·ti·des
Glouces·ter
Glouces·ter·shire
glove
  gloved
  glov·ing
glow

glow·er
glow·ing
glow·worm
glu·cose
glue
  glued
  glu·ing
glum
  glum·mer
  glum·mest
glut
  glut·ted
  glut·ting
glu·ten
glu·ti·nous
glut·ton
  glut·ton·ous
  glut·tony
glyc·er·in
  glyc·er·ine
  glyc·er·ol
gnarl
  gnarled
  gnarly
  gnarl·i·er
  gnarl·i·est
gnash
gnat
gnaw
  gnawed
  gnaw·ing
gneiss
gnome
gnu
gnus
goad·ed
go·a·head
goal·keep·er
goat·ee
goat·herd
goat·skin
gob·ble
  gob·bled
  gob·bling
gob·ble·dy·gook
gob·bler
go·be·tween
Go·bi
gob·let
gob·lin
go·cart
god·child
  god·chil·dren
  god·daugh·ter
  god·son
god·dess
god·fa·ther
god·head
Go·di·va
god·less
  god·less·ness
god·like
god·ly
  god·li·er
  god·li·est

god·li·ness
god·moth·er
god·par·ent
god·send
God·speed
Goeb·bels
Goe·thals
Goe·the
go·get·ter
gog·gle
  gog·gled
  gog·gling
gog·gle-eyed
gog·gles
go·ing
goi·ter
gold·brick
gold·en
gold·smith
Gol·go·tha
Go·li·ath
Go·mor·rah
Gom·pers
go·nad
gon·do·la
gon·do·lier
gon·er
gon·or·rhea
goo·ber
good-by
  good-bye
good-for-noth·ing
good-heart·ed
good·ish
good-look·ing
good·ly
  good·li·er
  good·li·est
good-na·tured
good·ness
Good·rich
good-tem·pered
goody
  good·ies
Good·year
goof-off
goofy
  goof·i·er
  goof·i·est
  goof·i·ness
goose·ber·ry
  goose·ber·ries
gore
  gored
  gor·ing
gorge
  gorged
  gorg·ing
gor·geous
  gor·geous·ly
  gor·geous·ness
gory
  gor·i·er
  gor·i·est
Go·shen

gos·ling
gos·pel
gos·sa·mer
  gos·sa·mery
  gos·sa·mer·i·er
  gos·sa·mer·i·est
gos·sip
  gos·sip·ing
  gos·sipy
Goth·am
Goth·ic
gouge
  gouged
  goug·ing
  goug·er
gou·lash
gourd
gour·mand
gour·met
  gour·mets
gout
  gouty
  gout·i·er
  gout·i·est
gov·ern
  gov·ern·a·ble
  gov·ern·ess
  gov·ern·ment
  gov·ern·men·tal
  gov·er·nor
  gov·er·nor·ship
gow·and
gowned
grab
  grabbed
  grab·bing
  grab·ber
grace
  graced
  grac·ing
  grace·ful
  grace·ful·ly
  grace·ful·ness
grace·less
gra·cious
gra·da·tion
grade
  grad·ed
  grad·ing
  grad·er
gra·di·ent
grad·u·al
  grad·u·al·ly
  grad·u·al·ness
grad·u·ate
  grad·u·at·ed
  grad·u·at·ing
  grad·u·a·tion
graf·fi·to
  graf·fi·ti
graft
  graft·age
  graft·er
  graft·ing
gra·ham

Grail
grain
grainy
  grain·i·er
  grain·i·est
  grain·i·ness
gram
gram·mar
  gram·mar·i·an
  gram·mat·i·cal
  gram·mat·i·cal·ly
Gra·na·da
gra·na·ry
  gra·na·ries
grand
  grand·ly
  grand·child
  grand·daugh·ter
gran·dee
gran·deur
grand·fa·ther
gran·dil·o·quence
  gran·dil·o·quent
gran·di·ose
  gran·di·ose·ly
grand·moth·er
grand·par·ent
Grand Rap·ids
grand·son
grand·stand
grange
  grang·er
gran·ite
  gra·nit·ic
gran·ny
  gran·nies
gran·u·lar
  gran·u·lar·i·ty
gran·u·late
  gran·u·lat·ed
  gran·u·lat·ing
  gran·u·la·tion
gran·ule
grape·fruit
grape·vine
graph·ic
  graph·i·cal
  graph·i·cal·ly
graph·ite
graph·ol·o·gy
  graph·ol·o·gist
grap·nel
grap·ple
  grap·pled
  grap·pling
  grap·pler
grasp·ing
grass
  grassy
  grass·i·er
  grass·i·est
  grass·hop·per
  grass·land
grate
  grat·ed

grat·ing
grate·ful
  grate·ful·ly
  grate·ful·ness
grat·i·fy
  grat·i·fied
  grat·i·fy·ing
  grat·i·fi·ca·tion
grat·ing
gra·tis
grat·i·tude
gra·tu·i·tous
  gra·tu·i·tous·ly
gra·tu·i·ty
  gra·tu·i·ties
grave
  graved
  grav·en
  grav·ing
  grav·er
  grav·est
  grave·ly
  grave·ness
grav·el
  grav·eled
  grav·el·ing
  grav·el·ly
  grav·en
  grave·stone
  grave·yard
grav·i·tate
  grav·i·tat·ed
  grav·i·tat·ing
  grav·i·ta·tion
  grav·i·ta·tion·al
grav·i·ty
  grav·i·ties
  grav·i·ta·tion
gra·vy
  gra·vies
gray
  gray·ly
  gray·ness
gray·ling
graze
  grazed
  graz·ing
grease
  greased
  greas·ing
greasy
  greas·i·er
  greas·i·est
  greas·i·ly
  greas·i·ness
great
  great·ly
  great·ness
Great Brit·ain
great·coat
great·heart·ed
Gre·cian
greedy
  greed·i·er
  greed·i·est

greed·i·ly
greed·i·ness
Greek
Gree·ley
green·back
green·ery
green·er·ies
green·gro·cer
green·gro·cery
green·gro·cer·ies
green·horn
green·house
green·hous·es
green·ing
green·ish
green·ish·ness
Green·land
green·sward
Green·wich
greet
greet·er
greet·ing
gre·gar·i·ous
gre·gar·i·ous·ly
gre·gar·i·ous·ness
Gre·go·ri·an
grem·lin
Gre·na·da
gren·a·dier
gren·a·dine
Gre·no·ble
grey
grey·ly
grey·ness
grid·dle
grid·dle·cake
grid·i·ron
grief
griev·ance
grieve
grieved
griev·ing
griev·ous
griev·ous·ly
grif·fin
grif·fon
grill
gril·lage
grille
grill·room
grim
grim·mer
grim·mest
grim·ly
grim·ness
grim·ace
grim·aced
grim·ac·ing
grime
grimed
grim·ing
grimy
grim·i·er
grim·i·est
grim·i·ly

grim·i·ness
grin
grinned
grin·ning
grin·ner
grind
ground
grind·ing
grind·er
grind·stone
grin·go
grin·gos
grip
gripped
grip·ping
gripe
griped
grip·ing
grip·er
grippe
Gri·sel·da
gris·ly
gris·li·er
gris·li·est
gris·li·ness
gris·tle
gris·tly
gris·tli·er
gris·tli·est
grit
grit·ted
grit·ting
grit·ty
grit·ti·er
grit·ti·est
grit·ti·ly
grit·ti·ness
griz·zled
griz·zly
griz·zli·er
griz·zli·est
griz·zlies
groan
groan·er
gro·cer
gro·cery
gro·cer·ies
grog·gy
grog·gi·er
grog·gi·est
grog·gi·ly
grog·gi·ness
groin
Gro·li·er
grom·met
groom
groove
grooved
groov·ing
groov·er
groovy
groov·i·er
groov·i·est
grope
groped

grop·ing
gros·grain
gross
gross·es
gross·ly
gross·ness
gro·tesque
gro·tesque·ly
gro·tesque·ness
grot·to
grot·toes
grot·tos
grouch
grouchy
grouch·i·er
grouch·i·est
ground·er
ground·less
ground·less·ly
ground·less·ness
ground·ling
ground·nut
ground·work
group·ie
grouse
groused
grous·ing
grous·er
grov·el
grov·eled
grov·el·ing
grov·el·er
grow
grew
grown
grow·ing
grow·er
growl
growl·er
grown·up
growth
grub
grubbed
grub·bing
grub·ber
grub·by
grub·bi·er
grub·bi·est
grub·stake
grub·staked
grub·stak·ing
grudge
grudged
grudg·ing
grudg·ing·ly
gru·el
gru·el·ing
grue·some
grue·some·ly
gruff
gruff·ly
gruff·ness
grum·ble
grum·bled
grum·bling

grum·bler
grumpy
grump·i·er
grump·i·est
grump·i·ly
grump·i·ness
Grun·dy
grunt
grunt·er
grunt·ing
Gua·dal·ca·nal
Gua·dal·qui·vir
Gua·de·loupe
gua·no
gua·nos
Gua·ra·ni
guar·an·tee
guar·an·teed
guar·an·tee·ing
guar·an·tor
guar·an·ty
guar·an·ties
guar·an·tied
guar·an·ty·ing
guard·ed
guard·ed·ly
guard·house
guard·i·an
guards·man
guards·men
Gua·te·ma·la
gua·va
gu·ber·na·to·ri·al
gudg·eon
Guern·sey
guer·ril·la
gue·ril·la
guess
guess·er
guess·work
guest
guf·faw
Gui·ana
guid·ance
guide
guid·ed
guid·ing
guide·book
guide·post
gui·don
guild·hall
guile
guile·ful
guile·ful·ly
guile·less
guile·less·ly
Guil·ford
guil·lo·tine
guil·lo·tined
guil·lo·tin·ing
guilt
guilt·less
guilt·less·ly
guilty
guilt·i·er

guilt·i·est
guilt·i·ly
guilt·i·ness
guin·ea
Guin·e·vere
guise
gui·tar
gui·tar·ist
gul·let
gul·li·ble
gul·li·bil·i·ty
gul·li·bly
Gul·li·ver
gul·ly
gul·lies
gul·lied
gul·ly·ing
gum
gummed
gum·ming
gum·bo
gum·bos
gum·drop
gum·my
gum·mi·er
gum·mi·est
gum·mi·ness
gump·tion
gum·shoe
gum·shoed
gum·shoe·ing
gun
gunned
gun·ning
gun·boat
gun·fight
gun·fight·er
gun·fire
gun·man
gun·men
gun·ner
gun·nery
gun·ny
gun·nies
gun·ny·bag
gun·pow·der
gun·shot
gun·smith
gun·stock
Gun·ther
gun·wale
gup·py
gup·pies
gur·gle
gur·gled
gur·gling
gu·ru
gush·er
gush·ing
gushy
gush·i·er
gush·i·est
gush·i·ness
gus·set
gus·ta·to·ry

gus·to
gusty
gust·i·er
gust·i·est
gust·i·ly
gust·i·ness
gut
gut·ted
gut·ting
Gu·ten·berg
Gut·ten·berg
gut·ter
gut·tur·al
gut·tur·al·ly
Guy·a·na
guz·zle
guz·zled
guz·zling
guz·zler
gym·na·si·um
gym·na·si·ums
gym·na·sia
gym·nast
gym·nas·tic
gym·nas·tics
gy·ne·col·o·gy
gy·ne·co·log·ic
gy·ne·co·log·i·cal
gy·ne·col·o·gist
gyp
gypped
gyp·ping
gyp·sum
gyp·sy
gyp·sies
gy·ral
gy·rate
gy·rat·ed
gy·rat·ing
gy·ra·tion
gy·ra·tor
gy·ra·to·ry
gyr·fal·con
gy·ro·com·pass
gy·roi·dal
gy·rom·e·ter
gy·ro·plane
gy·ro·scope
gy·ro·scop·ic
gy·ro·scop·i·cal·ly
gy·rose
gy·ro·sta·bi·liz·er
gy·ro·sta·tics
gy·rus
gyve
gyved
gyv·ing
Haar·lem
Hab·ak·kuk
ha·be·as cor·pus
hab·er·dash·er
hab·er·dash·ery
hab·er·dash·er·ies
ha·bil·i·ment
hab·it

hab·it·a·ble
hab·i·tat
hab·i·ta·tion
ha·bit·u·al
ha·bit·u·al·ly
ha·bit·u·al·ness
ha·bit·u·ate
ha·bit·u·at·ed
ha·bit·u·at·ing
ha·bit·u·a·tion
ha·bit·ué
ha·bit·u·és
ha·ci·en·da
ha·ci·en·das
hack·le
hack·led
hack·ling
hack·ney
hack·neyed
hack·saw
Ha·des
had·n't
hae·mo·glo·bin
hae·mo·phil·ia
Ha·ga·nah
Ha·gen
hag·gard
hag·gard·ly
hag·gle
hag·gled
hag·gling
hag·gler
hag·i·ol·o·gy
hag·i·ol·o·gies
hag·i·ol·o·gist
hag·rid·den
Hai·fa
hai·ku
hail·stone
hail·storm
hair·breadth
hair·brush
hair·cut
hair·do
hair·dress·er
hair·line
hair·pin
hair·rais·ing
hair·split·ter
hair·split·ting
hair·spring
hairy
hair·i·er
hair·i·est
Hai·ti
Ha·la·kah
hal·cy·on
hale
haled
hal·ing
half·back
half·baked
half·breed
half·caste
half·heart·ed

half·heart·ed·ly
half·hour
half·life
half·lives
half·mast
half·moon
half note
half step
half·tone
half·track
half·truth
half·way
half·wit
half·wit·ted
hal·i·but
Hal·i·fax
hal·i·to·sis
Hal·low·een
hal·le·lu·jah
hall·mark
hal·lo
hal·low
hal·lowed
Hal·low·een
hal·lu·ci·nate
hal·lu·ci·nat·ed
hal·lu·ci·nat·ing
hal·lu·ci·na·tion
hal·lu·ci·na·to·ry
hal·lu·cin·o·gen
hal·lu·cin·o·gen·ic
hall·way
ha·lo
ha·los
ha·loes
halt
halt·ing
halt·ing·ly
hal·ter
halve
halved
halv·ing
halves
hal·yard
Ham·burg
ham·burg·er
Ham·e·lin
Ham·il·ton
ham·let
Ham·mar·skjöld
ham·mer
ham·mer·head
ham·mer·less
Ham·mer·stein
ham·mock
Ham·mond
Ham·mu·ra·bi
ham·my
ham·mi·er
ham·mi·est
Hamp·den
ham·per
Hamp·shire
Hamp·ton
ham·ster

ham·string
ham·strung
ham·string·ing
Ham·tramck
Han·cock
hand·bag
hand·ball
hand·bill
hand·book
hand·cuff
hand·ed
Han·del
hand·ful
hand·fuls
hand·i·cap
hand·i·capped
hand·i·cap·ping
hand·i·cap·per
hand·i·craft
hand·i·ly
hand·i·ness
hand·i·work
hand·ker·chief
han·dle
han·dled
han·dling
han·dler
han·dle·bar
hand·made
hand·maid·en
hand·me·down
hand·out
hand·pick
hand·picked
hand·rail
hand·shake
hand·some
hand·som·er
hand·som·est
hand·some·ly
hand·some·ness
hand·spring
hand·to·hand
hand·to·mouth
hand·work
hand·writ·ing
handy
hand·i·er
hand·i·est
hand·y·man
hand·y·men
hang
hung
hanged
hang·ing
hang·ar
hang·dog
hang·er
hang·er·on
hang·man
hang·men
hang·nail
hang·out
hang·o·ver
hang·up

hank·er
Han·kow
Han·ni·bal
Ha·noi
Han·o·ver
han·som
Ha·nuk·kah
hap·haz·ard
  hap·haz·ard·ly
  hap·haz·ard·ness
hap·less
  hap·less·ly
hap·ly
hap·pen
hap·pen·ing
hap·pen·stance
hap·pi·ness
hap·py
  hap·pi·er
  hap·pi·est
  hap·pi·ly
hap·py-go-lucky
Haps·burg
ha·ra·ki·ri
ha·rangue
  ha·rangued
  ha·rang·uing
har·ass
  har·ass·ment
har·bin·ger
har·bor
hard-bit·ten
hard-boiled
hard-core
hard·en
  hard·en·er
hard-hat
hard-head·ed
hard-heart·ed
har·di·hood
har·di·ness
Har·ding
hard·ly
hard·pan
hard·ship
hard·tack
hard·top
hard·ware
hard·wood
har·dy
  har·di·er
  har·di·est
  har·di·ly
hare·brained
hare·lip
har·em
har·ken
Har·lem
har·le·quin
har·lot
  har·lot·ry
harm·ful
  harm·ful·ly
  harm·ful·ness
harm·less

harm·less·ly
harm·less·ness
har·mon·ic
har·mon·i·cal·ly
har·mon·i·ca
har·mon·ics
har·mo·ni·ous
  har·mo·ni·ous·ly
har·mo·nize
  har·mo·nized
  har·mo·niz·ing
har·mo·ny
  har·mo·nies
har·ness
harp·ist
har·poon
harp·si·chord
har·py
  har·pies
har·ri·dan
Har·ri·man
Har·ris·burg
Har·ri·son
har·row
har·row·ing
har·ry
  har·ried
  har·ry·ing
harsh
  harsh·ly
  harsh·ness
Hart·ford
har·um-scar·um
Har·vard
har·vest
har·ves·ter
Har·vey
has-been
hash·ish
hash·eesh
has·n't
has·sle
has·sled
has·sling
has·sock
has·ten
Has·tings
hast·y
  hast·i·er
  hast·i·est
  hast·i·ness
hatch·ery
  hatch·er·ies
hatch·et
hatch·way
hate
hat·ed
hat·ing
hat·er
hate·ful
  hate·ful·ly
  hate·ful·ness
ha·tred
hat·ter
haugh·ty

haugh·ti·er
haugh·ti·est
haugh·ti·ly
haugh·ti·ness
haul
haul·age
haunch
haunch·es
haunt·ed
haunt·ing
Haupt·mann
Hau·sa
hau·teur
Ha·va·na
ha·ven
have-nots
have·n't
Ha·ver·hill
hav·er·sack
haves
hav·oc
Ha·waii
hawk
  hawk·ish
haw·ser
Haw·thorne
Hay·dn
hay·loft
hay·mak·er
Hay·mar·ket
hay·mow
hay·seed
hay·stack
hay·wire
haz·ard
  haz·ard·ous
  haz·ard·ous·ly
  haz·ard·ous·ness
haze
hazed
haz·ing
ha·zel
ha·zel·nut
ha·zy
  ha·zi·er
  ha·zi·est
  ha·zi·ly
  ha·zi·ness
head·ache
head·band
head·dress
head·er
head·first
  head·fore·most
head·gear
head·hunt·er
head·ing
head·land
head·less
head·light
head·line
  head·lined
  head·lin·ing
head·long
head·mas·ter

head·mis·tress
head·most
head·on
head·piece
head·quar·ters
head·set
head·stone
head·strong
head·wait·er
head·wa·ters
head·way
head·wind
heady
 head·i·er
 head·i·est
 head·i·ly
 head·i·ness
heal·er
health·ful
 health·ful·ly
healthy
 health·i·er
 health·i·est
 health·i·ly
 health·i·ness
heaped
hear
heard
 hear·ing
 hear·er
heark·en
hear·say
hearse
heart·ache
heart·break
 heart·break·ing
 heart·brok·en
 heart·burn
 heart·en
heart·felt
hearth·stone
heart·less
 heart·less·ly
 heart·less·ness
heart·rend·ing
heart·sick
heart·strings
heart·to·heart
hearty
 heart·i·er
 heart·i·est
 heart·i·ly
 heart·i·ness
heat·ed
heat·er
heath
hea·then
heave
 heaved
 heav·ing
heav·en
heav·en·ly
heav·en·ward
 heav·en·wards
heavy

heav·i·er
heav·i·est
heav·i·ly
heav·i·ness
heav·y·du·ty
heav·y·hand·ed
heav·y·heart·ed
heav·y·weight
Hebe
He·brew
 He·bra·ic
 He·bra·i·cal·ly
Heb·ri·des
He·bron
heck·le
 heck·led
 heck·ling
 heck·ler
hec·tare
hec·tic
 hec·ti·cal·ly
hec·to·gram
hec·to·li·ter
hec·to·me·ter
hedge
 hedged
 hedg·ing
 hedg·er
he·don·ism
he·don·ist
he·do·nis·tic
hee·haw
hefty
 heft·i·er
 heft·i·est
He·gel
he·gem·o·ny
 he·gem·o·nies
 heg·e·mon·ic
he·gi·ra
Hei·del·berg
heif·er
height·en
 height·en·er
hei·nous
 hei·nous·ly
 hei·nous·ness
heir·ess
heir·loom
Hei·sen·berg
heist
Hel·e·na
hel·i·cop·ter
He·li·op·o·lis
He·li·os
he·li·um
he·lix
 hel·i·ces
 he·lix·es
hell·bent
hell·cat
Hel·len·ic
Hel·les·pont
hel·lion
hell·ish

hell·ish·ly
 hell·ish·ness
hel·lo
 hel·los
helm
 helm·less
hel·met
 hel·met·ed
helms·man
 helms·men
help·er
help·ful
 help·ful·ly
 help·ful·ness
help·ing
help·less
 help·less·ly
 help·less·ness
help·mate
Hel·sin·ki
hel·ter·skel·ter
Hel·ve·tia
hem
 hemmed
 hem·ming
he·man
 he·men
Hem·ing·way
hem·i·sphere
 hem·i·spher·ic
 hem·i·spher·i·cal
hem·lock
he·mo·glo·bin
he·mo·phil·ia
hem·or·rhage
 hem·or·rhaged
 hem·or·rhag·ing
 hem·or·rhag·ic
hem·or·rhoid
 hem·or·rhoi·dal
hemp·en
hem·stitch
hence·forth
hench·man
 hench·men
hench·man·ship
Hen·der·son
hen·na
hen·peck
hep·a·ti·tis
her·ald
 he·ral·dic
 her·ald·ry
 her·ald·ries
herb
 her·ba·ceous
 her·bage
her·biv·o·rous
her·cu·le·an
Her·cu·les
herd·er
herds·man
 herds·men
here·af·ter
he·red·i·tary

he·red·i·tar·i·ly
he·red·i·tar·i·ness
he·red·i·ty
he·red·i·ties
Her·e·ford
here·in
here·of
her·e·sy
her·e·sies
her·e·tic
he·ret·i·cal
he·ret·i·cal·ly
here·to
here·to·fore
here·up·on
here·with
her·it·a·ble
her·it·a·bil·i·ty
her·it·a·bly
her·it·age
her·maph·ro·dite
her·maph·ro·dit·ic
her·maph·o·dit·i·cal·ly
her·maph·ro·dit·ism
Her·mes
her·met·ic
her·met·i·cal
her·met·i·cal·ly
her·mit
her·mit·age
her·nia
her·ni·al
her·ni·a·tion
he·ro
he·roes
Her·od
He·ro·di·as
he·ro·ic
he·ro·i·cal
he·ro·i·cal·ly
her·o·in
her·o·ine
her·o·ism
her·on
her·ring·bone
her·ring·boned
her·ring·bon·ing
her·self
Hert·ford
Hert·ford·shire
hes·i·tant
hes·i·tan·cy
hes·i·tan·cies
hes·i·tance
hes·i·tant·ly
hes·i·tate
hes·i·tat·ed
hes·i·tat·ing
hes·i·tat·er
hes·i·ta·tor
hes·i·ta·tor
hes·i·tat·ing·ly
hes·i·ta·tion
Hes·per·i·des
Hes·per·us

Hes·sian
het·er·o·dox
het·er·o·doxy
het·er·o·ge·ne·ous
het·er·o·ge·ne·i·ty
het·er·o·ge·ne·ous·ness
het·er·o·ge·ne·ous·ly
het·er·o·sex·u·al
het·er·o·sex·u·al·i·ty
hew
hewed
hewn
hew·ing
hew·er
hex·a·gon
hex·ag·o·nal
hex·ag·o·nal·ly
hey·day
hey·dey
Hez·e·ki·ah
hi·a·tus
hi·a·tus·es
hi·ba·chi
hi·ber·nate
hi·ber·nat·ed
hi·ber·nat·ing
hi·ber·na·tion
Hi·ber·nia
hi·bis·cus
hic·cup
hic·cuped
hic·cup·ing
hid·den
hid·den·ness
hide
hid
hid·den
hid·ing
hid·er
hide·bound
hid·e·ous
hid·e·ous·ly
hid·e·ous·ness
hide·out
hi·er·ar·chy
hi·er·ar·chies
hi·er·ar·chal
hi·er·ar·chic
hi·er·ar·chi·cal
hi·er·ar·chi·cal·ly
hi·er·o·glyph·ic
hi·er·o·glyph·i·cal
hi·er·o·glyph
hi·er·o·glyph·i·cal·ly
hi·fi
high·ball
high·born
high·boy
high·brow
high·browed
high·brow·ism
high·er·up
high·fa·lu·tin
high·fa·lu·ting
high·flown

high·grade
high·hand·ed
high·hand·ed·ly
high·hand·ed·ness
high·hat
high·land
High·land·er
high·light
high·mind·ed
high·mind·ed·ly
high·mind·ed·ness
high·ness
high·pres·sure
high·pres·sured
high·pres·sur·ing
high school
high seas
high·spir·it·ed
high·spir·it·ed·ly
high·spir·it·ed·ness
high·strung
high·tail
high·ten·sion
high·toned
high·way
high·way·man
high·way·men
hi·jack
hi·jack·er
hi·jack·ing
hike
hiked
hik·ing
hik·er
hi·lar·i·ous
hi·lar·i·ous·ly
hi·lar·i·ous·ness
hi·lar·i·ty
hill·bil·ly
hill·bil·lies
hill·ock
hill·side
hill·top
hilly
hill·i·er
hill·i·est
Him·a·laya
him·self
Hin·den·burg
hin·der
hind·er·er
hind·most
hind·quar·ter
hin·drance
hind·sight
Hin·du
Hin·du·ism
Hin·du·stan
hinge
hinged
hing·ing
hint·er
hint·ing·ly
hin·ter·land
hipped

hip·pie
hip·po
 hip·pos
Hip·poc·ra·tes
hip·po·drome
Hip·pol·y·tus
hip·po·pot·a·mus
 hip·po·pot·a·mus·es
 hip·po·pot·a·mi
hire·ling
Hi·ro·hi·to
Hir·o·shi·ma
hir·sute
 hir·sute·ness
His·pa·nia
His·pan·ic
His·pan·i·o·la
hiss
 hiss·er
his·ta·mine
 his·ta·min·ic
his·to·ri·an
his·tor·ic
his·tor·i·cal
 his·tor·i·cal·ly
 his·tor·i·cal·ness
his·to·ry
 his·to·ries
his·tri·on·ic
 his·tri·on·i·cal
 his·tri·on·i·cal·ly
his·tri·on·ics
hit
 hit·ting
hit-and-run
hitch·er
hitch·hike
 hitch·hiked
 hitch·hik·ing
 hitch·hik·er
hith·er
hith·er·to
Hit·ler
Hit·tite
hive
 hived
 hiv·ing
hoary
 hoar·i·er
 hoar·i·est
 hoar·i·ness
hoard
 hoard·er
 hoard·ing
hoar·frost
hoarse
 hoarse·ly
hoars·en
 hoarse·ness
hoax
 hoax·er
hob·ble
 hob·bled
 hob·bling
hob·by

hob·bies
hob·by-horse
hob·gob·lin
hob·nail
hob·nailed
hob·nob
 hob·nobbed
 hob·nob·bing
ho·bo
 ho·boes
 ho·bos
 ho·bo·ism
Ho·bo·ken
hock·er
hock·ey
ho·cus-po·cus
hodge·podge
Hodg·kin's
hoe
 hoed
 hoe·ing
hoe·down
Hoff·mann
hog
 hogged
 hog·ging
 hog·gish
 hog·gish·ly
 hog·gish·ness
hogs·head
hog·tie
 hog·tied
 hog·ty·ing
hog·wash
Ho·hen·stau·fen
Ho·hen·zol·lern
hoi poi·loi
hoist·er
ho·kum
hol·der
hold·ing
hold·out
hold·o·ver
hold·up
hole
 holed
 hol·ing
 holey
hol·i·day
ho·li·ness
Hol·land
hol·ler
hol·low
 hol·low·ly
 hol·low·ness
hol·ly
 hol·lies
hol·ly·hock
Hol·ly·wood
hol·mi·um
hol·o·caust
ho·lo·gram
hol·o·graph
Hol·stein
hol·ster

ho·ly
 ho·li·er
 ho·li·est
 ho·lies
hom·age
hom·bre
 hom·bres
Hom·burg
home·com·ing
home·less
 home·less·ness
home·ly
 home·li·er
 home·li·est
 home·li·ness
home·made
hom·er
home·sick
 home·sick·ness
home·spun
home·stead
 home·stead·er
home·ward
 home·wards
home·work
homey
hom·i·er
 hom·i·est
 hom·i·ness
hom·i·cide
hom·i·let·ics
hom·i·ly
 hom·i·lies
hom·ing pi·geon
hom·i·ny
Ho·mo
ho·mo·ge·ne·ous
 ho·mo·ge·ne·i·ty
 ho·mo·ge·ne·ous·ly
 ho·mo·ge·ne·ous·ness
ho·mog·e·nize
 ho·meg·e·nized
 ho·mog·e·niz·ing
hom·o·graph
ho·mol·o·gous
 ho·mol·o·gy
 ho·mol·o·gies
hom·o·nym
 hom·o·nym·ic
hom·o·phone
 hom·o·phon·ic
Ho·mo sa·pi·ens
ho·mo·sex·u·al
 ho·mo·sex·u·al·i·ty
Hon·du·ras
hone
 honed
 hon·ing
hon·est
 hon·est·ly
hon·es·ty
 hon·es·ties
hon·ey
 hon·eys
 hon·eyed

hon·ied
hon·ey·ing
hon·ey·bee
hon·ey·comb
hon·ey·moon
hon·ey·moon·er
hon·ey·suck·le
hon·ey·suck·led
honk·y·tonk
Hon·o·lu·lu
hon·or
hon·or·a·ble
hon·or·a·bly
hon·o·rar·i·um
hon·o·rar·i·ums
hon·o·rar·ia
hon·or·ary
hon·or·if·ic
hood·ed
hood·lum
hoo·doo
hoo·doo·ism
hood·wink
hood·wink·er
hoo·ey
hoof
hoofs
hooves
hoofed
hooked
hook·er
hook·up
hoo·li·gan
hoo·li·gan·ism
hoop
hooped
hoop·like
hoop·la
hoo·ray
hoose·gow
Hoo·sier
hoot
hoot·er
hoot·ing·ly
Hoo·ver
hop
hopped
hop·ping
hope
hoped
hop·ing
hop·er
hope·ful
hope·ful·ly
hope·ful·ness
hope·less
hope·less·ly
hope·less·ness
hop·head
Hop·kins
hop·per
hop·scotch
Hor·ace
Ho·ra·tius
horde

hord·ed
hord·ing
Ho·reb
ho·ri·zon
hor·i·zon·tal
hor·i·zon·tal·ly
hor·mone
hor·mo·nal
horn
horned
horn·like
horny
horn·i·er
horn·i·est
hor·net
horn·swog·gle
horn·swog·gled
horn·swog·gling
ho·rol·o·gy
ho·rol·o·ger
ho·rol·o·gist
hor·o·scope
hor·ren·dous
hor·ren·dous·ly
hor·ri·ble
hor·ri·bly
hor·rid
hor·rid·ly
hor·rid·ness
hor·ri·fy
hor·ri·fied
hor·ri·fy·ing
hor·ri·fi·ca·tion
hor·ror
hors d'oeu·vre
hors d'oeu·vres
horse
hors·es
horsed
hors·ing
horse·back
horse·fly
horse·flies
horse·hair
horse·laugh
horse·man
horse·men
horse·man·ship
horse·wom·an
horse·wom·en
horse op·era
horse·play
horse·pow·er
horse·rad·ish
horse·shoe
horse·sho·er
horse·whip
horse·whipped
horse·whip·ping
hors·ey
horsy
hors·i·er
hors·i·est
hors·i·ly
hors·i·ness

hor·ta·to·ry
hor·ti·cul·ture
hor·ti·cul·tur·al
hor·ti·cul·tur·ist
ho·san·na
hose
hos·es
hosed
hos·ing
Ho·sea
ho·siery
hos·pice
hos·pi·ta·ble
hos·pi·ta·bly
hos·pi·tal
hos·pi·tal·i·ty
hos·pi·tal·i·ties
hos·pi·tal·i·za·tion
hos·pi·tal·ize
hos·pi·tal·ized
hos·pi·tal·iz·ing
hos·tage
hos·tel
hos·tel·ry
hos·tel·ries
host·ess
hos·tile
hos·tile·ly
hos·til·i·ty
hos·til·i·ties
hos·tler
hot
hot·ter
hot·test
hot·ly
hot·bed
hot·blood·ed
ho·tel
hot·head
hot·head·ed
hot·head·ed·ness
hot·house
hot·shot
Hot·ten·tot
Hou·di·ni
hound
hound·er
hour·glass
hour·ly
house
hous·es
housed
hous·ing
house·boat
house·bro·ken
house·break
house·broke
house·break·ing
house·fly
house·hold
house·hold·er
house·keep·er
house·keep·ing
house·maid
house·warm·ing

house·wife
house·wives
house·wife·ly
house·wif·ery
house·work
hous·ing
Hous·ton
hov·el
hov·eled
hov·el·ing
hov·er
hov·er·er
hov·er·ing
how·ev·er
how·itz·er
howl·er
how·so·ev·er
hoy·den
hoy·den·ish
hub·bub
huck·le·ber·ry
huck·le·ber·ries
huck·ster
hud·dle
hud·dled
hud·dling
hud·dler
Hud·son
Huer·ta
huffy
huff·i·er
huff·i·est
huff·i·ly
huff·i·ness
hug
hugged
hug·ging
hug·ger
huge
hug·er
hug·est
huge·ly
huge·ness
Hu·gue·not
hu·la
hulk·ing
hul·la·ba·loo
hum
hummed
hum·ming
hum·mer
hu·man
hu·man·ness
hu·mane
hu·mane·ly
hu·mane·ness
hu·man·ism
hu·man·ist
hu·man·is·tic
hu·man·i·tar·i·an
hu·man·i·tar·i·an·ism
hu·man·i·ty
hu·man·i·ties
hu·man·ize
hu·man·ized

hu·man·iz·ing
hu·man·i·za·tion
hu·man·iz·er
hu·man·kind
hu·man·ly
hum·ble
hum·bler
hum·blest
hum·bled
hum·bling
hum·ble·ness
hum·bly
Hum·boldt
hum·bug
hum·bugged
hum·bug·ging
hum·bug·ger
hum·bug·ger·y
hum·ding·er
hum·drum
hu·mer·us
hu·mid
hu·mid·ly
hu·mid·i·fy
hu·mid·i·fied
hu·mid·i·fy·ing
hu·mid·i·fi·er
hu·mid·i·ty
hu·mi·dor
hu·mil·i·ate
hu·mil·i·at·ed
hu·mil·i·at·ing
hu·mil·i·a·tion
hu·mil·i·ty
hum·ming bird
hum·mock
hum·mocky
hum·mock·i·er
hum·mock·i·est
hu·mor
hu·mor·ist
hu·mor·is·tic
hu·mor·ous
hu·mor·ous·ly
hu·mor·ous·ness
hump
humped
humpy
hump·i·er
hump·i·est
hump·back
hu·mus
hunch·back
hunch·backed
hun·dred
hun·dredth
hun·dred·weight
Hun·ga·ry
hun·ger
hun·gry
hun·gri·er
hun·gri·est
hun·gri·ly
hun·gri·ness
Hun·nish

Hun·nish·ness
hunt
hunt·er
hunt·ing
hunt·ress
hunts·man
hunts·men
Hun·ting·ton
hur·dle
hur·dled
hur·dling
hur·dler
hur·dy-gur·dy
hur·dy-gur·dies
hurl·er
hurl·y-burly
hurl·y-burl·ies
Hu·ron
hur·rah
hur·ri·cane
hur·ry
hur·ried
hur·ry·ing
hur·ried·ly
hur·ry·ing·ly
hurt·ful
hurt·ful·ly
hurt·ing
hur·tle
hur·tled
hur·tling
hus·band
hus·band·less
hus·band·ry
husk·er
husky
husk·i·er
husk·i·est
husk·i·ly
husk·i·ness
husk·ies
hus·sar
Huss·ite
hus·sy
huss·ies
hus·tings
hus·tle
hus·tled
hus·tling
hus·tler
hutch
Hux·ley
huz·zah
huz·za
hy·a·cinth
hy·brid
hy·brid·ism
hy·brid·ize
hy·brid·ized
hy·brid·iz·ing
hy·brid·i·za·tion
hy·dra
hy·dras
hy·drae
hy·dran·gea

hy·drant	hyp·no·tized	ice·man
hy·drate	hyp·no·tiz·ing	ice·men
hy·dra·ted	hy·po	ice-skate
hy·dra·ting	hy·po·chon·dria	ice-skat·ed
hy·dra·tion	hy·po·chon·dri·ac	ice-skat·ing
hy·dra·tor	hy·poc·ri·sy	ice-skat·er
hy·drau·lic	hy·poc·ri·sies	Ich·a·bod
hy·drau·li·cal·ly	hyp·o·crite	ich·nol·o·gy
hy·drau·lics	hy·po·der·mic	ich·no·log·i·cal
hy·dro·car·bon	hy·po·der·mic in·jec·tion	ich·thy·ol·o·gy
hy·dro·chlo·ric·ac·id	hy·po·sen·si·tize	ich·thy·o·log·i·cal
hy·dro·dy·nam·ics	hy·po·sen·si·tized	ich·thy·ol·o·gist
hy·dro·dy·nam·ic	hy·po·sen·si·tiz·ing	ici·cle
hy·dro·e·lec·tric	hy·po·ten·sion	ici·ly
hy·dro·gen	hy·pot·e·nuse	ici·ness
hy·drog·e·nous	hy·poth·e·cate	icon
hy·drol·y·sis	hy·poth·e·cat·ed	icon·o·clasm
hy·drol·y·ses	hy·poth·e·cat·ing	icon·o·clas·tic
hy·drom·e·ter	hy·poth·e·ca·tion	icon·o·clast
hy·dro·met·ric	hy·poth·e·ca·tor	icy
hy·dro·met·ri·cal	hy·poth·e·sis	ici·er
hy·drom·e·try	hy·poth·e·ses	ici·est
hy·dro·pho·bia	hy·poth·e·size	Ida·ho
hy·dro·plane	hy·poth·e·sized	idea
hy·dro·planed	hy·poth·e·siz·ing	ide·al
hy·dro·plan·ing	hy·po·thet·i·cal	ide·al·ness
hy·dro·pon·ics	hy·po·thet·i·cal·ly	ide·al·ism
hy·dro·pon·ic	hy·pox·e·mia	ide·al·ist
hy·dro·ther·a·py	hy·pox·ia	ide·al·is·tic
hy·dro·ther·a·pist	hyp·sog·ra·phy	ide·al·ize
hy·drous	hyp·som·e·ter	ide·al·ized
hy·drox·ide	hyp·som·e·try	ide·al·iz·ing
hy·drox·yl	hy·son	ide·al·i·za·tion
hy·dro·zo·an	hys·sop	ide·al·ly
hy·e·na	hys·ter·ec·to·my	idem
hy·giene	hys·ter·ec·to·mies	iden·ti·cal
hy·gi·en·ic	hys·ter·e·sis	iden·ti·cal·ly
hy·gi·en·i·cal·ly	hys·te·ria	iden·ti·cal·ness
hy·gien·ist	hys·ter·ic	iden·ti·fi·a·ble
hy·men	hys·ter·i·cal	iden·ti·fi·a·bly
hy·me·ne·al	hys·ter·i·cal·ly	iden·ti·fi·ca·tion
hy·me·ne·al·ly	hys·ter·ics	iden·ti·fy
hym·nal	iamb	iden·ti·fied
hy·per·bo·la	iambs	iden·ti·fy·ing
hy·per·bo·le	iam·bus	iden·ti·fi·er
hy·per·bo·lize	iam·bus·es	iden·ti·ty
hy·per·bo·lized	iam·bi	iden·ti·ties
hy·per·bo·liz·ing	iam·bic	ide·ol·o·gist
hy·per·bol·ic	iat·ric	ide·ol·o·gy
hy·per·crit·i·cal	Ibe·ria	ide·ol·o·gies
hy·per·crit·i·cal·ly	ibid	ides
hy·per·sen·si·tive	ibi·dem	id·i·o·cy
hy·per·sen·si·tive·ness	ibis	id·i·o·cies
hy·per·sen·si·tiv·i·ty	ibis·es	id·i·om
hy·per·ten·sion	ice	id·i·o·mat·ic
hy·per·thy·roid·ism	iced	id·i·o·mat·i·cal·ly
hy·phen	ic·ing	id·i·o·syn·cra·sy
hy·phen·ate	ice·bag	id·i·o·syn·cra·sies
hy·phen·at·ed	ice·berg	id·i·o·syn·crat·ic
hy·phen·at·ing	ice·boat	id·i·o·syn·crat·i·cal·ly
hyp·no·sis	ice·box	id·i·ot
hyp·not·ic	ice·cap	id·i·ot·ic
hyp·no·tism	ice-cold	id·i·ot·i·cal·ly
hyp·no·tist	ice cream	idle
hyp·no·tize	Ice·land	idler

idlest
idled
idling
idle·ness
idler
idly
idol
idol·a·try
idol·a·tries
idol·a·ter
idol·a·trous
idol·ize
idol·ized
idol·iz·ing
idol·i·za·tion
idol·iz·er
idyll
idyl·lic
idyl·lic·al·ly
if·fy
ig·loo
ig·loos
ig·ne·ous
ig·nite
ig·nit·ed
ig·nit·ing
ig·nit·er
ig·nit·a·ble
ig·nit·a·bil·i·ty
ig·ni·tion
ig·no·ble
ig·no·bil·i·ty
ig·no·ble·ness
ig·no·bly
ig·no·miny
ig·no·min·ies
ig·no·min·i·ous
ig·no·min·i·ous·ly
ig·no·min·i·ous·ness
ig·no·ra·mus
ig·no·rant
ig·no·rance
ig·no·rant·ly
ig·nore
ig·nored
ig·nor·ing
i·gua·na
Il·i·ad
ill-ad·vised
ill-ad·vis·ed·ly
ill-bred
il·le·gal
il·le·gal·i·ty
il·le·gal·ly
il·leg·i·ble
il·leg·i·bil·i·ty
il·leg·i·ble·ness
il·leg·i·bly
il·le·git·i·mate
il·le·git·i·ma·cy
il·le·git·i·ma·cies
il·le·git·i·mate·ly
ill-fat·ed
ill-fa·vored
ill-got·ten

il·lib·er·al
il·lic·it
il·lim·it·a·ble
Il·li·nois
il·lit·er·ate
il·lit·er·a·cy
il·lit·er·a·cies
ill·ness
il·log·i·cal
ill-starred
ill-tem·pered
ill-tem·pered·ly
ill-tem·pered·ness
ill-timed
il·lu·mi·nate
il·lu·mi·nat·ed
il·lu·mi·nat·ing
il·lu·mi·na·tor
il·lu·mi·na·tion
il·lu·mine
il·lu·mined
il·lu·min·ing
ill-use
ill-used
ill-us·ing
ill-us·age
il·lu·sion
il·lu·sive
il·lu·sive·ly
il·lu·sive·ness
il·lu·so·ry
il·lu·so·ri·ly
il·lu·so·ri·ness
il·lus·trate
il·lus·trat·ed
il·lus·trat·ing
il·lus·tra·tion
il·lus·tra·tive
il·lus·tra·tive·ly
il·lus·tra·tor
il·lus·tri·ous
il·lus·tri·ous·ly
il·lus·tri·ous·ness
Il·lyr·ia
im·age
im·aged
im·ag·ing
im·age·a·ble
im·ag·er
im·age·ry
im·age·ries
im·a·ge·ri·al
im·ag·i·na·ble
imag·i·na·ble·ness
imag·i·na·bly
im·ag·i·nary
im·ag·i·nar·ies
imag·i·nar·i·ly
imag·i·nar·i·ness
im·ag·i·na·tion
imag·i·na·tion·al
im·ag·i·na·tive
imag·i·na·tive·ly
imag·i·na·tive·ness
im·ag·ine

im·ag·ined
im·ag·in·ing
im·bal·ance
im·be·cile
im·be·cil·ic
im·be·cile·ly
im·be·cil·i·ty
im·bed
im·bed·ded
im·bed·ding
im·bibe
im·bibed
im·bib·ing
im·bib·er
im·bro·glio
im·bue
im·bued
im·bu·ing
im·i·ta·ble
im·i·tate
im·i·tat·ed
im·i·tat·ing
im·i·ta·tor
im·i·ta·tion
im·i·ta·tive
im·mac·u·late
im·mac·u·la·cy
im·mac·u·late·ness
im·mac·u·late·ly
im·ma·nent
im·ma·nence
im·ma·nen·cy
im·ma·nent·ly
im·ma·te·ri·al
im·ma·te·ri·al·ness
im·ma·te·ri·al·i·ty
im·ma·ture
im·ma·ture·ly
im·ma·ture·ness
im·ma·tu·ri·ty
im·meas·ur·a·ble
im·meas·ur·a·ble·ness
im·meas·ur·a·bly
im·me·di·a·cy
im·me·di·a·cies
im·me·di·ate
im·me·di·ate·ly
im·me·di·ate·ness
im·me·mo·ri·al
im·me·mo·ri·al·ly
im·mense
im·mense·ly
im·mense·ness
im·men·si·ty
im·merge
im·merged
im·merg·ing
im·mer·gence
im·merse
im·mersed
im·mers·ing
im·mer·sion
im·mi·grant
im·mi·grate
im·mi·grat·ed

im·mi·grat·ing
im·mi·gra·tion
im·mi·gra·tor
im·mi·nent
im·mi·nence
im·mo·bile
im·mo·bil·i·ty
im·mo·bi·lize
im·mo·bi·lized
im·mo·bi·liz·ing
im·mod·er·ate
im·mod·er·ate·ly
im·mod·er·ate·ness
im·mod·est
im·mod·est·ly
im·mod·es·ty
im·mo·late
im·mo·lat·ed
im·mo·lat·ing
im·mo·la·tion
im·mo·la·tor
im·mor·al
im·mor·al·ist
im·mo·ral·i·ty
im·mo·ral·i·ties
im·mor·al·ly
im·mor·tal
im·mor·tal·i·ty
im·mor·tal·ize
im·mor·tal·ized
im·mor·tal·iz·ing
im·mor·tal·ly
im·mov·a·ble
im·mov·a·bil·i·ty
im·mov·a·bly
im·mune
im·mu·ni·ty
im·mu·ni·ties
im·mu·nize
im·mu·nized
im·mu·niz·ing
im·mu·ni·za·tion
im·mu·nol·o·gy
im·mure
im·mured
im·mur·ing
im·mu·ta·ble
im·mu·ta·bil·i·ty
im·mu·ta·ble·ness
im·mu·ta·bly
im·pact
im·pac·tion
im·pact·ed
im·pair
im·pair·er
im·pair·ment
im·pala
im·pal·as
im·pal·ae
im·pale
im·paled
im·pal·ing
im·pale·ment
im·pal·er
im·pal·pa·ble

im·pal·pa·bil·i·ty
im·pal·pa·bly
im·pan·el
im·pan·eled
im·pan·el·ing
im·part
im·par·tial
im·par·ti·al·i·ty
im·par·tial·ness
im·par·tial·ly
im·pass·a·ble
im·pass·a·bil·i·ty
im·pass·a·ble·ness
im·pass·a·bly
im·passe
im·pas·si·ble
im·pas·si·bil·i·ty
im·pas·si·ble·ness
im·pas·si·bly
im·pas·sion
im·pas·sioned
im·pas·sioned·ly
im·pas·sioned·ness
im·pas·sive
im·pas·sive·ly
im·pas·sive·ness
im·pas·siv·i·ty
im·pa·tient
im·pa·tience
im·pa·tient·ly
im·peach
im·peach·a·ble
im·peach·ment
im·pec·ca·ble
im·pec·ca·bil·i·ty
im·pec·ca·bly
im·pe·cu·ni·ous
im·pe·cu·ni·ous·ly
im·pe·cu·ni·ous·ness
im·pede
im·ped·ed
im·ped·ing
im·ped·i·ment
im·pel
im·pelled
im·pel·ling
im·pend
im·pend·ing
im·pen·e·tra·bil·i·ty
im·pen·e·tra·ble
im·pen·e·tra·ble·ness
im·pen·e·tra·bly
im·pen·i·tent
im·pen·i·tence
im·pen·i·tent·ly
im·per·a·tive
im·per·a·tive·ly
im·per·a·tive·ness
im·per·cep·ti·ble
im·per·cep·ti·bil·i·ty
im·per·cep·ti·bly
im·per·cep·tive
im·per·cep·tive·ness
im·per·fect
im·per·fect·ly

im·per·fect·ness
im·per·fec·tion
im·pe·ri·al
im·pe·ri·al·ly
im·pe·ri·al·ism
im·pe·ri·al·ist
im·pe·ri·al·is·tic
im·pe·ri·al·is·ti·cal·ly
im·per·il
im·per·iled
im·per·il·ing
im·per·il·ment
im·pe·ri·ous
im·pe·ri·ous·ly
im·pe·ri·ous·ness
im·per·ish·a·ble
im·per·ish·a·bil·i·ty
im·per·ish·a·ble·ness
im·per·ish·a·bly
im·per·ma·nent
im·per·ma·nence
im·per·ma·nen·cy
im·per·ma·nent·ly
im·per·me·a·ble
im·per·me·a·bil·i·ty
im·per·me·a·ble·ness
im·per·me·a·bly
im·per·son·al
im·per·son·al·i·ty
im·per·son·al·i·ties
im·per·son·al·ly
im·per·son·ate
im·per·son·at·ed
im·per·son·at·ing
im·per·son·a·tion
im·per·son·a·tor
im·per·ti·nent
im·per·ti·nence
im·per·ti·nent·ly
im·per·turb·a·ble
im·per·turb·a·bly
im·per·vi·ous
im·per·vi·ous·ly
im·per·vi·ous·ness
im·pe·ti·go
im·pet·u·ous
im·pet·u·os·i·ty
im·pet·u·ous·ly
im·pet·u·ous·ness
im·pe·tus
im·pe·tus·es
im·pi·e·ty
im·pi·e·ties
im·pinge
im·pinged
im·ping·ing
im·pinge·ment
im·ping·er
im·pi·ous
im·pi·ous·ly
im·pi·ous·ness
im·plac·a·ble
im·plac·a·bil·i·ty
im·plac·a·ble·ness
im·plac·a·bly

im·plant
im·plan·ta·tion
im·plant·er
im·plau·si·ble
im·plau·si·bly
im·plau·si·bil·i·ty
im·ple·ment
im·ple·men·tal
im·ple·men·ta·tion
im·pli·cate
im·pli·cat·ed
im·pli·cat·ing
im·pli·ca·tion
im·plic·it
im·plic·it·ly
im·plic·it·ness
im·plode
im·plod·ed
im·plod·ing
im·plo·sion
im·plo·sive
im·plore
im·plored
im·plor·ing
im·plo·ra·tion
im·ply
im·plied
im·ply·ing
im·po·lite
im·po·lite·ly
im·po·lite·ness
im·pol·i·tic
im·pol·i·tic·ly
im·pon·der·a·ble
im·pon·der·a·bil·i·ty
im·pon·der·a·ble·ness
im·pon·der·a·bly
im·port
im·port·a·ble
im·port·er
im·por·tance
im·por·tant
im·por·tant·ly
im·por·ta·tion
im·por·tu·nate
im·por·tu·nate·ly
im·por·tune
im·por·tuned
im·por·tun·ing
im·pose
im·posed
im·pos·ing
im·pos·ter
im·po·si·tion
im·pos·si·ble
im·pos·si·bil·i·ty
im·pos·si·bil·i·ties
im·pos·si·bly
im·post
im·pos·tor
im·pos·ture
im·po·tent
im·po·tence
im·po·ten·cy
im·po·tent·ly

im·pound
im·pound·age
im·pov·er·ish
im·pov·er·ish·ment
im·prac·ti·ca·ble
im·prac·ti·ca·bil·i·ty
im·prac·ti·ca·ble·ness
im·prac·ti·ca·bly
im·prac·ti·cal
im·pre·cate
im·pre·cat·ed
im·pre·cat·ing
im·pre·ca·tion
im·preg·na·ble
im·preg·na·bil·i·ty
im·preg·na·ble·ness
im·preg·na·bly
im·preg·nate
im·preg·nat·ed
im·preg·nat·ing
im·preg·na·tion
im·preg·na·tor
im·pre·sa·rio
im·pre·sa·ri·os
im·press
im·press·er
im·press·i·ble
im·press·ment
im·pres·sion
im·pres·sion·ist
im·pres·sion·a·ble
im·pres·sion·a·bly
im·pres·sion·ism
im·pres·sion·ist
im·pres·sion·is·tic
im·pres·sive
im·pres·sive·ly
im·pres·sive·ness
im·pri·ma·tur
im·print
im·prin·ter
im·pris·on
im·pris·on·ment
im·prob·a·ble
im·prob·a·bil·i·ty
im·prob·a·ble·ness
im·prob·a·bly
im·promp·tu
im·prop·er
im·prop·er·ly
im·prop·er·ness
im·pro·pri·e·ty
im·pro·pri·e·ties
im·prove
im·proved
im·prov·ing
im·prov·a·bil·i·ty
im·prov·a·ble
im·prove·ment
im·prov·i·dent
im·prov·i·dence
im·prov·i·dent·ly
im·prov·i·sa·tion
im·prov·i·sa·tion·al
im·pro·vise

im·pro·vised
im·pro·vis·ing
im·pro·vis·er
im·pru·dent
im·pru·dence
im·pru·dent·ly
im·pugn
im·pugn·er
im·pulse
im·pul·sion
im·pul·sive
im·pu·ni·ty
im·pure
im·pure·ly
im·pure·ness
im·pu·ri·ty
im·pu·ri·ties
im·pute
im·put·ed
im·put·ing
im·pu·ta·ble
im·pu·ta·tion
im·put·a·tive
im·put·er
in·a·bil·i·ty
in·ac·ces·si·ble
in·ac·ces·si·bil·i·ty
in·ac·ces·si·ble·ness
in·ac·ces·si·bly
in·ac·cu·rate
in·ac·cu·rate·ly
in·ac·cu·ra·cy
in·ac·cu·ra·cies
in·ac·tion
in·ac·tive
in·ac·tive·ly
in·ac·tiv·i·ty
in·ad·e·quate
in·ad·e·qua·cy
in·ad·e·qua·cies
in·ad·e·quate·ly
in·ad·mis·si·ble
in·ad·mis·si·bly
in·ad·vert·ent
in·ad·vert·ence
in·ad·vert·en·cy
in·ad·vert·ent·ly
in·al·ien·a·ble
in·al·ien·a·bly
in·am·o·ra·ta
in·am·o·ra·tas
in·ane
in·ane·ly
in·ane·ness
in·an·i·ty
in·an·i·ties
in·an·i·mate
in·ap·pro·pri·ate
in·ap·pro·pri·ate·ly
in·ap·pro·pri·ate·ness
in·apt
in·ap·ti·tude
in·apt·ly
in·apt·ness
in·ar·tic·u·late

in·ar·tic·u·late·ly
in·ar·tic·u·late·ness
in·as·much as
in·at·ten·tion
in·at·ten·tive
in·at·ten·tive·ly
in·au·gu·ral
in·au·gu·rate
in·au·gu·rat·ed
in·au·gu·rat·ing
in·au·gu·ra·tion
in·aus·pi·cious
in·aus·pi·cious·ly
in·board
in·born
in·bred
in·breed
in·breed·ing
In·ca
in·cal·cu·la·ble
in·cal·cu·la·bly
in·can·des·cent
in·can·des·cence
in·can·des·cent·ly
in·can·ta·tion
in·ca·pa·ble
in·ca·pa·bly
in·ca·pac·i·tate
in·ca·pac·i·tat·ed
in·ca·pac·i·tat·ing
in·ca·pac·i·ty
in·ca·pac·i·ties
in·car·cer·ate
in·car·cer·at·ed
in·car·cer·at·ing
in·car·cer·a·tion
in·car·nate
in·car·nat·ed
in·car·nat·ing
in·car·na·tion
in·cen·di·a·ry
in·cen·di·a·ries
in·cense
in·censed
in·cens·ing
in·cen·tive
in·cep·tion
in·ces·sant
in·ces·sant·ly
in·cest
in·ces·tu·ous
in·ces·tu·ous·ly
in·ces·tu·ous·ness
in·cho·ate
in·cho·ate·ly
in·cho·ate·ness
in·ci·dence
in·ci·dent
in·ci·den·tal
in·ci·den·tal·ly
in·cin·er·ate
in·cin·er·at·ed
in·cin·er·at·ing
in·cin·er·a·tion
in·cin·er·a·tor

in·cip·i·ent
in·cip·i·ent·ly
in·cise
in·cised
in·cis·ing
in·ci·sion
in·ci·sive
in·ci·sive·ly
in·ci·sive·ness
in·ci·sor
in·cite
in·cit·ed
in·cit·ing
in·cite·ment
in·cit·er
in·clem·ent
in·clem·en·cy
in·clem·ent·ly
in·cli·na·tion
in·cline
in·clined
in·clin·ing
in·clin·er
in·clude
in·clud·ed
in·clud·ing
in·clud·a·ble
in·clu·sion
in·clu·sive
in·clu·sive·ly
in·clu·sive·ness
in·cog·ni·to
in·cog·ni·tos
in·co·her·ent
in·co·her·ence
in·co·her·ent·ly
in·come
in·com·ing
in·com·men·su·ra·ble
in·com·men·su·ra·bly
in·com·men·su·rate
in·com·men·su·rate·ly
in·com·mo·di·ous
in·com·pa·ra·ble
in·com·pa·ra·bly
in·com·pat·i·ble
in·com·pat·i·bil·i·ty
in·com·pat·i·bly
in·com·pe·tent
in·com·pe·tence
in·com·pe·ten·cy
in·com·pe·tent·ly
in·com·plete
in·com·plete·ly
in·com·plete·ness
in·com·ple·tion
in·com·pre·hen·si·ble
in·com·pre·hen·si·bly
in·com·pre·hen·sion
in·con·ceiv·a·ble
in·con·ceiv·a·bly
in·con·clu·sive
in·con·clu·sive·ly
in·con·clu·sive·ness
in·con·gru·ous

in·con·gru·ous·ly
in·con·gru·ous·ness
in·con·gru·i·ty
in·con·gru·i·ties
in·con·se·quen·tial
in·con·se·quen·tial·ly
in·con·sid·er·a·ble
in·con·sid·er·a·bly
in·con·sid·er·ate
in·con·sid·er·ate·ly
in·con·sid·er·ate·ness
in·con·sis·tent
in·con·sist·ent·ly
in·con·sol·a·ble
in·con·sol·a·ble·ness
in·con·sol·a·bly
in·con·spic·u·ous
in·con·spic·u·ous·ly
in·con·spic·u·ous·ness
in·con·stant
in·con·stan·cy
in·con·stan·cies
in·con·stant·ly
in·con·test·a·ble
in·con·test·a·bly
in·con·ti·nent
in·con·ti·nence
in·con·ti·nen·cy
in·con·ti·nent·ly
in·con·tro·vert·i·ble
in·con·ven·ience
in·con·ven·ien·cy
in·con·ven·ienced
in·con·ven·ienc·ing
in·con·ven·ient
in·con·ven·ient·ly
in·cor·po·rate
in·cor·po·rat·ed
in·cor·po·rat·ing
in·cor·po·ra·tion
in·cor·po·ra·tor
in·cor·po·re·al
in·cor·rect
in·cor·rect·ly
in·cor·ri·gi·ble
in·cor·ri·gi·bil·i·ty
in·cor·ri·gi·ble·ness
in·cor·ri·gi·bly
in·cor·rupt·i·ble
in·cor·rupt·i·bil·i·ty
in·cor·rupt·i·ble·ness
in·cor·rupt·i·bly
in·crease
in·creased
in·creas·ing
in·creas·a·ble
in·creas·ing·ly
in·cred·i·ble
in·cred·i·bil·i·ty
in·cred·i·ble·ness
in·cred·i·bly
in·cred·u·lous
in·cre·du·li·ty
in·cred·u·lous·ness
in·cred·u·lous·ly

in·cre·ment
in·cre·men·tal
in·crim·i·nate
in·crim·i·nat·ed
in·crim·i·nat·ing
in·crim·i·na·tion
in·crim·i·na·tor
in·crim·i·na·to·ry
in·crust
in·crus·ta·tion
in·cu·bate
in·cu·bat·ed
in·cu·bat·ing
in·cu·ba·tion
in·cu·ba·tor
in·cu·bus
in·cu·bus·es
in·cul·cate
in·cul·cat·ed
in·cul·cat·ing
in·cul·ca·tion
in·cul·ca·tor
in·cul·pate
in·cul·pat·ed
in·cul·pat·ing
in·cul·pa·tion
in·cum·bent
in·cum·ben·cy
in·cum·ben·cies
in·cum·bent·ly
in·cur
in·curred
in·cur·ring
in·cur·a·ble
in·cur·a·bil·i·ty
in·cur·a·ble·ness
in·cur·a·bly
in·cur·sion
in·cur·sive
in·debt·ed
in·debt·ed·ness
in·de·cent
in·de·cen·cy
in·de·cen·cies
in·de·cent·ly
in·de·ci·sion
in·de·ci·sive
in·de·ci·sive·ly
in·de·ci·sive·ness
in·deed
in·de·fat·i·ga·ble
in·de·fat·i·ga·bil·i·ty
in·de·fat·i·ga·ble·ness
in·de·fat·i·ga·bly
in·de·fen·si·ble
in·de·fen·si·bil·i·ty
in·de·fen·si·bly
in·def·i·nite
in·def·i·nite·ly
in·def·i·nite·ness
in·del·i·ble
in·del·i·bil·i·ty
in·del·i·ble·ness
in·del·i·bly
in·del·i·cate

in·del·i·ca·cy
in·del·i·cate·ness
in·del·i·cate·ly
in·dem·ni·fy
in·dem·ni·fied
in·dem·ni·fy·ing
in·dem·ni·fi·ca·tion
in·dem·ni·fi·er
in·dem·ni·ty
in·dem·ni·ties
in·dent
in·den·ta·tion
in·dent·ed
in·den·ture
in·den·tured
in·den·tur·ing
in·de·pend·ence
in·de·pend·en·cy
in·de·pend·ent
in·de·pend·ent·ly
in·de·scrib·a·ble
in·de·scrib·a·bil·i·ty
in·de·scrib·a·ble·ness
in·de·scrib·a·bly
in·de·struct·i·ble
in·de·struct·i·bil·i·ty
in·de·struct·i·ble·ness
in·de·struct·i·bly
in·de·ter·mi·nate
in·de·ter·mi·nate·ly
in·de·ter·mi·nate·ness
in·de·ter·mi·na·cy
in·de·ter·mi·na·tion
in·dex
in·dex·es
in·di·ces
in·dex·er
In·dia
In·di·an
In·di·ana
In·di·an·ap·o·lis
in·di·cate
in·di·cat·ed
in·di·cat·ing
in·di·ca·tion
in·dic·a·tive
in·dic·a·tive·ly
in·di·ca·tor
in·dic·a·tory
in·dict
in·dict·a·ble
in·dict·er
in·dict·or
in·dict·ment
In·dies
in·dif·fer·ent
in·dif·fer·ence
in·dif·fer·ent·ist
in·dif·fer·ent·ly
in·dig·e·nous
in·dig·e·nous·ly
in·dig·e·nous·ness
in·di·gent
in·di·gence
in·di·gent·ly

in·di·gest·i·ble
in·di·gest·i·bil·i·ty
in·di·gest·i·ble·ness
in·di·ges·tion
in·di·ges·tive
in·dig·nant
in·dig·nant·ly
in·dig·na·tion
in·dig·ni·ty
in·dig·ni·ties
in·di·go
in·di·gos
in·di·goes
in·di·rect
in·di·rec·tion
in·di·rect·ly
in·di·rect·ness
in·dis·creet
in·dis·creet·ly
in·dis·creet·ness
in·dis·crete
in·dis·cre·tion
in·dis·crim·i·nate
in·dis·crim·i·nate·ly
in·dis·crim·i·nate·ness
in·dis·crim·i·nat·ing
in·dis·crim·i·na·tion
in·dis·pen·sa·ble
in·dis·pen·sa·bil·i·ty
in·dis·pen·sa·ble·ness
in·dis·pen·sa·bly
in·dis·pose
in·dis·posed
in·dis·pos·ing
in·dis·po·si·tion
in·dis·sol·u·ble
in·dis·sol·u·bil·i·ty
in·dis·sol·u·ble·ness
in·dis·sol·u·bly
in·di·um
in·di·vid·u·al
in·di·vid·u·al·ly
in·di·vid·u·al·ism
in·di·vid·u·al·ist
in·di·vid·u·al·is·tic
in·di·vid·u·al·is·ti·cal·ly
in·di·vid·u·al·i·ty
in·di·vid·u·al·i·ties
in·di·vid·u·al·ize
in·di·vid·u·al·ized
in·di·vid·u·al·iz·ing
in·di·vid·u·al·i·za·tion
In·do-Chi·na
in·doc·tri·nate
in·doc·tri·nat·ed
in·doc·tri·nat·ing
in·doc·tri·na·tion
in·doc·tri·na·tor
in·do·lent
in·do·lence
in·do·lent·ly
in·dom·i·ta·ble
in·dom·i·ta·bil·i·ty
in·dom·i·ta·ble·ness
in·dom·i·ta·bly

In·do·ne·sia
in·door
in·doors
in·du·bi·ta·ble
  in·du·bi·ta·ble·ness
  in·du·bi·ta·bil·i·ty
  in·du·bi·tab·ly
in·duce
  in·duced
  in·duc·ing
  in·duce·ment
  in·duc·er
  in·duc·i·ble
in·duct
  in·duct·ee
  in·duc·tion
  in·duc·tive
in·dulge
  in·dulged
  in·dulg·ing
  in·dul·gence
  in·dul·gent
  in·dul·gent·ly
In·dus
in·dus·tri·al
  in·dus·tri·al·ly
  in·dus·tri·al·ness
  in·dus·tri·al·ism
  in·dus·tri·al·ize
  in·dus·tri·al·ized
  in·dus·tri·al·iz·ing
  in·dus·tri·al·i·za·tion
  in·dus·tri·al·ist
in·dus·tri·ous
  in·dus·tri·ous·ly
in·dus·try
  in·dus·tries
in·e·bri·ate
  in·e·bri·at·ed
  in·e·bri·at·ing
  in·e·bri·a·tion
  in·e·bri·e·ty
in·ed·u·ca·ble
in·ef·fa·ble
  in·ef·fa·bil·i·ty
  in·ef·fa·ble·ness
  in·ef·fa·bly
in·ef·fec·tive
  in·ef·fec·tive·ly
  in·ef·fec·tive·ness
in·ef·fec·tu·al
  in·ef·fec·tu·al·i·ty
  in·ef·fec·tu·al·ness
  in·ef·fec·tu·al·ly
in·ef·fi·cient
  in·ef·fi·cien·cy
  in·ef·fi·cien·cies
  in·ef·fi·cient·ly
in·el·i·gi·ble
  in·el·i·gi·bil·i·ty
  in·el·i·gi·bly
in·e·luc·ta·ble
in·ept
  in·ept·i·tude
  in·ept·ly

in·ept·ness
in·e·qual·i·ty
in·eq·ui·ta·ble
in·eq·ui·ty
in·eq·ui·ties
in·ert
  in·ert·ly
  in·ert·ness
in·er·tia
  in·er·tial
in·es·cap·a·ble
in·es·ti·ma·ble
  in·es·ti·ma·bly
in·ev·i·ta·ble
  in·ev·i·ta·bil·i·ty
  in·ev·i·ta·ble·ness
  in·ev·i·ta·bly
in·ex·haust·i·ble
  in·ex·haust·i·bil·i·ty
  in·ex·haust·i·ble·ness
  in·ex·haust·i·bly
in·ex·o·ra·ble
  in·ex·o·ra·bil·i·ty
  in·ex·o·ra·ble·ness
  in·ex·o·ra·bly
in·ex·pe·ri·ence
  in·ex·pe·ri·enced
in·ex·pert
  in·ex·pert·ly
  in·ex·pert·ness
in·ex·pi·a·ble
  in·ex·pi·a·ble·ness
  in·ex·pi·a·bly
in·ex·pli·ca·ble
  in·ex·pli·ca·bil·i·ty
  in·ex·pli·ca·ble·ness
  in·ex·pli·ca·bly
in·ex·press·i·ble
  in·ex·press·i·bil·i·ty
  in·ex·press·i·ble·ness
  in·ex·press·i·bly
in·ex·tin·guish·a·ble
  in·ex·tin·guish·a·bly
in·ex·tri·ca·ble
  in·ex·tri·ca·bil·i·ty
  in·ex·tri·ca·ble·ness
  in·ex·tri·ca·bly
in·fal·li·ble
  in·fal·li·bil·i·ty
  in·fal·li·ble·ness
  in·fal·li·bly
in·fa·mous
  in·fa·mous·ly
  in·fa·mous·ness
in·fa·my
  in·fa·mies
in·fan·cy
  in·fan·cies
in·fant
  in·fant·hood
  in·fant·like
in·fan·tile
  in·fan·tine
  in·fan·til·i·ty
in·fan·try

in·fan·tries
  in·fan·try·man
  in·fan·try·men
in·fat·u·ate
  in·fat·u·at·ed
  in·fat·u·at·ing
  in·fat·u·at·ed·ly
  in·fat·u·a·tion
in·fect
  in·fect·ed·ness
  in·fect·er
  in·fect·or
  in·fec·tion
in·fec·tious
  in·fec·tious·ly
  in·fec·tious·ness
  in·fec·tive
in·fer
  in·ferred
  in·fer·ring
  in·fer·a·ble
  in·fer·a·bly
  in·fer·ence
  in·fer·er
in·fe·ri·or
  in·fe·ri·or·i·ty
  in·fe·ri·or·ly
in·fer·nal
in·fer·no
  in·fer·nos
in·fest
  in·fes·ta·tion
  in·fest·er
in·fi·del
in·fi·del·i·ty
  in·fi·del·i·ties
in·field
  in·field·er
in·fight·ing
  in·fight·er
in·fil·trate
  in·fil·trat·ed
  in·fil·trat·ing
  in·fil·tra·tion
  in·fil·tra·tive
  in·fil·tra·tor
in·fi·nite
  in·fi·nite·ly
  in·fi·nite·ness
  in·fin·i·tude
in·fin·i·tes·i·mal
  in·fin·i·tes·i·mal·ly
in·fin·i·tive
  in·fin·i·tive·ly
in·fin·i·ty
  in·fin·i·ties
in·firm
  in·firm·ly
  in·firm·ness
in·fir·ma·ry
  in·fir·ma·ries
in·fir·mi·ty
  in·fir·mi·ties
in·flame
  in·flamed

in·flam·ing
in·flam·er
in·flam·ma·ble
in·flam·ma·bil·i·ty
in·flam·ma·ble·ness
in·flam·ma·bly
in·flam·ma·tion
in·flam·ma·to·ry
in·flate
in·flat·ed
in·flat·ing
in·flat·a·ble
in·flat·ed·ness
in·fla·tor
in·flat·er
in·fla·tion
in·fla·tion·ary
in·fla·tion·ism
in·fla·tion·ist
in·flect
in·flec·tion
in·flec·tion·al
in·flec·tion·al·ly
in·flec·tion·less
in·flec·tive
in·flec·tor
in·flex·i·ble
in·flex·i·bil·i·ty
in·flex·i·ble·ness
in·flex·i·bly
in·flict
in·flict·a·ble
in·flict·er
in·flict·or
in·flic·tion
in·flic·tive
in·flu·ence
in·flu·enced
in·flu·enc·ing
in·flu·ence·a·ble
in·flu·enc·er
in·flu·en·tial
in·flu·en·tial·ly
in·flu·en·za
in·flu·en·zal
in·flu·en·za-like
in·flux
in·form
in·formed
in·for·mer
in·for·mal
in·for·mal·i·ty
in·for·mal·ly
in·form·ant
in·for·ma·tion
in·for·ma·tion·al
in·for·ma·tive
in·for·ma·tive·ly
in·for·ma·tive·ness
in·for·ma·to·ry
in·frac·tion
in·fran·gi·ble
in·fran·gi·bil·i·ty
in·fran·gi·ble·ness
in·fran·gi·bly

in·fra·red
in·fra·struc·ture
in·fre·quent
in·fre·quen·cy
in·fre·quent·ly
in·fringe
in·fringed
in·fring·ing
in·fringe·ment
in·fring·er
in·fu·ri·ate
in·fu·ri·at·ed
in·fu·ri·at·ing
in·fu·ri·at·ing·ly
in·fu·ri·a·tion
in·fuse
in·fused
in·fus·ing
in·fus·er
in·fus·i·bil·i·ty
in·fus·i·ble
in·fu·sion
in·fu·sive
in·gen·ious
in·gen·ious·ly
in·gen·ious·ness
in·gé·nue
in·gé·nues
in·ge·nu·i·ty
in·gen·u·ous
in·gen·u·ous·ly
in·gen·u·ous·ness
In·ger·soll
in·gest
in·ges·tion
in·ges·tive
in·glo·ri·ous
in·glo·ri·ous·ly
in·glo·ri·ous·ness
in·got
in·grain
in·grained
in·grate
in·gra·ti·ate
in·gra·ti·at·ed
in·gra·ti·at·ing
in·gra·ti·a·tion
in·grat·i·tude
in·gre·di·ent
in·group
in·grow·ing
in·grown
in·growth
in·gulf
in·hab·it
in·hab·it·a·ble
in·hab·i·ta·tion
in·hab·it·er
in·hab·it·ed
in·hab·it·ant
in·hal·ant
in·ha·la·tion
in·ha·la·tor
in·hale
in·haled

in·hal·ing
in·hal·er
in·here
in·hered
in·her·ing
in·her·ence
in·her·ent
in·her·ent·ly
in·he·sion
in·her·it
in·her·i·tor
in·her·i·tance
in·hib·it
in·hib·i·tive
in·hib·i·to·ry
in·hib·i·ter
in·hib·it·or
in·hi·bi·tion
in·hos·pi·ta·ble
in·hos·pi·tal·i·ty
in·hu·man
in·hu·man·i·ty
in·hu·mane
in·im·i·cal
in·im·i·ta·ble
in·iq·ui·ty
in·iq·ui·ties
in·iq·ui·tous
in·i·tial
in·i·tialed
in·i·tial·ing
in·i·tial·ly
in·i·ti·ate
in·i·ti·at·ed
in·i·ti·at·ing
in·i·ti·a·tion
in·i·ti·a·tor
in·i·ti·a·tive
in·ject
in·jec·tion
in·jec·tor
in·ju·di·cious
in·junc·tion
in·junc·tive
in·jure
in·jured
in·jur·ing
in·ju·ri·ous
in·ju·ry
in·ju·ries
in·jus·tice
ink·blot
ink·ling
inky
ink·i·er
ink·i·est
in·laid
in·land
in·law
in·lay
in·laid
in·lay·ing
in·let
in·mate
in me·mo·ri·am

in·most
in·nards
in·nate
in·ner
in·ner·most
in·ner·sole
in·ner·vate
  in·ner·vat·ed
  in·ner·vat·ing
  in·ner·va·tion
in·nerve
  in·nerved
  in·nerv·ing
in·ning
inn·keep·er
in·no·cence
in·no·cent
  in·no·cent·ly
in·noc·u·ous
in·no·vate
  in·no·vat·ed
  in·no·vat·ing
  in·no·va·tion
  in·no·va·tive
  in·no·va·tor
in·nu·en·do
  in·nu·en·dos
  in·nu·en·does
in·nu·mer·a·ble
  in·nu·mer·ous
  in·nu·mer·a·bly
in·ob·serv·ance
  in·ob·serv·ant
  in·ob·serv·ant·ly
in·oc·u·lant
in·oc·u·late
  in·oc·u·lat·ed
  in·oc·u·lat·ing
  in·oc·u·la·tion
  in·oc·u·la·tor
in·oc·u·lum
in·of·fen·sive
in·op·er·a·ble
in·op·er·a·tive
in·op·por·tune
  in·op·por·tu·ni·ty
in·or·di·nate
in·pa·tient
in·pour
in·put
in·quest
in·qui·e·tude
in·quire
  in·quired
  in·quir·ing
  in·quir·er
in·quiry
  in·quir·ies
in·qui·si·tion
in·quis·i·tive
in·quis·i·tor
in·road
in·rush
in·sane
in·san·i·ty

in·san·i·ties
in·sa·tia·ble
in·sa·tia·bil·i·ty
in·sa·tia·bly
in·sa·ti·ate
in·scribe
in·scribed
in·scrib·ing
in·scrip·tion
in·scrip·tive
in·scru·ta·ble
in·scru·ta·bil·i·ty
in·scru·ta·bly
in·seam
in·sect
in·sec·ti·cide
  in·sec·ti·cid·al
in·se·cure
  in·se·cu·ri·ty
in·sem·i·nate
  in·sem·i·nat·ed
  in·sem·i·nat·ing
  in·sem·i·na·tion
in·sen·sate
in·sen·si·ble
in·sen·si·tive
  in·sen·si·tiv·i·ty
in·sen·ti·ent
in·sep·a·ra·ble
  in·sep·a·ra·bil·i·ty
  in·sep·a·ra·bly
in·sert
  in·sert·er
  in·ser·tion
in·set
  in·set·ting
in·shore
in·side
in·sid·er
in·sid·i·ous
in·sight
  in·sight·ful
in·sig·nia
in·sig·nif·i·cant
  in·sig·nif·i·cance
in·sin·cere
  in·sin·cer·i·ty
  in·sin·cer·i·ties
in·sin·u·ate
  in·sin·u·at·ed
  in·sin·u·at·ing
  in·sin·u·a·tor
  in·sin·u·a·tion
in·sip·id
  in·si·pid·i·ty
  in·sip·id·ness
in·sist
  in·sist·ence
  in·sist·ent
  in·sist·ent·ly
  in·sist·ing·ly
in·so·bri·e·ty
in·so·cia·ble
  in·so·cia·bil·i·ty
  in·so·cia·bly

in·so·far
in·sole
in·so·lent
  in·so·lence
in·sol·u·ble
  in·sol·u·bil·i·ty
  in·sol·u·bly
in·solv·a·ble
in·sol·vent
  in·sol·ven·cy
in·som·nia
  in·som·ni·ac
in·so·much
in·spect
in·spec·tion
in·spec·tor
in·spi·ra·tion
  in·spi·ra·tion·al
in·spire
in·spired
in·spir·ing
in·spir·it
in·sta·ble
  in·sta·bil·i·ty
in·stall
  in·stall·er
  in·stal·la·tion
  in·stall·ment
in·stance
in·stant
in·stan·ta·ne·ous
  in·stant·ly
in·state
  in·stat·ed
  in·stat·ing
  in·state·ment
in·stead
in·step
in·sti·gate
  in·sti·gat·ed
  in·sti·gat·ing
  in·sti·ga·tion
  in·sti·ga·tor
in·still
  in·stilled
  in·stil·ling
  in·stil·la·tion
in·stinct
in·stinc·tive
  in·stinc·tu·al
  in·stinc·tive·ly
in·sti·tute
  in·sti·tut·ed
  in·sti·tut·ing
  in·sti·tut·er
  in·sti·tu·tor
in·sti·tu·tion
in·sti·tu·tion·al
  in·sti·tu·tion·al·ism
  in·sti·tu·tion·al·ize
  in·sti·tu·tion·al·ized
  in·sti·tu·tion·al·iz·ing
in·struct
in·struc·tion
in·struc·tive

in·struc·tor
in·stru·ment
in·stru·men·tal
in·stru·men·ta·list
in·stru·men·ta·tion
in·sub·or·di·nate
in·sub·or·di·na·tion
in·sub·stan·tial
in·sub·stan·ti·al·i·ty
in·suf·fer·a·ble
in·suf·fer·a·bly
in·suf·fi·cient
in·suf·fi·cience
in·suf·fi·cien·cy
in·su·lar
in·su·lar·i·ty
in·su·late
in·su·lat·ed
in·su·lat·ing
in·su·la·tion
in·su·la·tor
in·su·lin
in·sult
in·sup·port·a·ble
in·sup·press·i·ble
in·sur·ance
in·sure
in·sured
in·sur·ing
in·sur·er
in·sur·gent
in·sur·gence
in·sur·gen·cy
in·sur·mount·a·ble
in·sur·rec·tion
in·sur·rec·tion·ary
in·sus·cep·ti·ble
in·tact
in·take
in·tan·gi·ble
in·tan·gi·bil·i·ty
in·tan·gi·ble·ness
in·tan·gi·bly
in·te·ger
in·te·gral
in·te·gral·ly
in·te·grate
in·te·grat·ed
in·te·grat·ing
in·te·gra·tion
in·te·gra·tion·ist
in·teg·ri·ty
in·tel·lect
in·tel·lec·tu·al
in·tel·lec·tu·al·ism
in·tel·lec·tu·al·ize
in·tel·lec·tu·al·ized
in·tel·lec·tu·al·iz·ing
in·tel·li·gence
in·tel·li·gent
in·tel·li·gent·ly
in·tel·li·gent·sia
in·tel·li·gi·ble
in·tel·li·gi·bil·i·ty
in·tel·li·bi·bly

in·tem·per·ance
in·tem·per·ate
in·tend
in·tend·er
in·tend·ed
in·tense
in·tense·ly
in·tense·ness
in·ten·si·fy
in·ten·si·fied
in·ten·si·fy·ing
in·ten·si·fi·ca·tion
in·ten·si·fi·er
in·ten·sion
in·ten·si·ty
in·ten·si·ties
in·ten·sive
in·ten·sive·ly
in·ten·sive·ness
in·tent
in·ten·tion
in·ten·tion·al
in·ten·tion·al·ly
in·ten·tioned
in·ter
in·terred
in·ter·ring
in·ter·ment
in·ter·act
in·ter·ac·tion
in·ter·ac·tive
in·ter·breed
in·ter·bred
in·ter·breed·ing
in·ter·cede
in·ter·ced·ed
in·ter·ced·ing
in·ter·ced·er
in·ter·cept
in·ter·cep·ter
in·ter·cept·or
in·ter·cep·tion
in·ter·cep·tive
in·ter·ces·sion
in·ter·change
in·ter·changed
in·ter·chang·ing
in·ter·change·a·ble
in·ter·change·a·bil·i·ty
in·ter·change·a·ble·ness
in·ter·change·a·bly
in·ter·col·le·gi·ate
in·ter·com
in·ter·com·mu·ni·cate
in·ter·com·mu·ni·cat·ed
in·ter·com·mu·ni·cat·ing
in·ter·com·mu·ni·ca·tion
in·ter·con·nect
in·ter·con·nec·tion
in·ter·con·ti·nen·tal
in·ter·course
in·ter·cul·tur·al
in·ter·cur·rent
in·ter·de·nom·i·na·tion·al
in·ter·de·nom·i·na·tion·al·ism

in·ter·de·part·men·tal
in·ter·de·pend·ent
in·ter·de·pend
in·ter·de·pend·ence
in·ter·de·pend·en·cy
in·ter·dict
in·ter·dic·tion
in·ter·dis·ci·pli·nary
in·ter·est
in·ter·est·ed
in·ter·est·ed·ly
in·ter·est·ing
in·ter·face
in·ter·fa·cial
in·ter·faith
in·ter·fere
in·ter·fered
in·ter·fer·ing
in·ter·fer·ence
in·ter·fer·er
in·ter·fer·ing·ly
in·ter·ga·lac·tic
in·ter·im
in·te·ri·or
in·ter·ject
in·ter·jec·tion
in·ter·jec·tion·al·ly
in·ter·jec·to·ry
In·ter·la·ken
in·ter·lay·er
in·ter·leaf
in·ter·leaves
in·ter·leave
in·ter·leaved
in·ter·leav·ing
in·ter·line
in·ter·lined
in·ter·lin·ing
in·ter·link
in·ter·lock
in·ter·lo·cu·tion
in·ter·loc·u·tor
in·ter·loc·u·to·ry
in·ter·lope
in·ter·loped
in·ter·lop·ing
in·ter·lop·er
in·ter·lude
in·ter·lu·nar
in·ter·lu·na·ry
in·ter·mar·ry
in·ter·mar·ried
in·ter·mar·ry·ing
in·ter·mar·riage
in·ter·me·di·ary
in·ter·me·di·ar·ies
in·ter·me·di·ate
in·ter·me·di·at·ed
in·ter·me·di·at·ing
in·ter·me·di·a·tion
in·ter·me·di·a·tor
in·ter·me·di·a·to·ry
in·ter·mi·na·ble
in·ter·min·gle
in·ter·min·gled

in·ter·min·gling
in·ter·mis·sion
in·ter·mis·sive
in·ter·mit
in·ter·mit·ted
in·ter·mit·ting
in·ter·mit·tence
in·ter·mit·ten·cy
in·ter·mit·tent
in·ter·mit·tent·ly
in·ter·mit·ting·ly
in·ter·mix
in·ter·mix·ture
in·tern
in·tern·ship
in·ter·nal
in·ter·nal·ly
in·ter·nal·ize
in·ter·nal·ized
in·ter·nal·iz·ing
in·ter·nal·i·za·tion
in·ter·na·tion·al
in·ter·na·tion·al·i·ty
in·ter·na·tion·al·ly
in·ter·na·tion·al·ize
in·ter·na·tion·al·ized
in·ter·na·tion·al·iz·ing
in·ter·na·tion·al·i·za·tion
in·ter·na·tion·al·ism
in·tern·ee
in·tern·ist
in·tern·ment
in·ter·of·fice
in·ter·pen·e·trate
in·ter·pen·e·tra·tion
in·ter·plan·e·tary
in·ter·play
in·ter·po·late
in·ter·po·lat·ed
in·ter·po·lat·ing
in·ter·po·la·tion
in·ter·po·la·tive
in·ter·po·la·tor
in·ter·pose
in·ter·posed
in·ter·pos·ing
in·ter·pos·er
in·ter·po·si·tion
in·ter·pret
in·ter·pret·a·ble
in·ter·pret·er
in·ter·pre·tive
in·ter·pre·ta·tion
in·ter·pre·ta·tion·al
in·ter·pre·ta·tive
in·ter·ra·cial
in·ter·re·late
in·ter·re·lat·ed
in·ter·re·lat·ing
in·ter·ro·gate
in·ter·ro·gat·ed
in·ter·ro·gat·ing
in·ter·ro·ga·tion
in·ter·ro·ga·tion·al
in·ter·rog·a·tive

in·ter·ro·ga·tor
in·ter·rupt
in·ter·rup·tion
in·ter·rup·tive
in·ter·rupt·er
in·ter·rupt·or
in·ter·scho·las·tic
in·ter·sect
in·ter·sec·tion
in·ter·space
in·ter·spaced
in·ter·spac·ing
in·ter·sperse
in·ter·spersed
in·ter·spers·ing
in·ter·sper·sion
in·ter·state
in·ter·stel·lar
in·ter·tid·al
in·ter·twine
in·ter·twined
in·ter·twin·ing
in·ter·ur·ban
in·ter·val
in·ter·vene
in·ter·vened
in·ter·ven·ing
in·ter·ven·er
in·ter·ve·nor
in·ter·ven·tion
in·ter·view
in·ter·view·er
in·ter·weave
in·ter·wove
in·ter·weav·ing
in·ter·wo·ven
in·tes·tate
in·tes·tine
in·tes·ti·nal
in·ti·mate
in·ti·mat·ed
in·ti·mat·ing
in·ti·mate·ly
in·ti·ma·tion
in·tim·i·date
in·tim·i·dat·ed
in·tim·i·dat·ing
in·tim·i·da·tion
in·tim·i·da·tor
in·ti·tle
in·ti·tled
in·ti·tling
in·to
in·tol·er·a·ble
in·tol·er·a·bly
in·tol·er·ant
in·tol·er·ance
in·tomb
in·to·mate
in·to·nat·ed
in·to·nat·ing
in·to·na·tion
in·tone
in·toned
in·ton·ing

in·ton·er
in·tox·i·cant
in·tox·i·cate
  in·tox·i·cat·ed
  in·tox·i·cat·ing
  in·tox·i·ca·tion
in·trac·ta·ble
  in·trac·ta·bil·i·ty
in·tra·mu·ral
  in·tra·mu·ral·ly
in·tran·si·gent
  in·tran·si·gence
  in·tran·si·gen·cy
in·tran·si·tive
in·tra·state
in·tra·u·ter·ine
in·tra·ve·nous
in·trench
in·trep·id
  in·tre·pid·i·ty
in·tri·cate
  in·tri·ca·cy
  in·tri·ca·cies
  in·tri·cate·ly
  in·tri·cate·ness
in·trigue
  in·trigued
  in·tri·guing
  in·tri·guer
in·trin·sic
  in·trin·si·cal
  in·trin·si·cal·ly
in·tro·duce
  in·tro·duced
  in·tro·duc·ing
  in·tro·duc·er
  in·tro·duc·tion
  in·tro·duc·to·ry
in·tro·spect
  in·tro·spec·tion
  in·tro·spec·tive
in·tro·ver·sion
  in·tro·ver·sive
in·tro·vert
  in·tro·vert·ed
in·trude
  in·trud·ed
  in·trud·ing
  in·trud·er
in·tru·sion
in·tru·sive
in·trust
in·tu·it
in·tu·i·tion
  in·tu·i·tion·al
in·tu·i·tive
in·un·date
  in·un·dat·ed
  in·un·dat·ing
  in·un·da·tion
  in·un·da·tor
in·ure
  in·ured
  in·ur·ing
in·vade

in·vad·ed
in·vad·ing
in·vad·er
in·va·lid
in·val·id
  in·va·lid·i·ty
in·val·i·date
  in·val·i·dat·ed
  in·val·i·dat·ing
  in·val·i·da·tion
  in·val·i·da·tor
in·va·lid·ism
in·val·u·a·ble
in·var·i·a·ble
  in·var·i·a·bil·i·ty
  in·var·i·a·ble·ness
in·var·i·ant
  in·var·i·ance
in·va·sion
in·va·sive
in·vec·tive
in·veigh
  in·veigh·er
in·vent
  in·vent·a·ble
  in·ven·tor
  in·ven·tion
  in·ven·tive
  in·ven·tive·ness
  in·ven·to·ry
  in·ven·to·ries
  in·ven·to·ried
  in·ven·to·ry·ing
In·ver·ness
in·verse
in·ver·sion
in·vert
  in·ver·te·brate
  in·vert·ed
in·vest
  in·ves·tor
in·ves·ti·gate
  in·ves·ti·gat·ed
  in·ves·ti·gat·ing
  in·ves·ti·ga·tion
  in·ves·ti·ga·tive
  in·ves·ti·ga·tor
in·ves·ti·ture
in·vest·ment
in·vet·er·ate
in·vid·i·ous
in·vig·or·ate
  in·vig·or·at·ed
  in·vig·or·at·ing
  in·vig·or·ant
  in·vig·or·a·tion
  in·vig·or·a·tor
in·vin·ci·ble
  in·vin·ci·bil·i·ty
  in·vin·ci·ble·ness
  in·vin·ci·bly
in·vi·o·la·ble
  in·vi·o·la·bil·i·ty
  in·vi·o·la·bly
in·vi·o·late

in·vis·i·ble
  in·vis·i·bil·i·ty
  in·vis·i·bly
in·vi·ta·tion
  in·vi·ta·tion·al
in·vite
  in·vit·ed
  in·vit·ing
  in·vit·er
in·vo·ca·tion
in·voice
in·voke
  in·voked
  in·vok·ing
in·vol·un·tary
  in·vol·un·tar·i·ly
  in·vol·un·tar·i·ness
in·vo·lute
in·vo·lu·tion
in·volve
  in·volved
  in·volv·ing
  in·volve·ment
  in·volv·er
in·vul·ner·a·ble
in·ward
  in·wards
  in·ward·ly
  in·ward·ness
in·weave
  in·wove
  in·weaved
  in·wov·en
  in·weav·ing
in·wrought
io·dine
ion
  ion·ic
ion·ize
  ion·ized
  ion·iz·ing
  ion·i·za·tion
  ion·iz·er
ion·o·sphere
io·ta
Io·wa
ip·so fac·to
Ips·wich
Ira·ni·an
iras·ci·ble
  iras·ci·bil·i·ty
  iras·ci·ble·ness
  iras·ci·bly
irate
Ire·land
ir·i·des·cent
  ir·i·des·cence
irid·i·um
iris
  iris·es
  ir·i·des
Irish
Irish·man
irk·some
iron

115

iron·er
iron·clad
iron-hand·ed
iron-heart·ed
iron·ic
iron·i·cal
Iron·sides
iron·smith
iron·stone
iron·ware
iron·work
iron·work·er
iro·ny
iro·nies
Ir·o·quois
ir·ra·di·ate
ir·ra·di·at·ed
ir·ra·di·at·ing
ir·ra·di·a·tion
ir·ra·di·a·ter
ir·rad·i·ca·ble
ir·ra·tion·al
ir·ra·tion·al·i·ty
ir·re·claim·a·ble
ir·rec·on·cil·a·ble
ir·rec·on·cil·a·bil·i·ty
ir·re·cov·er·a·ble
ir·re·duc·i·ble
ir·ref·u·ta·ble
ir·re·gard·less
ir·reg·u·lar
ir·reg·u·lar·i·ty
ir·rel·e·vant
ir·rel·e·vance
ir·rel·e·van·cy
ir·re·li·gion
ir·re·li·gious
ir·re·mis·si·ble
ir·re·mov·a·ble
ir·rep·a·ra·ble
ir·re·place·a·ble
ir·re·press·i·ble
ir·re·press·i·bil·i·ty
ir·re·press·i·bly
ir·re·proach·a·ble
ir·re·sist·i·ble
ir·re·sist·i·bil·i·ty
ir·res·o·lute
ir·res·o·lu·tion
ir·re·spec·tive
ir·re·spon·si·ble
ir·re·spon·si·bil·i·ty
ir·re·spon·sive
ir·re·spon·sive·ness
ir·re·triev·a·ble
ir·re·triev·a·bil·i·ty
ir·rev·er·ence
ir·rev·er·ent
ir·re·vers·i·ble
ir·re·vers·i·bil·i·ty
ir·re·vers·i·bly
ir·rev·o·ca·ble
ir·rev·o·ca·bil·i·ty
ir·ri·gate
ir·ri·gat·ed

ir·ri·gat·ing
ir·ri·ga·tion
ir·ri·ga·tor
ir·ri·ta·ble
ir·ri·ta·bil·i·ty
ir·ri·ta·ble·ness
ir·ri·tant
ir·ri·tate
ir·ri·tat·ed
ir·ri·tat·ing
ir·ri·ta·tion
ir·rupt
Ir·ving
Is·a·bel
Isa·iah
Is·car·i·ot
Ish·ma·el
Is·lam
is·lam·ic
Is·lam·ism
Is·lam·a·bad
is·land
is·land·er
isle
is·let
iso·bar
iso·bar·ic
Isoc·ra·tes
iso·gloss
iso·late
iso·lat·ed
iso·lat·ing
iso·la·tion
iso·la·tion·ism
iso·la·tion·ist
iso·met·ric
iso·met·ri·cal
ison·o·my
isos·ce·les
iso·therm
iso·ton·ic
iso·tope
iso·top·ic
Is·ra·el
Is·rae·li
Is·rae·lis
is·su·ance
is·sue
is·sued
is·su·ing
Is·tan·bul
isth·mus
Ital·ian
ital·ic
ital·i·cize
ital·i·cized
ital·i·ciz·ing
ital·i·ci·za·tion
It·a·ly
itch
itch·i·ness
itchy
item
item·ize
item·ized

item·iz·ing
it·er·ate
it·er·at·ed
it·er·at·ing
it·er·a·tion
it·er·a·tive
Ith·a·ca
itin·er·ant
itin·er·ary
itin·er·ar·ies
itin·er·ate
itin·er·at·ed
itin·er·at·ing
itin·er·a·tion
it'll
its
it's
Ivan
I've
ivied
ivo·ry
ivo·ries
ivy
ivies
Iz·mir
jab
jabbed
jab·bing
jab·ber
jab·ber·er
jack·al
jack·ass
jack·boot
jack·et
jack·et·ed
jack-ham·mer
jack-in-the-box
jack-in-the-box·es
jack·knife
jack·knives
jack·knifed
jack·knif·ing
jack-of-all-trades
jack-o'-lan·tern
jack·pot
jack rab·bit
Jack·son
Jack·son·ville
Ja·cob
Ja·co·bus
jac·o·net
jac·quard
jade
jad·ed
jad·ing
Jaf·fa
jag
jagged
jag·ging
jag·uar
jail·bird
jail·break
jail·er
Jai·pur
Ja·i·rus

116

ja·lopy
ja·lop·ies
jal·ou·sie
jam
jammed
jam·ming
jam·mer
Ja·mai·ca
jamb
jam·bo·ree
James·town
jan·gle
jan·gled
jan·gling
jan·gler
jan·gly
jan·i·tor
jan·i·to·ri·al
Jan·sen
Jan·u·ary
Ja·nus
Ja·pan
Jap·a·nese
Jap·a·nese bee·tle
Ja·pheth
jar
jar·ful
jarred
jar·ring
jar·di·niere
Ja·red
jar·gon
jas·mine
Ja·son
jaun·dice
jaun·diced
jaun·dic·ing
jaunt
jaun·ty
jaun·ti·er
jaun·ti·est
jaun·ti·ly
jaun·ti·ness
Ja·va
jave·lin
jaw·bone
jaw·break·er
Jay·cee
jay·walk
jay·walk·er
jazz
jazz·ist
jazz·man
jazzy
jazz·i·er
jazz·i·est
jazz·i·ly
jazz·i·ness
jeal·ous
jeal·ousy
jeal·ous·ies
jeer·er
Jef·fer·son
Je·ho·vah
Je·hu

Jek·yll
jel·li·fy
jel·li·fied
jel·li·fy·ing
Jell·o
jel·ly
jel·lies
jel·lied
jel·ly·ing
jel·ly·like
jel·ly·bean
jel·ly·fish
Je·mi·mah
jen·ny
jen·nies
jeop·ar·dy
jeop·ar·dize
jeop·ar·dized
jeop·ar·diz·ing
Jeph·thah
Jer·e·mi·ah
Jer·i·cho
jerk
jerk·er
jerk·i·ly
jerk·i·ness
jerky
jerk·i·er
jerk·i·est
jer·kin
Jer·o·bo·am
Je·rome
jer·ry·build
jer·ry·built
jer·ry·build·ing
jer·ry·build·er
jer·sey
Je·ru·sa·lem
jes·sa·mine
Jes·se
jest·er
jest·ing
Jes·u·it
Je·sus
jet
jet·ted
jet·ting
jet·lin·er
jet·port
jet·pro·pelled
jet·sam
jet·ti·son
jet·ty
jet·ties
jew·el
jew·eled
jew·el·ing
jew·el·er
jew·el·ry
Jew·ish
Jew·ry
jew's·harp
jews'·harp
Jez·e·bel·
jibe

jibed
jib·ing
jif·fy
jif·fies
jig
jigged
jig·ging
jig·ger
jig·gle
jig·gled
jig·gling
jig·gly
jig·saw
jilt·er
Jim Crow·ism
jim·dan·dy
jim·my
jim·mies
jim·mied
jim·my·ing
jin·gle
jin·gled
jin·gling
jinx
jit·ney
jit·neys
jit·ter
jit·ters
jit·tery
jit·ter·bug
jit·ter·bugged
jit·ter·bug·ging
Jo·ab
Jo·a·chim
job
jobbed
job·bing
job·ber
job·hold·er
jock·ey
jock·eys
jock·eyed
jock·ey·ing
jock·strap
jo·cose
jo·cos·i·ty
joc·u·lar
joc·u·lar·i·ty
joc·und
jo·cun·di·ty
jodh·pur
Jo·el
jog
jogged
jog·ging
jog·ger
jog·gle
jog·gled
jog·gling
Jo·han·nes·burg
John·son
John·ston
Johns·town
join·a·ble
join·er

joint
joint·ed
joint·ly
joist
joke
joked
jok·ing
joke·ster
jok·ing·ly
jok·er
Jo·li·et
jol·ly
jol·li·er
jol·li·est
jol·lied
jol·ly·ing
jolt
jolt·er
jolt·ing·ly
jolty
Jo·nah
Jon·a·than
jon·quil
Jop·lin
Jop·pa
Jor·dan
Jo·seph
Jo·se·phus
Josh·ua
Jo·si·ah
jos·tle
jos·tled
jos·tling
jos·tler
jot
jot·ted
jot·ting
joule
jour·nal
jour·nal·ism
jour·nal·ist
jour·nal·is·tic
jour·ney
jour·ney·man
jour·ney·men
joust
jo·vi·al
jo·vi·al·i·ty
jowl
jowled
jowly
joy·ful
joy·less
joy·ous
joy·ride
Jua·rez
ju·bi·lant
ju·bi·lance
ju·bi·lan·cy
ju·bi·la·tion
ju·bi·late
ju·bi·lat·ed
ju·bi·lat·ing
ju·bi·lee
Ju·dah

Ju·da·ism
Ju·da·ic
Ju·da·i·cal
Ju·das
Ju·dea
judge
judged
judg·ing
Judg·es
judg·ment
judg·men·tal
ju·di·cial
ju·di·ci·ary
ju·di·cious
Ju·dith
ju·do
jug
jugged
jug·ging
jug·ful
jug·ger·naut
jug·gle
jug·gled
jug·gling
jug·gler
Ju·go·sla·via
jug·u·lar
juice
juice·less
juic·er
juicy
juic·i·er
juic·i·est
juic·i·ly
juic·i·ness
ju·jit·su
juke·box
ju·lep
ju·li·enne
Ju·lius
Ju·ly
jum·ble
jum·bled
jum·bling
jum·bo
jum·bos
jump
jump·ing
jump·i·ness
jumpy
jump·er
jump-off
junc·tion
junc·ture
Ju·neau
jun·gle
jun·ior
ju·ni·per
junk
junk·man
junky
jun·ket
junk·ie
jun·ta
Ju·pi·ter

ju·ris·dic·tion
ju·ris·dic·tion·al
ju·ris·pru·dence
ju·ris·pru·dent
ju·ris·pru·den·tial
ju·rist
ju·ris·tic
ju·ror
ju·ry
ju·ries
ju·ry·man
just
just·ly
just·ness
jus·tice
jus·tice·less
jus·tice·like
jus·ti·fi·ca·tion
jus·ti·fy
jus·ti·fied
jus·ti·fy·ing
jus·ti·fi·a·ble
jus·tif·i·ca·to·ry
jut
jut·ted
jut·ting
jute
Jut·land
ju·ve·nes·cence
ju·ve·nes·cent
ju·ve·nile
ju·ve·nil·i·ty
jux·ta·pose
jux·ta·posed
jux·ta·pos·ing
jux·ta·po·si·tion
Kaa·ba
ka·bob
Ka·bul
Ka·byle
Kaf·fir
Kaf·ka
kai·ser
Kal·a·ma·zoo
ka·lei·do·scope
ka·lei·do·scop·ic
ka·lei·do·scop·i·cal
ka·mi·ka·ze
Ka·naka
kan·ga·roo
Kan·sas
ka·o·lin
ka·o·line
ka·pok
ka·put
Ka·ra·chi
kar·at
ka·ra·te
kar·ma
kar·mic
Kar·nak
Kash·mir
Ka·tan·ga
Kat·man·du
ka·ty·did

Ka·u·ai
kay·ak
kayo
  kay·os
kedge
  kedged
  kedg·ing
keel·haul
keel·son
keen·ly
  keen·ness
keep·ing
keep·sake
keg·ler
kelp
Ken·il·worth
Ken·ne·bec
Ken·ne·dy
ken·nel
  ken·neled
  ken·nel·ing
Ken·ny
ke·no
Ken·sing·ton
Kent·ish
Ken·tucky
Ke·nya
Ken·yon
Ke·o·kuk
Kep·ler
ker·a·tin
ker·chief
ker·mis
ker·nel
ker·o·sene
Ker·ry
kes·trel
ketch·up
ke·tone
ket·tle
ket·tle·drum
Ke·wee·naw·an
key
  keyed
key·board
key·hole
key·note
  key·not·ed
  key·not·ing
key·stone
khaki
  khak·is
kha·lif
khan
Khar·toum
Khru·shchev
Khy·ber
kib·butz
  kib·but·zim
kib·itz·er
ki·bosh
kick·back
kick·off
kid
  kid·dish

kid·dish·ness
kid·ded
kid·ding
kid·der
kid·nap
  kid·naped
  kid·napped
  kid·nap·ing
  kid·nap·ping
  kid·nap·er
  kid·nap·per
kid·ney
  kid·neys
Kier·ke·gaard
Ki·ga·la
Kil·i·man·ja·ro
Kil·ken·ny
Kil·lar·ney
kill·deer
kill·ing
kill·joy
kiln
kilo
  kil·os
kil·o·cy·cle
kil·o·gram
kil·o·me·ter
kil·o·ton
kil·o·watt
Kil·pat·rick
kilt
  kilt·er
Kim·ber·ley
ki·mo·no
kin·der·gar·ten
kind·heart·ed
  kind·heart·ed·ness
kin·dle
  kin·dled
  kin·dling
kind·ly
  kind·li·er
  kind·li·est
  kind·li·ness
kin·dred
kin·e·mat·ics
  kin·e·mat·ic
  kin·e·mat·i·cal
kin·e·scope
ki·net·ic
ki·net·ics
kin·folk
king·bird
king·bolt
king·dom
king·fish
king·fish·er
king·ly
  king·li·er
  king·li·est
  king·li·ness
king·pin
king·size
  king·sized
Kings·ley

Kings·ton
kinky
  kink·i·er
  kink·i·est
kins·folk
Kin·sha·sa
kin·ship
kins·man
  kins·men
  kins·wom·an
ki·osk
Kip·ling
kip·per
Kirch·hoff
kir·mess
kis·met
kiss·a·ble
kiss·er
kitch·en
  kitch·en·ette
  kitch·en·ware
kite
  kit·ed
  kit·ing
kitsch
kit·ten
  kit·ten·ish
  kit·ten·ish·ly
kit·ty
  kit·ties
  kit·ty·cor·ner
  Kit·ty·hawk
Ki·wa·nis
ki·wi
klatch
  klatsch
Kleen·ex
klep·to·ma·nia
  klep·to·ma·ni·ac
Klon·dike
knack
knap·sack
knave
  knav·ery
  knav·ish
  knav·ish·ly
knead
knee
  kneed
  knee·ing
  knee·cap
  knee-deep
kneel
  knelt
  kneeled
  kneel·ing
  kneel·er
  knee·pan
knell
knick·ers
knick·er·bock·ers
knick·knack
knife
  knives
  knifed

119

knif·ing
knife-like
knight
 knight·hood
 knight·ly
knight-er·rant
 knights-er·rant
knight-er·rant·ry
knit
 knit·ted
 knit·ting
 knit·ter
knob
 knobbed
 knob·by
 knob·bi·er
 knob·bi·est
knock
 knock·a·bout
 knock·down
 knock·er
 knock-knee
 knock-kneed
 knock-out
knoll
knot
 knot·ted
 knot·ting
 knot·less
 knot·like
 knot·ty
knot·hole
knout
know
 knew
 known
 know·ing
 know·a·ble
 know·er
 know-how
 know·ing·ly
 knowl·edge
 knowl·edge·a·ble
 know-noth·ing
 Knox·ville
knuck·le
 knuck·led
 knuck·ling
knurl
 knurled
 knurly
ko·a·la
ko·bold
Ko·dak
Ko·di·ak
ko·el
ko·gas·in
kohl·ra·bi
 kohl·ra·bies
ko·la
ko·lin·sky
 ko·lin·skies
kook
 kooky
 kook·i·er

kook·i·est
kook·a·bur·ra
ko·peck
Ko·ran
Ko·rea
Kor·sa·koff
ko·ru·na
ko·sher
kou·mis
kow·tow
kra·ken
Krem·lin
kreu·zer
krim·mer
Krish·na
kro·na
kro·ne
kryp·ton
Kua·la Lum·per
Ku·blai Khan
ku·dos
ku·miss
küm·mel
kum·quat
Kuo·min·tang
Ku·wait
Kwa·ja·lein
la·bel
 la·beled
 la·bel·ing
 la·bel·er
la·bi·al
 la·bi·al·ly
la·bi·ate
la·bi·o·den·tal
la·bi·um
la·bia
la·bor
 la·bor·er
lab·o·ra·to·ry
la·bored
la·bo·ri·ous
 la·bo·ri·ous·ly
 la·bo·ri·ous·ness
la·bor·sav·ing
Lab·ra·dor
La Bru·yère
la·bur·num
lab·y·rinth
 lab·y·rin·thine
 lab·y·rin·thi·an
lace
 laced
 lace·like
 lac·er
 lacy
 lac·i·er
 lac·i·est
Lac·e·de·mo·ni·an
lac·er·ate
 lac·er·at·ed
 lac·er·at·ing
 lac·er·a·tion
lace·wing
lach·es

lach·ry·mal
lach·ry·mose
 lach·ry·mose·ly
lac·ing
lack·a·dai·si·cal
 lack·a·dai·si·cal·ly
Lack·a·wan·na
lack·ey
 lack·eyed
 lack·ey·ing
lack·lus·ter
La·co·nia
la·con·ic
 la·con·i·cal·ly
lac·quer
 lac·quer·er
la·crosse
lac·tate
 lac·tat·ed
 lac·tat·ing
lac·ta·tion
lac·te·al
lac·tic
lac·tose
la·cu·na
 la·cu·nas
 la·cu·nae
lad·der
lad·die
lade
 lad·ed
 lad·en
 lad·ing
la·di·da
La·di·no
la·dle
 la·dled
 la·dling
la·dy
 la·dy·bug
 la·dy·fin·ger
 la·dy-in-wait·ing
 la·dy-kil·ler
 la·dy·like
 la·dy·love
 la·dy·ship
 la·dy's-slip·per
La·fay·ette
Laf·fite
La Fol·lette
La Fon·taine
lag
 lagged
 lag·ging
la·ger
lag·gard
la·gniappe
la·goon
La·gos
La Guar·dia
La·hore
la·ic
 la·i·cal
 la·i·cal·ly
lair

laird
lais·sez faire
la·i·ty
  la·i·ties
lake·side
lal·la·tion
la·lop·a·thy
lam
  lammed
  lam·ming
la·ma
La·ma·ism
  La·ma·ist
la·ma·sery
  la·ma·ser·ies
lam·baste
  lam·bast·ed
  lam·bast·ing
lam·bent
  lam·ben·cy
  lam·bent·ly
Lam·beth
lam·bre·quin
lamb·skin
lame
  lam·er
  lam·est
  lamed
  lam·ing
  lame·ly
  lame·ness
la·mé
la·mel·la
  la·mel·las
  la·mel·lae
  la·mel·lar
  lam·el·late
la·ment
  lam·en·ta·ble
  lam·en·ta·bly
  lam·en·ta·tion
lam·i·na
  lam·i·nae
  lam·i·nas
lam·i·nate
  lam·i·nat·ed
  lam·i·nat·ing
  lam·i·na·tion
lamp·black
lam·poon
lam·prey
  lam·preys
Lan·ark
Lan·ca·shire
Lan·cas·ter
lance
  lanced
  lanc·ing
  lance·like
Lan·ce·lot
lan·ce·o·late
lanc·er
lan·cet
lance·wood
lan·dau

land·ed
land·fall
land·hold·er
land·ing
land·la·dy
  land·la·dies
land·locked
land·lord
land·lub·ber
land·mark
land·own·er
  land·own·ing
  land·own·er·ship
land·scape
  land·scaped
  land·scap·ing
  land·scap·er
land·slide
lands·man
Land·sturm
land·ward
  land·wards
lang·syne
lan·guage
lan·guid
  lan·guid·ly
lan·guish
  lan·guish·ing
  lan·guish·ing·ly
lan·guor
  lan·guor·ous
  lan·guor·ous·ly
La·nier
lank·ness
lanky
  lank·i·er
  lank·i·est
  lank·i·ness
lan·o·lin
Lan·sing
Lan·ston
lan·tern
lan·tha·num
lan·yard
La·os
lap
  lapped
  lap·ping
  lap·per
la·pel
lap·ful
  lap·fuls
  laps·ful
lap·i·dary
  lap·i·dar·ies
lap·in
lap·is laz·u·li
La·place
Lap·land
lap·pet
lapse
  lapsed
  laps·ing
La·pu·ta
Lar·a·mie

lar·board
lar·ce·ny
  lar·ce·nies
  lar·ce·nous
larch
lar·der
La·res
large
  larg·er
  larg·est
  large·ness
large·ly
large-scale
lar·gess
lar·ghet·to
  lar·ghet·tos
larg·ish
lar·go
  lar·gos
lar·i·at
lark·spur
La Roche·fou·cauld
lar·rup
lar·va
  lar·vae
  lar·val
lar·yn·gi·tis
lar·ynx
  lar·ynx·es
la·ryn·ges
la·ryn·ge·al
las·civ·i·ous
  las·civ·i·ous·ly
  las·civ·i·ous·ness
la·ser
lash
  lash·ing
  lash·er
las·sie
las·si·tude
las·so
  las·sos
  las·soes
  las·so·er
last·ing
  last·ing·ly
last·ly
Las Ve·gas
latch·key
late
  lat·er
  lat·est
  late·ness
la·teen sail
late·ly
la·tent
  la·ten·cy
  la·tent·ly
lat·er·al
  lat·er·al·ly
la·tex
  la·tex·es
  lat·i·ces
lathe
lath·er

lath·er·er
lath·ery
lath·ing
Lat·in
Lat·in·A·mer·i·can
lat·i·tude
lat·i·tu·di·nal
lat·i·tu·di·nar·i·an
La·tium
La·to·na
la·trine
lat·ter
Lat·ter-day Saint
lat·tice
lat·ticed
lat·tic·ing
lat·tice·work
Lat·via
laud·a·ble
laud·a·bly
lau·da·num
laud·a·to·ry
laud·a·tive
Lau·der
laugh
laugh·er
laugh·ing·ly
laugh·a·ble
laugh·a·bly
laugh·ter
launch
launch·er
laun·der
laun·der·er
laun·dress
laun·der·ette
Laun·dro·mat
laun·dry
laun·dries
laun·dry·man
laun·dry·men
laun·dry·wom·an
laun·dry·wom·en
lau·re·ate
lau·rel
Lau·ren·tian
Lau·ri·er
Lau·sanne
la·va
lav·a·liere
lav·a·to·ry
lav·a·to·ries
lave
laved
lav·ing
lav·en·der
lav·ish
lav·ish·ly
lav·ish·ness
La·voi·sier
law-a·bid·ing
law·break·er
law·break·ing
law·ful
law·ful·ly

law·ful·ness
law·giv·er
law·giv·ing
law·less
law·less·ly
law·less·ness
law·mak·er
law·mak·ing
lawn
Law·rence
law·ren·ci·um
law·suit
law·yer
lax
lax·i·ty
lax·ly
lax·ness
lax·a·tive
lay·er
lay·ette
lay·man
lay·men
lay·off
lay·out
lay·o·ver
Laz·a·rus
laze
lazed
laz·ing
la·zy
la·zi·er
la·zi·est
la·zi·ly
la·zi·ness
la·zy·bones
lea
leach
lead
led
lead·ing
lead·en
lead·en·ly
lead·en·ness
lead·er
lead·er·less
lead·er·ship
leaf·age
leaf·less
leaf·stalk
leafy
leaf·i·er
leaf·i·est
leaf·i·ness
league
leagued
lea·guing
leak
leak·age
leak·i·ness
leaky
leak·i·er
leak·i·est
lean
lean·ly
lean·ness

lean·ing
lean-to
lean-tos
leap
leaped
leapt
leap·ing
leap·er
leap·frog
learn
learned
learnt
learn·ing
learn·er
learn·ed·ly
learn·ed·ness
lease
leased
leas·ing
leash
least·wize
least·ways
leath·er
leath·er·neck
leath·ery
leave
left
leav·ing
leav·er
leav·en
Leav·en·worth
leaves
leave-tak·ing
Leb·a·nese
Leb·a·non
lech·er
lech·er·ous
lech·er·ous·ly
lech·ery
lech·er·ies
lec·tern
lec·ture
lec·tured
lec·tur·ing
lec·tur·er
ledge
ledg·er
leech
leek
leer·ing·ly
leery
lee·ward
lee·way
left-hand·ed
left-hand·ed·ly
left-hand·ed·ness
left·ist
left·o·ver
left-wing
left-wing·er
leg
legged
leg·ging
leg·a·cy
leg·a·cies

le·gal
le·gal·ly
le·gal·ism
le·gal·ist
le·gal·is·tic
le·gal·i·ty
le·gal·i·ties
le·gal·ize
le·gal·ized
le·gal·iz·ing
le·gal·i·za·tion
leg·ate
leg·a·tee
le·ga·tion
le·ga·to
leg·end
leg·end·ary
leg·er·de·main
leg·gy
leg·gi·er
leg·gi·est
leg·horn
leg·i·ble
leg·i·bil·i·ty
leg·i·bly
le·gion
le·gion·ary
le·gion·ar·ies
le·gion·naire
leg·is·late
leg·is·lat·ed
leg·is·lat·ing
leg·is·la·tive
leg·is·la·tor
leg·is·la·tion
leg·is·la·ture
le·git
le·git·i·mate
le·git·i·mat·ed
le·git·i·mat·ing
le·git·i·ma·cy
le·git·i·mate·ly
le·git·i·mist
le·git·i·mize
le·git·i·mized
le·git·i·miz·ing
leg·ume
le·gu·mi·nous
Le·high
lei
leis
Leib·nitz
Leices·ter
Leip·zig
lei·sure
lei·sure·ly
lei·sure·li·ness
leit·mo·tif
lem·ming
lem·on
lem·on·ade
le·mur
lend
lent
lend·ing

lend·er
length
length·en
length·wise
lengthy
length·i·er
length·i·est
length·i·ly
length·i·ness
le·ni·ent
le·ni·ence
le·ni·en·cy
le·ni·ent·ly
Len·in
Len·in·grad
len·i·tive
len·i·ty
Len·ox
lens
Lent·en
len·til
len·to
Leo
Leom·in·ster
le·o·nine
leop·ard
leop·ard·ess
le·o·tard
Le·pan·to
lep·er
lep·i·dop·ter·ous
lep·re·chaun
lep·ro·sy
lep·rous
les·bi·an
les·bi·an·ism
le·sion
Le·sot·ho
les·see
less·en
less·er
les·son
les·sor
least
let·down
le·thal
le·thal·ly
leth·ar·gy
leth·ar·gies
le·thar·gic
le·thar·gi·cal
Le·the
let·ter
let·ter·er
let·tered
let·ter·head
let·ter·ing
let·ter·per·fect
let·ter·press
let·tuce
let·up
leu·ke·mia
leu·ko·cyte
Le·vant
Le·van·tine

lev·ee
lev·el
lev·eled
lev·el·ing
lev·el·er
lev·el·ly
lev·el·ness
lev·el·head·ed
lev·el·head·ed·ness
lev·er
lev·er·age
le·vi·a·than
Le·vi
Le·vis
lev·i·tate
lev·i·tat·ed
lev·i·tat·ing
lev·i·ta·tion
Le·vite
Le·vit·i·cus
lev·i·ty
levy
lev·ies
lev·ied
lev·y·ing
lewd
lewd·ly
lewd·ness
Lew·is
Lew·i·sohn
Lew·is·ton
Lew·is·town
lex·i·cog·ra·phy
lex·i·cog·ra·pher
lex·i·co·graph·ic
lex·i·co·graph·i·cal
lex·i·con
Lex·ing·ton
Ley·den
li·a·bil·i·ty
li·a·bil·i·ties
li·a·ble
li·ai·son
li·ar
li·ba·tion
li·bel
li·beled
li·bel·ing
li·bel·er
li·bel·ous
li·bel·ous·ly
lib·er·al
lib·er·al·ly
lib·er·al·ness
lib·er·al·ism
lib·er·al·i·ty
lib·er·al·i·ties
lib·er·al·ize
lib·er·al·ized
lib·er·al·iz·ing
lib·er·al·i·za·tion
lib·er·ate
lib·er·at·ed
lib·er·at·ing
lib·er·a·tion

lib·er·a·tor
Li·be·ria
lib·er·tar·i·an
lib·er·tine
lib·er·tin·ism
lib·er·ty
lib·er·ties
li·bid·i·nous
li·bid·i·nous·ly
li·bid·i·nous·ness
li·bi·do
li·bid·in·al
Li·bra
li·brar·i·an
li·brary
li·brar·ies
li·bret·to
li·bret·tos
li·bret·ist
Li·bre·ville
Lib·ya
li·cense
li·censed
li·cens·ing
li·cen·see
li·cens·er
li·cen·ti·ate
li·cen·tious
li·cen·tious·ly
li·cen·tious·ness
li·chee
li·chen
lic·it
lick·e·ty-split
lick·spit·tle
lic·o·rice
lid·ded
Lieb·frau·milch
Liech·ten·stein
Lie·der·kranz
lief
liege
lien
lieu
lieu·ten·an·cy
lieu·ten·an·cies
lieu·ten·ant
life·blood
life·boat
life·guard
life·less
life·less·ly
life·less·ness
life·like
life·line
lif·er
life·sav·er
life·size
life·style
life·time
life·work
lift-off
lig·a·ment
lig·a·ture
lig·a·tured

lig·a·tur·ing
light·en
light·er
light-fin·gered
light·foot·ed
light·foot·ed·ly
light·foot·ed·ness
light·head·ed
light·head·ed·ly
light·head·ed·ness
light·heart·ed
light·heart·ed·ly
light·heart·ed·ness
light·house
light·ing
light·ly
light-mind·ed
light-mind·ed·ly
light-mind·ed·ness
light·ning
light·weight
light-year
lig·nite
lig·nit·ic
like
liked
lik·ing
lik·a·ble
like·a·ble
lik·a·ble·ness
like·a·ble·ness
like·li·hood
like·ly
like·li·er
like·li·est
like-mind·ed
lik·en
like·ness
like·wise
lik·ing
li·lac
Lil·li·put
Lil·li·pu·tian
lilt·ing
lily
lil·ies
lil·y-liv·ered
li·ma
limb
lim·ber
lim·ber·ness
lim·bo
Lim·burg·er
lime
limed
lim·ing
limy
lim·i·er
lim·i·est
lime·like
lime·light
lime·light·er
lim·er·ick
lime·stone
lim·it

lim·it·a·ble
lim·i·ta·tive
lim·it·er
lim·it·less
lim·i·ta·tion
lim·it·ed
lim·it·ed·ly
lim·it·ed·ness
Li·moges
lim·ou·sine
limp
limp·er
limp·ing·ly
limp·ly
limp·ness
lim·pet
lim·pid
lim·pid·i·ty
lim·pid·ly
lim·pid·ness
lin·age
Lin·coln
Lind·bergh
lin·den
line
lined
lin·ing
lin·e·age
lin·e·al
lin·e·a·ment
lin·e·ar
lin·e·ar·ly
line·back·er
line·back·ing
line·man
line·men
lin·en
lin·er
line-up
lin·ger
lin·ger·er
lin·ger·ing·ly
lin·ge·rie
lin·go
lin·goes
lin·gua fran·ca
lin·gual
lin·gual·ly
lin·guist
lin·guis·tics
lin·guis·tic
lin·guis·ti·cal
lin·guis·ti·cal·ly
lin·i·ment
lin·ing
link
linked
link·er
link·age
lin·net
li·no·le·um
lin·seed
lint
linty
lint·i·er

lint·i·est
lin·tel
li·on
li·on·ess
li·on·like
Li·o·nel
li·on·heart·ed
li·on·ize
li·on·ized
li·on·iz·ing
li·on·i·za·tion
li·on·iz·er
Lip·pi
lip·py
lip·pi·er
lip·pi·est
lip·stick
liq·ue·fy
liq·ue·fied
liq·ue·fy·ing
liq·ue·fac·tion
liq·ue·fi·a·ble
liq·ue·fi·er
li·queur
liq·uid
li·quid·i·ty
liq·uid·ness
liq·uid·ly
liq·ui·date
liq·ui·dat·ed
liq·ui·dat·ing
liq·ui·da·tion
liq·ui·da·tor
liq·uor
Lis·bon
lisle
lisp
lisp·ing·ly
lis·some
lis·some·ly
lis·some·ness
list
list·ed
lis·ter
list·ing
lis·ten
lis·ten·er
Lis·ter
list·less
list·less·ly
list·less·ness
lit·a·ny
lit·a·nies
li·tchi
li·tchis
li·ter
lit·er·a·cy
lit·er·al
lit·er·al·i·ty
lit·er·al·ness
lit·er·al·ly
lit·er·ary
lit·er·ar·i·ly
lit·er·ar·i·ness
lit·er·ate

lit·er·ate·ly
lit·e·ra·ti
lit·er·a·ture
lithe
lithe·some
lithe·ly
lithe·ness
lith·i·um
lith·o·graph
li·thog·ra·pher
lith·o·graph·ic
lith·o·graph·i·cal·ly
li·thog·ra·phy
Lith·u·a·nia
lit·i·gate
lit·i·gat·ed
lit·i·gat·ing
lit·i·ga·tion
lit·i·ga·tor
lit·mus
lit·ter
lit·ter·bug
lit·tle
lit·tler
lit·tlest
lit·to·ral
lit·ur·gy
lit·ur·gies
lit·ur·gist
li·tur·gic
li·tur·gi·cal
liv·a·ble
live·a·ble
liv·a·ble·ness
live·a·ble·ness
live·li·hood
live·long
live·ly
live·li·er
live·li·est
live·li·ness
liv·en
liv·en·er
liv·er
Liv·er·pool
liv·er·wurst
liv·ery
liv·er·ies
liv·er·ied
liv·er·y·man
liv·er·y·men
live·stock
liv·id
li·vid·i·ty
liv·id·ness
liv·id·ly
liv·ing
liv·ing·ly
liv·ing·ness
Liv·ing·ston
liz·ard
lla·ma
lla·no
lla·nos
load

load·ed
load·er
loaf
loaves
loaf·er
loamy
loath
loath·ness
loathe
loathed
loath·ing
loath·ing·ly
loath·some
loath·some·ly
loath·some·ness
lob
lobbed
lob·bing
lob·by
lob·bies
lob·by·ist
lobe
lo·bar
lo·bate
lobed
lob·ster
lo·cal
lo·cal·ly
lo·cale
lo·cal·i·ty
lo·cal·i·ties
lo·cal·ize
lo·cal·ized
lo·cal·iz·ing
lo·cal·i·za·tion
lo·cate
lo·cat·ed
lo·cat·ing
lo·ca·tor
lo·ca·tion
loch
Loch·in·var
lock·a·ble
lock·er
lock·et
lock·jaw
lock·out
lock·smith
lock·up
lo·co
lo·co·mo·tion
lo·co·mo·tive
lo·co·weed
lo·cus
lo·ci
lo·cust
lo·cu·tion
lode·star
lode·stone
lodge
lodged
lodg·ing
lodg·er
lodg·ment
lofty

loft·i·er
loft·i·est
loft·i·ly
loft·i·ness
lo·gan·ber·ry
lo·gan·ber·ries
log·a·rithm
log·a·rith·mic
log·a·rith·mi·cal
log·a·rith·mi·cal·ly
log·book
loge
log·ger
log·ger·head
log·ic
lo·gi·cian
log·i·cal
log·i·cal·i·ty
log·i·cal·ly
log·i·cal·ness
lo·gis·tics
lo·gis·tic
lo·gis·ti·cal
log·jam
Lo·gos
log·roll·ing
log·roll
lo·gy
lo·gi·er
lo·gi·est
Lo·hen·grin
loin·cloth
loi·ter
loi·ter·er
lol·li·pop
Lom·bard
Lo·me
Lo·mond
Lon·don
Lon·don·der·ry
lone·ly
lone·li·er
lone·li·est
lone·li·ly
lone·li·ness
lon·er
lone·some
lone·some·ly
lone·some·ness
lon·gev·i·ty
Long·fel·low
long·hair
long·hand
long·ing
long·ing·ly
Lon·gi·nus
lon·gi·tude
lon·gi·tu·di·nal
lon·gi·tu·di·nal·ly
long·lived
long·lived·ness
long·play·ing
long·range
long·shore·man
long·shore·men

long·suf·fer·ing
long·suf·fer·ing·ly
long·term
long·wind·ed
long·wind·ed·ly
long·wind·ed·ness
long·wise
look·er·on
look·ers·on
look·out
loony
loon·i·er
loon·i·est
loon·ies
loon·i·ness
loop·hole
loop·holed
loop·hol·ing
loose
loos·er
loos·est
loosed
loos·ing
loose·ly
loose·ness
loos·en
loot·er
lop
lopped
lop·ping
lope
loped
lop·ing
lop·er
Lo·pez
lop·sid·ed
lop·sid·ed·ly
lop·sid·ed·ness
lo·qua·cious
lo·qua·cious·ly
lo·qua·cious·ness
lo·quac·i·ty
lo·quac·i·ties
lord·ly
lord·li·er
lord·li·est
lord·li·ness
lord·ship
lor·gnette
Lor·raine
lor·ry
lor·ries
Los An·ge·les
lose
lost
los·ing
los·a·ble
los·er
Los·sen
lot
lot·ted
lot·ting
Lo·thar·io
Lo·thar·i·os
lo·tion

lot·tery
lot·ter·ies
lot·to
lo·tus
lo·tus·es
lo·tus·eat·er
loud
loud·ly
loud·ness
loud·mouthed
loud·speak·er
Lou·i·si·ana
Lou·is·ville
lounge
lounged
loung·ing
loung·er
louse
lice
lousy
lous·i·er
lous·i·est
lous·i·ly
lous·i·ness
lout
lout·ish
lout·ish·ly
lout·ish·ness
lou·ver
lou·vered
Lou·vre
love
loved
lov·ing
lov·a·ble
love·a·ble
lov·a·bil·i·ty
lov·a·ble·ness
lov·a·bly
love·less
love·bird
love·lorn
love·ly
love·li·er
love·li·est
love·li·ness
lov·er
lov·ing
lov·ing·ly
lov·ing·ness
low·born
low·boy
low·brow
low·down
Low·ell
low·er
low·er·case
low·er·ing
low·er·ing·ly
low·ery
low·key
low·keyed
low·land
low·land·er
low·ly

low·li·er
low·li·est
low·li·ness
low-mind·ed
low-mind·ed·ly
low-mind·ed·ness
loy·al
loy·al·ist
loy·al·ly
loy·al·ty
loy·al·ties
Loy·o·la
loz·enge
Lu·an·da
lu·au
lub·ber
lub·ber·li·ness
lub·ber·ly
Lub·bock
Lu·beck
lu·bri·cant
lu·bri·cate
lu·bri·cat·ed
lu·bri·cat·ing
lu·bri·ca·tion
lu·bri·ca·tive
lu·bri·ca·tor
Lu·cerne
lu·cid
lu·cid·i·ty
lu·cid·ness
lu·cid·ly
Lu·cite
luck
luck·i·ly
luck·i·ness
lucky
luck·i·er
luck·i·est
lu·cra·tive
lu·cra·tive·ly
lu·cra·tive·ness
lu·cre
lu·cu·brate
lu·cu·brat·ed
lu·cu·brat·ing
lu·cu·bra·tion
lu·cu·bra·tor
lu·di·crous
lu·di·crous·ly
lu·di·crous·ness
Lud·wig
Luft·waf·fe
lug
lugged
lug·ging
lug·gage
lug·ger
lug·sail
lu·gu·bri·ous
lu·gu·bri·ous·ly
lu·gu·bri·ous·ness
luke·warm
luke·warm·ly
luke·warm·ness

lull·a·by
lull·a·bies
lum·ba·go
lum·bar
lum·ber
lum·ber·ing·ly
lum·ber·er
lum·ber·ing
lum·ber·jack
lum·ber·man
lum·ber·men
lu·men
lu·mens
lu·mi·na
lu·mi·nary
lu·mi·nar·ies
lu·mi·nes·cence
lu·mi·nes·cent
lu·mi·nous
lu·mi·nos·i·ty
lu·mi·nous·ly
lu·mi·nous·ness
lum·mox
lumpy
lump·i·er
lump·i·est
lump·i·ly
lump·i·ness
lu·na·cy
lu·na·cies
lu·nar
lu·nate
lu·na·tic
lunch
lunch·er
lunch·eon
lunch·room
lunge
lunged
lung·ing
lunk·head
lunk·head·ed
Lu·per·ca·lia
lu·pine
lurch
lure
lured
lur·ing
lu·rid
lu·rid·ly
lu·rid·ness
lurk
lurk·er
lurk·ing·ly
Lu·sa·ka
lus·cious
lus·cious·ly
lus·cious·ness
lush
lush·ly
lush·ness
Lu·si·ta·nia
lust
lust·ful
lust·ful·ly

lust·ful·ness
lus·ter
lus·ter·less
lus·trous
lus·trous·ly
lus·trous·ness
lusty
lust·i·er
lust·i·est
lust·i·ly
lust·i·ness
lu·te·ti·um
Lu·ther
Lu·ther·an
lut·ist
Lux·em·bourg
lux·u·ri·ant
lux·u·ri·ance
lux·u·ri·an·cy
lux·u·ri·ant·ly
lux·u·ri·ate
lux·u·ri·at·ed
lux·u·ri·at·ing
lux·u·ri·a·tion
lux·u·ri·ous
lux·u·ri·ous·ly
lux·u·ri·ous·ness
lux·u·ry
lux·u·ries
ly·cée
ly·ce·um
ly·ing
ly·ing-in
lymph
lym·phoid
lym·phat·ic
lynch
lynch·er
lynch·ing
lynx
lynx·es
lynx-eyed
Ly·ons
lyre
ly·ric
lyr·i·cal
lyr·i·cal·ly
lyr·i·cal·ness
lyr·i·cism
lyr·i·cist
ly·ser·gic
ly·sine
Ly·sol
ma·ca·bre
ma·ca·bre·ly
mac·ad·am
mac·ad·am·ize
mac·ad·am·ized
mac·ad·am·iz·ing
mac·ad·am·i·za·tion
Ma·cao
ma·caque
mac·a·ro·ni
mac·a·roon
Mac·Ar·thur

ma·caw
Mac·beth
mace
  maced
  mac·ing
Mac·e·do·nia
mac·er·ate
  mac·er·at·ed
  mac·er·at·ing
  mac·er·a·tion
  mac·er·a·tor
Mach
ma·chete
Ma·chia·vel·li
Mach·i·a·vel·li·an
  Mach·i·a·vel·li·an·ism
mach·i·nate
  mach·i·nat·ed
  mach·i·nat·ing
  mach·i·na·tion
  mach·i·na·tor
ma·chine
  ma·chined
  ma·chin·ing
  ma·chin·a·bil·i·ty
  ma·chin·a·ble
  ma·chine·like
  ma·chin·ery
  ma·chin·er·ies
  ma·chin·ist
Mac·ken·zie
mack·er·el
Mack·i·nac
mack·i·naw
mack·in·tosh
  mac·in·tosh
MacMil·lan
Ma·con
mac·ra·mé
mac·ro·cosm
  mac·ro·cos·mic
  mac·ro·cos·mi·cal·ly
ma·cron
mad
  mad·der
  mad·dest
  mad·ly
  mad·ness
Mad·a·gas·car
mad·am
  mes·dames
mad·ame
  mes·dames
Ma·da·ria·ga
mad·cap
mad·den
  mad·den·ing
  mad·den·ing·ly
Ma·dei·ra
mad·e·moi·selle
  mad·e·moi·selles
  mes·de·moi·selles
made-up
mad·house
Mad·i·son

mad·man
  mad·men
Ma·don·na
mad·ras
Ma·drid
mad·ri·gal
  mad·ri·gal·ist
Mae·ce·nas
mael·strom
maes·tro
Mae·ter·linck
Maf·e·king
Ma·fia
mag·a·zine
Mag·da·len
Mag·de·burg
Ma·gel·lan
ma·gen·ta
Mag·gio·re
mag·got
  mag·goty
Ma·gi
  Ma·gus
mag·ic
  mag·i·cal
  mag·i·cal·ly
ma·gi·cian
Ma·gi·not
mag·is·te·ri·al
  mag·is·te·ri·al·ly
  mag·is·te·ri·al·ness
mag·is·tra·cy
  mag·is·tra·cies
mag·is·trate
mag·ma
  mag·mas
  mag·ma·ta
  mag·mat·ic
Mag·na Car·ta
mag·nan·i·mous
  mag·nan·i·mous·ly
  mag·nan·i·mous·ness
  mag·na·nim·i·ty
  mag·na·nim·i·ties
mag·nate
mag·ne·sia
  mag·ne·sian
  mag·ne·si·um
mag·net
  mag·net·ic
  mag·net·i·cal·ly
  mag·net·ism
  mag·net·ize
  mag·net·ized
  mag·net·iz·ing
  mag·net·iz·a·ble
  mag·net·i·za·tion
  mag·net·iz·er
mag·ne·to
  mag·ne·tos
mag·ne·tom·e·ter
  mag·ne·to·met·ric
  mag·ne·tom·e·try
Mag·nif·i·cat
mag·nif·i·cent

mag·nif·i·cence
mag·nif·i·cent·ly
mag·ni·fy
  mag·ni·fied
  mag·ni·fy·ing
  mag·ni·fi·a·ble
  mag·ni·fi·ca·tion
  mag·ni·fi·er
mag·ni·tude
mag·no·lia
mag·num
mag·pie
mag·uey
Mag·yar
Ma·ha·bha·ra·ta
Ma·han
ma·ha·ra·jah
ma·ha·ra·ni
ma·hat·ma
  ma·hat·ma·ism
mah-jongg
ma·hog·a·ny
  ma·hog·a·nies
Ma·hom·et
ma·hout
Mah·rat·ta
maid·en
maid·en·hair
maid·en·head
maid·ser·vant
mail·a·ble
mail·box
mail·man
  mail·men
maim
  maim·er
Mai·mon·i·des
Main·er
main·land
  main·land·er
main·ly
main·mast
main·sail
main·spring
main·stream
main·tain
  main·tain·a·ble
main·te·nance
mai·tre d'hô·tel
  mai·tres d'hô·tel
maize
maj·es·ty
  maj·es·ties
ma·jes·tic
ma·jes·ti·cal
ma·jes·ti·cal·ly
ma·jol·i·ca
ma·jor
Ma·jor·ka
ma·jor-do·mo
  ma·jor-do·mos
ma·jor·i·ty
  ma·jor·i·ties
Ma·kas·sar
make

mak·a·ble
ma·ker
mak·ing
make-be·lieve
make·shift
make-up
Mal·a·bar
Ma·lac·ca
Mal·a·chi
mal·a·dapt·ed
mal·ad·just·ment
mal·ad·just·ed
mal·ad·min·is·ter
mal·ad·min·is·tra·tion
mal·a·droit
mal·a·droit·ly
mal·a·droit·ness
mal·a·dy
mal·a·dies
Mal·a·ga
Mal·a·gasy
ma·laise
mal·a·prop
mal·a·prop·ism
ma·lar·ia
ma·lar·i·al
ma·lar·i·an
ma·lar·i·ous
ma·lar·key
Mal·a·wi
Ma·laya
Ma·lay·sia
Mal·colm
mal·con·tent
Mal·dive
mal·e·dict
mal·e·dic·tion
mal·e·dic·to·ry
mal·e·fac·tion
mal·e·fac·tor
ma·lev·o·lent
ma·lev·o·lence
ma·lev·o·lent·ly
mal·fea·sance
mal·fea·sant
mal·for·ma·tion
mal·formed
mal·func·tion
Ma·li
mal·ice
ma·li·cious
ma·li·cious·ly
ma·li·cious·ness
ma·lign
ma·lign·er
ma·lign·ly
ma·lig·nant
ma·lig·nan·cy
ma·lig·nan·cies
ma·lig·nant·ly
Ma·lines
ma·lin·ger
ma·lin·ger·er
mal·lard
mal·le·a·ble

mal·le·a·bil·i·ty
mal·le·a·ble·ness
mal·let
mal·low
mal·nour·ished
mal·nu·tri·tion
mal·oc·clu·sion
mal·o·dor
mal·o·dor·ous
mal·o·dor·ous·ly
mal·o·dor·ous·ness
mal·prac·tice
mal·prac·ti·tion·er
malt
malty
malt·i·er
malt·i·est
Mal·ta
Mal·tese
mal·treat
mal·treat·ment
Mam·e·luke
mam·ma
ma·ma
mam·mal
mam·ma·li·an
mam·ma·ry
mam·ma·ries
mam·mon
mam·moth
mam·my
mam·mies
man
manned
man·ning
man·a·cle
man·a·cled
man·a·cling
man·age
man·aged
man·ag·ing
man·age·a·ble
man·age·a·bil·i·ty
man·age·a·ble·ness
man·age·a·bly
man·age·ment
man·ag·er
man·ag·er·ship
man·a·ge·ri·al
man·a·ge·ri·al·ly
Ma·na·gua
ma·ña·na
Ma·nas·sas
Ma·nas·seh
man·a·tee
Man·ches·ter
Man·chu·ko
Man·chu·ria
man·da·la
Man·da·lay
man·da·rin
man·date
man·dat·ed
man·dat·ing
man·da·to·ry

man·da·to·ries
man·da·to·ri·ly
Man·de·ville
man·di·ble
man·dib·u·lar
man·dib·u·lary
man·dib·u·late
man·do·lin
man·do·lin·ist
man·drake
man·drill
man-eat·er
man-eat·ing
Ma·net
ma·neu·ver
ma·neu·ver·a·bil·i·ty
ma·neu·ver·a·ble
ma·neu·ver·er
man·ful
man·ful·ly
man·ful·ness
man·ga·nese
mange
man·ger
man·gle
man·gled
man·gling
man·go
man·goes
man·gos
man·grove
man·gy
man·gi·er
man·gi·est
man·gi·ly
man·gi·ness
man·han·dle
man·han·dled
man·han·dling
Man·hat·tan
man·hole
man·hood
man-hour
man·hunt
man·hunt·er
ma·nia
man·ic
ma·ni·ac
ma·ni·a·cal
ma·ni·a·cal·ly
man·ic-de·pres·sive
Man·i·che·an
man·i·cure
man·i·cured
man·i·cur·ing
man·i·cur·ist
man·i·fest
man·i·fest·er
man·i·fest·ly
man·i·fes·ta·tion
man·i·fes·to
man·i·fes·tos
man·i·fes·toes
man·i·fold
man·i·fold·er

man·i·fold·ly
man·i·fold·ness
man·i·kin
man·a·kin
man·ni·kin
ma·nila
ma·nil·la
ma·nip·u·late
ma·nip·u·lat·ed
ma·nip·u·lat·ing
ma·nip·u·la·ble
ma·nip·u·la·tion
ma·nip·u·la·tive
ma·nip·u·la·tor
ma·nip·u·la·to·ry
Man·i·to·ba
man·kind
man·like
man·ly
man·li·er
man·li·est
man·li·ness
man·made
man·na
man·ne·quin
man·ner
man·nered
man·ner·ism
man·ner·ly
man·ner·li·ness
man·nish
man·of·war
men·of·war
ma·nom·e·ter
man·or
ma·no·ri·al
man·pow·er
man·sard
man·serv·ant
man·sion
man·sized
man·slaugh·ter
man·slay·er
man·slay·ing
man·tel
man·tle
man·til·la
man·tle
man·tled
man·tling
man·trap
Man·tua
man·u·al
man·u·al·ly
man·u·fac·ture
man·u·fac·tured
man·u·fac·tur·ing
man·u·fac·tur·a·ble
man·u·fac·tur·al
man·u·fac·tur·er
ma·nure
man·u·script
many
man·y·sid·ed
Mao Tse·tung

map
mapped
map·ping
map·per
ma·ple
mar
marred
mar·ring
ma·ra·ca
Mar·a·cai·bo
mar·a·schi·no
Ma·ra·tha
mar·a·thon
ma·raud
ma·raud·er
mar·ble
mar·bled
mar·bling
mar·ble·ize
mar·ble·ized
mar·ble·iz·ing
mar·bly
Mar·ble·head
Mar·burg
mar·cel
mar·celled
mar·cel·ling
march·er
mar·chion·ess
Mar·co·ni
Mar·co Po·lo
Mar·di gras
Ma·ren·go
mare's·tail
mar·ga·rine
mar·gin
mar·gi·nal
mar·gi·na·lia
mar·gin·al·i·ty
mar·gin·al·ly
mar·gin·ate
mar·gin·at·ed
mar·gin·at·ing
mar·gin·a·tion
Mar·got
mar·gue·rite
Ma·ria
Mar·i·co·pa
mar·i·cul·ture
mar·i·gold
ma·ri·jua·na
ma·rim·ba
ma·ri·na
mar·i·nade
mar·i·nad·ed
mar·i·nad·ing
mar·i·nate
mar·i·nat·ed
mar·i·nat·ing
mar·i·na·tion
ma·rine
mar·i·ner
Ma·ri·nist
mar·i·on·ette
Ma·ri·tain

mar·i·tal
mar·i·time
mar·jo·ram
marked
mark·ed·ly
mark·er
mar·ket
mar·ket·er
mar·ket·a·ble
mar·ket·a·bil·i·ty
mar·ket·ing
mar·ket·place
Mark·ham
mark·ing
marks·man
marks·men
marks·man·ship
Marl·bor·ough
mar·lin
Mar·lowe
mar·ma·lade
Mar·mi·on
mar·mo·set
mar·mot
ma·roon
mar·quee
Mar·quette
mar·quis
mar·quis·es
mar·quess
mar·quise
mar·quis·es
mar·riage
mar·riage·a·ble
mar·riage·a·bil·i·ty
mar·ried
mar·row
mar·rowy
mar·row·bone
mar·ry
mar·ried
mar·ry·ing
Mar·seilles
mar·shal
mar·shaled
mar·shal·ing
marsh·mal·low
marshy
marsh·i·er
marsh·i·est
marsh·i·ness
mar·su·pi·al
mar·tial
Mar·tian
mar·tin
Mar·ti·neau
mar·ti·ni
mar·ti·nis
Mar·ti·nique
mar·tyr
mar·tyr·ize
mar·tyr·ized
mar·tyr·iz·ing
mar·tyr·dom
mar·vel

mar·veled
mar·vel·ing
mar·vel·ous
mar·vel·ous·ly
Marx·ism
Marx·ist
Marx·i·an
Mary
Mary·land
mar·zi·pan
Ma·sa·ryk
mas·cara
mas·cot
mas·cu·line
mas·cu·line·ness
mas·cu·lin·i·ty
mas·cu·lin·ize
mas·cu·lin·ized
mas·cu·lin·iz·ing
Mas·eru
mash·er
mask
mask·like
masked
mas·och·ism
mas·och·ist
mas·och·is·tic
ma·son
ma·son·ic
Ma·son·ite
ma·son·ry
ma·son·ries
masque
mas·quer·ade
mas·quer·ad·ed
mas·quer·ad·ing
mas·quer·ad·er
Mas·sa·chu·setts
mas·sa·cre
mas·sa·cred
mas·sa·cring
mas·sa·crer
mas·sage
mas·saged
mas·sag·ing
mas·sag·er
mas·sag·ist
mas·seur
mas·seuse
mas·seus·es
mas·sive
mass·pro·duce
mass·pro·duced
mass·pro·duc·ing
mass·pro·duc·er
mass·pro·duc·tion
massy
mass·i·er
mass·i·est
mass·i·ness
mas·tec·to·my
mas·tec·to·mies
mas·ter
mas·ter·ful
mas·ter·mind

mas·ter·piece
mas·tery
mas·ter·ies
mast·head
mas·tic
mas·ti·cate
mas·ti·ca·ted
mas·ti·ca·ting
mas·ti·ca·ble
mas·ti·ca·tion
mas·ti·ca·tor
mas·tiff
mas·to·don
mas·toid
mas·tur·bate
mas·tur·bat·ed
mas·tur·bat·ing
mas·tur·ba·tion
mat
mat·ted
mat·ting
mat·a·dor
match·book
match·mak·er
match·mak·ing
mate
mat·ed
mat·ing
mate·less
ma·te·ri·al
ma·te·ri·al·ly
ma·te·ri·al·ism
ma·te·ri·al·ist
ma·te·ri·al·is·tic
ma·te·ri·al·is·ti·cal·ly
ma·te·ri·al·ize
ma·te·ri·al·ized
ma·te·ri·al·iz·ing
ma·te·ri·el
ma·ter·nal
ma·ter·nal·ism
ma·ter·nal·is·tic
ma·ter·nal·ly
ma·ter·ni·ty
ma·ter·ni·ties
math·e·mat·i·cal
math·e·mat·ic
math·e·mat·i·cal·ly
math·e·ma·ti·cian
math·e·mat·ics
Math·er
ma·tin
mat·in·al
mat·i·nee
ma·tri·arch
ma·tri·ar·chal·ism
ma·tri·ar·chy
ma·tri·ar·chies
mat·ri·cide
ma·tric·u·lant
ma·tric·u·late
ma·tric·u·lat·ed
ma·tric·u·lat·ing
ma·tric·u·la·tion
ma·tri·lin·e·al

mat·ri·mo·ny
mat·ri·mo·nies
mat·ri·mo·ni·al
ma·trix
ma·tri·ces
ma·trix·es
ma·tron
ma·tron·ly
mat·ter
Mat·ter·horn
mat·ter·of·course
mat·ter·of·fact
mat·ter·of·fact·ly
mat·ter·of·fact·ness
Mat·thew
Mat·thi·as
mat·ting
mat·tress
mat·u·rate
mat·u·rat·ed
mat·u·rat·ing
mat·u·ra·tion
ma·ture
ma·tu·ri·ty
mat·zo
mat·zoth
mat·zos
maud·lin
Ma·ui
Mau·re·ta·nia
Mau·ri·ti·us
mau·so·le·um
mau·so·le·ums
mau·so·lea
mauve
mav·er·ick
mawk·ish
max·im
max·i·mal
max·i·mal·ly
Max·i·mil·ian
max·i·mize
max·i·mized
max·i·miz·ing
max·i·mum
max·i·mums
max·i·ma
Ma·ya
may·be
May·day
may·flow·er
may·fly
may·flies
may·hem
may·on·naise
may·or
may·or·al
may·or·al·ty
may·or·al·ties
May·time
maze
mazed
maz·ing
ma·zy
ma·zi·er

ma·zi·est
ma·zi·ly
ma·zi·ness
Mba·ba·ne
Mc·Coy
McKin·ley
mead·ow
mead·ow·lark
mea·ger
 mea·ger·ly
 mea·ger·ness
meal·time
meal·worm
mealy
 meal·i·er
 meal·i·est
 meal·i·ness
meal·y-mouthed
mean
 mean·ing
 mean·ly
 mean·ness
me·an·der
mean·ing·ful
 mean·ing·ful·ly
mean·ing·less
 mean·ing·less·ly
 mean·ing·less·ness
meant
mean·time
mean·while
mea·sles
mea·sly
 mea·sli·er
 mea·sli·est
meas·ur·a·ble
 meas·ur·a·bil·i·ty
 meas·ur·a·bly
meas·ure
 meas·ur·er
meas·ured
 meas·ure·ment
meat-and-po·ta·toes
meaty
 meat·i·er
 meat·i·est
 meat·i·ness
mec·ca
me·chan·ic
me·chan·i·cal
 me·chan·i·cal·ly
me·chan·ics
mech·an·ism
mech·a·nis·tic
 mech·a·nis·ti·cal·ly
mech·a·nize
 mech·a·nized
 mech·a·niz·ing
 mech·a·ni·za·tion
 mech·a·niz·er
med·al
 med·aled
 med·al·ing
 me·dal·lic
 me·dal·lion

med·dle
 med·dled
 med·dling
 med·dler
 med·dle·some
Me·dea
me·dia
me·di·al
me·di·an
 me·di·an·ly
me·di·ate
 me·di·at·ed
 me·di·at·ing
 me·di·a·tion
 me·di·a·tive
 me·di·a·to·ry
 me·di·a·tor
med·ic
med·i·ca·ble
 med·i·ca·bly
Med·i·caid
med·i·cal
 med·i·cal·ly
me·dic·a·ment
Med·i·care
med·i·cate
 med·i·cat·ed
 med·i·cat·ing
 med·i·ca·tion
Med·i·ci
me·dic·i·nal
 me·dic·i·nal·ly
med·i·cine
 med·i·cined
 med·i·cin·ing
med·i·co
me·di·e·val
 me·di·e·val·ism
Me·di·na
me·di·o·cre
me·di·oc·ri·ty
 me·di·oc·ri·ties
med·i·tate
 med·i·tat·ed
 med·i·tat·ing
 med·i·tat·ing·ly
 med·i·ta·tor
med·i·ta·tion
 med·i·ta·tive
med·i·ter·ra·ne·an
me·di·um
 me·dia
 me·di·ums
med·ley
 med·leys
meet·ing
 meet·ing·house
meg·a·city
 meg·a·cit·ies
meg·a·cy·cle
meg·a·lo·ma·nia
 meg·a·lo·ma·ni·ac
 meg·a·lo·ma·ni·a·cal
meg·a·lop·o·lis
 meg·a·lo·pol·i·tan

meg·a·phone
 meg·a·phoned
 meg·a·phon·ing
meg·a·ton
meg·a·watt
mei·o·sis
 mei·ot·ic
mel·a·mine
mel·an·cho·lia
 mel·an·cho·li·ac
mel·an·choly
 mel·an·chol·ies
 mel·an·chol·ic
 mel·an·chol·i·cal·ly
 mel·an·chol·i·ty
 mel·an·chol·i·ness
Mel·a·ne·sia
mé·lange
mel·a·nin
mel·a·no·ma
 mel·a·no·mas
 mel·a·no·ma·ta
Mel·ba
Mel·bourne
Mel·chi·or
me·lee
mel·io·rate
 mel·io·rat·ed
 mel·io·rat·ing
 mel·io·ra·ble
 mel·io·ra·tion
 mel·io·ra·tor
mel·lif·lu·ous
 mel·lif·lu·ent
 mel·lif·lu·ous·ly
mel·low
me·lo·de·on
mel·o·dra·ma
 mel·o·dra·mat·ic
 mel·o·dra·mat·i·cal·ly
 mel·o·dra·mat·ics
mel·o·dy
 mel·o·dies
me·lod·ic
 me·lod·i·cal·ly
me·lo·di·ous
 me·lo·di·ous·ness
mel·on
Mel·rose
melt
 melt·ed
 melt·ing
 melt·a·bil·i·ty
 melt·a·ble
 melt·er
Mel·ville
mem·ber
 mem·bered
 mem·ber·less
 mem·ber·ship
mem·brane
 mem·bra·nous
me·men·to
 me·men·tos
 me·men·toes

Mem·non
memo
mem·oir
mem·o·ra·bil·ia
mem·o·ra·ble
mem·o·ra·bly
mem·o·ran·dum
mem·o·ran·dums
mem·o·ran·da
me·mo·ri·al
me·mo·ri·al·ly
me·mo·ri·al·ize
me·mo·ri·al·ized
me·mo·ri·al·iz·ing
me·mo·ri·al·i·za·tion
me·mo·ri·al·iz·er
me·mo·ri·al·ly
mem·o·rize
mem·o·rized
mem·o·riz·ing
mem·o·riz·a·ble
mem·o·ri·za·tion
mem·o·ry
mem·o·ries
Mem·phis
men·ace
men·aced
men·ac·ing
mé·nage
me·nag·er·ie
mend
mend·a·ble
men·da·cious
men·da·cious·ly
men·da·cious·ness
men·dac·i·ty
Men·del
men·de·le·vi·um
men·di·cant
me·ni·al
me·ni·al·ly
me·nin·ges
men·in·gi·tis
me·nis·cus
me·nis·cus·es
me·nis·ci
Men·no·nite
men·o·pause
men·o·pau·sal
me·nor·ah
men·sal
men·ses
men·stru·al
men·stru·a·tion
men·stru·ate
men·stru·at·ed
men·stru·at·ing
men·sur·a·ble
men·tal
men·tal·ly
men·tal·i·ty
men·tal·i·ties
men·thol
men·tho·lat·ed
men·tion

men·tion·a·ble
men·tion·er
men·tor
menu
me·ow
me·pro·ba·mate
mer·can·tile
mer·can·til·ism
mer·can·til·ist
mer·ce·nary
mer·ce·nar·ies
mer·ce·nar·i·ly
mer·cer·ize
mer·cer·ized
mer·cer·iz·ing
mer·chan·dise
mer·chan·dised
mer·chan·dis·ing
mer·chan·dis·er
mer·chant
mer·chant·man
mer·chant·men
mer·cu·ri·al
Mer·cu·ro·chrome
mer·cu·ry
mer·cu·ries
mer·cy
mer·cies
mer·ci·ful
mer·ci·ful·ly
mer·ci·less
mere·ly
mer·e·tri·cious
mer·e·tri·cious·ly
mer·e·tri·cious·ness
merge
merged
merg·ing
mer·gence
merg·er
Mer·i·den
me·rid·i·an
me·rid·i·o·nal
me·ringue
mer·it
mer·i·ted
mer·it·ed·ly
mer·it·less
mer·i·to·ri·ous
mer·maid
mer·man
mer·men
Mer·ri·mac
mer·ri·ment
mer·ry
mer·ri·er
mer·ri·est
mer·ri·ness
mer·ry-go-round
mer·ry·mak·er
mer·ry·mak·ing
me·sa
mes·cal
mes·dames
mes·de·moi·selles

mesh·work
me·si·al
mes·mer·ism
mes·mer·ic
mes·mer·i·cal·ly
mes·mer·ist
mes·mer·ize
mes·mer·ized
mes·mer·iz·ing
mes·mer·i·za·tion
mes·mer·iz·er
mes·o·morph
mes·o·mor·phic
mes·o·mor·phism
mes·o·mor·phy
me·son
Mes·o·po·ta·mia
mes·o·sphere
Meso·zo·ic
mes·quite
mess
mess·i·ly
mess·i·ness
messy
mess·i·er
mess·i·est
mes·sage
mes·sen·ger
Mes·si·ah
Mes·si·an·ic
mes·ti·zo
me·tab·o·lism
met·a·bol·ic
met·a·bol·i·cal
me·tab·o·lize
me·tab·o·lized
me·tab·o·liz·ing
met·al
met·aled
met·al·ing
met·al·ize
met·al·ized
met·al·iz·ing
me·tal·lic
me·tal·li·cal·ly
met·al·loid
met·al·lur·gy
met·al·lur·gic
met·al·lur·gi·cal
met·al·lur·gi·cal·ly
met·al·lur·gist
met·al·work
met·al·work·er
met·al·work·ing
met·a·mor·phism
met·a·mor·phic
met·a·mor·phose
met·a·mor·phosed
met·a·mor·phos·ing
met·a·mor·pho·sis
met·a·mor·pho·ses
met·a·phor
met·a·phor·ic
met·a·phor·i·cal
met·a·phys·ic

met·a·phys·ics
met·a·phys·i·cal
met·a·tar·sus
met·a·tar·si
met·a·tar·sal
met·a·zo·an
met·a·zo·al
met·a·zo·ic
mete
met·ed
met·ing
me·te·or
me·te·or·ic
me·te·or·ite
me·te·or·it·ic
me·te·or·oid
me·te·or·ol·o·gy
me·te·or·o·log·i·cal
me·te·or·o·log·i·cal·ly
me·te·or·ol·o·gist
me·ter
me·tre
me·ter-kil·o·gram-sec·ond
meth·a·done
meth·ane
meth·a·nol
meth·od
me·thod·i·cal
me·thod·i·cal·ly
Meth·od·ist
meth·od·ize
meth·od·ized
meth·od·iz·ing
meth·od·iz·er
meth·od·ol·o·gy
meth·od·ol·o·gies
meth·od·o·log·i·cal
meth·od·ol·o·gist
Me·thu·se·lah
me·tic·u·lous
me·tic·u·los·i·ty
me·tic·u·lous·ly
mé·tier
mé·tis
met·ric
met·ri·cal
met·ri·cal·ly
met·ri·fi·ca·tion
met·ro
met·ro·nome
met·ro·nom·ic
me·trop·o·lis
met·ro·pol·i·tan
met·ro·pol·i·tan·ism
Met·ter·nich
met·tle
met·tle·some
Mex·i·can
Mex·i·co
Mey·er·beer
mez·za·nine
mez·zo
Mi·ami
mi·as·ma
mi·as·mas

mi·as·ma·ta
mi·as·mal
mi·as·mat·ic
mi·as·mic
mi·ca
Mi·chel·an·ge·lo
Mich·i·gan
mi·crobe
mi·cro·bi·al
mi·cro·bi·an
mi·cro·bic
mi·cro·bi·ol·o·gy
mi·cro·bi·o·log·i·cal
mi·cro·bi·ol·o·gist
mi·cro·copy
mi·cro·cop·ies
mi·cro·cosm
mi·cro·cos·mos
mi·cro·cos·mic
mi·cro·cos·mi·cal
mi·cro·film
mi·cro·gram
mi·cro·groove
mi·crom·e·ter
mi·crom·e·try
mi·cro·mi·cron
mi·cro·mil·li·me·ter
mi·cron
mi·crons
mi·cra
mi·cro·or·gan·ism
mi·cro·phone
mi·cro·phon·ic
mi·cro·pho·to·graph
mi·cro·pho·to·graph·ic
mi·cro·pho·tog·ra·phy
mi·cro·read·er
mi·cro·scope
mi·cro·scop·ic
mi·cro·scop·i·cal
mi·cro·scop·i·cal·ly
mi·cros·co·py
mi·cros·co·pist
mi·cro·sec·ond
mi·cro·wave
Mi·das
mid·day
mid·dle
mid·dled
mid·dling
mid·dle-aged
mid·dle·man
mid·dle·men
mid·dle·most
mid·dle·weight
mid·dy
mid·dies
midg·et
Mid·i·an
mid·land
mid·line
Mid·lo·thi·an
mid·most
mid·night
mid·point

mid·riff
mid·sec·tion
mid·ship
mid·ship·man
  mid·ship·men
midst
mid·sum·mer
mid·term
mid·way
mid·wife
  mid·wives
mid·wife·ry
mid·year
mien
mighty
  might·i·er
  might·i·est
  might·i·ly
  might·i·ness
mi·graine
mi·grant
mi·grate
  mi·grat·ed
  mi·grat·ing
  mi·gra·tion
  mi·gra·tor
  mi·gra·to·ry
mi·la·dy
  mi·la·dies
Mi·lan
mild
  mild·ly
  mild·ness
mil·dew
  mil·dewy
mile·age
mil·er
mile·stone
mi·lieu
  mi·lieus
mil·i·tant
  mil·i·tan·cy
  mil·i·tant·ness
mil·i·ta·rism
  mil·i·ta·ris·tic
  mil·i·ta·ris·ti·cal·ly
  mil·i·ta·rize
  mil·i·ta·rized
  mil·i·ta·riz·ing
  mil·i·ta·ri·za·tion
mil·i·tary
  mil·i·tar·i·ly
mi·li·tia
milk
  milk·er
  milky
  milk·i·er
  milk·i·est
  milk·maid
  milk·man
  milk·men
  milk·weed
Mil·lay
mill·board
mil·len·ni·um

mil·len·nia
mil·len·ni·al
mill·er
mil·let
mil·li·am·pere
mil·li·bar
mil·li·gram
mil·li·li·ter
mil·li·me·ter
mil·li·mi·cron
mil·li·ner
mil·li·nery
mill·ing
mil·lion
  mil·lionth
mil·lion·aire
mil·li·sec·ond
mill·pond
mill·run
mill·stone
mill·stream
mi·lord
milt
Mil·wau·kee
mime
  mimed
  mim·ing
  mim·er
mim·e·o·graph
mim·ic
  mim·icked
  mim·ick·ing
  mim·i·cal
  mim·ick·er
mim·ic·ry
  mim·ic·ries
min·a·ble
mine·a·ble
min·a·ret
mince
  minced
  minc·ing
  minc·er
  minc·ing·ly
mince·meat
mind·ed
mind·less
  mind·less·ly
  mind·less·ness
min·er
mine·field
min·er·al
min·er·al·ize
  min·er·al·ized
  min·er·al·iz·ing
  min·er·al·i·za·tion
min·er·al·o·gy
  min·er·al·og·i·cal
  min·er·al·o·gist
min·e·stro·ne
mine·sweep·er
  mine·sweep·ing
min·gle
  min·gled
  min·gling

min·i·a·ture
  min·i·a·tur·ize
  min·i·a·tur·ized
  min·i·a·tur·iz·ing
  min·i·a·tur·i·za·tion
min·im
min·i·mal
  min·i·mal·ly
min·i·mize
  min·i·mized
  min·i·miz·ing
  min·i·mi·za·tion
  min·i·miz·er
min·i·mum
  min·i·mums
  min·i·ma
min·ing
min·ion
min·is·ter
  min·is·te·ri·al
min·is·trant
min·is·tra·tion
min·is·try
  min·is·tries
Min·ne·ap·o·lis
Min·ne·so·ta
min·now
mi·nor
mi·nor·i·ty
  mi·nor·i·ties
min·strel
mint·age
mint·er
min·u·end
mi·nus
mi·nus·cule
min·ute
  min·ut·ed
  min·ut·ing
mi·nute
  mi·nut·er
  mi·nut·est
min·ute·man
  min·ute·men
mi·nu·tia
  mi·nu·ti·ae
minx
mir·a·cle
mi·rac·u·lous
mi·rage
mire
  mired
  mir·ing
mir·ror
mirth
  mirth·ful
  mirth·ful·ly
  mirth·ful·ness
  mirth·less
mis·ad·ven·ture
mis·ad·vise
  mis·ad·vised
  mis·ad·vis·ing
mis·al·li·ance
mis·an·thrope

mis·an·thro·pist
mis·an·throp·ic
mis·an·throp·i·cal
mis·an·thro·py
mis·ap·ply
mis·ap·plied
mis·ap·ply·ing
mis·ap·pli·ca·tion
mis·ap·pre·hend
mis·ap·pre·hen·sion
mis·ap·pro·pri·ate
mis·ap·pro·pri·at·ed
mis·ap·pro·pri·at·ing
mis·ap·pro·pri·a·tion
mis·be·have
mis·be·haved
mis·be·hav·ing
mis·be·hav·er
mis·be·ha·vior
mis·cal·cu·late
mis·cal·cu·lat·ed
mis·cal·cu·lat·ing
mis·cal·cu·la·tion
mis·cal·cu·la·tor
mis·call
mis·car·riage
mis·car·ry
mis·car·ried
mis·car·ry·ing
mis·ce·ge·na·tion
mis·ce·ge·net·ic
mis·cel·la·ne·ous
mis·cel·la·ny
mis·cel·la·nies
mis·chance
mis·chief
mis·chie·vous
mis·chie·vous·ly
mis·chie·vous·ness
mis·ci·ble
mis·ci·bil·i·ty
mis·con·ceive
mis·con·ceived
mis·con·ceiv·ing
mis·con·ceiv·er
mis·con·cep·tion
mis·con·duct
mis·con·strue
mis·con·strued
mis·con·stru·ing
mis·con·struc·tion
mis·count
mis·cre·ant
mis·cue
mis·cued
mis·cu·ing
mis·deal
mis·dealt
mis·deal·ing
mis·deed
mis·de·mean·or
mis·di·rect
mis·di·rec·tion
mis·do
mis·did

mis·done
mis·do·ing
mis·em·ploy
mis·em·ploy·ment
mi·ser
mi·ser·li·ness
mi·ser·ly
mis·er·a·ble
mis·er·a·ble·ness
mis·er·a·bly
mis·ery
mis·er·ies
mis·fea·sance
mis·fire
mis·fired
mis·fir·ing
mis·fit
mis·fit·ted
mis·fit·ting
mis·for·tune
mis·giv·ing
mis·gov·ern
mis·gov·ern·ment
mis·guide
mis·guid·ed
mis·guid·ing
mis·guid·ance
mis·han·dle
mis·han·dled
mis·han·dling
mis·hap
mish·mash
mis·in·form
mis·in·form·ant
mis·in·form·er
mis·in·for·ma·tion
mis·in·ter·pret
mis·in·ter·pre·ta·tion
mis·in·ter·pret·er
mis·judge
mis·judged
mis·judg·ing
mis·judg·ment
mis·lay
mis·laid
mis·lay·ing
mis·lead
mis·led
mis·lead·ing
mis·lead·er
mis·man·age
mis·man·aged
mis·man·ag·ing
mis·man·age·ment
mis·match
mis·mate
mis·mat·ed
mis·mat·ing
mis·name
mis·named
mis·nam·ing
mis·no·mer
mi·sog·a·my
mi·sog·y·ny
mi·sog·y·nist

mi·sog·y·nous
mis·place
mis·placed
mis·plac·ing
mis·place·ment
mis·play
mis·print
mis·pri·sion
mis·prize
mis·prized
mis·priz·ing
mis·pro·nounce
mis·pro·nounced
mis·pro·nounc·ing
mis·pro·nun·ci·a·tion
mis·quote
mis·quot·ed
mis·quot·ing
mis·quo·ta·tion
mis·read
mis·read·ing
mis·rep·re·sent
mis·rep·re·sen·ta·tion
mis·rep·re·sen·ta·tive
mis·rule
mis·ruled
mis·rul·ing
mis·sal
mis·shape
mis·shaped
mis·shap·ing
mis·shap·en
mis·sile
miss·ing
mis·sion
mis·sion·ary
mis·sion·ar·ies
Mis·sis·sip·pi
mis·sive
Mis·sou·ri
mis·spell
mis·spelled
mis·spelt
mis·spel·ling
mis·spend
mis·spent
mis·spend·ing
mis·state
mis·stat·ed
mis·stat·ing
mis·state·ment
mis·step
mist
mist·i·ly
mist·i·ness
mis·tak·a·ble
mis·take
mis·took
mis·tak·en
mis·tak·ing
mis·tak·en·ly
mis·tak·en·ness
mis·tak·er
Mis·ter
mis·tle·toe

mis·tral
mis·treat
  mis·treat·ment
mis·tress
mis·tri·al
mis·trust
  mis·trust·ful
  mis·trust·ful·ly
  mis·trust·ing·ly
  mis·trust·ful·ness
misty
  mist·i·er
  mist·i·est
mis·un·der·stand
  mis·un·der·stood
  mis·un·der·stand·ing
mis·us·age
mis·use
  mis·used
  mis·us·ing
  mis·us·er
mis·val·ue
  mis·val·ued
  mis·val·u·ing
mi·ter
  mi·tre
mit·i·cide
  mit·i·cid·al
mit·i·gate
  mit·i·gat·ed
  mit·i·gat·ing
  mit·i·ga·tion
  mit·i·ga·tive
  mit·i·ga·tor
  mit·i·ga·to·ry
mi·to·sis
mi·tral
mit·ten
mix
  mixed
  mix·ing
mix·er
mix·ture
mix·up
Miz·pah
miz·zen
mne·mon·ic
mne·mon·ics
moa
Mo·ab·ite
mob
  mobbed
  mob·bing
  mob·bish
mo·bile
  mo·bil·i·ty
mo·bi·lize
  mo·bi·lized
  mo·bi·liz·ing
  mo·bi·li·za·tion
mob·ster
moc·ca·sin
mo·cha
mock
  mock·er

mock·ing·ly
mock·ery
  mock·er·ies
mock·ing·bird
mock-up
mod·al
  mo·dal·i·ty
  mod·al·ly
mod·el
  mod·eled
  mod·el·ing
  mod·el·er
mod·er·ate
  mod·er·at·ed
  mod·er·at·ing
  mod·er·ate·ly
  mod·er·ate·ness
mod·er·a·tion
mod·er·a·tor
  mod·er·a·tor·ship
mod·ern
mod·ern·ism
  mod·ern·ist
  mod·ern·ist·ic
mod·ern·ize
  mod·ern·ized
  mod·ern·iz·ing
  mod·ern·iz·er
  mod·ern·i·za·tion
mod·est
  mod·est·ly
  mod·es·ty
  mod·es·ties
mod·i·cum
mod·i·fi·ca·tion
mod·i·fy
  mod·i·fied
  mod·i·fy·ing
  mod·i·fi·a·ble
  mod·i·fi·er
mod·ish
  mod·ish·ly
  mod·ish·ness
mo·diste
mod·u·late
  mod·u·lat·ed
  mod·u·lat·ing
  mod·u·la·tion
  mod·u·la·tor
  mod·u·la·to·ry
mod·ule
mod·u·lar
mo·dus o·pe·ran·di
mo·dus vi·ven·di
mo·gul
mo·hair
Mo·ham·med
Mo·ham·med·an
  Mo·ham·med·an·ism
Mo·ha·ve
Mo·hawk
Mo·hi·can
moi·e·ty
  moi·e·ties
moil

moil·er
  moil·ing·ly
moi·ré
mois·ten
  moist·en·er
mois·ture
  mois·tur·ize
  mois·tur·ized
  mois·tur·iz·ing
  mois·tur·iz·er
mo·lar
mo·las·ses
mold
  mold·a·ble
  mold·er
mold·board
mold·ing
moldy
  mold·i·er
  mold·i·est
  mold·i·ness
mol·e·cule
mole·bill
mole·skin
mo·lest
  mo·les·ta·tion
  mo·lest·er
Mo·li·na
mol·li·fy
  mol·li·fied
  mol·li·fy·ing
  mol·li·fi·ca·tion
  mol·li·fi·er
  mol·li·fy·ing·ly
mol·lusk
mol·ly·cod·dle
  mol·ly·cod·dled
  mol·ly·cod·dling
Mo·lo·kai
Mo·lo·tov
molt
  moult
  molt·er
mol·ten
  mol·ten·ly
Mo·luc·ca
mo·lyb·de·num
mo·ment
mo·men·tary
  mo·men·tar·i·ly
  mo·men·tar·i·ness
mo·men·tous
  mo·men·tous·ly
  mo·men·tous·ness
mo·men·tum
Mon·a·co
mon·ad
  mo·nad·ic
  mo·nad·i·cal
  mo·nad·al
  mo·nad·i·cal·ly
mon·arch
  mo·nar·chal
  mo·nar·chal·ly
  mo·nar·chi·cal

mo·nar·chic
mo·nar·chi·cal·ly
mon·ar·chism
mon·ar·chist
mon·ar·chist·ic
mon·ar·chy
mon·ar·chies
mon·as·tery
mon·as·ter·ies
mon·as·te·ri·al
mo·nas·tic
mo·nas·ti·cal
mo·nas·ti·cal·ly
mo·nas·ti·cism
mon·au·ral
mon·au·ral·ly
Mon·day
Mo·net
mon·e·tary
mon·e·tar·i·ly
mon·e·tize
mon·e·tized
mon·e·tiz·ing
mon·e·ti·za·tion
mon·ey
mon·ey·chang·er
mon·eyed
mon·ied
mon·ey·mak·er
mon·ey·mak·ing
mon·ger
Mon·go·lia
Mon·gol·ism
mon·gol·oid
mon·goose
mon·goos·es
mon·grel
mon·i·ker
mon·ism
mon·ist
mo·nis·tic
mo·nis·ti·cal
mo·nis·ti·cal·ly
mo·ni·tion
mon·i·tor
mon·i·to·ri·al
monk
monk·ish
monk·ish·ly
mon·key
mon·keys
mon·keyed
mon·key·ing
mon·key·shines
Mon·mouth
mon·o·chro·mat·ic
mon·o·chro·mat·i·cal·ly
mon·o·chrome
mon·o·chro·mic
mon·o·chro·mi·cal
mon·o·chro·mi·cal·ly
mon·o·chrom·ist
mon·o·cle
mon·o·cled
mon·o·cli·nal

mon·o·cline
mon·o·cli·nal·ly
mon·o·cli·nous
mon·o·dist
mon·o·dy
mon·o·dies
mo·nod·ic
mo·noe·cious
mo·noe·cious·ly
mo·nog·a·my
mo·nog·a·mist
mo·nog·a·mous
mon·o·gram
mon·o·grammed
mon·o·gram·ming
mon·o·gram·mat·ic
mon·o·graph
mo·nog·ra·pher
mon·o·graph·ic
mon·o·lith
mon·o·logue
mon·o·log
mon·o·logu·ist
mon·o·log·ist
mon·o·ma·nia
mon·o·ma·ni·ac
mon·o·ma·ni·a·cal
mon·o·met·al·lism
mon·o·me·tal·lic
mo·no·mi·al
Mo·non·ga·he·la
mon·o·nu·cle·o·sis
mon·o·phon·ic
mon·o·plane
mo·nop·o·lize
mo·nop·o·lized
mo·nop·o·liz·ing
mo·nop·o·li·za·tion
mo·nop·o·liz·er
mo·nop·o·ly
mo·nop·o·lies
mon·o·rail
mon·o·so·di·um glu·ta·mate
mon·o·syl·lab·ic
mon·o·syl·lab·i·cal·ly
mon·o·syl·la·ble
mon·o·the·ism
mon·o·the·ist
mon·o·the·is·tic
mon·o·the·is·ti·cal·ly
mon·o·tone
mo·not·o·nous
mo·not·o·nous·ly
mo·not·o·nous·ness
mo·not·o·ny
mon·o·treme
mon·o·type
mon·o·typ·er
mon·o·typ·ic
mon·o·va·lent
mon·o·va·lence
mon·o·va·len·cy
mon·ox·ide
Mon·roe Doc·trine
Mon·ro·via

mon·sei·gneur
mes·sei·gneurs
mon·sieur
mes·sieurs
Mon·si·gnor
mon·si·gnors
mon·si·gno·ri
mon·soon
mon·ster
mon·stros·i·ty
mon·stros·i·ties
mon·strous
mon·strous·ly
mon·strous·ness
mon·tage
Mon·taigne
Mon·tana
Mon·te Car·lo
Mon·te·ne·grin
Mon·te·ne·gro
Mon·te·rey
Mon·ter·rey
Mon·tes·quieu
Mon·tes·so·ri
Mon·te·vi·deo
Mon·te·zu·ma
Mont·gol·fier
Mont·gom·ery
month·ly
month·lies
Mon·ti·cel·lo
Mont·mar·tre
Mont·pe·lier
Mon·tre·al
mon·u·ment
mon·u·men·tal
mon·u·men·tal·ly
mooch
mooch·er
moody
mood·i·er
mood·i·est
mood·i·ly
mood·i·ness
moon·beam
moon·light
moon·light·er
moon·light·ing
moon·scape
moon·shine
moon·shin·er
moon·stone
moon·struck
moony
moon·i·er
moon·i·est
moor·ing
Moor·ish
moot·ness
mop
mopped
mop·ping
mope
moped
mop·ing

mop·er
mop·ish
mop·pet
mo·raine
mo·rain·al
mo·rain·ic
mor·al
mor·al·ly
mo·rale
mor·al·ist
mor·al·is·tic
mo·ral·i·ty
mo·ral·i·ties
mor·al·ize
mor·al·ized
mor·al·iz·ing
mor·al·i·za·tion
mor·al·iz·er
mo·rass
mor·a·to·ri·um
mor·a·to·ri·ums
mor·a·to·ria
Mo·ra·vi·an
mo·ray
mor·bid
mor·bid·ly
mor·bid·i·ty
mor·bid·ness
mor·dant
mor·dan·cy
mor·dant·ly
Mor·de·cai
more·o·ver
mo·res
mor·ga·nat·ic
mor·ga·nat·i·cal·ly
Mor·gan·ton
Mor·gan·town
Mor·gen·thau
morgue
mor·i·bund
mo·ri·on
Mor·mon
Mor·mon·ism
morn·ing
morn·ing·glo·ry
morn·ing·glo·ries
Mo·ro
mo·roc·co
mo·ron
mo·ron·ic
mo·ron·i·cal·ly
Mo·roni
mo·rose
mo·rose·ly
mo·rose·ness
mor·pheme
Mor·phe·us
mor·phine
mor·phol·o·gy
mor·pho·log·ic
mor·pho·log·i·cal
mor·phol·o·gist
Mor·ris·town
mor·row

mor·sel
mor·tal
mor·tal·ly
mor·tal·i·ty
mor·tal·i·ties
mor·tar
mor·tar·board
mort·gage
mort·gaged
mort·gag·ing
mort·ga·gee
mort·ga·ger
mor·ti·cian
mor·ti·fy
mor·ti·fied
mor·ti·fy·ing
mor·ti·fi·ca·tion
mor·tise
mor·tised
mor·tis·ing
mort·main
mor·tu·ary
mor·tu·ar·ies
mo·sa·ic
Mos·cow
Mo·ses
mo·sey
mo·seyed
mo·sey·ing
Mos·lem
mosque
mos·qui·to
mos·qui·toes
mos·qui·tos
moss
moss·like
mossy
moss·i·er
moss·i·est
moss·back
most·ly
mo·tel
mo·tet
moth·ball
moth·eat·en
moth·er
moth·er·less
moth·er·hood
Moth·er Hub·bard
moth·er·in·law
moth·ers·in·law
moth·er·land
moth·er·ly
moth·er·li·ness
moth·er·of·pearl
mo·tif
mo·tile
mo·til·i·ty
mo·tion
mo·tion·less
mo·tion·less·ly
mo·tion·less·ness
mo·ti·vate
mo·ti·vat·ed
mo·ti·vat·ing

mo·ti·va·tion
mo·ti·va·tion·al
mo·tive
mot·ley
mo·tor
mo·tor·bike
mo·tor·boat
mo·tor·bus
mo·tor·cade
mo·tor·car
mo·tor court
mo·tor·cy·cle
mo·tor·cy·cled
mo·tor·cy·cling
mo·tor·cy·clist
mo·tor·ist
mo·tor·ize
mo·tor·ized
mo·tor·iz·ing
mo·tor·i·za·tion
mo·tor·man
mo·tor·men
mot·tle
mot·tled
mot·tling
mot·tler
mound
mount
mount·a·ble
mount·er
moun·tain
moun·tain·eer
moun·tain·ous
moun·te·bank
mount·ing
Mount Ver·non
mourn
mourn·er
mourn·ful
mourn·ful·ly
mourn·ful·ness
mourn·ing
mourn·ing·ly
mouse
moused
mous·ing
mous·er
Mous·sorg·sky
mous·tache
mousy
mous·i·er
mous·i·est
mouth
mouthed
mouth·er
mouth·ful
mouth·fuls
mouth·piece
mouthy
mouth·i·er
mouth·i·est
mouth·i·ness
mou·ton
mov·a·ble
mov·a·ble·ness

mov·a·bil·i·ty
mov·a·bly
move
moved
mov·ing
mov·er
move·ment
mov·ie
mow
mowed
mow·ing
mow·er
mox·ie
Mo·zam·bique
Mo·zart
mu·ci·lage
mu·ci·lag·i·nous
muck
mucky
muck·rake
muck·raked
muck·rak·ing
muck·rak·er
mu·cous
mu·cos·i·ty
mu·cus
mud
mud·ded
mud·ding
mud·dle
mud·dled
mud·dling
mud·dler
mud·dy
mud·di·er
mud·di·est
mud·di·ly
mud·di·ness
mu·ez·zin
muf·fin
muf·fle
muf·fled
muf·fling
muf·fler
muf·ti
mug
mugged
mug·ging
mug·ger
mug·gy
mug·gi·er
mug·gi·est
mug·gi·ness
mu·lat·to
mu·lat·toes
mul·ber·ry
mul·ber·ries
mulch
mu·le·teer
mul·ish
mul·ish·ly
mul·ish·ness
mul·let
mul·li·gan
mul·li·ga·taw·ny

mul·lion
mul·lioned
mul·ti·far·i·ous
mul·ti·far·i·ous·ly
mul·ti·far·i·ous·ness
mul·ti·lat·er·al
mul·ti·mil·lion·aire
mul·ti·ple
mul·ti·ple scle·ro·sis
mul·ti·pli·cand
mul·ti·pli·ca·tion
mul·ti·plic·i·ty
mul·ti·pli·er
mul·ti·ply
mul·ti·plied
mul·ti·ply·ing
mul·ti·pli·a·ble
mul·ti·tude
mul·ti·tu·di·nous
mul·ti·tu·di·nous·ly
mul·ti·tu·di·nous·ness
mum·ble
mum·bled
mum·bling
mum·bler
mum·bling·ly
Mum·bo Jum·bo
mum·mer
mum·mery
mum·mi·fy
mum·mi·fied
mum·mi·fy·ing
mum·mi·fi·ca·tion
mum·my
mum·mies
mum·mied
mum·my·ing
munch
munch·er
mun·dane
mun·dane·ly
Mu·nich
mu·nic·i·pal
mu·nic·i·pal·ly
mu·nic·i·pal·i·ty
mu·nif·i·cent
mu·nif·i·cence
mu·nif·i·cent·ly
mu·ni·tion
mu·ral
mu·ral·ist
mur·der
mur·der·er
mur·der·ess
mur·der·ous
mur·der·ous·ly
mur·der·ous·ness
mu·ri·at·ic ac·id
Mu·ril·lo
murky
murk·i·er
murk·i·est
murk·i·ly
murk·i·ness
mur·mur

mur·mur·er
mur·mur·ing
mur·mur·ing·ly
mur·rain
mus·cat
mus·ca·tel
mus·cle
mus·cled
mus·cling
mus·cle-bound
Mus·co·vite
mus·cu·lar
mus·cu·lar·i·ty
mus·cu·lar·ly
mus·cu·lar dys·tro·phy
mus·cu·la·ture
muse
mused
mus·ing
mus·er
mus·ing·ly
mu·se·um
mush
mushy
mush·i·er
mush·i·est
mush·i·ly
mush·i·ness
mush·room
mu·sic
mu·si·cal
mu·si·cal·ly
mu·si·cal·i·ty
mu·si·cal·ness
mu·si·cale
mu·si·cian
mu·si·cian·ship
musk
musky
musk·i·er
musk·i·est
musk·i·ness
mus·kel·lunge
mus·ket
mus·ket·eer
mus·ket·ry
musk·mel·on
Mus·ko·gee
musk·rat
mus·lin
muss
mussy
muss·i·er
muss·i·est
mus·sel
Mus·so·li·ni
mus·tache
mus·tang
mus·tard
mus·ter
mus·ty
mus·ti·er
mus·ti·est
mus·ti·ly
mus·ti·ness

mu·ta·ble
mu·ta·bil·i·ty
mu·ta·ble·ness
mu·ta·bly
mu·tant
mu·ta·tion
mu·tate
mu·tat·ed
mu·tat·ing
mu·ta·tion·al
mute
mut·ed
mut·ing
mute·ly
mute·ness
mu·ti·late
mu·ti·lat·ed
mu·ti·lat·ing
mu·ti·la·tion
mu·ti·la·tor
mu·ti·neer
mu·ti·ny
mu·ti·nies
mu·ti·nied
mu·ti·ny·ing
mu·ti·nous
mut·ter
mut·ter·er
mut·ter·ing·ly
mut·ton
mu·tu·al
mu·tu·al·i·ty
mu·tu·al·ly
muz·zle
muz·zled
muz·zling
muz·zler
My·ce·nae
my·col·o·gy
my·col·o·gist
my·na
my·nah
my·o·pia
my·op·ic
myr·i·ad
myr·mi·don
myrrh
myr·tle
my·self
mys·te·ri·ous
mys·te·ri·ous·ly
mys·te·ri·ous·ness
mys·tery
mys·ter·ies
mys·tic
mys·ti·cal
mys·ti·cal·ly
mys·ti·cal·ness
mys·ti·cism
mys·ti·fy
mys·ti·fied
mys·ti·fy·ing
mys·ti·fy·ing·ly
mys·ti·fi·ca·tion
mys·tique

myth
myth·ic
myth·i·cal
myth·i·cal·ly
myth·i·cist
myth·i·cize
my·thol·o·gy
my·thol·o·gies
myth·o·log·ic
myth·o·log·i·cal
my·thol·o·gist
nab
nabbed
nab·bing
na·bob
na·cre
na·cre·ous
na·dir
nag
nagged
nag·ging
nag·ger
nag·ging·ly
Na·ga·sa·ki
Na·go·ya
Na·hum
nail·er
Nai·ro·bi
na·ive
na·ive·ly
na·ive·ness
na·ive·te
na·ked
na·ked·ly
na·ked·ness
nam·by-pam·by
name
named
nam·ing
name·less
name·less·ly
name·less·ness
name·ly
name·sake
Na·mur
Na·nai·mo
nan·keen
nan·kin
Nan·king
nan·ny
nan·nies
Nan·tuck·et
Na·o·mi
nap
napped
nap·ping
nap·per
na·palm
nape
naph·tha
naph·tha·lene
Na·pi·er
nap·kin
Na·ples
Na·po·leon

nar·cis·sism
nar·cism
nar·cis·sist
nar·cis·sis·tic
nar·cis·sus
nar·cis·sus·es
nar·cis·si
nar·co·sis
nar·cot·ic
nar·cot·i·cal·ly
nar·co·tize
nar·co·tized
nar·co·tiz·ing
nar·is
nar·es
Nar·ra·gan·sett
nar·rate
nar·ra·ted
nar·ra·ting
nar·ra·tor
nar·ra·tion
nar·ra·tion·al
nar·ra·tive
nar·ra·tive·ly
nar·row
nar·row·ly
nar·row·ness
nar·row·mind·ed
nar·row·mind·ed·ly
nar·row·mind·ed·ness
Nar·va·ez
nary
na·sal
na·sal·i·ty
na·sal·ize
na·sal·ized
na·sal·iz·ing
na·sal·ly
nas·cent
nas·cence
nas·cen·cy
Nash·ville
Nas·sau
Nas·ser
na·stur·tium
nas·ty
nas·ti·er
nas·ti·est
nas·ti·ly
nas·ti·ness
na·tal
Natch·ez
na·tion
na·tion·hood
na·tion·al
na·tion·al·ly
na·tion·al·ism
na·tion·al·ist
na·tion·al·is·tic
na·tion·al·i·ty
na·tion·al·i·ties
na·tion·al·ize
na·tion·al·ized
na·tion·al·iz·ing
na·tion·al·i·za·tion

na·tion·wide
na·tive
na·tive·ly
na·tive·ness
na·tiv·i·ty
na·tiv·i·ties
nat·ty
nat·ti·er
nat·ti·est
nat·ti·ly
nat·ti·ness
nat·u·ral
nat·u·ral·ly
nat·u·ral·ness
nat·u·ral·ism
nat·u·ral·ist
nat·u·ral·is·tic
nat·u·ral·ize
nat·u·ral·ized
nat·u·ral·iz·ing
nat·u·ral·i·za·tion
na·ture
naught
naugh·ty
naugh·ti·er
naugh·ti·est
naugh·ti·ly
naugh·ti·ness
Nau·ru
nau·sea
nau·se·ate
nau·se·at·ed
nau·se·at·ing
nau·seous
nau·seous·ly
nau·seous·ness
nau·ti·cal
nau·ti·cal·ly
nau·ti·lus
nau·ti·lus·es
nau·ti·li
Nav·a·jo
na·val
Na·varre
na·vel
nav·i·ga·ble
nav·i·ga·bil·i·ty
nav·i·ga·ble·ness
nav·i·ga·bly
nav·i·gate
nav·i·gat·ed
nav·i·gat·ing
nav·i·ga·tion
nav·i·ga·tion·al
nav·i·ga·tor
na·vy
na·vies
Naz·a·rene
Naz·a·reth
Na·zi
Na·zis
Na·zism
Na·zi·ism
Ne·an·der·thal
Ne·a·pol·i·tan

near
near·ly
near·ness
near·by
Ne·arc·tic
near·sight·ed
near·sight·ed·ly
near·sight·ed·ness
neat
neat·ly
neat·ness
neb·bish
Ne·bo
Ne·bras·ka
Neb·u·chad·nez·zar
neb·u·la
neb·u·las
neb·u·lae
neb·u·lous
neb·u·lar
neb·u·lous·ly
neb·u·lous·ness
nec·es·sary
nec·es·sar·ies
nec·es·sar·i·ly
ne·ces·si·tate
ne·ces·si·ta·ted
ne·ces·si·ta·ting
ne·ces·si·ty
ne·ces·si·ties
neck·er·chief
neck·ing
neck·lace
neck·tie
ne·crol·o·gy
ne·crol·o·gies
nec·ro·man·cy
nec·ro·man·cer
ne·cro·sis
ne·crot·ic
nec·tar
nec·tar·ine
need·ful
need·ful·ly
need·ful·ness
nee·dle
nee·dled
nee·dling
nee·dle·like
nee·dler
nee·dle·point
need·less
need·less·ly
need·less·ness
nee·dle·work
nee·dle·work·er
needy
need·i·er
need·i·est
need·i·ness
ne'er·do·well
ne·far·i·ous
ne·far·i·ous·ly
ne·far·i·ous·ness
ne·gate

ne·ga·ted
ne·ga·ting
ne·ga·tion
neg·a·tive
neg·a·tive·ly
neg·a·tive·ness
neg·a·tiv·i·ty
neg·a·tiv·ism
ne·glect
ne·glec·ter
ne·glec·tor
ne·glect·ful·ness
ne·glect·ful
ne·glect·ful·ly
neg·li·gee
neg·li·gent
neg·li·gence
neg·li·gent·ly
neg·li·gi·ble
neg·li·gi·bly
neg·li·gi·bil·i·ty
ne·go·ti·a·ble
ne·go·ti·a·bil·i·ty
ne·go·ti·ate
ne·go·ti·at·ed
ne·go·ti·at·ing
ne·go·ti·a·tion
ne·go·ti·a·tor
Ne·gro
Ne·groes
Ne·groid
Ne·he·mi·ah
Neh·ru
neigh·bor
neigh·bor·ing
neigh·bor·ly
neigh·bor·li·ness
neigh·bor·hood
nei·ther
Nel·son
Nem·bu·tal
nem·e·sis
nem·e·ses
ne·o·clas·sic
ne·o·clas·si·cal
ne·o·clas·si·cism
ne·o·lith·ic
ne·ol·o·gism
ne·ol·o·gy
ne·on
ne·o·phyte
Ne·pal
ne·pen·the
ne·pen·the·an
neph·ew
ne·phri·tis
ne·phrit·ic
nep·o·tism
nep·o·tist
Nep·tune
Nep·tu·ni·an
nep·tu·ni·um
nerve
nerved
nerv·ing

nerve·less
nerve·less·ly
nerve·less·ness
nerve-rack·ing
nerve-wrack·ing
nerv·ous
nerv·ous·ly
nerv·ous·ness
nervy
nerv·i·er
nerv·i·est
nerv·i·ness
nes·tle
nes·tled
nes·tling
nes·tler
net
net·ted
net·ting
neth·er
Neth·er·lands
neth·er·most
net·tle
net·tled
net·tling
net·work
neu·ral
neu·ral·ly
neu·ral·gia
neu·ral·gic
neu·ras·the·nia
neu·ras·then·ic
neu·ri·tis
neu·rit·ic
neu·rol·o·gy
neu·ro·log·i·cal
neu·rol·o·gist
neu·ron
neu·ron·ic
neu·ro·sis
neu·ro·ses
neu·rot·ic
neu·rot·i·cal·ly
neu·ter
neu·tral
neu·tral·i·ty
neu·tral·ly
neu·tral·ism
neu·tral·ist
neu·tral·ize
neu·tral·ized
neu·tral·iz·ing
neu·tral·i·za·tion
neu·tral·iz·er
neu·tri·no
neu·tron
Ne·vada
nev·er
nev·er·more
nev·er·the·less
new
new·ish
new·ness
New·ark
new·born

New·burgh
New·cas·tle
new·com·er
New Del·hi
new·el
new·fan·gled
New·found·land
New·gate
New Guin·ea
New Hamp·shire
New Ha·ven
New Jer·sey
new·ly
new·ly·wed
New Mex·i·co
New Or·leans
New·port
news·boy
news·cast
news·cast·er
news·pa·per
news·pa·per·man
news·print
news·reel
news·stand
newsy
news·i·er
news·i·est
newt
New·ton
New Zea·land
nex·us
ni·a·cin
Ni·ag·a·ra
Ni·a·my
nib·ble
nib·bled
nib·bling
nib·bler
nib·lick
Nic·a·ra·gua
nice
nic·er
nic·est
nice·ly
nice·ness
Ni·cene
ni·ce·ty
ni·ce·ties
niche
Nich·o·las
nick·el
nick·el·o·de·on
nick·name
nick·named
nick·nam·ing
Ni·co·sia
nic·o·tine
nic·o·tin·ic
Nie·buhr
niece
Nietz·sche
nif·ty
nif·ti·er
nif·ti·est

Ni·ger
Ni·ge·ria
nig·gard
  nig·gard·li·ness
  nig·gard·ly
nigh
  nigh·er
  nigh·est
night·cap
night·dress
night·fall
night·gown
night·hawk
night·in·gale
night·ly
night·mare
  night·mar·ish
night·shade
night·shirt
night·time
ni·hil·ism
  ni·hil·ist
  ni·hil·is·tic
Ni·ke
nim·ble
  nim·bler
  nim·blest
  nim·ble·ness
  nim·bly
nim·bus
Nim·rod
nin·com·poop
nine·pins
nine·teen
  nine·teenth
nine·ty
  nine·ties
  nine·ti·eth
Nin·e·vah
nin·ny
  nin·nies
ninth
Ni·o·be
nip
  nipped
  nip·ping
nip·per
nip·ple
Nip·pon
nip·py
  nip·pi·er
  nip·pi·est
nir·va·na
Ni·sei
Nis·sen
nit
  nit·ty
  nit·ti·er
  nit·ti·est
ni·ter
nit·pick
ni·trate
  ni·trat·ed
  ni·trat·ing
  ni·tra·tion

ni·tra·tor
ni·tric
ni·tro·gen
ni·trog·e·nous
ni·tro·glyc·er·in
ni·trous ox·ide
nit·ty-grit·ty
nit·wit
No·a·chi·an
No·ah
No·bel
no·be·li·um
no·bil·i·ty
  no·bil·i·ties
no·ble
  no·bler
  no·blest
  no·ble·man
  no·ble·men
  no·ble·ness
  no·ble·wom·an
  no·ble·wom·en
  no·bly
no·body
noc·tur·nal
noc·turne
nod
  nod·ded
  nod·ding
  nod·der
node
  nod·al
nod·ule
  nod·u·lar
no·el
nog·gin
No·gu·chi
noise
  noised
  nois·ing
noise·less
  noise·less·ly
  noise·less·ness
noi·some
  noi·some·ly
  noi·some·ness
noisy
  nois·i·er
  nois·i·est
  nois·i·ly
  nois·i·ness
No·ko·mis
no·mad
  no·mad·ic
  no·mad·i·cal·ly
  no·mad·ism
nom de plume
  noms de plume
no·men·cla·ture
nom·i·nal
  nom·i·nal·ly
nom·i·nate
  nom·i·nat·ed
  nom·i·nat·ing
  nom·i·na·tion

nom·i·na·tor
nom·i·na·tive
nom·i·nee
non·age
nonce
non·cha·lant
  non·cha·lance
  non·cha·lant·ly
non·com
non·com·bat·ant
non·com·mit·tal
  non·com·mit·tal·ly
non·con·duc·tor
non·con·duc·ting
non·con·form·ist
  non·con·form·i·ty
non·de·script
non·en·ti·ty
  non·en·ti·ties
none·the·less
non·in·ter·ven·tion
  non·in·ter·ven·tion·ist
non·met·al
  non·me·tal·lic
non·pa·reil
non·par·ti·san
  non·par·ti·san·ship
non·plus
  non·plused
  non·plus·ing
non·prof·it
non·res·i·dent
  non·res·i·dence
  non·res·i·den·cy
  non·res·i·den·cies
non·re·stric·tive
non·sec·tar·i·an
non·sense
  non·sen·si·cal
  non·sen·si·cal·ly
non se·qui·tur
non·stop
non·sup·port
non·un·ion
  non·un·ion·ism
  non·un·ion·ist
non·vi·o·lence
  non·vi·o·lent
  non·vi·o·lent·ly
noo·dle
noon
noon·day
noon·time
noose
  noosed
  noos·ing
Nor·dic
Nor·folk
nor·mal
  nor·mal·cy
  nor·mal·i·ty
  nor·mal·ly
nor·mal·ize
  nor·mal·ized
  nor·mal·iz·ing

nor·mal·i·za·tion
Nor·man·dy
Norse·man
North Amer·i·ca
North·amp·ton
North Car·o·li·na
North Da·ko·ta
north·east
north·east·ern
north·east·er
north·east·er·ly
north·east·ward
north·east·ward·ly
north·er
nor·ther·ly
north·er·li·ness
north·ern
north·ern·most
north·ern·er
North·um·ber·land
North·um·bri·an
north·ward
north·wards
north·ward·ly
north·west
north·west·ern
north·west·er
north·west·ward
north·west·ward·ly
Nor·way
Nor·wich
nose
nosed
nos·ing
nose·gay
nos·tal·gia
nos·tal·gic
nos·tril
nos·trum
nosy
nos·i·er
nos·i·est
nos·i·ly
nos·i·ness
no·ta·ble
no·ta·ble·ness
no·ta·bil·i·ty
no·ta·bly
no·ta·rize
no·ta·rized
no·ta·riz·ing
no·ta·ri·za·tion
no·ta·ry
no·ta·ries
no·ta·tion
no·ta·tion·al
notch
notched
note
not·ed
not·ing
not·er
note·book
not·ed
not·ed·ly

not·ed·ness
note·wor·thy
note·wor·thi·ness
noth·ing
noth·ing·ness
no·tice
no·ticed
no·tic·ing
no·tice·a·ble
no·tice·a·bly
no·ti·fy
no·ti·fied
no·ti·fy·ing
no·ti·fi·ca·tion
no·ti·fi·er
no·tion
no·to·ri·ous
no·to·ri·ous·ly
no·to·ri·ous·ness
no·to·ri·e·ty
no-trump
Not·ting·ham
Not·ting·ham·shire
not·with·stand·ing
Nou·ak·chott
nought
nour·ish
nour·ish·er
nour·ish·ing
nour·ish·ment
no·va
no·vas
no·vae
No·va Sco·tia
nov·el
nov·el·ist
nov·el·is·tic
nov·el·ette
nov·el·ty
nov·el·ties
No·vem·ber
no·ve·na
no·ve·nae
nov·ice
no·vi·ti·ate
No·vo·cain
now·a·days
no·where
no·wise
nox·ious
nox·ious·ly
nox·ious·ness
noz·zle
nu·ance
nub·bin
nu·bile
nu·cle·ar
nu·cle·us
nu·cle·us·es
nu·clei
nude
nude·ly
nude·ness
nu·di·ty
nudge

nudged
nudg·ing
nudg·er
nud·ism
nud·ist
nug·get
nui·sance
null
nul·li·ty
nul·li·ties
nul·li·fy
nul·li·fied
nul·li·fy·ing
nul·li·fi·ca·tion
nul·li·fi·er
numb
numb·ly
numb·ness
numb·ing
numb·ing·ly
num·ber
num·ber·er
num·ber·less
numb·skull
nu·mer·al
num·er·al·ly
nu·mer·ate
nu·mer·at·ed
nu·mer·at·ing
nu·mer·a·tion
nu·mer·a·tor
nu·mer·i·cal
nu·mer·i·cal·ly
nu·mer·ous
nu·mer·ous·ly
nu·mer·ous·ness
nu·mis·mat·ics
nu·mis·mat·ic
nu·mis·mat·i·cal
nu·mis·ma·tist
num·skull
nun·cio
nun·ci·os
nun·nery
nun·ner·ies
nup·tial
nup·tial·ly
Nur·em·berg
nurse
nursed
nurs·ing
nurs·er
nurse·maid
nurs·ery
nurs·er·ies
nur·ture
nur·tured
nur·tur·ing
nur·tur·er
nut
nut·ted
nut·ting
nut·crack·er
nut·hatch
nut·meg

nu·tri·ent
nu·tri·ment
nu·tri·tion
nu·tri·tion·al
nu·tri·tion·al·ly
nu·tri·tion·ist
nu·tri·tious
nu·tri·tious·ly
nu·tri·tious·ness
nu·tri·tive
nu·tri·tive·ly
nu·tri·tive·ness
nut·shell
nut·ty
nut·ti·er
nut·ti·est
nut·ti·ness
nuz·zle
nuz·zled
nuz·zling
Ny·an·za
ny·lon
nymph
nym·phal
nym·pho·ma·nia
nym·pho·ma·ni·ac
oaf
oaf·ish
oaf·ish·ly
oaf·ish·ness
Oa·hu
oak·en
Oak·land
oa·kum
oar
oared
oars·man
oars·men
oar·lock
oa·sis
oa·ses
oat·en
oath
oat·meal
Oba·di·ah
ob·bli·ga·to
ob·bli·ga·tos
ob·du·rate
ob·du·ra·cy
ob·du·rate·ly
ob·du·rate·ness
Obe·ah
obe·di·ence
obe·di·ent
obe·di·ent·ly
obei·sance
obei·sant
ob·e·lisk
Ober·am·mer·gau
Ober·lin
Ober·on
obese
obese·ness
obes·i·ty
obey

obey·er
ob·fus·cate
ob·fus·ca·ted
ob·fus·ca·ting
ob·fus·ca·tion
obit
obit·u·ary
obit·u·ar·ies
ob·ject
ob·ject·less
ob·ject·or
ob·jec·tion
ob·jec·tion·a·ble
ob·jec·tion·a·ble·ness
ob·jec·tion·a·bly
ob·jec·tive
ob·jec·tive·ly
ob·jec·tive·ness
ob·jec·tiv·i·ty
ob·jur·gate
ob·jur·gat·ed
ob·jur·gat·ing
ob·jur·ga·tion
ob·jur·ga·to·ry
ob·late
ob·late·ly
ob·late·ness
ob·li·gate
ob·li·gat·ed
ob·li·gat·ing
ob·li·ga·tion
ob·lig·a·to·ry
oblige
obliged
oblig·ing
oblig·er
oblig·ing
oblig·ing·ly
oblig·ing·ness
ob·lique
ob·liqued
ob·liqu·ing
ob·lique·ly
ob·lique·ness
ob·liq·ui·ty
ob·lit·er·ate
ob·lit·er·at·ed
ob·lit·er·at·ing
ob·lit·er·a·tion
ob·lit·er·a·tive
ob·liv·i·on
ob·liv·i·ous
ob·liv·i·ous·ly
ob·liv·i·ous·ness
ob·long
ob·lo·quy
ob·lo·quies
ob·nox·ious
ob·nox·ious·ly
ob·nox·ious·ness
oboe
obo·ist
ob·scene
ob·scene·ly
ob·scene·ness

ob·scen·i·ty
ob·scen·i·ties
ob·scure
ob·scur·er
ob·scur·est
ob·scured .
ob·scur·ing
ob·scure·ly
ob·scure·ness
ob·scu·ri·ty
ob·scu·ri·ties
ob·se·qui·ous
ob·se·qui·ous·ly
ob·se·qui·ous·ness
ob·se·quy
ob·se·quies
ob·serv·a·ble
ob·serv·a·ble·ness
ob·serv·a·bly
ob·ser·vance
ob·ser·vant
ob·ser·vant·ly
ob·ser·va·tion
ob·ser·va·tion·al
ob·ser·va·to·ry
ob·ser·va·to·ries
ob·serve
ob·served
ob·serv·ing
ob·serv·ed·ly
ob·serv·er
ob·serv·ing·ly
ob·sess
ob·ses·sive
ob·ses·sive·ly
ob·ses·sion
ob·sid·i·an
ob·so·les·cent
ob·so·les·cence
ob·so·les·cent·ly
ob·so·lete
ob·so·lete·ness
ob·sta·cle
ob·ste·tri·cian
ob·stet·rics
ob·stet·ric
ob·stet·ri·cal
ob·stet·ri·cal·ly
ob·sti·nate
ob·sti·na·cy
ob·sti·na·cies
ob·sti·nate·ly
ob·sti·nate·ness
ob·strep·er·ous
ob·strep·er·ous·ly
ob·strep·er·ous·ness
ob·struct
ob·struc·tive
ob·struc·tor
ob·struc·tion
ob·struc·tion·ism
ob·struc·tion·ist
ob·tain
ob·tain·a·ble
ob·tain·er

ob·tain·ment
ob·trude
ob·trud·ed
ob·trud·ing
ob·trud·er
ob·tru·sion
ob·tru·sive
ob·tru·sive·ness
ob·tuse
ob·tuse·ly
ob·tuse·ness
ob·verse
ob·verse·ly
ob·vi·ate
ob·vi·at·ed
ob·vi·at·ing
ob·vi·a·tion
ob·vi·a·tor
ob·vi·ous
ob·vi·ous·ly
ob·vi·ous·ness
oc·ca·sion
oc·ca·sion·al
oc·ca·sion·al·ly
oc·ci·dent
oc·ci·den·tal
oc·clude
oc·clud·ed
oc·clud·ing
oc·clu·sive
oc·clu·sion
oc·cult
oc·cult·ly
oc·cult·ness
oc·cult·ism
oc·cult·ist
oc·cu·pan·cy
oc·cu·pan·cies
oc·cu·pant
oc·cu·pa·tion
oc·cu·pa·tion·al
oc·cu·pa·tion·al·ly
oc·cu·py
oc·cu·pied
oc·cu·py·ing
oc·cu·pi·er
oc·cur
oc·curred
oc·cur·ring
oc·cur·rence
oc·cur·rent
ocean
oce·an·ic
Oce·an·ia
oce·a·nog·ra·phy
oce·a·nog·ra·pher
oce·a·no·graph·ic
oce·a·no·graph·i·cal
oce·lot
ocher
ocher·ous
ochery
Ock·ham
o'clock
oc·ta·gon

oc·tag·o·nal
oc·tag·o·nal·ly
oc·ta·he·dron
oc·ta·he·drons
oc·ta·he·dra
oc·ta·he·dral
oc·tane
oc·tave
Oc·ta·vi·us
oc·ta·vo
oc·tet
Oc·to·ber
oc·to·ge·nar·i·an
oc·tog·e·nary
Oc·top·o·da
oc·to·pus
oc·u·lar
oc·u·lar·ly
oc·u·list
odd
odd·ly
odd·ness
odd·ball
odd·i·ty
odd·i·ties
Odes·sa
od·ic
odi·ous
odi·ous·ly
odi·ous·ness
odi·um
odom·e·ter
odor
odored
odor·less
odor·ous
odor·ous·ly
odor·ous·ness
odor·if·er·ous
odor·if·er·ous·ly
Odys·seus
od·ys·sey
Oed·i·pus com·plex
oed·i·pal
of·fal
off·beat
off·col·or
of·fend
of·fend·er
of·fense
of·fense·less
of·fen·sive
of·fen·sive·ly
of·fen·sive·ness
of·fer
of·fer·er
of·fer·ing
of·fer·to·ry
of·fer·to·ries
of·fer·to·ri·al
off·hand
off·hand·ed·ly
off·hand·ed·ness
of·fice
of·fice·hold·er

of·fic·er
of·fi·cial
of·fi·cial·ism
of·fi·cial·ly
of·fi·cial·dom
of·fi·ci·ate
of·fi·ci·at·ed
of·fi·ci·at·ing
of·fi·ci·a·tion
of·fi·ci·a·tor
of·fi·cious
of·fi·cious·ly
of·fi·cious·ness
off·ing
off·set
off·set·ting
off·shoot
off·shore
off·side
off·spring
off·stage
off-the-cuff
of·ten
of·ten·times
Ogal·la·la
Og·den
ogle
ogled
ogling
ogler
Ogle·thorpe
ogre
ogre·ish
Ohio
ohm
ohm·age
ohm·ic
ohm·me·ter
oil·cloth
oil·er
oil·skin
oily
oil·i·er
oil·i·est
oil·i·ness
oint·ment
Ojib·wa
Oke·fe·no·kee
Okie
Oki·na·wa
Okla·ho·ma
okra
old
old·er
old·est
old·en
old·ish
old·ness
old-fash·ioned
old·ster
old-time
old-tim·er
old-world
ole·ag·i·nous
ole·ag·i·nous·ly

ole·ag·i·nous·ness
oleo
ole·o·mar·ga·rine
ol·fac·tion
ol·fac·to·ry
ol·fac·to·ries
ol·i·gar·chy
ol·i·gar·chies
ol·i·gar·chic
ol·i·gar·chi·cal
ol·i·garch
ol·i·gop·o·ly
ol·ive
Ol·i·ver
Ol·i·vet
Olym·pia
Olym·pi·an
O·lym·pic
Olym·pus
Oma·ha
Omar Khay·yam
om·buds·man
om·buds·men
om·e·let
omen
om·i·nous
om·i·nous·ly
om·i·nous·ness
omis·sion
omit
omit·ted
omit·ting
om·ni·bus
om·ni·bus·es
om·nip·o·tence
om·nip·o·tent·ly
om·ni·pres·ent
om·ni·pres·ence
om·ni·pres·ent·ly
om·nis·cience
om·nis·cient
om·nis·cient·ly
om·niv·or·ous
om·niv·i·vore
om·niv·o·rous·ly
om·niv·o·rous·ness
onan·ism
onan·ist
onan·is·tic
once·o·ver
on·com·ing
Onei·da
on·er·ous
on·er·ous·ly
on·er·ous·ness
one·self
one·sid·ed
one·sid·ed·ly
one·sid·ed·ness
one·time
one·track
one·up·man·ship
one·way
on·go·ing
on·ion

on·ion·like
on·iony
on·ion·skin
on·line
on·look·er
on·look·ing
on·ly
on·o·mat·o·poe·ia
on·o·mat·o·poe·ic
on·o·mat·o·po·et·ic
on·o·mat·o·poe·i·cal·ly
on·o·mat·o·po·et·i·cal·ly
On·on·da·ga
on·rush
on·rush·ing
on·set
on·shore
on·slaught
On·tar·io
on·to
onus
on·ward
on·yx
oo·dles
ooze
oozed
ooz·ing
oo·zi·ness
oo·zy
oo·zi·er
oo·zi·est
opac·i·ty
opac·i·ties
opal
opal·es·cence
opal·es·cent
opaque
opaque·ly
opaque·ness
open
open·er
open·ly
open·ness
open·air
open·door
open·end
open·eyed
open·hand·ed
open·hand·ed·ly
open·hand·ed·ness
open house
open·ing
open·mind·ed
open·mind·ed·ly
open·mouthed
open ses·a·me
open·work
opera
op·er·at·ic
op·er·at·i·cal·ly
op·er·a·ble
op·er·a·bil·i·ty
op·er·a·bly
op·er·a glass·es
op·er·a house

op·er·ate
op·er·at·ed
op·er·at·ing
op·er·a·tion
op·er·a·tive
op·er·a·tive·ly
op·er·a·tive·ness
op·er·a·tor
op·er·et·ta
oph·thal·mic
oph·thal·mol·o·gist
oph·thal·mol·o·gy
oph·thal·mo·log·ic
opi·ate
opine
opined
opin·ing
opin·ion
opin·ion·at·ed
opin·ion·at·ed·ly
opin·ion·at·ed·ness
opi·um
opos·sum
Op·pen·hei·mer
op·po·nent
op·por·tune
op·por·tune·ly
op·por·tune·ness
op·por·tun·ism
op·por·tun·ist
op·por·tun·is·tic
op·por·tu·ni·ty
op·por·tu·ni·ties
op·pos·a·ble
op·pos·a·bil·i·ty
op·pose
op·posed
op·pos·ing
op·pos·er
op·pos·ing·ly
op·po·site
op·po·site·ly
op·po·site·ness
op·po·si·tion
op·po·si·tion·al
op·press
op·pres·si·ble
op·pres·sor
op·pres·sion
op·pres·sive
op·pres·sive·ly
op·pres·sive·ness
op·pro·bri·ous
op·pro·bri·ous·ly
op·pro·bri·ous·ness
op·pro·bri·um
op·tic
op·ti·cal
op·ti·cal·ly
op·ti·cian
op·tics
op·ti·mal
op·ti·mism
op·ti·mist
op·ti·mis·tic

op·ti·mis·ti·cal·ly
op·ti·mize
op·ti·mized
op·ti·miz·ing
op·ti·mi·za·tion
op·ti·mum
op·ti·ma
op·tion
op·tion·al
op·tion·al·ly
op·tom·e·trist
op·tom·e·try
op·to·met·ric
op·to·met·ri·cal
op·u·lent
op·u·lence
op·u·lent·ly
opus
ope·ra
opus·es
or·a·cle
orac·u·lar
orac·u·lar·i·ty
orac·u·lar·ly
oral
oral·ly
or·ange
or·ange·ade
or·ange·wood
orang·u·tan
orate
orat·ed
orat·ing
ora·tion
ora·tor
or·a·tor·i·cal
or·a·tor·i·cal·ly
or·a·to·rio
or·a·to·ri·os
or·a·to·ry
or·bic·u·lar
or·bic·u·late
or·bic·u·lar·i·ty
or·bic·u·lar·ly
or·bit
or·bit·al
or·bit·er
or·chard
or·ches·tra
or·ches·tral
or·ches·tral·ly
or·ches·trate
or·ches·trat·ed
or·ches·trat·ing
or·ches·tra·tion
or·chid
or·dain
or·dain·er
or·dain·ment
or·deal
or·der
or·dered
or·der·ly
or·der·li·ness
or·di·nal

or·di·nance
or·di·nar·i·ly
or·di·nary
or·di·nar·i·ness
or·di·na·tion
ord·nance
or·dure
oreg·a·no
Ore·gon
Ores·tes
or·gan
or·gan·dy
or·gan·ic
or·gan·i·cal·ly
or·gan·ism
or·gan·is·mal
or·gan·is·mic
or·gan·ist
or·gan·i·za·tion
or·gan·i·za·tion·al
or·gan·i·za·tion·al·ly
or·gan·ize
or·gan·ized
or·gan·iz·ing
or·gan·iz·a·ble
or·gan·iz·er
or·gasm
or·gas·mic
or·gi·as·tic
or·gi·as·ti·cal·ly
or·gy
or·gies
ori·ent
Ori·en·tal
ori·en·tal·ism
ori·en·tal·ist
ori·en·tal·ly
ori·en·tate
ori·en·tat·ed
ori·en·tat·ing
ori·en·ta·tion
or·i·fice
ori·ga·mi
Or·i·gen
orig·i·nal
orig·i·nal·i·ty
orig·i·nal·ly
orig·i·nate
orig·i·nat·ed
orig·i·nat·ing
orig·i·na·tion
orig·i·na·tor
orig·i·na·tive
orig·i·na·tive·ly
Ori·no·co
or·i·son
Or·lan·do
Or·leans
Or·lon
or·na·ment
or·na·men·tal
or·na·men·ta·tion
or·nate
or·nate·ly
or·nate·ness

or·nery
  or·ner·i·ness
or·ni·thol·o·gy
  or·ni·tho·log·ic
  or·ni·tho·log·i·cal
  or·ni·tho·log·i·cal·ly
  or·ni·thol·o·gist
oro·tund
  oro·tun·di·ty
or·phan
  or·phan·hood
or·phan·age
or·tho·don·tics
  or·tho·don·tic
  or·tho·don·tist
or·tho·dox
  or·tho·dox·ly
  or·tho·dox·ness
or·tho·doxy
  or·tho·dox·ies
or·tho·gen·ic
or·thog·o·nal
  or·thog·o·nal·ly
or·thog·ra·phy
  or·thog·ra·phies
  or·thog·ra·pher
  or·tho·graph·ic
  or·tho·graph·i·cal
  or·tho·graph·i·cal·ly
or·tho·pe·dics
  or·tho·pe·dic
  or·tho·pe·dist
Osa·ka
Os·car
os·cil·late
  os·cil·lat·ed
  os·cil·lat·ing
  os·cil·la·tion
  os·cil·la·tor
  os·cil·la·to·ry
os·cil·lo·scope
os·cu·late
  os·cu·lat·ed
  os·cu·lat·ing
  os·cu·la·tion
  os·cu·la·to·ry
Osh·kosh
Os·lo
os·mi·um
os·mose
  os·mosed
  os·mos·ing
os·mo·sis
  os·mot·ic
  os·mot·i·cal·ly
os·prey
os·si·fy
  os·si·fied
  os·si·fy·ing
  os·si·fi·er
Os·si·ning
os·ten·si·ble
  os·ten·si·bly
os·ten·sive
  os·ten·sive·ly

os·ten·ta·tion
  os·ten·ta·tious
  os·ten·ta·tious·ly
  os·ten·ta·tious·ness
os·te·op·a·thy
  os·te·o·path
  os·te·o·path·ic
  os·te·o·path·i·cal·ly
os·tra·cism
os·tra·cize
  os·tra·cized
  os·tra·ciz·ing
os·trich
Os·we·go
Othel·lo
oth·er
  oth·er·ness
  oth·er·wise
  oth·er world
  oth·er·world·ly
  oth·er·world·li·ness
oti·ose
  oti·ose·ly
  oti·os·i·ty
Ot·ta·wa
ot·ter
ot·to·man
Oua·ga·dou·gou
ought
Oui·da
Oui·ja
ounce
our·self
our·selves
oust·er
out·bid
  out·bid·den
  out·bid·ding
  out·bid·der
out·board
out·bound
out·brave
  out·braved
  out·brav·ing
out·break
out·build·ing
out·burst
out·cast
out·come
out·cry
  out·cries
out·dat·ed
out·dis·tance
  out·dis·tanced
  out·dis·tanc·ing
out·do
  out·did
  out·done
  out·do·ing
out·door
out·er
  out·er·most
  out·er space
out·face
  out·faced

out·fac·ing
out·field
  out·field·er
out·fit
  out·fit·ted
  out·fit·ting
  out·fit·ter
out·flank
out·fox
out·go
  out·went
  out·gone
  out·go·ing
out·grow
  out·grew
  out·grown
  out·grow·ing
out·growth
out·guess
out·ing
out·land·ish
  out·land·ish·ly
  out·land·ish·ness
out·last
out·law
  out·law·ry
out·lay
  out·laid
  out·lay·ing
out·let
out·line
  out·lined
  out·lin·ing
out·live
  out·lived
  out·liv·ing
out·look
out·ly·ing
out·mod·ed
out·num·ber
out-of-date
  out-of-date·ness
out·post
out·put
out·rage
  out·raged
  out·rag·ing
out·ra·geous
  out·ra·geous·ly
  out·ra·geous·ness
out·range
  out·ranged
  out·rang·ing
out·rank
out·rig·ger
out·right
out·run
  out·ran
  out·run·ning
out·sell
  out·sold
  out·sell·ing
out·set
out·shine
  out·shone

out·shin·ing
out·side
out·sid·er
out·skirts
out·smart
out·spo·ken
  out·spo·ken·ly
  out·spo·ken·ness
out·stand·ing
  out·stand·ing·ly
  out·stand·ing·ness
out·strip
  out·stripped
  out·strip·ping
out·ward
  out·wards
  out·ward·ly
  out·ward·ness
out·wear
  out·wore
  out·worn
  out·wear·ing
out·weigh
out·wit
  out·wit·ted
  out·wit·ting
ova
oval
  oval·ly
  oval·ness
ova·ry
  ova·ries
ovar·i·an
ovate
ova·tion
ov·en
over
over·act
over·age
over·all
over·alls
over·awe
  over·awed
  over·aw·ing
over·bear·ing
  over·bear·ing·ly
over·blown
over·board
over·build
  over·built
  over·build·ing
over·cast
over·charge
  over·charged
  over·charg·ing
over·coat
over·come
  over·came
  over·com·ing
  over·com·er
over·com·pen·sa·tion
  over·com·pen·sate
  over·com·pen·sat·ed
  over·com·pen·sat·ing
over·con·fi·dence

over·con·fi·dent
over·do
  over·did
  over·done
  over·do·ing
over·dose
  over·dos·age
  over·dosed
  over·dos·ing
over·draft
over·draw
  over·drew
  over·drawn
  over·draw·ing
over·drive
over·due
over·em·pha·sis
  over·em·pha·size
  over·em·pha·sized
  over·em·pha·sizing
over·es·ti·mate
  over·es·ti·mat·ed
  over·es·ti·mat·ing
  over·es·ti·ma·tion
over·flow
  over·flowed
  over·flown
  over·flowing
over·gen·er·ous
  over·gen·er·ous·ness
over·grow
  over·grew
  over·grown
  over·grow·ing
over·growth
over·hand
  over·hand·ed
over·hang
  over·hung
  over·hang·ing
over·haul
  over·haul·ing
over·head
over·hear
  over·heard
  over·hear·ing
over·joy
  over·joyed
over·kill
over·land
over·lap
  over·lapped
  over·lap·ping
over·lay
  over·laid
  over·lay·ing
over·look
over·lord
  over·lord·ship
over·ly
over·much
over·night
over·pass
over·play
over·pow·er

over·pow·er·ing
  over·pow·er·ing·ly
over·rate
  over·rat·ed
  over·rat·ing
over·reach
over·ride
  over·rode
  over·rid·den
  over·rid·ing
over·rule
  over·ruled
  over·rul·ing
over·run
  over·ran
  over·run·ning
over·seas
over·see
  over·saw
  over·seen
  over·see·ing
  over·se·er
over·sexed
over·shad·ow
over·shoe
over·shoot
  over·shot
  over·shoot·ing
over·sight
over·sim·pli·fy
  over·sim·pli·fied
  over·sim·pli·fy·ing
  over·sim·pli·fi·ca·tion
over·size
over·sleep
  over·slept
  over·sleep·ing
over·spread
  over·spread·ing
over·state
  over·stat·ed
  over·stat·ing
  over·state·ment
over·stay
over·step
  over·stepped
  over·step·ping
over·strung
over·stuff
overt
  overt·ly
over·take
  over·took
  over·tak·en
  over·tak·ing
over·tax
over·the·coun·ter
over·throw
  over·threw
  over·thrown
  over·throw·ing
over·time
over·tone
over·ture
over·turn

151

over·view
over·ween·ing
  over·ween·ing·ly
  over·ween·ing·ness
over·weight
over·whelm
  over·whelm·ing
  over·whelm·ing·ly
over·work
  over·worked
  over·work·ing
over·wrought
ovi·duct
ovip·a·rous
  ovip·ar·ous·ly
  ovip·ar·ous·ness
ovoid
  ovoi·dal
ovu·late
  ovu·lat·ed
  ovu·lat·ing
  ovu·la·tion
ovule
  ovu·lar
ovum
  ova
owe
  owed
  ow·ing
owl·ish
own·er
ox·al·ic ac·id
ox·bow
ox·en
ox·ford
ox·i·da·tion
  ox·i·da·tive
  ox·i·dant
ox·ide
ox·i·dize
  ox·i·dized
  ox·i·diz·ing
ox·y·a·cet·y·lene
ox·y·gen
ox·y·gen·ate
  ox·y·gen·at·ed
  ox·y·gen·at·ing
  ox·y·gen·a·tion
oys·ter
ozone
pab·u·lum
pace
  paced
  pac·ing
  pac·er
pace·mak·er
pa·cif·ic
pa·cif·i·ca·tion
  pa·cif·i·ca·tor
  pa·cif·i·ca·to·ry
pac·i·fi·er
pac·i·fism
  pac·i·fist
pac·i·fy
  pac·i·fied

pac·i·fy·ing
pack·age
  pack·ag·er
  pack·er
pack·et
pack·ing
pad
  pad·ded
  pad·ding
pad·dle
  pad·dled
  pad·dling
  pad·dler
pad·dock
pad·dy
  pad·dies
pad·lock
pae·an
  pe·an
pa·gan
  pa·gan·ism
page
  paged
  pag·ing
pag·eant
  pag·eant·ry
pag·i·nate
  pag·i·nat·ed
  pag·i·nat·ing
pa·go·da
pain
  pain·ful
  pain·less
  pain·less·ness
pain·kil·ler
pains·tak·ing
  pains·tak·ing·ly
paint·er
paint·ing
pais·ley
pa·jam·as
Pak·i·stan
pal·ace
pal·at·a·ble
  pal·at·a·bil·i·ty
  pal·at·a·bly
pal·ate
pa·la·tial
  pa·la·tial·ly
pal·a·tine
  pa·lat·i·nate
pa·lav·er
pale
  paled
  pal·ing
  pale·ly
  pale·ness
Pa·le·o·lith·ic
pa·le·on·tol·o·gy
  pa·le·on·to·log·ic
  pa·le·on·to·log·i·cal
  pa·le·on·tol·o·gist
Pa·ler·mo
Pal·es·tine
pal·ette

pal·imp·sest
pal·in·drome
pal·ing
pal·i·sade
  pal·i·sad·ed
  pal·i·sad·ing
pal·la·di·um
pall·bear·er
pal·let
pal·li·ate
  pal·li·at·ed
  pal·li·at·ing
  pal·li·a·tion
pal·lid
pal·lor
palm
  pal·ma·ceous
pal·mate
  pal·mate·ly
palm·er
palm·is·try
  palm·ist
palmy
  palm·i·er
  palm·i·est
pal·o·mi·no
  pal·o·mi·nos
Pa·los
pal·pa·ble
  pal·pa·bil·i·ty
  pal·pa·bly
pal·pate
  pal·pat·ed
  pal·pat·ing
  pal·pa·tion
pal·pi·tate
  pal·pi·tat·ed
  pal·pi·tat·ing
  pal·pi·ta·tion
pal·sy
  pal·sied
  pal·sy·ing
pal·ter
  pal·ter·er
pal·try
  pal·tri·er
  pal·tri·est
  pal·tri·ness
pam·pas
pam·pe·an
pam·per
  pam·per·er
pam·phlet
pan
  panned
  pan·ning
pan·a·ce·a
  pan·a·ce·an
pa·nache
Pan·a·ma
Pan-Amer·i·can
pan·cake
  pan·caked
  pan·cak·ing
pan·cre·as

pan·cre·at·ic
pan·dem·ic
pan·de·mo·ni·um
pan·der
Pan·do·ra
pan·el
  pan·eled
  pan·el·ing
  pan·el·ist
pang
pan·han·dle
  pan·han·dled
  pan·han·dling
pan·ic
  pan·icked
  pan·ick·ing
pan·nier
  pan·ier
pan·o·ply
  pan·o·plies
  pan·o·plied
pan·o·rama
  pan·o·ram·ic
  pan·o·ram·i·cal·ly
pan·sy
  pan·sies
pan·ta·loon
pan·the·ism
  pan·the·ist
  pan·the·is·tic
pan·the·on
pan·ther
pan·ties
pan·to·mime
  pan·to·mimed
  pan·to·mim·ing
  pan·to·mim·ic
  pan·to·mim·ist
pan·try
  pan·tries
pant·suit
pant·y·hose
pa·pa
pa·pa·cy
  pa·pa·cies
pa·pal
pa·per
  pa·per·er
  pa·pery
pa·per·back
pa·per·weight
pa·per·work
pa·pier·mâ·ché
pa·pil·la
  pa·pil·lae
pa·poose
pap·ri·ka
Pap·ua
pa·py·rus
par·a·ble
par·a·chute
  par·a·chut·ed
  par·a·chut·ing
  par·a·chut·ist
Par·a·clete

pa·rade
pa·rad·ed
pa·rad·ing
par·a·digm
par·a·dig·mat·ic
par·a·dise
par·a·di·si·a·cal
par·a·dox
par·a·dox·i·cal
par·af·fin
par·a·gon
par·a·graph
  par·a·graph·er
Par·a·guay
par·a·keet
par·al·lax
par·al·lac·tic
par·al·lel
  par·al·leled
  par·al·lel·ing
  par·al·lel·o·gram
pa·ral·y·sis
  pa·ral·y·ses
par·a·lyt·ic
par·a·lyze
  par·a·lyzed
  par·a·lyz·ing
Par·a·mar·i·bo
par·a·me·ci·um
par·a·med·ic
pa·ram·e·ter
par·a·mount
  par·a·mount·cy
  par·a·mount·ly
par·a·mour
par·a·noia
  par·a·noid
par·a·pet
par·a·pher·nal·ia
par·a·phrase
  par·a·phrased
  par·a·phras·ing
  par·a·phras·er
  par·a·phras·tic
par·a·ple·gia
  par·a·ple·gic
par·a·psy·chol·o·gy
par·a·site
  par·a·sit·ic
  par·a·sit·i·cal·ly
  par·a·sit·ism
par·a·sol
par·a·sym·pa·thet·ic
par·a·thi·on
par·a·troop·er
par·a·ty·phoid
par·boil
par·cel
  par·celed
  par·cel·ling
parch·ment
par·don
  par·don·a·ble
  par·don·a·bly
pare

pared
par·ing
par·e·gor·ic
par·ent
  pa·ren·tal
par·ent·age
pa·ren·the·sis
  pa·ren·the·ses
par·en·thet·ic
par·en·thet·i·cal
pa·re·sis
  pa·ret·ic
par·fait
pa·ri·ah
par·i·mu·tu·el
Par·is
par·ish
  pa·rish·ion·er
par·i·ty
par·ka
Par·kin·son
park·way
par·lance
par·lay
  par·layed
  par·lay·ing
par·ley
  par·leyed
  par·ley·ing
par·lia·ment
par·lia·men·tar·i·an
par·lia·men·ta·ry
par·lor
Par·ma
Par·me·san
pa·ro·chi·al
par·o·dy
  par·o·dies
  par·o·died
  par·o·dy·ing
pa·rod·ic
par·o·dist
pa·role
  pa·roled
  pa·rol·ing
pa·rot·id
par·ox·ysm
  par·ox·ys·mal
par·quet
  par·queted
  par·quet·ing
par·quet·ry
par·rot
  par·rot·like
  par·roty
par·ry
  par·ried
  par·ry·ing
parse
par·si·mo·ny
  par·si·mo·ni·ous
  par·si·mo·ni·ous·ly
  par·si·mo·ni·ous·ness
par·sley
pars·nip

par·son
par·son·age
par·take
  par·took
  par·tak·en
  par·tak·ing
  par·ta·ker
part·ed
par·the·no·gen·e·sis
Par·the·non
par·tial
  par·tial·ly
par·ti·al·i·ty
  par·ti·al·i·ties
par·tic·i·pant
par·tic·i·pate
  par·tic·i·pat·ed
  par·tic·i·pat·ing
  par·tic·i·pa·tion
  par·tic·i·pa·tive
par·ti·cip·i·al
par·ti·ci·ple
par·ti·cle
par·ti·col·ored
par·tic·u·lar
  par·tic·u·lar·ly
par·tic·u·lar·i·ty
  par·tic·u·lar·i·ties
par·tic·u·lar·ize
  par·tic·u·lar·ized
  par·tic·u·lar·iz·ing
par·tic·u·late
part·ing
par·ti·san
  par·ti·san·ship
par·tite
par·ti·tion
par·ti·tive
part·ly
part·ner
  part·ner·ship
par·tridge
  par·tridg·es
part·time
par·tu·ri·ent
par·tu·ri·tion
par·ty
  par·ties
par·ve·nu
Pas·a·de·na
pas·chal
pa·sha
pass·a·ble
pass·a·bly
pas·sage
pas·sage·way
Pas·sa·ic
pass·book
pas·sé
pas·sen·ger
pass·er·by
  pass·ers·by
pass·ing
pas·sion
  pas·sion·less

pas·sion·ate
  pas·sion·ate·ly
  pas·sion·ate·ness
pas·sive
pass·key
Pass·o·ver
pass·port
pass·word
pas·ta
paste
  pas·ted
  pas·ting
paste·board
pas·tel
Pas·teur
pas·teur·ize
  pas·teur·ized
  pas·teur·iz·ing
  pas·teur·i·za·tion
pas·tille
pas·time
pas·tor
pas·to·ral
pas·tor·ate
pas·tra·mi
pas·try
  pas·tries
pas·ture
  pas·tured
  pas·tur·ing
  pas·tur·age
pasty
past·i·er
past·i·est
pat
  pat·ted
  pat·ting
Pat·a·go·nia
Pa·taps·co
patch·work
patchy
  patch·i·er
  patch·i·est
pâ·té
  pâ·tés
pat·ent
  pa·ten·cy
  pat·ent·ly
pat·ent·ee
pat·er·nal
  pat·ter·nal·ly
pa·ter·nal·ism
pa·ter·ni·ty
Pat·er·son
pa·thet·ic
path·find·er
pa·thol·o·gy
  pa·thol·o·gies
  path·o·log·ic
  path·o·log·i·cal
  path·o·log·i·cal·ly
  pa·thol·o·gist
pa·thos
path·way
pa·tience

pa·tient
  pa·tient·ly
pat·i·na
pa·tio
pa·ti·os
pat·ois
pa·tri·arch
pa·tri·ar·chy
  pa·tri·ar·chies
pa·tri·cian
pat·ri·mo·ny
  pat·ri·mo·nies
pa·tri·ot
  pa·tri·ot·ic
  pa·tri·ot·i·cal·ly
  pa·tri·ot·ism
pa·trol
  pa·trolled
  pa·trol·ling
  pa·trol·ler
pa·trol·man
  pa·trol·men
pa·tron
  pa·tron·ess
pa·tron·age
pa·tron·ize
  pa·tron·ized
  pa·tron·iz·ing
  pa·tron·iz·ing·ly
pat·ro·nym·ic
pat·sy
  pat·sies
pat·ter
pat·tern
  pat·terned
Pat·ton
pat·ty
  pat·ties
pau·ci·ty
Paul·ist
paunch
  paunch·i·ness
  paunchy
  paunch·i·er
  paunch·i·est
pau·per
  pau·per·ism
pause
  paused
  paus·ing
  paus·er
pave
  paved
  pav·ing
  pav·er
pave·ment
pa·vil·ion
Pav·lov
pawn
  pawn·er
pawn·bro·ker
Paw·nee
pawn·shop
Paw·tuck·et
pay

paid
pay·ing
pay·ee
pay·er
pay·a·ble
pay·check
pay·load
pay·ment
pay·off
pay·roll
Pea·body
peace
peace·a·ble
  peace·a·bly
peace·ful
  peace·ful·ly
  peace·ful·ness
peace·mak·er
peace·time
peach
pea·cock
peak·ed
pea·nut
pearl
  pearly
Pear·son
Pea·ry
peas·ant
  peas·ant·ry
peaty
peb·ble
  peb·bled
  peb·bling
  peb·bly
pe·can
pec·ca·dil·lo
  pec·ca·dil·loes
  pec·ca·dil·los
peck·er
pec·tin
pec·to·ral
pec·u·late
  pec·u·lat·ed
  pec·u·lat·ing
  pec·u·la·tion
  pec·u·la·tor
pe·cu·liar
  pe·cu·liar·ly
  pe·cu·li·ar·i·ty
  pe·cu·li·ar·i·ties
  pe·cu·ni·ary
ped·a·gogue
  ped·a·gog
  ped·a·gog·ic
  ped·a·gog·i·cal
  ped·a·gog·i·cal·ly
  ped·a·go·gy
ped·al
  ped·aled
  ped·al·ing
ped·ant
  pe·dan·tic
  pe·dan·ti·cal·ly
  ped·ant·ry
ped·dle

ped·dled
ped·dling
ped·dler
ped·ler
ped·lar
ped·es·tal
pe·des·tri·an
  pe·des·tri·an·ism
pe·di·at·rics
  pe·di·at·ric
  pe·di·a·tri·cian
  pe·di·at·rist
ped·i·cure
  ped·i·cur·ist
ped·i·gree
  ped·i·greed
ped·i·ment
  ped·i·men·tal
  ped·i·ment·ed
pe·dom·e·ter
peep·hole
peer
  peer·age
  peer·ess
peer·less
  peer·less·ly
peeve
peeved
peev·ing
peev·ish
  pee·vish·ly
  pee·vish·ness
pee·wee
peg
  pegged
  peg·ging
Peg·a·sus
Pei·ping
pe·jo·ra·tive
  pe·jo·ra·tive·ly
Pe·king·ese
  Pe·ki·nese
pe·koe
Pe·la·gian
pel·i·can
pel·la·gra
pel·let
pell-mell
pel·lu·cid
  pel·lu·cid·i·ty
  pel·lu·cid·ness
  pel·lu·cid·ly
pelt·er
pelt·ry
pel·vis
  pel·vis·es
  pel·ves
  pel·vic
pem·mi·can
  pem·i·can
pen
  penned
  pen·ning
  pen·ner
  pe·nal

pe·nal·ize
  pe·nal·ized
  pe·nal·iz·ing
  pe·nal·i·za·tion
  pe·nal·ly
pen·al·ty
  pen·al·ties
pen·ance
pen·chant
pen·cil
  pen·ciled
  pen·cil·ing
pend·ant
pend·ent
  pend·en·cy
  pend·ent·ly
pend·ing
pen·du·lous
  pen·du·lous·ly
  pen·du·lous·ness
pen·du·lum
pen·e·tra·ble
  pen·e·tra·bil·i·ty
  pen·e·tra·ble·ness
  pen·e·tra·bly
pen·e·trate
  pen·e·trat·ed
  pen·e·trat·ing
  pen·e·tra·tive
  pen·e·tra·tion
pen·i·cil·lin
pen·in·su·la
  pen·in·su·lar
pe·nis
  pe·nes
  pe·nis·es
pe·nile
pe·ni·al
pen·i·tent
  pen·i·tence
  pen·i·ten·tial
  pen·i·ten·tial·ly
  pen·i·tent·ly
  pen·i·ten·tia·ry
  pen·i·ten·tia·ries
pen·knife
  pen·knives
pen·man·ship
pen·nant
pen·ni·less
pen·non
Penn·syl·va·nia
pen·ny
  pen·nies
pen·ny an·te
pen·ny pinch·er
  pen·ny pinch·ing
pen·ny·weight
pen·ny·wise
Pe·nob·scot
pe·nol·o·gy
  pe·no·log·i·cal
  pe·nol·o·gist
Pen·sa·co·la
pen·sion

pen·sion·a·ble
pen·sion·ary
pen·sion·ar·ies
pen·sion·er
pen·sive
pen·sive·ly
pen·sive·ness
pen·ta·gon
pen·tag·o·nal
pen·tag·o·nal·ly
pen·tam·e·ter
Pen·ta·teuch
pen·tath·lon
Pen·te·cost
Pen·te·cos·tal
pent·house
pent-up
pe·nult
pe·nul·ti·ma
pe·nul·ti·mate
pe·num·bra
pe·num·bras
pe·num·brae
pe·num·bral
pe·nu·ri·ous
pe·nu·ri·ous·ly
pe·nu·ri·ous·ness
pen·u·ry
Pen·zance
pe·on
pe·on·age
pe·o·ny
pe·o·nies
peo·ple
peo·pled
peo·pling
peo·pler
Pe·o·ria
pep
pepped
pep·ping
pep·per
pep·per·corn
pep·per·mint
pep·pery
pep·per·i·ness
pep·py
pep·pi·er
pep·pi·est
pep·pi·ness
pep·sin
pep·tic
per·am·bu·late
per·am·bu·lat·ed
per·am·bu·lat·ing
per·am·bu·la·tion
per·am·bu·la·to·ry
per·am·bu·la·tor
per an·num
per·cale
per cap·i·ta
per·ceive
per·ceived
per·ceiv·ing
per·ceiv·a·ble

per·ceiv·a·bly
per·cent
per·cent·age
per·cen·tile
per·cep·ti·ble
per·cep·ti·bil·i·ty
per·cep·ti·bly
per·cep·tion
per·cep·tion·al
per·cep·tu·al
per·cep·tu·al·ly
perch
perch·es
per·chance
per·co·late
per·co·lat·ed
per·co·lat·ing
per·co·la·tion
per·co·la·tor
per·cus·sion
per·cus·sion·ist
per di·em
per·di·tion
per·e·gri·nate
per·e·gri·nat·ed
per·e·gri·nat·ing
per·e·gri·na·tion
per·e·grine
per·emp·to·ry
per·emp·to·ri·ly
per·emp·to·ri·ness
per·en·ni·al
per·en·ni·al·ly
per·fect
per·fect·er
per·fect·ness
per·fect·i·ble
per·fect·i·bil·i·ty
per·fec·tive
per·fec·tive·ness
per·fec·tion
per·fec·tion·ist
per·fect·ly
per·fi·dy
per·fid·i·ous
per·fid·i·ous·ly
per·fid·i·ous·ness
per·fo·rate
per·fo·rat·ed
per·fo·rat·ing
per·fo·ra·tor
per·fo·ra·tion
per·force
per·form
per·form·a·ble
per·form·er
per·for·mance
per·fume
per·fumed
per·fum·ing
per·fum·er
per·fum·ery
per·fum·er·ies
per·func·to·ry
per·func·to·ri·ly

per·func·to·ri·ness
per·haps
Per·i·cles
per·i·gee
per·i·ge·al
per·i·ge·an
per·i·he·li·on
per·i·he·lia
per·il
per·iled
per·il·ing
per·il·ous
per·il·ous·ly
per·il·ous·ness
pe·rim·e·ter
per·i·met·ric
per·i·met·ri·cal
per·i·met·ri·cal·ly
pe·ri·od
pe·ri·od·ic
pe·ri·o·dic·i·ty
pe·ri·od·i·cal
pe·ri·od·i·cal·ly
per·i·pa·tet·ic
per·i·pa·tet·i·cal·ly
pe·riph·ery
pe·riph·er·ies
pe·riph·er·al
pe·riph·er·al·ly
per·i·phrase
per·i·scope
per·i·scopic
per·i·scop·i·cal
per·ish
per·ish·a·ble
per·ish·a·bil·i·ty
per·ish·a·ble·ness
per·ish·a·bly
per·i·stal·sis
per·i·stal·ses
per·i·stal·tic
per·i·style
per·i·to·ne·um
per·i·to·ne·ums
per·i·to·nea
per·i·to·ne·al
per·i·to·ni·tis
per·i·wig
per·i·win·kle
per·jure
per·jured
per·jur·ing
per·jur·er
per·ju·ry
per·ju·ries
perky
perk·i·er
perk·i·est
per·ma·nent
per·me·a·ble
per·me·a·bil·i·ty
per·me·a·bly
per·me·ate
per·me·at·ed
per·me·at·ing

per·me·a·tion
per·me·a·tive
per·mis·si·ble
  per·mis·si·bil·i·ty
  per·mis·si·bly
per·mis·sion
per·mis·sive
  per·mis·sive·ly
  per·mis·sive·ness
per·mit
  per·mit·ted
  per·mit·ting
  per·mit·ter
per·mu·ta·tion
per·ni·cious
  per·ni·cious·ly
  per·ni·cious·ness
Pe·ron
per·o·ra·tion
per·ox·ide
  per·ox·id·ed
  per·ox·id·ing
per·pen·dic·u·lar
  per·pen·dic·u·lar·i·ty
  per·pen·dic·u·lar·ly
per·pe·trate
  per·pe·trat·ed
  per·pe·trat·ing
  per·pe·tra·tion
  per·pe·tra·tor
per·pet·u·al
  per·pet·u·al·ly
per·pet·u·ate
  per·pet·u·at·ed
  per·pet·u·at·ing
  per·pet·u·a·tion
  per·pet·u·a·tor
per·pe·tu·i·ty
  per·pe·tu·i·ties
per·plex
  per·plexed
  per·plex·ing
  per·plex·ing·ly
  per·plex·ed·ly
  per·plex·i·ty
  per·plex·i·ties
per·qui·site
Per·ry·ville
per se
per·se·cute
  per·se·cut·ed
  per·se·cut·ing
  per·se·cu·tive
  per·se·cu·tor
  per·se·cu·tion
per·se·vere
  per·se·vered
  per·se·ver·ing
  per·se·ver·ance
  per·se·ver·ing·ly
Per·shing
Per·sia
per·si·flage
per·sim·mon
per·sist

per·sist·ence
per·sis·ten·cy
per·sist·ent
  per·sist·ent·ly
per·snick·ety
per·son
per·son·a·ble
per·son·age
per·son·al
per·son·al·i·ty
  per·son·al·i·ties
  per·son·al·ize
  per·son·al·ized
  per·son·al·iz·ing
per·son·al·ly
per·so·na non gra·ta
per·son·ate
  per·son·at·ed
  per·son·at·ing
  per·son·a·tion
  per·son·a·tor
per·son·i·fy
  per·son·i·fied
  per·son·i·fy·ing
  per·son·i·fi·ca·tion
  per·son·i·fi·er
per·son·nel
per·spec·tive
  per·spec·tive·ly
per·spi·ca·cious
  per·spi·ca·cious·ly
  per·spi·ca·cious·ness
  per·spi·cac·i·ty
per·spi·cu·i·ty
  per·spic·u·ous
  per·spic·u·ous·ly
per·spi·ra·tion
per·spire
  per·spired
  per·spir·ing
per·suade
  per·suad·ed
  per·suad·ing
  per·suad·a·ble
  per·suad·er
per·sua·sion
per·sua·sive
  per·sua·sive·ly
  per·sua·sive·ness
pert
  pert·ly
  pert·ness
per·tain
Perth·shire
per·ti·na·cious
  per·ti·na·cious·ly
  per·ti·na·cious·ness
  per·ti·nac·i·ty
per·ti·nent
  per·ti·nence
  per·ti·nen·cy
  per·ti·nent·ly
per·turb
  per·turb·a·ble
  per·tur·ba·tion

pe·ruke
pe·ruse
  pe·rused
  pe·rus·ing
  pe·rus·al
  pe·rus·er
per·vade
  per·vad·ed
  per·vad·ing
  per·vad·er
per·va·sion
per·va·sive
  per·va·sive·ly
  per·va·sive·ness
per·verse
  per·verse·ly
  per·verse·ness
  per·ver·si·ty
per·ver·sion
per·vert
  per·vert·ed
  per·vert·ed·ly
  per·vert·er
  per·vert·i·ble
per·vi·ous
  per·vi·ous·ness
pes·ky
  pes·ki·er
  pes·ki·est
  pesk·i·ly
  pesk·i·ness
pes·si·mism
  pes·si·mist
  pes·si·mis·tic
  pes·si·mis·ti·cal·ly
pes·ter
pest·hole
pest·i·cide
pes·tif·er·ous
  pes·tif·er·ous·ly
  pes·tif·er·ous·ness
pes·ti·lence
  pes·ti·len·tial
pes·ti·lent
  pes·ti·lent·ly
pes·tle
  pes·tled
  pes·tling
pet
  pet·ted
  pet·ting
  pet·ter
pet·al
  pet·aled
pet·cock
pe·ter
Pe·ters·burg
pet·i·ole
pe·tite
  pe·tite·ness
pet·it four
pe·ti·tion
  pe·ti·tion·ary
  pe·ti·tion·er
Pe·trarch

pet·rel
pet·ri·fy
 pet·ri·fied
 pet·ri·fy·ing
 pet·ri·fac·tion
pe·tro·chem·is·try
 pe·tro·chem·i·cal
Pet·ro·grad
pet·rol
pet·ro·la·tum
pe·trol·le·um
pet·ti·coat
pet·ti·fog
 pet·ti·fogged
 pet·ti·fog·ging
 pet·ti·fog·ger
 pet·ti·fog·gery
pet·tish
 pet·tish·ly
 pet·tish·ness
pet·ty
 pet·ti·er
 pet·ti·est
 pet·ti·ly
 pet·ti·ness
pet·u·lant
 pet·u·lance
 pet·u·lan·cy
 pet·u·lant·ly
pe·tu·nia
pew·ter
pe·yo·te
 pe·yo·tes
pha·e·ton
pha·lanx
 pha·lanx·es
 pha·lang·es
phal·lus
 phal·li
 phal·lus·es
 phal·lic
phan·tasm
 phan·tas·ma
 phan·tas·mal
 phan·tas·mic
phan·tas·ma·go·ria
 phan·tas·ma·go·ri·al
 phan·tas·ma·gor·ic
phan·ta·sy
 phan·ta·sies
phan·tom
phar·aoh
Phar·i·see
 phar·i·sa·ic
 phar·i·sa·i·cal
 phar·i·sa·ism
 phar·i·see·ism
phar·ma·ceu·ti·cal
 phar·ma·ceu·tic
 phar·ma·ceu·ti·cal·ly
phar·ma·ceu·tics
phar·ma·cist
phar·ma·col·o·gy
 phar·ma·co·log·ic
 phar·ma·co·log·i·ca

phar·ma·col·o·gist
phar·ma·co·poe·ia
 phar·ma·co·poe·ial
phar·ma·cy
 phar·ma·cies
Pha·ros
phar·ynx
 phar·yn·ges
 pha·ryn·ge·al
 pha·ryn·gal
phase
 phased
 phas·ing
 pha·sic
pheas·ant
phe·no·bar·bi·tal
phe·nol
 phe·nol·ic
phe·nom·e·non
 phe·nom·e·na
 phe·nom·e·nons
 phe·nom·e·nal
 phe·nom·e·nal·ly
phi·al
Phi Be·ta Kap·pa
Phil·a·del·phia
phi·lan·der
 phi·lan·der·er
phi·lan·thro·py
 phi·lan·thro·pies
 phil·an·throp·ic
 phil·an·throp·i·cal
 phil·an·throp·i·cal·ly
 phi·lan·thro·pist
phi·lat·e·ly
 phil·a·tel·ic
 phil·a·tel·i·cal
 phi·lat·e·list
phil·har·mon·ic
Phil·ip
Phi·lip·pi·ans
Phil·ip·pine
Phi·lis·tine
 Phi·lis·tin·ism
phil·o·den·dron
 phil·o·den·drons
 phil·o·den·dra
phi·lol·o·gy
 phi·lol·o·gist
 phi·lol·o·ger
phil·o·lo·gi·an
 phil·o·log·i·cal
 phil·o·log·ic
 phil·o·log·i·cal·ly
phi·los·o·pher
 phil·o·soph·i·cal
 phil·o·soph·ic
 phil·o·soph·i·cal·ly
phi·los·o·phize
 phi·los·o·phized
 phi·los·o·phiz·ing
 phi·los·o·phiz·er
phi·los·o·phy
 phi·los·o·phies
phil·ter

phil·tered
 phil·ter·ing
phle·bi·tis
 phle·bit·ic
phle·bot·o·my
 phle·bot·o·mist
phlegm
phleg·mat·ic
 phleg·mat·i·cal
 phleg·mat·i·cal·ly
phlox
pho·bia
 pho·bic
phoe·be
Phoe·ni·cia
phoe·nix
phone
 phoned
 phon·ing
pho·neme
 pho·ne·mic
pho·net·ics
 pho·net·ic
 pho·net·i·cal
 pho·net·i·cal·ly
phon·ic
 phon·ics
pho·no·graph
 pho·no·graph·ic
 pho·no·graph·i·cal·ly
pho·nol·o·gy
 pho·nol·o·gies
 pho·no·log·ic
 pho·no·log·i·cal
 pho·no·log·i·cal·ly
 pho·nol·o·gist
pho·ny
 pho·ni·er
 pho·ni·est
 pho·nies
 pho·ni·ness
phos·phate
phos·pho·res·cence
 phos·pho·resce
 phos·pho·resced
 phos·pho·resc·ing
 phos·pho·res·cent
 phos·pho·res·cent·ly
phos·pho·rus
pho·to
 pho·tos
pho·to·copy
 pho·to·cop·ies
 pho·to·cop·ied
 pho·to·cop·y·ing
pho·to·e·lec·tric
pho·to·en·grav·ing
pho·to·en·grave
 pho·to·en·graved
 pho·to·en·grav·er
pho·to·flash
pho·to·gen·ic
pho·to·graph
pho·tog·ra·pher
pho·tog·ra·phy

pho·to·graph·ic
pho·to·graph·i·cal
pho·to·graph·i·cal·ly
pho·to·gra·vure
pho·to·off·set
Pho·to·stat
  pho·to·stat·ed
  pho·to·stat·ing
  pho·to·stat·ic
pho·to·syn·the·sis
phrase
  phrased
  phras·ing
  phras·al
phra·se·ol·o·gy
phre·net·ic
phre·nol·o·gy
  phre·nol·o·gist
Phryg·i·an
phy·lac·tery
  phy·lac·ter·ies
phy·log·e·ny
  phy·lo·gen·e·sis
  phy·lo·ge·net·ic
  phy·lo·gen·ic
  phy·log·e·nist
phy·lum
phys·ic
  phys·icked
  phys·ick·ing
phys·i·cal
  phys·i·cal·ly
phy·si·cian
phys·ics
  phys·i·cist
phys·i·og·no·my
  phys·i·og·no·mies
  phys·i·og·nom·ic
  phys·i·og·nom·i·cal
  phys·i·og·no·mist
phys·i·og·ra·phy
  phys·i·og·ra·pher
  phys·i·o·graph·ic
  phys·i·o·graph·i·cal
phys·i·ol·o·gy
  phys·i·o·log·ic
  phys·i·o·log·i·cal
  phys·i·o·log·i·cal·ly
  phys·i·ol·o·gist
phys·i·o·ther·a·py
phy·sique
pi·a·nis·si·mo
pi·an·ist
pi·ano
  pi·an·os
pi·an·o·for·te
pi·az·za
pi·ca
pic·a·dor
Pic·ar·dy
pic·a·resque
Pi·cas·so
pic·a·yune
  pic·a·yun·ish
Pic·ca·dil·ly

pic·ca·lil·li
pic·co·lo
  pic·co·los
  pic·co·lo·ist
pick·ax
picked
pick·er·el
pick·et
  pick·et·er
pick·ing
pick·le
  pick·led
  pick·ling
pick·pock·et
pick·up
Pick·wick
picky
  pick·i·er
  pick·i·est
pic·nic
  pic·nicked
  pic·nick·ing
  pic·nick·er
pic·to·ri·al
  pic·to·ri·al·ly
pic·ture
  pic·tured
  pic·tur·ing
pic·tur·esque
  pic·tur·esque·ly
  pic·tur·esque·ness
pid·dle
  pid·dled
  pid·dling
pidg·in
pie·bald
piece
  piec·er
  piece·meal
  piece·work
  piece·work·er
pied
Pied·mont
pier
pierce
  pierced
  pierc·ing
  pierc·ing·ly
Pier·rot
pi·e·tism
  pi·e·tis·tic
  pi·e·tis·ti·cal
pi·e·ty
  pi·e·ties
pif·fle
pig
  pigged
  pig·ging
pi·geon
  pi·geon·hole
  pi·geon·holed
  pi·geon·hol·ing
  pi·geon·toed
pig·gish
  pig·gish·ly

pig·gish·ness
pig·gy·back
pig·head·ed
  pig·head·ed·ly
  pig·head·ed·ness
pig·ment
  pig·men·tary
  pig·men·ta·tion
pig·pen
pig·skin
pig·sty
  pig·sties
pig·tail
pike
  piked
  pik·ing
pik·er
pi·las·ter
Pi·late
pil·chard
pile
  piled
  pil·ing
pil·fer
  pil·fer·age
  pil·fer·er
pil·grim
  pil·grim·age
  pil·grim·aged
  pil·grim·ag·ing
pil·lage
  pil·laged
  pil·lag·ing
  pil·lag·er
pil·lar
pill·box
pil·lion
pil·lo·ry
  pil·lo·ries
  pil·lo·ried
  pil·lo·ry·ing
pil·low
pill·low·case
pi·lot
  pi·lot·age
  pi·lot·less
  pi·lot·house
pi·men·to
  pi·men·tos
pim·ple
  pim·pled
  pim·ply
pin
  pinned
  pin·ning
pin·a·fore
pi·ña·ta
pince·nez
pin·cers
pinch
  pinch·er
pinch·beck
pin·cush·ion
Pin·dar
pine

pine-like
piney
pined
pin-ing
pin-e-al
pine-ap-aple
pin-feath-er
pin-feath-ered
pin-feath-ery
pin-fold
pin-head
pin-head-ed
pin-hole
pin-ion
pink-eye
pink-ie
pinko
pink-os
pink-oes
pin-na
pin-nas
pin-nae
pin-nal
pin-na-cle
pin-na-cled
pin-na-cling
pin-nate
pin-nate-ly
pin-na-tion
pi-noch-le
pi-noc-le
pin-point
pin-prick
pin-set-ter
pin-tail
pin-tailed
pin-tle
pin-to
pin-tos
pin-up
pin-wheel
pin-worm
pi-o-neer
pi-ous
pi-ous-ly
pi-ous-ness
pip
pipped
pip-ping
pipe-line
pipe-lined
pipe-lin-ing
pip-er
pip-ing
pip-it
pip-pin
pip-squeak
pi-quant
pi-quan-cy
pi-quant-ness
pi-quant-ly
pique
piqued
pi-quing
pi-qué

pi-ra-cy
pi-ra-cies
Pi-rae-us
pi-ra-nha
pi-rate
pi-rat-ed
pi-rat-ing
pi-rat-i-cal
pi-rat-i-cal-ly
pi-rogue
pir-ou-ette
pir-ou-et-ted
pir-ou-et-ting
Pi-sa
Pis-ces
pis-ci-cul-ture
pis-ta-chio
pis-ta-chi-os
pis-til
pis-til-late
pis-tol
pis-toled
pis-tol-ing
pis-ton
pit
pit-ted
pit-ting
pitch-black
pitch-blende
pitch-er
pitch-fork
pitchy
pitch-i-er
pitch-i-est
pit-e-ous
pit-e-ous-ly
pit-e-ous-ness
pit-fall
pith
pithy
pith-i-er
pith-i-est
pith-i-ly
pith-i-ness
pit-i-a-ble
pit-i-a-ble-ness
pit-i-a-bly
pit-i-ful
pit-i-ful-ly
pit-i-ful-ness
pit-i-less
pit-i-less-ly
pit-i-less-ness
pit-man
pit-men
pit-tance
Pitts-burgh
pi-tu-i-tar-y
pi-tu-i-tar-ies
Pi-us
pity
pit-ies
pit-ied
pit-y-ing
pit-y-ing-ly

piv-ot
piv-ot-al
piv-ot-al-ly
pix-i-lat-ed
pixy
pix-ie
pix-ies
piz-za
Pi-zar-ro
piz-ze-ri-a
piz-zi-ca-to
plac-a-ble
plac-a-bil-i-ty
plac-a-bly
plac-ard
pla-cate
pla-cat-ed
pla-cat-ing
pla-cat-er
pla-ca-tion
pla-ca-tive
pla-ca-to-ry
place
placed
plac-ing
pla-ce-bo
pla-ce-bos
pla-ce-boes
place-ment
pla-cen-ta
pla-cen-tas
pla-cen-tae
pla-cen-tal
plac-er
plac-id
pla-cid-i-ty
plac-id-ness
plac-id-ly
plack-et
pla-gia-rism
pla-gia-rist
pla-gia-ris-tic
pla-gia-rize
pla-gia-rized
pla-gia-riz-ing
pla-gia-riz-er
pla-gia-ry
pla-gia-ries
plague
plagued
pla-guing
pla-guer
pla-guy
pla-guey
pla-gui-ly
plaid
plain
plain-ly
plain-ness
plain-clothes man
plain-song
plain-spo-ken
plain-tiff
plain-tive
plain-tive-ly

plain·tive·ness
plait
plait·ing
plan
planned
plan·ning
plan·less
plan·ner
plane
planed
plan·ing
plan·er
plan·et
plan·e·tar·i·um
plan·e·tar·i·ums
plan·e·tar·ia
plan·e·tary
plan·e·toid
plan·ish
plan·ish·er
plank·ing
plank·ton
plank·ton·ic
plant
plant·a·ble
plant·like
Plan·tag·e·net
plan·tain
plan·ta·tion
plant·er
plaque
plasm
plas·ma
plas·mic
plas·mat·ic
plas·ter
plas·ter·er
plas·ter·ing
plas·ter·work
plas·ter·board
plas·tered
plas·tic
plas·ti·cal·ly
plas·tic·i·ty
plas·ti·ciz·er
plat
plat·ted
plat·ting
plate
plat·ed
plat·ing
plat·er
pla·teau
pla·teaus
pla·teaux
plate·ful
plate·fuls
plate·let
plat·form
plat·i·num
plat·i·tude
plat·i·tu·di·nal
plat·i·tu·di·nous
plat·i·tu·di·nize
plat·i·tu·di·nized

plat·i·tu·di·niz·ing
Pla·to
pla·ton·ic
pla·ton·i·cal·ly
pla·toon
plat·ter
plat·y·pus
plat·y·pus·es
plat·y·pi
plau·dit
plau·si·ble
plau·si·bil·i·ty
plau·si·ble·ness
plau·si·bly
play·act
play·act·ing
play·back
play·bill
play·boy
play·er
play·ful
play·ful·ly
play·ful·ness
play·go·er
play·ground
play·house
play·hous·es
play·let
play·mate
play·off
play·pen
play·thing
play·time
play·wright
pla·za
plea
plead
plead·ed
plead·ing
plead·a·ble
plead·er
pleas·ant
pleas·ant·ly
pleas·ant·ness
pleas·ant·ry
pleas·ant·ries
please
pleased
pleas·ing
pleas·ing·ly
pleas·ing·ness
pleas·ur·a·ble
pleas·ur·a·ble·ness
pleas·ur·a·bly
pleas·ure
pleat
pleat·ed
pleat·er
plebe
ple·be·ian
pleb·i·scite
pledge
pledged
pledg·ing
pledg·ee

pledg·er
ple·na·ry
plen·i·po·ten·ti·ar·y
plen·i·po·ten·ti·ar·ies
plen·i·tude
plen·te·ous
plen·te·ous·ly
plen·ti·ful
plen·ti·ful·ly
plen·ty
pleth·o·ra
ple·thor·ic
pleu·ra
pleu·rae
pleu·ral
pleu·ri·sy
pleu·rit·ic
plex·us
plex·us·es
pli·a·ble
pli·a·bil·i·ty
pli·a·ble·ness
pli·a·bly
pli·ant
pli·an·cy
pli·ant·ness
pli·ant·ly
pli·ca·tion
pli·ers
plight
plink
plod
plod·ded
plod·ding
plod·der
plop
plopped
plop·ping
plot
plot·ted
plot·ting
plot·ter
plow
plow·a·ble
plow·er
plow·man
plow·share
pluck
pluck·er
plucky
pluck·i·er
pluck·i·est
pluck·i·ly
pluck·i·ness
plug
plugged
plug·ging
plug·ger
plum·age
plumb·er
plumb·ing
plume
plumed
plum·ing
plume·like

plumy
plum·i·er
plum·i·est
plum·met
plump
plump·er
plump·ly
plump·ness
plun·der
plun·der·er
plun·der·ous
plunge
plunged
plung·ing
plung·er
plunk·er
plu·ral
plu·ral·ly
plu·ral·ize
plu·ral·ized
plu·ral·iz·ing
plu·ral·ism
plu·ral·ist
plu·ral·is·tic
plu·ral·i·ty
plu·ral·i·ties
plush
plush·i·ness
plushy
plush·i·er
plush·i·est
Plu·tarch
Plu·to
plu·toc·ra·cy
plu·toc·ra·cies
plu·to·crat
plu·to·crat·ic
plu·to·ni·um
plu·vi·al
ply
plied
ply·ing
Plym·outh
ply·wood
pneu·mat·ic
pneu·mat·i·cal·ly
pneu·mat·ics
pneu·mo·nia
pneu·mon·ic
poach
poach·er
Po·ca·hon·tas
pock·et
pock·et·book
pock·et·ful
pock·et·knife
pock·et·knives
pock·mark
pock·marked
pod
pod·ded
pod·ding
pod·like
podgy
podg·i·er

podg·i·est
po·di·a·trist
po·di·a·try
po·di·um
po·dia
po·di·ums
Po·dunk
po·em
po·et·ic
po·et·i·cal
po·et·i·cal·ly
po·e·sy
po·e·sies
po·et
po·et·ess
po·et·ize
po·et·ized
po·et·iz·ing
po·et·iz·er
po·et lau·re·ate
po·ets lau·re·ate
po·et·ry
po·go
po·grom
poign·ant
poign·an·cy
poig·nant·ly
poin·set·tia
point-blank
point·ed
point·ed·ly
point·ed·ness
point·er
poin·til·lism
poin·til·list
point·less
Poi·ret
poise
poised
pois·ing
poi·son
poi·son·er
poi·son·ing
poi·son·ous
poi·son·pen
Poi·tiers
poke
poked
pok·ing
pok·er
poky
pok·i·er
pok·i·est
pok·i·ly
pok·i·ness
Po·land
po·lar
Po·lar·is
po·lar·i·ty
po·lar·i·ties
po·lar·i·za·tion
po·lar·ize
po·lar·ized
po·lar·iz·ing
po·lar·iz·a·ble

po·lar·iz·er
Po·lar·oid
pole
poled
pol·ing
pole·less
pole·cat
po·lem·ic
po·lem·i·cal
po·lem·i·cal·ly
po·lem·i·cist
po·lem·ics
pole·star
po·lice
po·liced
po·lic·ing
pol·i·cy
pol·i·cies
pol·i·cy·hold·er
po·lio
pol·i·o·my·e·li·tis
pol·ish
pol·ish·er
po·lite
po·lite·ly
po·lite·ness
pol·i·tic
po·lit·i·cal
po·lit·i·cal·ly
pol·i·ti·cian
po·lit·i·cize
po·lit·i·cized
po·lit·i·ciz·ing
pol·i·tick
pol·i·tick·er
pol·i·tics
pol·i·ty
pol·i·ties
pol·ka
pol·kaed
pol·ka·ing
poll
poll·ee
poll·er
pol·len
pol·li·nate
pol·li·nat·ed
pol·li·nat·ing
pol·li·na·tion
pol·li·na·tor
pol·li·wog
poll·ster
pol·lu·tant
pol·lute
pol·lut·ed
pol·lut·ing
pol·lu·ter
pol·lu·tion
Pol·ly·an·na
po·lo
po·lo·ist
pol·o·naise
po·lo·ni·um
pol·ter·geist
pol·y·an·dry

162

pol·y·an·drous
pol·y·chro·mat·ic
pol·y·chrome
pol·y·es·ter
pol·y·eth·yl·ene
po·lyg·a·mist
po·lyg·a·my
po·lyg·a·mous
pol·y·glot
pol·y·gon
po·lyg·o·nal
po·lyg·o·nal·ly
pol·y·graph
pol·y·graph·ic
po·lyg·y·ny
po·lyg·y·nous
pol·y·he·dron
pol·y·he·drons
pol·y·he·dra
pol·y·he·dral
pol·y·mer
pol·y·mer·ize
pol·y·mer·ized
pol·y·mer·iz·ing
po·lym·er·ism
po·lym·er·i·za·tion
pol·y·mor·phism
pol·y·mor·phic
pol·y·mor·phous
Poly·ne·sia
pol·y·no·mi·al
pol·yp
pol·y·phon·ic
po·lyph·o·ny
pol·y·sty·rene
pol·y·syl·lab·ic
pol·y·syl·lab·i·cal·ly
pol·y·syl·la·ble
pol·y·tech·nic
pol·y·the·ism
po·y·the·ist
pol·y·the·is·tic
pol·y·the·is·ti·cal
pol·y·un·sat·u·rat·ed
pom·ace
po·made
po·mad·ed
po·mad·ing
pome·gran·ate
Pom·er·a·nia
pom·mel
pom·meled
pom·mel·ing
pom·pa·dour
Pom·peii
Pom·pey
pom·pon
pomp·ous
pom·pos·i·ty
pom·pous·ly
pom·pous·ness
Pon·ce
Pon·ce de Le·ón
pon·cho
pon·der

pon·der·a·ble
pon·der·er
pon·der·ous
pon·der·ous·ly
pon·der·ous·ness
pon·iard
Pon·ti·ac
pon·tiff
pon·tif·i·cal
pon·tif·i·cal·ly
pon·tif·i·cate
pon·tif·i·cat·ed
pon·tif·i·cat·ing
Pon·tius
pon·toon
po·ny
po·nies
po·nied
po·ny·ing
po·ny·tail
poo·dle
pool·room
poor
poor·ish
poor·ly
poor·ness
pop·corn
pop·ery
pop·ish
pop·eyed
pop·gun
pop·in·jay
pop·lar
pop·lin
Po·po·ca·te·petl
pop·per
pop·py
pop·pies
pop·pied
pop·py·cock
pop·u·lace
pop·u·lar
pop·u·lar·ly
pop·u·lar·i·ty
pop·u·lar·ize
pop·u·lar·ized
pop·u·lar·iz·ing
pop·u·lar·i·za·tion
pop·u·lar·iz·er
pop·u·late
pop·u·lat·ed
pop·u·lat·ing
pop·u·la·tion
pop·u·lism
pop·u·list
pop·u·lous
pop·u·lous·ly
por·ce·lain
por·cine
por·cu·pine
pore
pored
por·ing
pork·er
por·nog·ra·phy

por·nog·ra·pher
por·no·graph·ic
por·no·graph·i·cal·ly
po·rous
po·ros·i·ty
po·rous·ly
po·rous·ness
por·poise
por·pois·es
por·ridge
port·a·ble
port·a·bil·i·ty
port·a·bly
por·tage
por·taged
por·tag·ing
por·tal
Port-au-Prince
por·tend
por·tent
por·ten·tous
por·ter
por·ter·house
port·fo·lio
port·fo·li·os
port·hole
Por·tia
por·ti·co
por·ti·coes
por·ti·cos
por·tion
por·tion·less
Port·land
port·ly
port·li·er
port·li·est
port·li·ness
por·trait
por·trait·ist
por·trai·ture
por·tray
por·tray·er
por·tray·al
Ports·mouth
Por·tu·gal
Por·tu·guese
pose
posed
pos·ing
Po·sei·don
pos·er
po·seur
pos·it
po·si·tion
po·si·tion·al
po·si·tion·er
pos·i·tive
pos·i·tive·ly
pos·i·tive·ness
pos·i·tiv·ism
pos·i·tron
pos·se
pos·sess
pos·ses·sor
pos·sessed

pos·ses·sion
pos·ses·sive
  pos·ses·sive·ly
  pos·ses·sive·ness
pos·si·bil·i·ty
pos·si·ble
pos·si·bly
pos·sum
post·age
post·box
post·date
  post·dat·ed
  post·dat·ing
post·er
pos·te·ri·or
  pos·te·ri·or·i·ty
pos·ter·i·ty
post·grad·u·ate
post·haste
post·hu·mous
  post·hu·mous·ly
post·lude
post·man
  post·men
post·mark
post·mas·ter
  post·mis·tress
post me·rid·i·em
post·mor·tem
post·na·sal
post·na·tal
  post·na·tal·ly
post·paid
post·par·tum
post·pone
  post·poned
  post·pon·ing
  post·pon·a·ble
  post·pone·ment
  post·pon·er
post·script
pos·tu·lant
pos·tu·late
  pos·tu·lat·ed
  pos·tu·lat·ing
  pos·tu·la·tion
  pos·tu·la·tor
pos·ture
  pos·tured
  pos·tur·ing
  pos·tur·al
  pos·tur·er
post·war
po·sy
  po·sies
pot
  pot·ted
  pot·ting
po·ta·ble
pot·ash
po·tas·si·um
po·ta·to
  po·ta·toes
pot·bel·ly
  pot·bel·lied

pot·boil·er
po·tent
  po·ten·cy
  po·tent·ly
  po·ten·tate
po·ten·tial
  po·ten·ti·al·i·ty
  po·ten·tial·ly
pot·hole
po·tion
pot·luck
Po·to·mac
pot·pour·ri
Pots·dam
pot·sherd
pot·tage
pot·ter
pot·tery
  pot·ter·ies
pot·ty
  pot·ties
  pot·ty-chair
pouch
  pouched
  pouchy
  pouch·i·er
  pouch·i·est
Pough·keep·sie
poul·tice
  poul·ticed
  poul·tic·ing
poul·try
pounce
  pounced
  pounc·ing
pound·age
pound-fool·ish
pour
  pour·a·ble
  pour·er
pout
pov·er·ty
  pov·er·ty-strick·en
pow·der
  pow·dery
Pow·ell
pow·er
  pow·er·boat
  pow·er·ful
  pow·er·ful·ly
  pow·er·ful·ness
  pow·er·house
  pow·er·less
Pow·ha·tan
pow·wow
prac·ti·ca·ble
  prac·ti·ca·bil·i·ty
  prac·ti·ca·ble·ness
  prac·ti·ca·bly
prac·ti·cal
  prac·ti·cal·i·ty
  prac·ti·cal·ly
prac·tice
  prac·ticed
  prac·ti·tion·er

prae·di·al
pre·di·al
prag·mat·ic
  prag·mat·i·cal
  prag·mat·i·cal·ly
  prag·mat·i·cal·ness
prag·ma·tism
prag·ma·tist
  prag·ma·tis·tic
prai·rie
praise
  praised
  prais·ing
  prais·er
praise·wor·thy
  praise·wor·thi·ly
  praise·wor·thi·ness
pra·line
prance
  pranced
  pranc·ing
  pranc·er
prank
  prank·ish
  prank·ster
prate
  prat·ed
  prat·ing
  prat·er
  prat·ing·ly
prat·fall
prat·tle
  prat·tled
  prat·tling
  prat·tler
  prat·tling·ly
prawn
  prawn·er
prayer
pray·er
  prayer·ful
preach
  preach·er
preach·i·fy
  preach·i·fied
  preach·i·fy·ing
preach·ment
preachy
  preach·i·er
  preach·i·est
pre·ad·o·les·cence
  pre·ad·o·les·cent
pre·am·ble
pre·ar·range
  pre·ar·ranged
  pre·ar·rang·ing
  pre·ar·range·ment
pre·as·signed
pre·can·cel
  pre·can·celed
  pre·can·cel·ing
  pre·can·cel·la·tion
pre·car·i·ous
  pre·car·i·ous·ly
  pre·car·i·ous·ness

pre·cau·tion
pre·cau·tion·ary
pre·cede
pre·ced·ed
pre·ced·ing
prec·e·dence
prec·e·dent
pre·cept
pre·cep·tive
pre·cep·tor
pre·cep·to·ri·al
pre·ces·sion
pre·ces·sion·al
pre·cinct
pre·cious
pre·ci·os·i·ty
pre·cious·ness
prec·i·pice
pre·cip·i·tous
pre·cip·i·tant
pre·cip·i·tant·ly
pre·cip·i·tant·ness
pre·cip·i·tate
pre·cip·i·tat·ed
pre·cip·i·tat·ing
pre·cip·i·ta·tive
pre·cip·i·ta·tor
pre·cip·i·ta·tion
pre·cip·i·tous
pre·cip·i·tous·ly
pre·cip·i·tous·ness
pré·cis
pre·cise
pre·cise·ness
pre·ci·sion
pre·ci·sion·ist
pre·clude
pre·clud·ed
pre·clud·ing
pre·clu·sion
pre·clu·sive
pre·co·cious
pre·co·cious·ly
pre·co·cious·ness
pre·coc·i·ty
pre·cog·ni·tion
pre·cog·ni·tive
pre·con·ceive
pre·con·ceived
pre·con·ceiv·ing
pre·con·cep·tion
pre·cook
pre·cur·sor
pre·cur·so·ry
pre·date
pred·a·tor
pred·a·to·ry
pred·a·to·ri·ly
pre·dawn
pred·e·ces·sor
pre·des·ti·nate
pre·des·ti·nat·ed
pre·des·ti·nat·ing
pre·des·ti·na·tion
pre·des·tine

pre·des·tined
pre·des·tin·ing
pre·de·ter·mine
pre·de·ter·mined
pre·de·ter·min·ing
pre·de·ter·mi·na·tion
pred·i·ca·ble
pred·i·ca·bil·i·ty
pre·dic·a·ment
pred·i·cate
pred·i·cat·ed
pred·i·cat·ing
pred·i·ca·tion
pred·i·ca·tive
pre·dict
pre·dict·a·ble
pre·dict·a·bly
pre·dict·a·bil·i·ty
pre·dic·tion
pre·dic·tive
pre·di·lec·tion
pre·dis·po·si·tion
pre·dis·pose
pre·dis·posed
pre·dis·pos·ing
pre·dom·i·nant
pre·dom·i·nance
pre·dom·i·nan·cy
pre·dom·i·nate
pre·dom·i·nat·ed
pre·dom·i·nat·ing
pre·dom·i·na·tion
pre·em·i·nent
pre·em·i·nence
pre·empt
pre·emp·tor
pre·emp·tion
pre·emp·tive
preen·er
pre·ex·ist
pre·ex·ist·ence
pre·ex·ist·ent
pre·fab·ri·cate
pre·fab·ri·cat·ed
pre·fab·ri·cat·ing
pre·fab·ri·ca·tion
pref·ace
pref·aced
pref·ac·ing
pref·a·to·ry
pre·fer
per·ferred
pre·fer·ring
pre·fer·rer
pref·er·a·ble
pref·er·a·ble·ness
pref·er·a·bil·i·ty
pref·er·a·bly
pref·er·ence
pref·er·en·tial
pref·er·en·tial·ly
pre·fer·ment
pre·fix
pre·flight
pre·form

preg·na·ble
preg·na·bil·i·ty
preg·nan·cy
preg·nan·cies
preg·nant
pre·heat
pre·hen·sile
pre·hen·sil·i·ty
pre·his·tor·ic
pre·his·to·ry
pre·judge
pre·judged
pre·judg·ing
pre·judg·er
pre·judg·ment
prej·u·dice
prej·u·diced
prej·u·dic·ing
prej·u·di·cial
prej·u·di·cial·ly
prej·u·di·cial·ness
prel·ate
prel·ate·ship
prel·a·ture
pre·lim·i·nary
pre·lim·i·nar·ies
pre·lim·i·nar·i·ly
prel·ude
prel·ud·ed
prel·ud·ing
pre·ma·ture
pre·ma·ture·ness
pre·ma·tu·ri·ty
pre·med·i·cal
pre·med·i·tate
pre·med·i·tat·ed
pre·med·i·tat·ing
pre·med·i·ta·tor
pre·med·i·tat·ed·ly
pre·med·i·ta·tive
pre·med·i·ta·tion
pre·men·stru·al
pre·mier
pre·mier·ship
pre·miere
prem·ise
prem·ised
prem·is·ing
pre·mi·um
pre·mo·ni·tion
pre·mon·i·to·ry
pre·mon·i·to·ri·ly
pre·na·tal
pre·na·tal·ly
pre·oc·cu·pa·tion
pre·oc·cu·py
pre·oc·cu·pied
pre·oc·cu·py·ing
prep·a·ra·tion
pre·par·a·to·ry
pre·par·a·to·ri·ly
pre·pare
pre·pared
pre·par·ing
pre·par·er

pre-par-ed-ness
pre-pay
pre-paid
pre-pay-ing
pre-pay-ment
pre-plan
pre-planned
pre-plan-ning
pre-pon-der-ant
pre-pon-der-ance
pre-pon-der-an-cy
pre-pon-der-ant-ly
pre-pon-der-ate
pre-pon-der-at-ed
pre-pon-der-at-ing
pre-pon-der-at-ing-ly
pre-pon-der-a-tion
prep-o-si-tion
prep-o-si-tion-al
pre-pos-sess
pre-pos-sess-ing
pre-pos-sess-ing-ly
pre-pos-ter-ous
pre-puce
pre-pu-tial
pre-re-cord
pre-req-ui-site
pre-rog-a-tive
pres-age
pres-aged
pres-ag-ing
pres-ag-er
Pres-by-te-ri-an
Pres-by-te-ri-an-ism
pres-by-tery
pres-by-ter-ies
pre-school
pre-scribe
pre-scribed
pre-scrib-ing
pre-scrib-er
pre-script
pre-scrip-tion
pre-scrip-tive
pre-sea-son
pres-ence
pre-sent
pre-sent-er
pres-ent
pre-sent-a-ble
pre-sent-a-bil-i-ty
pre-sent-a-ble-ness
pre-sent-a-bly
pres-en-ta-tion
pres-ent-day
pres-ent-ly
pre-serv-a-tive
pre-serve
pre-served
pre-serv-ing
pre-serv-a-ble
pres-er-va-tion
pre-serv-er
pre-side
pre-sid-ed

pre-sid-ing
pre-sid-er
pres-i-den-cy
pres-i-den-cies
pres-i-dent
pres-i-den-tial
press-board
press-ing
pres-sure
pres-sured
pres-sur-ing
pres-su-rize
pres-su-rized
pres-su-riz-ing
pres-su-riz-er
pres-sur-i-za-tion
press-work
pres-ti-dig-i-ta-tion
pres-ti-dig-i-ta-tor
pres-tige
pres-tig-ious
pres-to
pre-sum-a-ble
pre-sum-a-bly
pre-sume
pre-sumed
pre-sum-ing
pre-sum-er
pre-sump-tion
pre-sump-tive
pre-sump-tu-ous
pre-sup-pose
pre-sup-posed
pre-sup-pos-ing
pre-sup-po-si-tion
pre-tend
pre-tend-ed
pre-tend-er
pre-tense
pre-ten-sion
pre-ten-tious
pre-ten-tious-ness
pre-test
pre-text
Pre-to-ria
pret-ti-fy
pret-ti-fied
pret-ti-fy-ing
pret-ti-fi-ca-tion
pret-ty
pret-ties
pret-tied
pret-ty-ing
pret-ti-ly
pret-ti-ness
pret-ty-ish
pret-zel
pre-vail
pre-vail-ing
prev-a-lent
prev-a-lence
pre-vent
pre-vent-a-ble
pre-vent-a-bil-i-ty
pre-vent-er

pre-ven-tion
pre-view
pre-vi-ous
pre-war
prey
prey-er
price-less
prick-er
prick-le
prick-ly
prick-li-er
prick-li-est
prick-li-ness
pride
prid-ed
prid-ing
pride-ful
pri-er
priest
priest-ess
priest-hood
priest-ly
priest-li-er
priest-li-est
priest-li-ness
prig
prig-gish
prim
prim-mer
prim-mest
primmed
prim-ming
prim-ness
pri-ma-cy
pri-ma-cies
pri-ma don-na
pri-ma don-nas
pri-mal
pri-ma-ri-ly
pri-ma-ry
pri-mar-ies
pri-mate
prime
primed
prim-ing
prime me-rid-i-an
prim-er
pri-me-val
prim-i-tive
pri-mo-gen-i-tor
pri-mo-gen-i-ture
pri-mor-di-al
pri-mor-di-al-ly
primp
prim-rose
prince-ly
prince-li-er
prince-li-est
prince-li-ness
prin-cess
Prince-ton
prin-ci-pal
prin-ci-pal-ly
prin-ci-pal-i-ty
prin-ci-pal-i-ties

prin·ci·ple
prin·ci·pled
print·a·ble
print·ing
print-out
pri·or
 pri·or·ate
pri·or·ess
pri·or·i·ty
 pri·or·i·ties
pri·ory
 pri·or·ies
prism
 pris·mat·ic
 pris·mat·i·cal·ly
pris·on
pris·on·er
pris·sy
 pris·si·er
 pris·si·est
 pris·si·ly
 pris·si·ness
pris·tine
pri·va·cy
pri·vate
pri·va·tion
priv·et
priv·i·lege
 priv·i·leged
 priv·i·leg·ing
privy
 priv·ies
 priv·i·ly
prize
 prized
 priz·ing
prize-fight
 prize-fight·er
 prize-fight·ing
prob·a·bil·i·ty
 prob·a·bil·i·ties
prob·a·ble
 prob·a·bly
pro·bate
 pro·bat·ed
 pro·bat·ing
pro·ba·tion
 pro·ba·tion·al
 pro·ba·tion·ary
 pro·ba·tion·al·ly
pro·ba·tion·er
pro·ba·tive
probe
 probed
 prob·ing
 prob·er
prob·lem
prob·lem·at·ic
 prob·lem·at·i·cal
pro·bos·cis
 pro·bos·cis·es
 pro·bos·ci·des
pro·ce·dure
 pro·ce·dur·al
 pro·ce·dur·al·ly

pro·ceed
pro·ceed·ing
pro·ceeds
proc·ess
pro·ces·sion
pro·ces·sion·al
pro·claim
 pro·claim·er
proc·la·ma·tion
pro·cliv·i·ty
 pro·cliv·i·ties
pro·cras·ti·nate
 pro·cras·ti·nat·ed
 pro·cras·ti·nat·ing
 pro·cras·ti·na·tion
 pro·cras·ti·na·tor
pro·cre·ate
 pro·cre·at·ed
 pro·cre·at·ing
 pro·cre·a·tion
 pro·cre·a·tive
 pro·cre·a·tor
Pro·crus·tes
proc·tor
 proc·to·ri·al
proc·u·ra·tor
 proc·u·ra·to·ri·al
 proc·u·ra·tor·ship
pro·cure
 pro·cured
 pro·cur·ing
 pro·cur·a·ble
 pro·cur·ance
 pro·cure·ment
 pro·cur·er
prod
 prod·ded
 prod·ding
 prod·der
prod·i·gal
 prod·i·gal·i·ty
 prod·i·gal·ly
pro·di·gious
 pro·di·gious·ness
prod·i·gy
 prod·i·gies
pro·duce
 pro·duced
 pro·duc·ing
 pro·duc·er
prod·uct
 pro·duc·tion
 pro·duc·tive
 pro·duc·tive·ness
 pro·duc·tiv·i·ty
pro·fane
 pro·faned
 pro·fan·ing
 pro·fan·a·to·ry
 pro·fane·ness
 pro·fan·er
 pro·fan·i·ty
pro·fess
 pro·fessed
 pro·fess·ed·ly

pro·fes·sion
pro·fes·sion·al
 pro·fes·sion·al·ism
pro·fes·sion·al·ize
 pro·fes·sion·al·ized
 pro·fes·sion·al·iz·ing
pro·fes·sor
 pro·fes·so·ri·al
 pro·fes·so·ri·al·ly
 pro·fes·sor·ship
prof·fer
 prof·fer·er
pro·fi·cien·cy
pro·fi·cient
pro·file
 pro·filed
 pro·fil·ing
prof·it
 prof·it·less
prof·it·a·ble
 prof·it·a·bil·i·ty
 prof·it·a·ble·ness
 prof·it·a·bly
prof·it·eer
prof·li·gate
 prof·li·ga·cy
pro·found
pro·fun·di·ty
 pro·fun·di·ties
pro·fuse
pro·fu·sion
pro·gen·i·tor
prog·e·ny
 prog·e·nies
pro·ges·ter·one
prog·no·sis
 prog·no·ses
prog·nos·tic
prog·nos·ti·cate
 prog·nos·ti·cat·ed
 prog·nos·ti·cat·ing
 prog·nos·ti·ca·tion
 prog·nos·ti·ca·tive
 prog·nos·ti·ca·tor
pro·gram
 pro·grammed
 pro·gram·ming
 pro·gramed
 pro·gram·ing
 pro·gram·mer
 pro·gram·er
prog·ress
pro·gres·sion
pro·gres·sive
 pro·gres·siv·ism
pro·hib·it
pro·hi·bi·tion
 pro·hi·bi·tion·ist
pro·hib·i·tive
pro·ject
pro·jec·tile
pro·jec·tion
 pro·jec·tion·ist
pro·jec·tive
 pro·jec·tive·ly

pro·jec·tiv·i·ty
pro·jec·tor
pro·le·tar·i·at
pro·le·tar·i·an
pro·lif·er·ate
pro·lif·er·at·ed
pro·lif·er·at·ing
pro·lif·er·a·tion
pro·lif·er·a·tive
pro·lif·ic
pro·lif·i·ca·cy
pro·lif·ic·ness
pro·lif·i·cal·ly
pro·lix
pro·lix·i·ty
pro·lix·ly
pro·lix·ness
pro·logue
pro·logued
pro·log·uing
pro·long
pro·lon·ga·tion
pro·long·er
prom·e·nade
prom·e·nad·ed
prom·e·nad·ing
prom·e·nad·er
Pro·me·theus
prom·i·nence
prom·i·nent
prom·i·nent·ly
pro·mis·cu·i·ty
pro·mis·cu·i·ties
pro·mis·cu·ous
pro·mis·cu·ous·ly
pro·mis·cu·ous·ness
prom·ise
prom·ised
prom·is·ing
prom·is·a·ble
prom·is·er
prom·ise·ful
prom·is·so·ry
prom·on·to·ry
prom·on·to·ries
pro·mote
pro·mot·ed
pro·mot·ing
pro·mot·a·ble
pro·mot·er
pro·mo·tion
pro·mo·tive
prompt
prompt·er
prompt·ly
prompt·ness
prom·ul·gate
prom·ul·gat·ed
prom·ul·gat·ing
prom·ul·ga·tion
prone
prong
pro·noun
pro·nounce
pro·nounced

pro·nounc·ing
pro·nounce·a·ble
pro·nounce·er
pro·nounce·ment
pron·to
pro·nun·ci·a·tion
proof
proof·read
proof·read·ing
proof·read·er
prop
propped
prop·ping
prop·a·gan·da
prop·a·gan·dist
prop·a·gan·dis·tic
prop·a·gan·dis·ti·cal·ly
prop·a·gan·dism
prop·a·gan·dize
prop·a·gan·dized
prop·a·gan·diz·ing
prop·a·gate
prop·a·gat·ed
prop·a·gat·ing
prop·a·ga·tive
prop·a·ga·tor
prop·a·ga·tion
prop·a·ga·tion·al
pro·pane
pro·pel
pro·pelled
pro·pel·ling
pro·pel·lant
pro·pel·ler
pro·pen·si·ty
pro·pen·si·ties
prop·er
prop·er·ly
prop·er·ness
prop·er·ty
prop·er·ties
prop·er·tied
prop·er·ty·less
proph·e·cy
proph·e·cies
proph·e·sy
proph·e·sied
proph·e·sy·ing
proph·e·si·er
proph·et
pro·phet·ic
pro·phet·i·cal
pro·phet·i·cal·ly
pro·phy·lax·is
pro·pin·qui·ty
pro·pi·ti·ate
pro·pi·ti·at·ed
pro·pi·ti·at·ing
pro·pi·ti·a·tion
pro·pi·ti·a·to·ry
pro·pi·tious
pro·pi·tious·ly
pro·po·nent
pro·por·tion
pro·por·tion·a·ble

pro·por·tion·a·bly
pro·por·tion·al
pro·por·tion·al·i·ty
pro·por·tion·ate
pro·por·tion·at·ed
pro·por·tion·at·ing
pro·pos·al
pro·pose
pro·posed
pro·pos·ing
pro·pos·er
prop·o·si·tion
pro·o·si·tion·al
pro·pound
pro·pound·er
pro·pri·e·tary
pro·pri·e·tar·ies
pro·pri·e·tor
pro·pri·e·tor·ship
pro·pri·e·ty
pro·pri·e·ties
pro·pul·sion
pro·pul·sive
pro·rate
pro·rat·ed
pro·rat·ing
pro·ra·tion
pro·sa·ic
pro·sa·i·cal·ly
pro·sa·ic·ness
pro·scribe
pro·scribed
pro·scrib·ing
pro·scrib·er
pro·scrip·tion
pro·scrip·tive
prose
prosed
pros·ing
pros·e·cute
pros·e·cut·a·ble
pros·e·cu·tion
pros·e·cu·tor
pros·pect
pros·pec·tor
pro·spec·tive
pro·spec·tus
pros·per
pros·per·i·ty
pros·per·ous
pros·tate
pros·the·sis
pros·the·ses
pros·thet·ic
pros·thet·i·cal·ly
pros·thet·ics
pros·the·tist
pros·tho·don·tics
pros·tho·don·tist
pros·ti·tute
pros·ti·tut·ed
pros·ti·tut·ing
pros·ti·tu·tion
pros·ti·tu·tor
pros·trate

pros·trat·ed
pros·trat·ing
pros·tra·tion
pros·tra·tor
pros·tra·tive
prosy
pros·i·er
pros·i·est
pros·i·ly
pros·i·ness
pro·tag·o·nist
pro·te·an
pro·tect
pro·tect·ing
pro·tec·tive
pro·tec·tive·ly
pro·tec·tive·ness
pro·tec·tor
pro·tec·tion
pro·tec·tion·ism
pro·tec·tion·ist
pro·tec·tor·ate
pro·té·gé
pro·tein
pro·test
Prot·es·tant
Prot·es·tant·ism
prot·es·ta·tion
pro·tist
pro·tis·tan
pro·to·col
pro·ton
pro·to·plasm
pro·to·plas·mic
pro·to·type
pro·to·ty·pal
pro·to·typ·ic
pro·to·zo·an
pro·to·zo·ic
pro·tract
pro·trac·tion
pro·trac·tive
pro·trac·tile
pro·trac·tor
pro·trude
pro·trud·ed
pro·trud·ing
pro·trud·ent
pro·tru·si·ble
pro·tru·sion
pro·tru·sive
pro·tu·ber·ance
pro·tu·ber·ant
proud
proud·ly
proud·ness
prove
proved
prov·en
prov·ing
prov·a·ble
prov·a·bly
prov·er
Pro·ven·cal
Prov·ence

prov·erb
pro·ver·bi·al
pro·ver·bi·al·ly
pro·vide
pro·vid·ed
pro·vid·ing
pro·vid·a·ble
pro·vid·er
prov·i·dence
prov·i·den·tial
prov·i·dent
prov·ince
Prov·ince·town
pro·vin·cial
pro·vin·ci·al·i·ty
pro·vin·cial·ly
pro·vin·cial·ist
pro·vin·cial·ize
pro·vin·cial·ized
pro·vin·cial·iz·ing
pro·vin·cial·ism
pro·vi·sion
pro·vi·sion·er
pro·vi·sion·al
pro·vi·sion·ary
prov·o·ca·tion
pro·voc·a·tive
pro·voc·a·tive·ly
pro·voc·a·tive·ness
pro·voke
pro·voked
pro·vok·ing
pro·vok·ing·ly
prov·ost
prow·ess
prowl
prowl·er
prox·i·mal
prox·i·mate
prox·i·mate·ly
prox·im·i·ty
proxy
prox·ies
prude
pru·dence
pru·dent
pru·den·tial
prud·ery
prud·er·ies
prud·ish
prune
pruned
prun·ing
prun·er
pru·ri·ent
pru·ri·ence
pru·ri·en·cy
Prus·sia
Prus·sian
pry
pried
pry·ing
pry·er
pri·er
psalm·book

psalm·ist
Psal·ter
pseu·do
pseu·do·nym
pseu·don·y·mous
pseu·do·preg·nan·cy
pseu·do·preg·nant
pseu·do·sci·ence
pseu·do·sci·en·tif·ic
pshaw
psil·o·cy·bin
pso·ri·a·sis
pso·ri·at·ic
psych
psyched
psych·ing
Psy·che
psych·e·del·ic
psy·chi·a·trist
psy·chi·a·try
psy·chi·at·ric
psy·chi·at·ri·cal·ly
psy·chic
psy·chi·cal
psy·chi·cal·ly
psy·cho
psy·cho·a·nal·y·sis
psy·cho·an·a·lyt·ic
psy·cho·an·a·lyt·i·cal
psy·cho·an·a·lyst
psy·cho·an·a·lyze
psy·cho·an·a·lyzed
psy·cho·an·a·lyz·ing
psy·cho·bi·ol·o·gy
psy·cho·bi·o·log·ic
psy·cho·bi·o·log·i·cal
psy·cho·bi·ol·o·gist
psy·cho·dra·ma
psy·cho·dy·nam·ic
psy·cho·dy·nam·i·cal·ly
psy·cho·dy·nam·ics
psy·cho·gen·e·sis
pry·cho·ge·net·ic
psy·cho·ge·net·i·cal·ly
psy·cho·gen·ic
psy·cho·gen·i·cal·ly
psy·cho·log·i·cal
psy·cho·log·ic
psy·cho·log·i·cal·ly
psy·chol·o·gist
psy·chol·o·gy
psy·cho·mo·tor
psy·cho·neu·ro·sis
psy·cho·neu·ro·ses
psy·cho·neu·rot·ic
psy·cho·path
psy·cho·pa·thol·o·gy
psy·cho·pa·thol·o·gist
psy·cho·path·o·log·ic
psy·cho·path·o·log·i·cal
psy·chop·a·thy
psy·cho·path·ic
psy·cho·path·i·cal·ly
psy·cho·sis
psy·cho·ses

psy·chot·ic
psy·chot·i·cal·ly
psy·cho·so·mat·ic
psy·cho·so·mat·i·cal·ly
psy·cho·ther·a·py
psy·cho·ther·a·peu·tics
psy·cho·ther·a·peu·tic
psy·cho·ther·a·peu·ti·cal·ly
psy·cho·ther·a·pist
Ptol·e·my
pto·maine
pu·ber·ty
pu·bes·cence
pu·bes·cen·cy
pu·bes·cent
pu·bic
pub·lic
pub·lic·ly
pub·lic·ness
pub·li·ca·tion
pub·li·cist
pub·li·ci·ty
pub·li·cize
pub·li·cized
pub·li·ciz·ing
pub·lish
pub·lish·a·ble
pub·lish·er
Puc·ci·ni
puce
puck·er
pud·ding
pud·dle
pud·dled
pud·dling
pudgy
pudg·i·er
pudg·i·est
pudg·i·ness
pueb·lo
pueb·los
pu·er·ile
pu·er·il·i·ty
Puer·to Ri·co
puff
puff·i·ness
puffy
puff·i·er
puff·i·est
puff·er
pu·gil·ism
pu·gil·ist
pu·gil·is·tic
pug·na·cious
pug·na·cious·ness
pug·nac·i·ty
puke
puked
puk·ing
Pu·las·ki
Pul·itz·er
pull·back
pul·let
pul·ley
Pull·man

pull·out
pull·o·ver
pul·mo·nary
pulp
pulp·i·ness
pulpy
pulp·i·er
pulp·i·est
pul·pit
pulp·wood
pul·sate
pul·sat·ed
pul·sat·ing
pul·sa·tion
pul·sa·tor
pul·sa·to·ry
pulse
pulsed
puls·ing
pul·ver·ize
pul·ver·ized
pul·ver·iz·ing
pul·ver·iz·a·ble
pul·ver·i·za·tion
pul·ver·iz·er
pu·ma
pu·mas
pum·ice
pu·mi·ceous
pum·mel
pum·meled
pum·melled
pum·mel·ing
pum·mel·ling
pump
pump·a·ble
pump·er
pum·per·nick·el
pump·kin
pun
punned
pun·ning
punch
punch·er
punch-drunk
punchy
punch·i·er
punch·i·est
punc·tu·al
punc·tu·al·i·ty
punc·tu·al·ly
punc·tu·al·ness
punc·tu·ate
punc·tu·at·ed
punc·tu·at·ing
punc·tu·a·tor
punc·tu·a·tion
punc·ture
punc·tured
punc·tur·ing
punc·tur·a·ble
pun·dit
pun·gent
pun·gen·cy
pun·gent·ly

Pu·nic
pun·ish
pun·ish·a·ble
pun·ish·ment
pu·ni·tive
pun·ster
punt·er
pu·ny
pu·ni·er
pu·ni·est
pu·ni·ness
pup
pupped
pup·ping
pu·pa
pu·pae
pu·pas
pu·pal
pu·pate
pu·pat·ed
pu·pat·ing
pu·pa·tion
pu·pil
pu·pil·ar
pu·pil·lary
Pu·pin
pup·pet
pup·pet·eer
pup·pet·ry
pup·pet·ries
pup·py
pup·pies
pup·py·ish
pur·chase
pur·chased
pur·chas·ing
pur·chas·a·ble
pur·chas·er
Pur·due
pure
pure·ly
pure·ness
pu·rée
pu·réed
pu·rée·ing
pur·ga·tive
pur·ga·to·ry
pur·ga·to·ries
pur·ga·to·ri·al
purge
purged
purg·ing
purg·er
pu·ri·fy
pu·ri·fied
pu·ri·fy·ing
pu·ri·fi·ca·tion
pu·ri·fi·er
Pu·rim
pur·ism
pur·ist
pu·ris·tic
pu·ri·tan
pu·ri·tan·i·cal
pu·ri·tan·i·cal·ly

pu·ri·ty
purl
pur·loin
  pur·loin·er
pur·ple
  pur·pled
  pur·pling
  pur·plish
pur·port
  pur·port·ed
  pur·port·ed·ly
pur·pose
  pur·posed
  pur·pos·ing
  pur·pose·ful
  pur·pose·ful·ly
  pur·pose·ly
  pur·pos·ive
purse
  pursed
  purs·ing
  purs·er
pur·su·ant
pur·sue
  pur·sued
  pur·su·ing
  pur·su·er
pur·suit
pur·sy
  pur·si·er
  pur·si·est
  pur·si·ness
pu·ru·lent
  pu·ru·lence
  pu·ru·len·cy
  pu·ru·lent·ly
pur·vey
  pur·vey·or
  pur·vey·ance
pur·view
pushy
  push·i·er
  push·i·est
  push·i·ly
  push·i·ness
push·cart
push·o·ver
pu·sil·lan·i·mous
  pu·sil·la·nim·i·ty
  pu·sil·lan·i·mous·ly
pussy
  puss·ies
puss·y·foot
puss·y·wil·low
pus·tule
  pus·tu·lar
  pus·tu·late
put
  put·ting
pu·ta·tive
  pu·ta·tive·ly
put-on
pu·tre·fac·tion
pu·tre·fy
  pu·tre·fied

pu·tre·fy·ing
pu·trid
  pu·trid·i·ty
  pu·trid·ness
putt
  putt·ed
  putt·ing
put·ter
  put·ter·er
put·ty
  put·tied
  put·ty·ing
put-up
puz·zle
  puz·zled
  puz·zling
  puz·zler
  puz·zle·ment
Pyg·ma·lion
Pyg·my
  Pyg·mies
py·lon
P'yong·yang
pyr·a·mid
  py·ram·i·dal
Pyr·a·mus
pyre
Pyr·e·nees
Py·rex
py·ric
py·ro·ma·nia
  py·ro·ma·ni·ac
  py·ro·ma·ni·a·cal
py·rom·e·ter
  py·rom·e·try
py·ro·tech·nics
  py·ro·tech·nic
  py·ro·tech·ni·cal
Pyr·rhic
Pyr·rhus
Py·thag·o·ras
py·thon
Qa·ter
quack·ery
  quack·er·ies
Quad·ra·ges·i·ma
quad·ran·gle
  quad·ran·gu·lar
quad·rant
  quad·ran·tal
quad·ra·phon·ic
quad·rate
  quad·rat·ed
  quad·rat·ing
quad·rat·ic
  quad·rat·i·cal·ly
quad·rat·ics
quad·ra·ture
quad·ri·lat·er·al
qua·drille
quad·ril·lion
  quad·ril·lionth
quad·roon
quad·ru·ped
  quad·ru·pe·dal

quad·ru·ple
  quad·ru·pled
  quad·ru·pling
quad·ru·plet
quad·ru·pli·cate
  quad·ru·pli·cat·ed
  quad·ru·pli·cat·ing
quaff
  quaff·er
quag·mire
  quag·mired
  quag·miry
quail
  quail-like
quaint
quake
  quaked
  quak·ing
Quak·er
qual·i·fi·ca·tion
qual·i·fied
  qual·i·fied·ly
qual·i·fy
  qual·i·fy·ing
  qual·i·fi·a·ble
  qual·i·fi·er
quar·i·ta·tive
qual·i·ty
  qual·i·ties
qualm
  qualm·ish
quan·da·ry
  quan·da·ries
quan·ti·fi·er
quan·ti·fy
  quan·ti·fied
  quan·ti·fy·ing
  quan·ti·fi·a·ble
  quan·ti·fi·ca·tion
quan·ti·ta·tive
quan·ti·ty
  quan·ti·ties
quan·tum
  quan·ta
quar·an·tine
  quar·an·tin·a·ble
quar·rel
  quar·reled
  quar·rel·ing
  quar·rel·er
  quar·rel·some
quar·ri·er
quar·ry
  quar·ries
  quar·ried
  quar·ry·ing
quart
quar·ter
  quar·ter·back
  quar·ter·deck
  quar·ter·ing
  quar·ter·ly
  quar·ter·lies
  quar·ter·mas·ter
quar·tet

quartz
quash
qua·si
qua·ter·nary
quat·rain
qua·ver
 quav·er·ing·ly
 qua·very
quay
quea·sy
 quea·si·er
 quea·si·est
 quea·si·ly
 quea·si·ness
Que·bec
queen
 queen·li·ness
 queen·ly
Queens·ber·ry
Queens·land
queer
quell
 quell·er
Que·moy
quench
 quench·a·ble
 quench·er
Quen·tin
quer·u·lous
que·ry
 que·ries
 que·ried
 que·ry·ing
quest
 quest·er
 quest·ing·ly
ques·tion
 ques·tion·er
 ques·tion·a·ble
 ques·tion·a·ble·ness
 ques·tion·a·bil·i·ty
 ques·tion·a·bly
 ques·tion·naire
queue
 queued
 queu·ing
Que·zon
quib·ble
 quib·bled
 quib·bling
 quib·bler
quick
quick·en
 quick·en·er
quick-freeze
 quick-froze
 quick-fro·zen
 quick-freez·ing
quick·ie
quick·lime
quick·sand
quick·sil·ver
quick-tem·pered
quick-wit·ted
 quick-wit·ted·ly

quick-wit·ted·ness
qui·es·cent
 qui·es·cence
qui·et
 qui·et·ly
 qui·et·ness
 qui·et·er
qui·e·tude
quill
quilt
 quilt·er
 quilt·ing
quince
Quin·cy
qui·nine
Quin·qua·ges·i·ma
Quin·ta·na
quin·tes·sence
 quin·tes·sen·tial
quin·tet
quin·til·lion
 quin·til·lionth
quin·tu·ple
 quin·tu·pled
 quin·tu·pling
 quin·tu·plet
quip
 quipped
 quip·ping
 quip·pish
 quip·ster
quirk
 quirk·i·ly
 quirk·i·ness
 quirky
 quirk·i·er
 quirk·i·est
quis·ling
quit
 quit·ted
 quit·ting
 quit·claim
quite
Qui·to
quits
quit·ter
quiv·er
quix·ot·ic
 quix·ot·i·cal
 quix·ot·i·cal·ly
quiz
 quiz·zes
 quizzed
 quiz·zing
 quiz·zer
quiz·zi·cal
 quiz·zi·cal·ly
quoin
quoit
quon·dam
Quon·set
quo·rum
quo·ta
quot·a·ble
 quot·a·bil·i·ty

quo·ta·tion
quote
 quot·ed
 quot·ing
quo·tid·i·an
quo·tient
Ra·bat
rab·bet
 rab·bet·ed
 rab·bet·ing
rab·bi
rab·bis
rab·bin·i·cal
 rab·bin·i·cal·ly
rab·bit
rab·ble
 rab·bled
 rab·bling
Rab·e·lais
rab·id
 rab·id·ly
ra·bies
Ra·bin·o·witz
race
 raced
 rac·ing
race·course
race·horse
ra·ceme
rac·er
race·track
ra·chis
 ra·chis·es
 rach·i·des
ra·cial
 ra·cial·ly
Ra·cine
rac·ism
 ra·cial·ism
rac·ist
rack·et
 rack·et·eer
rac·on·teur
racy
 rac·i·er
 rac·i·est
 rac·i·ly
 rac·i·ness
ra·dar
Rad·cliffe
ra·di·al
 ra·di·al·ly
ra·di·ance
 ra·di·an·cy
ra·di·ant
 ra·di·ant·ly
ra·di·ate
 ra·di·at·ed
 ra·di·at·ing
ra·di·a·tion
ra·di·a·tor
rad·i·cal
 rad·i·cal·ly
 rad·i·cal·ism
ra·dio

ra·di·os
ra·di·oed
ra·di·o·ing
ra·di·o·ac·tive
ra·di·o·ac·tiv·i·ty
ra·di·o·fre·quen·cy
ra·di·o·gram
ra·di·o·graph
ra·di·og·ra·phy
ra·di·ol·o·gy
ra·di·ol·o·gist
rad·ish
ra·di·um
ra·di·us
ra·di·us·es
ra·don
raf·fia
raf·fish
raf·fle
raf·fled
raf·fling
raft·er
rag
ragged
rag·ging
rag·a·muf·fin
rage
raged
rag·ing
rag·ing·ly
rag·ged
rag·ged·ly
rag·ged·ness
rag·man
rag·time
rag·weed
raid·er
rail·ing
rail·lery
rail·ler·ies
rail·road
rail·road·er
rail·road·ing
rail·way
rai·ment
rain·bow
rain·coat
rain·drop
rain·fall
Rai·nier
rainy
rain·i·er
rain·i·est
rain·i·ly
rain·i·ness
raise
raised
rais·ing
rais·er
rai·sin
Raj·put
rake
raked
rak·ing
rak·er

rake-off
rak·ish
rak·ish·ly
rak·ish·ness
Ra·leigh
ral·ly
ral·lied
ral·ly·ing
ral·lies
ram
rammed
ram·ming
ram·mer
Ram·a·dan
ram·ble
ram·bled
ram·bling
ram·bler
ram·bunc·tious
ram·i·fi·ca·tion
ram·i·fy
ram·i·fied
ram·i·fy·ing
ram·page
ram·paged
ram·pag·ing
ramp·ant
ram·pan·cy
ram·pant·ly
ram·part
ram·rod
ram·shack·le
ranch·er
ran·cid
ran·cid·i·ty
ran·cid·ness
ran·cor
ran·cor·ous
Ran·dolph
ran·dom
ran·dom·ly
ran·dom·ness
range
ranged
rang·ing
rang·er
Ran·goon
rangy
rang·i·er
rang·i·est
rang·i·ness
ran·kle
ran·kled
ran·kling
ran·sack
ran·som
rant·er
rap
rapped
rap·ping
ra·pa·cious
ra·pa·cious·ly
ra·pac·i·ty
rape
rap·ist

Raph·a·el
rap·id
ra·pid·i·ty
rap·id·ly
rap·id·ness
rap·id·fire
ra·pi·er
rap·ine
Rap·pa·han·nock
rap·port
rap·proche·ment
rap·scal·lion
rap·ture
rap·tur·ous
rap·tur·ous·ly
rap·tur·ous·ness
rare
rar·er
rar·est
rare·bit
rar·e·fy
rar·e·fied
rar·e·fy·ing
rar·e·fac·tion
rar·e·fied
rare·ly
rar·i·ty
rar·i·ties
ras·cal
ras·cal·i·ty
ras·cal·ly
rash
rash·ly
rash·ness
rasp
rasp·ing·ly
raspy
rasp·i·er
rasp·i·est
rasp·ber·ry
Ras·pu·tin
rat
rat·ted
rat·ting
rat·a·ble
ratch·et
rate
rat·ed
rat·ing
rath·er
rat·i·fy
rat·i·fied
rat·i·fy·ing
rat·i·fi·ca·tion
rat·i·fi·er
ra·tio
ra·tios
ra·ti·oc·i·na·tion
ra·tion
ra·tion·al
ra·tion·al·i·ty
ra·tion·al·ly
ra·tion·ale
ra·tion·al·ism
ra·tion·al·ist

ra·tion·al·is·tic
ra·tion·al·is·ti·cal·ly
ra·tion·al·ize
ra·tion·al·ized
ra·tion·al·iz·ing
ra·tion·al·i·za·tion
ra·tion·al·iz·er
rat·line
rat·tan
rat·tle
  rat·tled
  rat·tling
rat·tle·brain
rat·tler
rat·tle·snake
rat·tle·trap
rat·ty
  rat·ti·er
  rat·ti·est
rau·cous
rau·cous·ly
raun·chy
  raun·chi·er
  raun·chi·est
rav·age
  rav·aged
  rav·ag·ing
  rav·ag·er
rave
  raved
  rav·ing
  rav·er
rav·el
  rav·eled
  rav·el·ing
  rav·el·er
ra·ven
Ra·ven·na
rav·en·ous
  rav·en·ous·ly
ra·vine
ra·vi·o·li
rav·ish
  rav·ish·ment
  rav·ish·ing
raw
  raw·ness
raw·boned
raw·hide
ray·on
raze
  razed
  raz·ing
  raz·er
ra·zor
raz·zle-daz·zle
re·act
re·ac·tive
re·ac·tion
re·ac·tion·ary
  re·ac·tion·ar·ies
re·ac·ti·vate
  re·ac·ti·vat·ed
  re·ac·ti·vat·ing
re·ac·tor

read·a·ble
  read·a·bil·i·ty
read·a·ble·ness
read·a·bly
read·er
read·ing
re·ad·just
  re·ad·just·ment
ready
  read·i·er
  read·i·est
  read·ied
  read·y·ing
  read·i·ly
  read·i·ness
read·y-made
re·a·gent
re·al
re·al·ism
re·al·ist
re·al·is·tic
re·al·is·ti·cal·ly
re·al·i·ty
  re·al·i·ties
re·al·ize
  re·al·ized
  re·al·iz·ing
  re·al·iz·a·ble
  re·al·i·za·tion
re·al·ly
realm
Re·al·tor
re·al·ty
ream·er
re·an·i·mate
  re·an·i·mat·ed
  re·an·i·mat·ing
  re·an·i·ma·tion
reap·er
re·ap·pear
  re·ap·pear·ance
  re·ap·por·tion·ment
  re·ap·por·tion
rear ad·mir·ral
re·arm
  re·ar·ma·ment
re·ar·range
  re·ar·ranged
  re·ar·rang·ing
  re·ar·range·ment
rear·ward
rea·son
rea·son·er
rea·son·a·ble
  rea·son·a·bil·i·ty
  rea·son·a·ble·ness
  rea·son·a·bly
rea·son·ing
re·as·sem·ble
  re·as·sem·bled
  re·as·sem·bling
  re·as·sem·bly
re·as·sume
  re·as·sump·tion
re·as·sure

re·as·sured
re·as·sur·ing
re·as·sur·ance
re·as·sur·ing·ly
re·bate
re·bat·ed
re·bat·ing
re·bat·er
Re·bec·ca
reb·el
re·bel
re·belled
re·bel·ling
re·bel·lion
re·bel·lious
re·bel·lious·ly
re·bel·lious·ness
re·birth
re·born
re·bound
re·buff
re·build
re·built
re·build·ing
re·buke
re·buked
re·buk·ing
re·buk·er
re·bus
re·bus·es
re·but
re·but·ted
re·but·ting
re·but·ter
re·but·tal
re·cal·ci·trant
re·cal·ci·trance
re·cal·ci·tran·cy
re·call
re·cant
re·can·ta·tion
re·ca·pit·u·late
re·ca·pit·u·lat·ed
re·ca·pit·u·lat·ing
re·ca·pit·u·la·tion
re·cap·ture
re·cap·tured
re·cap·tur·ing
re·cede
re·ced·ed
re·ced·ing
re·ceipt
re·ceiv·a·ble
re·ceive
re·ceived
re·ceiv·ing
re·ceiv·er
re·ceiv·er·ship
re·cent
re·cent·ly
re·cen·cy
re·cent·ness
re·cep·ta·cle
re·cep·tion
re·cep·tion·ist

re·cep·tive
re·cep·tive·ly
re·cep·tive·ness
re·cep·tiv·i·ty
re·cess
re·ces·sion
re·ces·sion·ary
re·ces·sion·al
re·ces·sive
re·charge
re·charged
re·charg·ing
Re·ci·fe
rec·i·pe
re·cip·i·ent
re·cip·i·ence
re·cip·i·en·cy
re·cip·ro·cal
re·cip·ro·cal·ly
re·cip·ro·cate
re·cip·ro·cat·ed
re·cip·ro·cat·ing
re·cip·ro·ca·tion
re·cip·ro·ca·tive
rec·i·proc·i·ty
rec·it·al
rec·i·ta·tion
rec·i·ta·tive
re·cite
re·cit·ed
re·cit·ing
reck·less
reck·less·ly
reck·less·ness
reck·on
reck·on·ing
re·claim
rec·la·ma·tion
re·cline
re·clined
re·clin·ing
re·clin·er
re·cluse
rec·og·ni·tion
re·cog·ni·zance
rec·og·nize
rec·og·nized
rec·og·niz·ing
rec·og·niz·a·ble
rec·og·niz·a·bly
re·coil
re·coil·less
re·col·lect
rec·ol·lect
rec·ol·lec·tion
rec·om·mend
rec·om·mend·a·ble
rec·om·mend·er
rec·om·men·da·tion
rec·om·pense
rec·om·pensed
rec·om·pens·ing
rec·on·cile
rec·on·ciled
rec·on·cil·ing

rec·on·cil·a·ble
rec·on·cil·a·bly
rec·on·cil·er
rec·on·cil·i·a·tion
rec·on·cile·ment
rec·on·dite
re·con·di·tion
re·con·firm
re·con·nais·sance
re·con·noi·ter
re·con·noi·tered
re·con·noi·ter·ing
re·con·sid·er
re·con·sid·er·a·tion
re·con·struct
re·con·struc·tion
re·cord
re·cord·er
re·cord·ing
re·count
re·count
re·coup
re·course
re·cov·er
re·cov·ery
re·cov·er·ies
re·cre·ant
re·cre·ate
re·cre·at·ed
re·cre·at·ing
re·cre·a·tion
rec·re·a·tion
rec·re·a·tion·al
re·crim·i·nate
re·crim·i·nat·ed
re·crim·i·nat·ing
re·crim·i·na·tion
re·crim·i·na·tive
re·crim·i·na·to·ry
re·cruit
re·cruit·er
re·cruit·ment
rec·tal
rec·tan·gle
rec·tan·gu·lar
rec·ti·fi·er
rec·ti·fy
rec·ti·fied
rec·ti·fy·ing
rec·ti·fi·a·ble
rec·ti·fi·ca·tion
rec·ti·lin·e·ar
rec·ti·tude
rec·tor
rec·to·ry
rec·to·ries
rec·tum
rec·tums
rec·ta
re·cum·bent
re·cum·ben·cy
re·cum·bent·ly
re·cu·per·ate
re·cu·per·at·ed
re·cu·per·at·ing

re·cu·per·a·tion
re·cu·per·a·tive
re·cur
re·curred
re·cur·ring
re·cur·rence
re·cur·rent
red
red·der
red·dest
red·ness
red·bird
red·blood·ed
red·breast
red·den
red·dish
re·dec·o·rate
re·dec·o·rat·ed
re·dec·o·rat·ing
re·dec·o·ra·tion
re·ded·i·cate
re·ded·i·cat·ed
re·ded·i·cat·ing
re·ded·i·ca·tion
re·deem
re·deem·a·ble
re·deem·er
re·demp·tion
re·demp·tive
red·hand·ed
red·hot
re·di·rect
re·di·rec·tion
red·let·ter
red·neck
re·do
re·did
re·done
re·do·ing
red·o·lent
red·o·lence
red·o·len·cy
re·dou·ble
re·dou·bled
re·dou·bling
re·doubt·a·ble
re·doubt·a·bly
re·dound
re·dress
red·start
re·duce
re·duced
re·duc·ing
re·duc·er
re·duc·i·ble
re·duc·tion
re·dun·dant
re·dun·dance
re·dun·dan·cy
re·dun·dan·cies
re·dun·dant·ly
re·du·pli·cate
re·du·pli·cat·ed
re·du·pli·cat·ing
re·dup·li·ca·tion

red·wood
re·echo
  re·ech·oed
  re·ech·o·ing
  re·ech·oes
reedy
  reed·i·er
  reed·i·est
  reed·i·ness
reef·er
re·e·lect
  re·e·lec·tion
re·em·pha·size
  re·em·pha·sized
  re·em·pha·siz·ing
re·en·force
  re·en·forced
  re·en·forc·ing
  re·en·force·ment
re·en·list
  re·en·list·ment
re·en·ter
  re·en·trance
re·en·try
  re·en·tries
re·es·tab·lish
  re·es·tab·lish·ment
re·ex·am·ine
  re·ex·am·ined
  re·ex·am·in·ing
  re·ex·am·i·na·tion
re·fec·to·ry
  re·fec·to·ries
re·fer
  re·ferred
  re·fer·ring
  re·fer·a·ble
  re·fer·ral
ref·er·ee
  ref·er·eed
  ref·er·ee·ing
ref·er·ence
  ref·er·enced
  ref·er·enc·ing
ref·er·en·dum
  ref·er·en·dums
  ref·er·en·da
ref·er·ent
re·fill
  re·fill·a·ble
re·fine
  re·fined
  re·fin·ing
  re·fine·ment
re·fin·ery
  re·fin·er·ies
re·fin·ish
re·fit
  re·fit·ted
  re·fit·ting
re·flect
  re·flec·tion
  re·flec·tive
  re·flec·tive·ly
  re·flec·tive·ness

re·flec·tor
re·flex
re·flex·ive
re·for·est
  re·for·est·a·tion
re·form
  re·formed
  re·form·er
  re·form·ist
Ref·or·ma·tion
re·form·a·to·ry
  re·form·a·to·ries
  re·form·a·tive
re·fract
  re·frac·tive
  re·frac·tion
  re·frac·to·ry
  re·frac·to·ri·ly
  re·frac·to·ri·ness
re·frain
re·fresh
  re·fresh·ing
  re·fresh·er
  re·fresh·ment
re·frig·er·ant
re·frig·er·ate
  re·frig·er·at·ed
  re·frig·er·at·ing
  re·frig·er·a·tion
  re·frig·er·a·tor
re·fu·el
ref·uge
ref·u·gee
re·ful·gent
  re·ful·gence
re·fund
re·fur·bish
re·fus·al
re·fuse
  re·fused
  re·fus·ing
ref·use
re·fute
  re·fut·ed
  re·fut·ing
  re·fut·a·ble
ref·u·ta·tion
re·gain
re·gal
  re·gal·ly
re·gale
  re·galed
  re·gal·ing
re·ga·lia
re·gard
  re·gard·ful
  re·gard·ing
  re·gard·less
  re·gard·less·ly
re·gat·ta
re·gen·cy
  re·gen·cies
re·gen·er·ate
  re·gen·er·at·ed
  re·gen·er·at·ing

re·gen·er·a·cy
re·gen·er·a·tion
re·gen·er·a·tive
re·gent
re·gime
reg·i·men
reg·i·ment
  reg·i·men·tal
  reg·i·men·ta·tion
re·gion
re·gion·al
  re·gion·al·ly
reg·is·ter
  reg·is·tered
  reg·is·trant
reg·is·trar
  reg·is·tra·tion
reg·is·try
  reg·is·tries
Re·gnault
re·gress
  re·gres·sion
  re·gres·sor
re·gret
  re·gret·ted
  re·gret·ting
  re·gret·ta·ble
  re·gret·ta·bly
  re·gret·ter
  re·gret·ful
  re·gret·ful·ly
  re·gret·ful·ness
reg·u·lar
  reg·u·lar·i·ty
reg·u·late
  reg·u·lat·ed
  reg·u·lat·ing
  reg·u·la·tive
  reg·u·la·tor
  reg·u·la·to·ry
reg·u·la·tion
re·gur·gi·tate
  re·gur·gi·tat·ed
  re·gur·gi·tat·ing
  re·gur·gi·ta·tion
re·ha·bil·i·tate
  re·ha·bil·i·tat·ed
  re·ha·bil·i·tat·ing
  re·ha·bil·i·ta·tion
  re·ha·bil·i·ta·tive
re·hash
re·hears·al
re·hearse
  re·hearsed
  re·hears·ing
  re·hears·er
Re·ho·bo·am
Re·ho·both
Reichs·tag
reign
re·im·burse
  re·im·bursed
  re·im·burs·ing
  re·im·burse·ment
rein

re·in·car·na·tion
rein·deer
re·in·force
  re·in·forced
  re·in·forc·ing
  re·in·force·ment
re·in·state
  re·in·stat·ed
  re·in·stat·ing
  re·in·state·ment
re·it·er·ate
  re·it·er·at·ed
  re·it·er·at·ing
  re·it·er·a·tion
re·ject
  re·jec·tion
re·joice
  re·joiced
  re·joic·ing
  re·joic·er
  re·joic·ing·ly
re·join
  re·join·der
re·ju·ve·nate
  re·ju·ve·nat·ed
  re·ju·ve·nat·ing
  re·ju·ve·na·tion
  re·ju·ve·na·tor
re·kin·dle
  re·kin·dled
  re·kin·dling
re·lapse
  re·lapsed
  re·laps·ing
  re·laps·er
re·late
  re·lat·ed
  re·lat·ing
  re·lat·er
  re·lat·or
re·la·tion
  re·la·tion·al
  re·la·tion·ship
rel·a·tive
  rel·a·tive·ly
  rel·a·tiv·i·ty
re·lax
  re·lax·a·tion
re·lay
  re·laid
  re·lay·ing
re·lay
  re·layed
  re·lay·ing
re·lease
  re·leased
  re·leas·ing
  re·leas·a·ble
  re·leas·er
rel·e·gate
  rel·e·gat·ed
  rel·e·gat·ing
  rel·e·ga·tion
re·lent
  re·lent·less

rel·e·vant
rel·e·vance
rel·e·van·cy
rel·e·vant·ly
re·li·a·ble
  re·li·a·bil·i·ty
  re·li·a·ble·ness
  re·li·a·bly
re·li·ance
re·li·ant
rel·ic
re·lief
re·lieve
  re·lieved
  re·liev·ing
  re·liev·a·ble
  re·liev·er
re·li·gion
re·li·gi·os·i·ty
re·li·gious
re·lin·quish
rel·ish
re·live
  re·lived
  re·liv·ing
re·lo·cate
  re·lo·cat·ed
  re·lo·cat·ing
  re·lo·ca·tion
re·luc·tance
re·luc·tant
re·ly
  re·lied
  re·ly·ing
re·main
  re·main·der
re·mand
re·mark
  re·mark·a·ble
  re·mark·a·ble·ness
  re·mark·a·bly
Re·marque
Rem·brandt
re·me·di·a·ble
re·me·di·al
rem·e·dy
  rem·e·dies
  rem·e·died
  rem·e·dy·ing
re·mem·ber
  re·mem·brance
re·mind
  re·mind·er
Rem·ing·ton
rem·i·nisce
  rem·i·nisced
  rem·i·nisc·ing
  rem·i·nis·cence
  rem·i·nis·cent
re·miss
re·mis·sion
re·mit
  re·mit·ted
  re·mit·ting
  re·mit·tance

rem·nant
re·mod·el
re·mon·strance
re·mon·strate
  re·mon·strat·ed
  re·mon·strat·ing
re·morse
  re·morse·ful
  re·morse·ful·ly
  re·morse·less
re·mote
  re·mot·er
  re·mot·est
re·mount
re·mov·a·ble
re·mov·al
re·move
  re·moved
  re·mov·ing
re·mu·ner·ate
  re·mu·ner·at·ed
  re·mu·ner·at·ing
  re·mu·ner·a·tion
  re·mu·ner·a·tive
Re·mus
ren·ais·sance
Re·nan
re·nas·cence
re·nas·cent
rend
  rend·ed
  rend·ing
ren·der
ren·dez·vous
  ren·dez·voused
  ren·dez·vous·ing
ren·di·tion
ren·e·gade
re·nege
  re·neged
  re·neg·ing
re·new
re·new·al
ren·net
Re·no
Re·noir
re·nounce
  re·nounced
  re·nounc·ing
ren·o·vate
  ren·o·vat·ed
  ren·o·vat·ing
  ren·o·va·tion
re·nown
re·nowned
rent·al
re·nun·ci·a·tion
re·or·gan·i·za·tion
re·or·gan·ize
  re·or·gan·ized
  re·or·gan·iz·ing
re·pair
  re·pair·man
  re·pair·men
rep·a·ra·ble

rep·a·ra·tion
rep·ar·tee
re·past
re·pa·tri·ate
  re·pa·tri·at·ed
  re·pa·tri·at·ing
  re·pa·tri·a·tion
re·pay
  re·paid
  re·pay·ing
  re·pay·ment
re·peal
re·peat
  re·peat·a·ble
  re·peat·ed
re·peat·er
re·pel
  re·pelled
  re·pel·ling
re·pel·lent
re·pent
  re·pent·ance
  re·pent·ant
re·per·cus·sion
rep·er·toire
rep·er·to·ry
  rep·er·to·ries
rep·e·ti·tion
  rep·e·ti·tious
re·pet·i·tive
re·place
  re·placed
  re·plac·ing
  re·place·a·ble
re·place·ment
re·plen·ish
re·plete
  re·ple·tion
rep·li·ca
re·ply
  re·plied
  re·ply·ing
  re·plies
re·port
re·port·ed·ly
re·port·er
  rep·or·to·ri·al
re·pose
  re·posed
  re·pos·ing
  re·pose·ful
re·pos·i·tory
  re·pos·i·tor·ies
re·pos·sess
  re·pos·ses·sion
rep·re·hend
rep·re·hen·si·ble
rep·re·sent
rep·re·sen·ta·tion
rep·re·sent·a·tive
re·press
  re·pres·sion
re·prieve
  re·prieved
  re·priev·ing

rep·ri·mand
re·print
re·pris·al
re·proach
  re·proach·ful
rep·ro·bate
  rep·ro·ba·tion
re·pro·duce
  re·pro·duced
  re·pro·duc·ing
  re·pro·duc·tion
  re·pro·duc·tive
re·proof
re·prove
  re·proved
  re·prov·ing
rep·tile
  rep·til·i·an
re·pub·lic
  re·pub·li·can
  re·pub·li·can·ism
re·pu·di·ate
  re·pu·di·at·ed
  re·pu·di·at·ing
  re·pu·di·a·tion
re·pug·nance
  re·pug·nan·cy
  re·pug·nant
re·pulse
  re·pulsed
  re·puls·ing
re·pul·sion
re·pul·sive
rep·u·ta·ble
  rep·u·ta·bly
  rep·u·ta·bil·i·ty
rep·u·ta·tion
re·pute
  re·put·ed
  re·put·ing
  re·put·ed·ly
re·quest
req·ui·em
re·quire
  re·quired
  re·quir·ing
  re·quire·ment
req·ui·site
req·ui·si·tion
re·quit·al
re·quite
  re·quit·ed
  re·quit·ing
re·run
  re·run·ning
re·sale
re·scind
res·cue
  res·cued
  res·cu·ing
  res·cu·er
re·search
  re·search·er
re·sem·blance
re·sem·ble

re·sem·bled
re·sem·bling
re·sent
  re·sent·ful
re·sent·ment
res·er·va·tion
re·serve
  re·served
  re·serv·ing
  re·serv·ist
res·er·voir
re·set
  re·set·ting
re·side
  re·sid·ed
  re·sid·ing
res·i·dence
  res·i·den·cy
  res·i·den·cies
res·i·dent
  res·i·den·tial
re·sid·u·al
res·i·due
re·sign
  res·ig·na·tion
  re·signed
re·sil·ient
  re·sil·ience
  re·sil·ien·cy
res·in
  res·in·ous
re·sist
  re·sist·er
  re·sist·i·ble
re·sist·ance
re·sist·ant
re·sist·less
re·sis·tor
res·o·lute
  res·o·lu·tion
re·solve
  re·solved
  re·solv·ing
res·o·nance
res·o·nant
res·o·nate
  res·o·nat·ed
  res·o·nat·ing
  res·o·na·tor
re·sort
re·sound
  re·sound·ing
  re·sound·ing·ly
re·source
  re·source·ful
  re·source·ful·ly
  re·source·ful·ness
re·spect
  re·spect·ful
  re·spect·ful·ly
  re·spect·ful·ness
re·spect·a·ble
  re·spect·a·bil·i·ty
re·spect·ing
re·spec·tive

178

re·spec·tive·ly
res·pi·ra·tion
res·pi·ra·to·ry
res·pi·ra·tor
re·spire
  re·spired
  re·spir·ing
res·pite
re·splend·ent
  re·splend·ence
re·spond
re·spond·ent
re·sponse
re·spon·si·bil·i·ty
  re·spon·si·bil·i·ties
re·spon·si·ble
re·spon·sive
res·tau·rant
rest·ful
res·ti·tu·tion
res·tive
rest·less
res·to·ra·tion
re·stor·a·tive
re·store
  re·stored
  re·stor·ing
re·strain
re·straint
re·strict
  re·strict·ed
  re·strict·ed·ly
re·stric·tion
re·stric·tive
re·sult
  re·sult·ant
re·sume
  re·sumed
  re·sum·ing
ré·su·mé
re·sump·tion
re·sur·gent
  re·sur·gence
res·ur·rect
res·ur·rec·tion
re·sus·ci·tate
  re·sus·ci·tat·ed
  re·sus·ci·tat·ing
  re·sus·ci·ta·tion
  re·sus·ci·ta·tor
re·tail
  re·tail·er
re·tain
re·tain·er
re·take
  re·took
  re·tak·en
  re·tak·ing
re·tal·i·ate
  re·tal·i·at·ed
  re·tal·i·at·ing
  re·tal·i·a·tion
  re·tal·i·a·to·ry
re·tard
  re·tard·ant

re·tar·da·tion
re·tard·ed
re·ten·tion
re·ten·tive
ret·i·cent
  ret·i·cence
ret·i·na
  ret·i·nas
  ret·i·nae
  ret·i·nal
ret·i·nue
re·tire
  re·tired
  re·tir·ing
re·tire·ment
re·tool
re·tort
re·touch
re·trace
  re·traced
  re·trac·ing
re·tract
  re·trac·tion
  re·trac·tor
re·trac·tile
re·tread
re·treat
re·trench
  re·trench·ment
re·tri·al
ret·ri·bu·tion
re·trieve
  re·trieved
  re·triev·ing
  re·triev·er
ret·ro·ac·tive
ret·ro·grade
  ret·ro·grad·ed
  ret·ro·grad·ing
ret·ro·gress
  ret·ro·gres·sion
  ret·ro·gres·sive
ret·ro·rock·et
ret·ro·spect
  ret·ro·spec·tion
  ret·ro·spec·tive
re·turn
re·turn·a·ble
re·turn·ee
Reu·ben
re·un·ion
re·u·nite
  re·u·nit·ed
  re·u·nit·ing
rev
  revved
  rev·ving
re·vamp
re·veal
rev·eil·le
rev·el
  rev·el·er
rev·e·la·tion
rev·el·ry
  rev·el·ries

re·venge
  re·venged
  re·veng·ing
re·venge·ful
rev·e·nue
rev·e·nu·er
re·ver·ber·ate
  re·ver·ber·at·ed
  re·ber·ver·at·ing
  re·ver·ber·a·tion
re·vere
  re·vered
  re·ver·ing
rev·er·ence
  rev·er·enced
  rev·er·enc·ing
rev·er·end
rev·er·ent
rev·er·en·tial
rev·er·ie
re·ver·sal
re·verse
  re·versed
  re·vers·ing
  re·vers·i·ble
re·ver·sion
re·vert
re·view
  re·view·er
re·vile
  re·viled
  re·vil·ing
re·vise
  re·vised
  re·vis·ing
re·vi·sion
  re·vi·sion·ist
  re·vi·sion·ism
re·viv·al
  re·viv·al·ist
re·vive
  re·vived
  re·viv·ing
rev·o·ca·ble
rev·o·ca·tion
re·voke
  re·voked
  re·vok·ing
re·volt
rev·o·lu·tion
  rev·o·lu·tion·ary
  rev·o·lu·tion·ar·ies
  rev·o·lu·tion·ist
  rev·o·lu·tion·ize
  rev·o·lu·tion·ized
  rev·o·lu·tion·iz·ing
  rev·o·lu·tion·iz·er
re·volve
  re·volved
  re·volv·ing
  re·volv·er
re·vue
re·vul·sion
re·ward
re·write

179

re·wrote
re·writ·ten
re·writ·ing
Rey·kja·vik
Rey·nard
Reyn·olds
rhap·sod·ic
rhap·sod·i·cal
rhap·sod·i·cal·ly
rhap·so·dize
rhap·so·dized
rhap·so·diz·ing
rhap·so·dy
rhap·so·dies
rhap·so·dist
rhea
Rhen·ish
rhe·ni·um
rhe·o·stat
rhe·sus
rhet·o·ric
rhe·tor·i·cal
rhet·o·ri·cian
rheum
rheu·mat·ic
rheu·mat·i·cal·ly
rheu·ma·tism
rhine·stone
rhi·no
rhi·noc·er·os
rhi·noc·er·os·es
rhi·zome
Rhode Is·land
Rho·de·sia
rho·di·um
rho·do·den·dron
rhom·bic
rhom·boid
rhom·boi·dal
rhom·bus
rhom·bus·es
rhom·bi
rhu·barb
rhyme
rhymed
rhym·ing
rhyme·ster
rhythm
rhyth·mic
rhyth·mi·cal
rhyth·mi·cal·ly
rib
ribbed
rib·bing
rib·ald
rib·ald·ry
rib·ald·ries
rib·bon
ri·bo·fla·vin
rib·bo·nu·cle·ic
rice
riced
ric·ing
Riche·lieu
rich·es

Rich·mond
rich·ness
Rich·ter
rick·ets
rick·ety
rick·et·i·er
rick·et·i·est
rick·et·i·ness
rick·shaw
ric·o·chet
rid
rid·ded
rid·ding
rid·dance
rid·dle
rid·dled
rid·dling
ride
rode
rid·den
rid·ing
rid·er
ridge
ridged
ridg·ing
ridge·pole
rid·i·cule
rid·i·culed
rid·i·cul·ing
ri·dic·u·lous
rif·fle
rif·fled
rif·fling
riff·raff
ri·fle
ri·fled
ri·fling
rig
rigged
rig·ging
Ri·ga
rig·ger
right·eous
right·ful
right·hand
right·hand·ed
right·ism
right of way
rig·id
ri·gid·i·ty
rig·ma·role
rig·or
rig·or·ous
rile
riled
ril·ing
rim
rimmed
rim·ming
rime
rimed
rim·ing
rim·er
ring·er
ring·lead·er

ring·let
ring·mas·ter
ring·side
ring·worm
rinse
rinsed
rins·ing
Rio de Ja·nei·ro
Rio Grande
ri·ot
ri·ot·ous
rip
ripped
rip·ping
rip·per
ri·par·i·an
rip·en
rip·off
rip·ple
rip·pled
rip·pling
rip·saw
rip·tide
rise
rose
ris·en
ris·ing
ris·er
ris·i·ble
ris·i·bil·i·ty
risky
risk·i·er
risk·i·est
risk·i·ness
ris·qué
rit·u·al
rit·u·al·ism
rit·u·al·ist
rit·u·al·is·tic
rit·u·al·is·ti·cal·l
ritzy
ritz·i·er
ritz·i·est
ri·val
ri·val·ry
ri·val·ries
riv·er
riv·er·side
riv·et
riv·et·er
riv·i·er·a
riv·u·let
Ri·yadh
roach·es
road·bed
road·block
road·run·ner
road·side
road·ster
road·way
Ro·a·noke
roast·er
rob
robbed
rob·bing

rob·ber
rob·bery
rob·ber·ies
robe
robed
rob·ing
Robes·pierre
rob·in
Rob·in·son Cru·soe
ro·bot
ro·bust
Ro·cham·beau
Ro·chelle
Roch·es·ter
rock-and-roll
rock-bound
Rock·e·fel·ler
rock·er
rock·et
rock·et·ry
Rock·ford
Rock·ies
rock-ribbed
rocky
rock·i·er
rock·i·est
rock·i·ness
ro·co·co
ro·dent
ro·deo
ro·de·os
Ro·din
roe·buck
roent·gen
rog·er
rogue
ro·guish
ro·guish·ly
ro·guish·ness
ro·guery
ro·guer·ies
roist·er
roll·er
roll·er bear·ing
roll·er coast·er
roll·er-skate
roll·er-skat·ed
roll·er-skat·ing
roll·er-skat·er
rol·lick
rol·lick·ing
roll·ing mill
roll·ing pin
Röl·vaag
ro·ly-po·ly
ro·ly-po·lies
ro·maine
Ro·man
ro·mance
ro·manced
ro·manc·ing
Ro·man·esque
Ro·ma·nia
ro·man·tic
ro·man·ti·cism

ro·man·ti·cist
ro·man·ti·cize
ro·man·ti·cized
ro·man·ti·ciz·ing
Rom·a·ny
Ro·meo
romp·er
roof·ing
roof·tree
rook·ery
rook·er·ies
rook·ie
room·er
room·ful
room·mate
roomy
room·i·er
room·i·est
room·i·ly
room·i·ness
Roo·se·velt
roost·er
root·stock
rope
roped
rop·ing
ropy
rop·i·er
rop·i·est
rop·i·ness
Roque·fort
Ror·schach
Ro·sa·rio
ro·sa·ry
ro·sa·ries
ro·se·ate
rose-bud
rose-col·ored
rose·mary
rose·mar·ies
Ro·set·ta
ro·sette
rose·wood
Rosh Ha·sha·nah
ros·in
Ros·set·ti
ros·ter
ros·trum
ros·tra
ros·trums
rosy
ros·i·er
ros·i·est
ros·i·ly
ros·i·ness
rot
rot·ted
rot·ting
ro·ta·ry
ro·ta·ries
ro·tate
ro·tat·ed
ro·tat·ing
ro·ta·tion
ro·tis·ser·ie

ro·tor
rot·ten
Rot·ter·dam
ro·tund
ro·tun·di·ty
ro·tun·di·ties
ro·tun·da
r ou·é
Rou·en
rouge
rouged
roug·ing
rough·age
rough-and-tum·ble
rough·en
rough-hew
rough-hewed
rough-hewn
rough-hew·ing
rough-house
rough·neck
rough·rid·er
rough·shod
rou·lette
round·a·bout
round·ed
round·er
Round·head
round·ish
round-shoul·dered
round·up
rouse
roused
rous·ing
rous·er
roust
roust·a·bout
rout
route
rout·ed
rout·ing
rout·er
rou·tine
rou·tin·ize
rou·tin·ized
rou·tin·iz·ing
rove
roved
rov·ing
rov·er
row·boat
row·dy
row·dies
row·di·er
row·di·est
row·di·ly
row·di·ness
row·lock
roy·al
roy·al·ly
roy·al·ist
roy·al·ty
roy·al·ties
rub
rubbed

rub·bing
rub·ber
rub·bery
rub·ber·ize
rub·ber·ized
rub·ber·iz·ing
rub·ber·neck
rub·bish
rub·bishy
rub·ble
rub·bly
rub·bli·er
rub·bli·est
rub·down
ru·bel·la
Ru·bens
ru·be·o·la
Ru·bi·con
ru·bi·cund
ru·bid·i·um
Ru·bin·stein
ru·bric
ru·by
ru·bies
ruck·sack
ruck·us
rud·der
rud·dy
rud·di·er
rud·di·est
rud·di·ly
rud·di·ness
rude
rud·er
rud·est
rude·ly
rude·ness
ru·di·ment
ru·di·men·tal
ru·di·men·ta·ry
rue
rued
ru·ing
rue·ful
rue·ful·ly
rue·ful·ness
ruff
ruffed
ruf·fi·an
ruf·fle
ruf·fled
ruf·fling
Rug·by
rug·ged
rug·ged·ly
rug·ged·ness
ru·in
ru·in·a·tion
ru·in·ous
rule
ruled
rul·ing
rul·er
Ru·ma·nia
rum·ba

rum·baed
rum·ba·ing
rum·ble
rum·bled
rum·bling
rum·bler
rum·bly
ru·mi·nant
ru·mi·nate
ru·mi·nat·ed
ru·mi·nat·ing
ru·mi·na·tion
ru·mi·na·tor
rum·mage
rum·maged
rum·mag·ing
rum·mag·er
rum·my
rum·mies
ru·mor
ru·mor·mon·ger
rum·ple
rum·pled
rum·pling
rum·pus
run
run·ning
run·a·bout
run·a·round
run·a·way
run·down
run·in
run·ner
run·ner·up
run·ny
run·ni·er
run·ni·est
run·off
run-of-the-mill
run·on
runt
runty
runt·i·er
runt·i·est
run·through
run·way
rup·ture
rup·tured
rup·tur·ing
ru·ral
ru·ral·ly
ru·ral·ize
ru·ral·ized
ru·ral·iz·ing
ru·ral·i·za·tion
rus·set
Rus·sia
Rus·sian rou·lette
rus·tic
rus·ti·cate
rus·ti·cat·ed
rus·ti·cat·ing
rus·ti·ca·tion
rus·ti·ca·tor
rus·tic·i·ty

rus·tic·i·ties
rus·tle
rus·tled
rus·tling
rus·tler
rust·proof
rusty
rust·i·er
rust·i·est
rust·i·ly
rust·i·ness
rut
rut·ted
rut·ting
ru·ta·ba·ga
ru·the·ni·um
ruth·less
ruth·less·ly
ruth·less·ness
Rut·land
rut·ty
rut·ti·er
rut·ti·est
Rwan·da
Sab·a·oth
Sab·bath
Sab·bat·i·cal
sa·ber
sa·ber-toothed
sa·ble
sab·o·tage
sab·o·taged
sab·o·tag·ing
sab·o·teur
sa·bra
Sac·a·ga·wea
sac·cha·rine
sac·er·do·tal
sa·chet
sack·cloth
sack·ful
sack·fuls
sack·ing
sac·ra·ment
sac·ra·men·tal
Sac·ra·men·to
sa·cred
sa·cred·ly
sa·cred·ness
sac·ri·fice
sac·ri·ficed
sac·ri·fic·ing
sac·ri·fic·er
sac·ri·fi·cial
sac·ri·lege
sac·ri·le·gious
sac·ro·il·i·ac
sac·ro·sanct
sac·ro·sanc·ti·ty
sac·ro·sanct·ness
sac·rum
sac·rums
sac·ra
sa·cral
sad

182

sad·der
sad·dest
sad·ly
sad·ness
sad·den
sad·dle
sad·dled
sad·dling
sad·dle·backed
sad·dle·bag
Sad·du·cee
sad·ism
sad·ist
sa·dis·tic
sa·dis·ti·cal·ly
sad·o·mas·o·chism
sad·o·mas·o·chist
sa·fa·ri
sa·fa·ris
safe
saf·er
saf·est
safe·con·duct
safe·crack·er
safe·crack·ing
safe·de·pos·it
safe·guard
safe·keep·ing
safe·ty
safe·ties
safe·ty match
safe·ty pin
safe·ty valve
safe·ty zone
saf·flow·er
saf·fron
sag
sagged
sag·ging
sa·ga
sa·ga·cious
sa·gac·i·ty
sage
sag·er
sag·est
sage·ly
sage·ness
sage·brush
Sag·i·naw
Sag·it·ta·ri·us
Sag·ue·nay
Sai·gon
sail·boat
sail·cloth
sail·er
sail·fish
sail·ing
sail·or
saint
saint·hood
saint·ship
Saint Ber·nard
saint·ed
saint·ly
saint·li·er

saint·li·est
saint·li·ness
Sai·pan
sa·ke
Sa·kha·lin
sal·a·ble
sale·a·ble
sal·a·bil·i·ty
sal·a·bly
sa·la·cious
sal·ad
Sal·a·man·ca
sal·a·man·der
sa·la·mi
Sal·a·mis
sal·a·ry
sal·a·ries
Sa·lem
Sa·ler·no
sales·man
sales·men
sales·man·ship
sales·per·son
sales·peo·ple
sales·room
sa·li·ent
sa·li·ence
sa·li·en·cy
sa·li·ent·ly
sa·li·ent·ness
sa·line
sa·lin·i·ty
Salis·bury
sa·li·va
sal·i·vary
sal·i·vate
sal·i·vat·ed
sal·i·vat·ing
sal·i·va·tion
sal·low
sal·low·ish
sal·ly
sal·lies
sal·lied
sal·ly·ing
salm·on
Sa·lo·me
sa·lon
Sa·lon·i·ka
sa·loon
salt·cel·lar
salt·ed
sal·tine
salt·shak·er
salt·wa·ter
salt·wort
salty
salt·i·er
salt·i·est
salt·i·ness
sa·lu·bri·ous
Sa·lu·ki
sal·u·tary
sal·u·ta·tion
sa·lu·ta·to·ry

sa·lu·ta·to·ries
sa·lute
sa·lut·ed
sa·lut·ing
sa·lut·er
Sal·va·dor
sal·vage
sal·vaged
sal·vag·ing
sal·vage·a·ble
sal·vag·er
sal·va·tion
Sal·va·tion Ar·my
salve
salved
salv·ing
sal·vor
sal·vo
sal·vos
sal·voes
Salz·burg
Sa·mar·ia
Sa·mar·i·tan
Samar·kand
sam·ba
sam·baed
sam·ba·ing
same·ness
Sa·moa
sam·o·var
sam·ple
sam·pled
sam·pling
sam·pler
sam·pling
Sam·son
San·aa
San An·to·nio
san·a·to·ri·um
San·cho
sanc·ti·fy
sanc·ti·fied
sanc·ti·fy·ing
sanc·ti·fi·ca·tion
sanc·ti·fi·er
sanc·ti·mo·ny
sanc·ti·mo·ni·ous
sanc·tion
sanc·tion·a·ble
sanc·tion·er
sanc·ti·ty
sanc·ti·ties
sanc·tu·ary
sanc·tu·ar·ies
sanc·tum
sanc·ta
san·dal
san·dal·wood
sand·bag
sand·bagged
sand·bag·ging
sand·bag·ger
sand·bank
sand·blast
sand·box

Sand·burg
sand·cast
 sand·cast·ed
 sand·cast·ing
San Di·e·go
sand·lot
sand·man
 sand·men
San Do·min·go
sand·pa·per
sand·pi·per
sand·stone
sand·storm
sand·wich
sandy
 sand·i·er
 sand·i·est
 sand·i·ness
sane
 san·er
 san·est
 sane·ly
 sane·ness
San·for·ize
 san·for·ized
 san·for·iz·ing
San Fran·cis·co
sang·froid
san·gui·nary
san·guine
 san·guine·ly
 san·guine·ness
San·he·drin
san·i·tar·i·um
 san·i·tar·i·ums
 san·i·tar·ia
san·i·tary
 san·i·ta·ri·ly
san·i·ta·tion
san·i·tize
 san·tized
 san·i·tiz·ing
san·i·ty
San Joa·quin
San Mar·i·no
San Sal·va·dor
San Se·bas·tian
San·skrit
San·ta An·na
San·ta Bar·ba·ra
San·ta Claus
San·ta Fe
San·ta Ma·ria
San·ta·ya·na
San·ti·a·go
San·to Do·min·go
São Pau·lo
sap
 sapped
 sap·ping
sap·head
 sap·head·ed
sa·pi·ent
 sa·pi·ence
 sa·pi·en·cy

sap·less
sap·ling
sa·pon·i·fy
 sa·pon·i·fied
 sa·pon·i·fy·ing
sap·per
sap·phire
sap·phism
sap·py
 sap·pi·er
 sap·pi·est
 sap·pi·ness
sap·suck·er
sap·wood
Sar·a·cen
Sa·ra·je·vo
sa·ran
Sar·a·so·ta
Sar·a·to·ga
sar·casm
 sar·cas·tic
 sar·cas·ti·cal·ly
sar·co·ma
 sar·co·mas
 sar·co·ma·ta
sar·coph·a·gus
 sar·coph·a·gi
 sar·coph·a·gus·es
sar·dine
Sar·din·ia
sar·don·ic
 sar·don·i·cal·ly
sar·gas·sum
sa·ri
 sa·ris
sa·rong
sar·sa·pa·ril·la
sar·to·ri·al
sa·shay
Sas·katch·e·wan
sas·sa·fras
sas·sy
 sas·si·er
 sas·si·est
Sa·tan
sa·tan·ic
 sa·tan·i·cal
sa·tan·ism
 sa·tan·ist
satch·el
sate
 sat·ed
 sat·ing
sa·teen
sat·el·lite
sa·ti·a·ble
 sa·ti·a·bly
 sa·ti·a·bil·i·ty
 sa·ti·a·ble·ness
sa·ti·ate
 sa·ti·at·ed
 sa·ti·at·ing
 sa·ti·a·tion
sa·ti·e·ty
sat·in

sat·iny
sat·ire
sa·tir·i·cal
 sa·tir·i·cal·ly
sat·i·rist
sat·i·rize
 sat·i·rized
 sat·i·riz·ing
 sat·i·riz·er
sat·is·fac·tion
sat·is·fac·to·ry
 sat·is·fac·to·ri·ly
sat·is·fy
 sat·is·fied
 sat·is·fy·ing
 sat·is·fi·a·ble
 sat·is·fi·er
 sat·is·fy·ing·ly
sat·u·ra·ble
sat·u·rate
 sat·u·rat·ed
 sat·u·rat·ing
 sat·u·ra·tion
Sat·ur·day
Sat·urn
sat·ur·na·lia
sat·ur·nine
sa·tyr
 sa·tyr·ic
sauce
 sauced
 sauc·ing
 sau·cer
 sau·cy
 sau·ci·er
 sau·ci·est
 sau·ci·ly
 sau·ci·ness
Sau·di
sau·er·bra·ten
sau·er·kraut
Sault Sainte Ma·rie
sau·na
saun·ter
 saun·ter·er
sau·sage
 sau·sage·like
sau·té
 sau·téed
 sau·tée·ing
sav·age
 sav·age·ness
 sav·age·ry
 sav·age·ries
sa·van·na
Sa·van·nah
sa·vant
save
 saved
 sav·ing
 sav·er
sav·ior
sa·vior-faire
sa·vor
 sa·vor·er

sa·vory
sa·vor·i·er
sa·vor·i·est
sa·vor·i·ly
sa·vor·i·ness
sav·vy
sav·vied
sav·vy·ing
sav·vi·er
sav·vi·est
saw·buck
saw·dust
sawed-off
saw·horse
saw·mill
saw-toothed
saw·yer
Sax·on
Sax·o·ny
sax·o·phone
sax·o·phon·ist
say
said
say·ing
say·a·ble
say·er
say-so
scab
scabbed
scab·bing
scab·bard
scab·by
scab·bi·er
scab·bi·est
scab·bi·ness
sca·bies
scaf·fold
scaf·fold·ing
sca·lar
scal·a·wag
scald
scald·ing
scale
scaled
scal·ing
scale·less
scale·like
scal·i·ness
scal·lion
scal·lop
scal·lop·er
scalp
scalp·er
scal·pel
scaly
scal·i·er
scal·i·est
scal·i·ness
scamp
scamp·er
scan
scanned
scan·ning
scan·ner
scan·dal

scan·dal·ize
scan·dal·ized
scan·dal·iz·ing
scan·dal·iz·er
scan·dal·i·za·tion
scan·dal·mon·ger
scan·dal·ous
Scan·di·na·via
Scan·di·na·vi·an
scan·sion
scant
scant·ness
scan·ties
scanty
scant·i·er
scant·i·est
scant·i·ly
scant·i·ness
scape·goat
scape·grace
scap·u·la
scap·u·las
scap·u·lae
scar
scarred
scar·ring
scarce
scarce·ness
scar·ci·ty
scare
scared
scar·ing
scar·er
scare·crow
scare·mon·ger
scarf
scarfs
scarves
scarf·less
scarf·like
scarf·skin
scar·i·fy
scar·i·fied
scar·i·fy·ing
scar·i·fi·ca·tion
scar·let
scarp
scary
scar·i·er
scar·i·est
scat
scat·ted
scat·ting
scathe
scathed
scath·ing
scathe·less
scat·o·log·i·cal
scat·ter
scat·ter·a·ble
scat·ter·er
scat·ter·brain
scat·ter·brained
scav·enge
scav·enged

scav·eng·ing
scav·en·ger
sce·nar·io
sce·nar·i·os
sce·nar·ist
scen·ery
scen·er·ies
sce·nic
sce·ni·cal
scent
scent·ed
scep·ter
scep·tered
scep·ter·ing
sched·ule
sched·uled
sched·ul·ing
sched·u·lar
sche·ma
sche·ma·ta
sche·mat·i·cal·ly
sche·ma·tize
sche·ma·tized
sche·ma·tiz·ing
scheme
schem·er
schem·ing
scher·zo
scher·zos
scher·zi
schism
schis·mat·ic
schis·mat·i·cal
schist
schizo
schiz·os
schiz·oid
schiz·o·phre·nia
schiz·o·phren·ic
schle·miel
schmaltz
schmaltzy
schmo
schnapps
schnau·zer
schnit·zel
Schnitz·ler
schnook
schnor·kel
schnoz·zle
schol·ar
schol·ar·ly
schol·ar·li·ness
schol·ar·ship
scho·las·tic
scho·las·ti·cal
scho·las·ti·cism
school board
school·boy
school bus
school·child
school·chil·dren
school·girl
school·house
school·ing

school-marm
school-mas-ter
school-mate
school-mis-tress
school-room
school-teach-er
 school-teach-ing
school-work
schoon-er
Scho-pen-hauer
Schu-bert
Schu-mann
schuss
schwa
Schweit-zer
sci-at-ic
sci-at-i-ca
sci-ence
sci-en-tif-ic
 sci-en-tif-i-cal-ly
sci-en-tist
scim-i-tar
scin-tig-ra-phy
scin-til-la
scin-til-lant
scin-til-late
 scin-til-lat-ed
 scin-til-lat-ing
 scin-til-la-tion
sci-on
scis-sor
scis-sors
scle-ra
 scle-rot-i-ca
scle-ro-sis
 scle-ro-ses
scle-rot-ic
scle-rous
scoff
 scoff-er
 scoff-ing-ly
scold
 scold-er
 scold-ing
scol-lop
sconce
scone
scoop
 scoop-er
 scoop-ful
scoot-er
scope
scorch
 scorched
 scorch-ing
scorch-er
score
 scored
 scor-ing
 score-less
 scor-er
 score-board
score-keep-er
scorn
 scorn-er

scorn-ful
scorn-ful-ness
Scor-pio
scor-pi-on
Scotch
Scotch-I-rish
Scotch-man
 Scotch-men
scot-free
Scot-land Yard
Scots-man
 Scots-men
scot-tie
Scot-tish
Scot-tish ter-ri-er
scoundrel
 scoun-drel-ly
scour
 scour-er
scourge
 scourged
 scourg-ing
 scourg-er
 scour-ings
scout-ing
scout-mas-ter
scowl
 scowl-er
scrab-ble
 scrab-bled
 scrab-bling
 scrab-bler
scrag
 scragged
 scrag-ging
 scrag-gly
 scrag-gli-er
 scrag-gli-est
 scrag-gy
 scrag-gi-er
 scrag-gi-est
scram
 scrammed
 scram-ming
scram-ble
 scram-bled
 scram-bling
 scram-bler
Scran-ton
scrap
 scrapped
 scrap-ping
scrap-book
scrape
 scraped
 scrap-ing
 scrap-a-ble
 scrap-er
 scrap-per
 scrap-py
 scrap-pi-er
 scrap-pi-est
 scrap-pi-ly
 scrap-pi-ness
scratch

scratch-a-ble
scratch-er
scratchy
scratch-i-er
scratch-i-est
scratch-i-ly
scratch-i-ness
scrawl
scrawl-er
scrawly
scrawl-i-er
scrawl-i-est
scrawny
scrawn-i-er
scrawn-i-est
scrawn-i-ness
scream-er
scream-ing-ly
screech
screech-er
screen
screen-a-ble
screen-er
screen-ing
screen-play
screw
screw-ball
screw-driv-er
screwy
screw-i-er
screw-i-est
scrib-ble
scrib-bled
scrib-bling
scrib-bler
scribe
scribed
scrib-ing
scrib-al
scrim
scrim-mage
scrim-maged
scrim-mag-ing
scrim-mag-er
scrimpy
scrimp-i-er
scrimp-i-est
script
scrip-tur-al
scrip-ture
script-writ-er
scroll-work
scrooge
scro-tum
scro-ta
scro-tums
scro-tal
scrounge
scroung-er
scrub
scrubbed
scrub-bing
scrub-ber
scrub-by
scrub-bi-er

scrub·bi·est
scrub·wom·an
scrub·wom·en
scruffy
scruff·i·er
scruff·i·est
scrump·tious
scru·ple
scru·pled
scru·pling
scru·pu·lous
scru·pu·los·i·ty
scru·pu·lous·ness
scru·pu·lous·ly
scru·ta·ble
scru·ti·nize
scru·ti·nized
scru·ti·niz·ing
scru·ti·niz·er
scru·ti·niz·ing·ly
scru·ti·ny
scru·ti·nies
scu·ba
scud
scud·ded
scud·ding
scuf·fle
scuf·fled
scuf·fling
scul·lery
scul·ler·ies
sculp·tor
sculp·tress
sculp·ture
sculp·tured
sculp·tur·ing
sculp·tur·al
scum
scummed
scum·ming
scur·ri·lous
scur·ril·i·ty
scur·ril·i·ties
scur·ry
scur·ried
scur·ry·ing
scur·ries
scur·vy
scur·vi·er
scur·vi·est
scur·vi·ly
scur·vi·ness
scut·tle
scut·tled
scut·tling
scut·tle·butt
Scyl·la
scythe
scythed
scyth·ing
sea·bed
Sea·bee
sea·board
sea·coast
sea·drome

sea·far·ing
sea·far·er
sea·food
sea·fowl
sea·go·ing
sea·go·er
sea·green
sea gull
sea horse
seal
seal·er
sea lam·prey
sea legs
sea lev·el
seal·ing wax
sea li·on
seal·skin
seam
seam·er
seam·like
sea·maid
sea·man
sea·men
sea·man·ship
seam·stress
seamy
seam·i·er
seam·i·est
seam·i·ness
sé·ance
sea ot·ter
sea·plane
sea·port
sea·quake
search
search·a·ble
search·er
search·ing
search·light
search war·rant
sea·scape
sea ser·pent
sea·shell
sea·shore
sea·sick·ness
sea·sick
sea·side
sea·son
sea·son·er
sea·son·a·ble
sea·son·al
sea·son·al·ly
sea·son·ing
seat·ing
Se·at·tle
sea ur·chin
sea wall
sea·ward
sea·way
sea·weed
sea·wor·thy
sea·wor·thi·ness
se·ba·ceous
se·cant
se·cede

se·ced·ed
se·ced·ing
se·ced·er
se·ces·sion
se·ces·sion·ist
se·clude
se·clud·ed
se·clud·ing
se·clud·ed·ly
se·clud·ed·ness
se·clu·sion
se·clu·sive
sec·ond
sec·ond·ary
sec·ond·ar·i·ly
sec·ond-best
sec·ond-class
sec·ond-guess
sec·ond-hand
sec·ond-rate
sec·ond-sto·ry man
se·cre·cy
se·cre·cies
se·cret
sec·re·tar·i·at
sec·re·tary
sec·re·tar·ies
sec·re·tar·i·al
se·crete
se·cret·ed
se·cret·ing
se·cre·tion
se·cre·tive
se·cre·to·ry
se·cre·to·ries
sec·tar·i·an
sec·tar·i·an·ism
sec·tion
sec·tion·al
sec·tor
sec·to·ri·al
sec·u·lar
sec·u·lar·ism
sec·u·lar·ize
sec·u·lar·ized
sec·u·lar·iz·ing
sec·u·lar·i·za·tion
sec·u·lar·iz·er
se·cure
se·cured
se·cur·ing
se·cur·a·ble
se·cure·ness
se·cur·er
se·cu·ri·ty
se·cu·ri·ties
se·dan
se·date
se·dat·ed
se·dat·ing
se·date·ness
se·da·tion
sed·a·tive
sed·en·tary
sed·en·tar·i·ness

sedge
sed·i·ment
 sed·i·men·tal
 sed·i·men·ta·ry
 sed·i·men·ta·tion
se·di·tion
 se·di·tion·ary
se·di·tious
se·duce
 se·duced
 se·duc·ing
 se·duc·er
 se·duc·i·ble
 se·duce·a·ble
 se·duc·tion
 se·duce·ment
 se·duc·tive
 se·duc·tive·ness
sed·u·lous
 se·du·li·ty
 sed·u·lous·ness
seed·bed
seed·case
seed·ling
seed·pod
seedy
 seed·i·er
 seed·i·est
 seed·i·ly
 seed·i·ness
see·ing
seek
 sought
 seek·ing
seem·ing
 seem·ing·ness
seem·ly
 seem·li·er
 seem·li·est
 seem·li·ness
seep
 seepy
 seep·i·er
 seep·i·est
 seep·age
se·er
 seer·ess
 seer·suck·er
see·saw
seethe
 seethed
 seeth·ing
seg·ment
 seg·men·tal
 seg·men·tary
 seg·men·ta·tion
seg·re·gate
 seg·re·gat·ed
 seg·re·gat·ing
 seg·re·ga·tion
 seg·re·ga·tion·ist
sei·gneur
seine
 seined
 sein·ing

seis·mic
 seis·mal
 seis·mi·cal
 seis·mi·cal·ly
seis·mo·graph
 seis·mog·ra·pher
 seis·mo·graph·ic
 seis·mog·ra·phy
seis·mol·o·gy
 seis·mo·log·ic
 seis·mo·log·i·cal
 seis·mol·o·gist
seize
 seized
 seiz·ing
 seiz·er
 sei·zure
sel·dom
se·lect
 se·lect·ed
 se·lec·tor
 se·lec·tion
 se·lec·tive
 se·lec·tiv·i·ty
se·le·ni·um
self-a·base·ment
self-ab·ne·ga·tion
self-a·buse
self-ad·dressed
self-ag·gran·dize·ment
 self-ag·gran·diz·ing
self-as·sur·ance
 self-as·sured
self-cen·tered
 self-cen·tered·ness
self-col·lect·ed
self-com·mand
self-com·posed
self-con·fessed
self-con·fi·dence
 self-con·fi·dent
self-con·scious
 self-con·scious·ness
self-con·tained
self-con·trol
 self-con·trolled
self-cor·rect·ing
self-crit·i·cism
 self-crit·i·cal
self-de·cep·tion
 self-de·cep·tive
self-de·fense
self-de·ni·al
 self-de·ny·ing
self-de·ter·mi·na·tion
 self-de·ter·min·ing
self-dis·ci·pline
 self-dis·ci·plined
self-ed·u·cat·ed
 self-ed·u·ca·tion
self-ef·fac·ing
self-em·ployed
 self-em·ploy·ment
self-es·teem
self-ev·i·dent

self-ev·i·dence
self-ex·plan·a·to·ry
self-ex·pres·sion
 self-ex·pres·sive
self-ful·fill·ment
 self-ful·fill·ing
self-gov·ern·ment
 self-gov·erned
 self-gov·ern·ing
self-help
self·hood
self-im·age
self-im·por·tance
 self-im·por·tant
self-im·posed
self-im·prove·ment
self-in·duced
self-in·dul·gence
 self-in·dul·gent
self-in·flict·ed
self-in·ter·est
 self-in·ter·est·ed
self·ish
 self·ish·ness
self-know·ledge
self·less
 self·less·ness
self-love
 self-lov·ing
self-made
self-per·pet·u·at·ing
 self-per·pet·u·a·tion
self-pity
 self-pit·y·ing
self-pol·li·na·tion
self-pos·sessed
 self-pos·sess·ed·ly
 self-pos·ses·sion
self-pres·er·va·tion
self-pro·pelled
 self-pro·pel·ling
self-re·al·i·za·tion
self-re·li·ance
 self-re·li·ant
self-re·spect
 self-re·spect·ing
self-re·straint
 self-re·strain·ing
self-right·eous
 self-right·eous·ness
self-sac·ri·fice
 self-sac·ri·fic·ing
self-same
self-sat·is·fied
 self-sat·is·fac·tion
 self-sat·is·fy·ing
self-serv·ice
 self-serv·ing
self-start·er
 self-start·ing
self-styled
self-suf·fi·cient
 self-suf·fic·ing
 self-suf·fi·cien·cy
self-sup·port

188

self-sup·port·ing
self-taught
self-will
self-willed
sell
  sold
  sell·ing
sell·er
sell-out
Selt·zer
sel·vage
  sel·vaged
se·man·tics
  se·man·tic
  se·man·ti·cal
  se·man·ti·cal·ly
sem·a·phore
  sem·a·phored
  sem·a·phor·ing
sem·blance
se·men
se·mes·ter
sem·i·an·nu·al
  sem·i·an·nu·al·ly
sem·i·ar·id
sem·i·au·to·mat·ic
sem·i·cir·cle
  sem·i·cir·cu·lar
sem·i·clas·si·cal
  sem·i·clas·sic
sem·i·co·lon
sem·i·con·duc·tor
  sem·i·con·duct·ing
sem·i·con·scious
  sem·i·con·scious·ness
sem·i·de·tached
sem·i·fi·nal
  sem·i·fi·nal·ist
sem·i·flu·id
sem·i·for·mal
sem·i·gloss
sem·i·liq·uid
sem·i·month·ly
sem·i·nal
  sem·i·nal·ly
sem·i·nar
sem·i·nary
  sem·i·nar·ies
  sem·i·nar·i·an
Sem·i·nole
sem·i·of·fi·cial
  sem·i·of·fi·cial·ly
sem·i·per·ma·nent
sem·i·per·me·a·ble
sem·i·pre·cious
sem·i·pri·vate
sem·i·pro·fes·sion·al
sem·i·pro
sem·i·pub·lic
sem·i·skilled
sem·i·sol·id
Sem·ite
Se·mit·ic
Sem·i·tism
sem·i·trail·er

sem·i·trop·ics
  sem·i·trop·ic
  sem·i·trop·i·cal
sem·i·vow·el
sem·i·week·ly
  sem·i·week·lies
sem·i·year·ly
sen·a·ry
sen·ate
sen·a·tor
  sen·a·tor·ship
  sen·a·to·ri·al
  sen·a·to·ri·al·ly
send-off
Sen·e·ca
Sen·e·gal
se·nile
  se·nil·i·ty
sen·ior
  sen·ior·i·ty
sen·na
Sen·nach·er·ib
se·ñor
  se·ñors
  se·ño·ra
  se·ño·ri·ta
sen·sate
sen·sa·tion
  sen·sa·tion·al
  sen·sa·tion·al·ly
  sen·sa·tion·al·ism
sense
  sensed
  sens·ing
sense·less
  sense·less·ness
sen·si·bil·i·ty
  sen·si·bil·i·ties
sen·si·ble
  sen·si·ble·ness
  sen·si·bly
sen·si·tive
  sen·si·tiv·i·ty
  sen·si·tiv·i·ties
sen·si·tize
  sen·si·tized
  sen·si·tiz·ing
  sen·si·ti·za·tion
  sen·si·tiz·er
sen·sor
sen·so·ry
  sen·so·ri·al
sen·su·al
  sen·su·al·i·ty
  sen·su·al·ly
  sen·su·al·ism
  sen·su·al·ist
  sen·su·al·ize
  sen·su·al·ized
  sen·su·al·iz·ing
  sen·su·al·i·za·tion
sen·su·ous
sen·tence
  sen·tenced
  sen·tenc·ing

sen·tient
sen·ti·ment
sen·ti·men·tal
  sen·ti·men·tal·ly
  sen·ti·men·tal·i·ty
  sen·ti·men·tal·i·ties
  sen·ti·men·tal·ist
  sen·ti·men·tal·ize
  sen·ti·men·tal·ized
  sen·ti·men·tal·iz·ing
  sen·ti·men·ta·li·za·tion
sen·ti·nel
  sen·ti·neled
  sen·ti·nel·ing
sen·try
  sen·tries
se·pal
se·paled
se·palled
sep·a·ra·ble
  sep·a·ra·bil·i·ty
  sep·a·ra·bly
sep·a·rate
  sep·a·rat·ed
  sep·a·rat·ing
  sep·a·rate·ness
  sep·a·ra·tion
  sep·a·ra·tist
  sep·a·ra·tism
  sep·a·ra·tive
  sep·a·ra·tor
se·pia
sep·sis
sep·ses
Sep·tem·ber
sep·ten·ni·al
sep·tet
sep·tic
  sep·ti·cal·ly
  sep·tic·i·ty
sep·ti·ce·mia
  sep·ti·ce·mic
sep·tu·a·ge·nar·i·an
Sep·tu·a·gint
sep·tum
sep·ta
sep·tu·ple
  sep·tu·pled
  sep·tu·pling
sep·ul·cher
  sep·ul·chered
  sep·ul·cher·ing
  se·pul·chral
se·quel
se·quence
se·quent
se·quen·tial
  se·quen·tial·ly
se·ques·ter
  se·ques·tered
  se·ques·tra·ble
  se·ques·tra·tion
se·quin
  se·quined
se·quoia

189

se·ra·pe
ser·aph
ser·aphs
ser·a·phim
se·raph·ic
Ser·bia
ser·e·nade
ser·e·nad·ed
ser·e·nad·ing
ser·e·nad·er
ser·en·dip·i·ty
ser·en·dip·i·tous
se·rene
se·rene·ness
se·ren·i·ty
se·ren·i·ties
serf
serge
ser·geant
ser·geant at arms
ser·geant ma·jor
se·ri·al
se·ri·al·ly
se·ri·al·ist
se·ri·al·i·za·tion
se·ri·al·ize
se·ri·al·ized
se·ri·al·iz·ing
se·ries
se·ri·ous
se·ri·ous·ly
se·ri·ous·ness
se·ri·ous-mind·ed
se·ri·ous-mind·ed·ly
ser·mon
ser·mon·ize
ser·mon·ized
ser·mon·iz·ing
ser·mon·iz·er
se·rol·o·gy
se·ro·log·ic
se·ro·log·i·cal
se·rol·o·gist
se·rous
ser·pent
ser·pen·tine
ser·rate
ser·rat·ed
ser·rat·ing
ser·ra·tion
se·rum
se·rums
se·ra
serv·ant
serve
served
serv·ing
serv·er
serv·ice
serv·iced
serv·ic·ing
serv·ice·a·ble
serv·ice·a·bil·i·ty
serv·ice·a·ble·ness
serv·ice·a·bly

serv·ice·man
ser·vile
ser·vil·i·ty
ser·vile·ness
ser·vi·tude
ser·vo·mech·an·ism
ses·a·me
ses·qui·cen·ten·ni·al
ses·sion
set·back
set-in
set·off
set·tee
set·ter
set·ting
set·tle
set·tled
set·tling
set·tle·ment
set·tler
set-to
set·up
sev·en
sev·enth
sev·en·teen
sev·en·teenth
sev·en·ty
sev·en·ti·eth
sev·er
sev·er·a·bil·i·ty
sev·er·a·ble
sev·er·al
sev·er·al·ly
sev·er·al·fold
sev·er·ance
se·vere
se·ver·er
se·ver·est
se·vere·ness
se·ver·i·ty
se·ver·i·ties
Se·ville
sew·age
Sew·ard
sew·er
sew·er·age
sew·ing
sew·ing ma·chine
sex·less
sex·less·ness
sex·ol·o·gy
sex·o·log·i·cal
sex·ol·o·gist
sex·tant
sex·tet
sex·ton
sex·tu·ple
sex·tu·pled
sex·tu·pling
sex·tu·plet
sex·u·al
sex·u·al·ly
sex·u·al·i·ty
sexy
sex·i·er

sex·i·est
sex·i·ness
shab·by
shab·bi·er
shab·bi·est
shab·bi·ly
shab·bi·ness
shack·le
shack·led
shack·ling
shack·ler
shade
shad·ed
shad·ing
shade·less
shad·ow
shad·ow·er
shad·ow·like
shad·ow·box
shad·owy
shady
shad·i·er
shad·i·est
shad·i·ly
shad·i·ness
shaft·ing
shag
shagged
shag·ging
shag·ged
shag·like
shag·bark
shag·gy
shag·gi·er
shag·gi·est
shag·gi·ly
shag·gi·ness
shake
shak·en
shak·ing
shake·down
shak·er
Shake·speare
Shake·spear·e·an
shake-up
shaky
shak·i·er
shak·i·est
shak·i·ly
shak·i·ness
shal·lot
shal·low
shal·low·ness
sham
shammed
sham·ming
sha·man
sha·man·ism
sha·man·ist
sham·bles
shame
shamed
sham·ing
shame·faced
shame·fac·ed·ly

shame-fac-ed-ness
shame-ful
  shame-ful-ly
shame-less
  shame-less-ly
  shame-less-ness
sham-mer
sham-my
sham-poo
  sham-pooed
  sham-poo-ing
  sham-poo-er
sham-rock
shang-hai
  shang-haied
  shang-hai-ing
Shan-gri-la
Shan-non
shan-tey
  shan-teys
shan-ty
  shan-ties
shan-ty-town
shape
  shaped
  shap-ing
  shap-a-ble
  shap-er
shape-less
shape-ly
  shape-li-er
  shape-li-est
  shape-li-ness
share
  shared
  shar-ing
  shar-er
share-crop-per
  share-crop
  share-cropped
  share-crop-ping
share-hold-er
shark-skin
Shar-on
sharp-en
  sharp-en-er
sharp-er
sharp-eyed
sharp-ie
sharp-shoot-er
  sharp-shoot-ing
sharp-tongued
sharp-wit-ted
  sharp-wit-ted-ly
  sharp-wit-ted-ness
Shas-ta
shat-ter
shat-ter-proof
shave
  shaved
  shav-en
  shav-ing
  shav-er
shawl
Shaw-nee

sheaf
sheaves
shear
  sheared
  shear-ing
  shear-er
sheath
  sheath-less
  sheath-like
sheathe
  sheathed
  sheath-ing
  sheath-er
sheave
  sheaved
  sheav-ing
She-ba
she-bang
shed
  shed-ding
sheen
  sheeny
  sheen-i-er
  sheen-i-est
sheep-dog
sheep-herd-er
  sheep-herd-ing
sheep-ish
sheep-shear-ing
  sheep-shear-er
sheep-skin
sheer
  sheer-ly
  sheer-ness
sheet-ing
Shef-field
sheik
shelf
  shelves
shell
  shelled
  shell-like
shel-ly
shel-ler
shel-lac
  shel-lacked
  shel-lack-ing
shell-fire
shell-fish
shell-shocked
shel-ter
  shel-ter-er
shelve
  shelved
  shelv-ing
Shen-an-do-ah
she-nan-i-gan
shep-herd
  shep-herd-ess
Sher-a-ton
sher-bet
Sher-i-dan
sher-iff
Sher-lock
Sher-man

sher-ry
  sher-ries
Sher-wood
Shet-land
shib-bo-leth
shield
  shield-er
shift
  shift-er
  shift-ing-ness
shift-less
shifty
  shift-i-er
  shift-i-est
  shift-i-ly
  shift-i-ness
shi-ly-shal-ly
  shil-ly-shal-lied
  shil-ly-shal-ly-ing
Shi-loh
shim-mer
  shim-mery
  shim-mer-i-er
  shim-mer-i-est
shim-my
  shim-mies
  shim-mied
  shim-my-ing
shin
  shinned
  shin-ning
shin-bone
shin-dig
shine
  shined
  shone
  shin-ing
shin-er
shin-gle
  shin-gled
  shin-gling
  shin-gler
  shin-gles
  shin-ing
  shin-ing-ly
shin-ny
  shin-nied
  shin-ny-ing
shiny
  shin-i-er
  shin-i-est
  shin-i-ness
ship
  shipped
  ship-ping
ship-pa-ble
ship-board
ship-build-er
  ship-build-ing
ship-mate
ship-ment
ship-per
ship-shape
ship-wreck
ship-yard

shirk
  shirk·er
shirt·tail
shirt·waist
shish ke·bab
shiv·er
  shiv·ery
  shiv·er·i·er
  shiv·er·i·est
shoal
shock·er
shock·ing
shod·dy
  shod·dies
  shod·di·er
  shod·di·est
  shod·di·ly
  shod·di·ness
shoe·horn
shoe·lace
shoe·mak·er
sho·er
shoe·string
shoo·in
shoot
  shot
  shoot·ing
  shoot·er
shop
  shopped
  shop·ping
shop·keep·er
shop·lift·er
  shop·lift·ing
shop·per
shop·talk
shop·worn
shore
  shore·line
short
  short·ly
  short·ness
short·age
short·change
  short·changed
  short·chang·ing
  short·chang·er
short·com·ing
short·cut
  short·cut·ting
short·en
  short·en·er
short·en·ing
short·hand
  short·hand·ed
  short·hand·ed·ly
  short·hand·ed·ness
short·lived
short·sight·ed
  short·sight·ed·ly
  short·sight·ed·ness
short·tem·pered
short·term
short·wave
short·wind·ed

Sho·sho·ne
shot·gun
  shot·gunned
  shot·gun·ning
shoul·der
shoul·der blade
shout·er
shout·ing
shove
  shoved
  shov·ing
  shov·er
shov·el
  shov·eled
  shov·el·ing
  shov·el·er
  shov·el·ful
show
  showed
  shown
  show·ing
show·bill
show·boat
show·case
  show·cased
  show·cas·ing
show·down
show·er
  show·ery
show·man
  show·men
  show·man·ship
show·off
show·piece
show·place
show·room
showy
  show·i·er
  show·i·est
  show·i·ly
  show·i·ness
shrap·nel
shred
  shred·ded
  shred·ding
  shred·der
Shreve·port
shrew
  shrew·like
shrewd
  shrewd·ly
  shrewd·ness
shrew·ish
Shrews·bury
shriek
shrill
  shril·ly
  shrill·ness
shrimp
shrine
  shrined
  shrin·ing
shrink
  shrunk·en
  shrink·a·ble

shrink·er
shrink·age
shriv·el
  shriv·eled
  shriv·el·ing
Shrop·shire
shroud
Shrove·tide
shrub·bery
  shrub·ber·ies
shrub·by
  shrub·bi·er
  shrub·bi·est
shrug
  shrugged
  shrug·ging
shuck·er
shud·der
  shud·dery
shuf·fle
  shuf·fled
  shuf·fling
  shuf·fler
shuf·fle·board
shun
  shunned
  shun·ning
  shun·ner
shunt
  shunt·er
shut·down
shut·eye
shut·in
shut·off
shut·out
shut·ter
shut·tle
  shut·tled
  shut·tling
  shut·tle·like
shy
  shi·er
  shi·est
  shy·er
  shy·est
  shied
  shy·ing
  shy·ness
Shy·lock
shy·ster
Si·am
Si·a·mese
Si·be·ria
sib·i·lant
  sib·i·lance
sib·ling
sic
  sicked
  sick·ing
sick·bed
sick·en
  sick·en·ing
sick·ish
sick·le
sick·ly

sick·li·er
sick·li·est
sick·li·ness
sick·ness
sick·room
side·arm
side·board
side·burns
side·car
sid·ed
side·kick
side·light
side·line
side·lined
side·lin·ing
side·long
side·show
side·split·ting
side·step
side·stepped
side·step·ping
side·swipe
side·swiped
side·swip·ing
side·track
side·walk
side·wall
side·ward
side·ways
sid·ing
si·dle
si·dled
si·dling
siege
Si·ena
si·en·na
si·er·ra
Si·er·ra Le·one
Si·er·ra Ma·dre
Si·er·ra Ne·vad·as
si·es·ta
sieve
sieved
siev·ing
sift·er
sift·ings
sigh·er
sight·ed
sight·less
sight·ly
sight·read
sight·read·ing
sight·see·ing
sight·see·er
sig·nal
sig·naled
sig·nal·ing
sig·nal·er
sig·nal·man
sig·nal·men
sig·na·to·ry
sig·na·to·ries
sig·na·ture
sign·board
sig·net

sig·nif·i·cance
sig·nif·i·cant
sig·ni·fi·ca·tion
sig·ni·fy
sig·ni·fied
sig·ni·fy·ing
sig·ni·fi·a·ble
sig·ni·fi·er
sign·post
si·tage
si·lence
si·lenced
si·lenc·ing
si·lenc·er
si·lent
Si·le·sia
sil·hou·ette
sil·hou·et·ted
sil·hou·et·ting
sil·ica
sil·i·con
sil·i·cone
silk·en
silk·like
silk·weed
silk·worm
silky
silk·i·er
silk·i·est
silk·i·ly
silk·i·ness
sil·ly
sil·li·er
sil·li·est
sil·li·ly
sil·li·ness
si·lo
si·los
si·loed
si·lo·ing
silt
silt·ta·tion
silty
silt·i·er
silt·i·est
sil·ver
sil·ver·fish
sil·ver·smith
sil·ver·tongued
sil·ver·ware
sil·very
sil·ver·i·ness
Sim·e·on
sim·i·an
sim·i·lar
sim·i·lar·i·ty
sim·i·lar·i·ties
sim·i·le
si·mil·i·tude
sim·mer
si·mon·ize
si·mon·ized
si·mon·iz·ing
Si·mon Le·gree
sim·pa·ti·co

sim·per
sim·per·er
sim·per·ing·ly
sim·ple
sim·pler
sim·plest
sim·ple·ness
sim·ple·mind·ed
sim·ple·mind·ed·ness
sim·ple·ton
sim·plex
sim·plic·i·ty
sim·plic·i·ties
sim·pli·fy
sim·pli·fied
sim·pli·fy·ing
sim·pli·fi·ca·tion
sim·pli·fi·er
sim·plism
sim·plis·tic
sim·plis·ti·cal·ly
sim·ply
sim·u·late
sim·u·lat·ed
sim·u·lat·ing
sim·u·la·tion
sim·u·la·tive
sim·u·la·tor
si·mul·cast
si·mul·cast·ing
si·mul·ta·ne·ous
si·mul·ta·ne·ous·ness
si·mul·ta·ne·i·ty
sin
sinned
sin·ning
Si·nai
Sin·bad
sin·cere
sin·cer·i·ty
si·ne·cure
si·ne qua non
sin·ew
sin·ewy
sin·ful
sin·ful·ly
sin·ful·ness
sing
sing·ing
sing·a·ble
Sing·a·pore
singe
singed
singe·ing
sing·er
sin·gle
sin·gled
sin·gling
sin·gle·ness
sin·gle·breast·ed
sin·gle·hand·ed
sin·gle·hand·ed·ly
sin·gle·hand·ed·ness
sin·gle·mind·ed
sin·gle·mind·ed·ly

sin·gle-mind·ed·ness
sin·gle-space
sin·gle-spaced
sin·gle-spac·ing
sin·gle·ton
sin·gle-track
sin·gly
sing·song
sin·gu·lar
sin·gu·lar·i·ty
sin·gu·lar·i·ties
sin·is·ter
sin·is·ter·ness
sink·a·ble
sink·er
sink·hole
sin·less
sin·ner
sin·u·ate
sin·u·at·ed
sin·u·at·ing
sin·u·ous
sin·u·os·i·ty
sin·u·ous·ness
si·nus
si·nus·i·tis
sip
sipped
sip·ping
sip·per
si·phon
sire
sired
sir·ing
si·ren
sir·loin
sis·sy
sis·sies
sis·si·fied
sis·sy·ish
sis·ter
sis·ter·li·ness
sis·ter·ly
sis·ter·hood
sis·ter-in-law
sis·ters-in-law
si·tar
sit-in
Sit·ka
sit·ter
sit·ting
sit·u·ate
sit·u·at·ed
sit·u·at·ing
sit·u·a·tion
six-pack
six-shoot·er
six·teen
six·teenth
sixth
six·ty
six·ti·eth
siz·a·ble
siz·a·ble·ness
siz·a·bly

size
sized
siz·ing
siz·zle
siz·zled
siz·zling
siz·zler
skate
skat·ed
skat·ing
skat·er
ske·dad·dle
ske·dad·dled
ske·dad·dling
skein
skel·e·ton
skel·e·tal
skep·tic
skep·ti·cal
skep·ti·cism
sketch
sketch·er
sketch·book
sketchy
sketch·i·er
sketch·i·est
sketch·i·ly
sketch·i·ness
skew·er
skew·ness
ski
skied
ski·ing
ski·er
skid
skid·ded
skid·ding
skid·der
skilled
skil·let
skill·ful
skill·ful·ly
skill·ful·ness
skim
skimmed
skim·ming
skim·mer
skimp
skimp·i·ly
skimp·i·ness
skimp·ing·ly
skimp·y
skimp·i·er
skimp·i·est
skin
skinned
skin·ning
skin-deep
skin-dive
skin-dived
skin-div·ing
skin-div·er
skin·flint
skin·less
skin·ner

skin·ny
skin·ni·er
skin·ni·est
skin·tight
skip·per
skir·mish
skir·mish·er
skirt·er
skirt·ing
skit·ter
skit·tish
skiv·vy
skiv·vies
skoal
skul·dug·ger·y
skulk·er
skull·cap
skunk
sky
skies
skied
sky·ing
sky-blue
sky·cap
sky·div·ing
sky-high
sky·lark
sky·light
sky·line
sky·rock·et
sky·scrap·er
sky·ward
sky·way
sky·writ·ing
sky·writ·er
slab
slabbed
slab·bing
slack
slack·ness
slack·en
slack·er
slack-jawed
slake
slaked
slak·ing
sla·lom
slam
slammed
slam·ming
slam-bang
slan·der
slan·der·er
slan·der·ous
slang
slang·i·ly
slang·i·ness
slangy
slang·i·er
slang·i·est
slant
slant·ways
slant·wise
slap
slapped

slap·ping
slap·per
slap·dash
slap·hap·py
slap·hap·pi·er
slap·hap·pi·est
slap·stick
slasher
slash·ing
slat
slat·ted
slat·ting
slate
slat·ed
slat·ing
slate·like
slaty
slat·i·er
slat·i·est
slath·er
slat·tern
slat·tern·li·ness
slat·tern·ly
slaugh·ter
slaugh·ter·er
slaugh·ter·house
slave
slaved
slav·ing
slav·er
slav·ery
Slav·ic
slav·ish
sla·vish·ly
sla·vish·ness
slay
slain
slay·ing
slay·er
slea·zy
slea·zi·er
slea·zi·est
slea·zi·ly
slea·zi·ness
sled
sled·ded
sled·ding
sled·der
sledge
sledged
sledg·ing
sleek
sleek·er
sleek·ness
sleep·er
sleep·less
sleep·less·ness
sleep·walk
sleep·walk·er
sleep·walk·ing
sleepy
sleep·i·er
sleep·i·est
sleep·i·ly
sleep·i·ness

sleep·y·head
sleet
sleety
sleet·i·ness
sleeve
sleeved
sleev·ing
sleeve·less
sleigh
sleigh·er
sleight
slen·der
slen·der·ness
slen·der·ize
slen·der·ized
slen·der·iz·ing
sleuth
slice
sliced
slic·ing
slic·er
slick·er
slick·ness
slide
slid
slid·ing
slid·er
slight
slight·er
slight·ing
slim
slim·mer
slim·mest
slimmed
slim·ming
slim·ness
slime
slimed
slim·ing
slimy
slim·i·er
slim·i·est
slim·i·ly
slim·i·ness
sling·er
sling·shot
slinky
slink·i·er
slink·i·est
slip
slipped
slip·ping
slip·cov·er
slip·knot
slip·on
slip·o·ver
slip·page
slip·per
slip·pery
slip·per·i·er
slip·per·i·est
slip·per·i·ness
slip·py
slip·shod
slip·stick

slip·up
slit
slit·ting
slit·ter
slith·er
slith·ery
sliv·er
sliv·er·er
sliv·er·like
slob·ber
slob·ber·er
slob·ber·ing·ly
sloe·eyed
slo·gan
slo·gan·eer
slop
slopped
slop·ping
slope
sloped
slop·ing
slop·er
slop·py
slop·pi·er
slop·pi·est
slop·pi·ly
slop·pi·ness
sloshy
slosh·i·er
slosh·i·est
slot
slot·ted
slot·ting
sloth
sloth·ful
sloth·ful·ly
sloth·ful·ness
slouch
slouch·er
slouch·i·ly
slouch·i·ness
slouchy
slouch·i·er
slouch·i·est
slough
sloughy
slough·i·er
slough·i·est
slough·i·ness
Slo·vak
Slo·vak·ia
slov·en
slov·en·ly
slov·en·li·ness
slow·down
slow·mo·tion
slow·poke
slow·wit·ted
sludge
sludgy
sludg·i·er
sludg·i·est
slug
slugged
slug·ging

slug·ger
slug·gard
 slug·gard·li·ness
slug·gish
 slug·gish·ness
sluice
 sluiced
 sluic·ing
slum
 slummed
 slum·ming
 slum·mer
slum·ber
 slum·ber·er
 slum·ber·ous
slur
 slurred
 slur·ring
slush
 slush·i·ness
 slushy
 slush·i·er
 slush·i·est
slut
 slut·tish
sly
 sli·er
 sly·er
 sli·est
 sly·est
 sly·ly
 sli·ly
 sly·ness
smack·er
smack·ing
small-mind·ed
 small-mind·ed·ness
small·pox
small-time
 small-tim·er
smart
 smart·ness
smart al·eck
 smart-al·ecky
smart·en
smarty
smash·er
smash·ing
smash-up
smat·ter
 smat·ter·er
 smat·ter·ing
smear
 smear·er
smeary
 smear·i·er
 smear·i·est
 smear·i·ness
smell
 smelled
 smel·ling
 smell·er
 smelly
 smell·i·er
 smell·i·est

smelt
smelt·er
 smelt·ery
smid·gen
smile·
 smil·er
 smil·ing·ly
smirch
smirk
 smirk·er
 smirk·ing·ly
smite
 smote
 smit·ten
 smit·ing
 smit·er
smith·er·eens
Smith·so·ni·an
smit·ten
smock·ing
smog·gy
 smog·gi·er
 smog·gi·est
smoke
 smoked
 smok·ing
 smoke·less
 smoke·house
 smok·er
 smoke·stack
 smok·ing jack·et
 smoky
 smok·i·er
 smok·i·est
 smok·i·ly
 smok·i·ness
smol·der
smooth
 smooth·er
 smooth·ness
 smooth·en
 smooth·ie
smoth·er
 smoth·ery
 smoth·er·i·er
 smoth·er·i·est
smudge
 smudged
 smudg·ing
 smudg·i·ly
 smudg·i·ness
 smudgy
 smudg·i·er
 smudg·i·est
smug
 smug·ger
 smug·gest
 smug·ly
 smug·ness
smug·gle
 smug·gled
 smug·gling
 smug·gler
smut
 smut·ted

smut·ting
smut·ty
 smut·ti·er
 smut·ti·est
 smut·ti·ly
 smut·ti·ness
Smyr·na
sna·fu
 sna·fued
 sna·fu·ing
snag
 snagged
 snag·ging
 snag·gy
 snag·gi·er
 snag·gi·est
 snag·gle·tooth
 snag·gle·teeth
 snag·gle·toothed
snail
 snail-like
 snail-paced
snake
 snaked
 snak·ing
 snake-like
 snak·i·ly
 snake·bite
 snake·skin
 snaky
 snak·i·er
 snak·i·est
 snak·i·ness
snap
 snapped
 snap·ping
 snap·back
 snap·drag·on
 snap·per
 snap·pish
 snap·pish·ness
 snap·py
 snap·pi·er
 snap·pi·est
 snap·pi·ly
 snap·pi·ness
 snap·shot
snare
 snared
 snar·ing
 snar·er
snarl
 snarl·er
 snarly
 snarl·i·er
 snarl·i·est
snatch
 snatch·er
 snatchy
 snatch·i·er
 snatch·i·est
 snatch·i·ly
snaz·zy
 snaz·zi·er
 snaz·zi·est

sneak·er
sneak·ing
sneaky
  sneak·i·er
  sneak·i·est
  sneak·i·ly
  sneak·i·ness
sneer
  sneer·er
  sneer·ing·ly
sneeze
  sneezed
  sneez·ing
  sneez·er
  sneezy
  sneez·i·er
  sneez·i·est
snick·er
snif·fle
  snif·fled
  snif·fling
  snif·fler
  snif·fy
  snif·fi·er
  snif·fi·est
  snif·fi·ly
  snif·fi·ness
sniff·ish
snif·ter
snip
  snipped
  snip·ping
  snip·per
snipe
  sniped
  snip·ing
  snip·er
snip·py
  snip·pi·er
  snip·pi·est
  snip·pi·ly
  snip·pi·ness
snitch·er
sniv·el
  sniv·eled
  sniv·el·ing
  sniv·el·er
snob
  snob·bery
  snob·bish
  snob·bish·ness
snoop
  snoopy
  snoop·i·er
  snoop·i·est
  snoop·er
snooty
  snoot·i·er
  snoot·i·est
  snoot·i·ly
  snoot·i·ness
snooze
  snoozed
  snooz·ing
  snooz·er

snore
  snored
  snor·ing
  snor·er
snor·kel
snort
  snort·er
snot·ty
  snot·ti·er
  snot·ti·est
snout
  snout·ed
  snouty
  snout·i·er
  snout·i·est
snow·ball
snow·blow·er
snow·bound
snow·cap
snow·drift
snow·fall
snow·flake
snow·man
  snow·men
snow·mo·bile
snow·plow
snow·shoe
  snow·shoed
  snow·shoe·ing
snow·suit
snow·white
snowy
  snow·i·er
  snow·i·est
  snow·i·ly
  snow·i·ness
snub
  snubbed
  snub·bing
  snub·ber
  snub·by
  snub·bi·er
  snub·bi·est
  snub·bi·ness
snub-nosed
snuf·fle
  snuf·fled
  snuf·fling
  snuf·fler
  snuf·fly
  snuf·fli·er
  snuf·fli·est
snuffy
  snuff·i·er
  snuff·i·est
  snuff·i·ness
snug
  snug·ger
  snug·gest
  snugged
  snug·ging
  snug·ly
  snug·ness
snug·gle
  snug·gled

snug·gling
soak
  soak·age
  soak·er
  soak·ing·ly
so-and-so
soap·box
soap·suds
soapy
  soap·i·er
  soap·i·est
  soap·i·ly
  soap·i·ness
soar·er
sob
  sobbed
  sob·bing
  sob·ber
so·ber
  so·ber·ing·ly
  so·ber·ness
so·bri·e·ty
so·bri·quet
so-called
soc·cer
so·cia·ble
  so·cia·bil·i·ty
  so·cia·ble·ness
  so·cia·bly
so·cial
  so·ci·al·i·ty
  so·cial·ly
so·cial·ism
so·cial·ist
  so·cial·is·tic
  so·cial·is·ti·cal·ly
so·cial·ite
so·cial·ize
  so·cial·ized
  so·cial·iz·ing
  so·cial·i·za·tion
  so·cial·iz·er
so·ci·e·ty
  so·ci·e·ties
  so·ci·e·tal
so·ci·o·ec·o·nom·ic
so·ci·ol·o·gy
  so·ci·o·log·i·cal
  so·ci·ol·o·gist
so·ci·o·po·lit·i·cal
sock·et
Soc·ra·tes
sod
  sod·ded
  sod·ding
so·da
so·dal·i·ty
  so·dal·i·ties
sod·den
  sod·den·ness
so·di·um
Sod·om
sod·omy
so·ev·er
so·fa

So·fia
soft
  soft·ness
soft·ball
soft·boiled
sof·ten
  sof·ten·er
soft·head·ed
soft·heart·ed
  soft·heart·ed·ness
soft·ped·al
  soft·ped·aled
  soft·ped·al·ing
soft·shell
soft·shoe
soft·spo·ken
soft·ware
soft·wood
softy
  sof·ties
sog·gy
  sog·gi·er
  sog·gi·est
  sog·gi·ly
  sog·gi·ness
soi·rée
so·journ
  so·journ·er
sol·ace
  sol·aced
  sol·ac·ing
  sol·ac·er
so·lar
so·lar·i·um
  so·lar·i·ums
  so·lar·ia
so·lar·ize
  so·lar·ized
  so·lar·iz·ing
  so·lar·i·za·tion
sol·der
  sol·der·er
sol·dier
  sol·diery
sol·e·cism
sole·ly
sol·emn
  sol·emn·ly
  sol·emn·ness
so·lem·ni·ty
  so·lem·ni·ties
sol·em·nize
  sol·em·nized
  sol·em·niz·ing
  sol·em·ni·za·tion
sole·ness
so·lic·it
  so·lic·i·ta·tion
so·lic·i·tor
so·lic·i·tous
  so·lic·i·tous·ness
so·lic·i·tude
sol·id
  so·lid·i·ty
  sol·id·ness

sol·i·dar·i·ty
  sol·i·dar·i·ties
so·lid·i·fy
  so·lid·i·fied
  so·lid·i·fy·ing
  so·lid·i·fi·ca·tion
so·lil·o·quize
  so·lil·o·quized
  so·lil·o·quiz·ing
  so·lil·o·quist
  so·lil·o·quy
  so·lil·o·quies
sol·i·taire
sol·i·tary
  sol·i·tar·ies
  sol·i·tar·i·ly
  sol·i·tar·i·ness
sol·i·tude
so·lo
  so·loed
  so·lo·ing
  so·lo·ist
Sol·o·mon
So·lon
sol·stice
sol·u·ble
  sol·u·bil·i·ty
  sol·u·ble·ness
  sol·u·bly
sol·ute
so·lu·tion
solve
  solved
  solv·ing
  solv·a·ble
  solv·a·bil·i·ty
  solv·a·ble·ness
  solv·er
sol·vent
  sol·ven·cy
So·ma·li
so·mat·ic
so·ma·to·type
som·ber
  som·ber·ly
  som·ber·ness
som·bre·ro
  som·bre·ros
some·body
  some·bod·ies
some·day
some·how
some·one
some·place
som·er·sault
Som·er·set
Som·er·ville
some·thing
some·time
some·times
some·way
some·what
some·where
som·nam·bu·late
  som·nam·bu·lat·ed

som·nam·bu·lat·ing
som·nam·bu·lant
som·nam·bu·la·tion
som·nam·bu·lism
som·nam·bu·list
som·no·lent
som·no·lence
som·no·len·cy
so·nar
so·na·ta
song·bird
song·fest
song·ster
song·stress
song·writ·er
son·ic
son-in-law
  sons-in-law
son·net
son·net·eer
son·ny
  son·nies
So·no·ra
so·no·rous
so·nor·i·ty
  so·no·rous·ness
soon·er
soothe
soothed
sooth·ing
sooth·er
sooth·say·er
  sooth·say·ing
sooty
  soot·i·er
  soot·i·est
  soot·i·ly
  soot·i·ness
sop
sopped
sop·ping
So·phia
soph·ist
soph·ism
so·phis·tic
so·phis·ti·cal
so·phis·ti·cate
  so·phis·ti·cat·ed
  so·phis·ti·cat·ing
  so·phis·ti·ca·tion
  so·phis·ti·ca·tor
soph·ist·ry
  soph·ist·ries
Soph·o·cles
soph·o·more
soph·o·mor·ic
  soph·o·mor·i·cal
  soph·o·mor·i·cal·ly
sop·o·rif·ic
sop·py
  sop·pi·er
  sop·pi·est
so·prano
  so·pran·os
Sor·bonne

sor·cer·er
sor·cer·ess
sor·cery
sor·cer·ies
sor·cer·ous
sor·did
sor·did·ness
sore
sor·er
sor·est
sore·ly
sore·ness
sore·head
sore·head·ed
sor·ghum
so·ror·i·ty
so·ror·i·ties
sor·rel
sor·row
sor·row·er
sor·row·ful
sor·ry
sor·ri·er
sor·ri·est
sor·ri·ly
sor·ri·ness
sort·a·ble
sort·er
sor·tie
so·so
sot
sot·ted
sot·tish
sot·tish·ness
sot·to vo·ce
sou·bri·quet
souf·flé
souf·fléed
sought
soul·ful
soul·ful·ly
soul·ful·ness
soul·less
soul·search·ing
sound
sound·a·ble
sound·ly
sound·ness
sound·box
sound·er
sound·ing
sound·less
sound·less·ly
sound·less·ness
sound·proof
soupy
soup·i·er
soup·i·est
sour
sour·ish
sour·ness
sour·ball
source
souse
soused

sous·ing
South·amp·ton
south·bound
South Car·o·li·na
South Da·ko·ta
south·east
south·east·er
south·east·er·ly
south·east·ern
south·east·ward
south·east·ward·ly
south·er
south·er·ly
south·ern
south·ern·most
south·ern·er
South·ern Hem·i·sphere
south·paw
south·ward
south·ward·ly
South·wark
south·west
south·west·er
south·west·er·ly
south·west·ern
south·west·ern·er
south·west·ward
south·west·ward·ly
sou·ve·nir
sov·er·eign
sov·er·eign·ty
sov·er·eign·ties
so·vi·et
sow·er
soy·bean
space
spaced
spac·ing
space·less
spac·er
Space·Age
space·craft
space·man
space·men
space·ship
space·walk
spa·cious
spa·cious·ness
Spack·le
spack·led
spack·ling
spade
spad·ed
spad·ing
spade·ful
spad·er
spade·work
spa·ghet·ti
span
spanned
span·ning
span·gle
span·gled
span·gling
Span·iard

span·iel
Span·ish
spank·er
spank·ing
spar
sparred
spar·ring
spare
spared
spar·ing
spar·er
spar·est
spare·a·ble
spare·ness
spar·er
spare·rib
spar·ing
spar·ing·ness
spark·er
spar·kle
spar·kled
spar·kling
spar·kler
spar·row
spar·row·grass
sparse
spars·er
spars·est
sparse·ness
Spar·ta
Spar·tan
spasm
spas·mod·ic
spas·mod·i·cal
spas·mod·i·cal·ly
spas·tic
spas·ti·cal·ly
spat
spat·ted
spat·ting
spa·tial
spa·cial
spa·ti·al·i·ty
spa·tial·ly
spat·ter
spat·u·la
spawn
speak
spok·en
speak·ing
speak·a·ble
speak·easy
speak·eas·ies
speak·er
speak·er·ship
spear·er
spear·head
spear·mint
spe·cial
spe·cial·ly
spe·cial·ist
spe·cial·ize
spe·cial·ized
spe·cial·iz·ing
spe·cial·i·za·tion

spe·cial·ty
spe·cial·ties
spe·cie
spe·cies
spec·i·fi·a·ble
spe·cif·ic
spe·cif·i·cal·ly
spec·i·fic·i·ty
spec·i·fi·ca·tion
spec·i·fy
spec·i·fied
spec·i·fy·ing
spec·i·fi·er
spec·i·men
spe·cious
spe·ci·os·i·ty
spe·ci·os·i·ties
spe·cious·ness
speck·le
speck·led
speck·ling
spec·ta·cle
spec·ta·cled
spec·tac·u·lar
spec·tac·u·lar·ly
spec·ta·tor
spec·ter
spec·tral
spec·tro·scope
spec·tro·scop·ic
spec·tro·scop·i·cal
spec·tros·co·py
spec·trum
spec·tra
spec·trums
spec·u·late
spec·u·lat·ed
spec·u·lat·ing
spec·u·la·tion
spec·u·la·tor
spec·u·ia·tive
speech·i·fy
speech·i·fied
speech·i·fy·ing
speech·less
speech·less·ness
speed
speed·ed
speed·ing
speed·er
speed·ster
speed·boat
speed·boat·ing
speed·om·e·ter
speed-up
speed·way
speedy
speed·i·er
speed·i·est
speed·i·ly
speed·i·ness
spe·le·ol·o·gy
spe·le·ol·o·gist
spell
spelled

spell·ing
spell·bind
spell·bound
spell·bind·ing
spell·bind·er
spell·er
spe·lun·ker
spend
spent
spend·ing
spend·a·ble
spend·er
spend·thrift
sper·ma·ceti
sper·mat·ic
sper·ma·to·zo·on
sper·ma·to·zo·a
sper·ma·to·zo·ic
spew·er
sphag·num
sphere
sphered
spher·ing
spher·ic
sphe·ric·i·ty
spher·i·cal
spher·i·cal·ly
sphe·roid
sphe·roi·dal
sphinc·ter
sphinc·ter·al
sphinc·ter·ic
sphinx
sphinx·es
sphin·ges
spice
spiced
spic·ing
spi·cule
spic·u·lar
spic·u·late
spicy
spic·i·er
spic·i·est
spic·i·ly
spic·i·ness
spi·der
spi·dery
spiel
spiel·er
spi·er
spiffy
spiff·i·er
spiff·i·est
spiff·i·ness
spig·ot
spike
spiked
spik·ing
spiky
spik·i·er
spik·i·est
spill
spilled
spill·ing

spil·lage
spill·way
spin
spun
spin·ning
spin·ach
spi·nal
spi·nal·ly
spin·dle
spin·dled
spin·dling
spin·dle·legs
spin·dle·leg·ged
spin·dly
spin·dli·er
spin·dli·est
spine·less
spin·et
spin·na·ker
spin·ner
spin·ning wheel
spin-off
spi·nose
spi·nous
Spi·no·za
spin·ster
spiny
spin·i·ness
spi·ra·cle
spi·ral
spi·raled
spi·ral·ing
spi·ral·ly
spire
spired
spir·ing
spir·it
spir·it·ed
spir·it·ism
spir·it·ist
spir·it·less
spir·it·less·ness
spir·i·tous
spir·it·u·al
spir·it·u·al·ly
spir·it·u·al·ism
spir·it·u·al·ist
spir·it·u·al·is·tic
spir·it·u·al·i·ty
spir·it·u·al·i·ties
spir·it·u·al·ize
spir·it·u·al·ized
spir·it·u·al·iz·ing
spir·it·u·al·i·za·tion
spir·it·u·ous
spir·it·u·os·i·ty
spi·ro·chete
spit
spat
spit·ting
spit·ter
spite
spit·ed
spit·ing
spite·ful

spit·fire
spit·tle
spit·toon
splash
  splash·er
  splashy
  splash·i·er
  splash·i·est
  splash·i·ly
  splash·i·ness
splash·board
splash·down
splat·ter
splay·foot
  splay·feet
  splay·foot·ed
spleen
  spleen·ful
splen·did
splen·dif·er·ous
sple·net·ic
splice
  spliced
  splic·ing
  splic·er
splin·ter
  splin·tery
split
  split·ting
  split·a·ble
  split·ter
split·lev·el
split·sec·ond
splotch
  splotchy
  splotch·i·er
  splotch·i·est
splurge
  splurged
  splurg·ing
splut·ter
  splut·ter·er
spoil
  spoiled
  spoil·ing
  spoil·age
  spoil·er
spoil·sport
Spo·kane
spoke
  spoked
  spok·ing
spo·ken
spokes·man
  spokes·men
  spokes·wom·an
  spokes·wom·en
sponge
  sponged
  spong·ing
spong·er
spon·gy
  spon·gi·er
  spon·gi·est
  spon·gi·ness

spon·sor
  spon·sor·ship
spon·ta·ne·i·ty
  spon·ta·ne·i·ties
spon·ta·ne·ous
  spon·ta·ne·ous·ly
  spon·ta·ne·ous·ness
spook
  spook·ish
  spooky
  spook·i·er
  spook·i·est
  spook·i·ly
  spook·i·ness
spoon·er·ism
  spoon·er·is·tic
spoon-fed
spoon-feed
  spoon-feed·ing
spoon·ful
  spoon·fuls
spo·rad·ic
  spo·rad·i·cal
  spo·rad·i·cal·ly
spo·ran·gi·um
  spo·ran·gia
spore
  spored
  spor·ing
sport
  sport·er
  sport·ful
  sport·ful·ly
  sport·ful·ness
sport·ing
  sport·ing·ly
spor·tive
sports·cast
  sports·cast·er
sports·man
  sports·men
  sports·wom·an
  sports·wom·en
  sports·man·like
  sports·man·ly
  sports·man·ship
sports·wear
sports·writ·er
sporty
  sport·i·er
  sport·i·est
  sport·i·ly
  sport·i·ness
spot
  spot·ted
  spot·ting
  spot·less
  spot·less·ly
  spot·less·ness
spot·light
  spot·ter
  spot·ty
  spot·ti·er
  spot·ti·est
  spot·ti·ly

  spot·ti·ness
spouse
spout·er
sprained
sprawl·er
spray
  spray·er
spread
  spread·ing
spread-ea·gle
  spread-ea·gled
  spread-ea·gling
spread·er
sprig
  sprigged
  sprig·ging
spright·ly
  spright·li·er
  spright·li·est
  spright·li·ness
spring
  spring·ing
spring·board
spring-clean·ing
Spring·field
spring·time
springy
  spring·i·er
  spring·i·est
  spring·i·ly
  spring·i·ness
sprin·kle
  sprin·kled
  sprin·kling
  sprink·ler
sprint
  sprint·er
sprock·et
spruce
  spruc·er
  spruc·est
  spruced
  spruc·ing
spry
  spry·er
  spry·est
  spry·ly
  spry·ness
spue
  spued
  spu·ing
spume
  spumed
  spum·ing
  spum·ous
spunky
  spunk·i·er
  spunk·i·est
  spunk·i·ly
  spunk·i·ness
spur
  spurred
  spur·ring
spu·ri·ous
  spu·ri·ous·ness

spurner
spurt
  spurt·er
  spur·tive
sput·nik
sput·ter
  sput·ter·er
spu·tum
  spu·ta
spy
  spies
  spied
  spy·ing
  spy·glass
squab·ble
  squab·bled
  squab·bling
squad·ron
squal·id
  squal·id·ly
  squal·id·ness
squall
  squally
  squall·i·er
  squall·i·est
squal·or
squan·der
  squan·der·er
square
  squared
  squar·ing
  square·ly
  square·ness
  square-dance
  square-danced
  square-danc·ing
squar·ish
  squar·ish·ly
squash
  squash·er
  squash·es
squashy
  squash·i·er
  squash·i·est
  squash·i·ly
  squash·i·ness
squat
  squat·ted
  squat·ting
  squat·ly
  squat·ness
squat·ter
squat·ty
  squat·ti·er
  squat·ti·est
squawk
  squawk·er
  squawky
  squawk·i·er
  squawk·i·est
squeak
  squeak·er
  squeak·ing·ly
  squeaky
  squeak·i·er

squeak·i·est
squeal
  squeal·er
squeam·ish
  squeam·ish·ly
  squeam·ish·ness
squee·gee
squeeze
  squeezed
  squeez·ing
  squeez·er
squelch
  squelch·er
squib
squid
squig·gle
  squig·gled
  squig·gling
squint
  squint·er
  squint·ing·ly
  squinty
  squint·i·er
  squint·i·est
  squint-eyed
squire
  squired
  squir·ing
squirm
  squirmy
  squirm·i·er
  squirm·i·est
squir·rel
squirt
  squirt·er
squish
  squishy
  squish·i·er
  squish·i·est
stab
  stabbed
  stab·bing
  stab·ber
sta·bil·i·ty
  sta·bil·i·ties
sta·bi·lize
  sta·bi·lized
  sta·bi·liz·ing
  sta·bi·li·za·tion
  sta·bi·liz·er
sta·ble
  sta·bled
  sta·bling
stac·ca·to
stack·er
sta·di·um
staff·er
Staf·ford
stag
  stagged
  stag·ging
stage
  staged
  stag·ing
  stage-coach

stage·hand
stage-struck
stag·ger
  stag·ger·er
  stag·ger·ing
stag·nant
  stag·nan·cy
stag·nate
  stag·nat·ed
  stag·nat·ing
  stag·na·tion
stagy
  stag·i·er
  stag·i·est
  stag·i·ly
  stag·i·ness
staid·ness
stain
  stain·a·ble
  stained
  stain·er
  stained-glass
  stain·less
stair·case
stair·way
stair·well
stake
  staked
  stak·ing
stake·hold·er
sta·lac·tite
sta·lag·mite
stale
  stal·er
  stal·est
  staled
  stal·ing
  stale·ness
stale·mate
  stale·mat·ed
  stale·mat·ing
Sta·lin
Sta·lin·grad
Sta·lin·ism
stalk
  stalked
  stalky
  stalk·i·er
  stalk·i·est
  stalled
stal·lion
stal·wart
  stal·wart·ness
sta·men
  sta·mens
  stam·i·na
Stam·ford
stam·i·na
stam·mer
  stam·mer·ing·ly
stam·pede
  stam·ped·ed
  stam·ped·ing
  stam·ped·er
  stam·ped·ing·ly

stamp·er
stance
stand
  stand·ing
  stand·er
stand·ard
stand·ard·ize
  stand·ard·ized
  stand·ard·iz·ing
  stand·ard·i·za·tion
stand·by
stand·ee
stand·in
Stan·dish
stand·off·ish
  stand·off·ish·ness
stand·out
stand·pipe
stand·point
stand·still
sta·nine
Stan·ton
stan·za
  stan·za·ic
sta·pes
  sta·pes
  sta·ped·es
  sta·pe·di·al
staph·y·lo·coc·cus
sta·ple
  sta·pled
  sta·pling
  sta·pler
star
  starred
  star·ring
  star·less
  star·like
star·board
star·dom
stare
  stared
  star·ing
  star·er
star·fish
star·gaze
  star·gazed
  star·gaz·ing
star·let
star·light
star·ling
star·ry
  star·ri·er
  star·ri·est
  star·ri·ly
  star·ri·ness
star·ry·eyed
star-span·gled
start·er
star·tle
  star·tled
  star·tling
  star·tling·ly
star·va·tion
starve

starved
starv·ing
sta·sis
sta·ses
state
  stat·ed
  stat·ing
  stat·a·ble
state·craft
state·hood
state·less
  state·less·ness
state·ly
  state·li·er
  state·li·est
state·ment
Stat·en Is·land
state·room
state·side
states·man
  states·men
  states·man·like
  states·man·ship
stat·ic
stat·ics
sta·tion
sta·tion·ary
sta·tion·er
sta·tion·ery
stat·ism
  stat·ist
sta·tis·tic
  sta·tis·ti·cal
  sta·tis·ti·cal·ly
stat·is·ti·cian
sta·tis·tics
sta·tor
stat·u·ary
  stat·u·ar·ies
stat·ue
stat·u·esque
stat·u·ette
stat·ure
sta·tus
stat·ute
staunch
stave
  staved
  stav·ing
stay
  stayed
  stay·ing
  stay·er
stead·fast
  stead·fast·ly
  stead·fast·ness
steady
  stead·i·er
  stead·i·est
  stead·ied
  stead·y·ing
  stead·i·ly
  stead·i·ness
steal
  stol·en

steal·ing
steal·er
stealth
stealthy
  stealth·i·er
  stealth·i·est
  stealth·i·ly
  stealth·i·ness
steam·boat
steam·er
steam·fit·ter
  steam·fit·ting
steam·roll·er
steam·ship
steamy
  steam·i·er
  steam·i·est
  steam·i·ly
  steam·i·ness
ste·a·tite
sted·fast
steel·head
steel·works
  steel·work·er
steely
  steel·i·er
  steel·i·est
  steel·i·ness
steel·yard
steep
  steep·ly
  steep·ness
steep·en
stee·ple
stee·ple·chase
  stee·ple·chas·er
stee·ple·jack
steer
  steer·a·ble
  steer·er
steer·age
stein
stel·lar
Stel·lite
stem
  stemmed
  stem·ming
stem·less
stem·ware
stem·wind·er
  stem·wind·ing
stench
stenchy
  stench·i·er
  stench·i·est
sten·cil
  sten·ciled
  sten·cil·ing
ste·nog·ra·pher
ste·nog·ra·phy
sten·o·graph·ic
sten·o·graph·i·cal·ly
sten·to·ri·an
step
  stepped

step·ping
step·broth·er
step·child
step·child·ren
step·daugh·ter
step·fa·ther
step·lad·der
step·moth·er
step·par·ent
stepped-up
step·ping·stone
step·sis·ter
step·son
ster·eo
ster·e·os
ster·e·o·phon·ic
ster·e·o·phon·i·cal·ly
ster·e·o·scope
ster·e·o·scop·ic
ster·e·o·type
ster·e·o·typed
ster·e·o·typ·ing
ster·ile
ste·ril·i·ty
ster·i·lize
ster·i·lized
ster·i·liz·ing
ster·i·li·za·tion
ster·i·li·zer
ster·ling
stern
stern·ly
stern·ness
ster·num
ster·na
ster·nums
stern-wheel·er
ster·oid
steth·o·scope
steth·o·scop·ic
Steu·ben
Steu·ben·ville
ste·ve·dore
ste·ve·dored
ste·ve·dor·ing
Ste·ven·son
stew·ard
stew·ard·ess
Stew·art
stick·er
stick·ing
stick-in-the-mud
stick·le·back
stick·ler
stick·pin
stick-up
sticky
stick·i·er
stick·i·est
stick·i·ly
stick·i·ness
stiff
stiff·ly
stiff·ness
stiff·en

stiff·en·er
stiff-necked
sti·fle
sti·fled
sti·fling
sti·fler
sti·fling·ly
stig·ma
stig·mas
stig·ma·ta
stig·ma·tic
stig·mat·i·cal·ly
stig·ma·tize
stig·ma·tized
stig·ma·tiz·ing
stig·ma·ti·za·tion
sti·let·to
sti·let·tos
sti·let·toes
still-birth
still-born
still·ness
stilt·ed
stilt·ed·ly
stim·u·lant
stim·u·late
stim·u·lat·ed
stim·u·lat·ing
stim·u·la·tion
stim·u·la·tive
stim·u·lus
stim·u·li
sting
sting·ing
sting·er
sting·ing·ly
stin·gy
stin·gi·er
stin·gi·est
stin·gi·ly
stin·gi·ness
stink
stink·ing
stink·er
stinky
stink·i·er
stink·i·est
stint·er
sti·pend
stip·ple
stip·pled
stip·pling
stip·u·late
stip·u·lat·ed
stip·u·lat·ing
stip·u·la·tion
stip·u·la·to·ry
stir
stirred
stir·ring
stir·ring·ly
Stir·ling
stir·rup
stitch
stitch·er

stock·ade
stock·ad·ed
stock·ad·ing
stock·brok·er
stock·hold·er
Stock·holm
stock·ing
stock·pile
stock·piled
stock·pil·ing
Stock·ton
stocky
stock·i·er
stock·i·est
stock·i·ly
stock·i·ness
stock·yard
stodgy
stodg·i·er
stodg·i·est
stodg·i·ly
stodg·i·ness
sto·ic
sto·i·cal
stoke
stoked
stok·ing
stok·er
stol·id
sto·lid·i·ty
stol·id·ly
sto·ma
sto·ma·ta
sto·mas
stom·ach
stom·ach·er
stone
stoned
ston·ing
stone-deaf
Stone·henge
stone·ma·son
stone·ma·son·ry
stone·wall
stony
ston·i·er
ston·i·est
ston·i·ly
ston·i·ness
stop
stopped
stop·ping
stop·gap
stop·light
stop·o·ver
stop·page
stop·per
stop·watch
stor·age
store
stored
stor·ing
store·house
store·keep·er
store·room

sto·ried
stormy
storm·i·er
storm·i·est
storm·i·ly
storm·i·ness
story
sto·ries
sto·ry·ing
sto·ry·book
sto·ry·tell·er
sto·ry·tell·ing
stout
stout·ly
stout·ness
stout-heart·ed
stove
stoved
stov·ing
stove·pipe
stow·age
stow·a·way
stra·bis·mus
strad·dle
strad·dled
strad·dling
strad·dler
strafe
strafed
straf·ing
strag·gle
strag·gled
strag·gling
strag·gler
strag·gly
strag·gli·er
strag·gli·est
straight·a·way
straight-edge
straight·en
straight·en·er
straight·for·ward
straight·for·ward·ly
straight·way
strain·er
strait·en
strait·jack·et
strait-laced
strange
strang·er
strang·est
strange·ly
strange·ness
stran·ger
stran·gle
stran·gled
stran·gling
stran·gler
stran·gu·la·tion
stran·gu·late
stran·gu·lat·ed
stran·gu·lat·ing
strap
strapped
strap·ping

strap·less
strat·a·gem
stra·te·gic
stra·te·gi·cal·ly
strat·e·gy
strat·e·gies
strat·e·gist
Strat·ford
strat·i·fi·ca·tion
strat·i·fy
strat·i·fied
strat·i·fy·ing
stra·to·cu·mu·lus
strat·o·sphere
strat·o·spher·ic
stra·tum
stra·ta
stra·tums
stra·tus
stra·ti
straw·ber·ry
straw·ber·ries
stray·er
stray·ing
streak
streaky
streak·i·er
streak·i·est
stream·er
stream·line
stream·lined
stream·lin·ing
street·car
street·walk·er
street·walk·ing
strength·en
strength·en·er
stren·u·ous
stren·u·os·i·ty
stren·u·ous·ly
strep·to·coc·cus
strep·to·coc·ci
strep·to·coc·cal
strep·to·coc·cic
strep·to·my·cin
stress
stress·ful
stress·ful·ly
stress·less
stress·less·ness
stretch
stretch·a·bil·i·ty
stretch·a·ble
stretch·er
strew
strewed
strew·ing
stria
stri·ae
stri·ate
stri·at·ed
stri·at·ing
strick·en
strict
strict·ly

strict·ness
stric·ture
stride
strid·den
strid·ing
stri·dent
strid·u·la·tion
strife
strife·ful
strife·less
strike
strick·en
strik·ing
strike·less
string
strung
string·ing
strin·gent
strin·gen·cy
strin·gent·ly
stringy
string·i·er
string·i·est
string·i·ness
strip
stripped
strip·ping
stripe
striped
strip·ing
strip·ling
strip·per
strip·tease
strip·teas·er
strive
strove
striv·en
striv·ing
stro·bo·scope
stro·bo·scop·ic
stro·bo·scop·i·cal·ly
stroke
stroked
strok·ing
stroll·er
strong
strong·ish
strong·ly
strong·ness
strong-arm
strong·box
strong·hold
strong-mind·ed
strong-mind·ed·ly
strong-mind·ed·ness
stron·ti·um
stron·tic
strop
stropped
strop·ping
struc·tural
struc·tur·al·ly
struc·ture
struc·tured
struc·tur·ing

struc·ture·less
strug·gle
strug·gled
strug·gling
strug·gler
strum
strum·mer
strum·pet
strut
strut·ted
strut·ting
strych·nine
strych·nia
strych·nic
stub
stubbed
stub·bing
stub·by
stub·bi·er
stub·bi·est
stub·ble
stub·bled
stub·bly
stub·bli·er
stub·bli·est
stub·born
stub·born·ly
stub·born·ness
stuc·co
stuc·coes
stuc·cos
stuc·coed
stuc·co·ing
stuck-up
stud
stud·ded
stud·ding
Stu·de·bak·er
stu·dent
stud·ied
stud·ied·ly
stud·ied·ness
stu·dio
stu·di·os
stu·di·ous
stu·di·ous·ly
stu·di·ous·ness
study
stud·ies
stud·ied
stud·y·ing
stuff·er
stuff·ing
stuffy
stuff·i·er
stuff·i·est
stuff·i·ly
stuff·i·ness
stul·ti·fy
stul·ti·fied
stul·ti·fy·ing
stul·ti·fi·ca·tion
stul·ti·fi·er
stum·ble
stum·bled

stum·bling
stum·bler
stum·bling·ly
stump
stump·er
stumpy
stump·i·er
stump·i·est
stun
stunned
stun·ning
stunt
stunt·ed
stunt·ed·ness
stu·pe·fy
stu·pe·fied
stu·pe·fy·ing
stu·pe·fac·tion
stu·pe·fi·er
stu·pe·fy·ing·ly
stu·pen·dous
stu·pen·dous·ly
stu·pen·dous·ness
stu·pid
stu·pid·i·ty
stu·pid·ly
stu·pid·ness
stu·por
stu·por·ous
stur·dy
stur·di·er
stur·di·est
stur·geon
stut·ter
stut·ter·er
stut·ter·ing·ly
Stutt·gart
Stuy·ve·sant
style
styled
styl·ing
styl·er
styl·ish
styl·ish·ly
styl·ish·ness
styl·ist
sty·lis·tic
sty·lis·ti·cal
sty·lis·ti·cal·ly
styl·ize
styl·ized
styl·iz·ing
styl·i·za·tion
styl·iz·er
sty·lus
sty·lus·es
sty·li
sty·mie
sty·mies
sty·mied
sty·mie·ing
styp·tic
styp·ti·cal
styp·tic·i·ty
Sty·ro·foam

suave
suave·ly
suave·ness
swav·i·ty
sub
subbed
sub·bing
sub·al·tern
sub·arc·tic
sub·as·sem·bly
sub·as·sem·blies
sub·as·sem·bler
sub·base·ment
sub·chas·er
sub·class
sub·com·mit·tee
sub·con·scious
sub·con·scious·ly
sub·con·scious·ness
sub·con·ti·nent
sub·con·ti·nen·tal
sub·con·tract
sub·con·trac·tor
sub·cul·ture
sub·cul·tur·al
sub·cu·ta·ne·ous
sub·cu·ta·ne·ous·ly
sub·deb·u·tante
sub·di·vide
sub·di·vid·ed
sub·di·vid·ing
sub·di·vid·a·ble
sub·di·vid·er
sub·di·vi·sion
sub·di·vi·sion·al
sub·due
sub·dued
sub·du·ing
sub·du·a·ble
sub·du·al
sub·du·er
sub·en·try
sub·en·tries
sub·freez·ing
sub·group
sub·head
sub·hu·man
sub·ject
sub·jec·tion
sub·jec·tive
sub·jec·tive·ly
sub·jec·tive·ness
sub·jec·tiv·i·ty
sub·join
sub·ju·gate
sub·ju·gat·ed
sub·ju·gat·ing
sub·ju·ga·tion
sub·ju·ga·tor
sub·junc·tive
sub·lease
sub·leased
sub·leas·ing
sub·let
sub·let·ting

sub·li·mate
  sub·li·mat·ed
  sub·li·mat·ing
  sub·li·ma·tion
sub·lime
  sub·lim·er
  sub·lim·est
  sub·limed
  sub·lim·ing
  sub·lime·ly
  sub·lime·ness
  sub·lim·er
sub·lim·i·nal
  sub·lim·i·nal·ly
sub·lim·i·ty
  sub·lim·i·ties
sub·ma·chine
sub·mar·gin·al
sub·ma·rine
sub·merge
  sub·merged
  sub·merg·ing
  sub·mer·gence
  sub·mer·gi·ble
sub·merse
  sub·mersed
  sub·mers·ing
  sub·mer·sion
sub·mers·i·ble
sub·mi·cro·scop·ic
sub·mis·sion
sub·mis·sive
  sub·miss·ive·ly
  sub·miss·ive·ness
sub·mit
  sub·mit·ted
  sub·mit·ting
sub·nor·mal
  sub·nor·mal·i·ty
sub·or·di·nate
  sub·or·di·nat·ed
  sub·or·di·nat·ing
  sub·or·di·nate·ly
  sub·or·di·nate·ness
  sub·or·di·na·tion
  sub·or·di·na·tive
sub·orn
  sub·or·na·tion
  sub·orn·er
sub·poe·na
  sub·poe·naed
  sub·poe·na·ing
sub·scribe
  sub·scribed
  sub·scrib·ing
  sub·scrib·er
sub·scrip·tion
sub·se·quent
  sub·se·quence
  sub·se·quent·ly
  sub·se·quent·ness
sub·ser·vi·ent
  sub·ser·vi·ence
  sub·ser·vi·en·cy
  sub·ser·vi·ent·ly

sub·side
  sub·sid·ed
  sub·sid·ing
  sub·sid·ence
sub·sid·i·ary
  sub·sid·i·ar·ies
sub·si·dize
  sub·si·dized
  sub·si·diz·ing
  sub·si·di·za·tion
  sub·si·diz·er
sub·si·dy
  sub·si·dies
sub·sist
sub·sist·ence
sub·soil
sub·son·ic
sub·stance
sub·stand·ard
sub·stan·tial
  sub·stan·ti·al·i·ty
  sub·stan·tial·ly
  sub·stan·tial·ness
sub·stan·ti·ate
  sub·stan·ti·at·ed
  sub·stan·ti·at·ing
  sub·stan·ti·a·tion
  sub·stan·ti·a·tive
sub·stan·tive
  sub·stan·ti·val
  sub·stan·ti·val·ly
  sub·stan·tive·ly
  sub·stan·tive·ness
sub·sti·tute
  sub·sti·tut·ed
  sub·sti·tut·ing
  sub·sti·tut·able
  sub·sti·tu·tion
  sub·sti·tu·tion·al
  sub·sti·tu·tion·al·ly
  sub·sti·tu·tion·ary
sub·stra·tum
  sub·stra·ta
  sub·stra·tums
sub·struc·ture
sub·sume
  sub·sumed
  sub·sum·ing
  sub·sum·a·ble
  sub·sump·tive
  sub·sump·tion
sub·teen
sub·tend
sub·ter·fuge
sub·ter·ra·ne·an
  sub·ter·ra·ne·ous
  sub·ter·ra·ne·an·ly
  sub·ter·ra·ne·ous·ly
sub·ti·tle
sub·tle
  sub·tle·ness
  sub·tle·ty
  sub·tle·ties
  sub·tly
sub·tract

sub·tract·er
sub·trac·tion
sub·trac·tive
sub·tra·hend
sub·trop·i·cal
sub·trop·ic
sub·trop·ics
sub·urb
sub·ur·ban
sur·ur·ban·ite
sub·ur·bia
sub·ver·sion
sub·ver·sion·ary
sub·ver·sive
sub·ver·sive·ly
sub·ver·sive·ness
sub·vert
sub·vert·er
sub·way
suc·ceed
suc·ceed·er
suc·cess
suc·cess·ful·ly
suc·cess·ful·ness
suc·ces·sion
suc·ces·sion·al
suc·ces·sion·al·ly
suc·ces·sive
suc·ces·sive·ly
suc·ces·sive·ness
suc·ces·sor
suc·cinct
suc·cinct·ly
suc·cinct·ness
suc·cor
suc·cor·er
suc·co·tash
suc·cu·bus
suc·cu·bi
suc·cu·lent
suc·cu·lence
suc·cu·len·cy
suc·cu·lent·ly
suc·cumb
suck·er
suck·le
suck·led
suck·ling
Su·cre
su·crose
suc·tion
Su·dan
sud·den
sud·den·ly
sud·den·ness
sudsy
suds·i·er
suds·i·est
sue
sued
su·ing
su·er
suede
su·et
su·ety

Su·ez
suf·fer
suf·fer·a·ble
suf·fer·a·ble·ness
suf·fer·a·bly
suf·fer·er
suf·fer·ing
suf·fer·ing·ly
suf·fer·ance
suf·fice
suf·ficed
suf·fic·ing
suf·fic·er
suf·fi·cien·cy
suf·fi·cien·cies
suf·fi·cient
suf·fi·cient·ly
suf·fix
suf·fo·cate
suf·fo·cat·ed
suf·fo·cat·ing·
suf·fo·cat·ing·ly
suf·fo·ca·tion
suf·fo·ca·tive
Suf·folk
suf·frage
suf·fra·gette
suf·fuse
suf·fused
suf·fus·ing
suf·fu·sion
suf·fu·sive
sug·ar
sug·ar·less
sug·ar·like
sug·ary
sug·ar·i·er
sug·ar·i·est
sug·ar-coat
sug·gest
sug·gest·er
sug·gest·i·ble
sug·gest·i·bil·i·ty
sug·ges·tion
sug·ges·tive
sug·ges·tive·ly
sug·ges·tive·ness
su·i·cide
su·i·cid·ed
su·i·cid·ing
su·i·cid·al
suit·a·ble
suit·a·bil·i·ty
suit·a·ble·ness
suit·a·bly
suit·case
suite
suit·ing
suit·or
sul·fa
sul·fa·nil·a·mide
sul·fate
sul·fide
sul·fur
sul·fu·ric

sul·fur·ous
  sur·fur·ous·ly
  sul·fur·ous·ness
sulky
  sulk·i·er
  sulk·i·est
  sulk·i·ly
  sulk·i·ness
sul·len
  sul·len·ly
  sul·len·ness
Sul·li·van
sul·ly
  sul·lied
  sul·ly·ing
sul·tan
  sul·tan·ic
sul·tana
  sul·tan·ess
sul·tan·ate
sul·try
  sul·tri·er
  sul·tri·est
  sul·tri·ly
  sul·tri·ness
sum
  summed
  sum·ming
su·mac
Su·ma·tra
sum·ma·rize
  sum·ma·rized
  sum·ma·riz·ing
  sum·ma·ri·za·tion
  sum·ma·riz·er
  sum·mar·ist
sum·ma·ry
  sum·ma·ries
  sum·mar·i·ly
  sum·mar·i·ness
sum·ma·tion
  sum·ma·tion·al
sum·mer
  sum·mery
sum·mer·house
sum·mit
sum·mon
  sum·mon·er
sum·mons
  sum·mons·es
sump·tu·ary
sump·tu·ous
  sump·tu·ous·ly
  sump·tu·ous·ness
sun
  sunned
  sun·ning
sun·bathe
  sun·bathed
  sun·bath·ing
  sun·bath·er
sun·beam
sun·bon·net
sun·burn
  sun·burned

sun·burnt
  sun·burn·ing
sun·dae
Sun·day
sun·der
  sun·der·ance
sun·di·al
sun·down
sun·dries
sun·dry
sun·fish
sun·flow·er
sun·glass·es
sunk·en
sun·light
sun·lit
sun·ny
  sun·ni·er
  sun·ni·est
  sun·ni·ly
  sun·ni·ness
sun·rise
sun·set
sun·shine
  sun·shiny
sun·spot
sun·stroke
sun·up
sup
  supped
  sup·ping
su·per
su·per·a·bun·dant
  su·per·a·bun·dance
  su·per·a·bun·dant·ly
su·per·an·nu·ate
  su·per·an·nu·at·ing
  su·per·an·nu·at·ed
  su·per·an·nu·a·tion
su·perb
  su·perb·ly
  su·perb·ness
su·per·car·go
  su·per·car·goes
su·per·charge
  su·per·charged
  su·per·charg·ing
  su·per·charg·er
su·per·cil·i·ous
  su·per·cil·i·ous·ly
  su·per·cil·i·ous·ness
su·per·e·go
su·per·e·rog·a·to·ry
su·per·fi·cial
  su·per·fi·ci·al·i·ty
  su·per·fi·ci·al·i·ties
  su·per·fi·cial·ly
  su·per·fi·cial·ness
su·per·fine
su·per·flu·ous
  su·per·flu·i·ty
  su·per·flu·i·ties
  su·per·flu·ous·ly
  su·per·flu·ous·ness
su·per·high·way

su·per·hu·man
su·per·hu·man·i·ty
su·per·hu·man·ly
su·per·hu·man·ness
su·per·im·pose
su·per·im·posed
su·per·im·pos·ing
su·per·im·po·si·tion
su·per·in·tend
su·per·in·tend·ence
su·per·in·tend·en·cy
su·per·in·tend·ent
su·pe·ri·or
su·pe·ri·or·i·ty
su·pe·ri·or·ly
su·per·la·tive
su·per·la·tive·ly
su·per·la·tive·ness
su·per·man
su·per·mar·ket
su·per·nal
su·per·nal·ly
su·per·nat·u·ral
su·per·nat·u·ral·ism
su·per·nat·u·ral·ly
su·per·nat·u·ral·ness
su·per·nu·mer·ary
su·per·nu·mer·ar·ies
su·per·pow·er
su·per·scribe
su·per·scribed
su·per·scrib·ing
su·per·scrip·tion
su·per·script
su·per·sede
su·per·sed·ed
su·per·sed·ing
su·per·sed·er
su·per·son·nic
su·per·son·i·cal·ly
su·per·star
su·per·sti·tion
su·per·sti·tious
su·per·sti·tious·ly
su·per·sti·tious·ness
su·per·struc·ture
su·per·vene
su·per·vened
su·per·ven·ing
super·ven·tion
su·per·vise
su·per·vised
su·per·vis·ing
su·per·vi·sion
su·per·vi·sor
su·per·vi·so·ry
su·pine
su·pine·ly
su·pine·ness
sup·per
sup·plant
sup·plan·ta·tion
sup·plant·er
sup·ple
sup·pler

sup·plest
sup·ple·ness
sup·ple·ment
sup·ple·men·tal
sup·ple·men·ta·ry
sup·ple·men·ta·tion
sup·pli·ant
sup·pli·ant·ly
sup·pli·cant
sup·pli·cate
sup·pli·cat·ed
sup·pli·cat·ing
sup·pli·ca·tion
sup·pli·ca·to·ry
sup·ply
sup·plied
sup·ply·ing
sup·plies
sup·pli·er
sup·port
sup·port·a·ble
sub·port·a·ble·ness
sup·port·a·bly
sup·port·er
sup·port·ive
sup·pose
sup·posed
sup·pos·ing
sup·pos·a·ble
sup·pos·a·bly
sup·pos·ed·ly
sup·po·si·tion
sup·po·si·tion·al
sup·po·si·tion·al·ly
sup·pos·i·to·ry
sup·press
sup·press·i·ble
sup·pres·sion
sup·pres·sor
sup·pu·rate
sup·pu·rat·ed
sup·pu·rat·ing
sup·pu·ra·tion
sup·pu·ra·tive
su·pra·re·nal
su·prem·a·cy
su·prem·a·cies
su·prem·a·cist
su·preme
su·preme·ly
su·preme·ness
sur·cease
sur·charge
sur·charged
sur·charg·ing
sur·cin·gle
sure
sur·er
sur·est
sure·ly
sure·ness
sure-fire
sure-foot·ed
sure-foot·ed·ly
sure·ty

sure·ties
sure·ty·ship
surf
surfy
surf·i·er
surf·i·est
sur·face
sur·faced
sur·fac·ing
sur·face·less
sur·fac·er
surf·board
surf·board·er
sur·feit
sur·feit·er
surge
surged
surg·ing
sur·geon
sur·gery
sur·ger·ies
sur·gi·cal
sur·gi·cal·ly
Su·ri·nam
sur·ly
sur·li·er
sur·li·est
sur·li·ly
sur·li·ness
sur·mise
sur·mised
sur·mis·ing
sur·mount
sur·mount·a·ble
sur·name
sur·pass
sur·pass·a·ble
sur·pass·ing
sur·pass·ing·ly
sur·plice
sur·plus
sur·plus·age
sur·prise
sur·prised
sur·pris·ing
sur·pris·al
sur·pris·er
sur·pris·ing·ly
sur·re·al·ism
sur·re·al·ist
sur·re·al·is·tic
sur·re·al·is·ti·cal·ly
sur·ren·der
sur·rep·ti·tious
sur·rep·ti·tious·ly
sur·rep·ti·tious·ness
sur·rey
sur·reys
sur·ro·gate
sur·ro·gat·ed
sur·ro·gat·ing
sur·round
sur·round·er
sur·round·ing
sur·tax

sur·veil·lance
sur·veil·lant
sur·vey
sur·vey·ing
sur·vey·or
sur·viv·al
sur·vive
sur·vived
sur·viv·ing
sur·vi·vor
sus·cep·ti·ble
sus·cep·ti·bil·i·ty
sus·cep·ti·ble·ness
sus·cep·ti·bly
sus·pect
sus·pend
sus·pend·er
sus·pense
sus·pense·ful
sus·pen·sion
sus·pi·cion
sus·pi·cious
sus·pi·cious·ly
sus·pi·cious·ness
Sus·que·han·na
Sus·sex
sus·tain
sus·tain·a·ble
sus·tain·er
sus·tain·ment
sus·te·nance
su·ture
su·tured
su·tur·ing
su·tur·al
su·tur·al·ly
Su·va
su·ze·rain
su·ze·rain·ty
svelte
svelte·ly
svelte·ness
swab
swabbed
swab·bing
swab·ber
Swa·bia
swad·dle
swad·dled
swad·dling
swag·ger
swag·ger·er
swag·ger·ing
swag·ger·ing·ly
swain
swain·ish
swain·ish·ness
swal·low
swal·low·er
swal·low·tail
swa·mi
swa·mis
swamp
swampy
swamp·i·er

swamp·i·est
swamp·i·ness
swank
swank·i·ly
swank·i·ness
swanky
swank·i·er
swank·i·est
swan's-down
swap
swapped
swap·ping
sward
swarthy
swarth·i·er
swarth·i·est
swarth·i·ness
swash·buck·ler
swash·buck·ling
swas·ti·ka
swat
swat·ted
swat·ting
swat·ter
swathe
swathed
swath·ing
sway
sway·a·ble
sway·er
sway·back
sway·backed
Swa·zi·land
swear
swore
swear·ing
swear·er
swear·word
sweat
sweat·ed
sweat·ing
sweat·i·ly
sweat·i·ness
sweat·less
sweaty
sweat·i·er
sweat·i·est
sweat·er
sweat-shop
Swe·den
sweep
swept
sweep·ing
sweep·er
sweep·ing·ly
sweep·ing·ness
sweep·stakes
sweet
sweet·ish
sweet·ly
sweet·ness
sweet·bread
sweet·bri·er
sweet·en
sweet·en·er

sweet·en·ing
sweet·heart
sweet·meat
sweet-talk
swell
swelled
swoll·en
swell·ing
swell·head
swel·ter
swel·ter·ing
swel·ter·ing·ly
swerve
swerved
swerv·ing
swift
swift·ly
swift·ness
swig
swigged
swig·ging
swig·ger
swill
swill·er
swim·ming
swim·ming·ly
swin·dle
swin·dled
swin·dling
swin·dler
swine
swin·ish
swing
swing·ing
swing·a·ble
swing·er
swipe
swiped
swip·ing
swirl
swirl·ing·ly
swirly
swirl·i·er
swirl·i·est
swish
swish·er
swish·ing·ly
swishy
swish·i·er
swish·i·est
switch
switch·er
switch·blade
switch·board
switch-hit·ter
Switz·er·land
swiv·el
swiv·eled
swiv·el·ing
swiz·zle
swoon
swoon·er
swoon·ing·ly
swoop·er
swop

swopped
swop·ping
sword
sword·like
sword·fish
sword·play
sword·play·er
swords·man
swords·men
swords·man·ship
syc·a·more
syc·o·phant
syc·o·phan·cy
syc·o·phan·tic
syc·o·phan·ti·cal
syc·o·phan·ti·cal·ly
Syd·ney
syl·lab·ic
syl·lab·i·cate
syl·lab·i·cat·ed
syl·lab·i·cat·ing
syl·lab·i·ca·tion
syl·lab·i·fy
syl·lab·i·fied
syl·lab·i·fy·ing
syl·lab·i·fi·ca·tion
syl·la·ble
syl·la·bled
syl·la·bling
syl·la·bus
syl·la·bus·es
syl·la·bi
syl·lo·gism
syl·lo·gis·tic
sylph·like
syl·van
sym·bi·o·sis
sym·bi·ot·ic
sym·bi·ot·i·cal·ly
sym·bol
sym·bol·ic
sym·bol·i·cal
sym·bol·ism
sym·bol·ist
sym·bol·ize
sym·bol·ized
sym·bol·iz·ing
sym·bol·i·za·tion
sym·bol·iz·er
sym·me·try
sym·me·tries
sym·met·ric
sym·met·ri·cal
sym·pa·thet·ic
sym·pa·thet·i·cal·ly
sym·pa·thize
sym·pa·thized
sym·pa·thiz·ing
sym·pa·thiz·er
sym·pa·thiz·ing·ly
sym·pa·thy
sym·pa·thies
sym·pho·ny
sym·pho·nies
sym·phon·ic

sym·po·si·um
sym·po·sia
sym·po·si·ums
symp·tom
symp·to·mat·ic
symp·to·mat·i·cal
symp·to·mat·i·cal·ly
syn·a·gogue
syn·a·gog·al
syn·a·gog·i·cal
syn·apse
sync
synced
sync·ing
syn·chro·nism
syn·chro·nis·tic
syn·chro·nis·ti·cal
syn·chro·nis·ti·cal·ly
syn·chro·nize
syn·chro·nized
syn·chro·niz·ing
syn·chro·ni·za·tion
syn·chro·niz·er
sny·chro·nous
syn·chro·nous·ly
syn·chro·nous·ness
syn·co·pate
syn·co·pat·ed
syn·co·pat·ing
syn·co·pa·tion
syn·co·pa·tor
syn·di·cate
syn·di·cat·ed
syn·di·cat·ing
syn·di·ca·tion
syn·di·ca·tor
syn·drome
syn·drom·ic
syn·od
syn·od·al
syn·o·nym
syn·o·nym·ic
syn·o·nym·i·cal
syn·o·nym·i·ty
syn·on·y·mous
syn·on·y·mous·ly
syn·on·y·my
syn·on·y·mies
syn·op·sis
syn·op·ses
syn·op·ti·cal
syn·tac·tic
syn·tac·ti·cal
syn·tac·ti·cal·ly
syn·tax
syn·the·sis
syn·the·ses
syn·the·sist
syn·the·size
syn·the·sized
syn·the·siz·ing
syn·thet·ic
syn·thet·i·cal
syn·thet·i·cal·ly
syph·i·lis

syph·i·lit·ic
Syr·a·cuse
Syr·ia
Syr·i·ac
sy·ringe
 sy·ringed
 sy·ring·ing
syr·up
 syr·upy
 syr·up·i·er
 syr·up·i·est
sys·tem
 sys·tem·at·ic
  sys·tem·at·i·cal
  sys·tem·at·i·cal·ly
  sys·tem·at·ic·ness
 sys·tem·a·tize
  sys·tem·a·tized
  sys·tem·a·tiz·ing
  sys·tem·a·ti·za·tion
  sys·tem·a·tiz·er
 sys·tem·ic
  sys·tem·i·cal·ly
 sys·to·le
  sys·tol·ic
tab
 tabbed
 tab·bing
tab·by
 tab·bies
tab·er·na·cle
 tab·er·nac·u·lar
ta·ble
 ta·bled
 ta·bling
tab·leau
 tab·leaux
 tab·leaus
ta·ble·cloth
ta·ble d'hôte
ta·ble·land
ta·ble·spoon
 ta·ble·spoon·ful
 ta·ble·spoon·fuls
tab·let
ta·ble·ware
tab·loid
ta·boo
 ta·booed
 ta·boo·ing
ta·bor
tab·u·lar
 tab·u·lar·ly
tab·u·late
 tab·u·lat·ed
 tab·u·lat·ing
 tab·u·la·tion
 tab·u·la·tor
ta·chom·e·ter
tac·it
 tac·it·ly
 tac·it·ness
tac·i·turn
 tac·i·tur·ni·ty
tack

tacked
 tack·ing
 tack·er
tack·le
 tack·led
 tack·ling
 tack·ler
tacky
 tack·i·er
 tack·i·est
 tack·i·ness
ta·co
 ta·cos
Ta·co·ma
tact
 tact·ful
 tact·ful·ly
 tact·ful·ness
 tact·less
tac·ti·cal
tac·tics
 tac·ti·cian
tac·tile
 tac·til·i·ty
tad·pole
taf·fe·ta
taf·fy
tag
 tagged
 tag·ging
Ta·ga·log
Ta·hi·ti
Ta·hoe
tail
 tailed
 tail·er
 tail·less
 tail·like
tail·gate
 tail·gat·ed
 tail·gat·ing
tail·light
tai·lor
 tai·lored
 tai·lor·ing
tai·lor-made
tail·piece
tail·spin
tail·wind
taint
 taint·less
Tai·pei
Tai·wan
take
 tak·en
 tak·ing
 tak·er
take·off
 tak·ing
 tak·ing·ly
 tak·ing·ness
tal·cum
tale·bear·er
 tale·bear·ing
tal·ent

tal·ent·ed
tales·man
 tales·men
tal·is·man
 tal·is·mans
 tal·is·man·ic
 tal·is·man·i·cal
 tal·is·man·i·cal·ly
talk
 talk·er
talk·a·tive
 talk·a·tive·ly
 talk·a·tive·ness
talk·ie
talk·ing·to
talky
 talk·i·er
 talk·i·est
tall
 tall·ish
 tall·ness
Tal·la·has·see
Tal·ley·rand
tal·low
 tal·lowy
 tal·low·i·er
 tal·low·i·est
tal·ly
 tal·lies
 tal·lied
 tal·ly·ing
tal·ly·ho
Tal·mud
 Tal·mud·ic
 Tal·mud·i·cal
 Tal·mud·ism
 Tal·mud·ist
tal·on
 tal·oned
Ta·los
ta·ma·le
tam·a·rack
tam·a·rind
tam·bou·rine
tame
 tam·er
 tam·est
 tamed
 tam·ing
 tam·a·ble
 tame·ly
 tameness
 tam·er
Tam·ma·ny
tam·o'·shan·ter
Tam·pa
tam·per
 tam·per·er
Tam·pi·co
tan
 tanned
 tan·ning
 tan·nish
tan·a·ger
Tan·a·gra

Ta·nan·a·rive
tan·bark
tan·dem
tang
 tangy
 tang·i·er
 tang·i·est
Tan·gan·yi·ka
tan·gent
 tan·gen·cy
tan·gen·tial
tan·ge·rine
tan·gi·ble
 tan·gi·bil·i·ty
 tan·gi·ble·ness
 tan·gi·bly
Tan·gier
tan·gle
 tan·gled
 tan·gling
 tan·gle·ment
 tan·gly
 tan·gli·er
 tan·gli·est
tan·go
 tan·goed
 tan·go·ing
tank·age
tank·ard
tank·er
tan·nery
 tan·ner·ies
tan·nin
tan·ta·lize
 tan·ta·lized
 tan·ta·liz·ing
 tan·ta·liz·ing·ly
tan·ta·lum
tan·ta·mount
tan·trum
Tan·zan·ia
Tao·ism
 Tao·ist
tap
 tapped
 tap·ping
tape
 taped
 tap·ing
 tap·er
 tape·like
ta·per
 ta·per·er
 ta·per·ing·ly
tape·re·cord
tap·es·try
 tap·es·tries
 tap·es·tried
 tap·es·try·ing
tape·worm
tap·i·o·ca
ta·pir
tap·room
tap·root
tar

tarred
tar·ring
tar·an·tel·la
ta·ran·tu·la
ta·ran·tu·las
ta·ran·tu·lae
tar·dy
tar·di·er
tar·di·est
tar·di·ly
tar·di·ness
tar·get
tar·iff
Tar·king·ton
tar·nish
tar·nish·a·ble
ta·ro
ta·ros
tar·pau·lin
tar·pon
tar·ry
tar·ried
tar·ry·ing
tar·ries
tar·ry
tar·ri·er
tar·ri·est
tar·sal
tar·sus
tar·si
tart
tart·ly
tart·ness
tar·tan
tar·tar
tar·tar·ic
tar·tar·ous
Tar·ta·ry
task·mas·ter
Tas·ma·nia
tas·sel
tas·seled
tas·sel·ing
taste
tast·ed
tast·ing
taste·ful
taste·ful·ly
taste·ful·ness
taste·less
taste·less·ly
taste·less·ness
tast·er
tasty
tast·i·er
tast·i·est
tast·i·ly
tast·i·ness
tat
tat·ted
tat·ting
tat·ter
Ta·tar
tat·tered
tat·tle

tat·tled
tat·tling
tat·tler
tat·tle·tale
tat·too
tat·toos
tat·tooed
tat·too·ing
tat·too·er
tat·too·ist
taunt
taunt·er
taunt·ing·ly
Taun·ton
taupe
Tau·rus
taut
taut·ly
taut·ness
tau·tol·o·gy
tau·to·log·i·cal
tau·to·log·i·cal·ly
tav·ern
taw·dry
taw·dri·er
taw·dri·est
taw·dri·ly
taw·ny
taw·ni·er
taw·ni·est
taw·ni·ness
tax
tax·a·bil·i·ty
tax·a·ble
tax·er
tax·a·tion
taxi
tax·ies
tax·ied
tax·i·ing
tax·i·cab
tax·i·der·my
tax·i·der·mic
tax·i·der·mist
tax·i·me·ter
tax·on·o·my
tax·o·nom·i·cal
tax·o·nom·i·cal·ly
tax·on·o·mist
tax·pay·er
T-bone
Tchai·kov·sky
teach
taught
teach·ing
teach·a·ble
teach·a·ble·ness
teach·a·bil·i·ty
teach·er
tea·cup
teak
teak·wood
tea·ket·tle
team·mate
team·ster

team·work
tea·pot
tear
  teary
  tear·i·er
  tear·i·est
tear·drop
tear·ful
  tear·ful·ly
  tear·ful·ness
tear·gas
tea·room
tease
  teased
  teas·ing
  teas·er
  teas·ing·ly
tea·sel
  tea·seled
  tea·sel·ing
tea·spoon
  tea·spoon·ful
tech·ne·ti·um
tech·ni·cal
  tech·ni·cal·ly
tech·ni·cal·ness
tech·ni·cal·i·ty
tech·ni·cian
Tech·ni·col·or
tech·nique
tech·noc·ra·cy
  tech·noc·ra·cies
  tech·no·crat
  tech·no·crat·ic
tech·nol·o·gy
  tech·no·log·i·cal
  tech·no·log·ic
  tech·nol·o·gist
Te·cum·seh
te·di·ous
  te·di·ous·ly
  te·di·ous·ness
te·di·um
tee
  teed
  tee·ing
teen-ag·er
tee·ny
  tee·ni·er
  tee·ni·est
tee·pee
tee·ter
tee·ter·board
teethe
  teethed
  teeth·ing
tee·to·tal
  tee·to·tal·er
  tee·to·tal·ist
  tee·to·tal·ism
  tee·to·tal·ly
Te·gu·ci·gal·pa
teg·u·ment
Te·he·ran
Teh·ran

Te·huan·te·pec
Tel Aviv
tel·e·cast
  tel·e·cast·ing
  tel·e·cast·er
tel·e·com·mu·ni·ca·tion
tel·e·gram
tel·e·graph
  te·leg·ra·pher
  tel·e·graph·ic
  tel·e·graph·i·cal
te·leg·ra·phy
te·lep·a·thy
  tel·e·path·ic
  tel·e·path·i·cal·ly
  tel·lep·a·thist
tel·e·phone
  tel·e·phoned
  tel·e·phon·ing
  tel·e·phon·er
  tel·e·phon·ic
te·leph·o·ny
tel·e·pho·to
tel·e·pho·tog·ra·phy
  tel·e·pho·to·graph·ic
tel·e·scope
  tel·e·scoped
  tel·e·scop·ing
  tel·e·scop·ic
  tel·e·scop·i·cal
tel·e·thon
Tel·e·type
  tel·e·typed
  tel·e·typ·ing
  tel·e·typ·ist
tel·e·type·writ·er
tel·e·vise
  tel·e·vised
  tel·e·vis·ing
tel·e·vi·sion
tell·er
tell·ing
  tell·ing·ly
tell·tale
tel·lu·ri·um
Tel·star
tem·blor
te·mer·i·ty
tem·per
  tem·per·a·bil·i·ty
  tem·per·a·ble
  tem·per·er
tem·pera
tem·per·a·ment
tem·per·a·ment·al
tem·per·ance
tem·per·ate
  tem·per·ate·ly
  tem·per·ate·ness
tem·per·a·ture
tem·pered
tem·pest
tem·pes·tu·ous
  tem·pes·tu·ous·ly
  tem·pes·tu·ous·ness

tem·plate
tem·ple
 tem·pled
 tem·ple·like
tem·po
 tem·pos
 tem·pi
tem·po·ral
 tem·por·al·i·ty
 tem·po·ral·ly
 tem·po·ral·ness
tem·po·rary
 tem·po·rar·i·ly
 tem·po·rar·i·ness
tem·po·rize
 tem·po·ri·za·tion
 tem·po·riz·er
 tem·po·riz·ing·ly
tempt
 tempt·a·ble
 temp·ta·tion
 tempt·er
 tempt·ing
 tempt·ress
ten·a·ble
 ten·a·bil·i·ty
 ten·a·ble·ness
 ten·a·bly
te·na·cious
 te·na·cious·ly
 te·na·cious·ness
 te·nac·i·ty
ten·ant
 ten·an·cy
 ten·an·cies
 ten·ant·a·ble
 ten·ant·less
ten·den·cy
 ten·den·cies
ten·den·tious
 ten·den·tious·ly
 ten·den·tious·ness
ten·der
 ten·der·ly
 ten·der·ness
ten·der·foot
ten·der·ize
 ten·der·ized
 ten·der·iz·ing
 ten·der·iz·er
ten·der·loin
ten·don
ten·dril
Ten·e·brae
ten·e·ment
 ten·e·men·ta·ry
ten·et
Ten·nes·see
ten·nis
Ten·ny·son
ten·on
ten·or
ten·pins
tense
 tens·er

tens·est
tensed
 tens·ing
 tense·ly
 tense·ness
 ten·si·ty
ten·sile
 ten·sil·i·ty
ten·sion
 ten·sion·al
 ten·sion·less
 ten·sive
ten·ta·cle
 ten·ta·cled
 ten·tac·u·lar
ten·ta·tive
 ten·ta·tive·ly
 ten·ta·tive·ness
ten·ter·hook
tenth·ly
ten·u·ous
 ten·u·ous·ly
 ten·u·ous·ness
ten·ure
 ten·u·ri·al
 ten·u·ri·al·ly
te·pee
tep·id
 te·pid·i·ty
 tep·id·ness
te·qui·la
ter·cen·te·nary
 ter·cen·te·nar·ies
 ter·cen·ten·ni·al
ter·cet
ter·ma·gant
 ter·ma·gant·ly
ter·mi·na·ble
ter·mi·nal
 ter·mi·nal·ly
ter·mi·nate
 ter·mi·nat·ed
 ter·mi·nat·ing
 ter·mi·na·tion
 ter·mi·na·tive
 ter·mi·na·tive·ly
 ter·mi·na·tor
ter·mi·nol·o·gy
 ter·mi·nol·o·gies
 ter·mi·no·log·i·cal
 ter·mi·no·log·i·cal·ly
ter·mi·nus
 ter·mi·nus·es
 ter·mi·ni
ter·mite
ter·race
 ter·raced
 ter·rac·ing
ter·ra cot·ta
ter·ra fir·ma
ter·rain
ter·ra·pin
ter·rar·i·um
 ter·rar·ia
 ter·rar·i·ums

218

Ter·re Haute
ter·res·tri·al
 ter·res·tri·al·ly
ter·ri·ble
 ter·ri·ble·ness
 ter·ri·bly
ter·ri·er
ter·rif·ic
 ter·rif·i·cal·ly
ter·ri·fy
 ter·ri·fied
 ter·ri·fy·ing
 ter·ri·fy·ing·ly
ter·ri·to·ry
 ter·ri·to·ri·al
ter·ror
 ter·ror·less
ter·ror·ism
 ter·ror·ist
 ter·ror·is·tic
 ter·ror·less
ter·ror·ize
 ter·ror·ized
 ter·ror·iz·ing
 ter·ror·i·za·tion
 ter·ror·iz·er
ter·ry
 ter·ries
terse
 ters·er
 ters·est
 terse·ly
 terse·ness
ter·ti·ary
Ter·tul·lian
tes·sel·lat·ed
 tes·sel·late
 tes·sel·lat·ing
 tes·sel·la·tion
tes·ta·ment
tes·tate
tes·ta·tor
 tes·ta·trix
 tes·ta·tri·ces
tes·ti·cle
 tes·tic·u·lar
tes·ti·fy
 tes·ti·fied
 tes·ti·fy·ing
 tes·ti·fi·er
tes·ti·mo·ni·al
tes·ti·mo·ny
 tes·ti·mo·nies
tes·tis
 tes·tes
tes·tos·ter·one
tes·ty
 tes·ti·er
 tes·ti·est
 tes·ti·ly
 tes·ti·ness
tet·a·nus
te·tan·ic
 te·tan·i·cal
tête-à-tête

teth·er
tet·ra·eth·yl
tet·ra·he·dron
 tet·ra·he·drons
 tet·ra·he·dra
 tet·ra·he·dral
te·tral·o·gy
 te·tral·o·gies
Teu·ton
Teu·ton·ic
Tex·ar·kana
Tex·as
text·book
tex·tile
tex·tu·al
tex·ture
 tex·tur·al
 tex·tur·al·ly
 tex·tured
Thack·er·ay
Thai·land
thal·a·mus
 tha·lam·ic
 tha·lam·i·cal·ly
Tha·les
thal·li·um
thal·lo·phyte
 thal·lo·phyt·ic
thal·lus
 thal·li
 thal·lus·es
thank
 thank·er
thank·ful
 thank·ful·ly
 thank·ful·ness
thank·less
 thank·less·ly
 thank·less·ness
thanks·giv·ing
thatch
 thatch·ing
 thatch·er
thaw
the·a·ter
 the·a·tre
the·at·ri·cal
 the·at·ri·cal·ism
 the·at·ri·cal·i·ty
 the·at·ri·cal·ly
the·ism
 the·ist
 the·is·tic
 the·is·ti·cal
 the·is·ti·cal·ly
theme
 the·mat·ic
 the·mat·i·cal·ly
them·selves
thence·forth
the·oc·ra·cy
 the·oc·ra·cies
 the·o·crat
 the·o·crat·ic
 the·o·crat·i·cal

this·tle
　this·tly
this·tle·down
thith·er
Thom·as
tho·rax
　tho·rax·es
　tho·ra·ces
　tho·rac·ic
tho·ri·um
thorn
　thorn·less
　thorn·like
thorny
　thorn·i·er
　thorn·i·est
　thorn·i·ness
thor·ough
　thor·ough·ly
　thor·ough·ness
thor·ough·bred
thor·ough·fare
thor·ough·go·ing
thought·ful
　thought·ful·ly
　thought·ful·ness
thought·less
　thought·less·ly
　thought·less·ness
thou·sand
　thou·sandth
thrall
　thrall·dom
thrash·er
thrash·ing
thread
　thread·er
　thread·less
　thread·like
thread·bare
　thread·bare·ness
thready
　thread·i·er
　thread·i·est
　thread·i·ness
threat·en
　threat·en·er
　threat·en·ing·ly
three-deck·er
three-di·men·sion·al
three·fold
three-ring
three·score
three·some
thren·o·dy
　thren·o·dies
　thre·no·di·al
　thren·o·dist
thresh·er
thresh·old
thrift·less
thrift·shop
thrifty
　thrift·i·er
　thrift·i·est

thrift·i·ly
thrift·i·ness
thrill
　thrill·ful
　thrill·ing
　thrill·ing·ly
thril·ler
thrive
　thrived
　thriv·ing
　thriv·er
　thriv·ing·ly
throat
　throat·ed
throaty
　throat·i·er
　throat·i·est
　throat·i·ly
　throat·i·ness
throb
　throbbed
　throb·bing
　throb·ber
throm·bo·sis
　throm·bo·ses
throne
　throned
　thron·ing
　throne·less
throt·tle
　throt·tled
　throt·tling
　throt·tler
through·out
through·way
throw
　throw·ing
　throw·er
throw·a·way
throw·back
thrum
　thrummed
　thrum·ming
　thrum·mer
thrust
　thrust·ing
　thrust·er
thru·way
thud
　thud·ded
　thud·ding
thug
　thug·gery
　thug·gism
　thug·gish
thu·li·um
thumb
　thumb·less
　thumb·like
thumb·nail
thumb·screw
thumb·tack
thump·ing
thun·der
　thun·der·er

this·tle
 this·tly
this·tle·down
thith·er
Thom·as
tho·rax
 tho·rax·es
 tho·ra·ces
 tho·rac·ic
tho·ri·um
thorn
 thorn·less
 thorn·like
thorny
 thorn·i·er
 thorn·i·est
 thorn·i·ness
thor·ough
 thor·ough·ly
 thor·ough·ness
thor·ough·bred
thor·ough·fare
thor·ough·go·ing
thought·ful
 thought·ful·ly
 thought·ful·ness
thought·less
 thought·less·ly
 thought·less·ness
thou·sand
 thou·sandth
thrall
 thrall·dom
thrash·er
thrash·ing
thread
 thread·er
 thread·less
 thread·like
thread·bare
 thread·bare·ness
thready
 thread·i·er
 thread·i·est
 thread·i·ness
threat·en
 threat·en·er
 threat·en·ing·ly
three-deck·er
three-di·men·sion·al
three·fold
three-ring
three·score
three·some
thren·o·dy
 thren·o·dies
 thre·no·di·al
 thren·o·dist
thresh·er
thresh·old
thrift·less
thrift·shop
thrifty
 thrift·i·er
 thrift·i·est

thrift·i·ly
thrift·i·ness
thrill
 thrill·ful
 thrill·ing
 thrill·ing·ly
thril·ler
thrive
 thrived
 thriv·ing
 thriv·er
 thriv·ing·ly
throat
 throat·ed
throaty
 throat·i·er
 throat·i·est
 throat·i·ly
 throat·i·ness
throb
 throbbed
 throb·bing
 throb·ber
throm·bo·sis
 throm·bo·ses
throne
 throned
 thron·ing
 throne·less
throt·tle
 throt·tled
 throt·tling
 throt·tler
through·out
through·way
throw
 throw·ing
 throw·er
 throw·a·way
 throw·back
thrum
 thrummed
 thrum·ming
 thrum·mer
thrust
 thrust·ing
 thrust·er
thru·way
thud
 thud·ded
 thud·ding
thug
 thug·gery
 thug·gism
 thug·gish
thu·li·um
thumb
 thumb·less
 thumb·like
 thumb·nail
 thumb·screw
 thumb·tack
thump·ing
thun·der
 thun·der·er

thun·der·bolt
thun·der·clap
thun·der·cloud
thun·der·head
thun·der·ous
 thun·der·ous·ly
thun·der·show·er
thun·der·storm
thun·der·struck
Thur·ber
Thurs·day
thwack·er
thwart
thyme
 thym·ic
thy·mus
 thy·mic
thy·roid
 thy·roid·less
thy·self
ti·ara
Ti·ber
Ti·be·ri·as
Ti·bet
tib·ia
 tib·i·ae
 tib·i·as
tick·er
tick·et
tick·ing
tick·le
 tick·led
 tick·ling
tick·ler
tick·lish
 tick·lish·ly
 tick·lish·ness
tick·tack·toe
Ti·con·der·o·ga
ti·dal
tid·bit
tid·dly·winks
tide
 tid·ed
 tid·ing
tide·land
tide·wa·ter
ti·dings
ti·dy
 ti·di·er
 ti·di·est
 ti·di·ly
 ti·di·ness
tie
 tied
 ty·ing
tie-in
tie·pin
tier
Tier·ra del Fue·go
tie-up
ti·ger
 ti·ger·ish
 ti·ger·like
tight

tight·ly
tight·ness
tight·en
 tight·en·er
tight-fist·ed
tight-lipped
tight·rope
tight·wad
ti·gress
Ti·gris
til·de
tile
 tiled
 til·ing
till
 till·a·ble
 till·er
till·age
tilt
 tilt·er
tim·ber
tim·bered
tim·ber line
tim·ber wolf
tim·bre
Tim·buk·tu
time
 timed
 tim·ing
time·card
time-hon·ored
time·keep·er
 time·keep·ing
time·less
 time·less·ly
 time·less·ness
time-out
time·piece
tim·er
time·serv·er
 time·serv·ing
time-share
 time-shared
 time-shar·ing
time·ta·ble
time·worn
tim·id
 tim·id·ly
 tim·id·i·ty
 tim·id·ness
tim·ing
tim·or·ous
 tim·or·ous·ly
 tim·or·ous·ness
tim·o·thy
tim·pa·ni
 tim·pa·nist
tin
 tinned
 tin·ning
tinc·ture
 tinc·tured
 tinc·tur·ing
tin·der
tin·der·box

tin·foil
tinge
  tinged
  tinge·ing
tin·gle
  tin·gled
  tin·gling
  tin·gling·ly
  tin·gly
  tin·gli·er
  tin·gli·est
tink·er
tin·kle
  tin·kled
  tin·kling
tin·ny
  tin·ni·er
  tin·ni·est
  tin·ni·ly
  tin·ni·ness
tin·sel
  tin·seled
  tin·sel·ing
  tin·sel·ly
tint
  tint·er
  tint·ing
  tint·less
tin·tin·nab·u·lar
  tin·tin·nab·u·la·tion
tin·type
ti·ny
  ti·ni·er
  ti·ni·est
  ti·ni·ly
  ti·ni·ness
tip
  tipped
  tip·ping
  tip·less
  tip·pa·ble
  tip·per
tip-off
Tip·pe·ca·noe
Tip·pe·rary
tip·ple
  tip·pled
  tip·pling
  tip·pler
tip·ster
tip·sy
  tip·si·er
  tip·si·est
  tip·si·ly
  tip·si·ness
tip·toe
  tip·toed
  tip·to·ing
tip·top
ti·rade
Ti·ra·ne
tire
  tired
  tir·ing
  tire·less

tire·less·ly
  tire·less·ness
tire·some
  tire·some·ly
  tire·some·ness
Tish·chen·ko
tis·sue
ti·tan
ti·tan·ic
  ti·tan·i·cal·ly
ti·ta·ni·um
tithe
  tithed
  tith·ing
  tith·a·ble
  tithe·less
ti·tian
Ti·ti·ca·ca
tit·il·late
  tit·il·lat·ed
  tit·il·lat·ing
  tit·il·la·tion
  tit·il·la·tive
ti·tle
  ti·tled
  ti·tling
tit·mouse
  tit·mice
Ti·to·ism
tit·ter
  tit·ter·er
  tit·ter·ing·ly
tit·tle
tit·u·lar
  tit·u·lar·ly
tiz·zy
  tiz·zies
toad·stool
toady
  toad·ies
  toad·ied
  toad·y·ing
  toad·y·ism
toast·er
toast·mas·ter
  toast·mis·tress
to·bac·co
  to·bac·cos
  to·bac·co·nist
To·ba·go
to·bog·gan
  to·bog·gan·er
  to·bog·gan·ist
Tocque·ville
toc·sin
to·day
tod·dle
  tod·dled
  tod·dling
  tod·dler
tod·dy
  tod·dies
to-do
toed
toe·hold

223

toe·less
toe·nail
tof·fee
to·ga
  to·gas
  to·gae
to·geth·er
  to·geth·er·ness
tog·gle
  tog·gled
  tog·gling
To·go
toil·er
toi·let
toi·let·ry
toil·some
  toil·some·ly
  toil·some·ness
To·kay
to·ken
To·kyo
To·le·do
tol·er·a·ble
  tol·er·a·ble·ness
  tol·er·a·bil·i·ty
  tol·er·a·bly
tol·er·ance
tol·er·ant
  tol·er·ant·ly
tol·er·ate
  tol·er·at·ed
  tol·er·at·ing
  tol·er·a·tion
  tol·er·a·tive
  tol·er·a·tor
toll·booth
toll·gate
toll·house
toll·way
Tol·stoy
tol·u·ene
tom·a·hawk
to·ma·to
  to·ma·toes
tomb
  tomb·less
  tomb·like
tom·boy
  tom·boy·ish
  tom·boy·ish·ness
tomb·stone
tom·cat
tom·fool·ery
  tom·fool·er·ies
to·mor·row
tom·tit
tom-tom
to·nal·i·ty
  to·nal·i·ties
tone
  ton·al
  ton·al·ly
  tone·less
  tone·less·ly
  tone·less·ness

tone-deaf
Ton·ga
tongue
tongue-in-cheek
tongue-lash
  tongue-lash·ing
tongue-tied
ton·ic
  ton·i·cal·ly
to·night
ton·nage
ton·sil
  ton·sil·lar
  ton·sil·lec·to·my
  ton·sil·lec·to·mies
  ton·sil·li·tis
  ton·so·ri·al
ton·sure
  ton·sured
  ton·sur·ing
tool·box
tool·house
tool·mak·er
  tool·mak·ing
tool·room
tooth·ache
  tooth·achy
tooth·brush
tooth·less
  tooth·less·ly
  tooth·less·ness
tooth·paste
tooth·pick
tooth·some
  tooth·some·ly
  tooth·some·ness
toothy
  tooth·i·er
  tooth·i·est
  tooth·i·ly
  tooth·i·ness
top
  topped
  top·ping
to·paz
top·coat
tope
  toped
  top·ing
To·pe·ka
top·flight
top-heavy
to·pi
  to·pis
to·pi·ary
  to·pi·ar·ies
top·ic
top·i·cal
top·i·cal·i·ty
  top·i·cal·i·ties
top·knot
top·less
top·most
top·notch
  top·notch·er

224

to·pog·ra·phy
  to·pog·ra·phies
  to·pog·ra·pher
  top·o·graph·i·cal
  top·o:graph·i·cal·ly
top·ping
top·ple
  top·pled
  top·pling
top·se·cret
top·soil
top·sy·tur·vy
  top·sy·tur·vies
  top·sy·tur·vi·ly
  top·sy·tur·vi·ness
toque
To·rah
torch·bear·er
torch·light
tor·e·a·dor
to·re·ro
  to·re·ros
to·rii
tor·ment
  tor·ment·ing·ly
  tor·men·tor
tor·na·do
  tor·na·does
  tor·na·dos
  tor·nad·ic
To·ron·to
tor·pe·do
  tor·pe·does
  tor·pe·doed
  tor·pe·do·ing
tor·pid
  tor·pid·i·ty
  tor·pid·ly
tor·por
torque
Tor·rens
tor·rent
  tor·ren·tial
  tor·ren·tial·ly
tor·rid
  tor·rid·i·ty
  tor·rid·ness
  tor·rid·ly
tor·sion
  tor·sion·al
  tor·sion·al·ly
tor·so
  tor·sos
  tor·si
torte
tor·til·la
  tor·til·las
tor·tois
  tor·toise·shell
tor·to·ni
tor·tu·ous
  tor·tu·ous·ly
  tor·tu·ous·ness
tor·ture
  tor·tured

tor·tur·ing
tor·tur·a·ble
tor·tured·ly
tor·tur·er
tor·ture·some
toss·er
toss·up
to·tal
  to·taled
  to·tal·ing
to·tal·i·tar·i·an
  to·tal·i·tar·i·an·ism
to·tal·i·ty
  to·tal·i·ties
to·tal·i·za·tor
to·tal·ly
tote
  tot·ed
  tot·ing
  tot·er
to·tem
  to·tem·ic
  to·tem·ism
  to·tem·ist
  to·tem·is·tic
tot·ter
  tot·ter·er
  tot·ter·ing
  tot·ter·ing·ly
tou·can
touch
  touch·a·ble
  touch·a·ble·ness
  touch·er
  touch·down
  tou·ché
  touched
  touch·ing
  touch·ing·ly
  touch·ing·ness
  touch·stone
  touch-tone
touch-type
  touch-typed
  touch-typ·ing
  touch-typ·ist
touchy
  touch·i·er
  touch·i·est
  touch·i·ly
  touch·i·ness
tough
  tough·ly
  tough·ness
tough·en
  tough·en·er
Tou·lon
Tou·louse
tou·pee
tour de force
  tours de force
tour·ism
tour·ist
tour·ma·line
tour·na·ment

tour·ni·quet
tou·sle
 tou·sled
 tou·sling
Tous·saint
tout·er
tow·age
to·ward
tow·el
 tow·eled
 tow·el·ing
tow·er
 tow·ered
 tow·er·ing
tow·head
 tow·head·ed
tow·line
town·ship
towns·man
 towns·men
towns·peo·ple
tow·path
tow·rope
tox·e·mia
tox·ic
 tox·i·cal
 tox·i·cal·ly
tox·ic·i·ty
 tox·ic·i·ties
tox·i·col·o·gy
 tox·i·co·log·i·cal
 tox·i·co·log·i·cal·ly
 tox·i·col·o·gist
tox·in
tox·oid
toy·like
trace
 traced
 trac·ing
 trace·a·ble
 trace·a·ble·ness
 trace·a·bly
 trace·less
 trac·er
trac·ery
 trac·er·ies
tra·chea
 tra·che·ae
 tra·che·as
 tra·che·al
tra·che·ot·o·my
 tra·che·ot·o·mies
tra·cho·ma
track·age
track·er
trac·ta·ble
 trac·ta·bil·i·ty
 trac·ta·ble·ness
 trac·ta·bly
trac·tion
 trac·tion·al
 trac·tive
trac·tor
trade
 trad·ed

trad·ing
trade-in
trade·mark
trad·er
trades·man
 trades·men
trade·wind
trad·ing post
tra·di·tion
 tra·di·tion·less
 tra·di·tion·al
 tra·di·tion·al·ism
 tra·di·tion·al·ist
 tra·di·tion·al·ly
tra·duce
 tra·duced
 tra·duc·ing
 tra·duce·ment
 tra·duc·er
Tra·fal·gar
traf·fic
 traf·ficked
 traf·fick·ing
 traf·fick·er
tra·ge·di·an
trag·e·dy
 trag·e·dies
trag·ic
 trag·i·cal
 trag·i·cal·ly
 trag·i·cal·ness
trail·blaz·er
 trail·blaz·ing
trail·er
trail·er camp
train
 train·a·ble
 train·er
 train·ing
 train·man
 train·men
traipse
 traipsed
 traips·ing
trai·tor
 trai·tor·ous
 trai·tor·ous·ly
tra·jec·to·ry
 tra·jec·to·ries
tram·mel
 tram·meled
 tram·mel·ing
 tram·mel·er
tramp·er
tram·ple
 tram·pled
 tram·pling
 tram·pler
tram·po·line
 tram·po·lin·er
 tram·po·lin·ist
trance
tran·quil
 tran·quil·li·ty
 tran·quil·ly

tran·quil·ness
tran·quil·ize
  tran·quil·ized
  tran·quil·iz·ing
tran·quil·iz·er
trans·act
  trans·ac·tor
trans·ac·tion
  trans·ac·tion·al
trans·al·pine
trans·at·lan·tic
trans·ceiv·er
tran·scend
  tran·scend·ent
tran·scen·den·tal
  tran·scen·den·tal·ly
  tran·scen·den·tal·ism
trans·con·ti·nen·tal
tran·scribe
  tran·scribed
  tran·scrib·ing
  tran·scrib·er
tran·script
tran·scrip·tion
  tran·scrip·tion·al
  tran·scrip·tive
tran·sept
  tran·sep·tal
  tran·sep·tal·ly
trans·fer
  trans·ferred
  trans·fer·ring
  trans·fer·al
  trans·fer·a·ble
  trans·fer·ence
trans·fig·ure
  trans·fig·ured
  trans·fig·ur·ing
  trans·fig·ure·ment
  trans·fig·u·ra·tion
trans·fix
  trans·fixed
  trans·fix·ing
  trans·fix·ion
trans·form
  trans·form·a·ble
  trans·for·ma·tion
  trans·form·a·tive
trans·form·er
trans·fuse
  trans·fused
  trans·fus·ing
  trans·fus·a·ble
  trans·fu·sion
trans·gress
  trans·gres·sive
  trans·gres·sor
  trans·gres·sion
tran·sient
  tran·sient·ly
tran·sis·tor
tran·sis·tor·ize
  tran·sis·tor·ized
  tran·sis·tor·iz·ing
trans·it

tran·si·tion
  tran·si·tion·al
  tran·si·tion·al·ly
tran·si·tive
  tran·si·tive·ly
  tran·si·tive·ness
  tran·si·tiv·i·ty
tran·si·to·ry
  tran·si·to·ri·ly
  tran·si·to·ri·ness
trans·late
  trans·lat·ed
  trans·lat·ing
  trans·lat·a·bil·i·ty
  trans·lat·a·ble
  trans·lat·or
trans·la·tion
  trans·la·tion·al
  trans·la·tive
trans·lit·er·ate
  trans·lit·er·at·ed
  trans·lit·er·at·ing
  trans·lit·er·a·tion
trans·lu·cent
  trans·lu·cence
  trans·lu·cen·cy
  trans·lu·cent·ly
trans·mi·grate
  trans·mi·grat·ed
  trans·mi·grat·ing
  trans·mi·gra·tion
  trans·mi·gra·tor
  trans·mi·gra·to·ry
trans·mis·sion
  trans·mis·si·bil·i·ty
  trans·mis·siv·i·ty
  trans·mis·si·ble
  trans·mis·sive
trans·mit
  trans·mit·ted
  trans·mit·ting
  trans·mit·ta·ble
  trans·mit·tal
trans·mit·ter
trans·mute
  trans·mut·ed
  trans·mut·ing
  trans·mut·er
  trans·mut·a·ble·ness
  trans·mut·a·bil·i·ty
  trans·mut·a·bly
  trans·mu·ta·tion
  trans·mut·a·ble
trans·na·tion·al
trans·o·ce·an·ic
tran·som
  tran·somed
trans·pa·cif·ic
trans·par·ent
  trans·par·en·cy
  trans·par·en·cies
  trans·par·ent·ly
  trans·par·ent·ness
tran·spire
  tran·spired

tran·spir·ing
trans·plant
  trans·plant·a·ble
  trans·plan·ta·tion
  trans·plant·er
tran·spon·der
trans·port
  trans·port·a·bil·i·ty
  trans·port·a·ble
  trans·port·er
trans·por·ta·tion
trans·pose
  trans·posed
  trans·pos·ing
  trans·pos·a·ble
  trans·po·si·tion
Trans·vaal
trans·verse
  trans·verse·ly
trans·ves·tism
  trans·ves·tite
Tran·syl·va·nia
trap
  trapped
  trap·ping
tra·peze
  tra·pez·ist
tra·pe·zi·um
  tra·pe·zi·ums
  tra·pe·zia
trap·e·zoid
  trap·e·zoi·dal
trap·pings
Trap·pist
trap·shoot·ing
  trap·shoot·er
trash
  trash·i·ly
  trash·i·ness
  trashy
  trash·i·er
  trash·i·est
trau·ma
  trau·mas
  trau·ma·ta
  trau·mat·ic
  trau·mat·i·cal·ly
tra·vail
tra·vel
  tra·veled
  tra·vel·ing
  trav·el·er
trav·e·logue
  trav·e·log
trav·erse
  trav·ersed
  trav·ers·ing
  tra·vers·a·ble
  tra·vers·al
  tra·vers·er
trav·es·ty
  trav·es·ties
  trav·es·tied
  trav·es·ty·ing
trawl·er

treach·er·ous
  treach·er·ous·ly
  treach·er·ous·ness
treach·ery
  treach·er·ies
trea·cle
  trea·cly
  trea·cli·er
  trea·cli·est
tread
  trod·den
  tread·ing
  tread·er
trea·dle
tread·mill
trea·son
  trea·son·a·ble
  trea·son·ous
  trea·son·a·bly
treas·ure
  treas·ured
  treas·ur·ing
  treas·ur·a·ble
treas·ur·er
  treas·ur·er·ship
treas·ure-trove
treas·ury
  treas·ur·ies
treat
  treat·a·ble
  treat·er
trea·tise
treat·ment
trea·ty
  trea·ties
tre·ble
  tre·bled
  tre·bling
  tre·bly
tre·foil
  tre·foiled
trek
  trekked
  trek·king
  trek·ker
trel·lis
trem·ble
  trem·bled
  trem·bling
  trem·bler
  trem·bly
  trem·bli·er
  trem·bli·est
  trem·bling·ly
tre·men·dous
  tre·men·dous·ly
  tre·men·dous·ness
trem·o·lo
  trem·o·los
trem·or
  trem·or·ous
trem·u·lous
  trem·u·lous·ly
  trem·u·lous·ness
trench·ant

trench·an·cy
trench·ant·ly
trench·er·man
trench·er·men
trendy
trend·i·er
trend·i·est
Tren·ton
tre·pan
tre·panned
tre·pan·ning
trep·an·a·tion
tre·phine
tre·phined
tre·phin·ing
treph·i·na·tion
trep·i·da·tion
tres·pass
tres·pass·er
tres·tle
tri·ad
tri·ad·ic
tri·ad·i·cal·ly
tri·al
tri·an·gle
tri·an·gu·lar
tri·an·gu·lar·i·ty
tri·an·gu·lar·ly
tri·an·gu·late
tri·an·gu·lat·ed
tri·an·gu·lat·ing
tri·an·gu·la·tion
tribe
trib·al
tribes·man
tribes·men
trib·u·la·tion
tri·bu·nal
trib·une
trib·une·ship
trib·u·nate
trib·u·tary
trib·u·tar·ies
trib·u·tar·i·ly
trib·ute
tri·ceps
tri·cep·ses
trich·i·no·sis
trick·ery
trick·er·ies
trick·le
trick·led
trick·ling
trick·ster
tricky
trick·i·er
trick·i·est
trick·i·ly
trick·i·ness
tri·col·or
tri·col·ored
tri·cus·pid
tri·cy·cle
tri·dent
tri·den·tate

tri·den·tal
tri·di·men·sion·al
tri·di·men·sion·al·i·ty
tri·en·ni·al
tri·en·ni·al·ly
tri·en·ni·um
tri·en·ni·ums
tri·en·nia
tri·fle
tri·fled
tri·fling
trif·ler
tri·fling·ly
tri·fling·ness
tri·fo·cals
tri·fo·li·ate
trig·ger
trig·ger·less
trig·ger·hap·py
trig·ger·man
trig·ger·men
trig·o·nom·e·try
trig·o·no·met·ric
trig·o·no·met·ri·cal
trig·o·no·met·ri·cal·ly
tril·lion
tril·lionth
tri·lo·bite
tril·o·gy
tril·o·gies
trim
trimmed
trim·ming
trim·mer
trim·mest
trim·ly
trim·ness
tri·mes·ter
tri·mes·tral
tri·mes·tri·al
tri·month·ly
Trin·i·dad
tri·ni·tro·tol·u·ene
Trin·i·ty
Trin·i·ties
trin·ket
trio
tri·os
trip
tripped
trip·ping
trip·ping·ly
tri·par·tite
tri·par·tite·ly
tri·par·ti·tion
trip·ham·mer
tri·ple
tri·pled
tri·pling
tri·ply
tri·plet
trip·li·cate
trip·li·cat·ed
trip·li·cat·ing
trip·li·ca·tion

tri·pod
 trip·o·dal
 tri·pod·ic
Trip·o·li
trip·tych
tri·sect
 tri·sec·tion
 tri·sec·tor
trite
 trite·ly
 trite·ness
trit·u·rate
 trit·u·rat·ed
 trit·u·rat·ing
 trit·u·ra·ble
 trit·u·ra·tor
tri·umph
 tri·um·phal
 tri·um·phal·ly
 tri·um·phant
 tri·um·phant·ly
tri·um·vir
 tri·um·vi·ral
 tri·um·vi·rate
triv·et
triv·ia
triv·i·al
 triv·i·al·i·ty
 triv·i·al·i·ties
 triv·i·al·i·za·tion
 triv·i·al·ly
tri·week·ly
 tri·week·lies
tro·che
trog·lo·dyte
 trog·lo·dyt·ic
troi·ka
Tro·jan
troll
 troll·er
trol·ley
 trol·leys
 trol·leyed
 trol·ley·ing
trol·lop
Trol·lope
trom·bone
 trom·bon·ist
troop·er
tro·phy
 tro·phies
trop·ic
trop·i·cal
 trop·i·cal·ly
tro·pism
 tro·pis·tic
trop·o·sphere
 trop·o·spher·ic
trot
 trot·ted
 trot·ting
trot·ter
trou·ba·dour
trou·ble
 trou·bled

trou·bling
 trou·bler
trou·ble·mak·er
trou·ble·shoot·er
trou·ble·some
trough
 trough·like
trounce
 trounced
 trounc·ing
troupe
 trouped
 troup·ing
 troup·er
trou·sers
trous·seau
 trous·seaux
 trous·seaus
trow·el
 trow·el·er
tru·an·cy
 tru·an·cies
 tru·ant·ry
tru·ant
truck·age
truck·er
truck·ing
truck·load
truc·u·lent
 truc·u·lence
 truc·u·lent·ly
trudge
 trudged
 trudg·ing
 trudg·er
true
 tru·er
 tru·est
 true·ness
true-blue
true·love
truf·fle
tru·ism
 tru·is·tic
tru·ly
trump
 trump·er
trum·pet
 trum·pet·like
 trum·pet·er
trun·cate
 trun·cat·ed
 trun·cat·ing
 trun·ca·tion
trun·cheon
 trun·cheoned
trun·dle
 trun·dled
 trun·dling
 trun·dler
truss·er
trust
 trust·er
 trust·less
trus·tee

230

trus·teed
trus·tee·ing
trus·tee·ship
trust·ful
trust·ful·ly
trust·wor·thy
trust·wor·thi·ly
trust·wor·thi·ness
trusty
trust·i·er
trust·i·est
trust·i·ness
truth·ful
truth·ful·ly
truth·ful·ness
try
tried
try·ing
try·out
tryst
tset·se
T-shirt
Tshom·be
T-square
tsu·na·mi
tub
tubbed
tub·bing
tu·ba
tu·bas
tu·bae
tu·bal
tub·by
tub·bi·er
tub·bi·est
tub·bi·ness
tube
tubed
tub·ing
tube·less
tu·ber
tu·ber·cle
tu·ber·cu·lar
tu·ber·cu·lar·ly
tu·ber·cu·lin
tu·ber·cu·lo·sis
tu·ber·cu·lous
tu·ber·ous
tu·bu·lar
tu·bule
tuck·er
tuck-point
tuck-point·er
tuck-point·ing
Tuc·son
Tu·dor
Tues·day
tuf·fet
tuft
tuft·er
tufty
tuft·i·er
tuft·i·est
tug-boat
tu·i·tion

tu·i·tion·al
tu·lip
Tul·sa
tum·ble
tum·bled
tum·bling
tum·ble-down
tum·bler
tum·ble·weed
tu·mid
tu·mid·i·ty
tum·my
tum·mies
tu·mor
tu·mor·ous
tu·mult
tu·mul·tu·ous
tu·mul·tu·ous·ly
tu·mul·tu·ous·ness
tu·na
tun·a·ble
tun·dra
tune
tuned
tun·ing
tune·ful
tune·less
tun·er
tune-up
tung·sten
tu·nic
Tu·nis
Tu·ni·sia
tun·nel
tun·neled
tun·nel·ing
tun·nel·er
tur·ban
tur·baned
tur·bid
tur·bid·i·ty
tur·bid·ness
tur·bine
tur·bo
tur·bos
tur·bo·car
tur·bo·charg·er
tur·bo·fan
tur·bo·jet
tur·bo·pro·pel·ler
tur·bo·su·per·charg·er
tur·bot
tur·bu·lence
tur·bu·len·cy
tur·bu·lent
tu·reen
tur·gid
tur·gid·i·ty
tur·gid·ness
Tu·rin
Tur·ke·stan
tur·key
tur·keys
Turk·ish
tur·mer·ic

tur·moil
turn·a·bout
turn·a·round
Turn·bull
turn·coat
turn·down
turn·er
turn·ing
tur·nip
turn·key
turn·off
turn·out
turn·o·ver
turn·pike
turn·stile
turn·ta·ble
turn·up
tur·pen·tine
  tur·pen·tined
  tur·pen·tin·ing
tur·pi·tude
tur·quoise
tur·ret
tur·tle
tur·tle·dove
tur·tle·neck
Tus·ca·loo·sa
Tus·ca·ny
tusk
  tusked
  tusk·er
Tus·ke·gee
tus·sive
tus·sle
  tus·sled
  tus·sling
tu·te·lage
tu·tor
  tu·tor·ship
tu·tor·age
tu·to·ri·al
tut·ti·frut·ti
tu·tu
tux·e·do
twad·dle
twain
twang
  twangy
  twang·i·er
  twang·i·est
tweed
  tweedy
  tweed·i·er
  tweed·i·est
  tweed·i·ness
tweet·er
tweez·ers
  tweeze
  tweezed
  tweez·ing
twelve
  twelfth
twen·ty
  twen·ties
  twen·ti·eth

twen·ty-one
twid·dle
  twid·dled
  twid·dling
  twid·dler
twig
  twig·gy
  twig·gi·er
  twig·gi·est
twi·light
twilled
twin
  twinned
  twin·ning
twine
  twined
  twin·ing
twinge
  twinged
  twing·ing
twin·kle
  twin·kled
  twin·kling
  twin·kler
twirl
  twirl·er
  twirly
  twirl·i·er
  twirl·i·est
twist·er
twit
  twit·ted
  twit·ting
twitch·er
twit·ter
  twit·ter·er
  twit·tery
two-bit
two-di·men·sion·al
two-faced
  two-fac·ed·ly
  two-fac·ed·ness
two-fist·ed
two-sid·ed
  two-sid·ed·ness
two·some
two-step
  two-stepped
  two-step·ping
two-time
  two-timed
  two-tim·ing
two-way
ty·coon
tym·bal
tym·pan·ic
type
  typed
  typ·ing
  typ·a·ble
type·cast
type·face
type·script
type·set·ter
  type·set

type·set·ting
type·write
  type·wrote
  type·writ·ten
  type·writ·ing
type·writ·er
ty·phoid
ty·phoon
ty·phus
typ·i·cal
  typ·ic
  typ·i·cal·ly
  typ·i·cal·ness
  typ·i·cal·i·ty
typ·i·fy
  typ·i·fied
  typ·i·fy·ing
  typ·i·fi·ca·tion
typ·ist
ty·po
ty·pog·ra·phy
  ty·pog·ra·pher
  ty·po·graph·ic
  ty·po·graph·i·cal
  ty·po·graph·i·cal·ly
ty·ran·ni·cal
  ty·ran·nic
  ty·ran·ni·cal·ly
tyr·an·nize
  tyr·an·nized
  tyr·an·niz·ing
  tyr·an·niz·er
tyr·an·ny
  tyr·an·nies
ty·rant
ty·ro
Ty·ro·le·an
Uban·gi
ubiq·ui·tous
  ubiq·ui·tary
  ubiq·ui·tous·ly
  ubiq·ui·tous·ness
ubiq·ui·ty
U-boat
ud·der
Ugan·da
ug·ly
  ug·li·er
  ug·li·est
  ug·li·ly
  ug·li·ness
ukase
Ukraine
uku·le·le
Ulan Ba·tor
Ul·bricht
ul·cer
  ul·cer·ous
ul·cer·ate
  ul·cer·at·ed
  ul·cer·at·ing
  ul·cer·a·tion
ul·na
  ul·nae
  ul·nas

ul·nar
ul·ster
ul·te·ri·or
  ul·te·ri·or·ly
ul·ti·mate
  ul·ti·mate·ly
  ul·ti·mate·ness
ul·ti·ma·tum
  ul·ti·ma·tums
  ul·ti·ma·ta
ul·tra
ul·tra·con·serv·a·tive
ul·tra·high
ul·tra·ma·rine
ul·tra·son·ic
ul·tra·vi·o·let
ul·u·late
  ul·u·lat·ed
  ul·u·lat·ing
  ul·u·lant
  ul·u·la·tion
Ulys·ses
um·bel
  um·bel·lar
  um·bel·late
  um·bel·lat·ed
  um·bel·late·ly
um·ber
um·bil·i·cal
um·bra
  um·bras
  um·brae
um·brage
  um·bra·geous
  um·bra·geous·ly
  um·bra·geous·ness
um·brel·la
Um·bri·an
u·mi·ak
um·laut
um·pire
  um·pired
  um·pir·ing
ump·teen
  ump·teenth
un·a·bashed
  un·a·bash·ed·ly
un·a·ble
un·a·bridged
un·ac·cep·ta·ble
  un·ac·cept·ed
un·ac·com·pa·nied
un·ac·count·a·ble
  un·ac·count·a·ble·ness
  un·ac·count·a·bly
un·ac·cus·tomed
un·ac·quaint·ed
un·a·dorned
un·a·dul·ter·at·ed
  un·a·dul·ter·at·ed·ly
un·ad·vised
  un·ad·vis·ed·ly
  un·ad·vis·ed·ness
un·af·fect·ed
  un·af·fect·ed·ly

un·af·fect·ed·ness
un·a·fraid
un·A·mer·i·can
unan·i·mous
una·nim·i·ty
unan·i·mous·ly
unan·i·mous·ness
un·an·swer·a·ble
un·an·swer·a·bly
un·an·swered
un·ap·pe·tiz·ing
un·ap·pre·ci·at·ed
un·ap·pre·ci·a·tive
un·ap·proach·a·ble
un·ap·proach·a·ble·ness
un·ap·proach·a·bly
un·ap·proached
un·armed
un·a·shamed
un·asked
un·a·spir·ing
un·as·sail·a·ble
un·as·sail·a·ble·ness
un·as·sail·a·bly
un·as·sailed
un·at·tached
un·at·tain·a·ble
un·at·tained
un·at·tend·ed
un·au·thor·ized
un·a·vail·a·ble
un·a·vail·a·bil·i·ty
un·a·vail·a·bly
un·a·void·a·ble
un·a·void·a·bil·i·ty
un·a·void·a·ble·ness
un·a·void·a·bly
un·a·ware
un·a·ware·ness
un·a·wares
un·backed
un·bal·anced
un·bar
un·barred
un·bar·ring
un·bear·a·ble
un·bear·a·ble·ness
un·bear·a·bly
un·beat·en
un·beat·a·ble
un·be·com·ing
un·be·com·ing·ly
un·be·com·ing·ness
un·be·lief
un·be·liev·a·ble
un·be·liev·a·bly
un·be·liev·er
un·be·liev·ing
un·be·liev·ing·ly
un·be·liev·ing·ness
un·bend
un·bend·ed
un·bend·ing
un·bend·ing·ly
un·bend·ing·ness

un·bi·ased
un·bi·ased·ly
un·bid·den
un·bind
un·bound
un·bind·ing
un·blem·ished
un·bolt
un·bolt·ed
un·born
un·bos·om
un·bound
un·bound·ed
un·bound·ed·ly
un·bound·ed·ness
un·bowed
un·break·a·ble
un·bri·dle
un·bri·dled
un·bri·dling
un·bro·ken
un·bro·ken·ly
un·buck·le
un·buck·led
un·buck·ling
un·bur·den
un·but·ton
un·but·toned
un·called-for
un·can·ny
un·can·ni·er
un·can·ni·est
un·can·ni·ly
un·can·ni·ness
un·cap
un·capped
un·cap·ping
un·ceas·ing
un·ceas·ing·ly
un·ceas·ing·ness
un·cer·e·mo·ni·ous
un·cer·e·mo·ni·ous·ly
un·cer·e·mo·ni·ous·ness
un·cer·tain
un·cer·tain·ly
un·cer·tain·ness
un·cer·tain·ty
un·cer·tain·ties
un·chal·lenged
un·change·a·ble
un·change·a·bly
un·changed
un·chang·ing
un·char·i·ta·ble
un·char·i·ta·ble·ness
un·char·i·ta·bly
un·chart·ed
un·chris·tian
un·cir·cum·cised
un·civ·il
un·civ·il·ly
un·civ·i·lized
un·class·i·fi·a·ble
un·clas·si·fied
un·cle

un·clean
  un·clean·ly
  un·clean·ness
un·clear
un·cloak
un·clothe
  un·clothed
  un·cloth·ing
un·clut·tered
un·coil
un·com·fort·a·ble
  un·com·fort·a·ble·ness
  un·com·fort·a·bly
un·com·mit·ted
un·com·mon
  un·com·mon·ly
  un·com·mon·ness
un·com·mu·ni·ca·tive
  un·com·mu·ni·ca·tive·ly
  un·com·mu·ni·ca·tive·ness
un·com·pre·hend·ing
un·com·pro·mis·ing
  un·com·pro·mised
  un·com·pro·mis·ing·ly
  un·com·pro·mis·ing·ness
un·con·cern
un·con·cerned
  un·con·cern·ed·ly
  un·con·cern·ed·ness
un·con·di·tion·al
  un·con·di·tion·al·ly
un·con·firmed
un·con·nect·ed
  un·con·nect·ed·ly
  un·con·nect·ed·ness
un·con·quer·a·ble
  un·con·quered
un·con·scion·a·ble
  un·con·scion·a·ble·ness
  un·con·scion·a·bly
un·con·scious
  un·con·scious·ly
  un·con·scious·ness
un·con·sti·tu·tion·al
  un·con·sti·tu·tion·al·i·ty
  un·con·sti·tu·tion·al·ly
un·con·strained
un·con·test·ed
un·con·trol·la·ble
  un·con·trol·la·bly
  un·con·trolled
un·con·ven·tion·al
  un·con·ven·tion·al·i·ty
  un·con·ven·tion·al·ly
un·count·ed
un·cou·ple
  un·cou·pled
  un·cou·pling
un·couth
  un·couth·ly
  un·couth·ness
un·cov·er
  un·cov·ered
unc·tion
unc·tu·ous

unc·tu·os·i·ty
unc·tu·ous·ness
unc·tu·ous·ly
un·curl
un·cut
un·daunt·ed
  un·daunt·ed·ly
  un·daunt·ed·ness
un·de·ceive
  un·de·ceived
  un·de·ceiv·ing
  un·de·ceiv·a·ble
un·de·cid·ed
  un·de·cid·ed·ly
  un·de·cid·ed·ness
un·de·fined
  un·de·fin·a·ble
un·de·mon·stra·tive
  un·de·mon·stra·tive·ly
  un·de·mon·stra·tive·ness
un·de·ni·a·ble
  un·de·ni·a·ble·ness
  un·de·ni·a·bly
  un·de·nied
un·de·pend·a·ble
  un·de·pend·a·bil·i·ty
  un·de·pend·a·ble·ness
un·der
un·der·a·chiev·er
  un·der·a·chiev·ment
un·der·act
un·der·age
un·der·arm
un·der·bel·ly
  un·der·bel·lies
un·der·brush
un·der·car·riage
un·der·charge
  un·der·charged
  un·der·charg·ing
un·der·class·man
  un·der·class·men
un·der·clothes
un·der·coat
un·der·cov·er
un·der·cur·rent
un·der·cut
  un·der·cut·ting
un·der·de·vel·oped
  un·der·de·vel·op·ing
un·der·dog
un·der·done
un·der·es·ti·mate
  un·der·es·ti·mat·ed
  un·der·es·ti·mat·ing
  un·der·es·ti·ma·tion
un·der·foot
un·der·gar·ment
un·der·go
  un·der·went
  un·der·gone
  un·der·go·ing
un·der·grad·u·ate
un·der·ground
un·der·growth

un·der·hand
un·der·hand·ed
  un·der·hand·ed·ly
  un·der·hand·ed·ness
un·der·lie
 un·der·lay
 un·der·lain
 un·der·ly·ing
un·der·line
 un·der·lined
 un·der·lin·ing
un·der·ling
un·der·mine
 un·der·mined
 un·der·min·ing
 un·der·min·er
un·der·most
un·der·neath
un·der·pants
un·der·pass
un·der·pin·ning
un·der·priv·i·leged
un·der·rate
 un·der·rat·ed
 un·der·rat·ing
un·der·score
 un·der·scored
 un·der·scor·ing
un·der·sea
un·der·sec·re·tary
 un·der·sec·re·tar·ies
un·der·sell
 un·der·sold
 un·der·sell·ing
 un·der·sell·er
un·der·shirt
un·der·shot
un·der·side
un·der·signed
un·der·stand
 un·der·stood
 un·der·stand·ing
 un·der·stand·a·bil·i·ty
 un·der·stand·a·ble
 un·der·stand·a·bly
 un·der·stand·ing·ly
un·der·state
 un·der·stat·ed
 un·der·stat·ing
 un·der·state·ment
un·der·stood
un·der·study
 un·der·stud·ied
 un·der·stud·y·ing
 un·der·stud·ies
un·der·take
 un·der·took
 un·der·tak·en
 un·der·tak·ing
 un·der·tak·er
un·der·the·coun·ter
un·der·tone
un·der·tow
un·der·wa·ter
un·der·wear

un·der·weight
un·der·world
un·der·write
 un·der·wrote
 un·der·writ·ten
 un·der·writ·ing
 un·der·writ·er
un·de·sir·a·ble
 un·de·sir·a·bil·i·ty
 un·de·sir·a·ble·ness
 un·de·sir·a·bly
un·de·ter·mined
un·dies
un·dip·lo·mat·ic
 un·dip·lo·mat·i·cal·ly
un·dis·ci·plined
un·dis·closed
un·dis·posed
un·dis·tin·guished
un·di·vid·ed
un·do
 un·did
 un·done
 un·do·ing
 un·do·er
un·doubt·ed
 un·doubt·ed·ly
 un·doubt·ing
un·dress
 un·dressed
 un·dress·ing
Und·set
un·due
un·du·lant
un·du·late
 un·du·lat·ed
 un·du·lat·ing
 un·du·la·tion
un·du·ly
un·dy·ing
un·earth
un·earth·ly
 un·earth·li·ness
un·easy
 un·eas·i·er
 un·eas·i·est
 un·ease
 un·eas·i·ly
 un·eas·i·ness
un·em·ployed
un·em·ploy·ment
un·e·qual
 un·e·qual·ly
 un·e·qualed
un·e·quiv·o·cal
 un·e·quiv·o·cal·ly
un·err·ing
 un·err·ing·ly
un·eth·i·cal
 un·eth·i·cal·ly
un·e·ven
 un·e·ven·ly
 un·e·ven·ness
un·ex·cep·tion·a·ble
 un·ex·cep·tion·a·ble·ness

un·ex·cep·tion·a·bly
un·ex·pect·ed
un·ex·pect·ed·ly
un·ex·pect·ed·ness
un·fail·ing
un·fail·ing·ly
un·fail·ing·ness
un·faith·ful
un·faith·ful·ly
un·faith·ful·ness
un·fa·mil·iar
un·fa·mil·i·ar·i·ty
un·fa·mil·iar·ly
un·fast·en
un·fas·ten·a·ble
un·fas·ten·er
un·fath·om·a·ble
un·fa·vor·a·ble
un·fa·vor·a·ble·ness
un·fa·vor·a·bly
un·feel·ing
un·feel·ing·ly
un·feel·ing·ness
un·feigned
un·feign·ed·ly
un·fet·ter
un·fet·tered
un·fin·ished
un·fit
un·fit·ly
un·fit·ness
un·fit·ting
un·flat·ter·ing
un·flinch·ing
un·flinch·ing·ly
un·fold
un·for·get·ta·ble
un·for·get·ta·bly
un·for·giv·a·ble
un·for·tu·nate
un·for·tu·nate·ly
un·for·tu·nate·ness
un·found·ed
un·found·ed·ness
un·friend·ly
un·friend·li·er
un·friend·li·est
un·friend·li·ness
un·frock
un·furl
un·gain·ly
un·gain·li·ness
un·gird
un·gird·ed
un·gird·ing
un·glazed
un·god·ly
un·god·li·er
un·god·li·est
un·god·li·ness
un·gov·ern·a·able
un·gov·ern·a·ble·ness
un·gov·ern·a·bly
un·gra·cious
un·gra·cious·ly

un·gra·cious·ness
un·gram·mat·i·cal
un·gram·mat·i·cal·l
un·grate·ful
un·grate·ful·ly
un·grate·ful·ness
un·guard·ed
un·guard·ed·ly
un·guard·ed·ness
un·guent
un·gu·late
un·ham·pered
un·hand
un·handy
un·hand·i·er
un·hand·i·est
un·hap·py
un·hap·pi·er
un·hap·pi·est
un·hap·pi·ly
un·hap·pi·ness
un·harmed
un·healthy
un·health·i·er
un·health·i·est
un·health·i·ly
un·health·i·ness
un·heard
un·heed·ed
un·heed·ful
un·heed·ing
un·hinge
un·hinged
un·hing·ing
un·hitch
un·ho·ly
un·ho·li·er
un·ho·li·est
un·ho·li·ly
un·ho·li·ness
un·hook
un·horse
un·horsed
un·hors·ing
un·hur·ried
un·hurt
uni·cam·er·al
uni·cam·er·al·ly
uni·cel·lu·lar
uni·corn
uni·fi·ca·tion
uni·form
uni·formed
uni·form·i·ty
uni·form·ly
uni·form·ness
uni·fy
uni·fied
uni·fy·ing
uni·fi·er
uni·lat·er·al
uni·lat·er·al·ism
uni·lat·er·al·ly
un·im·ag·i·na·ble
un·im·paired

un·im·peach·a·ble
  un·im·peach·a·bly
un·im·por·tance
  un·im·por·tant
un·im·proved
un·in·hib·it·ed
  un·in·hib·it·ed·ly
un·in·ter·est·ed
  un·in·ter·est·ing
un·ion
un·ion·ism
  un·ion·ist
un·ion·ize
  un·ion·ized
  un·ion·iz·ing
  un·ion·i·za·tion
unique
  unique·ly
  unique·ness
uni·son
unit
Uni·tar·i·an
unite
  unit·ed
  unit·ing
  unit·er
uni·ty
  uni·ties
uni·valve
  uni·valved
  uni·val·vu·lar
uni·ver·sal
  uni·ver·sal·i·ty
  uni·ver·sal·ly
  uni·ver·sal·ness
Uni·ver·sal·ist
uni·ver·sal·ize
  uni·ver·sal·ized
  uni·ver·sal·iz·ing
uni·verse
uni·ver·si·ty
  uni·ver·si·ties
un·just
  un·just·ly
  un·just·ness
un·kempt
un·kind
  un·kind·ness
un·kind·ly
  un·kind·li·er
  un·kind·li·est
  un·kind·li·ness
un·known
un·law·ful
  un·law·ful·ly
  un·law·ful·ness
un·learn
  un·learned
  un·learn·ing
un·learn·ed
  un·learn·ed·ly
un·leash
un·less
un·let·tered
un·like

un·like·ness
un·like·ly
  un·like·li·er
  un·like·li·est
  un·like·li·ness
un·lim·ber
un·lim·it·ed
un·load
  un·load·er
un·lock
un·looked-for
un·loose
  un·loosed
  un·loos·ing
  un·loos·en
un·lucky
  un·luck·i·er
  un·luck·i·est
  un·luck·i·ly
  un·luck·i·ness
un·make
  un·made
  un·mak·ing
  un·mak·er
un·man
  un·manned
  un·man·ning
un·mask
un·mean·ing
  un·mean·ing·ly
  un·mean·ing·ness
un·men·tion·a·ble
un·mer·ci·ful
  un·mer·ci·ful·ly
un·mis·tak·a·ble
  un·mis·tak·a·bly
un·mit·i·gat·ed
  un·mit·i·gat·ed·ly
un·nat·u·ral
  un·nat·u·ral·ly
  un·nat·u·ral·ness
un·nec·es·sary
  un·nec·es·sar·i·ly
un·nerve
  un·nerved
  un·nerv·ing
un·num·bered
un·ob·jec·tion·a·ble
un·or·gan·ized
un·pack
un·par·al·leled
un·par·don·a·ble
un·pleas·ant
  un·pleas·ant·ly
  un·pleas·ant·ness
un·plumbed
un·pop·u·lar
  un·pop·u·lar·i·ty
  un·pop·u·lar·ly
un·prec·e·dent·ed
  un·prec·e·dent·ed·ly
un·prin·ci·pled
un·print·a·ble
un·pro·fes·sion·al
  un·pro·fes·sion·al·ly

un-qual-i-fied
  un-qual-i-fied-ly
un-ques-tion-a-ble
  un-ques-tion-a-bly
un-ques-tioned
un-quote
  un-quot-ed
  un-quot-ing
un-rav-el
  un-rav-eled
  un-rav-el-ing
  un-rav-el-ment
un-read
un-re-al
un-rea-son-a-ble
  un-rea-son-a-ble-ness
  un-rea-son-a-bly
un-rea-son-ing
un-re-fined
un-re-gen-er-ate
un-re-lat-ed
un-re-lent-ing
  un-re-lent-ing-ly
un-re-mit-ting
un-re-serve
  un-re-served
  un-re-serv-ed-ly
  un-re-serv-ed-ness
un-rest
un-ri-valed
un-roll
un-ruf-fled
un-ru-ly
  un-ru-li-er
  un-ru-li-est
  un-ru-li-ness
un-sad-dle
  un-sad-dled
  un-sad-dling
un-said
un-sa-vory
un-say
  un-say-ing
un-scathed
un-schooled
un-scram-ble
  un-scram-bled
  un-scram-bling
un-screw
un-scru-pu-lous
  un-scru-pu-lous-ly
  un-scru-pu-lous-ness
un-seal
un-sea-son-a-ble
  un-sea-son-a-ble-ness
  un-sea-son-a-bly
un-seat
un-seem-ly
  un-seem-li-ness
un-set-tle
  un-set-tled
  un-set-tling
un-sheathe
  un-sheathed
  un-sheath-ing

un-shod
un-sight-ly
  un-sight-li-er
  un-sight-li-est
  un-sight-li-ness
un-skilled
un-skill-ful
  un-skill-ful-ly
  un-skill-ful-ness
un-snap
  un-snapped
  un-snap-ping
un-snarl
un-so-phis-ti-cat-ed
  un-so-phis-ti-cat-ed-ly
  un-so-phis-ti-cat-ed-ness
  un-so-phis-ti-ca-tion
un-sound
  un-sound-ly
  un-sound-ness
un-spar-ing
  un-spar-ing-ly
  un-spar-ing-ness
un-speak-a-ble
  un-speak-a-bly
un-sta-ble
  un-sta-ble-ness
  un-sta-bly
un-steady
  un-stead-i-er
  un-stead-i-est
  un-stead-i-ly
un-stop
  un-stopped
  un-stop-ping
un-strung
un-stud-ied
un-sung
un-tan-gle
  un-tan-gled
  un-tan-gling
un-taught
Un-ter-mey-er
un-think-a-ble
un-think-ing
  un-think-ing-ly
un-ti-dy
  un-ti-di-er
  un-ti-di-est
  un-ti-di-ly
  un-ti-di-ness
un-tie
  un-tied
  un-ty-ing
un-til
un-time-ly
  un-time-li-ness
un-to
un-told
un-touch-a-ble
  un-touch-a-bly
un-to-ward
  un-to-ward-ly
  un-to-ward-ness
un-truth

un·tu·tored
un·used
un·u·su·al
  un·u·su·al·ly
  un·u·su·al·ness
un·ut·ter·a·ble
  un·ut·ter·a·bly
un·var·nished
un·veil
un·wary
  un·war·i·ly
  un·war·i·ness
un·well
un·whole·some
  un·whole·some·ly
  un·whole·some·ness
un·wieldy
  un·wield·i·ness
un·will·ing
  un·will·ing·ly
  un·will·ing·ness
un·wind
  un·wound
  un·wind·ing
un·wise
  un·wise·ly
un·wit·ting
  un·wit·ting·ly
un·wont·ed
  un·wont·ed·ly
  un·wont·ed·ness
un·wor·thy
  un·wor·thi·ly
  un·wor·thi·ness
un·wrap
  un·wrapped
  un·wrap·ping
un·yield·ing
up-and-com·ing
up-and-down
up·beat
up·braid
  up·braid·er
  up·braid·ing
  up·braid·ing·ly
up·bring·ing
up·com·ing
up·coun·try
up·date
  up·dat·ed
  up·dat·ing
up·end
up·grade
  up·grad·ed
  up·grad·ing
up·heav·al
up·heave
  up·heaved
  up·heav·ing
up·hill
up·hold
  up·held
  up·hold·ing
  up·hold·er
up·hol·ster

up·hol·ster·er
up·hol·stery
up·hol·ster·ies
up·keep
up·land
up·lift
up·most
up·on
up·per
up·per-class
up·per·class·man
  up·per·class·men
up·per·cut
  up·per·cut·ting
up·per·most
up·pish
  up·pish·ly
  up·pish·ness
up·pi·ty
up·raise
  up·raised
  up·rais·ing
up·rear
up·right
  up·right·ly
  up·right·ness
up·ris·ing
up·roar
up·roar·i·ous
  up·roar·i·ous·ly
  up·roar·i·ous·ness
up·root
  up·root·er
up·set
  up·set·ting
up·shot
up·side
up·stage
  up·staged
  up·stag·ing
up·stairs
up·stand·ing
  up·stand·ing·ness
up·start
up·state
up·stream
up·swing
up·take
up-to-date
  up-to-date·ness
up·town
up·trend
up·turn
up·ward
  up·ward·ly
  up·ward·ness
Ural
Ura·nia
ura·ni·um
Ura·nus
ur·ban
ur·bane
  ur·bane·ly
  ur·bane·ness
ur·ban·i·ty

ur·ban·ize
  ur·ban·ized
  ur·ban·iz·ing
  ur·ban·i·za·tion
ur·chin
urea
  ure·al
  ure·ic
ure·mia
  ure·mic
ure·ter
ure·thra
  ure·thrae
  ure·thras
  ure·thral
urge
  urged
  urg·ing
  urg·er
  urg·ing·ly
ur·gent
  ur·gen·cy
  ur·gen·cies
  ur·gent·ly
Uri·ah
uric
uri·nal
uri·nal·y·sis
  uri·nal·y·ses
uri·nary
  uri·nar·ies
uri·nate
  uri·nat·ed
  uri·nat·ing
  uri·na·tion
urine
urol·o·gy
  uro·log·ic
  uro·log·i·cal
  urol·o·gist
Uru·guay
us·a·ble
  us·a·ble·ness
  us·a·bly
  us·a·bil·i·ty
us·age
use
  used
  us·ing
  us·er
use·ful
  use·ful·ly
  use·ful·ness
use·less
  use·less·ly
  use·less·ness
ush·er
usu·al
  usu·al·ly
  usu·al·ness
usurp
  usurp·pa·tion
  usurp·er
usu·ry
  usu·ries

usu·rer
usu·ri·ous
Utah
uten·sil
uter·us
  uteri
Uti·ca
util·i·tar·ian
util·i·ty
  util·i·ties
uti·lize
  uti·lized
  uti·liz·ing
  uti·liz·a·ble
  uti·li·za·tion
  uti·liz·er
ut·most
Uto·pia
  Uto·pi·an
ut·ter
  ut·ter·a·ble
  ut·ter·er
  ut·ter·ance
  ut·ter·most
uvu·la
  uvu·las
  uvu·lae
  uvu·lar
ux·o·ri·ous
  ux·o·ri·ous·ly
  ux·o·ri·ous·ness
va·can·cy
  va·can·cies
va·cant
  va·cant·ly
  va·cant·ness
va·cate
  va·cat·ed
  va·cat·ing
va·ca·tion
  va·ca·tion·less
vac·ci·nate
  vac·ci·nat·ed
  vac·ci·nat·ing
  vac·ci·na·tion
vac·cine
vac·il·late
  vac·il·lat·ed
  vac·il·lat·ing
  vac·il·la·tion
  vac·il·la·tor
va·cu·i·ty
  va·cu·i·ties
vac·u·ous
  vac·u·ous·ly
  vac·u·ous·ness
vac·u·um
  vac·u·ums
  vac·ua
  vac·u·um-packed
Va·duz
vag·a·bond
  vag·a·bond·age
  vag·a·bond·ish
  vag·a·bond·ism

va·gary
va·gar·ies
va·gar·i·ous
va·gar·i·ous·ly
va·gi·na
va·gi·nas
va·gi·nae
vag·i·nal
va·grant
va·gran·cy
va·gran·cies
va·grant·ly
vague
vague·ly
vague·ness
vain
vain·ly
vain·ness
vain·glo·ry
vain·glo·ries
vain·glo·ri·ous
vain·glo·ri·ous·ly
vain·glo·ri·ous·ness
val·ance
val·anced
val·e·dic·tion
val·e·dic·to·ri·an
val·e·dic·to·ry
val·e·dic·to·ries
va·lence
va·len·cy
Va·len·cia
val·en·tine
val·et
Val·hal·la
val·iant
val·iant·ly
val·iant·ness
val·id
val·id·ly
val·id·ness
val·i·date
val·i·dat·ed
val·i·dat·ing
val·i·da·tion
va·lid·i·ty
va·lid·i·ties
va·lise
Val·let·ta
val·ley
val·leys
Val·ois
val·or
val·or·ous
val·or·ous·ly
val·or·ous·ness
Val·pa·rai·so
val·u·a·ble
val·u·a·ble·ness
val·u·a·bly
val·u·a·tion
val·u·a·tion·al
val·ue
val·ued
val·u·ing

val·ue·less
val·ue·less·ness
val·u·er
valve
valve·less
val·vu·lar
va·moose
vam·pire
vam·pir·ic
vam·pir·ism
va·na·di·um
Van Bu·ren
Van·cou·ver
van·dal
van·dal·ism
van·dal·ize
van·dal·ized
van·dal·iz·ing
Van·der·bilt
Van·dyke
vane
vaned
vane·less
van·guard
va·nil·la
van·ish
van·ish·er
van·i·ty
van·i·ties
van·quish
van·quish·a·ble
van·quish·er
van·tage
vap·id
va·pid·i·ty
vap·id·ness
vap·id·ly
va·por
va·por·er
va·por·ish
va·por·ish·ness
va·por·ize
va·por·ized
va·por·iz·ing
va·por·i·za·tion
va·por·iz·er
va·por·ous
va·por·ous·ly
va·que·ro
va·que·ros
var·i·a·ble
var·i·a·bil·i·ty
var·i·a·ble·ness
var·i·a·bly
var·i·ance
var·i·ant
var·i·a·tion
var·i·a·tion·al
var·i·a·tion·al·ly
var·i·col·ored
var·i·cose
var·ied
var·ied·ness
var·i·e·gate
var·i·e·gat·ed

var·i·e·gat·ing
var·i·e·ga·tion
var·i·e·ga·tor
va·ri·e·tal
va·ri·e·tal·ly
va·ri·e·ty
va·ri·e·ties
var·i·ous
var·i·ous·ly
var·i·ous·ness
var·nish
var·nish·er
var·si·ty
var·si·ties
vary
var·ied
var·y·ing
var·i·er
var·y·ing·ly
vas·cu·lar
vas·cu·lar·i·ty
vas·ec·to·my
vas·ec·to·mies
Vas·e·line
vas·o·mo·tor
vas·sal
vas·sal·age
vast·ness
vat
vat·ted
vat·ting
Vat·i·can
vaude·ville
vault
vault·ed
vault·er
vault·ing
vaunt
vaunt·er
vaunt·ing·ly
vec·tor
vec·to·ri·al
veer·ing
veg·e·ta·ble
veg·e·tal
veg·e·tar·i·an
veg·e·tar·i·an·ism
veg·e·tate
veg·e·tat·ed
veg·e·tat·ing
veg·e·ta·tion
veg·e·ta·tion·al
veg·e·ta·tion·less
veg·e·ta·tive
ve·he·ment
ve·he·mence
ve·he·men·cy
ve·hi·cle
ve·hic·u·lar
veil
veiled
veil·ing
vein
veiny
vein·i·er

vein·i·est
vein·ing
Ve·las·quez
vel·lum
ve·loc·i·ty
ve·loc·i·ties
vel·our
ve·lum
ve·la
vel·vet
vel·vet·ed
vel·vet·een
vel·vety
vel·vet·i·er
vel·vet·i·est
ve·nal
ve·nal·i·ty
ve·nal·ly
ve·na·tion
ve·na·tion·al
vend·er
vend·or
ven·det·ta
vend·i·ble
vend·i·bil·i·ty
ve·neer
ve·neer·er
ve·neer·ing
ven·er·a·ble
ven·er·a·bil·i·ty
ven·er·a·ble·ness
ven·er·a·bly
ven·er·ate
ven·er·a·tion
ven·er·a·tor
ve·ne·re·al
Ve·ne·tian
Ven·e·zu·e·la
venge·ance
venge·ful
venge·ful·ness
ve·ni·al
ve·ni·al·i·ty
ve·ni·al·ness
ve·ni·al·ly
Ven·ice
ven·i·son
ven·om
ven·om·ous
ven·om·ous·ness
ve·nous
ve·nous·ly
ve·nous·ness
vent
vent·ed
vent·ing
ven·ti·late
ven·ti·lat·ed
ven·ti·lat·ing
ven·ti·la·tion
ven·ti·la·tor
ven·tral
ven·tral·ly
ven·tri·cle
ven·tril·o·quism

ven·tri·lo·qui·al
ven·tril·o·quist
ven·tril·o·quize
ven·tril·o·quized
ven·tril·o·quiz·ing
ven·ture
ven·ture·some
ven·ture·some·ness
ven·tur·ous
ven·tur·ous·ness
Ve·nus
ve·ra·cious
ve·ra·cious·ness
ve·rac·i·ty
ve·rac·i·ties
Ve·ra·cruz
ve·ran·da
ver·bal
ver·bal·ly
ver·bal·ize
ver·bal·ized
ver·bal·iz·ing
ver·bal·i·za·tion
ver·bal·iz·er
ver·ba·tim
ver·bi·age
ver·bose
ver·bose·ness
ver·bos·i·ty
ver·bo·ten
ver·dant
ver·dan·cy
Ver·di
ver·dict
ver·di·gris
Ver·dun
ver·dure
ver·dured
ver·dur·ous
verge
verged
verg·ing
Ver·gil
ver·i·fi·ca·tion
ver·i·fy
ver·i·fied
ver·i·fy·ing
ver·i·fi·a·bil·i·ty
ver·i·fi·a·ble·ness
ver·i·fi·a·ble
ver·i·fi·er
ver·i·si·mil·i·tude
ver·i·ta·ble
ver·i·ta·ble·ness
ver·i·ta·bly
ver·i·ty
ver·i·ties
Ver·meer
ver·meil
ver·mic·u·lar
ver·mic·u·late
ver·mic·u·lat·ed
ver·mi·fuge
ver·mil·ion
ver·min

ver·min·ous
Ver·mont
ver·mouth
ver·nac·u·lar
ver·nac·u·lar·ism
ver·nal
ver·nal·ly
Ver·non
Ver·ra·za·no
Ver·sailles
ver·sa·tile
ver·sa·tile·ness
ver·sa·til·i·ty
versed
ver·si·fy
ver·si·fied
ver·si·fy·ing
ver·si·fi·er
ver·si·fi·ca·tion
ver·sion
ver·sion·al
ver·sus
ver·te·bra
ver·te·brae
ver·te·bral
ver·te·bral·ly
ver·te·brate
ver·tex
ver·tex·es
ver·ti·ces
ver·ti·cal
ver·ti·cal·i·ty
ver·ti·cal·ness
ver·ti·cal·ly
ver·ti·go
ver·ti·goes
ver·tig·i·nes
ves·i·cant
ves·i·ca·to·ry
ves·i·ca·to·ries
ves·i·cate
ves·i·cat·ed
ves·i·cat·ing
ves·i·ca·tion
ves·i·cle
ve·sic·u·lar
ves·pers
ves·sel
ves·tal
vest·ed
ves·ti·bule
ves·ti·buled
ves·ti·bul·ing
ves·tib·u·lar
ves·tige
ves·tig·i·al
ves·tig·i·al·ly
vest·ment
vest-pock·et
ves·try
ves·tries
Ve·su·vi·us
vet
vet·ted
vet·ting

vet·er·an
vet·er·i·nar·i·an
vet·er·i·nary
ve·to
  ve·toed
  ve·to·ing
  ve·to·er
vex
  vex·er
  vex·ing·ly
vex·a·tion
vex·a·tious
vexed
via
vi·a·ble
  vi·a·bil·i·ty
vi·a·bly
vi·a·duct
vi·al
vi·and
vi·brant
  vi·bran·cy
vi·brate
  vi·brat·ed
  vi·brat·ing
vi·bra·tion
vi·bra·to
  vi·bra·tos
vi·bra·tor
vi·bra·to·ry
vi·bur·num
vic·ar
  vic·ar·ship
vic·ar·age
vi·car·i·ous
  vi·car·i·ous·ly
  vi·car·i·ous·ness
vice ad·mi·ral
vice con·sul
  vice-con·su·lar
  vice-con·su·late
  vice-con·sul·ship
vice pres·i·dent
  vice-pres·i·den·cy
  vice-pres·i·den·cies
  vice-pres·i·den·tial
vice·roy
  vice·roy·al
vice ver·sa
Vi·chy
vi·cin·i·ty
  vi·cin·i·ties
vi·cious
  vi·cious·ly
  vi·cious·ness
vi·cis·si·tude
Vicks·burg
vic·tim
vic·tim·ize
  vic·tim·ized
  vic·tim·iz·ing
  vic·tim·i·za·tion
  vic·tim·iz·er
vic·tor
Vic·to·ri·an

Vic·to·ri·an·ism
vic·to·ri·ous
  vic·to·ri·ous·ly
  vic·to·ri·ous·ness
vic·to·ry
  vic·to·ries
Vic·tro·la
vict·ual
vi·cu·ña
vid·eo
vid·e·o·tape
  vid·e·o·taped
  vid·e·o·tap·ing
vie
  vied
  vy·ing
  vi·er
Vi·en·na
Vien·tiane
Vi·et Nam
Vi·et·nam·ese
view·er
view·less
view·point
vig·il
vig·i·lance
vig·i·lant
vig·i·lan·te
vi·gnette
vig·or
vig·or·ous
  vig·or·ous·ly
vi·king
vile
  vil·er
  vil·est
vil·i·fy
  vil·i·fied
  vil·i·fy·ing
  vil·i·fi·ca·tion
vil·la
vil·lage
vil·lain
vil·lain·ous
  vil·lain·ous·ly
  vil·lain·ous·ness
vil·lainy
  vil·lain·ies
vil·lein
vil·lous
vil·lus
  vil·li
Vin·cennes
vin·ci·ble
  vin·ci·bil·i·ty
vin·di·cate
  vin·di·cat·ed
  vin·di·cat·ing
  vin·di·ca·tion
  vin·di·ca·tor
vin·dic·tive
  vin·dic·tive·ly
  vin·dic·tive·ness
vin·e·gar
vin·e·gary

vine·yard
vi·nous
vin·tage
vint·ner
vi·nyl
vi·ol
vi·o·la
  vi·o·list
vi·o·la·ble
  vi·o·la·bil·i·ty
vi·o·late
  vi·o·lat·ed
  vi·o·lat·ing
  vi·o·la·tor
vi·o·la·tion
vi·o·lence
vi·o·lent
vi·o·let
vi·o·lin
  vi·o·lin·ist
vi·o·lon·cel·lo
  vi·o·lon·cel·list
vi·per
vi·ra·go
  vi·ra·goes
  vi·ra·gos
vi·ral
vir·eo
  vir·e·os
Vir·gil
vir·gin
  vir·gin·al
  vir·gin·al·ly
Vir·gin·ia
vir·gin·i·ty
vir·gule
vir·ile
  vi·ril·i·ty
vi·rol·o·gy
  vi·rol·o·gist
vir·tu·al
  vir·tu·al·ly
vir·tue
vir·tu·os·i·ty
  vir·tu·os·i·ties
vir·tu·o·so
  vir·tu·o·sos
  vir·tu·o·si
  vir·tu·o·sic
vir·tu·ous
  vir·tu·ous·ly
  vir·tu·ous·ness
vir·u·lence
  vir·u·len·cy
vir·u·lent
vi·rus
  vi·rus·es
vi·sa
vis·age
vis·à·vis
vis·cera
vis·cer·al
vis·cid
  vis·cid·i·ty
  vis·cid·ly

vis·cid·ness
vis·cos·i·ty
  vis·cos·i·ties
vis·count
  vis·count·cy
  vis·count·ship
vis·count·ess
vis·cous
vis·i·bil·i·ty
  vis·i·bil·i·ties
vis·i·ble
Vis·i·goth
vi·sion
vi·sion·ary
  vi·sion·ar·ies
vis·it
vis·i·tant
vis·it·a·tion
vis·it·ing
vis·i·tor
vi·sor
vis·ta
Vis·tu·la
vis·u·al
  vis·u·al·ly
vis·u·al·ize
  vis·u·al·ized
  vis·u·al·iz·ing
  vis·u·al·i·za·tion
vi·tal
vi·tal·i·ty
  vi·tal·i·ties
vi·tal·ize
  vi·tal·ized
  vi·tal·iz·ing
  vi·tal·i·za·tion
vi·tals
vi·ta·min
vi·ti·ate
  vi·ti·at·ed
  vi·ti·at·ing
  vi·ti·a·tion
vit·re·ous
  vit·re·os·i·ty
vit·ri·fy
  vit·ri·fied
  vit·ri·fy·ing
  vit·ri·fi·a·ble
  vit·ri·fi·ca·tion
vit·ri·ol
  vit·ri·ol·ic
vi·tu·per·ate
  vi·tu·per·at·ed
  vi·tu·per·at·ing
  vi·tu·per·a·tion
vi·va
vi·va·cious
vi·vac·i·ty
  vi·vac·i·ties
viv·id
viv·i·fy
  viv·i·fied
  viv·i·fy·ing
  viv·i·fi·ca·tion
vi·vip·ar·ous

viv·i·sec·tion
vix·en
vi·zier
vi·zor
Vlad·i·vos·tok
vo·cab·u·lar·y
  vo·cab·u·lar·ies
vo·cal
vo·cal·ic
vo·cal·ist
vo·cal·ize
  vo·cal·ized
  vo·cal·iz·ing
  vo·cal·i·za·tion
vo·ca·tion
vo·ca·tion·al
vo·cif·er·ous
vod·ka
voice
  voiced
  voic·ing
voice·less
voice·print
void·a·ble
vol·a·tile
  vol·a·til·i·ty
voi·can·ic
  vol·can·i·cal·ly
vol·ca·no
  vol·ca·noes
  vol·ca·nos
Vol·ga
Vol·go·grad
vo·li·tion
vol·ley
  vol·leys
  vol·leyed
  vol·ley·ing
vol·ley·ball
Vol·ta
volt·age
vol·ta·ic
Vol·taire
volt·me·ter
vol·u·ble
  vol·u·bly
  vol·u·bil·i·ty
vol·ume
vo·lu·mi·nous
  vo·lu·mi·nous·ly
  vo·lu·mi·nous·ness
vol·un·tary
  vol·un·tar·i·ly
vol·un·teer
vo·lup·tu·ary
  vo·lup·tu·ar·ies
vo·lup·tu·ous
vom·it
voo·doo
  voo·doos
voo·doo·ism
  voo·doo·ist
  voo·doo·is·tic
vo·ra·cious
  vo·rac·i·ty

vor·tex
  vor·tex·es
  vor·ti·ces
vo·ta·ry
  vo·ta·ries
vote
  vot·ed
  vot·ing
vot·er
vo·tive
vouch·er
vouch·safe
  vouch·safed
  vouch·saf·ing
vow·el
voy·age
  voy·aged
  voy·ag·ing
  voy·ag·er
vo·ya·geur
vo·yeur
  vo·yeur·ism
  voy·eur·is·tic
Vul·can
vul·can·ite
vul·can·ize
  vul·can·ized
  vul·can·iz·ing
  vul·can·i·za·tion
vul·gar
vul·gar·ism
vul·gar·i·ty
  vul·gar·i·ties
vul·gar·ize
  vul·gar·ized
  vul·gar·iz·ing
  vul·gar·i·za·tion
vul·gate
vul·ner·a·ble
  vul·ner·a·bil·i·ty
  vul·ner·a·bly
vul·pine
vul·ture
vul·va
  vul·vae
  vul·vas
Wa·bash
wab·ble
  wab·bled
  wab·bling
wacky
  wack·i·er
  wack·i·est
  wack·i·ly
  wack·i·ness
wad
  wad·ded
  wad·ding
wad·dle
  wad·dled
  wad·dling
  wad·dler
  wad·dly
  wad·dli·er
  wad·dli·est

wade
  wad·ed
  wad·ing
wad·er
wa·fer
waf·fle
wag
  wagged
  wag·ging
  wag·ger
  wag·gish
wage
  waged
  wag·ing
wa·ger
wag·gery
  wag·ger·ies
wag·gle
  wag·gled
  wag·gling
Wag·ner
wag·on
wag·on·er
Wai·ki·ki
wain·scot
  wain·scot·ing
wain·wright
waist·band
waist·coat
waist·line
wait·er
wait·ing
wait·ress
waive
  waived
  waiv·ing
waiv·er
wake
  waked
  wok·en
  wak·ing
wake·ful
  wake·ful·ly
  wake·ful·ness
wak·en
Wal·den
Wal·do
Wal·dorf
wale
  waled
  wal·ing
walk·a·way
walk·er
walk·ie·talk·ie
walk·out
walk·o·ver
walk·up
walk·way
wal·la·by
  wal·la·bies
Wal·la·chia
wall·board
wal·let
wall·eye
wall·eyed

wall·flow·er
Wal·loon
wal·lop
wall·pa·per
wall·to·wall
wal·nut
Wal·pole
wal·rus
  wal·rus·es
Wal·tham
Wal·ton
wam·pum
wan
  wan·ner
  wan·nest
  wan·ness
wan·der
wan·der·lust
wane
  waned
  wan·ing
wan·gle
  wan·gled
  wan·gling
  wan·gler
want·ing
wan·ton
wap·i·ti
  wap·i·ties
war
  warred
  war·ring
war·ble
  war·bled
  war·bling
war·bler
war·den
  war·den·ship
ward·er
ward·robe
ware·house
war·fare
war·head
war·horse
war·like
war·lock
warm
  warm·er
  warm·est
warm·blood·ed
warm·heart·ed
war·mong·er
warmth
warn·ing
war·path
war·rant
war·ran·ty
  war·ran·ties
war·ren
war·ri·or
War·saw
war·ship
war·time
War·wick
wary

248

war·i·er
war·i·est
war·i·ly
war·i·ness
wash·a·ble
wash·ba·sin
wash·board
wash·bowl
wash·cloth
wash·er
wash·ing
Wash·ing·ton
wash·out
wash·room
wash·stand
wash·tub
was·n't
wasp
  wasp·ish
  wasp·ish·ly
  wasp·ish·ness
was·sail
Was·ser·mann test
wast·age
waste
  wast·ed
  wast·ing
  waste·ful
  waste·ful·ly
  waste·ful·ness
waste·bas·ket
waste·land
waste·pa·per
wast·er
wast·rel
watch·dog
watch·ful
watch·man
  watch·men
watch·tow·er
watch·word
wa·ter
wat·er·buck
Wa·ter·bury
wa·ter·col·or
wa·ter·course
wa·ter·cress
wa·ter·fall
wa·ter·fowl
wa·ter·front
wa·ter·less
wa·ter lev·el
wa·ter lily
  wa·ter lil·ies
wa·ter line
wa·ter·logged
Wa·ter·loo
wa·ter main
wa·ter·man
  wa·ter·men
wa·ter·mark
wa·ter·mel·on
wa·ter moc·ca·sin
wa·ter·proof
wa·ter·re·pel·lent

wa·ter·shed
wa·ter·side
wa·ter·ski
  wa·ter·skied
  wa·ter·ski·ing
wa·ter·spout
wa·ter·tight
wa·ter·way
wa·ter·works
wa·tery
watt·age
watt·hour
wat·tle
  wat·tled
  wat·tling
Wau·ke·gan
Wau·sau
wave
  waved
  wav·ing
wave·length
wave·let
wa·ver
Wa·ver·ley
wav·y
  wav·i·er
  wav·i·est
  wav·i·ly
  wav·i·ness
wax
  waxed
  wax·ing
wax·en
wax·wing
wax·work
waxy
  wax·i·er
  wax·i·est
  wax·i·ness
way·far·er
  way·far·ing
way·lay
  way·laid
  way·lay·ing
way·side
way·ward
weak·en
weak·kneed
weak·ling
weak·ly
  weak·li·er
  weak·li·est
  weak·li·ness
weak·mind·ed
weak·ness
wealthy
  wealth·i·er
  wealth·i·est
  wealth·i·ly
  wealth·i·ness
wean
weap·on
weap·on·ry
wear
  wear·ing

wea·ri·some
wea·ry
  wea·ri·er
  wea·ri·est
  wea·ried
  wea·ry·ing
  wea·ri·ly
  wea·ri·ness
wea·sel
weath·er
weath·er·beat·en
weath·er·cock
weath·er·glass
weath·er·ing
weath·er·man
  weath·er·men
weath·er·proof
weath·er·vane
weave
  weaved
  wov·en
  weav·ing
weav·er
web
  webbed
  web·bing
web·foot
  web·foot·ed
Web·ster
wed·ding
wedge
  wedged
  wedg·ing
Wedg·wood ware
wed·lock
Wednes·day
weedy
  weed·i·er
  weed·i·est
week·day
week·end
week·ly
weep·ing
wee·vil
weigh
weight
weighty
  weight·i·er
  weight·i·est
  weight·i·ly
  weight·i·ness
weird
  weird·er
  weird·est
wel·come
  wel·comed
  wel·com·ing
wel·fare
well·be·ing
well·born
well·bred
well·dis·posed
well·done
well·found·ed
well·groomed

well·ground·ed
Wel·ling·ton
well·known
well·mean·ing
well·nigh
well·off
well·read
well·spo·ken
well·spring
well·thought·of
well·timed
well·to·do
well·wish·er
well·worn
Welsh·man
wel·ter
wel·ter·wright
Wen·ces·laus
were·wolf
  were·wolves
Wes·ley
Wes·sex
west·bound
West·ches·ter
west·er·ly
west·ern
west·ern·er
West·ern Hem·i·sphere
west·ern·ize
  west·ern·ized
  west·ern·iz·ing
  west·ern·i·za·tion
west·ern·most
West In·dies
West·ing·house
West·min·ster
West·more·land
West·pha·lia
West Vir·gin·ia
west·ward
wet
  wet·ter
  wet·test
wet·back
Wey·mouth
whale
  whaled
  whal·ing
whale·boat
whale·bone
whal·er
wharf
  wharves
Whar·ton
what·ev·er
what·not
what·so·ev·er
wheal
wheat·en
whee·dle
  whee·dled
  whee·dling
  whee·dler
wheel and ax·le
wheel·bar·row

wheel·chair
wheeled
wheel·house
Wheel·ing
wheel·wright
wheeze
  wheezed
  wheez·ing
wheezy
  wheez·i·er
  wheez·i·est
  wheez·i·ly
  wheez·i·ness
whelm
whelp
whence·so·ev·er
where·a·bouts
where·as
where·by
where·fore
where·in
where·on
where·so·ev·er
where·to
where·up·on
wher·ev·er
where·with
where·with·al
wher·ry
  wher·ries
whet
  whet·ted
  whet·ting
wheth·er
whet·stone
which·ev·er
whim·per
whim·si·cal
whim·sy
  whim·sies
whine
  whined
  whin·ing
whin·ny
  whin·nied
  whin·ny·ing
  whin·nies
whip
  whipped
  whip·ping
whip·lash
whip·per·snap·per
whip·pet
whip·poor·will
whir
  whirred
  whir·ring
whirl·i·gig
whirl·pool
whirl·wind
whisk·er
whis·key
  whis·ky
  whis·keys
  whis·kies

whis·per
whist
whis·tle
  whis·tled
  whis·tling
whis·tler
white
  whit·er
  whit·est
  whit·ish
white-col·lar
white·fish
whit·en
white·wash
white wa·ter
whith·er
whit·ing
Whit·man
Whit·sun·day
Whit·sun·tide
Whit·ti·er
whit·tle
  whit·tled
  whit·tling
  whit·tler
whiz
  whizzed
  whiz·zing
  whiz·zes
whoa
who·ev·er
whole·heart·ed
whole·sale
  whole·saled
  whole·sal·ing
  whole·sal·er
whole·some
whole-wheat
whol·ly
whom·ev·er
whom·so·ev·er
whoop·ing
whop·per
whop·ping
whorled
whose·so·ev·er
who·so·ev·er
Wich·i·ta
wick·ed
wick·er
wick·er·work
wick·et
wide
  wid·er
  wid·est
wide-a·wake
wide-eyed
wid·en
wide·spread
widg·eon
wid·ow
wid·ow·er
wid·ow·hood
width
wield·er

wieldy
wie·ner
wig·gle
  wig·gled
  wig·gling
  wig·gly
  wig·gli·er
  wig·gli·est
wig·gler
wig·wag
  wig·wagged
  wig·wag·ging
wig·wam
wild·cat
  wild·cat·ted
  wild·cat·ting
wild·cat strike
Wil·der
wil·der·ness
wild·fire
wild·fowl
wild-goose chase
wild·life
wild·wood
wile
  wiled
  wil·ing
  wil·i·ly
  wil·i·ness
  wily
  wil·i·er
  wil·i·est
Wil·helms·ha·ven
Wilkes-Bar·re
Wil·lam·ette
willed
will·ful
Wil·liams·burg
wil·lies
will·ing
will-o'-the-wisp
wil·low
wil·lowy
wil·ly-nil·ly
Wil·ming·ton
wim·ble
wim·ple
win
  win·ning
wince
  winced
  winc·ing
Win·ches·ter
wind
  wound
  wind·ing
wind·bag
wind·break
wind·ed
Win·der·mere
wind·fall
wind·flow·er
wind·jam·mer
wind·lass
wind·mill

win·dow
win·dow·pane
win·dow-shop
  win·dow-shopped
  win·dow-shop·ping
  win·dow-shop·per
wind·pipe
wind·row
wind·shield
Wind·sor
wind·storm
wind·up
wind·ward
windy
  wind·i·er
  wind·i·est
  wind·i·ly
  wind·i·ness
wine
  wined
  win·ing
win·ery
  win·er·ies
Wine·sap
wine·skin
winged
wing·span
wing·spread
Win·ne·ba·go
win·ner
win·ning
Win·ni·peg
win·now
Wins·low
win·some
Win·ston-Sa·lem
win·ter
win·ter·green
win·ter·ize
  win·ter·ized
  win·ter·iz·ing
  win·ter·i·za·tion
win·try
  win·tri·er
  win·tri·est
  win·ter·y
  win·tri·ly
  win·tri·ness
wipe
  wiped
  wip·ing
wire-haired
wire·less
wire·tap
  wire·tapped
  wire·tap·ping
  wire·tap·per
wir·ing
wiry
  wir·i·er
  wir·i·est
  wir·i·ly
  wir·i·ness
Wis·con·sin
wis·dom

wise
  wis·er
  wis·est
wise·a·cre
wise·crack
wish·bone
wish·ful
wish·y-washy
wisp
  wispy
  wisp·i·er
  wisp·i·est
wis·te·ria
wist·ful
witch·craft
witch·ery
  witch·er·ies
witch·ing
with·draw
  with·drew
  with·drawn
  with·draw·ing
with·draw·al
with·er
  with·ered
  with·er·ing
with·hold
  with·held
  with·hold·ing
with·in
with·out
with·stand
  with·stood
  with·stand·ing
wit·less
wit·ness
wit·ted
wit·ti·cism
wit·ting
  wit·ting·ly
wit·ty
  wit·ti·er
  wit·ti·est
  wit·ti·ly
  wit·ti·ness
wiz·ard
  wiz·ard·ly
  wiz·ard·ry
wiz·en
  wiz·ened
wob·ble
  wob·bled
  wob·bling
  wob·bly
  wob·bli·er
  wob·bli·est
woe·be·gone
woe·ful
wolf·hound
wolf·ram
Wol·sey
wol·ver·ine
wom·an
  wom·en
  wom·an·like

wom·an·ly
  wom·an·li·ness
wom·an·hood
wom·an·ish
wom·an·kind
womb
wom·bat
wom·en·folk
won·der
  won·der·ful
  won·der·land
  won·der·ment
won·drous
wont·ed
wood·bine
wood·chuck
wood·cock
wood·craft
wood·cut
  wood·cut·ter
wood·ed
wood·en
wood·land
wood·man
  wood·men
wood·peck·er
wood·pile
wood·shed
woods·man
  woods·men
Wood·stock
woodsy
  woods·i·er
  woods·i·est
wood·wind
wood·work
woody
  wood·i·er
  wood·i·est
woo·er
wool·en
wool·gath·er·ing
  wool·gath·er
  wool·gath·er·er
wool·ly
  wool·li·er
  wool·li·est
  wool·li·ness
wool·ly-head·ed
Wool·worth
woozy
  wooz·i·er
  wooz·i·est
  wooz·i·ly
  wooz·i·ness
Worces·ter
Worces·ter·shire
word·book
word·ing
word·less
  word·less·ly
  word·less·ness
Words·worth
wordy
  word·i·er

word·i·est
word·i·ly
word·i·ness
work·a·ble
work·a·bil·i·ty
work·a·day
work·bench
work·book
work·day
worked-up
work·er
work·horse
work·house
work·ing
work·ing·man
work·ing·men
work·man
work·men
work·man·like
work·man·ship
work·out
work·room
work·shop
work·ta·ble
world·ly
world·li·er
world·li·est
world·li·ness
world·ly-wise
world-wea·ry
world-wide
worm-eat·en
worm·wood
wormy
worm·i·er
worm·i·est
worn-out
wor·ri·some
wor·ry
wor·ried
wor·ry·ing
wor·ries
wor·ri·er
wor·ry·wart
wors·en
wor·ship
wor·ship·ful
wor·sted
worth·less
worth·while
wor·thy
wor·thi·er
wor·thi·est
wor·thi·ly
wor·thi·ness
would-be
would·n't
wound·ed
wraith
wran·gle
wran·gled
wran·gling
wran·gler
wrap
wrapped

wrap·ping
wrap·per
wrath·ful
wreak
wreath
wreathe
wreathed
wreath·ing
wreck·age
wreck·er
wrench
wres·tle
wres·tled
wres·tling
wretch·ed
wrig·gle
wrig·gled
wrig·gling
wrig·gly
wrig·gli·er
wrig·gli·est
wrig·gler
wring
wrung
wring·ing
wring·er
wrin·kle
wrin·kled
wrin·kling
wrin·kly
wrin·kli·er
wrin·kli·est
wrist·band
write
wrote
writ·ten
writ·ing
write-in
writ·er
writhe
writhed
writh·ing
wrong·do·er
wrong·do·ing
wronged
wrong·ful
wrong-head·ed
wrought
wry
wri·er
wri·est
wry·ly
Wur·tem·berg
Wyc·liffe
Wy·lie
Wy·o·ming
Xa·ve·ri·an
Xav·i·er
X-chro·mo·some
xe·bec
xe·non
xen·o·pho·bia
Xen·o·phon
Xer·xes
Xmas

X-ray
  x-ray
xy-lem
xy-lo-phone
  xy-lo-phon-ist
Xy-ris
yacht
yacht-ing
yachts-man
  yachts-men
Yah-weh
yak
yam
Yang-tze
yank
Yan-kee
Ya-oun-dé
yap
  yapped
  yap-ping
yard-age
yard-arm
yard-mas-ter
yard-stick
yarn
yar-row
yawn
Y-chro-mo-some
vca
year-book
year-ling
year-long
year-ly
yearn
  yearn-ing
year-round
yeast
yeasty
  yeast-i-er
  yeast-i-est
yel-low
  yel-low-ish
yel-low-bird
yel-low fe-ver
yel-low-ham-mer
yel-low jack-et
Yel-low-stone
yelp
Yem-en
yen
  yenned
  yen-ning
yeo-man
  yeo-men
ye-shi-va
  ye-shi-vas
yes-ter-day
yes-ter-year
yeti
yew
Yid-dish
yield
yield-ing
yip
  yipped

yip-ping
yo-del
yo-deled
yo-del-ing
yo-del-er
yo-ga
  yo-gic
yo-gi
  yo-gis
yo-gurt
yoke
  yoked
  yok-ing
yo-kel
Yo-ko-ha-ma
yolk
Yom Kip-pur
yon-der
Yon-kers
yore
York-shire
Yo-sem-i-te
young
young-ling
young-ster
Youngs-town
your-self
  your-selves
youth-ful
yowl
Yo-Yo
yt-ter-bi-um
yt-tri-um
Yu-ca-tan
yuc-ca
Yu-go-slav-ia
Yu-kon
yule-tide
yum-my
  yum-mi-er
  yum-mi-est
Zach-a-ri-ah
Zam-be-si
Zam-be-zi
Zam-bia
za-ny
  za-nies
  za-ni-er
  za-ni-est
  za-ni-ly
  za-ni-ness
Zan-zi-bar
Zea-land
zeal-ot
zeal-ous
Zeb-e-dee
ze-bra
  ze-bras
ze-bu
Zech-a-ri-ah
Zen-ger
ze-nith
zeph-yr
zep-pe-lin
ze-ro

255

ze·ros
ze·roes
zest
zesty
zest·i·er
zest·i·est
zig·zag
zig·zagged
zig·zag·ging
zinc
Zin·fan·del
zing
zin·nia
Zi·on
Zi·on·ism
Zi·on·ist
zip
zipped
zip·ping
zip·per
zip·py
zip·pi·er
zip·pi·est

zir·con
zir·co·ni·um
zith·er
zo·di·ac
zo·di·a·cal
Zom·ba
zom·bie
zom·bi
zon·al
zone
zoned
zon·ing
zoo
zoos
zo·ol·o·gy
zo·o·log·i·cal
zo·o·log·i·cal·ly
zo·ol·o·gist
zuc·chi·ni
Zu·rich
zwie·back
Zwing·li
zy·gote